Forbes
MediaGuide
500

1993

Forbes MediaGuide 500

Jude Wanniski
Editor

Kathy McNamara
Executive Editor

Patricia M. Koyce
Senior Editor

Wylie H. Nash
Art Director

Richard Doyle
Associate Editor

Timothy A. Meis
Associate Editor

Skye Wilson
Associate Editor

Karolyn M. Necco
Director of Research

Michael Conley
Matthew Wanniski
Research Assistants

Ronald deLaRosa
S. Malcolm Macdonald
G. Kathleen Pizar
Proofreaders

Malcolm S. Forbes, Jr.
Chairman

Timothy C. Forbes
President

Scott Masterson
**Vice President and
General Manager**

Elizabeth L. Williams
**Director of Consumer
Marketing**

Carlos A. Aguilar
Production Director

Forbes MediaGuide 500 is published annually by Forbes Inc. ©1993 by Forbes Inc. Editorial correspondence should be sent to MediaGuide, P.O. Box 762, Bedminster, NJ 07921. Subscriptions correspondence should go to MediaGuide Subscriptions Dept. c/o Forbes Inc., 60 Fifth Ave., New York, NY 10011.
ISSN: 1067-4918
ISBN: 08281-9950-7

T. O. C.

Editor's Letter
by Jude Wanniski 3

MAJOR STORIES
A Three-Way Race
by Patricia M. Koyce 6

A World Turned Upside Down
by Richard Doyle 11

Europe 1992: A Dream Dissolves
by Kathy McNamara 17

THE BEST STORIES & COLUMNS OF 1992
Business 25
Commentary 28
Foreign 32
General 36
Political 40

THE RATING GUIDE 45

THE HIGHEST RATED JOURNALISTS OF 1992 46

JOURNALIST RATINGS
Business 50
Commentators 115
Foreign 151
National Security 212
Science/Health/Environment 234
Society & Politics 247

PUBLICATIONS AND SYNDICATES 298

INDEX 301

EDITOR'S LETTER

By Jude Wanniski

There has never been anything like *MediaGuide*—either in its old form or in its new incarnation as *Forbes MediaGuide 500* and *MediaGuide Quarterly*. The novelty of the initiative rests on the idea that information about the world around us, "news," has never traveled so rapidly in such volume as in this global, computer age. The quality of the work produced by those responsible for the data flow—reporters, commentators and editors—has never been quite as important.

In an earlier era, when the tempo of life was restricted by the relatively glacial pace of the information flow, journalists were far less important to the process. Almost anyone who could type with two fingers could land a job as a reporter. The work was considered a "trade," and wages rarely exceeded those of a carpenter. College degrees were rare. Only a handful of pundits achieved celebrity status. Because the "news" was simple and the dispatches formulaic, the only distinguishing characteristic among competing "newshounds" was speed. The "scoop" or "newsbeat" was all-important.

In today's high-speed, high-tech world, journalism has become a profession. Many of its practitioners are better known to the general public than the political and business leaders who make the news. Cub reporters routinely have several college degrees and are expected to handle topics of profound complexity. At the national level, the incomes and net worth of a great many leading journalists rival those of professional athletes. The premium is no longer on speed, but perspective, distinctiveness and flair. If yesterday's newshound was a short-order cook, today's journalist is expected to be a gourmet chef, satisfying the most refined tastes of today's consumers of news, a national population of educated news connoisseurs. In many ways, the Fourth Estate has become the First.

The initial *MediaGuide* goes back eight years, work getting under way in 1985 and the launch coming a year later. As a concept, though, the idea of an annual review and assessment of the print media's performance stretches back more than 30 years to my days as a graduate student in journalism at UCLA. First loves make deep impressions, and my many years as a journalist left me with a deep and abiding passion for the printed word, a passion that has remained long after my leaving the profession. The motivation for *MediaGuide* was the desire to produce a standard whereby excellence in this arena could be identified and acknowledged. My ambition was to produce for the journalism profession a kind of *Michelin Guide* to the media. The best reporters and columnists would be rated annually, similar to the ratings of Europe's top restaurants conducted by *Michelin* each year. After all, criticism in any endeavor is absolutely essential for excellence.

Criticism becomes of greater importance when the endeavor becomes more complex, more sophisticated. Today, the demands of the computer age and the widening debates over the course of society that stem from this technological change require journalistic cadres of great expertise. Acutely aware of the powers and perils of the press, A. J. Liebling once declared "... it is evil that men anywhere be forced to depend, for the information on which they must govern their lives, on the caprice of anybody at all. There should be a great, free, living stream of information and equal access to it for all." Hyperbole aside, we agree. Yet, there is also a tyranny that prevails when quantity predominates over quality. How do you know what to read in this seemingly news-saturated environment, when more and more information comes hurtling at you? As news consumers we must be discriminating, if only to have the information necessary to participate productively in the democratic and free-market processes that guide our nation.

If we could read only one newspaper or periodical to be adequately informed, which would it be? The answer is that no such publication exists. Each has its strengths and weaknesses. The most serious consumers of news treat the entire media as one giant databank. The intent of *MediaGuide Quarterly* is to provide access to the most useful and provocative information that this database has to offer. *MediaGuide 500*, as an annual supplement, complements that effort by offering a quality check on the most influential journalists who contribute to the database.

The need for a means of distilling quality out of the sea of information certainly has occurred to others over the years, but not until *MediaGuide* has there ever been any attempt to create such a product. Only recently has the press been writing about itself. Most major publications now have a "media beat," with a full-time reporter covering other newspapers and periodicals, and not only the business news of the communications industry, but also the politics of the profession. It has been a healthy and necessary development that accommodates the times. Systematic criticism of the profession's performance did not exist, however. There do exist ideologically-oriented watchdog organizations and newsletters, like Accuracy In Media (AIM), MediaWatch (MW), and Fairness And Accuracy In Media (FAIR), which search for and identify partisan biases within the media. *MediaGuide*, on the other hand, searches for excellence.

When *MediaGuide* first appeared in 1986, there were legitimate questions from within the profession as to whether our criteria might be ideologically tilted, whether we defined excellence as "orthodoxy," and whether we could judge without partisanship. A declaration of our intention and goal was simply not sufficient; judgment had to be withheld until the consumers could examine and absorb several editions of the product. The profession and other users of *MediaGuide* had to see over a period of time a commitment to professionalism, the systematic weeding out on our part of any bias in our evaluations and the consistent application of the profession's own standards for judging excellence. There could be no arbitrariness, no hidden agenda. It took time, as we expected, but with the acquisition of *MediaGuide* by Forbes Inc., its credibility within the profession has been formally acknowledged.

The only annual, systematic assessment of the nation's most important journalists, *MediaGuide 500* is indeed one of a kind. An even more ambitious undertaking is *MediaGuide Quarterly*, which will appear on newsstands this coming fall. The *Quarterly* will be an exceedingly informative and entertaining periodical devoted to the global political economy. Its vantage point will be just a little bit higher than any other periodical published today, as it will view the world through the prism of the print media *as a whole*. Each issue will contain several essay length treatments on topics the editors deem to be sufficiently important and encompassing to engage the most refined tastes for information. Instead of assigning a reporter to tackle the subject as he or she would for *Newsweek, Fortune* or *The New York Times, MediaGuide Quarterly* will ask a specialist in the topic to present the state of the art by assessing the collective wisdom to be found in the media universe and beyond. The whole, we think, can easily be greater than the sum of its parts. Readers of *MediaGuide Quarterly* will feel themselves informed at a greater depth and with a higher degree of confidence than they possibly could by relying on a few random sources. The *Quarterly* will do so by drawing on the *exclusive* expertise we have developed over these past eight years in evaluating the strengths and weaknesses of the news media.

To whom will *MediaGuide Quarterly* and *MediaGuide 500* appeal? Everyone who takes seriously news of public affairs. These publications will assist us in grappling with the complexities of the information age, and they will do so with all the wit and excitement that naturally accompany the exploration of a world of knowledge. *MediaGuide*, there has never been anything quite like it.

Jude Wanniski

MAJOR STORIES OF 1992

THE THREE-WAY PRESIDENTIAL RACE

A WORLD TURNED UPSIDE DOWN

EUROPE 1992: A DREAM DISSOLVES

A THREE-WAY RACE
The Media vs. the Candidates vs. the Voters
by Patricia M. Koyce

The 1992 presidential election, easily the most extraordinary three-way political contest of the century, challenged the established political press corps as never before. The incumbent Republican, who in 1991 enjoyed stunning approval ratings in the opinion polls and seemed certain of re-election, dissolved like a snowman in spring. A citizen billionaire appeared from nowhere, drafted into the race by a television audience, and for a few improbable weeks took command. The Democratic nominee, the early press darling, was relegated to a distant third due to scorching revelations about his character, then quickly leaped to the fore as the amateur from Texas cracked up with breathtaking suddenness and dropped out to re-evaluate. It was, indeed, a zany contest, which frequently overwhelmed a political press that clung to tradition. From this perspective, as we watched the news media watch it all, the most unusual aspect of this election year was the profound shift in the way the electorate chose to receive its political information.

Some called the development "New News," a term coined by Jon Katz in "Rock, Rap and Movies Bring You the News," *Rolling Stone* 3-5. Katz described a culture in which the public would receive news primarily through infotainment. "Straight news—the Old News," he said, "is pooped, confused and broke." While his view overstated the case, it came as close as anything we saw to summing up in the vernacular an important phenomenon: frustrated by the alliance of a failing political establishment and the establishment press, the masses have been turning to unconventional sources to exchange information and shape the political process.

In "The Growing Irrelevance of Journalists," 10-23, *Washington Post* columnist Richard Harwood quoted NYU professor Jay Rosen who explained: "If journalists cannot convince the rest of us that they...are worth listening to, that they add something to public discourse that would be missing if they were not there, then the press will lose an asset of inestimable value." Just as the press has long been a watchdog of the government, rapid advances in technology now permit the electorate to become watchdogs of the press by presenting an unfiltered account of our political mechanisms and the people who run them. Voters are all too often finding a troubling gap between what they experience firsthand and what they learn through the prism of the media.

To get undistilled information, voters turned in astonishing numbers to forums where they could experience the candidates directly: radio and TV interview and call-in shows, op-eds, infomercials, books by the candidates, and, of course, televised debates. When the candidates wisely exploited this trend, journalists accused them of taking the easy way out, of skirting the media's "tough questions." The candidates said they were just trying to make sure their messages reached the people. Both positions held merit.

There were, of course, penetrating questions from the press among the hundreds of thousands asked during the course of the interminable campaign. All too often, though, the material that came through to the electorate from the political press focused in excruciating detail on matters that were once relegated to the supermarket tabloids: Bill Clinton's libido, his draft records, his student travels to Moscow, Paul Tsongas's medical history, President George Bush's shopping excursions, Ross Perot's private detectives, Jerry Brown's "moonbeam" stereotype, and Pat Buchanan's alleged anti-Semitism. Yes, there's a place for such detail in a presidential campaign and political mudslinging has long been the American way, but with the myriad of electronic and print news sources quantity has been increasingly driving out quality in long-established venues. The electorate, clearly trying to regain control of its political destiny, made its demands known in original ways this year.

In "Ask a Silly Question," *The New Republic* 7-6, Michael Kinsley compares a Bush press conference to a Perot two-hour call-in session on NBC's "Today Show" and notes that "the most striking difference between the two sets of questions, of course, is that the pros are obsessed with process while the amateurs are obsessed with substance." Yet, while admitting he would be "hard-put to argue that on balance the insider professionals with press passes dangling from their necks asked better questions than the amateurs who got through to 'Today's' 800 number," Kinsley fudges: "I do not subscribe to today's fashionable pseudo-populism, which holds that all wisdom lies with ordinary citizens, who are rightly outraged at all those out-of-touch, inside the Beltway cultural elitists who are wrecking the country, etc. etc. etc." Indeed, Kinsley's comments reflect the creeping arrogance that guides the analysis of the established political media. The high priests of political journalism posture as if they possess more certain knowledge of governance than the poor louts who buy their papers and periodicals and view their programs.

Part of the problem, we surmise, is that the political press has increasingly attached itself to the permanent class of political pros who have become "scientific" in telling us what the masses want, through elaborate opinion polls, focus groups, and mass mailings that target the lowest common denominator. After the 1988 election, this establishment process concluded that Bush had won the election by gutter tactics and jingoism, Willie Horton and the flag. In '92, the same alliance of press and pros made similar assumptions about the electorate, and the people, fed up, turned to sources that involved no middleman. Candidates discovered the efficiency of programs such as "Larry King Live," "Donahue," C-Span's relentless cameras, and what Perot introduced as the "electronic town hall." Eventually all the major candidates would appear on King's show, a first for the genre. High ratings for Perot's infomercials and biographic film led Clinton to follow suit with his own rendition, airing election eve. Albert Gore's *Earth in the Balance* and Perot's *United We Stand*, slung together after his summer hiatus, went right to the bestseller lists. Different policy proposals in pamphlet form, such as Tsongas's "An Economic Call to Arms" and Clinton's "Putting People First," were hot items. Once the electorate got an unedited glimpse of the candidates, the floodgates opened. As Jonathan Alter put it in his *Washington Monthly* essay, "How Phil Donahue Came to Manage the '92 Campaign," 6-92: "At their best, Phil, Larry and Brian Lamb's C-Span interviews are as democratic as American media politics gets."

One of the clearest signs that the Fourth Estate wasn't getting the point of this revolt was its anointing of Bill Clinton as the front-runner well before a single primary vote had been cast. Having scientifically concluded in 1991 that it was practically impossible for anyone to beat George Bush, the political press told the voters that Governor Clinton was the best of the Democratic lot, and it seemed we might as well dispense with the election. It was this discouraging atmosphere that became the impetus for the Perot campaign, as desperate voters reached out for a genuine outsider to break up this game.

The Washington Post's Howard Kurtz provided a handy inventory of where things stood early in the year with "In Quadrennial Rite, Press Bestows Front Runner Status: It's Clinton," 1-12: "'The person to beat' (USA Today); 'on a roll' (Los Angeles Times); 'the putative Democratic front-runner' (Washington Post columnist Jim Hoagland); 'at least a nominal front-runner' ([Sun columnist Jack] Germond); 'the likely front-runner' (U.S.News & World Report); and 'the contender with the most polished message and the sharpest organization' (The Wall Street Journal)." Our favorite was Margaret Carlson's description in "Bill Clinton: Front Runner by Default," *Time* 12-30-91: Clinton as "Doogie Howser, succeeding at everything he tried."

With the prestige of the political press committed to this horse, all other entries faced an automatic handicap. As Eleanor Clift put it in "Character Questions," *Newsweek* 2-10: "The press is willing to cut Clinton some slack because they like him—and what he has to say.

He is a policy wonk in tune with a younger generation of Democrats eager to take the party beyond the liberal stereotype."

Support for Clinton came at the expense of Clinton's Democratic primary challengers in the form of less coverage, less serious coverage or outright negative coverage, depending on the news source. At *The New York Times*, the political writers in the Washington bureau for the most part performed competently and even-handedly. It was the powers that be in New York that seemed obsessed with electing Clinton, massaging news, opinions and headlines to that end from start to finish.

Political historians will marvel at the way the *Times* handled Jerry Brown's campaign, for example. Early on, when Brown's campaign seemed no threat to Clinton, the *Times* applauded when he unveiled a flat-tax proposal as the primary plank in his economic platform. Its chief economic editorial writer, Michael Weinstein, had studied under one of the California economists who had developed the idea. In the signed editorial "The Beauty of the Flat Tax," 3-9, Weinstein saluted Stanford economist Robert Hall, who co-authored the proposal "that forms the basis for Mr. Brown's flat tax." But when Brown began accumulating primary victories and was surging in New York with the flat tax as *the* issue, the *Times* denounced Brown's version in advance of the New York primary in "Fairness and a Flat Tax," by Steven Greenhouse 3-26, and the editorial "Mr. Brown's Flat Tax Tilted," 3-27. The paper also cited an "impartial" study purporting to show that the proposal was deeply flawed. Brown was swamped by the chorus. The only journalist to point out that the "impartial" study was done by a Washington lobby with direct ties to the Clinton campaign was Alexander Cockburn, *The Nation* columnist, who also demonstrated that the study contained manipulated statistics.

While the established political press is not about to go the way of the dinosaur, it is in danger of becoming trivial.

"Why the Left Should Support the Flat Tax," *WSJ* 4-2, co-authored by economist Robert Pollin, destroyed the Citizens for Tax Justice's (CTJ) "double counting" arguments. After Clinton secured the nomination, the *Times* returned to support the flat-tax idea in an editorial, "Why Stop at a Flatter Tax?" 8-11: "If the Republicans wanted boldness, all they had to do was adapt Mr. Brown's plan, correcting its glaring but remediable errors. That could produce a plan that's truly pro-growth." But when Clinton showed no interest in the idea, it was no longer mentioned.

The New York editors of the *Times* also contrived another economic factoid, perhaps inadvertently at first, one that seemed to clinch the Clinton argument that during the Reagan/Bush years the rich got richer and the poor poorer. The Page One misinformation, in early March, was trumpeted gleefully by Clinton for the duration of the campaign, resounding throughout the press as a repudiation of Reaganomics. It began when Sylvia Nasar, a PhD economist in the New York office, reported as *fact* MIT economist Paul Krugman's assessment of a CBO income data survey which *alleged*, "Even Among the Well-Off, the Richest Got Richer: Data Show Top 1% Got 60% of the Gain in the 80s Boom," 3-5. Just as the *Times* failed to note the connection of the CTJ and the Clinton campaign, Nasar failed to inform *Times* readers that Krugman was a partisan Democrat and Clinton advisor. The story contained no independent judgment of the Krugman assessment of the CBO study; Nasar didn't even check Krugman's arithmetic. Nor did we learn that the CBO data encompasses 1977–89, which includes the Carter years. When the CBO issued a press release the following day, protesting the misinterpretation of its data, not a word could be found of this correction in the "newspaper of record." *The Wall Street Journal* addressed the question in an editorial, "CBO Sues for Divorce," 5-11, in which the writer noted that the CBO data used could lead to vastly different conclusions depending on the calculations. The *Journal* reported that "in response to the Krugman-Times efforts, [CBO director Robert Reischauer] recently took the extraordinary step of issuing an eight-page memo 'to clarify some of the confusion surrounding the meaning and derivation of estimates reported in the original New York Times article.' He also warned about the 'limitations to analyses of incomes.' Yet while Mr. Krugman made page one, Mr. Reischauer's caveats somehow aren't deemed news fit to print." Instead, the *Times* had played politics with the issue in "The Rich Get Richer And What to Do About It," 4-19, an editorial proudly announcing Clinton was "[inciting] voters with his favorite statistic: The richest one percent of families got 60 percent of the increase in average family income between 1977 and 1989."

Nasar massaged yet another study to reinforce this theme in "Fed Gives New Evidence of 80's Gains by Richest," 4-21. This article was based on the 1989 Survey of Consumer Finances, the most comprehensive source on family income available, and more importantly, a source which dealt solely with the period 1982–89. Once again, though, she juggled numbers and concepts to support the headline, with no attempt to clear her assertions with independent sources, let alone Reagan or Bush economists. In her 5-11 article, "However You Slice the Data the Richest Did Get Richer," the reason why was shamelessly evident: "When Bill Clinton wants to galvanize his audience, he thunders from the podium that the top 1 percent of families got 60 percent of the gains from economic growth during the 1980's.... Governor Clinton, the likely Democratic Presidential nominee, had been searching for months for facts to illustrate his claim that America's middle class benefited little from 12 years of Republican rule. The explosion of riches at the top struck him as a perfect vehicle....' He was reading the paper that morning and went crazy,' said Dee Dee Myers, the campaign's press secretary, referring to a New York Times article in March that reported on the wildly disproportionate gains of the top 1 percent. 'The story proved a point he had been trying to make for months, so he added the statistic to his repertoire.'"

The mass media, for all its crowing over Bush's breaking of the "No New Taxes" pledge, scrupulously avoided mention of the inescapable fact that the Bush administration had abandoned the growth strategy of the Reagan years, which was in large part why he was elected, in favor of old-fashioned budget control in collaboration with the Democratic establishment. So smug had the press elite become in its certainty that the voters did not know what was best for them, that they frequently insisted George Bush should never have made his "read my lips" pledge in the first place. There were exceptions, as in Paul Gigot's columns in *The Wall Street Journal* and Paul Craig Roberts in *The Washington Times*. The Beltway bible *National Journal* also weighed in with Jonathan Rauch's "The Regulatory President," 11-30-91, citing Bush's replacement of many of Reagan's free enterprise policies with restrictive regulations reminiscent of the Carter years. Coupled with the tax increases of the 1990 budget deal with Congress, Bush's policies were obviously counter to those that led to the Reagan boom.

By the fall, the press corps had positioned the election as a referendum on Reaganomics, rather than Bush's execution of Reaganomics. In the *Washington Post* series "The Mortgage on America," Steven Mufson lumped together the national debt and the Reagan-Bush policies. We find that "an entire era of reckoning has arrived" in "Debt Spree Leaves a Painful Legacy," 9-27. With "The Political Path to a Debt Crisis," 9-28, Mufson simply blames Reagan and Bush, without examining the dynamics of the boom he condemns as responsible for the deficit. Even when the economic news was good, it wasn't good enough. As the figures improved, noted Jonathan Peterson, Republicans would use the 2.7% rise in third-quarter GDP "as evidence of a long-awaited economic turnaround and trumpeted the findings at their campaign stops," in "Economy Grows at a Brisk 2.7%," *Los Angeles Times* 10-28.

A serious study of economic history can teach us much, but instead the political press establishment gave us the facts that fit their agenda. It was no wonder that Clinton and Tsongas wrote their own lengthy, detailed pamphlets laying out their economic plans, so that no one could distort their record. It was also no wonder that "10,000 copies of 'An Economic Call to Arms' were gone in the first day of printing," according to Tsongas's secretary Diane Ossinger. Ross Perot ran half-hour infomercials with bland, technical charts. He went into great detail about the country's economic situation. And the audience ate it up. An estimated 20 million viewers tuned into his first infomercial. According to Neilsen, this half-hour averaged a 12.2 rating/20 share nationally, slightly higher than the 12.0 rating/20 share average of the opening National League playoff game between the Atlanta Braves and Pittsburgh Pirates. Clearly, the voters were looking for facts, and they weren't finding enough of them in the press.

Since any critical scrutiny of Bush's record threatened to break the link with Reaganomics, the media focused on the man, who it claimed "just didn't get it." Beginning with Bush's trip to J.C. Penney's in late 1991, the press portrayed him as sadly out of touch with today's world. Instead of Desert Storm's fearless leader, Bush was portrayed as an amiable, aloof buffoon. In "Bush Encounters the Supermarket, Amazed," *NYT* 2-5, Andrew Rosenthal has Bush awed over "an electronic pad used to detect check forgeries," and a new generation of electronic scanners, which Rosenthal noted had been in use since 1980. The network news on Bush was also negative. According to a Center for Media and Public Affairs study, a whopping 71 percent of the comments about Bush on the national evening news were disapproving, as opposed to 48 percent for Clinton and 55 percent for Ross Perot.

More than any other candidate, Ross Perot was the subject of the media's ire. When Perot returned to the campaign in the fall, after withdrawing in July, the establishment political media made no attempt to hide its feelings. Thomas B. Rosenstiel articulated their sentiments perfectly in "Reporters See Perot as Object of Derision," *LAT* 10-7. "He's Back," 10-12, *Time* announced hauntingly, while *Newsweek* editorialized, "Ego Trip," 10-12. Bush played on this press-created theme by saying Perot had "some nutty ideas." Ultimately, concluded *Time*'s Michael Kramer, "Don't Waste Your Vote," 11-2. But even after Perot's exit from the race and all his bad press, 20 percent of the U.S. population decided to "waste" their vote on Perot; as a result he remains a potent political force in this country. Either the electorate ignored the onslaught of bad press, or they simply rejected it, coming to a different conclusion after watching Perot's infomercials and talk-show appearances. Perot, more than any of the three candidates, defined himself for the voters through direct communication that bypassed the establishment political press.

Jon Katz put it well in "The Plugged-In Voter," *RS* 12-10/24: "Reporters, did, in fact, hate Perot's candidacy, a stinging rebuke to them and their impact on politics.... Everything he promised to do to politics he did to the media, breaking open the decades-old monopoly they have had over presidential politics.... Perot paid dearly for his gall. The press attacked him continuously from the moment it was clear how he intended to run his campaign.... He was cast as a dangerous and troubled man ... a monomaniac, a paranoid and a liar. That we still don't know which Perot was real—the Caligula of the early and late campaign or the sensible, homespun CEO of the debates, shows how frantic and unnerved journalists were by his renegade candidacy."

Indeed, Stephen Holmes and Doron P. Levin were casting him as a man of mystery in April, with "A Man Who Says He Wants to Be Savior, If He's Asked," *NYT* 4-13. Sidney Blumenthal hammered away at the Texan in such *New Republic* essays as "The Mission," 7-6, alleging without concrete evidence that, "according to a reliable eyewitness," Perot had his children followed, their friends investigated, and "has forced his children to cut off close relationships, personally threatening to 'ruin the lives' of certain friends he didn't like."

The establishment media covered Perot because the public demanded it at the most basic level. Not connected to any independent party, Perot's willingness to serve, revealed on "Larry King Live," 2-20, spawned a grassroots movement so powerful it could not be ignored. His well-funded United We Stand America movement successfully navigated the bureaucracy to get Perot on the ballot in all 50 states. Without similar clout or economic resources, independent party candidates became political footnotes. Andre Marrou, Libertarian party candidate, was mentioned only four times in the *NYT*, most prominently in William Safire's "The Fourth Man," 10-22, and Francis X. Clines's "He's on Every State Ballot, If Not on Every Voter's Lips," 10-28. But these stories came *very* late in the campaign. There was *no* mention of Marrou in the *Times* from February to October. *The Washington Post* was generous, mentioning Marrou fourteen times. Despite the fact that this candidate was on the ballot in all 50 states, just as Perot was, the mainstream press had decided that voters did not need to know about him or his proposals. Even three candidates were too many to cover.

This does not mean there were no serious or outstanding efforts. There were many selections that challenged the perspective of the electorate and/or altered the debate. As the media was proclaiming Clinton the front-runner, Rowland Evans and Robert Novak weighed in with their evaluation of how Mario Cuomo's decision not to run and the Democratic party's centrist drift would aid Clinton in "Clinton the Front-Runner," *WP* 1-3. Rather than anointing Clinton, the pair considered the political dynamic at work, crafting a scenario that played out with astonishing accuracy. Paul Craig Roberts, a PhD economist, has grown steadily more effective as a syndicated columnist and handed Bush an issue that might have saved his campaign with "Instant Way to Cut Capital Gains Tax?" *The Washington Times* 1-22, an idea debated behind the scenes until nearly election day. Before the GOP convention, in "'A Figure of Genuine Pathos,'" *WP* 7-29, conservative columnist George Will asked the unthinkable: should Bush even be running? Bob Woodward crafted a strong indictment of the Bush administration's handling of economic policy with the series "Making Choices," *WP* 10-4, 10-5, 10-6, 10-7, detailing the disarray at Treasury and OMB at a crucial time. And William Safire's striking analysis of Bush's "inordinate fear of running without solid support from the far right" was unmatched, "Bush's Gamble," *NYT Magazine* 10-18.

While the established political press is not about to go the way of the dinosaur, it is in danger of becoming trivial. In their efforts to shape the debate, to play the advocate—no matter how well intentioned—journalists have drifted from their most important function as providers of news. In many cases they have hindered the flow of information and thus the political process that they purport to defend. As information means power, the electorate will continue to seek out more reliable alternatives. As we look back on the media's coverage of the 1992 campaign, Richard Harwood's advice to his fellow journalists in "The Growing Irrelevance of Journalists," 10-23, rings in our ears: "something is happening here that is not trivial. It deserves our attention."

A WORLD TURNED UPSIDE DOWN
by Richard Doyle

For the world at large, 1992 was a miserable year for political leadership. This was supposed to be the first year of a New World Order, with the victorious winners of the Cold War at least moving toward fresh rules-of-the-road to handle regional conflicts. This was to be the first year of market economics in Russia—with the Soviet Union dissolved, a newly-elected democratic president in charge, and the introduction January 1 of economic "shock therapy" to jolt Russia and the republics toward capitalism.

It was also going to be the brave, new year of Europe, with the finishing touches for monetary union and economic integration in place.

Instead, there was frustration or failure on almost every front, from one end of the year to the other. The Cold War was over, but the international environment was as perilous as ever, and in some ways more so. It was certainly more complicated, posing an entire new set of challenges for the press, and the government and institutions it covers. The press corps was as confused and as helpless in this tricky new environment as were the presidents, prime ministers and parliaments.

While the former Soviet Union has not yet exploded into the sort of nuclear-tinged civil war many were fearing as it plunged into the unknown, the "shock therapy" produced so few results and so much agony that by year's end President Boris Yeltsin and his reform government were forced to retrace their steps. In Europe, the timetable for political and economic integration had to be scrapped as the Maastricht treaty was rejected at the grassroots, first by the people of Denmark, then by general consensus. It did not help that Germany, the central actor in the new monetary scenario, chose 1992 to deflate its currency, dragging everyone else into further economic stagnation. While its weakened European neighbors and the United Nations watched in paralysis, the former Yugoslavia slid once again into a new round of savage civil warfare following Bosnia and Herzegovina's Declaration of Independence. Third World countries such as Haiti, Somalia, Liberia, and Cambodia, which once figured prominently in the calculations of Cold War strategists, struggled to cope, unsuccessfully, with economic deprivation and political chaos. Indeed, it was a year of awesome challenge for the world's leaders, as well as the journalists chronicling their successes and failures.

Yet with all of the international crises demanding attention, the United States began the year in what many observers felt was almost an isolationist mode. The New World Order took a distant backseat to the U.S. presidential campaign, which had less foreign policy discussion than any in memory. President George Bush, Governor Bill Clinton and Mr. Ross Perot generally ignored foreign policy, except to argue all year about whether the U.S. or Mexico would gain more from a free-trade agreement. BBC correspondent John Simpson, in "The Closing of the American Media," *The Spectator* 7-18, argued that "In the 30 years during which I have visited the United States regularly, I have never found it quite as self-absorbed as it is today." He heaped scorn on the U.S. press, both broadcast and print, for neglecting international news except when it concerned America or Americans directly. NBC's Tom Brokaw told reporter Bill Carter in "Networks Cutting Back on Foreign Coverage," *The New York Times* 6-10, that with the end of the Cold War "the whole nation started turning inward, with the main concerns being about what's going on inside our own borders."

There were, of course, exceptions. In the early spring, former President Richard Nixon tried to jump-start a debate within the nation's political circles and op-ed pages on aid to Russia. Nixon circulated a memo among foreign policy elites lambasting President Bush's handling of the post-Soviet Union, calling the aid offered thus far "penny ante," and warning that if Yeltsin fell, the biggest political question of the 1990s would be "Who Lost Russia?" The memo quickly found its way into the press. *NYT* "Foreign Affairs" columnist Leslie H. Gelb, in "Nixon's Tricky Crusade," 3-13, labeled Nixon "the Old Trickster," and complained about "foreign policy mandarins who...seem perpetually more interested in Russia than Amer-

If shocking TV images dictate foreign policy, the Information Age will degenerate into the Age of Misinformation.

ica." However, as fellow *Times* columnist William Safire wrote at the time of a key Russian parliamentary session and President-elect Bill Clinton's "economic summit," in "Kozyrev's Wake-up Slap," *NYT* 12-17: "No stunting going on in Little Rock is more important to the job future of Americans than the reformers' success in Moscow."

For the most part, though, the Western press was content to report on the saga from Moscow within the old Cold War parameters. Boris Yeltsin and his reform architect, Finance Minister Yegor Gaidar, were "good guys" struggling against reactionary "hard liners." There was also the "tough road to capitalism" theme that declared that the hardships borne by the Russians were "necessary steps."

We cannot remember a single notable dispatch from the press professionals in Moscow that left the slightest possibility that the shock therapy being administered was not what the patient required. A line from a *Washington Post* editorial, "Price Shock in Russia," 1-5, seemed to set the tone of Russian coverage in 1992: "Serious economic reform always begins harshly." Occasionally a dissenting voice would be heard in an op-ed essay or column. Former Czechoslovakian Deputy Prime Minister Valtr Komarek, in "Shock Therapy and Its Victims," *NYT* 1-5, wrote that "shock therapy is out of touch with reality," and "ignores the impact of such an approach on the vast educated, skilled classes of Eastern Europe." *New York* "Bottom Line" columnist Christopher Byron, in "Save the Bear," 1-13, argued that "what Russia and its sister republics really need to get this crisis behind them is a package of monetary and financial reforms to stabilize the ruble before the situation gets completely out of hand."

There was virtually nothing with a Russian dateline in 1992 that came close to testing the assumptions of how to go about managing a conversion from a command to a market economy. The press contingent in Moscow *en masse* assured us that Gaidar's critics in the Russian parliament were simply opposed to reform. When in December, Yeltsin was forced to remove Gaidar, and nothing dire occurred, the press had to scramble to find a new context. An article early in the year, by *WP* bureau chief Michael Dobbs, briefly lit up the sky. There had been warnings that freeing prices on January 1 would lead to immediate chaos, absent a preliminary currency reform. No such chaos occurred. We learned why in the 10 Best selection "Officials, Not Market, Still Set Prices," *WP* 1-3, in which Dobbs takes the trouble to ask a manager of State Grocery No. 2: "How do you set prices now that they have been 'freed' by the Russian government?" The grocer's reply: "The same as before.... I pick up the phone and make a call." Former *WP* Moscow correspondent David Remnick, in the 10 Best selection "The Trial of the Old Regime," *The New Yorker* 11-30, was able to capture the malaise gripping the country by observing the on-going trial of the country's former communist bosses. *Barron's* correspondent Maggie Mahar, in such dispatches as "Economic Miracle or Catastrophe?" 1-13, and "Wolf at the Door," 10-19, provided far more interesting insights about the Russian plight than other journalists who merely quoted the same old insider sources.

The deteriorating situation in Russia was the subject of cover stories in two of the leading newsweeklies at the end of the year, in the 12-7 issues of both *U.S. News & World Report* and *Time*. Both magazines painted a Chekovian portrait of a nation struggling to come to grips with loss and despair. Underpinning both reports was the faith of the Western press corps that the conversion to market capitalism would require large infusions of cash from Western taxpayers. But whereas *USNWR* was at best fatalistic about the prospects of Western aid, noting that incoming President Bill Clinton would have to deal with the "false hopes and misconceptions on both sides," *Time* Editor at Large Strobe Talbott, who has been nominated by Clinton as ambassador at large and special adviser to the Secretary of State on the new independent states, argued in "A Miracle Wrapped in Danger," that "if the U.S. is going to reap domestic dividends from the end of the cold war, Clinton must help Yeltsin prevail on his own home front." We became exhausted reading assessments of whether a few billion dollars in such aid would be forthcoming.

Reporting on the momentous changes occurring in China's political economy was slightly better, if only because the evidence of the fastest-growing economy in the world could hardly have been missed. The last of the communist superpowers was somehow successfully converting to entrepreneurial capitalism without vast infusions of foreign aid. Instead, vast amounts of investment capital were pouring in from ethnic Chinese abroad and from foreign investors. There were attempts, at least, to figure out why, and we were pleased with some of the results. In the best single piece of reporting on China all year, the 10 Best selection "When China Wakes," *The Economist* 11/28-12/4, Jim Rohwer asserts without overstatement that if China's economic potential is unleashed "the world is in for the biggest change since the industrial revolution." Orville Schell and Todd Lappin, in "Underwriting Communism in China," *WP* 3-18, summed up the situation sharply when they observed that "In a macabre way, [China's] political system has demonstrated an astonishing talent for grafting laissez-faire branches onto an old and despotic Leninist trunk."

This assessment seemed fair enough, but we were still disappointed by our search for analysis on the political dynamics in Beijing. As in Moscow, the press contingent seemed to require "good guys" and "hardliners" to convey a sense of what was unfolding. When in November, the new Governor of Hong Kong, Christopher Patten, challenged Beijing over the path of Hong Kong's reversion to the mainland, the entire press corps dutifully leaped to his defense, having found a "good guy." Indeed, *Time*, which had named Chinese leader Deng Xiaoping as its "Man of the Year," in 1978 and 1985, named Patten as a runner-up for "Man of the Year" in 1992, writing in "Hong Kong's Brash Viceroy," 1/4-93, that Patten had "challenged the status quo with a limited but novel plan to widen democratic representation." What their readers missed was any sense of the underlying commercial interests involved. Indeed, the position of the Beijing government—that these matters had already been resolved—was hardly to be found in the U.S. press.

Clearly, nailing down stories on China was not always that easy. Beat reporters, from time to time, had to put up with harassment from state security officials, especially when testing the limits. *WP* Beijing bureau chief Lena Sun experienced such harassment first hand and recounted the experience in "Beijing Authorities Harass Reporter," 5-18. However, correspondents such as Sun, Nicholas D. Kristof of *NYT*, James McGregor of *The Wall Street Journal*, David Holley of the *Los Angeles Times*, and Uli Schmetzer of the *Chicago Tribune* were often able to bypass the restrictions and capture vignettes of daily life in the Chinese capital, and in China's southeast provinces where the reforms were taking place.

At times, the daily reporters captured the nuances of the ongoing political debate taking place behind the scenes, but it was only at year's end, with the conclusion of the 14th Party Congress, that a full perspective could be offered. In the best essay on Chinese politics in 1992, Roderick MacFarquhar, in "Deng's Last Campaign," *The New York Review of Books* 12-17, documented how the year-long policy battle was being driven by a combination of ideological differences, personal animosities and raw ambition; the participants engaging in long-running battles that had their origins in the days of the Cultural Revolution—and earlier. Consequently, MacFarquhar concluded, while Deng and the reformers won a major victory by all appearances, "clearly Deng does not think [the reform program has become entrenched] or he would not have left the bridge table to tour the country. He knows from CCP history that realism has never been an obstacle to determined ideologues convinced of their rectitude."

From the very beginning of 1992, when *The New Yorker*, reported in "The Talk of the Town," 1-6, that "Many Somalis ask the obvious question: If the world can pay so much attention to Yugoslavia, why does it ignore what is happening in their country?" to the very end, when *Time*, on its 12-21 cover, asked the question: "Clinton's first foreign challenge: If Somalia, why not Bosnia?" Somalia and the former Yugoslavia were at the forefront of international coverage and of concerns of policymakers. More than once the question was raised if a causal effect was involved. What is certain is that, as Gerald B. Helman and Steven R. Ratner documented in "Saving Failed States," *Foreign Policy* Winter 1992-93, "Civil Strife, government breakdown, and economic privation are creating more and more modern *debellatios*, the term used in describing the destroyed German state after World War II."

As *The New Yorker* suggested, both the former Yugoslavia and Somalia were ongoing stories all year, but both exploded into public consciousness in August, when the TV networks, with CBS and the "MacNeil/Lehrer NewsHour" in the lead, began airing footage of the victims of the Somalian famine. Then the news broke of so-called "death camps" being set up by the Serbs in Bosnia and Herzegovina. It was a print reporter, Roy Gutman, Europe correspondent of New York's *Newsday*, who, in "Survivors Tell of Captivity, Mass Slaughters in Bosnia," 8-2, first broke the story of the nightmarish conditions of incarceration in a former iron-mining complex at Omarska. Several days later a crew from the British network ITN visited Omarska and another Serb camp at Trnopolje. The horrifying footage, which was replayed on U.S. television and given prominent space in the periodical press, created, in the words of John Newhouse in "The Diplomatic Round," *TNY* 8-24, the "trap known as the CNN curve: a torrent of pictures of dismembered or tortured innocents could create pressure for using whatever it took to halt the violence, but then another torrent of pictures, this one of body bags containing young soldiers being unloaded in home ports, could create a reverse spin and, with it, political retribution."

Coverage of the civil war in Bosnia posed both professional challenges and physical dangers for journalists, including the presence of snipers and gunmen who seemed to target journalists in an unprecedented way. In November, the New York-based Committee to Protect Journalists reported that at least 26 journalists had been killed covering the fighting in the former Yugoslavia since the summer of 1991. One victim, ABC News producer David Kaplan, was killed in a van, the bullet coming through the letters "T" and "V" taped on the side. Anna Husarska, in "News From Hell," *TNY* 10-5, detailed why "All those who have reported from here, even seasoned war correspondents, agree that Sarajevo is the most dangerous assignment they've ever had." For one thing, there are the snipers, "who are allegedly paid five hundred German marks for each journalist hit."

A professional challenge to journalists covering Bosnia was placing the news in proper context. Charles Lane, in "When Is It Genocide?" *Newsweek* 8-17, wondered if "there [would] have been such a furor over the war in Bosnia last week if New York Newsday had not used the phrase 'death camps' in its front-page headline?" Lane went on to write of the necessity of "drawing a distinction between genocide and ethnic and tribal war." Occasionally there would be an article offering the Serbian perspective on the war, such as "Paranoid and Vengeful, Serbs Claim Their War Is to Right Old Wrongs," 9-18, by Roger Thurow and Tony Horwitz *WSJ*, and "History Is Another Recruit in the Balkan War," *NYT* 11-15, by Stephen Kinzer, but these were rare. As the international landscape increasingly is marked by ethnic feuds and nationalist warfare that have roots stretching back into the Middle Ages, reporters will need to cover the full dimensions of the story without condoning the actions of either side or engaging in any sort of "moral equivalency." They must enable news consumers to fully understand the situation as they and their governments debate whether to become militarily involved.

The so-called "CNN curve" also was at work in Somalia as footage from that star-crossed nation assumed a regular slot on the evening news and was the subject of gut-wrenching photo-spreads in the newsweeklies. However, it was in print reporting, through the efforts of Jane Perlez of the *NYT*, Michael Hiltzik of the *LAT*, Keith B. Richburg of the *WP* and Rick Lyman of *The Philadelphia Inquirer* that the full story behind the largely-manmade disaster of Somalia emerged. Hiltzik, the *LAT*'s Nairobi bureau chief, scored a 10 Best selection with "Somalia—Anatomy of a Famine," 9-24, in which he fully outlines how the famine came about through the breakdown of Somalia's political economy: "'Drought doesn't kill people, politics does,' said William Garvelink, a disaster specialist. . . . In Somalia, in 1991–92, civil strife and government collapse played the role that government interference did in 1980s Ethiopia. The factional fighting that followed Siad Barre's ouster restricted the nomad's movement, trapping them in waterless locations where their herds died. Fighting drove farmers off their land, separating them from their stocks and undermining crop output. In the past years, authorities could have responded to localized hunger by moving grain in or importing food from abroad, as is being done in Zambia and Zimbabwe, southern African countries hit this year by unprecedented drought. But with Siad Barre's departure, there was no longer any government in Somalia."

In late November, President Bush, speaking of the "shocking images" Americans, evidently including himself, had been witnessing, announced to the surprise of almost everyone that he was sending nearly 30,000 U.S. troops to Somalia to ensure the delivery of relief supplies and to restore some sort of order. Leslie H. Gelb, in "Shoot to Feed Somalia," *NYT* 11-19, revealed that on 11-20 the White House was going to hold a meeting in which "key Bush aides" were going to recommend U.S. intervention in Somalia. Gelb also reported that "disaster relief expert" Fred Cuny was also calling for U.S. troops to move in immediately and establish a security zone in southern Somalia. Cuny's call for U.S. military intervention was echoed the next day in an Anthony Lewis column, "Action or Death," *NYT* 11-20. Reporting on the behind-the-scenes activity surrounding the decision, in "The Path to Intervention," *WP* 12-6, Don Oberdorfer wrote that Cuny, who had advised AID on the U.S. military relief effort for the Kurds in northern Iraq, had also advised the State Department on the necessity for at least 2,500 troops shortly before the 11-20 meeting: "At the time, this was considered a very bold proposal." In the end, the decision received almost universal support from both the U.S. public and press, only a few observers, such as Henry Kissinger, in "Somalia: Reservations," *WP* 12-13, offering even cautious dissent.

The press did struggle briefly with the complex issues raised by such a humanitarian intervention, but it seemed difficult for them to be too critical. Observers questioning the propriety of using the military for ostensibly humanitarian purposes were few. Jim Hoagland, in "On Somalia, a Mysterious Decision," *WP* 12-3, argued that "Neither ease nor guilt is sufficient reason for a nation to engage its military force abroad, during hostilities."

At dawn, Somalia time, December 9, the U.S. Marines came ashore, "storming beaches heavily defended by cameramen," in the sardonic words of *TE* 12-12. Indeed, the heavy presence of journalists on the beach was the most controversial aspect of Operation Restore Hope. The Pentagon expressed dismay and claimed that the bright lights of the TV cameras would have jeopardized the lives of the Navy Seals had they encountered resistance. The press responded by claiming the military had invited the coverage and had issued no warning about TV lights. However, as Howard Rosenberg observed in "It's Only Show in Town for Single-Minded Newscasters," *LAT* 12-10: "If a journalist has to be specifically told about the dangers of turning on lights during a military operation executed in darkness, then he or she hasn't got enough smarts even to be there."

But increasingly, "he or she" will be there. ABC diplomatic correspondent Barrie Dunsmore, in "Military's Photo Op 'Got Out of Hand,'" *USA Today* 12-10, told Johanna Neuman that "[Somalia] is the culmination of the dream of every TV news executive since he first sent the first TV reporter, with a silent black and white film camera, to Vietnam in the early '60s.... It's now possible to have live —in living color—a military invasion."

Chicago Tribune Washington columnist Clarence Page, appearing on "The MacNeil/Lehrer NewsHour" 12-7, noted that we were entering an age of "video-driven foreign policy." Thomas L. Friedman, in "Clinton Inherits Conflicts That Don't Follow Rules," *NYT* 12-13, commented that "indeed, without a Soviet Union to compel and define American engagement abroad, CNN in some ways is taking its place."

Of course, an argument could be made that the role of the press, especially TV, in determining policy has been overblown. Indeed, Jonathan Alter, in "Did the Press Push Us Into Somalia?" *Newsweek* 12-21, did make that argument strongly, contending that TV may be structurally incapable of covering the full complexities of the post-Cold War world: "On TV, Somalia is larger than Russia, China and Europe combined right now; when the troops leave, it will disappear altogether."

Presidents, parliaments, people, and the press are just now sorting out their roles in a world which is undergoing breathtaking ideological and technological changes. Are these changes outracing man's ability to adapt to them? At times in 1992 it seemed so. If international coverage becomes driven solely by hardware, then the "New Information Age" will exist in name only, for information without understanding is misinformation, at best. As the crises in Somalia and the former Yugoslavia illustrate, issues of war and peace are literally hanging in the balance. For the press, both print and broadcast, the challenge of the post-Cold War, satellite-linked new world, is not just to capture and convey images of the victims of tribal warfare or U.S. soldiers in action, but to illuminate the stories behind the pictures and to give equal attention to important stories which do not easily lend themselves to photo-ops. The press must place *all* the planet's significant events in context. This is the only way news consumers and policymakers will be equipped to meet the challenges of today's fast-moving world. The events of 1992 suggest that if American foreign policy is driven by video, then the "new world order" may become one in which the press, public, and policymakers simply react to events overseas, finding themselves faced with a Hobson's choice of either doing nothing or sending troops in great numbers. Like the public, journalists have been empowered by the technological advances of the last several years, but their uneven performance in 1992 does not imply they will always use this new power wisely.

EUROPE 1992: A DREAM DISSOLVES
by Kathy McNamara

The United States was scheduled to hold elections in 1992. It did and a new president was elected. Europe was supposed to be integrated in 1992. It was not, and the dream of European unity turned into a frazzle of bickering and confusion. From this side of the Atlantic, the turnabout from carefully planned harmony to chaotic dissension seemed inexplicable. In the span of a single year, Europe signed a treaty at Maastricht that provided for the key link of monetary union, then saw all this handiwork dissolve in what appeared to be a popular rejection of Maastricht. What had gone wrong? We searched for answers.

Certainly the press, both in the U.S. and Europe, had not prepared us for the dramatic reversal that would take place after the treaty was signed. But gradually, the people and the media began to examine the implications of a monetary union dominated by a single central bank in Germany, which had coincidentally been turning inward to deal with its own domestic problems of integration. As in the United States, where the presidential election was thrown into confusion by a popular intervention on the part of a surprise third-party candidate, Europe '92 broke down at the hands of elite, un-elected Eurocrats who hadn't bothered to consult the ordinary people whose future was at stake. The first rumblings of discontent surfaced in spring elections throughout the Continent, followed by an outright rejection of the treaty by the Danes. With blinders on, the Eurocrats tried to force "unity" forward, but wild swings in the European currency markets in advance of a referendum in France derailed these plans. By the slimmest of margins, the French electorate endorsed Maastricht, but the feeble "*oui*" was universally interpreted as a popular demand for the Ruling Establishment to return to the drawing board.

Though late, the political press corps ably interpreted the popular consternation. The economic and financial press corps, though, seemed uncertain of the meaning behind the alarm bells being sounded by Europe's financial markets throughout the year. Black Wednesday, the day when Britain left the European Exchange Rate Mechanism after Europe's currencies began tumbling like so many dominoes, was the culmination of powerful political and economic forces that had been pushing and pulling the tectonic plates of the EC for many years. In the aftermath, economic writers on both sides of the Atlantic scrambled to explain the seemingly unexplainable. How could Britain, with very low inflation and a budget surplus, be forced out of the ERM at the same time as Italy, with its excessive inflation and deficits? The financial press groped and stretched for rationales. Just as it could not cope with the crosscurrents in the United States, with the dollar sinking amid relative calm on Wall Street, the financial press scratched its head as interest rates in Sweden soared into the triple digits and as London shares leapt joyously when the pound was cut loose from the ERM. Similarly, millions of words were written on the first serious economic decline in Japan in more than forty years, but the best analysis the press could give us on the dramatic downturn was that the Japanese had simply run out of steam. It was a year in which the realities of the global economy turned conventional economic wisdom on its head. The press searched among the pool of familiar economic wise men and standard interpretations. The handy answer frequently pulled off the shelf was that economic distress around the world was due to the chickens coming home to roost on the "excesses of the '80s" and the Reagan years. Obviously, there was much more to the story.

At the epicenter of the European crisis was the Maastricht treaty. Soon after it was signed, in a "burst of Euro-ardor," as Peter Gumbel of *The Wall Street Journal* put it, there were already voices questioning the manner in which the treaty was being forced forward. Gumbel noted the growing discontent, in "Europe's Spirits Over Unity Begin to Sink," *WSJ* 3-24: "Reasons for the backlash vary, but the dissidents all share an uneasiness about losing control of their national affairs on the road to monetary union." For one thing, the cost of unification was becoming apparent just as the benefits were being questioned, a development noted in *National Review*'s "The Week" column, 4-27: "Jacques Delors, EC Commission president, has announced that the transition will cost the Community an additional $75 billion in member-state contributions over five years; he and others have bruited about the idea of letting the EC levy taxes directly on individuals or businesses. This was greeted, appropriately, with howls. *Le Figaro* said it best: 'We pay tax to the city, we pay tax to the county, we pay tax to the region, we pay tax to the nation, and now we must pay tax to Europe; why not to the United Nations as well?'" The Deutschemark's position as the anchor currency added to concerns about economic and political autonomy—sentiments expressed quite bluntly in a London *Spectator* editorial, "The Giant Stumbles," 1-25: "We should blame our own government for locking us into a system in which one country can so easily sway the rest, and where the process of domination is glorified as the achievement of 'unity.'"

Indeed, because of the currency issue, Germany was the fulcrum on which European unity balanced. Almost nine months before Black Wednesday, in "Which Market Is Wrong," *Barron's* 1-6, Randall Forsyth recognized the pressures that were already building: "The Bundesbank will hold the key to European bond market returns.... Other European central banks would prefer to lower rates as their economies slow. But they have been forced to hold their interest rates up, or actually raise them in some cases, in order to maintain their currencies' values vs. the mark. . . . The conflict between maintaining tight monetary policy, as dictated by the ERM, or easing policy, as domestic economics would dictate, is growing. Moreover, it's spilling over into the political realm." A more prescient assessment we did not find.

Had European leaders listened to their electorates early in the year, they would have known well before events came to a head that they were taking the wrong road. Across the Continent, voters were becoming increasingly frustrated. As Britain contemplated its choices in the April 9 election, *The Economist* quipped, "May the worst lot lose." In Italy, the Christian Democrats polled their lowest totals in post-war history, 29% in the April elections. French voters in the March cantonal election rejected the ruling Socialists, forcing the resignation of PM Edith Cresson. Germany's Christian Democrats and Social Democrats were both trounced in the April state elections. The *Süddeutsche Zeitung* editorialized on 4-7: "If anything gives rise to dourness, it is not the difficult-to-calculate behavior of the citizenry, but rather the unwillingness of the political class to learn any lessons from it."

European politicians were still not getting the message. By mid-year, the Danish vote against the treaty in a national referendum on June 2 became the first of many tremors leading to Black Wednesday. The political press, for its part, was beginning to understand the gravity of the problem, as David Marsh of the *Financial Times* made clear in his 10 Best selection, "Out of Step with the People," 6-9: "[The Danish vote] has focused attention on an apparent lack of democratic backing for the goal of greater European integration. . . . The squalls unleashed by the Danish 'No' are, however, clearly not just about European integration. Voters are showing discontent over European policies partly, it seems, as a means of expressing wider irritation with the political parties which govern them. . . . During the months before the Maastricht agreement in December last year, there was in most EC countries astonishingly little public debate on the exact nature of the institutional and economic changes planned by the EC."

European leaders vowed to push forward despite the Danish "setback," a mistake Noel Malcolm critiqued in "Heads in the Sand," *The Spectator* 7-20: "The perfect symbol for the European Community at this crucial moment in its history: an ostrich with its head in the sand. . . . What had gone wrong in Denmark? The first error was to allow the Danish people to find out what was in the treaty. Half a million copies were printed, and they sold out within a week. 'It is a mistake to let people see the treaty,' said one prominent member of the European Parliament, the French socialist Jean-Pierre Cot; 'they will only misunderstand it.' But many Danes seem to have understood it all too well. . . . If a single common theme emerges, it is that millions of ordinary voters feel that they have not been properly represented or even consulted."

Forsyth's predictions were coming true—the conflict between domestic economic pressures and the constraints of the ERM were growing and spreading into the political sector. In addition, the rush toward monetary union as required by Maastricht had generated a destructive anti-inflation zealotry on the part of European policymakers and central bankers. Inflation had become "the lodestar of policy" as one journalist put it. And, as in the U.S., "deficit" had become a dirty word. It did not matter if the deficit resulted from one-time productive investment expenditures by a government, as in the case of Germany, or if it was the outcome of government waste. In the press, as in Europe's policy circles, deficits were Deficits, with a capital D for the Drag they placed on the real economy. As Deficit and Inflation Reduction became the focal point of fiscal and monetary planning, Austerity was the mantra that could be heard across the land. Tax rates went up, interest rates were raised, budgets were cut. Indeed, several countries greatly reduced inflation and deficits. A fact that was touted often in the press, in such articles as "The End of Inflation?" *TE* 2-22: "In the OECD countries inflation is now hovering around its 1960s level of 3-4%." Unfortunately, we saw extremely little discussion anywhere on the continuing decline in the price of gold and other sensitive commodities, *especially in Deutschemark*, although this has always been a sure signal of *deflation*— a squeeze on debtors that invites recession.

Because of this lapse, the press corps flocked to the answer preferred by the Eurocrats: blame it on German unity. As Alan Riding put it in "The High Cost of Unity," *The New York Times* 9-17: "The crisis is rooted in the high cost of German unification, which is driving up German interest rates at a time when other European countries need lower rates to help them out of their economic slowdown." We were told Chancellor Helmut Kohl had struck a "Faustian" bargain and now had to pay the price with harsh fiscal and monetary policies. Even the *Journal*, one of the few papers to recognize the drop of commodity prices in Europe, editorialized in "Money System Overload," 9-18: "Germany's problems can be dated to mid-1990, when Helmut Kohl over-ruled Bundesbank President Karl Otto Poehl and handed East Germans the gift of one powerful west mark for each puny east mark (or at least a large share of them). This was followed by very large commitments from Bonn to invest in the rehabilitation of East Germany..." The sympathy in the press for this explanation, based on its assumption that *the Bundesbank always knows best*, contributed to the political frictions and financial turbulence that were at the heart of Europe's problems. Despite the evidence that the Maastricht treaty had become a "straight jacket," as Margaret Thatcher put it, European leaders vowed to press onward no matter what the cost.

Why should the press bother to challenge, or even understand, the assumptions of conventional wisdom?

In July, we saw further signs that Germany's austerity measures were radiating distress throughout the Continent and across the Channel. On the anniversary of tax hikes on income (7.5%) and gasoline (37%) enacted in 1991, Bonn boosted the withholding tax on investment income by 5%, effective January 1, 1993. Interest from bank accounts would be taxed at 30%, and income from bonds and over-the-counter stocks at 35%. Also on January 1, the Value Added Tax rate would increase to 15% from 14%. In the U.S. press, at least, there was barely consideration given to the implications of these measures. A tiny "World Wire" blurb in the *WSJ*, "German Tax Spurs Cash Flight," 8-4, was about the best we saw: "German savers transferred an estimated 3 billion to 3.5 billion marks ($2.03 billion to $2.37 billion) each month to bank accounts in Luxembourg...before new taxes take effect next year. And the pace of such transfers is expected to increase, the weekly *Der Spiegel* said." In another news blurb in the *Journal*, "Spain Aims Tax Boosts at Deficit," 7-22, we saw the pain spreading in this German-led recession: "Spain's cabinet, in a move that would reverse most of last January's tax cuts...agreed to increase income tax rates in the highest bracket to 56% from 53% and in the lowest tax bracket to 18.5% from 18%, retroactive to January. . . . The government also agreed to raise the average rate of value-added tax to 15% from 13%." There was even talk of harmonizing European corporate tax rates, an idea that *TE*, 3-21, said would "simply mean that everyone had the same distortion." Europe was in the grip of tax fever.

The best analysis of the situation came late in the year from Stanford economist Ronald McKinnon, who outlined the distortions created by Germany's deflation on the op-ed page of the *FT* in "Why German Policy

Hurts at Home as Well as Abroad," 9-7: "The Bundesbank's mandate is to stabilize the level of German prices.... Consequently, if the German monetary authorities are to ease their policies, they must be convinced that they are violating their own mandate. And that is precisely what I believe the Bundesbank is doing. Present German monetary policy is unnecessarily tight for stabilizing domestic prices in the longer term. By implication, the German and world economies are experiencing unnecessary financial trauma." Indeed, an easing by the Bundesbank on September 14 brought global relief in the financial markets until it became clear that it was merely a token gesture. The currency crisis that culminated in Black Wednesday and the crack-up of Maastricht was underway, only a week after McKinnon's analysis made it into print.

Because the financial press had been so ardent in its backing of the Eurocrats going into Black Wednesday, its post-crisis efforts to explain what had gone wrong seemed especially feeble. Normally astute commentators such as Samuel Brittan of *FT* spilled plenty of ink trying to make sense of what had occurred. Brittan a strong supporter of the ERM, wrote in "Devaluation Threat—How '92 Differs," 9-17, that he had supported the devaluation of the pound in 1964 but could not support this one: "There is... one big difference in policies between now and then. When the Wilson government came to office in 1964, it was asked to choose between restricting domestic demand and devaluing the pound. It chose neither and tried to muddle through by overseas borrowing, income policies and marginal industrial intervention. By contrast the Major government is committed—like the French Socialist government—to a monetary and fiscal policy which gives top priority to maintaining the ERM parity rather than to 'growth' objectives." Here and throughout the financial press, there was practically no recognition that the British "devaluation" that snapped the ERM had correctly broken the Bank of England's chain to the Bundesbank's deflation. Why else would the London financial market have jumped for joy? In the U.S., we had expected the *Journal* to keep us informed on such issues, but the paper had joined the Eurocrat parade. George Melloan, editorial page editor of the *Journal's* European edition, had committed himself to the Maastricht treaty early on. Consequently, he continuously pooh-poohed those who questioned the logic of pound-Deutschemark link, in such columns as "Major Is Right to Resist the Coin Clippers," 7-27, and "Monetary Jitters: Deja Vu All Over Again," 8-31.

In Japan, the sun was also setting on a practically uninterrupted era of economic growth dating to the early 1950s. The persistent decline of the Tokyo stock market that had begun two years earlier was now creating staggering problems for Japan's industrial and financial establishment, as shrinking asset values eroded the collateral base of the Tokyo banks. There were plenty of stories to describe the anguish of these developments, but the press corps utterly failed to explain why Japan, which had been held up as a shining example of the glories of national industrial planning, had suddenly lost its magic.

We had thought that the political pressures on Japan from the other industrial nations must be at the heart of its problems, for the pressures had been explicitly aimed at suppressing the vitality of its economic machine. In 1988, the U.S. had passed a trade act designed to cripple Japan. The measure essentially required Japan to deflate its currency and puncture the value of its capital assets if it wished to keep open its U.S. export market. Japan's ruling elite, further weakened by a subsequent series of political scandals, buckled under to the incessant demands of U.S. Treasury Secretary Nicholas Brady. An effective doubling of the capital gains tax on real estate, to satisfy the U.S., took effect in 1990 just as the market decline began in earnest. Brady's aim was to reduce Japan's trade surplus with the United States, in the mistaken belief that this would strengthen the U.S. economy and enhance President Bush's chances for re-election. The process had the opposite effect, as Japan's weakened economy led to fewer purchases abroad and increased disgorging of products at distressed prices.

The Orwellian idea that a collapse in asset values could be *a good thing* implanted itself so thoroughly that the Establishment press treated it as axiomatic. An editorial in *FT* of June 18 smugly praised the Bank of Japan's undertaking "to deflate Japan's frighteningly large asset market bubble." Robert Samuelson told us in "Japan's Bubble Bursts," *The Washington Post* 3-18, that "Japan's problems are mostly self-inflicted. An orgy of easy credit and speculation drove the economy into a frenzied boom that's now collapsing." But there was a whole part of the story that was being missed in these shallow rhetoric-fests.

In April, the Nikkei stood as high as 18,436, but then Secretary Brady met with the G-7 finance ministers. Their deliberations produced a communiqué on April 27 that insisted upon an appreciation of the yen. The Nikkei promptly tumbled 2,000 points, threatening the capital requirements of Japanese banks. By May 12, the Nikkei had struggled back above the 18,000 level as the government took counter measures to save the banks. On that day, Treasury Undersecretary David Mulford, Brady's enforcer in Japan, told the Senate Banking Committee that the G-7 had to take additional steps to address Japan's trade surplus, that "in particular, we will have to watch the value of the yen." The yen soared against the dollar, and Japanese stocks crashed. On June 11, Mulford praised the yen's rise as "appropriate," and the Japanese market went into another tailspin.

Across the ocean, the U.S. dollar was trading at record lows against the Deutschemark and the yen. But no one seemed able to explain why two of the largest economies in the world with the two "strongest" currencies, Japan and Germany, were careening toward recession while the U.S. with its "weak" currency was beginning to emerge from a long recession. Like so many events this year, the paradoxes were striking. The major economic powers of the increasingly interconnected global economy seemed to be going their separate ways. The "transatlantic contrast," as *The Economist* described it in its 8-29 issue, raised other issues: "The dollar has plunged, and no American seems to give a hang. Yet Europeans are grimly determined to keep their places in the exchange-rate mechanism (ERM), regarding devaluation as a disgrace. Why this difference? Surely, in logic, both views cannot be right? Alas for logic, the answer is they can, at least in the short term." As the press grappled with its own illogic, the shallowness of this commentary was the rule, not the exception. Peter Passell of the *NYT*, a former economics professor who has one of the most influential posts in journalism, gave us this profound explanation in "Bonn Punches, the Dollar Rolls," 8-27: "Just why the dollar chose this month to head south is anyone's guess."

Instead of guessing, Passell and others might have been paying attention to what was happening at the Federal Reserve, the central bank of the world's superpower. For the past two decades, Wall Street had been focused upon "the money supply." Since 1979, the Fed had been trying to manage the quantity of dollars in the system, while shifting to different definitions of what constitutes "money." Bond markets ebbed and flowed with weekly reports of the "Ms." In 1992, Fed Chairman Alan Greenspan advised the Congress that he had little confidence in this process, news that should have alerted the press that it was time to shift its perspective. What happened? The financial press corps was asleep at the wheel.

The news was reported, but matter-of-factly, as in Rick Wartzman's account in the *WSJ*, "Fed Is Leaning Toward Cutting Money Target," 7-23, in which Wartzman reports that Greenspan has told Congress that, as far as he is concerned, there is little connection between the "Ms" and inflation and growth, that "a couple of years ago, both of those relationships broke down." This was a stunning repudiation of the monetarist concepts that had been central in guiding policy, but the press corps, as well as the economics profession, acted as if nothing had changed. We did not see much more discussion of this new monetary course until Fed Governor

Wayne Angell clarified the shift on PBS's "Nightly Business Report" on September 9: "The Federal Reserve prefers to have sound money, and sound money generally means that the currency will be stable against gold, commodities and generally, against other currencies, if those currencies are also stable against those same commodities."

The Fed was shifting away from a "quantity rule" toward a "price rule" in managing the dollar's value. This was as profound a change as a turn from east to west, and by taking this change into account, with the slightest effort the press corps could have made sense of what was happening in Europe and Japan. But once again the press corps was asleep at the wheel. The clearest explanation of the change came not from financial writers, but from Paul Gigot, a political writer, in his *WSJ* column of 11-27, "Clinton Will Find Angells of Mercy at the Fed," a 10 Best selection which explains why Greenspan and Angell have been "the two Fed governors who look most closely at the price of gold." If a reader looked beyond the editorial page of the *Journal* for this historic change, he would not find it. Nor would there be a clue at *The New York Times*, *The Washington Post*, or the periodical press. It just didn't happen.

The chronic disbelief in the establishment press that the price of gold might be a better market signal than the "Ms" was not countered even by President Bush. In September, after Black Wednesday, Bush revived the idea, first elevated by Treasury Secretary James Baker III in September 1987, of tying all the world's currencies together, solving questions of who should ease and who should tighten via "an independent arbiter," the price of a commodity basket that would include gold. The idea sank like a stone. Those few journalists who gave it any play at all cast it as insignificant or of questionable value. Peter Norman of *FT* in "US Puts Commodities Index at Centre-Stage," 9-22, went so far as to say: "There is also a suspicion that the US as a leading producer of primary commodities and gold would benefit from the scheme more than other industrial countries."

Cynicism and lethargy were the flip sides of the coin of economic and financial journalism in 1992. Everyone knows why the world is in such an economic mess, so why bother trying to challenge, or even to understand, the assumptions of conventional wisdom? The dream of Europe '92 dissolves, an unbeatable American President is defeated, the Japanese juggernaut is dead in the water, and the best that our economic philosophers in the Fourth Estate can provide by way of guidance is the assurance that illogic has its own logic. Can the sun rise in the west and the east? Only in the short run, *The Economist* assures us.

THE BEST STORIES & COLUMNS OF 1992

For the seventh consecutive year, the *MediaGuide* highlights ten individual efforts by print journalists in each of five categories: Business, Commentary, Foreign, General and Political. The articles in each category are listed in *alphabetical* order, *not* in the order in which we might rank them. For this year's edition of the 10 Best, we reviewed thousands of articles, constantly refining the list, to make the final 50 selections. As in previous years, we have also invited editors to nominate selections from their publications.

There is no other award in U.S. print journalism where the judges have read as much at the time of publication or where the judges consist exclusively of consumers of news, instead of professional peers. As a result, some selections are chosen on the basis of timeliness, some because they stand the test of time, still others because they challenge our perspectives, or answer our questions when no one else could. In order to do justice to the works cited, we have added comments following each citation, further defining the material's distinctiveness.

BUSINESS

"Gillette Holds its Edge by Endlessly Searching for a Better Shave"
12-10-92
Lawrence Ingrassia
The Wall Street Journal

Part of an ongoing front-page series, Ingrassia's vivid profile of Gillette Co. is the best of business journalism, a veritable trip to the company's operations and through its history, in which we learn precisely why Gillette currently has a 72% market share in the U.S. and a dazzling global presence. What Ingrassia discovers as the key to this success is the passion, bordering on obsession, with which Gillette employees pursue the perfect shave, and the technology necessary to achieve it. At one manufacturing and research plant "some 200 volunteers... come to work unshaven each day. They troop to the second floor and enter small booths with a sink and mirror, where they take instructions from technicians on the other side of a small window: try this blade or shaving cream or this aftershave, then answer questionnaires." Ever since a market-share threat from Wilkinson Sword in 1962, Gillette has been mad about research: "'We test the blade edge, the blade guard, the angle of the blades, the balance of the razor, the length, the heft, the width,' explains Donald Chaulk, vice president of the shaving technology laboratory. 'What happens to the chemistry of the skin? What happens to the hair when you pull it? What happens to the follicle? We own the face. We know more about shaving than anybody. I don't think obsession is too strong a word.' He pauses. 'I've got to be careful. I don't want to sound crazy.'"

"Guilty"
4-13-92
Michele Galen with Alice Cuneo and David Greising
BusinessWeek

This article was the only place we saw such a detailed exploration of the charge, promoted by Vice President Dan Quayle and others, that too much litigation is stifling U.S. business. The *BW* team finds that some companies are "shunning domestic markets out of fear of product-liability suits. Biomet Inc. sells spinal implants for back problems virtually all over the world—with one glaring exception. 'We don't feel confident in the U.S, with such a product,' says Dane A. Miller, CEO of the Warsaw (Ind.) orthopedics company. 'Our legal system in America is totally out of control.'" In addition, Galen and crew not only offer numerous creative solutions being embraced by corporate America, but also explore the impact such creative options are having on business profits. For instance, policy at Motorola Inc. dictates that in-house lawyers must seek all possible alternatives to court, and if they still want to go to trial they "must fill out a form estimating legal costs, likely damages, and chances of victory. 'The form is so onerous that they gladly work out an alternative settlement rather than screw around with that form,' says General Counsel Richard H. Weise.... If that sounds like an unproductive use of an attorney's time, think again. Since starting the program in 1984, alternative dispute-resolution techniques have slashed Motorola's litigation costs by as much as 75%."

"How Well Run Is the Federal Government?"
10-27-92
Katherine Barrett and Richard Greene
Financial World

Amid record-high disillusionment with Beltway bureaucracy, someone finally undertakes a comprehensive analysis of the federal government from a management perspective. This isn't about where to spend tax dollars, but "how government can more efficiently deliver the services to which it's already committed." As the duo explains, much about the government's management strategies makes political sense, not common sense. "'It's very hard to convince the policymakers... that financial management is critical,' says Frank Hodsoll, the man directly in charge of the M in OMB.... 'The promotion prospects at the average agency are not based on financial management. They're based on issues. When a person says, "I got three laws enacted to do such and so," everybody says "Hurrah." But nobody pays much attention to seeing if the laws actually worked.'" We find out what changes have been undertaken, which federal agencies are making the grade, and what reforms may be ahead. Senate Bill 20, for instance, would, according to Sen. William Roth (R-DE), "require that . . . each agency publish an annual program performance report, showing what was actually accomplished versus planned objectives. . . . The legislation also requires the incorporation of measurable goals into the federal budget itself—what is referred to as 'performance-based budgeting.' This is what changes a budget from being largely a political document into a real policy-making and management tool."

"Investors at Risk: The Dark Side of the Brokerage Business"
7-1-92 through 7-5-92
Scot J. Paltrow
Los Angeles Times

Caveat emptor, let the buyer beware, is the theme of this exhaustive investigation of securities brokers' dealings with customers. This is consumer-watchdog journalism at its finest. Paltrow does an enormous amount of research for this eye-opening five-part series, uncovering indicting evidence of unethical and even illegal behavior by members of some of the nation's most prestigious stock brokerage houses. More importantly, Paltrow, with scalpel-like precision, dissects the inefficiencies of the industry's self-regulatory policies. "William McLucas, the [SEC] enforcement chief, claims that investors can help protect themselves . . . by . . . calling a toll-free hot line set up last October by the National Assn. of Securities Dealers. . . . But an investigation by the *Times* shows that the NASD's 800 number is often worse than no information at all. Operators routinely give out false or misleading information, giving a clean bill of health to brokers who have records of judgements against them for harming customers. . . . The hot line's failure to give out complete and accurate information raises questions about the SEC, which under the Penny Stock Reform Act of 1990 is supposed to supervise the NASD's implementation of the hot line. . . . Interviews with SEC officials show that they are not aware of how the hot line is actually operating. The SEC, for example, apparently is not aware that the NASD refuses to disclose arbitration awards against brokers and that it sometimes falsely states that there are none."

"Should Business Fear Clinton?"
7-16-92
John Merline and
Thomas McArdle
Investor's Business Daily

In the last few years *Investor's Daily* has increasingly nudged itself to the center of discussion on critical questions of economic policy—without an editorial page and without turning its reporters loose to grind their own axes for ideological agendas. Merline and McArdle have been two of the most effective at simply asking the right questions and allowing the exploration for answers to range as far and wide as is necessary to deliver the goods to their readers. The headline in this front-page leader is just what we wanted, when we wanted it, and the story beneath it presented enough information on the leanings of Clintonomics to permit us to answer the question ourselves, with the journalists remaining at a safe distance. They begin by noting that Clinton's rhetoric and the Democratic platform recognize "the value of a healthy, growing private enterprise system." In roaming through specific proposals, though, they find "new mandates, regulations and taxes that could heap significant new costs onto businesses, dampening the growth he seeks." An accompanying chart from a GOP source indicates that total business profits in 1991 were $189.7 billion while Clinton's health care, worker training and new taxes would cut $125.2 billion from that. They take us through the ballpark estimates with enough detachment to persuade us the analysis is serious, non-partisan and non-ideological, the type of information upon which daily investors must rely.

"U.S. Cars Come Back"
11-16-92
Alex Taylor III
Fortune

Taylor pens what is likely to become *the* definitive press account of the auto industry in the '80s and early '90s. At the very least, this is the most ambitious attempt we've seen to analyze this crucial industry's successes and failures. More accurately, it is a remarkable history of a remarkable industry, a book of knowledge condensed into an article. "Detroit's biggest collective failure has been its unwillingness to confront the threat from Japan. Instead, the industry has adopted a Maginot-line mentality.... The import restraints [of 1981], still in effect, never worked as intended. In their first years they served only to limit supply, not depress demand.... The restraint agreements led to two other, more significant developments, neither fully anticipated by Detroit. Honda was once the only Japanese manufacturer to try assembling cars in the U.S. After the first restraint agreement, to circumvent the import ceiling, six other Japanese automakers joined in. ... The second unintended consequence was the upscale Japanese auto. Given the incentive to maximize the profit on each car shipped, the Japanese decided to export more expensive automobiles." Going a step deeper into the story, Taylor studies the Big Three's individual ups and downs. He nails Lee Iacocca for the "violent swings of fortune" that have marked his tenure at Chrysler and extracts an important revelation from new GM chief Jack Smith, who divulges that the much heralded '84 GM restructuring "really didn't work that well."

"What Did Pop Expect to Happen When He Gave the Kid His Credit Card?"
9-28-92
Gretchen Morgenson
Forbes

Revealing Part II of the S&L crisis, in which "the government looks for scapegoats," Morgenson's shocking exposé makes clear that the FDIC is "a government agency utterly out of control, terrorizing innocent bystanders and frequently costing the taxpayers far more in legal fees than it is recovering." She has plenty of proof that this taxpayer-financed "witch-hunt" helps no one but the private law firms hired by the government. "No matter how absurd their claims, they can bill the taxpayer for their time on these professional liability cases, at $200 an hour and up. Total cost? Well over $100 million of the FDIC and Resolution Trust Corp.'s legal budget..." One of the many stories of abuse she offers is the tale of appraiser Lawrence Brown who was included in a suit for allegedly overvaluing six properties for a subsidiary of Pacific Savings Bank which failed in 1989. "Never mind that four of the six appraisals were made months and in one case a year *after* Pacific had financed the properties . . . Brown was sued for $28 million.... Brown died two years ago... His insurer has had to pay $400,000 in legal bills. In 1991, after two years of litigation, a U.S. district court judge in California threw out the case, ruling that the FDIC's law firm . . . had never proved

that the appraisals it said were negligently prepared by Brown were prepared by him at all. Not to be stopped, the agency has appealed.... Cost to the FDIC...about $400,000, with more to come.... Recovery to the taxpayer: zero."

"Which Market Is Wrong?"
1-6-92
Randall W. Forsyth
Barron's

Almost nine months before the currency crisis shook Europe, Forsyth offered some stunningly prescient observations on potential hot spots ahead in the world bond and currency markets. "The Bundesbank will hold the key to European bond market returns. . . . Other European central banks would prefer to lower rates as their economies slow. But they have been forced to hold their interest rates up, or actually raise them in some cases, in order to maintain their currencies' values vs. the mark. . . . The conflict between maintaining tight monetary policy, as dictated by the ERM, or easing policy, as domestic economies would dictate, is growing. Moreover, it's spilling over into the political realm. Nowhere is that more evident than in the U.K., where the economy remains mired in recession. While rates there have been slashed more than four percentage points in the past year, they remain in double digits. Prime Minister John Major's government would wish to cut rates further, ahead of the general election that must be called this spring at the latest. But the constraints of the ERM preclude cuts at this time. Devaluation would permit interest-rate cuts but would be embarrassing for Major, who pushed for Britain to enter the ERM when he was Chancellor of the Exchequer. . . . Similar, if less stark, conflicts between domestic and international demands on monetary policy play out throughout the Continent." It is only with an impressive understanding of his beat that Forsyth can have such surprising foresight.

"Why the Price Wars Never End"
3-23-92
Bill Saporito
Fortune

Every once in a while we come upon a piece of journalism that enables us to view an important trend from an entirely new perspective. Saporito's virtually flawless report on the price wars does just that—and more. He quotes an impressive array of sources, including George Wydo, Borden's president of snack foods: "'The snack war is going to continue. And the reason is that everybody has too much money in fixed assets to get out. We probably have more than $500 million. . . . Who's going to write those assets off?' The academics call that a barrier to exit. And barriers are now so high in some industries that capacity keeps running when it shouldn't." We walked away from Saporito's analysis understanding that such forces, including Chapter 11 bankruptcy protection for a growing number of competitors, are changing the way manufacturers, retailers and even the service industry do business. "For makers of consumer products, the danger of a price war is that brand equity—so expensive to build—erodes, and products become commodities. . . . Consider Porsche, the yuppie dream machine that has as much brand equity as it does horsepower. Sales are idling, stalled by a change in values and competition from less expensive Japanese high-performance vehicles. Says David Aaker, professor of marketing strategy at the University of California at Berkeley and author of *Managing Brand Equity*: 'Porsche has equity but no sales. What do you do—pack it in? Go downscale? Or weather the storm?' Welcome to the prisoner's dilemma of pricing."

"You Can't Get There From Here"
7-6-92
Peter Brimelow and
Leslie Spencer
Forbes

This is an article Carol Browner should read as she takes the reins at the EPA. Much more than just another environmental story, this enlightening essay deftly analyzes how the EPA's "command-and-control" bureaucracy is doing little for the environment in which most Americans live, while swallowing an increasingly large chunk of the paychecks they depend on: "The EPA's staff has quadrupled since 1970. Its inflation-adjusted spending has gone up ten times. . . . In 1990 the agency estimated that complying with its pollution-control regulations was costing Americans $115 billion a year, or a remarkable 2.1% of GNP, versus 0.9% in 1972. . . . Put it this way: Because of pollution controls, every American is paying on average about $450 more in taxes and higher prices." The authors offer creative alternatives to the present confusion: "There is an environmental policy ideally suited to the American way: the development of property rights and the common law of tort. . . . Of course, relying on common law to protect the environment would deprive Congress of some of its powers to grant and withhold favors, cost thousands of bureaucrats their jobs and power, and spoil the games played by lots of business people. But isn't the limiting of government control over people's lives an important part of what America is all about?"

COMMENTARY

"Baker's Guilty Knowledge"
6-22-92
"'Not in the System'"
6-25-92
"Digging Deeper in Iraqgate"
7-6-92
"A Smoking Gun?"
9-10-92
William Safire
The New York Times

As with his columns last year that helped to topple John Sununu, Safire's work on the relationship between Saddam Hussein's Iraq and the Bush administration prior to the Persian Gulf War had a tremendous impact on Washington politics. We cite the most damning columns from a portfolio characterized by Safire's relentless pursuit of the entire story. In "Baker's Guilty Knowledge," Safire sounds the alarm on the administration's relationship with Iraq, citing the 10-13-89 memo of foreign service officer Frank Lemay, which outlined the likelihood that Saddam Hussein was diverting agriculture subsidies and credits to acquire "sensitive" nuclear technology. Safire follows up by discovering the memo was marked "'Not in the System,'" meaning it was removed from the normal channels. He describes "a mosaic of cover-up: first, in State's perverting the use of Agriculture's farm-export guarantees; second, in Commerce doctoring documents to mislead Congress; finally, in the Department of Justice delaying prosecution of a huge Iraqi fraud." As Bush scrambled for cover on "CBS This Morning," claiming ignorance of the Lemay memo, Safire builds a convincing case with "Digging Deeper in Iraqgate," that, indeed, George Bush could not possibly not have known. And he seems to find "A Smoking Gun?" with a memo dated 10-26-89 to James Baker from John Kelly, head of State's Near East Bureau, and Abraham Sofaer, Legal Counsel. "The idea was to pervert the grain credits program...and turn it into a backdoor foreign aid source."

"Clinton Will Find Angells of Mercy at the Fed"
11-27-92

Paul A. Gigot
The Wall Street Journal

With this "Potomac Watch" column, Gigot insightfully reveals the importance of the Reagan-Bush Federal Reserve Board to the Clinton administration. "With an improving economy, [Clinton] can moderate any short-term 'stimulus' plan—proposing just enough to get some credit for growth without spooking financial markets. Democrats, recalling the Carter Inflation, tend to think of the Fed in horror. But Mr. Clinton may come to think of even this Republican Fed as his best friend. Its presence reassures investors that another round of inflation isn't imminent. Such reassurance in turn gives Mr. Clinton more leeway to implement his budget ideas." Here, he credits the Fed's policy of price level targeting, the brainchild of Fed Gov. Wayne Angell, for keeping inflation at bay. To Clinton's further benefit, Gigot positions the goal of the Fed as returning "to the halcyon days of zero inflation. 'Inflation is cheating,' says the man whose Fed term expires in 1994. If markets believe the Fed is serious about stable prices, they'll damp inflation expectations and interest rates will fall. Growth will bloom. Mr. Angell admits the Fed blundered in the mid-1980s when it ignored rising gold prices that heralded an inflation rebound; the recession was in part a price of correcting that mistake. Let's hope Mr. Clinton was paying attention." This incisive discussion of the political *and* economic aspects of the Federal Reserve is *essential* reading for the new administration.

"The Crack-Up"
10-1-92

Jim Squires
Rolling Stone

When Ross Perot re-entered the race in October, he ran his campaign his way, unglamorous infomercials and all. We find out why from Squires, in the only analysis of Perot's withdrawal that made sense. From his post as media advisor to the Perot campaign, the former *Chicago Tribune* editor reveals how the campaign was sabotaged from within, as Perot handler and GOP consultant Ed Rollins steadfastly refused to "Let Perot Be Perot." Squires aptly captures the flaw of the poor fit between Rollins and the Perot campaign. "Perot . . . did not know that among his new hires was a man with a self-image bigger than Perot's own, someone so drenched in the big-money, showbiz brand of modern presidential politics that he personified the very system Perot was challenging." We find here ample evidence of Perot's dedication to his family and his own standards, and his increasing frustration as the campaign got away from him. Squires places the blame firmly on Rollins and his mechanical plans to market the candidate as politician, despite Perot's popularity as a Beltway outsider and Texas populist with the grass-roots movement he inspired. In the end, the only avenue for Perot to control the campaign was to terminate it, Squires reveals, so damaging were Rollins's leaks to the news media and destructive television appearances on "behalf" of the candidate. By trying to fit a round peg into a square hole, Rollins torpedoed Perot's initial campaign.

"'A Figure of Genuine Pathos'"
7-29-92

George F. Will
The Washington Post

This Tory conservative made the first, and the strongest, call for George Bush to step down from the nomination for a second term. Like Will's "lapdog" column in *Newsweek* four years earlier, "'A Figure of Genuine Pathos'" cuts deeply at George Bush, and at precisely the right moment. Will puts into words what a great many GOP leaders were thinking but were unable to say publicly. The column itself became a milestone in the campaign. Its arguments pervaded political discussion right to the very end. Will uses Bush's record to cast his second candidacy as a no-win proposition: "If he runs he almost certainly will lose, perhaps in a landslide that does considerable damage to his party. If he wins, his second term almost certainly will be even worse than most second terms, worse even than his first. . . . He should not run because he has no reason to, other than an ambition eerily disconnected from any agenda." Will's exceedingly perceptive evaluation of Bush and his primary conviction helped to change the tone of debate over the GOP ticket as much as any other assertion this year: "[His conviction] is that he should be president. He is now a figure of genuine pathos because he is bewildered by the fact that more is expected of him than what has hitherto sufficed, his belief that people like him should administer things."

"Heather Has a Message"
8-17-92

John Leo
U.S.News & World Report

The "On Society" columnist offers an authoritative discussion of multiculturalism in the New York City public school system. The debate raged over the addition of *Heather Has Two Mommies*, a story of lesbians becoming parents through artificial insemination, to the first-grade teacher's guide. The argument culminated in the suspension of a Queens school board in December. Leo excellently defines the difficulty. "Schools can promote respect for all children without endorsing all the different beliefs, lifestyles or orientations found in their homes." But rather than promoting the traditional pluralism embraced by public schools, Leo argues, the city has folded to the pressures from the politically correct by instructing teachers that they "must 'be aware of varied family structures, including gay or lesbian parents,' and 'Children must be taught to acknowledge the positive aspects of each type of household.' A line is being crossed here; in fact, a brand new ethic is descending upon the city's public school system. The traditional civic virtue of tolerance (if gays want to live together, it's their own business) has been replaced with a new ethic requiring approval and endorsement (if gays want to live together, we must 'acknowledge the positive aspects' of their way of life)." He exceptionally outlines the danger of this shift. "This [controversy] touches off a destructive battle over public norms at a time when the schools desperately need to focus on academics, not intergroup warfare." Leo is a voice of reason on this explosive issue.

"NAACP: Time for a Change"
2-19-92
"When People Feel They Don't Matter"
5-4-92

William Raspberry
The Washington Post

Raspberry was the voice of record on black America this year, clarifying and crystallizing our perceptions of the complex problems facing African-Americans. Before the explosions in Los Angeles, he sensed changes in the wind, and put the National Association for the Advancement of Colored People on the margin, arguing strenuously that its mandate must shift from pursuing legal solutions to economic solutions. "For [Ben] Hooks's generation the major threat to black progress was racism," but with civil rights legislation in place, he asserts, "the big threat to our progress—to our *survival*—is now more internal than external, and mostly beyond the reach of legislation and court decrees.... Our civil rights generals are still fighting the last war—demanding that the government create and fund the programs we need, that the courts protect our interests.... What might the new directions be? For me, the answer is easy: Our children and economic development." After the riots, when others asked "Why?" Raspberry provided insight into the psychology of the inner city, which, he says, "is full of young black men who don't register on society's screen except when they are hurting someone else or threatening to. The most consistent message they hear is: You don't matter." He examines events with exceptional clarity, defining the riots as "a rampage by a berserk man whose rage is triggered by his having been reminded, once again, that he doesn't matter.... Picture what it must be like to matter only as a source of present or potential violence, and then to be told to forgo violence, because it 'only hurts your cause.' Try to imagine what it must feel like to know that the closest anyone will come to respecting you is to be afraid of you."

"No Womb for Debate"
7-27-92
Fred Barnes
The New Republic
With this essay, Barnes moves the dialogue beyond the conventional on abortion by revealing the growing fault lines within the Democratic party on this divisive issue. Rather than buying the traditional notion of an ideological monolith on abortion, Barnes identifies Democratic pro-lifers, most prominently Governor Robert Casey of Pennsylvania, and goes on to place the party's refusal to address dissent on the issue within the context of national politics. Gov. Casey, notes Barnes, "disputes the conventional wisdom that being aggressively pro-choice helps Democrats (or Republicans, for that matter). The opposite is true, he says. Sure, polls show that Americans are pro-choice by a 3-to-1 margin or better, but that's only half the story. Most pro-choicers are queasy about abortion on demand, favor some restrictions, and don't automatically vote for pro-choice candidates. In fact, pro-life voters are more likely to vote based on the single issue of abortion. Thus, the electoral edge in many states goes to the anti-abortion side. One more thing. Millions of these pro-lifers are Democrats." Barnes examines how the party hierarchy is working to shut Casey and his arguments out, despite the idea that "what Democratic abortion opponents are asking for is not an abandonment of the Democrats' position in favor of a woman's right to choose. What they want is for the party to merely give up its extreme disinclination to say anything critical of abortion. ...[Casey would] settle for a rejection of abortion on demand." A revealing analysis.

"Odd Way to Choose a President"
1-28-92
David S. Broder
The Washington Post
As allegations about Bill Clinton surfaced in the tabloid press and bubbled over into the mainstream media, the dean of the political press corps makes the definitive case for leaving the infidelity question out of the campaign. With Broder's thirty-something years of experience covering Washington politics, his powerful critique of the press corps on this issue is particularly stinging. He draws this important distinction: "Gary Hart was different. The conduct that drove him from the race in 1987 was current, it was flagrant, it violated the promises he had made to his closest political associates—and it suggested a reckless imprudence and disregard of consequences that clearly did raise questions about his fitness for the presidency. When the press is confronted by such behavior in a presidential candidate, it has no choice but to report it. But the press has no such obligation to go rummaging in the closets of White House contenders for any past indiscretions that may fall out. As the Clinton case and others show, it is terribly difficult to resolve the is-

sues of motivation, evidence and conflicting recollection that attend such past relationships—and politicians are easily victimized by people seeking to settle old scores. More important, the ransacking of personal histories diverts journalism from what is far more important—the examination of past performance in public office and the scrutiny of current policy positions."

"The Real Story Goes Beyond Black and White"
5-18-92
Virginia I. Postrel
Los Angeles Times

Reason editor Postrel explodes the mythology perpetuated by politicians and the media in the aftermath of the Los Angeles riots, terming the official, polarized representation of events as a "cheap thrill" that served to confirm prejudices rather than further understanding. She explains for those of us in the balcony that "Parts of the official story are true. Black Angelenos are indeed angry about the King verdict and about a justice system that seems quick to deem blacks to be criminals and slow to protect them from crime, official and otherwise. Gangs have indeed wreaked havoc on South Los Angeles. Korean-owned stores were indeed targeted by many rioters. White and Asian motorists were indeed singled out for beatings by black mobs. But the riots were multiracial, television viewers could see plenty of whites among the rioters smashing downtown, and Latinos among those hauling away furniture, food and other loot from ravaged stores. The victims, too, came in all colors, as did the cleaning crews. To suggest otherwise is not only to grossly distort the truth but to further the fear and bigotry that led to the beating of Rodney King, to the verdicts and the riots." Postrel appropriately deems that clear comprehension of these events is vital to the progress of race relations: "Disturbing the official story makes understanding what happened harder. But real understanding requires that we start with the truth, not a morality play where you can tell the players by the colors of their masks."

"Taxonomy"
8-31-92
Michael Kinsley
The New Republic

Kinsley, ever on the alert for Republican malfeasance, is first to reveal the specious nature of GOP charges that Bill Clinton raised taxes 128 times during his 12-year tenure as Arkansas governor. Even the Republicans had difficulty settling on a figure, "like Joe McCarthy counting Communists in the State Department." Kinsley effectively torpedoes the "hilariously shoddy" list derived from a compendium issued by Clinton's 1990 gubernatorial rival, Sheffield Nelson. "Item No. 46 is a 1987 law lengthening the season for dog racing. This is apparently a 'tax increase' on the theory that a longer season increases state gambling revenues. No. 48 is a $500 license fee for abortion clinics. Does the GOP really object to this burden on commerce? Other supposed tax increases either never took effect (No. 71) or replaced another tax of equal size (No. 117). A fuel tax increase is counted as two because it applies to both gasoline and diesel. A general booze tax weighs in at *five* if you count categories like wine coolers separately—as they do." In addition, Kinsley uncovers tax *cuts* enacted by the Democratic governor. "These include such George Bush favorites as a tax credit for businesses hiring employees in enterprise zones and a tax break for capital gains. They also include a general cut last year that reduced or eliminated income taxes on 374,000 low-income Arkansas citizens." He rounds out this devastating assessment with salient data on Bush's tax record, including the 1990 tax reform, which adds up to 73 increases in and of itself by the GOP methodology. After this column, the GOP soft-pedaled the issue.

FOREIGN

"Army Uses Terror to Widen Grip Over Haiti"
2-16-92
"Haiti's Poor Hit Hardest by Embargo"
8-3-92
Nathaniel Sheppard
Chicago Tribune

It was all too easy at times to lose sight of what was going on in Haiti, despite that beleaguered nation's proximity to our shores. But Sheppard, Latin American correspondent for the *Trib*, never failed to shake our consciences and document the evident failure of U.S. policy toward Haiti. These two reports were particular standouts. Just as the U.S. was returning Haitian refugees to their home shores, the enterprising Sheppard, in "Army Uses Terror..." travels into the remote villages of northwestern Haiti where deposed President Jean-Bertrand Aristide received some of his biggest electoral support. There he documents firsthand the repression former Aristide supporters were suffering, despite Washington's protestations to the contrary. "Residents gave chilling accounts of hiding in the steep hillsides as troops sacked and then torched their tin-roof wooden homes." While getting the story, Sheppard and another reporter were detained by the section chief and his paramilitary thugs, who, with the backing of the army, have created a "feudal system in which the section chief is lord." The section chief wanted to kill Sheppard and his companion "as a warning to others who might come here," but Sheppard survived and, several months later, filed "Haiti's Poor..." This concise, yet comprehensive report brings us up-to-date on the devastation the embargo is bringing to the Haitian economy, while merchants backing the military regime "have found the embargo to be a source of windfall profits."

"The Battle for the West Bank"
4-5-92
Ethan Bronner
The Boston Globe Magazine

Just as we had thought we had read more than we would ever need to know about the occupied territories we came across this remarkable *Globe Magazine* article which made us feel we were reading about the West Bank for the first time. Other reporters have covered the story of increased Israeli settlements in recent years, but only Bronner, Middle East correspondent for the *Globe*, puts the story in full political and cultural perspective. In doing so, he captures the true historical forces at work which may make the settlements permanent. The Israelis, Bronner reveals here, actually began winning "The Battle for the West Bank" about five years ago when Jewish settlers started moving in by the thousands onto ground declared Israeli "state land," and built modern urban complexes. Almost overnight, we learn, settlers went from being a national joke, compared to the "Jerusalem faithful who are patiently sewing priestly gowns for the arrival of the Messiah," into being part of the national fabric. "Suddenly, it seems, your doctor, your plumber, your neighbor's cousin, live on a settlement." The settlers also assumed the mantle of the country's rural pioneering founders. We learn first-hand of the human implications of this development in this impeccably balanced report, Bronner capturing the voices of both the settlers and the Palestinians they are displacing. As for the larger picture, Bronner knowingly warns that the stateless Palestinians could become "one more tribe that—like the Kurds, like the Cherokee and Apache, for that matter—fell off the train of history."

"The Last Battleground"
4-26-92
Steve Coll
The Washington Post

The world may have thought it was putting the Cold War behind it in 1992, but in this superior *Magazine* cover story, Coll reminds us that the conflict was more than just a game in which the playing board can now be neatly folded up and packed away. Traveling to Afghanistan as that country's bloody civil war nears its end, Coll, the *WP*'s former South Asia correspondent, reports that "Kabul after the Cold War is a strange, sparse landscape of human, material and ideological ruin." It is the ideological ruin Coll is most interested in, the true debris of the last battleground of the Cold War. Coll talks to no victorious rebels here, he's interested in the losers, the "zealots, professionals, cynics, timeservers—who gave the best years of their lives to a cause now completely discredited." Former leaders such as Babrak Karmel and Najibullah sit in their offices and dens trying to come to terms with the wreckage that emerged from their youthful idealism to make Afghanistan a more modern, equalitarian society, while rockets whiz overhead. Their outlook, and Coll's observant, historically informed prose, create a memorable portrait of the human side of one of the Cold War's most violent conflicts, a "Soviet generation's Spain," in the words of one Red Army officer as quoted by a Bulgarian ambassador. "Certitude," Coll writes at one point, "belongs to the victors." Writing from a land where the only certainty is more human suffering, Coll reminds us of the price of victory.

"New, Virulent Strains of Hatred in the Balkans and Beyond"
5-3-92

John F. Burns
The New York Times

This essay by the *NYT*'s Toronto bureau chief is foreign reporting at its finest, a breathtaking summation of what has led the world to its current state of affairs and where it might be heading, and why. "The ghost of [Gavrilo] Princip is abroad, and those it threatens may include millions who know nothing of the historic grievances of Bosnian Serbs." With this knowing reference to the assassin of Archduke Franz Ferdinand, Burns brilliantly captures the biggest threat to world stability in the post-Cold War era: the ability of determined minorities to rock the very pillars of international order to express their grievances. Burns has seen enough of the world to know that societies, both east and west, face varying degrees of their own Yugoslavia, and that "to blame Communism for the malevolent resurgence of ancient currents is too comfortable a conclusion." Burns provocatively draws a connection between the "nobility [of] the idea of uniting peoples across the divides of culture and faith," through the principles of Marxism and the popular idea today of uniting people through free trade, free markets, and human rights. He then draws on the words of Vaclav Havel to warn that "universalist answers to the problems of human history," may fail to "respond adequately to human needs," resulting in groups like the Serbs asserting their rights at the expense of others. "But if there is another lesson here, it may be, as in Los Angeles, that no nation can rest easy as long as any community feels that it lacks guarantees of an equal spot in the sun."

"Officials, Not Market, Still Set Prices"
1-3-92

Michael Dobbs
The Washington Post

Russia's era of free-market capitalism was to be heralded in by the "Big Bang" of freeing prices. Dobbs's superbly-written dispatch was the best on-the-scene report we saw which revealed why the Big Bang was really more of a Big Whimper. "How do you set prices now that they have been 'freed' by the Russian government?" Dobbs, *WP* Moscow bureau chief, asks the manager of State Grocery No. 2. "'The same as before,'" is the reply. "'I pick up the phone and make a call.'" With a fine sense of irony, Dobbs deftly evokes the dead hand of bureaucracy accompanying Russia's move to a "market" economy, which has left shopkeepers thumbing through 12-page booklets listing the new prices and regulations creating "free contract prices" set by "supply and demand." Along with memorably evoking the grimy state stores which are still short of consumer goods, Dobbs also steps back to capture the bigger picture of why "The Russian economy remains an economy of scarcity." By retaining control of distribution, the state has created "a chronic shortage not only of goods and natural resources, but also of Western-style entrepreneurs with an eye for economic detail." Meanwhile, foreshadowing the year to come, the black market has been booming and officials still keep portraits of Lenin in their offices. "Yeltsin seems a temporary phenomenon," one tells Dobbs. "I don't think we will go back to communism, but I figure there's no point in changing the portrait on my wall until we really know where we are headed."

"Out of Step With the People"
6-9-92

David Marsh
Financial Times

Anybody looking for the reason why the promise of Maastricht in late 1991 went sour in 1992 would do well to start here. In this masterful analytic written shortly after the

Maastricht Treaty's defeat at the hands of the Danish voters, Marsh draws on his own deep understanding of the European political scene and the viewpoints of opinion molders and opinion pollsters. He illuminates how the goals of western European political leaders floundered "on an apparent lack of democratic backing for the goal of greater European integration proclaimed at the EC summit in the Netherlands six months ago." Marsh makes a key distinction here, drawing on the EC's "Eurobarometer" of public opinion among the member nations to document that while people "appear generally satisfied with the achievements of the European Community so far . . . they favour a slowdown in further changes while they digest those which are already taking place." This is most prevalent in Germany, Marsh writes, which is pivotal to any European integration but where doubts are already evident in spring of 1992. "Decisions are being forced through too fast," is the quote from Prof. Elisabeth Noelle-Neumann, head of the Allensbach Institute and "the doyenne of European opinion pollsters." Whither Europe? Observing the growing trend of antipathy toward mainstream political institutions throughout Europe, Marsh leaves us with the troubling thought: "if the people cannot trust the politicians, who else is there to lead them towards an integrated, stable and prosperous continent?"

"Outsiders"
4-9-92
Ian Buruma
The New York Review of Books

History seemed to be returning to Germany with a special vengeance this year, as xenophobic violence under the shadow of fascistic trappings was on the rise. We found the most sophisticated analysis of this chilling trend here in Buruma's concise, sensitive essay. A former cultural editor of the *Far Eastern Economic Review* and a Fellow of the Wissenschaftskolleg in Berlin in the Spring of '92, Buruma moves beyond easy political or economic explanations to get to the heart of darkness threatening Germany's social fabric, basing citizenship on the existentialist question of who is and who is not "naturally" a German. The debate over immigration policy in Germany is frozen, Buruma explains, as the mainstream left and right act out of reflex to protect the rights of immigrants and ethnic Germans seeking asylum, respectively. Consequently, the country has failed to come to grips with the basic question of having *ethnicity* at the core of German citizenship. Buruma has little use for the multicultural platitudes advanced by the Left, either, observing that "to answer these questions by dreaming of organic communities, as though human beings were plants, can only give a spurious air of respectability to the chauvinist *vox populi* in the soccer stadiums." Only when Germans of all ideologies see their community as one of freely associating individuals, not as components of an idealized, inclusive *volk*, will Germany no longer be such an "outsider" to the world, and to itself.

"Somalia—Anatomy of a Famine"
9-24-92
Michael A. Hiltzik
Los Angeles Times

Hiltzik, Nairobi bureau chief for the *LAT*, sets out to prove here that "Famine is not a natural phenomenon but a man-made one," and succeeds in a report which stayed with us long after we read it. Just as hunger can lead to starvation by breaking down the body's natural systems, so political mismanagement, in the case of Ethiopia, or political anarchy, in the case of Somalia, can allow drought and a year of bad crops to break down a country's agricultural and market systems, resulting in mass famine. "In areas as marginal as rural Somalia," Hiltzik writes, "a family's entitlement—in this case, enough food to sustain life—can be suddenly put out of reach, even amid abundance." Thus, Somalian markets still stock food while thousands of rural Somalians line up and die in refugee camps. "But when a famine is permitted to progress as far as Somalia's, relief efforts may continue to undermine the recovery of markets." Besides the destruction to Somalia's political economy, Hiltzik is also graphic on the toll starvation is taking on the Somalian population, warning that there may be more Somalia's ahead. "I find an incredible explosion of [man-made] disasters around the world," Hiltzik quotes the UN undersecretary general for humanitarian affairs at one point. With Washington's decision late in the year to send more than 20,000 troops to safeguard relief efforts, Hiltzik's article left us wondering if Somalia would become the paradigm of military intervention in the 1990s.

"The Trial of the Old Regime"
11-30-92
David Remnick
The New Yorker

This was the year the bills of history came due in the former Soviet Union and nobody documented Russia's struggle to pay better than Remnick in this remarkable piece of reportage. Former Moscow correspondent for *The Washington Post*, Remnick takes us into a remodelled meeting room in the Central Committee Complex to portray a "historical sideshow... a judicial battle over the life, death, and potential resurrection of the Communist Party." Through Remnick's eyes, we witness "tired men in bad suits," who once ruled one of the world's largest empires, railing about the lack of democracy in post-communist Russia and blaming the collapse of the system on Mikhail Gorbachev, Boris Yeltsin, and other leaders they suspect of being on the CIA's payroll. Remnick meets the prosecutors and, thorough them, is able to glimpse some of the Kremlin's biggest secrets. Included is a transcript of the key Politburo meeting where Gorbachev is elevated to General Secretary. "His performance, even on the page, is worthy of Machiavelli's demands for a would-be prince." As for Gorbachev today, Remnick finds him a King Lear figure, denouncing the "shitty trial" while the Yeltsin government chips away at his privileges. Remnick is well aware that it is the post-communist regime which is really on trial in 1992, and he vividly depicts the political and economic malaise gripping Russia. "Moscow seems filled now with demagogues who would be czar." In a land where history can turn the mighty and the powerful into non-entities overnight, Remnick powerfully reminds us that the verdict is still out on the democrats.

"When China Wakes"
11-28-92
Jim Rohwer
The Economist

China's explosive economic growth was perhaps the biggest international story of 1992, but the bulk of the coverage we saw reminded us of the efforts of blind men trying to describe an elephant. Then, late in the year, came this breathtaking survey in *TE*. Opening with Napoleon's famous warning to "Let China sleep," the knowledgeable Rohwer alertly zeroes in on the key question: "Can China's economy go on doing what it has done ever since Deng Xiaoping began unshackling it in 1978?" To answer this, Rohwer walks us through the staggering changes Deng unleashed (apparently unintentionally) when he began implementing agricultural reforms 14 years ago. This, Rohwer writes, was the true economic "Big Bang" which ultimately resulted in a country with more than a fifth of the world's population finding itself only "a mere generation behind the East Asian tigers." Masterfully utilizing charts, figures, statistics and quotes, Rohwer takes us from the "commanding heights" of Chinese industry to the astonishing success of the "township and village enterprises" (TVEs) to the role foreign investment has played, to document how China's reforms have worked in practice: "A modest change, introduced with a narrow aim, releases undreamed-of energies that hijack the process and sweep it along with their own pace and logic." But will the reforms sweep away the Communist Party? Not even Rohwer knows the answer to that question, preferring only to pass along a warning to Western leaders: "After advising it to let China sleep, Napoleon went on to add that 'when China wakes it will shake the world.'"

GENERAL

"Confessions of an Investigative Reporter"
3-92
Christopher Georges
The Washington Monthly

Georges, a former CNN investigative reporter himself, explodes the myth of the Watergate investigative reporter. "While there is much worthy of praise in the national media's investigative reporting, in one area, perhaps the most important one, we...are woefully lacking. A close examination of major institutional scandals within government and business in recent years, HUD, the S&Ls, Wedtech, Salomon Brothers, BCCI, corruption at the Chicago commodities exchange, the Ill Wind defense contractor scandal, and so on, reveals that it wasn't the national press that exposed wrongdoing, but the government itself or, in a few cases, the regional or trade press." One reason, says Georges, is a direct result of Watergate: a government more aware of and better able to police itself. But he does not excuse journalism: "...as thorough as government investigators might be, there are plenty of stories that they miss, like Iran-contra. Investigative journalists might be going out in search of those elusive stories. Instead, most take the easier path, becoming increasingly dependent on the inmates' notion of what's wrong with the asylum." He even takes it a step further in terms of accountability and journalistic responsibility in this stinging critique. "By launching our own independent investigations of large institutions, we have the opportunity not just to reveal problems within the system, but to help *fix* them before the bailout bill reaches $500 billion or the *Challenger* explodes."

"Conning the Media"
8-31-92
Christopher Byron
New York

Byron offers more evidence that *Time* is dead as its "scoop" on Pan Am 103 turns out to be erroneous. ABC and NBC were also duped, but Byron centers on *Time* as the most journalistically irresponsible with its cover story, "The Untold Story of Pan Am 103," 4-27, written by Roy Rowan and supervised by John Stacks. "*Time* had very little to rely on at all beyond three basic sources of information. They were (1) [Lester] Coleman, (2) a private investigator named Juval Aviv, who once worked for Pan Am," and Pan Am's lawyers. Byron dismisses the lawyers as partial, and he destroys the credibility of Coleman and Aviv by thoroughly reviewing their checkered résumés. *Time*, says Byron, knew the story to be questionable, despite a search for "credible sources to help shoot the story down" in the Washington bureau, and warnings from its members (including Stanley Cloud), the story ran. Byron tells us why with an eye-opening look at the corporate culture after the Time Warner merger. "Historically, nothing has been more important to the editors of *Time* than their control over the stories that wind up in the magazine's pages. But the story on Pan Am 103 did not originate with any editor or writer at *Time*. Rather, it evolved from a 'development deal' that began with Juval Aviv, the ex-Pan Am investigator, and Warner Books, a division of Warner Communications.... There could eventually be a book, but before the book was published, there could be a series of spinoff articles and exposés that would appear as 'scoops' in *Time* magazine. Laurence Kirshbaum, president of Warner Books, confirms this was the deal." *Caveat emptor.*

"Dolphin Courtship: Brutal, Cunning and Complex"
2-18-92
Natalie Angier
The New York Times

As with her Pulitzer Prize winning work on animal behavior in 1990 and her 10 Best selection for last year's "Pit Viper's Life: Bizarre, Gallant and Venomous," 10-15-91, Angier scores again with a delightful, well-balanced and comprehensively-researched dispatch on the habits of dolphins. Her work on animal behavior is irresistible and, like the substantial portion of her portfolio, definitive. This essay dispels much of the mythology surrounding dolphin behavior in a readable, entertaining manner. "As much as puppies or pandas or even children, dolphins are universally beloved. They seem to cavort and frolic at the least provocation, their mouths are fixed in what looks like a state of perpetual merriment, and their behavior and enormous brains suggest an intelligence approaching that of humans—or even, some might argue, surpassing it. Dolphins are turning out to be exceedingly clever, but not in the loving, utopian-socialist manner that sentimental Flipperophiles might have hoped." She details the complex socialization and habits of these creatures with grace and ease, bringing to life a subject which, in the hands of another less enthusiastic reporter, might be dull and unimaginatively presented.

"Heart Attack Study Adds to the Cautions About Iron in the Diet"
9-8-92
David Stipp
The Wall Street Journal

In this solid leder, Stipp tells us nearly everything we've ever needed or wanted to know about this mineral but were afraid to ask. "Researchers studying heart disease, the country's No. 1 killer, have over the years narrowed the main risk factors down to a well-known handful: smoking, hypertension, lack of exercise, high cholesterol. But before long people may be hearing that they need to worry about one more thing: iron. A study to be published today in *Circulation*, a journal of the American Heart Association, found a close parallel between the levels of iron in the body and the chances of having a heart attack. Indeed, it suggested that iron levels have a closer association with heart attacks than does any other cardiac risk factor except smoking." Here Stipp outlines different studies and findings that would seem to corroborate the notion that too much iron isn't a good idea. He is careful to put his sources up front, as well as to emphasize the preliminary nature of the findings. We appreciate his trim navigation and clear elucidation of the scientific aspects of the story, presenting his information in a straightforward manner. Despite the public service nature of the dispatch, Stipp avoids hawking or hyping the results of this Finnish study, and we come away enriched.

"In the Shooting Gallery: Addicts and AIDS"
9-27-92 through 9-30-92
Barry Bearak
Los Angeles Times

Bearak goes into a Brooklyn, N.Y., shooting gallery to pen this devastating portrait of the tortured lives of heroin addicts. While the subject has been treated before, Bearak makes it more current and all the more poignant, as some "fiends" wait fearfully for the results of HIV tests and others try vainly to circumnavigate the maze of bureaucracy to get into city-funded treatment programs. Because he makes no judgment, we get full-blooded images of the people in the gallery, rather than cardboard caricatures. "She was five months pregnant, and her belly had not yet outgrown a streetwalker's skirts. Lourdes Pabon, 28 and comely, made more money than most on the Flushing Avenue stroll.... Drugs kept her from her gloominess. She could shoot up and then there she was, in the broad daylight of simply being, without a messy life to muddle things. Heroin was such a relief that way, and so nice generally, except that it always wore off and the scramble for more seemed to go on forever." He makes us cognizant of the gravity of the situation. "The nation has an estimated 1 million injecting drug users, and in recent years they have not only been responsible for 34% of all newly reported AIDS cases, they have also been the main cause of the epidemic's spread to the heterosexual population."

"The Media & The LAPD: From Coziness to Conflict"
5-24-92 through 5-28-92
David Shaw
Los Angeles Times

With this stunning series on the complicated relationship between the Los Angeles Police Department and the media, Shaw, the *Times* media analyst, provides the definitive examination of the coverage of the Rodney Glen King story. He ventures way into the past, all the way back to the city's gunslinging days, to lay the groundwork for the complexities of today's adversarial relationship between the media, both local and national, and the department. In the 5-24 and 5-25 analyses, he cites decisive turning points in the relationship such as the Watts riots and the advent of television, which became a visual forum for both the police and critics of the LAPD. Using this rich history as a guide, he moves onto the high point of the series in the 5-26 article, providing a tough dissection of his paper's record in reporting racial incidents involving police abuse. This sharp evaluation provides numerous case studies of the *Times* and other area publications' handling of such issues. He broadens this discussion to other media with two exceptional essays on 5-27 and 5-28, posing important questions about the impact media coverage had on the Rodney King affair. "Of greater concern is the question of whether the media, by the very nature of their coverage, contributed significantly to a widespread assumption that the officers were guilty and would be convicted—an assumption that helped fuel the rage, shock and violent reaction of so many when the officers were not convicted." This sterling examination capped the *Times*'s exceptional coverage of King and the riots.

"Support Grows for Vitamins as Roadblocks to Heart Disease"
9-22-92
Gina Kolata
The New York Times

After the panic over cholesterol levels several years ago, Kolata provides a valuable public service with this dispatch that updates us on the issue by explaining in clear terms how vitamins may help avert heart disease by preventing cholesterol from clumping after oxidation. The impact of this information is tremendous in terms of changing one's diet and vitamin intake as she illuminates how cholesterol, "a substance that is a constituent of every cell's membranes and that is completely inert when mixed with cells in the laboratory, elicit[s] bumps and lesions on the slick linings of artery walls. Findings from basic research said that the answer lay in oxidation; cholesterol must be oxidized, made rancid, before it does its damage. Once cholesterol is oxidized, it acts like a lure, drawing other cells to it, precipitating a snowball of reactions that culminate in an artery-clogging plaque. The more cholesterol around, the more damage is done. Now researchers are finding that they can easily stymie the oxidation process and defuse cholesterol. Drugs and minerals like selenium can block oxidation, and, even better, so can vitamins, including vitamins E, C, and beta carotene, a parent molecule of vitamin A that colors vegetables yellow and orange." She catalogues the research most readably, maintaining an appropriate emphasis on the developmental nature of the findings. As should be the case with the best dispatches on such issues, we *learn* from this superb treatment.

"Their Malcolm, My Problem"
12-92
Gerald Early
Harper's

The director of African and Afro-American Studies at Washington University takes us on the poignant, painfully honest journey of a soul—his own and that of black America. He struggles to come to terms with the contradictions of his life experience: as a youth in a racist world where Malcolm X's message empowered and inspired, and as a middle-class American who has come to view Malcolm's nationalist cries as destructive. "So here I am, caught between my daughters, who find my race lessons tiresome, and my students, who think me somehow insufficiently black. I need look no farther than Malcolm, old ally and new nemesis, to find the source of this ambiguity. Malcolm embodied contradiction. He preached the importance of Africa, yet he was the most American of men. His autobiography is the quintessential Horatio Alger tale of the self-created individual." The honesty and depth of Early's search for balance makes this an essay all Americans should read. "Malcolm preached the necessity of being African at the complete expense of our American selves, a love of the misty past at the cost of our actual lives, our triumphs, our sufferings in the New World and as modern people.... Our profound past of being African, which we must never forget, must be balanced by the complex fate of being American, which we can never deny or, worse, evade. For we must accept who and what we are and the forces and conditions that have made us this, not as defeat or triumph, not in shame or with grandiose pride, but as the tangled, strange, yet poignant and immeasurable record of an imperishable human presence."

"What Do We Get for Our School Dollars?"
10-12-92
Janet Novack
Forbes

"In all the current furor about education in the U.S., too much attention gets paid to the size of school budgets and too little to how those budgets are spent." With this in mind, Novack takes us on a highly-educational tour of the suburbs around Dayton, Ohio, where we peer into the inner workings of schools in "archetypal Middle America." "What we did not find here was much waste. But maybe we did find a clue as to why the increase in spending on education in this country has not be followed by rising education results." What we discover is that "For all the talk in the 1980s about 'back to basics,' the lack of focus shows up right from the first grade, both in spending and the pupil's day. . . . On a typical day, after lunch, recess, snack, and art, music or gym, the second-grade teachers have at most four hours to teach their charges." In addition, Novack explains, "What the teachers teach is increasingly mandated from above on political grounds and influenced by what grant money is available." Complains one teacher: "'There is more and more being put on teachers that should be done in the home—sex education, drugs, self-esteem.' Yet Dayton's own congressman, Democrat Tony Hall, has been pushing a bill to create a national commission to recommend how schools should teach character values. Wonderful again, but is that what schools are supposed to do?" As the debate over how to educate the nation's children steamrolls ahead, educators and policymakers would be advised to stop and ponder Novack's eye-opening analysis.

"Why Did Robin Peeler Die?"
6-7-92
"Paying Dearly for Privatization"
6-14-92
Eileen McNamara
The Boston Globe Magazine

In this shocking two-part series examining health care in the Massachusetts prison system, staff writer McNamara goes inside the Massachusetts Correctional Institution for women at Framingham and reveals the details of how women are dying at the prison, taking Robin Peeler, a 32-year-old shoplifter-drug addict, as a case in point. Three months after Peeler's death, the causes are still "undetermined," with speculation ranging from a heart attack to drug overdose, though her autopsy showed no signs of illegal drugs in her system. McNamara shrinks from nothing in detailing the apparent inadequacy of health care at the facility as the state contracts with a Ft. Lauderdale firm, Emergency Medical Systems Associates, to provide care for the entire prison system. " . . . The physician hired to run the Health Services Unit [at MCI-Framingham] has an emergency room background, with no experience in gynecology, obstetrics or HIV infection in women. 'He's an expert in emergency medicine, and that's what you need in a prison,' [EMS program director Dr. Henry] Phipps says of Dr. Andrew Mitchell. 'He can handle OB-GYN, and let's face it, we are right now in the middle of an explosion of knowledge about AIDS. No one is an expert.' That attitude disturbs some of those who work with inmates at Framingham. 'This is a prison for women, and no one thinks it's important that they know anything about women's health?' asks Jo-Anna Rorie, the nurse-midwife." This is an informative, disturbing portrait that gained currency as a minute subset of the debate over state-run health services.

POLITICAL

"Bush's Gamble"
10-18-92
William Safire
The New York Times Magazine

Although others handled President Bush's economic missteps better, Safire's striking analysis of Bush's "inordinate fear of running without solid support from the far right" was matched by none. Here, Safire captures "the mode-changing Jekyll-Hyde Bush." "Nobody ever says, 'Let Bush be Bush,' because nobody can be sure what that would be." Safire crystallized the political ramifications of this split personality, especially as it manifested itself at the Republican convention which pandered to the far right: "Result: the righteous right thinks of him as a vehicle to be used while the reasonable right thinks of him as a traitor to his kind. That accounts for the crack, 'His support may be narrow, but it runs shallow . . .'" His analysis is uncannily accurate; his prose impressively fluid. "Conservatives who cast a grudging vote for Clinton will be 'Bushed Republicans': conservative women turned off in droves by the party platform's unequivocal anti-abortion stand; hawkish males tired of a spent Administration; . . . and right-wingers of all feathers troubled by a candidate who presents himself as Mr. Nice Guy clanking about in far-right armor." As Safire notes, this is an extremely subjective essay from a longtime conservative who is now thinking the unthinkable: "That's where the Bush campaign leaves me and my ilk . . . Neither Perot nor staying home is an option. We will closely watch Bush reveal himself in the final weeks, cock a skeptical ear to the Clinton call and make a decision inside the voting booth—putting a clothespin in our pocket just in case."

"Clinton the Front-Runner"
1-3-92
Rowland Evans & Robert Novak
The Washington Post

Few journalists had a handle on the political dynamic at work this election year or pin-pointed Bill Clinton's centrist campaign strategy so precisely, or so early in the year, as did Evans & Novak. The duo's ability to provide prescient, clear-eyed analysis remains unmatched. In the aftermath of the Democratic party's flirtation with an indecisive Mario Cuomo, the duo discerns that the "wholly unintended beneficiary" of Cuomo's decision not to run is "the Democratic candidate who irks him most"—Gov. Bill Clinton. "There is a strong vein of opinion among the [Democratic] party faithful that Bush is beatable, but not by another in the McGovern-Mondale-Dukakis sequence tied to liberal special interests. Clinton, who is his own best strategist, consciously picked a fight with the politically pugnacious [Mario] Cuomo to show how different he is from that parade of melancholy standard-bearers." As the year progressed, the pair's razor-sharp assessment of Clinton's staying power played out on the national scene: "If he loses Feb. 18 [in New Hampshire primary] he still has the spate of southern primaries to fall back. All this poses a nightmare scenario for the Bush camp, which has long acknowledged Clinton to be the one Democrat capable of breaking the Republican hammerlock on the South's electoral votes but which smugly adds that he is just not liberal enough to be nominated. That betrays GOP ignorance of what is going on inside the Democratic Party."

"His Master's Voice"
10-92
Marjorie Williams
Vanity Fair

Perhaps James Baker III played the power behind the throne too well by half, carefully crafting positive news about himself through highly controlled "leaks," according to this revealing profile. But when the clothes were stripped off the President this campaign year, Baker found himself naked as well, and no one served up the head of Bush's Richelieu as did Marjorie Williams, a former correspondent for *The Washington Post*. "After weeks of talking to friends and colleagues who had dressed him up in humanitarian garb, I was stunned how frankly Baker seemed to wear his true manner: he was one of the least warm human beings I had ever met, a high-performance engine uninterested in pretending to be anything else." From Baker's early ties to George Bush, to his achievements as Secretary of State, we learn the influence he has had over the recent presidencies: "Baker's ability to survive is also closely tied to his ideological neutrality." Williams' most notable salvo is her assessment of the heretofore unchallenged contention that Baker was the master diplomatic pragmatist. She sheds light on his numerous missteps including his coddling of Mikhail Gorbachev as the U.S.S.R. fell apart, as well as his pre-war policies toward Iraq, an image problem that he overcame, according to Williams, by hanging U.S. Ambassador April Glaspie out to dry for his own misreading of Hussein's intentions. Williams keenly observes that "Bush needs you to like him; Baker wants you to respect him."

"Instant Way to Cut Capital Gains Tax?"
1-22-92
Paul Craig Roberts
The Washington Times

With this thunderbolt column early in the political year, Roberts pushed an idea into public discussion that occupied the Bush administration, on and off, throughout the re-election campaign. Roberts, who on tax policy had been a decisively influential U.S. Treasury economist in the early Reagan years and is now a widely-read syndicated columnist, argues that Bush, who had been unsuccessful for three years running in persuading the Democratic Congress to cut the capital gains tax, could effectively do so by executive order, with the stroke of a regulatory pen at Treasury. Roberts explained that the definition of capital gains is not governed by statute, but by regulation, and thus "the president can cut the capital gains tax rate simply by exercising his authority to change the regulatory definition to index capital gains for inflation." Soon after, Roberts was summoned to the White House to explain the idea. A host of lawyers in and out of government debated the pros and cons for weeks, until the idea was rejected, only to surface again when Secretary of State James Baker III became White House chief-of-staff in September. The Roberts idea blossomed again at Baker's urging and for a while seemed as if it would fly, effectively liberating trillions of dollars of inflated gains trapped by Beltway gridlock. With Wall Street holding its breath, the idea was killed again by Justice Department lawyers. Roberts, though, had demonstrated the Power of One to trigger an important policy debate.

"An Israeli Contract With a U.S. Company Leads to Espionage"
1-17-92
"U.S. Firms Are Linked to an Israeli General at Heart of a Scandal"
1-20-92
"Roles of Ex-Pentagon Officials at Jewish Group Show Clout of Cold Warrior, Pro-Israel Network"
1-22-92
Edward T. Pound and David Rogers
The Wall Street Journal

At a time of increasing tension between the U.S. and Israel, Pound and Rogers explore the more curious idiosyncracies of this traditionally close, but complex alliance. In their dramatic 1-17 scoop, the pair gains access to the contents of an arbiters' February 1991 sealed decision on the Recon case which involved espionage charges against three Air Force officers from Israel who had been working at the U.S. plant which had been contracted to build a top-secret airborne spy-camera system for Israel. "The panel ruled that the Israeli agents had indeed used 'elaborate subterfuges' to steal some of the company's plans for the spy camera, which, the arbiters said, was considered by the Israeli government to be 'very important to its national security interest.' . . . The case establishes for apparently the first time in a U.S. legal proceeding that Israel stole high-tech secrets from an American company." Another investigative coup on 1-20 reveals that the Dotan affair, which led to the imprisonment of Israeli brigadier general Rami Dotan for skimming millions of dollars in U.S. military aid, "could prove to be as much an American scandal as an Israeli one." Finally, the 1-22 report, provides a revealing look at the "tight little circle [which] illustrates an enduring network of Cold War conservatives and pro-Israel interests in Washington."

"Making Choices: Bush's Economic Record"
10-4-92 through 10-7-92
Bob Woodward
The Washington Post

Few stories this year created as much consternation within the administration as did this highly-detailed exposé of the behind-the-scene infighting over economic policy and Bush's reversal on his "no new tax" pledge. The administration considered the information leaked by well-placed anonymous inside sources crippling to its re-election efforts and the highest form of personal treason in the gentlemen's White

House. The article undermined any perception of the White House economic team working as a unit. There was much speculation that OMB director Richard Darman was a key source for the exposé. "Bush did not entirely trust Darman. For years Bush had told others that he suspected Darman had leaked unfavorable information about him during the Reagan presidency." Indeed, Darman appears to have his fingerprints all over the report; "Analyzing his own mistakes, Darman told others that he worried he had made a 'Faustian bargain,' selling his soul and his skills as he went along with questionable policies in exchange for power. Darman reasoned that if he left office, quit, gave up power, he would never have a chance to put the federal budget on a path of deficit reduction. But if he stayed and Bush were re-elected, he could salvage his credibility, he has told others, and this time it would be different. But recently, according to associates, Darman has been struggling with the choices he has made, and even asked 'if I am kidding myself.'" In the end, though, Darman is cast as a self-serving traitor, and President Bush as a bystander to the carnage.

"The President's Understudy"
1-5-92 through 1-10-92
and 1-12-92
*David S. Broder and
Bob Woodward
The Washington Post*

So talked about was the Broder/Woodward examination of the Vice President that former President Richard Nixon quipped the pair were merely inflating Quayle to knock him down come the '96 presidential race. Indeed, this in-depth study of Dan Quayle, the man and the myth, took on even more weight as Republicans looked beyond their political defeat in November. Many of the article's enlightening observations took on new importance, such as the observation in the 1-5 report that "Dan Quayle has proved himself to be a skillful player of the political game, with a competitive drive that has been underestimated repeatedly by his rivals." Perhaps most insightful were the two 1-7 pieces on the '88 election, in which the pair reveals the confusion that surrounded the announcement of Quayle as George Bush's running mate. As Quayle became the victim of a press feeding frenzy, Broder and Woodward review the disorganization that compounded Quayle's inexperience as a national candidate. "...Marilyn Quayle lays the blame entirely on the Bush operative. 'They should have been ready to go with papers on exactly who Dan was,' she said recently. 'All of his accomplishments in the Senate.... They should have lined up his colleagues in the Senate.... Nobody was lined up. There was nothing tangible to hand to a member of the press. So people were scrounging...'" A stellar piece of political journalism.

"Profiles: Outsider"
2-3-92, 2-10-92 and 2-17-92
*Marshall Frady
The New Yorker*

If you think you know Jesse Jackson, forget it, until you read this book-length essay. Frady, who spent an enormous amount of time travelling with and studying his subject, files the definitive political and personal portrait of the Rev. Jackson. This stunning three-part series allows us to get to know the enigmatic Jackson in three-dimensional detail, making other, earlier profiles seem like cardboard caricatures. "One needn't be an admirer of Jackson's to recognize that he is possibly the most original figure ever to have arrived at such an importance in the contest for the Presidency. He emerged as something like the Muhammad Ali of Presidential politics, not only in his fondness for prancing rhyme but as a spectacular and irrepressible virtuoso of ego." But page after page, Jackson speaks for himself, on race, on his political career, his childhood, his religion, his ambition and his drive to unite voters behind the Democratic party. We see Jackson the consummate politician, revelling emotionally in the spotlight as he negotiates for the release of the hostages from Kuwait. Then Frady recalls: "And then I saw that—out of the witness of any camera, all by himself in the dark—he was still weeping. Sobbing soundlessly but so deeply and unstoppably that when I went back to congratulate him and asked what might be the significance of how things had turned out—the sort of question he usually could not resist expatiating on—he could not reply. Could not speak. He simply went on weeping." Taken together, these three reports provide extraordinary insight into the complexities of Jackson's life and personality.

"U.S. Strategy Plan Calls for Insuring No Rivals Develop" 3-8-92
"Pentagon Drops Goal of Blocking New Superpowers" 5-24-92
Patrick E. Tyler
The New York Times

With his 3-8 article Tyler shocked the nation by revealing the draft of a broad and highly controversial new policy statement from the Pentagon: "The Defense Department asserts that America's political and military mission in the post-cold-war era will be to insure that no rival superpower is allowed to emerge in Western Europe, Asia or the territory of the former Soviet Union." Tyler's impressive analytical skills enhance the article. "The document is conspicuously devoid of references to collective action through the United Nations," and "What is most important, [the document] says, is 'the sense that the world order is ultimately backed by the U.S.'" The draft was widely criticized by the White House and in foreign capitals. In fact, so contentious was the nature of Tyler's disclosure that by May the Pentagon had revised the documents, an event Tyler depicted in his 5-24 article. In this follow-up, we also learn more about Tyler's source for the original leak, "an Administration official who believes the debate on post-cold-war strategy should be conducted in public." The impact of the leak led to the deletion of language "from an earlier document advocating the perpetuation of a one-superpower world..." Tyler's tenacious pursuit of the story provided a high-water mark in his field for cleanly written, influential reporting.

"33 Days That Defined a Candidate" 7-12-92
Curtis Wilkie
The Boston Globe Magazine

Among the numerous documents written from reporters given unprecedented access to Bill Clinton's campaign this year, Wilkie's account of the wounded front-runner's trial by fire in the New Hampshire primary proved the most exceptional. Appearing just before the Democratic National Convention, this article provided a detailed portrait of Clinton as an indefatigable campaigner who persevered through a roller coaster primary campaign that began strongly, encountered a devastating plunge of 20 percent in the polls following revelations about extramarital affairs and possible draft evasion, and staged a dramatic comeback. "Then, on January 16, a blemish appeared like the first, faint signs of a malignancy. It was a Thursday, the day of the week that became known as 'garbage day' in the Clinton campaign, for it was on Thursdays that advance copies of *Star*, a national tabloid, were released ...Maintaining a smile and an air of bemusement, Clinton followed a preordained plan. He described the story as old and false and ridiculed the source, dismissing *Star* as a newspaper 'that says Martians walk on earth and cows have human heads.'" Wilkie's inclusion of seemingly peripheral trivia creates a telling, multidimensional feature: "For want of an office, Clinton took over the men's room at the airport. The governor perched on a lavatory, and his aides huddled around him, pondering what course to take next."

THE RATING GUIDE

Inclusion in the *MediaGuide 500*, regardless of the stars received, is an indication of a journalist's prominence in the Big Leagues of print journalism. However, even at the top, there is a range of quality which we attempt to define through specific criteria. Ratings are based on work written between January 1, 1992, and December 31, 1992. We cite at least four articles in each write-up, though we read and evaluate many more. The basic standards for reporters are those generally accepted by the profession: fairness, accuracy and balance (objectivity), plus three additional measures which define excellence: depth of reporting and analysis, writing ability and the consistency with which quality work is produced. For commentators, the criteria includes depth of insight and information, presentation and soundness of argumentation (persuasive ability), and the consistency with which quality work is produced.

(—)
Failing most criteria.

½★
Failing the secondary criteria on one or more counts.

★
Good. Reporters: professional.
Commentators: worth trying.

★½
Good/very good.
Very good inconsistently.

★★
Very good. In reporters, above average reporting and writing, average analytical skills. In commentators, generally interesting content and presentation.

★★½
Very good/excellent. Above average consistency.

★★★
Excellent. In reporters, superior reporting and writing, above average in analytical skills. In commentators, very strong presentation, frequent insights.

★★★½
Excellent/exceptional. Approaching the very best.

★★★★
Exceptional. In reporters, loftily objective, pacesetters for the profession in reporting and writing, penetrating analytical skills, always worth reading. In commentators, pacesetters for the profession, must reading for insights, a consistently well-defined point of view.

THE HIGHEST RATED JOURNALISTS OF 1992

★★★★

Dempsey, Judy	*Financial Times*	Foreign
Evans & Novak	*Creators Syndicate*	Commentary
Morrocco, John D.	*Aviation Week & Space Technology*	National Security
Roberts, Paul Craig	*The Washington Times*	Commentary
Safire, William	*The New York Times*	Commentary
Tanner, James	*The Wall Street Journal*	Business
Waldmeir, Patti	*Financial Times*	Foreign

★★★½

Angier, Natalie	*The New York Times*	Science
Bacon, Kenneth H.	*The Wall Street Journal*	Business
Burns, John F.	*The New York Times*	Foreign
Dobrzynski, Judith H.	*BusinessWeek*	Business
Fineman, Mark	*Los Angeles Times*	Foreign
Gigot, Paul	*The Wall Street Journal*	Commentary
Gilder, George	*Forbes*	Business
Harden, Blaine	*The Washington Post*	Foreign
Hoagland, Jim	*The Washington Post*	Commentary
Ingersoll, Bruce	*The Wall Street Journal*	Business
Keller, Bill	*The New York Times*	Foreign
Lippman, Thomas W.	*The Washington Post*	Business
Loomis, Carol J.	*Fortune*	Business
Mahar, Maggie	*Barron's*	Business
Marsh, David	*Financial Times*	Foreign
Raspberry, William	*The Washington Post*	Commentary
Sanger, David E.	*The New York Times*	Foreign
Starr, Barbara	*Jane's Defence Weekly*	National Security
Taylor, Alex, III	*Fortune*	Business
Truell, Peter	*The Wall Street Journal*	Business

Tyler, Patrick E.	*The New York Times*	National Security
Vatikiotis, Michael	*Far Eastern Economic Review*	Foreign
Williams, Carol J.	*Los Angeles Times*	Foreign
Williams, Juan	*The Washington Post*	Society & Politics
Wrubel, Robert	*Financial World*	Business

★★★

Andrews, Edmund L.	*The New York Times*	Business
Baker, Russell	*The New York Times*	Commentary
Barnes, Fred	*The New Republic*	Commentary
Bartley, Robert L.	*The Wall Street Journal*	Commentary
Blumenthal, Sidney	*The New Yorker*	Commentary
Brimelow, Peter	*Forbes*	Business
Brittan, Samuel	*Financial Times*	Business
Broder, David S.	*The Washington Post*	Commentary
Bronner, Ethan	*The Boston Globe*	Foreign
Brownstein, Ronald	*Los Angeles Times*	Society & Politics
Carey, John	*BusinessWeek*	Business
Charen, Mona	*Creators Syndicate*	Commentary
Cook, James	*Forbes*	Business
Coy, Peter	*BusinessWeek*	Business
Cullison, A. E.	*The Journal of Commerce*	Foreign
de Briganti, Giovanni	*Defense News*	National Security
Darlin, Damon	*The Wall Street Journal*	Foreign
Drogin, Bob	*Los Angeles Times*	Foreign
Easterbrook, Gregg	*Newsweek, The Atlantic*	Society & Politics
Fields, Suzanne	*The Washington Times*	Commentary
Forsyth, Randall W.	*Barron's*	Business
Fraser, Damien	*Financial Times*	Foreign
Friedman, Thomas L.	*The New York Times*	National Security
Georges, Christopher	*The Washington Monthly*	Society & Politics
Greenfield, Meg	*Newsweek, The Washington Post*	Commentary
Grenier, Richard	*The Washington Times*	Commentary
Gupta, Udayan	*The Wall Street Journal*	Business

Harwood, Richard	*The Washington Post*	Society & Politics
Henriques, Diana B.	*The New York Times*	Business
Hiltzik, Michael A.	*Los Angeles Times*	Foreign
Holley, David	*Los Angeles Times*	Foreign
Ibrahim, Youssef M.	*The New York Times*	Foreign
Jameson, Sam	*Los Angeles Times*	Foreign
Kamm, Henry	*The New York Times*	Foreign
Kaye, Lincoln	*Far Eastern Economic Review*	Foreign
Kristol, Irving	*The Wall Street Journal*	Commentary
Lamb, Christina	*Financial Times*	Foreign
Leo, John	*U.S. News & World Report*	Commentary
Leopold, George	*Defense News*	National Security
Levin, Doron P.	*The New York Times*	Business
Lewis, Anthony	*The New York Times*	Commentary
Lewis, Paul	*The New York Times*	National Security
Mallet, Victor	*Financial Times*	Foreign
Mathews, Jay	*Newsweek, The Washington Post*	Society & Politics
McArdle, Thomas	*Investor's Business Daily*	Business
Merline, John	*Investor's Business Daily*	Society & Politics
Moberg, David	*In These Times*	Business
Morgenson, Gretchen	*Forbes*	Business
Mortimer, Edward	*Financial Times*	Commentary
O'Brian, Bridget	*The Wall Street Journal*	Business
Opall, Barbara	*Defense News*	National Security
Oppenheimer, Andres	*The Miami Herald*	Foreign
Ozanne, Julian	*Financial Times*	Foreign
Pasztor, Andy	*The Wall Street Journal*	National Security
Pollack, Andrew	*The New York Times*	Foreign
Postrel, Virginia I.	*Reason*	Commentary
Proctor, Paul	*Aviation Week & Space Technology*	National Security
Reinhold, Robert	*The New York Times*	Society & Politics
Richburg, Keith B.	*The Washington Post*	Foreign
Salwen, Kevin G.	*The Wall Street Journal*	Business
Saporito, Bill	*Fortune*	Business

Sawyer, Kathy	*The Washington Post*	Science
Schlesinger, Jacob M.	*The Wall Street Journal*	Foreign
Schmemann, Serge	*The New York Times*	Foreign
Schrage, Michael	*Los Angeles Times*	Business
Sciolino, Elaine	*The New York Times*	National Security
Seligman, Daniel	*Fortune*	Commentary
Shaw, David	*Los Angeles Times*	Society & Politics
Sheppard, Nathaniel, Jr.	*Chicago Tribune*	Foreign
Shogren, Elizabeth	*Los Angeles Times*	Foreign
Silverberg, David	*Defense News*	National Security
Sowell, Thomas	*Forbes*	Commentary
Tanzer, Andrew	*Forbes*	Foreign
Thomas, Paulette	*The Wall Street Journal*	Business
Wagstyl, Stefan	*Financial Times*	Foreign
Wilford, John Noble	*The New York Times*	Science
Woodward, Bob	*The Washington Post*	Society & Politics
Zachary, G. Pascal	*The Wall Street Journal*	Business

★ BUSINESS ★

Alan Abelson
Barron's
★½

Editor. We suggest that when you launch into an Abelson column you get your yucks in the first few paragraphs, then skip directly to the end where you'll find a meaty stock tidbit or two. According to news reports in December, Abelson, an icon at the weekly, had been asked to step down as editor, but continue his "Up & Down Wall Street" column. The outcome of this news was still unclear at year's end. What is clear, though, is that Abelson consistently sacrifices content for style. Take his 2-3 column in which he says George Bush's politesse shined through in his State of the Union address: "... there was nothing in his entire speech... to offend hard times..." We're dying, but we're still waiting for substantive analysis. His analysis of macroeconomic issues is also weak. For instance, in the 4-13 column, he makes gentle sport of Federal Reserve chairman Alan Greenspan whose "ardor" for easy money "tends to swell especially during those years in which... presidents are elected." Maybe, but with inflation dropping throughout 1992, perhaps readers deserved a serious assessment of the Fed's tactics. We do find some valuable information in his 6-8 essay, although it's buried in column four: "We agree... that the price behavior of [gold] for the past couple of years accurately portrayed the absence of inflationary pressures.... But we don't think that undermines our case. For we believe that gold is about to regain some luster. Who laughed?" Well, we did, especially after gold closed down substantially in 1992. But, we genuinely appreciated his evaluation. We also valued his 9-14 column, an effective critique of the dollar-bashing crowd in D.C. But after dozens of knee-slappers on Bill Clinton's economic summit, Abelson's 12-14 column provides little more than his standard bearish line.

George Anders
The Wall Street Journal
★★

A veteran on Wall Street, Anders has a new book out on KKR, *Merchants of Debt*. As the book indicates, his forté is dealmaking, and though the deals he covers now aren't as hot as those of the go-go '80s, Anders manages to bring plenty of enthusiasm to his reports. He's in top form for "Insilco Debt Plan Gets Merrill Lynch Off the Hot Seat," 5-5, uncovering the story behind Insilco Inc.'s emergence from bankruptcy: "As part of the transaction, Goldman acknowledges, it signed a confidential one-page agreement with Merrill concerning the bonds. Goldman won't say what was in the agreement. But other Insilco creditors believe it amounted to an assurance that Goldman, as an Insilco creditor, wouldn't press litigation against Merrill before the Texas company was ready to emerge from bankruptcy." As Sunbeam weighs an IPO, Anders takes a quick, but perceptive look at the company's short, but profitable history in "Investors Steinhardt and Mutual Series Aim for Over $1 Billion in Sunbeam-Oster Offering," 7-31, then compares the proposed offering price against those of competitors such as Black & Decker. Though the story of ex-Drexelite Leon Black's return to finance has been told elsewhere, Anders gives us new detail on Black's startup of Apollo Investment in "Ex-Official of Drexel Restructures Firms It Loaded Up With Debt," 3-16. Joined by co-writer Paul Ingrassia for "Roger Smith Wanted a Quiet Retirement; He Didn't

50 MEDIAGUIDE

Get One," 11-13, the duo provides an enjoyable leder on the complexities of running a small business, complexities which Roger Smith, retired chairman of GM, discovered firsthand when he got involved as part-time chairman of a small company called Rubatex. Anders isn't nearly as strong on economics as he is on dealmaking. He's much too general in "Germany's Rates Cut Is Likely to Boost Europe's Stock, Bond Markets Right Away," 9-14, and though his contribution to a special anniversary report on the '87 crash, "Trading Moves Blamed in Crash of 1987 Tamed," 10-16, is better, it provides only flashes of new information.

Edmund L. Andrews
The New York Times
★★★

"Patents" columnist. A beat journalist who does his homework, Andrews always furthers our understanding of technology issues. His most cutting-edge work is on the burgeoning telecommunications industry, where he constantly scans the horizon for technological and investment opportunities. But no matter how exciting the advancement, he steadies his enthusiasm with professional composure, candidly assessing the promise and pitfalls of each technology without stifling our excitement. "Cable TV Battling Phone Companies," 3-29, is a perfect example of his thorough analysis. Here he assesses, with plentiful examples, the "inevitable" collision between these two important and lucrative industries: "In the last year, 30 cable television companies have obtained Federal licenses to build experimental wireless telephone networks." In "Networks Receive Approval to Buy Local Cable Units," 6-19, Andrews expertly walks us through the ins and outs of important legislation, and looks down the road to explain how this bill is likely to "hasten a basic realignment of the television industry." His Sunday "Business" lead, "Mr. Tough Guy in Telecommunications," 8-23, brings together all aspects of the Sprint story: the changing environment in which the company now competes, its operational problems, and the CEO's grand vision for the future. Andrews's work on the controversial cable TV legislation kept us thoroughly up-to-date with such competent reports as "Cable TV Regulation Battle Heats Up Before Showdown," 9-16, an impeccably balanced evaluation that gets to the heart of the debate, and "Senate Sends Bush Bill to Regulate Price of Cable TV," 9-23, in which he foresees the override of President Bush's veto and does a fine job of balancing the economic and political implications of the bill. The same perceptive reporting characterizes "Phone Policy Starts to Blur," 11-9, a crystal-clear look at the significance of AT&T's bid to acquire one-third of McCaw Cellular Communications Inc., which would give AT&T a strong presence in the Baby Bells' local telephone markets.

Stuart Auerbach
The Washington Post

Far from being a pacesetter, Auerbach approaches the international trade beat with little enthusiasm. Rather than trying to capture the amazing dynamic that pushes the flow of goods and capital from one country to another, he gives us bare bones updates—a trade barrier here, two tariffs there, etc. He doesn't do justice to this important and exciting beat. Filing from Singapore for "Bush Stresses U.S. Commitment to Asia," 1-5, Auerbach offers standard reporting on Bush's trip and the region's fears about NAFTA, but he clearly lingers with the press pool for this assignment. Though he covers all the bases on Minolta's alleged infringement on three Honeywell patents in "Honeywell Wins $96 Million Judgement Against Minolta," 2-8, much of the information is attributed to wire services. He misses an opportunity to truly examine the post-Cold War repositioning taking place within Cocom in "U.S., Germany Want Ex-Soviet Nations in Cocom," 5-31, getting just the basics on James Baker's efforts to bring the former Soviet Union into the fold of an institution "that once kept Western technology away from Moscow and its Eastern European allies . . . " GATT should be one of the most important stories on Auerbach's trade beat, but his coverage of the issue is lackluster at best, as displayed in "Little Progress Seen on Global Trade Pact," 7-5. What could have been a crucial report on the G-7 meeting in Munich turns out to be a bland collection of generic observations culled from press briefings: "If the summit leaders fail to give strong political impetus to the almost six-year effort to reinvigorate world trade laws, analysts say they fear there will be an escalation of trade tensions, a greater movement to regional trading blocs and a loss of economic growth." This is not news. More run-of-the-mill reporting characterizes "Gephardt Draws Line on Trade Pact," 7-28, on the House majority leader's calls for funding of environmental protection and worker training through NAFTA. He's only slightly more thorough in "Hopes Fade for Trade Agreement," 12-18, a mediocre analysis of the dismal prospects for concluding GATT negotiations before Clinton takes office.

Kenneth H. Bacon
The Wall Street Journal
★★★½

Banking. Though his work is not as consistently vigorous as last year, Bacon remains one of the finest journalists on this complex beat. He typically leaves no stone unturned in his efforts to scrutinize the status quo and assess the latest legislative and regulatory proposals for this troubled industry. His finest work this year, "Fannie Mae Expected to Escape an Attempt at Tighter Regulation," 6-19, offers an in-depth look at the privileged position of this lending organization. Bacon does a superb job of revealing how the current regulatory environment is causing private banks to sell rather than hold mortgages: "Their financial strength has enabled Fannie Mae and Freddie Mac to provide a steady stream of mortgage finance during a decade when thousands of banks and thrifts failed.... As a result the residential mortgage markets are becoming increasingly federalized..." As a result of this article, we're able to read between the lines of his succinct follow-up, "Senate Bill Setting New Requirements on Fannie Mae, Freddie Mac Is Passed," 7-2, which reports on new capital standards being imposed on the two lending organization: "After working hard to shape the bill, Fannie Mae and Freddie Mac supported the measure." Typical of his expert daily beat reporting are "FDIC Testing Cheaper Ways to Save Banks," 3-2, an insightful report on the FDIC's controversial new methods for structuring takeovers of failed banks, and "FDIC Delays Increase in Fee for Insurance," 4-8, in which Bacon turns a mundane FDIC announcement into a study of the complexities of bank policymaking in an election year. Joined by co-writer Steven Lipin for "Under New Bank Law, More Large Depositors Face Losses in Failures," 10-22, we're offered a useful exploration of the dilemmas surrounding the FDIC's attempts to reduce the cost of bank failures by limiting federal insurance to $100,000. He gives us a lot to chew on in "Clinton Economic Appointments Raise Questions About Possible Conflicts in Dealings With RTC," 12-16, a balanced and well-sourced evaluation of the problems that could arise from the professional connections of appointees Robert Rubin and Roger Altman.

Howard Banks
Forbes
★★½

Assistant managing editor. Banks is writing less this year as his management responsibilities increase and he moves toward the top of the masthead. We still watch for his byline as it always promises sturdy analysis, especially on aerospace issues. His pithy contribution to *Forbes*'s "Annual Report on American Industry," "Aerospace & Defense," 1-6, provides a compact overview of what lies ahead for these industries, and showcases Banks's impressive grasp of industry trends: "Spending on space is expected to reach $31.8 billion in 1992.... In 1992 [SDI] will soak up about $4 billion.... This will benefit companies such as Lockheed, Martin Marietta, Hughes Aircraft and Rockwell International." Positing in "The World's Most Competitive Economy," 3-30, that gloom, right or wrong, sells papers and buys votes,

Banks questions the U.S.'s current economic pessimism. We appreciate his optimism and credible analysis of the export boom. He's much less upbeat for "Dwindling Hopes," 6-8, a candid look at the "tough days" ahead for McDonnell Douglas and its proposed MD-12 airliner. By the end of this systematic assessment, we understand his pessimism fully. Continuing the theme in "The Thin Line," 10-12, Banks serves up a savvy profile of Boeing Chairman Frank Shrontz and the reasons for his split, optimistic/pessimistic personality: "Looking ahead, Shrontz knows that commercial aviation in the 1990s is going to be a lot tougher than it was in the 1980s. Boeing's union leaders, on the other hand, will be focusing on today's bright figures and demanding big pay increases the company cannot afford if it is to remain competitive." Banks is at his best in this business profile genre, as further evinced in "Good-Bye to Cost Plus," 11-23, a concrete evaluation of Germany's Deutsche Aerospace. The report provides a fine contrast of this company's profit-oriented environment to the rest of Europe's highly-subsidized aerospace industry.

William P. Barrett
Forbes
★★

Contributing editor. Though still inconsistent, Barrett is getting back to the kind of useful reporting we appreciated a few years ago. He's still attracted to the unusual, but he's weaving useful investment angles into his offbeat tales more often these days. For instance, he shows us the practical and profitable side of a morbid industry in "Doctors of Death," 12-7, a dispassionate profile of publicly-traded CAPX which provides money to terminally ill patients by buying their life insurance policies: "In financial terms, the sooner the patient dies, the higher CAPX's return on its capital." Family feuds are a favorite topic for Barrett. "Soured Blood," 6-8, for instance, gives the behind-the-scenes scoop on the brother vs. sister battle for control of American Maize-Products: "A victory by the sister could put American Maize-Products in play. Suitors exist." On the other hand, "Splitting Heirs," 3-30, is the type of quick, gossipy read that airs dirty laundry on the warring heirs of the W.T. Waggoner Estate, but doesn't inform on the financial implications of the feud. When the Texas-based Barrett goes wildcatting for information on a particular company or issue—watch out—he's likely to strike black gold as he did in several business profiles this year. "We're the Only One Left," 2-17, is chock-full of valuable data and information for media investors interested in William Dean Singleton's MediaNews Group. Barrett gives the low-down on the company's financial success amid industry retrenching, providing an impartial assessment of the job done by a man "who gets a dreadful word-of-mouth within the business." He turns a dry and complicated topic, publicly registered limited partnership interests, into an engaging and informative read in "Flypaper Securities," 6-22. Written in the first person, he tells of his own maddening encounter with this complex investment. In "Testing for Money," 7-6, he explains how Underwriters Laboratories Inc., which practically monopolizes the safety testing industry, has turned its controversial tax-exempt status into quite a marketing tool.

Aaron Bernstein
BusinessWeek
★★½

"The Workplace" editor. Having started on this beat during the corporate restructuring of the mid-'80s, Bernstein views labor-management relations through a practical profit/loss prism. He is a competent reporter who remains balanced on a beat that invites bias. He's keen on the repositioning going on between labor and management at AT&T in "What's the Right Choice for AT&T?" 4-13, informing us that the company's acquisition of other non-union companies such as NCR has become a flash point for tensions. In his perceptive "GE's Hard Lesson: Pay Cuts Can Backfire," 8-10, we learn why one GE unit has decided that capitalizing on the productivity of U.S. workers might be more profitable than sending jobs to low-wage countries. Though the program is still too new to judge its success, we appreciate Bernstein's exploration of the idea. He's not nearly as strong on broad employment trends. In fact, we think he has the equation wrong in "The Self-Employed Start Trading In Their Shingles," 11-30, an analysis of the reasons many self-employed workers are heading back to corporate America. Bernstein and his sources seem surprised the recession didn't spur self-employment: "The economy shed 1.3 million jobs from the third quarter of 1990 to the first quarter of 1991.... That sent plenty of managers going into business for themselves. It all fit neatly into a longer-term trend toward white-collar self-employment, which grew by 30% from 1982 to 1991..." But how could the constricting economic environment of the '90s provide the necessary capital and work opportunities that incubated the trend in the '80s? His work on labor relations in the sports business is quite good, as illustrated in "Baseball May Be About to Get Creamed," 12/30/91-1/6/92, a very strong dissection of the technical bargaining breakdown that is leading to soaring pay for players and lower profits for team owners. He's also comprehensive on the legal battle over free agency in "Football's Owners May Be Sacked by a Jury," 6-22.

Harry Bernstein
Los Angeles Times
★

Labor. You'd never know that there were two sides to labor-management debates after reading a Bernstein column. He holds an unshakable opinion that all management is inherently anti-worker. But even though his work is blatantly one-sided, he does provide a useful window on labor's concerns, and this election year he was especially informative on the presidential candidates' inclinations toward labor's interests. Early on, Bernstein viewed Bill Clinton as the friendliest to labor, though he urges the Arkansas governor to be more outspoken on labor issues in "Clinton Can't Afford to Lose Unions," 6-23. Though jabs at the executive suite pepper "How Unions Might Revive Under Clinton," 12-22, this well-informed assessment of President-elect Clinton's emerging cabinet is full of insights: "Labor unions might rightly expect a sympathetic ear in the White House since, under Clinton's close friend, [Robert] Reich, the Labor Department will become a major player.... Yet... the [Economic Policy Institute] board member who will be the next labor secretary... knows few labor leaders and has rarely dealt with specific problems of unions." More typical of Bernstein's polemics, though, are the comments found in "Attempting to Help the Working Poor," 1-21: "Rare acts of local government decency can only help a relatively few people...However, when they threaten to cost some wealthy corporate executives a few bucks, their lobbyists can usually block them." And here's the type of ineffectual belligerence he offers on the Caterpillar strike, in "Others Stand to Gain From Cat Fight," 4-14: "The odds are that Caterpillar Inc.'s immoral threat to devastate the lives of its 13,000 striking workers... will fail." The free-trade pact is another target. As Smith Corona Corp. moves operations to Mexico, Bernstein, in "Free Trade Pact to Hurt U.S. Workers," 8-18, screeches that "Workers here [in the U.S.] are told to accept miserable wages and job conditions." He provides only one example of such abuse.

John M. Berry
The Washington Post
★ ½

As a key player on the *Post*'s economic team, Berry has access to all the important Beltway players. Regrettably, he more often relies on his own impulses and fails to capitalize on this asset. Though he can be relied upon to provide a fair and accurate account of the Fed chairman's testimony to Congress or the latest economic policy pronouncement, his analysis of economic data is simply too general to enhance our understanding of complex topics such as monetary policy, unemployment, economic growth, etc. For example, just as consumers and businesses are finally digging out of their heavy debt loads, he writes "From Fast Living to Slow Growth," 1-12, a behind-the-curve assessment characterized by vague generalizations. He's much more specific covering Fed chairman Alan Greenspan's testimony before Congress in "Greenspan Faces Barrage of Senators' Complaints," 1-30, where we found numerous key quotes not given play elsewhere. Refreshingly, his "Fed Moves to Bolster Banks' Net," 2-19, is free of the political undertones that tainted many of the reports on the reduction of bank reserve requirements. Tracking the latest blip on the economic screen, Berry offers shallow analysis in "Housing Starts Plunge," 5-20, allowing the easy-money crowd to gripe as if monetary policy were solely to blame for the plunge in housing starts. Similarly, Berry's interpretation of the latest unemployment figures, in "Jobless Rate Rose to 7.5 Pct. in May," 6-6, gives us only conventional generalizations on the fundamentals of this phenomenon. His analysis is much sturdier in "Fed Faces Growing Pressure on Rates," 6-30, recognizing how Bush's Fed bashing could further complicate interest rate reductions. "Recovery Sputtered in Spring," 7-31, is merely a collection of political reactions to the low economic growth figures, Berry making no effort to challenge the assumptions of his sources, allowing them to take control of the story. He adequately updates us on the latest data out of the Beltway's economic statistics mill in "Consumer Spending Rise Surprises Economists," 12-24, but skims over important issues such as the staying power of this trend.

Marcia Berss
Forbes
★★

Chicago, senior editor. Although she may not have as much flair as other *Forbes* writers, Berss compensates with razor-sharp reporting and carefully-considered analysis. This year, though, we noticed a tendency to put the optimism into overdrive, a shift that detracts from her record of measured evaluation and drops her a notch in our rating. Berss is a bit too impressed with the changes Michael Bozic has brought about at Hills Department Stores in "A Turnaround Is the Best Revenge," 8-3, losing sight of the fact that the company is still in bankruptcy. A query of the talented CEO's plans to handle business after the protections of Chapter 11 are lifted would have been appreciated. Her upbeat profile of the chairman of the consistently profitable National Bank of Detroit, "Bank by Fisher," 4-13, teaches us a great deal about how Carl Fisher has successfully navigated the treacherous waters of lending since the Great Depression. Berss brings drama to the seemingly mundane world of school supplies in "Mr. School Tools," 11-23, chronicling the tale of Bruce Shapiro and his struggle to build Creative Works into the $3 million company it is today. It's an inspiring entrepreneurial tale that reads like *The Little Engine That Could*, but Berss doesn't adequately consider the company's future prospects. More typical of her work from previous years is the proficient "Back to Basics," 3-2, a thorough inspection of First Chicago Corp. and its pragmatic new chief executive, Richard Thomas. By the end of the piece, we have a sturdy handle on the troubled bank's prospects for survival and growth. "This Isn't Ross Perot and GM," 6-8, is also Berss at her best: concise, comprehensive and balanced. Here, she speculates on whether the Hormel family is loosening its grip on cash-rich, debt-light Geo. A. Hormel & Co. This article was surely relished by stock analysts in the food sector. Her zesty profile of the hard-nosed CEO of Guardian Industries, "Nice Guys Finish Last," 7-6, neatly weaves in issues that concern the big players in the monopolistic glass-making industry.

Alan S. Blinder
BusinessWeek
★½

"Economic Viewpoint" columnist. The Gordon S. Rentschler Memorial Professor of Economics at Princeton served as an economic adviser to Bill Clinton during the campaign, and accepted a position with the new administration's Council of Economic Advisors in early January. We turn to Blinder's byline not because it guarantees cutting-edge analysis, but because it holds the possibility of a unique angle from a well-connected player. Nonetheless, he penned a number of ill-considered arguments this year. While he offers a provocative proposal to chop off a chunk of the federal debt in "Let's Start the New Year by Cutting the Debt Load," 1-13, he fails to consider the long-term ramifications of calling government bonds in order to refinance at today's lower interest rates. There is no consideration here of the inevitability that bond holders, accustomed to calls being a remote possibility, now will factor in the increased risk by raising prices. He's much more instructive in "America's Trade Gap Isn't Made in Japan," 4-6, an exceptional dissection of popular myths surrounding U.S. trade with Japan. Blinder makes clear that our trade deficit doesn't cause unemployment, is almost gone, and wasn't made in Japan. "Bounced Checks? That's Not the Real Problem," 5-4, a list of Blinder's proposal to clean up Congress, is mostly a spin-off of ideas we've read elsewhere. Although Blinder purports to construct an argument for labor-oriented economic policies in "We Should Focus on Human Capital, Not Capital," 7-27, this is really an argument against capital-oriented policies that tells us little about the policies Blinder supports. Equally frail are his arguments in "Clintonomics: Figure the Merits Along With the Math," 9-21, an unconvincing rebuttle of the Republican charge that Clinton's economic programs are going to cost two million jobs. Blinder argues that counting paid maternity leave and health insurance as taxes is misleading since "you simply took from one to give to the other." This sounds precisely like a redistribution tax to us. Better, but still somewhat muddled, is his argument that inflation in the service sector is a result of market forces, in "Why the Cost of Services Is Soaring," 11-16.

Peter Brimelow
Forbes
★★★

Senior editor. Make no mistake about it, Brimelow's conservative, supply-side inclinations shape most of his articles. But he packs his perspectives with so much enlightening history and credible data, that no matter what your political or economic beliefs, you learn something. His major strength is making sense out of complex economic statistics, as he does skillfully in "It Can Be Done," 1-6. Taking us back to the Britain of 1891, he reveals how government spending was brought from more than 30 percent to a only 7.3 percent of GNP without abandoning the poor. In "The Fracturing of America," 3-30, he effectively explores the counter-conventional ideas of Manhattan Institute's Linda Chavez, who argues that static median-income and other statistics don't reflect the progress the U.S. Hispanic community has made toward assimilation. He doesn't fare as well in "An Interview With Milton Friedman," 8-17, allowing the Nobel prize-winning economist to take control of the discussion, failing to challenge or probe Friedman's statements to a deeper level. There are few journalists in the U.S. who have as firm a grasp of Canadian politics as Brimelow. He's hard-hitting on the Quebec question in "Agreeing to Disagree," 3-2, thoroughly inspecting the GDP numbers and concluding that separation might not impact Quebec's economy, however, for the rest of Canada, the ultimate question "may not be whether Quebec should secede—but whether it should be expelled." In much the same vein, but with a much harsher tone, "Oh? Canada?" *National Review* 11-30, drives home the eviction theme: "It's what the Czechs are doing with the Slovaks right now, a parallel so striking that almost no Canadians seem to have been informed about it." Economic considerations guide Brimelow's coverage of other international stories, such as "Can Israel Go It Alone?" 5-11. But this was merely a broad skim of this troubled economy. Joined by co-writer Leslie Spencer for "'You Can't Get There From Here,'" 7-6, a 10 Best selection, we're offered a highly-effective critique of the EPA's "command-and-control" bureaucracy.

Samuel Brittan
Financial Times

Assistant editor. Like most of the analysts trying to make sense out of the complex forces that erupted into the European currency crisis,

Brittan was overwhelmed. His analysis of this major story yielded much less than we expect from such a gifted analyst. Overall, though, Brittan remains an especially valuable resource. Unlike so many, he understands the crucial intersection of politics and economics and has a strong grasp of its history. Prescient in "Plenty of Headroom in the UK Economy," 4-23, Brittan advises: "I would . . . shelve any attempt to narrow the UK's ERM bands from 6 per cent to the normal 2¼ per cent this year. . . . With narrow bands, either the UK has to stick with German-type interest rates; or it has to . . . leave the ERM . . . " While the ideologues align themselves with the Yes or No factions in the Maastricht debate, Brittan chooses a more market-oriented perspective. He cheers the Danish rejection in "Emu: Time to Go Back to Evolutionary Approach," 6-11, calling the result "a tonic for those of us who are much keener on the exchange rate mechanism (ERM) than economic and monetary union…" But cognizant of the economic pressures that would accompany a French No vote, he offers an especially sharp analysis on the forces rattling Europe, in "Case for Danish No and French Yes," 9-10: "There is a good technical argument . . . that the German monetary indicator, M3, is giving misleading signals. . . . I doubt, however, if the Bundesbank will stick to M3 for scholastic reasons, once it decides that recession is a greater threat than inflation." But as the currency crisis hits home, Brittan offers a surprisingly weak argument that the Bank of England should have defended the pound, in "Devaluation Threat—How '92 Differs," 9-17. He mentions nothing of the commodity deflation, asserting feebly that if the ERM "is thrown off-course this time, it will have been by a combination of political and market events, having little to do with market fundamentals." His thoughtful essay on Asia, "Eastward, Look, the Land Is Bright," 12-10, sees the region's exponential growth as an opportunity not to be squandered.

John A. Byrne
BusinessWeek
★★

The journalist who four years ago asked his editors if he could undertake a ranking of business schools, continues to pen insightful studies of MBA programs. Overall, though, his body of work is less incisive this year. As always, his annual "The Best B Schools," 10-26, which rates the top 20 business schools, is packed with insights on failures, successes and changes. Unfortunately, "Calling in the Consultants—to the Classroom," 11-16, a study of the U. of Texas, which has been dropped from the list, is too focused on the revamping of student recruitment, and doesn't explore important curriculum and staffing issues. Also disappointing is "Can Ethics Be Taught? Harvard Gives it the Old College Try," 4-6, a mere snapshot of Harvard's attempt to integrate ethics into its business curriculum. We learn of structural changes such as the hiring of more professors, but Byrne doesn't go into the classroom where the effort will ultimately succeed or fail. Executive compensation is another topic Byrne tracks closely, as in his impressive introduction to *BW*'s "Executive Compensation Scoreboard," "What, Me Overpaid? CEOs Fight Back," 5-4, which is even-handed on this hot topic and goes in depth on the latest, rather surprising, pay trends: "Last year marked one of those rare occasions when the average boss's compensation failed to outstrip the paychecks of white-collar professionals, whose pay rose by 5.1%…" On other issues, Byrne's portfolio is mixed. His commentary during the breast implant crisis, "Here's What to Do Next, Dow Corning," 2-24, takes the form of an open letter to CEO Keith McKennon, whose company is at the center of the controversy. Byrne urges McKennon to win over the court of public opinion, but some of his suggestions are impractical: "If patients come with reports from physicians who document problems caused by implants, write out the checks —even accepting some claims without full evidence." And his update on Tom Peters, author of *In Search of Excellence*, "Ever in Search of a New Take on Excellence," 8-31, is engaging, but should have probed more fully the management guru's latest ideas.

Christopher Byron
New York
★★½

"The Bottom Line" columnist. A vigorous reporter, Byron is clearly better on the politics of economic policy than the actual economics. When Byron sets his sights on an issue, however, he usually hits the target. In fact, he receives a 10 Best citation for a report completely out of his normal purview, "Conning the Media," 8-31, a painstakingly researched investigation. Byron reveals how *Time*, ABC and NBC were duped into believing the conspiracy theory of "rogue journalist" Lester Coleman, who claimed that the U.S. government had a hand in the bombing of Pan Am flight 103. Back on his regular beat, he zeroes in on Bush's indecisive handling of the health care issue in "Medicine Man," 1-20, laying bare Bush's lack of "vision" here. His muscular critique of the bankrupt tax-and-spend ideology gushing from both sides of the aisle, "Chapter Eleven," 3-2, effectively punches holes in the election-year tax bills being batted around. Ever cognizant of the partisan posturing behind economic policymaking, Byron offers a robust critique of the balanced-budget amendment in "Balancing Act," 6-8. His sources advise that some in Congress "support the amendment... because they see it as a risk-free vote—enabling them to appear politically correct on the deficit issue while secretly and cynically hoping that the states will fail to ratify the amendment once Congress approves it." It's when Byron ventures into hardcore economic analysis that his work is inconsistent. "Strike Up the Bonds," 2-24, for example, advises readers to invest in long-term bonds because growth is inflationary and there's no sign of growth ahead. He fails to confront the arguments of those who point out that historically, the fastest growing economies are those with the least inflation. His worst economic analysis of the year, "Slowly Submerging Nation," 8-24, is full of insupportable gloom and doom, and he embraces without question his sources' claims: "The U.S. is no longer the pacesetter of economic growth. Rather, it has become what might be termed a newly submerging nation, mired in a bog of long-term structural decline... " He's better for "Zone Offense," 5-25, which illustrates how "enterprise zones" are helping cities.

John Carey
BusinessWeek
★★★

Washington. Carey possesses a rare blend of expertise that enables him to look at science and technology projects in the broader context of the political and business considerations that guide their development. In a mere two-page report, "One Stepper Forward for Sematech," 6-8, he captures the ins and outs of an entire industry and explains how the Sematech consortium's new microlithographic gear, "a critical link in the technological food chain of the $31 billion semiconductor industry," could help the U.S. rebound in chip-making technology. He introduces us to the practical applications of a fairly new and complex mathematical theory in "'Wavelets' Are Causing Ripples Everywhere," 2-3: "The technique could help detect stealthy submarines, provide cruise missiles or autos with detailed maps, and enable phone lines to carry movies and other video images more efficiently." Though we usually have all our questions answered in a Carey report, his update on the Human Genome Project, "This Genetic Map Will Lead to a Pot of Gold," 3-2, is a rare disappointment. He tells us how the NIH has opened up a potential can of worms by trying to patent the genes discovered, but doesn't fully analyze the problem which ultimately may dictate the project's value to biotech companies. He's instructive when he focuses on the political aspects of his beat, as in "Is the NIH's Doctor In? You'd Better Believe It," 5-18, a full-toned profile of the NIH's new "unconventional bureaucrat," Dr. Bernadine P. Healy, who has ruffled plenty of feathers her first year on the job. And "Big Worries for Big Science," 7-6, a thoughtful assessment of the June 17 Congressional vote to kill the Superconducting Supercollider: "Science is a tempting target at a time when the Los Angeles riots and other problems have put social programs at the top of the agenda."

Laurie P. Cohen
The Wall Street Journal
★★

Cohen should stay away from legal cases and concentrate on her growing area of strength —Wall Street deals. Her contributions to the "Heard on the Street" column are some of her best reports. Occasionally, though, Cohen reveals her old tendency to take sides as she did while covering the Michael Milken saga. For example, in "Billionaires Battle Over Rockettes Accord," 1-29, she comes down heavily on the side of the wealthy Pritzkers of Chicago in their legal battle with the Rockefellers over a Radio City Rockettes contract. Similarly, in "How the SEC Caught Edward Downe Using Insider Information," co-written by Alexandra Peers 6-8, she and Peers diminish the impact of their impressive investigative footwork by relying heavily on the prosecution's sources. On deal-making, her analysis is much more balanced and useful, as in "Pied Piper of Biotech Keeps Followers Happy With Cut-Rate Stock," 5-7, a careful examination of David Blech's practice of granting cheap or "founders" stock to brokers, board members and investment bankers. Cohen is cautious not to accuse, but does press on the ethics questions raised by his approach: "Mr. Blech says he doles out warrants to brokers because '. . . this is a way of inducing [brokers] to work on our deals.' . . . However, in some cases, investors may not be aware that brokers pushing Blech's stocks have potentially lucrative warrants in their pockets." Plenty of meaty details enhance her solid investment analysis in "Former Dissidents Who Won Todd Shipyards Find a New Group Is Trying to Rock the Boat," 7-9, on the second proxy battle in less than a year for Todd Shipyards' chairman and CEO Burton Borman. She visits the former chief of Salomon Brothers for "Gone From Salomon 16 Months, Gutfreund Finds Life Frustrating," 12-4, an atmospheric read about a power broker whose command and world was taken away from him after the Treasury bond trading scandal. Her engaging "That Frightening Month Is Here Again," 10-6, explores some of the quirkier theories as to why October is such a bad month for investing in stocks.

James Cook
Forbes
★★★

Executive editor. After sixteen years with *Forbes*, Cook has announced his retirement. We will miss his novel and probing profiles which not only explore the internal dynamics of companies, but also measure company performance against the industry and global economy in which each company competes. With risk and debt being cast as taboo in much of the mainstream financial press, Cook goes against the grain in "Betting the Farm," 1-6, offering an eye-opening anecdote of how calculated risk-taking paid off big for the Ciron Corp. "Strong Hands at the Helm," 3-16, is a precise, no-nonsense appraisal of shipping company OMI Corp., Cook looking at OMI head Jack Goldstein's record over the past six years and seeing a sharp financial strategist with the ability to navigate some of the rough waters ahead. In "Heads I Win, Tails I Also Win," 7-6, he precisely explains why Sahara Resorts' Paul Lowden is building niche markets instead of mega-casinos, and how this tactic could pay off in a saturated market. By far his best analysis of the year, "A Mailman's Lot Is Not a Happy One," 4-27, is one of the most complete and intelligent dissections of the U. S. Postal Services' operations we've read. Forget the ideological arguments in the public versus private debate, Cook gives us hardcore numbers and examples of the areas where the USPS has become more efficient and where it still carries the financial ball and chain of government bureaucracy. Occasionally, Cook dabbles in environmental issues. He doesn't try to hide his belief that capitalism augments environmental protection in such stories as "New Growth," 6-8. Nevertheless, even environmental extremists will be forced to ponder this sound analysis of the benefits of

Stone Container Corp.'s profit-based reforestation of Costa Rica. And "The Ghosts of Christmas Yet to Come," 6-22, is extremely enlightening on *Beyond the Limits*, a book by "enviro-socialists" which causes Cook to ask: How did genuine concern about the environment translate into anticapitalism?

Alison Leigh Cowan
The New York Times
★★½

Accounting. Cowan brings life and enthusiasm to what some would consider a drab subject. The majority of her work this year is devoted to executive compensation issues. She does a fine job of bringing new information to this much-discussed issue. Though controversial compensation expert Graef Crystal has been profiled often, Cowan's "The Gadfly C.E.O.'s Want to Swat," 2-2, is one of the more developed versions we've seen. Also on executive compensation, her highly-informative "Board Room Back-Scratching," 6-2, raises possible conflict of interest issues for outside directors: "Until a year ago one of the outside directors who helped set the pay for Goodrich's chief executive, John D. Ong, was Joseph A. Pichler, the chief executive of the Kroger Company—whose compensation committee included Mr. Ong as an outside director. Thus, Mr. Pichler's $890,370 pay for 1991 was partly determined by a man whose own $905,113 pay Mr. Pichler helped set." Cowan is careful to note that this does not constitute impropriety. She investigates subtle pressure tactics that organizations like the Business Roundtable are using to muzzle compensation consultants who talk to the press or regulators, in "Executives Are Fuming Over Data on Their Pay," 8-25. And in "Untying the Executive Pay Tangle," 9-18, she teaches us about Gerber Products Co.'s innovative attempts to make their executive-pay system more understandable. The program is being called "a model of corporate candor." We found "The New Letdown: Making Partner," 4-1, to be very interesting reading on why making partner doesn't hold the appeal it once did: "Offered a partnership, some people are thinking twice—and some are even saying no thanks, deciding that the prospect of a higher salary and the improved status do not offset the greater exposure to lawsuits and the firm's financial problems."

Peter Coy
BusinessWeek
★★★

Technology editor. The head of *BW*'s impressive technology team is a lightning rod for future trends, especially in the telecommunications industry. While he's highly enthusiastic about the technological innovations he encounters, he's doesn't forget that he works for a business magazine. In other words, he keeps his eye on the bottom line. Coy does quite a bit of work on the role that giant AT&T will play in the future. For instance, "Twin Engines," 1-20, is very strong on CEO Bob Allen's attempts to create "a global information powerhouse by putting together a set of resources that no other company can match: a sophisticated worldwide network to carry voice and data, plus the equipment to run it, plus the devices that hook up to it.... Put them under one roof, the Allen theory goes, and you can build complex, networked information systems that surpass anything available..." Coy is careful to question how Allen's synergy will "translate into revenue growth and earnings." In the same vein, "AT&T Is Strutting its Stuff in Consumer Goods," 7-6, is the telling story of how AT&T consumer products division turned itself around and became a profitable, competitive arm of the company. "AT&T Smacks a Double," 10-26, is a compact piece on how Universal Card Services became one of two AT&T units to win the Malcolm Baldrige National Quality Awards. Keeping an eye on larger industry trends, Coy explains why cellular phone companies have weathered their first recession in fine style, in "Not Just a Yuppie Toy," 2-24. He makes clear the next challenge will be meeting the clients' technological demands with heavy investment spending. In "IBM Needs a New Network—But Not Too New," 4-20, he examines the prospects that IBM will strike the "delicate balance" necessary to successfully modernize its 18-year-old Systems Network Architecture. Providing numerous illuminating case studies, Coy sculpts a highly informative report on corporate attempts to align information systems with corporate goals in "The New Realism in Office Systems," 6-15.

John Crudele
New York Post
½★

Business columnist. A journalist whose work we once respected, Crudele has gone native since joining the *Post* and now simply thrives on conspiracy theories. Unfortunately, it's *chutzpah*, more than an understanding of the market dynamic, that carries his column and some of his more outrageous theories. Two days after the election, Crudele lands on the front page with "Hey, Bill . . . George Cooked the Books," *The New York Post* 11-5, a weak piece of investigative reporting if we've ever seen one. He says a "reliable source" told him that in September the word was that the unemployment figures were supposed to rise; instead they dropped just before the election. This is supposed to be responsible journalism? Another mysterious source surfaces for "GOP Source Says Stocks Being Manipulated," *San Francisco Examiner* 8-28. With virtually no evidence except word from his "source with strong contacts in the Republican Party" and observations from a few traders, he feels comfortable with his conclusions. We, however, do not. Just as the economy is turning the corner, he sets the scene for a stock market decline in "Wall St. Finds Economy a Downer," *Chicago Sun-Times* 6-15, a very unconvincing evaluation from the kitchen-sink school of journalism. Though his assertion in "Why the Fed Can't Stop the Recession," *Seattle Post-Intelligencer* 2-12, that the Fed "botched" its rate cut is highly questionable, Crudele does have a point when he says that "Since last year, a minority of experts have believed the Fed's power to end this recession was limited . . ." And in "Pssst, Bill, Here's Some Advice You Really Need," *NYP* 12-18, he offers sappy street-corner advice to the President-elect: "Bill, nuke the government's statistics gatherers. Forget the economic data being produced by Washington. It's wrong. Misleading. Screwy. And it could be dangerous if it gets in policy makers' brains. . . . Instead, hang around with corporate leaders and suck in all the anecdotal information you can."

Susan Dentzer
U.S. News & World Report
★★

Senior writer. Dentzer has good reporting instincts that impress us more than ever this year. But she still lacks the expertise to adequately flesh out the pros and cons of the important economic policy recommendations she gathers. This year those prescriptives came mainly from the presidential candidates. Refreshingly, though, her work is not weighed down by the heavy political and economic ideology that often taints coverage of this subject. We appreciated "America's Investment Crisis," 2-24, one of the first places we saw a serious comparison of the presidential candidates' proposals regarding investment capital. Though she doesn't scrutinize each candidate's approach as closely as we'd like, at least she gets the information out there. She's more incisive in "Can Either Fix the Economy?" 3-16, positing that despite attempts at "product differentiation," Democratic presidential contenders Paul Tsongas and Bill Clinton are "fraternal twins. . . . There are noticeable differences between the two—but the gene pool is the same." She supplies plenty of examples to support her case. Contradicting economist Paul Krugman's widely-cited assertions that Reaganomics was responsible for a growing gap between rich and poor, Dentzer reveals, in "The Wealth of Nations," 5-4, that "Rather than being a purely American problem, the [UN Development Program] report asserts, the growing gap is a world-wide trend. And far from being limited to the excess-ridden '80s, such income disparities actually have more than doubled over the past 30 years." "Why Workers Have Little to Cheer," 8-17, is a broad skim of both Bush's and Clinton's ideas on job creation. After reviewing the various arguments, she concludes that neither has a solid plan in place. Post-election, she asserts, in "Clinton's Big Test," 11-23, that the new president's biggest challenge will be the nation's health care problems. She reviews Clinton's "managed competition" plan in depth, observing that "there are . . . concerns that Clinton hasn't quite got the basic recipe right—partly because his plan entails far more regulation than even many advocates of managed competition think is desirable."

Kathleen Deveny
The Wall Street Journal
★★

A writer with style and enthusiasm, Deveny wrote the premier article for the *Journal*'s new "Marketscan" column which assesses the latest data gathered from checkout scanners. Though the first piece, "Stingy Shoppers Stir Up Supermarkets," 9-22, deals with a subject that isn't as fresh or specific as we'd have expected—the impact the growing hordes of discount shoppers are having on supermarkets—her other "Marketscan" columns are quite provocative. "Despite AIDS and Safe-Sex Exhortations, Sales of Condoms in U.S. Are Lackluster," 11-24, for example, takes on the taboo from a marketing perspective: " . . . units sales of condom packages in drugstores and supermarkets increased only 5% so far this year . . . far below the 40% to 50% annual gains manufacturers saw during the late 1980s." As the column hits its stride, so does Deveny with "Firms See a Fat Opportunity in Catering to Americans' Quest for 'Easy' Lunches," 11-3, which gives us the lowdown on an important trend for food companies—lunch takers' infatuation with "self-contained lunch items." She notes that even though many such products have failed, "the prize for capturing even a tiny segment of the carried-lunch market is so large that many marketers remain undaunted." She takes an interesting and informative look at the quandary perfume makers face, as buyers move away from department stores to discount outlets, in "Red and Navy Will Mingle With Scent of Pine and Potpourri This Christmas," 12-22. Marketers, she reports, fear that moving their products to less prestigious stores could ruin brand equity. With "RJ Reynolds Takes on the AMA, Defending Joe Camel Cartoon Ad," 2-5, she provides an info-rich snapshot of RJR's attempts to defend its Joe Camel ad campaign against anti-smoking activists. She warns that the aggressive PR efforts could backfire as Philip Morris's did a few years ago. As teeth whiteners become one of the fastest-growing drugstore categories, Deveny studies the promise and pitfalls of this niche in "Lure of a Lovelier Smile Prompts a Rush to Buy Do-It-Yourself Teeth Whiteners," 7-6, warning a shakeout isn't far off as so many competitors are crowding in.

Judith H. Dobrzynski
BusinessWeek
★★★½

Senior editor. Dobrzynski is clearly energized by the year's flurry of corporate activism. Her frequent commentaries on corporate governance issues are always on the cutting edge and evince a keen awareness of the importance of shareholder activism in the post-takeover era. Although she's careful not to gloat over GM CEO Robert Stempel's downfall, she absolutely oozes enthusiasm for the precedent this ouster sets, in "A GM Postmortem: Lessons for Corporate America," 11-9: "Independent directors have succeeded takeovers as agents of change. Executives who relaxed because takeovers dwindled, thanks to their push for state antitakeover laws and their use of poison pills and other devices, must realize that they didn't shut off market forces." And "A Wake-Up Call for Corporate Boards," 4-20, explains why GM's needed shake-up "could help reverse Corporate America's slide." In "CEO Pay: Something Should Be Done—But Not by Congress," 2-3, she spies the pitfalls of Congressional intervention: "The way Corporate America pays its executives does need revamping. . . . But turning CEO pay into a political issue is pure folly. Since virtually all pay schemes can be manipulated, the solution lies in exposing the process to shareholders and thus to the market." She thoroughly examines the effectiveness of shareholders' latest tactic in the war for more influence—withholding votes from would-be board members—in "A Ground Swell Builds for 'None of the Above,'" 5-11. Dobrzynski had a bird's-eye view for "A Sweeping Prescription for Corporate Myopia," 7-6, serving as a member of a panel advising academic researchers on U.S. competitiveness. The essay is packed with meaty assessments of the causes of corporate insularity. As usual, she comes through with a sophisticated, highly-instructive opinion on the SEC's new proxy rules in "An October Surprise That Has Shareholders Cheering," 11-2, laying out precisely how the changes will give shareholders a stronger voice.

Thomas G. Donlan
Barron's
★★½

Editorial page editor. Assuming the position of his long-time predecessor, Robert Bleiberg, Donlan continues to undergo the challenging transition from reporter to opinion-maker. What we hope lies ahead are more commentaries like "Superfund or Superflop," 5-4, an extremely articulate and persuasive dissection of what is wrong with the Superfund Act: "By assigning liability without limit to everyone involved, it assures that the least costly course of action for property owners and dumpers is to try to pass the buck—to file suit against every imaginable other party." Yet, a look at other commentaries in his portfolio reveals that the quality of his arguments is far from consistent. For example, there's nothing especially fresh in "Hangover Remedies," 1-6, in which he blames the eastern media establishment for low consumer confidence and echoes criticism of President Bush for taking the CEOs of GM, Ford, and Chrysler with him to Japan. Several other commentaries seem surprisingly run-of-the-mill as well, including "Rockets and Duds," 7-13, an unsatisfying rummage through the "rubble of the legislative season," which reads like a laundry list. "Insurance Failure," 9-14, walks us through the First Executive story (with a few glaring omissions), and leads us to a lukewarm conclusion: "If states must regulate insurance companies, they should set meaningful capital requirements, but free-wheeling competition among companies would better expose the cold relationship between risk and reward." He enriches "Exorcising Insull," 3-2, a well-constructed argument for reform of the Public Utility Holding Company Act of 1935, with plenty of historical insight. And "The Gathering in Little Rock," 12-14, packs an editorial punch reminiscent of Bleiberg: "A government with an investment strategy must quit tinkering with the tax code.... It should provide even-handed distribution of tax rates, with few exemptions. To pick an example unfortunately dear to Clinton's heart, an investment tax credit is not a true incentive to investment, it's just a handout that distorts capital markets."

Peter C. Du Bois
Barron's
★★½

Foreign editor. Du Bois has all the ingredients to turn "The International Trader" column he pens into a must read. He has a broad network of international sources, he's cognizant of how the integral connection between politics and economics impacts markets, and, with more and more investors exploring international and emerging markets, the future looks bright for this type of column. Du Bois's main shortcoming is that he does not challenge those he interviews. His chat with Frankfurt-based Heinz J. Hockmann, chief investment officer of Commerzbank, "German Strategist Sounds Illiquidity Alarm," 3-2, for example, is disappointing. Hockmann compares what he calls liquid and illiquid markets, i.e., Germany vs. Mexico, but such labeling shows a lack of knowledge about Germany's creeping illiquidity which is bound to impact stocks at some point. Du Bois could have challenged Hockmann's basic assumptions. For investors taking a look at Thailand, Du Bois's "Thai Crisis —It Ain't Over Yet," 5-25, is valuable reading which provides a telling portrait of the country's political economy. As Japan prepares to announce its economic bailout plan for the economy, Du

Bois assesses the impact rather superficially in "Tokyo Stocks Soar on Rescue Plan," 8-31. One of his more conventional assessments of the year, "Bullish for the Markets," 9-21, explains unsatisfactorily the currency shakeout and the boost it should give equities. Only at the very end do we find some worthwhile observations from Henry B. W. de Vismes of Citibank: "I believe that [the Bundesbank's] Sept. 13 promise to cut rates was likely due to their realization that the German economy is in trouble. They wanted to gloss over this move by allowing Italy to devalue." In addition to his work on foreign investments, Du Bois keeps a close eye on the domestic art market. His articles on this subject have been upbeat throughout the year and in his year-end "Graphic Recovery," 12-21, he documents the trend with plenty of tangible examples.

Esther Dyson
Forbes
★

"Random Access" columnist. Though Dyson's work has improved a bit, she still needs to tone down the techno-speak and play more to her investment-minded audience. We were intrigued by her "Who Pays for Data?" 2-3, an interesting read on one entrepreneur's proposal "to create an advertiser-supported home fax network, Home-Fax, that would offer free fax machines to individuals willing to release certain information about themselves to HomeFax, which would then pass on targeted pitches from advertisers." She takes a sophisticated look at Digital Equipment Corp. in "Re-creating DEC," 3-30: "'For the first time,' says [David] Stone [Vice president of software engineering], 'we realize we have to separate the business into two models. Hardware is a commodity where you need high market share and low R&D. Software is different. You need to spend twice as much, maybe 15% of revenues, on R&D, and you need to treat it as a high-value-added service. We were giving away our expertise to sell hardware, and other [hardware] people could undercut our price because they didn't have all the software costs.'" She needed more development to drive home her ideas on custom-tailored software in "Software With a Personality," 6-22. "End of Customer Chaos," 8-3, on the other hand, is a snappy little profile of David Buchanan and his wife, who decided that "If the 1980s was the decade to streamline the factory, the 1990s would be the decade to streamline the sales office." The result was the development of several successful "hot-selling" software products to do just that. We get the lowdown on who's positioned to exploit the latest software niche in "Workflow," 11-23: "We've always had the ability to build workflow if we really wanted. What's new is the tools to do so easily, so it's possible to respond flexibly and handle new situations. Microsoft, so to speak, has bricks and mortar; Lotus has prefab rooms and blueprints."

Jack Egan
U.S. News & World Report
★½

"On Money" columnist. Although Egan is rarely ahead of the curve, he is at least not as far behind as many of his fellow investment columnists. He typically hits trends as the wave is cresting. We always glean an interesting tidbit or two from his practical assessments. He's best on specific investments rather than the market's ebb and flow. In "Why Not Index Capital Gains?" 2-17, Egan makes clear that when it comes to indexing capital gains against inflation, support is bipartisan: "Supporters range from conservative economist Milton Friedman to Sen. Bob Kerrey, the presidential hopeful from Nebraska. Friedman likes indexing because, as he declares, 'No one can claim that indexing is inequitable.' He favors eliminating capital-gains taxes entirely, as Germany has done. Short of that, taxing only real gains would be 'a more effective long-term reform' than merely lowering the capital-gains rate." His tough assessment of Latin American markets, "Investments With a Latin Flavor," 4-27, indicates that their record-breaking days might be over: "'The opportunities you had six months ago in Latin America have largely disappeared, and the Asian markets now seem to present better value,' notes Josephine Jimenez, a portfolio manager..." Also worthwhile is his examination of the vulnerabilities of leveraged closed-end municipal bond funds, "A Rush to Climb Aboard Risky Funds," 6-29: "A rise in interest rates that would cut 10 percent off a closed-end fund's net asset value could reduce its market price by, say, 20 percent." His sources are skeptical of the rally in bank stocks in "Bank Stocks Are Where the Money Is," 8-3, hinting that "most of the good news already has been discounted..." One source recommends stocks from a handful of banks that he feels "can not only recover but also prosper, as opposed to the many banks that can recover but then will only stagnate." Egan is much less sure of his footing on macroeconomic stories such as "Watching for the Next Big Crash," 10-5. Though there's no bad advice here, there's nothing especially fresh, either.

Stuart Elliott
The New York Times
★★

"Advertising" columnist. Elliott steps into Randall Rothenberg's shoes at a full run. We saw literally hundreds of articles from him this first year on the job. He brings a business sense to this beat that Rothenberg did not possess, a plus for ad execs looking for the news on the latest campaign thrown into review. Though it's too early to be completely sure, we sense a lot of potential for this beat under Elliott's stewardship. The information he imparts in "Mercedes Is Scali's Redemption," 2-26, answers all our questions on the dumping of McCaffrey & McCall by Mercedes-Benz North America after thirteen years. The implications for winner Scali, McCabe, Sloves are made crystal clear: "The victory in the Mercedes review is expected to mean that cash-short WPP Group in London, which owns Scali, will end offers to sell the agency." Another possible agency switch is the subject of "Oldsmobile May Drop Ad Agency," 9-21. After 25 years with Leo Burnett, this major account is considering a change which "is likely to set off a frenzy among the nation's agencies." And giving that extra insight, Elliott observes: "Emblematic of G.M.'s abandonment of business as usual was the appointment in July of Philip Guarascio as general manager of marketing and advertising for North America. Mr. Guarascio and his staff will serve as consultants on the review...." He lands on the front page with "Top Health Official Demands Abolition of 'Joe Camel' Ads," 3-10, a professionally-balanced and thorough report on this contentious case. Smart and compact is the way we describe "Realigning the Pieces at Omnicom," 5-6, on Omnicom's somewhat confusing attempts to reorganize: "The upshot of all this—for now, anyway—is merger between Tracy-Locke, the nations 23rd-largest agency, with billings of around $400 million, and No. 5 DDB Needham, based in New York, with billings of $5 billion worldwide." On the creative side, he takes a mildly-engaging look at how Warner Brothers is peddling "Batman Returns" in "A Sequel Is Coming! WHAM? POW?... SELL!" 6-9, which has turned out to be "one of the trickiest tasks in marketing: trying to generate bat hoopla without it deteriorating into bat hype."

Paul Farhi
The Washington Post
★★

Farhi, who earned a 10 Best citation last year for his profile of FCC chairman Alfred C. Sikes, is a strong beat reporter. He has a keen eye for the cutting-edge financial and economic particulars that shape today's increasingly important and complex telecommunications stories. He opens 1992 with a three-part series, "The Cable Colossus," 1-22, 1-23, 1-24, which was cited in *Congressional Record* as the Senate began debate on a comprehensive bill to re-regulate cable TV prices and other aspects of the industry. Farhi's series provides an instructive overview of the major issues early in the legislative process. His follow-up, "Senate Approves Bill Reregulating Cable TV," 2-1, is concise, balanced and thorough on the bill's forward motion, and offers an interesting snapshot of things to come: "Bush has threatened to veto a cable bill. Supporters of cable legislation in the

House and Senate questioned whether the threat was meaningful, given that Bush would risk voters' ire by vetoing a consumer bill in the middle of an election year." Even more interesting is the reaction from the cable industry: "'There's a responsible way to regulate and an irresponsible way. This goes too far,' said John Hendricks, founder and chief executive of the Bethesda-based Discovery Channel. 'The capital markets are going to dry up for us.'" As the bill moves forward, Farhi keeps us up-to-date, with competent reports such as, "House Passes Bill to Reimpose Price Restraints on Cable TV," 7-27. In the aftermath of the cable bill's passage, his "Cable TV Rates Rise Ahead of Law," 12-7, updates us thoroughly, although he's a little rough on cable operators here, his sources accusing them of "trying to beat the deadline for the imposition of new federal price restraints." Compact and complete reporting characterizes "AT&T Announces System to Expand Cable Offerings," 5-5, on AT&T's announcement that it has developed a "digital video compression" system that will enable cable television operators to offer as many as 500 channels by 1994.

Christopher Farrell
BusinessWeek
★★

Economics editor. As a department editor, Farrell contributes to numerous important *BW* cover stories, but most carry too many bylines to be assessed as Farrell's own work. He dabbles solo in numerous economic topics from free trade to poverty, though he rarely sinks his teeth into a subject. We keep an eye on his byline because, occasionally, he drives home an important point. For example, he constructs razor-sharp arguments to boost the case for free trade in his commentary, "America Needs Protection From the Protectionists," 2-10: "Overseas trade has contributed about 30% of real growth in the economy since the trade deficit peaked in 1986." After the L.A. riots, he embarks on a discussion of the underclass through the prism of three books on the subject in "American Gridlock: The State of the Underclass," 5-18. His reviews of *Two Nations* by Andrew Hacker, *The Dispossessed* by Jacqueline Jones and *Rethinking Social Policy* by Christopher Jencks, lead to a timely and thought-provoking analysis of poverty in America. Also intellectually engaging is his discussion of the social and economic forces reshaping the American family in "Where Have All the Families Gone?" 6-29. Though we don't agree with all of his conclusions, the statistics he cites are compelling: "The percentage of white children living with one parent has almost tripled, to 19.2% during the past three decades, and it has more than doubled among blacks, to 54.8%." His commentary in support of a fiscal stimulus package, "Yes, Spur the Economy With Public Spending," 9-21, is disappointing: "The 1930s showed that without concerted government action, an economy can stagnate for years with growth and employment at very low levels. Is it worth risking a latter-day replay of those conditions for the sake of fiscal orthodoxy?" This call seems to contradict his conclusion in "A Liberal Reworking of Liberal Ideas," 11-23, that liberals' "old cry for government to solve any problem is hardly a whisper today."

Tim W. Ferguson
The Wall Street Journal
★★½

"Business World" columnist. Finally finding his footing after several hit-or-miss years with this column, Ferguson's work has improved markedly, with his analysis finally taking us someplace. He seems invigorated, his writing more resolute. He's highly-instructive for "Pension Funds as Yeast for Rising Companies," 4-21, an enthusiastic exploration of one corporate finance group's attempts to attract cash-rich pension funds to the risky "non-investment grade" sector which is having plenty of trouble finding capital amid economic stagnation. Ferguson apparently has had enough in "What's Shaken in L.A.? Not the Governing Complacency," 7-7, as he lambastes government at all levels for destroying the California and national economies with policies that invite recession. There's plenty of verve and vigor in this feisty and fairly well-substantiated attack. Packed with poignant observations from the business battleground, his "Why 'Growth Companies' Aren't Picking Up the Slack," 9-22, sheds light on the "dread" that makes even dynamic small companies reluctant to hire: "It's all part of a drive to minimize fixed costs and debt in a deflationary setting." "Programming for Professors, if Cable Survives the Midterm," 2-11, is a telling profile of Robert Chitester, who wants to bring his "Idea Channel" to cable "to illuminate the primary 'schools of thought.'" Ferguson reveals how legislation to re-regulate cable threatens such innovation. Although he could have fleshed out the issues more in "Whittle's Lesson Plan for the Public Schools," 6-2, this is a refreshing look at what's ahead if for-profit schools take off as innovator Christopher Whittle envisions. In anticipation of Lloyd Bentsen's appointment as Treasury Secretary, Ferguson offers a worthwhile analysis of the man he calls "Loophole Lloyd," in "Was Tax Reform Just an Invitation to Start Over?" 12-8: "Mr. Bentsen's general regard for using the tax code to direct . . . the economy is the most important thing to keep in mind about the career-capping assignment he's due to be given this week."

James Flanigan
Los Angeles Times
★★

Business columnist. Though we've seen improvement in Flanigan's work in the last two years, it's clear he doesn't handle economic issues with the same aplomb that characterizes his coverage of business. His analysis is superficial at best for "Politics or No, Economy Will Rebound in '92," 1-1, Flanigan ignoring the fact that inflammatory political rhetoric can result in ill-conceived, election-year legislation. Also unsatisfying was "As Some Ridicule U.S., Japanese Having Own Economic Troubles," 2-5, in which Flanigan blames the deflation of Japan's "real estate bubble" for that country's economic woes. Though there's some truth to his analysis, there's much left unexplained here, such as how the country's tax structure has impacted the situation. His evaluation is very narrow-minded in "Raise Taxes or Lower U.S. Lifestyles," 4-1, in which he contends that Americans have high expectations, but aren't willing to pay higher taxes. He fails to consider any possibility that tax rates may have already passed a point of diminishing returns. He lands an interview with Ross Perot for "Perot Details His Plan to Mend U.S. Economy," 6-5, guiding the Texan through a number of interesting subjects. This was one of the few places we saw Perot's views on capgains expressed: "'I've got to give you a reason to take money out of Treasury bills to invest in a high-risk, wildcatting venture,' Perot explained." He's more critical of the presidential contender in "Perot's Bitter Medicine for Debt an Old Recipe," 9-30, favoring the familiar standby of public spending over Perot's austerity measures. There's more creative thinking in "Clinton Has it Harder Than Postwar Predecessors," 11-5, in which Flanigan asserts that without the Baby Boomers, Clinton's challenge is different: "His predecessors had to find jobs for new entrants to the work force, but the new Administration's task 'will be retraining old entrants to equip them for this new, changing economy,' says Prof. Daniel Mitchell of UCLA . . ."

Jerry Flint
Forbes
★★

Senior editor. The 30-year veteran of Detroit was a bit off kilter in this dramatic year for the Big Three. Probably his most perplexing, and yet most courageous article of the year was "The Case for Protection," 2-17. The article opens with an editorial disclaimer: "Arguments for protection generally get a chilly reception at *Forbes*." Flint, however, obviously holds enough clout to venture onto this unholy ground and ask: "What type of protection would save the industry? Action that would push down Japanese car imports and push up prices. A variety of methods would work—directed import cuts, quotas, dumping charges and even the creation of dockside red tape." We found it especially odd, then, to read his "Detroit Takes the Offensive," 9-28, later in the year. In this very upbeat report, Flint writes: "If GM gives up more market share, as in the 1980s, it will probably be won by Ford and Chrysler, not the Japanese. Detroit, having grown flabby and complacent, took a terrible pounding. It survived it and kept punching. Now the other side is catching the haymakers. Think about that when you hear the doomsayers whine that Americans can't compete." How could one journalist have written both of these pieces? Also well below Flint's usual standard is "One More Chance?" 8-17, an inconclusive article in which Flint asks: "Can American consumers be developing a Buy American habit?" An interesting question, but Flint never gives us a solid answer. The balance of Flint's work, though, is more typical of his strong performance in years past. In "Platform Madness," 1-20, he takes us down to the basics of platform automobile production, revealing how GM is trimming the number of workers and platforms to get the fat out and keep profitability up. Also strong is "Baby Steps," 4-13, on GM's plans to produce a minivan in the U.S. for export to Europe, a move which Flint believes may be a sign of things to come: "The U.S. . . . has become a very cost-competitive production site." He gives us the lowdown on how Ford made its way back to black ink in "Follow That Ford," 4-27, providing an impressive balance of stats and well-sourced analysis.

Randall W. Forsyth
Barron's
★★★

Capital markets editor and "Current Yield" columnist. Though we often do not agree with Forsyth, his assessments, amid the plethora of pedestrian speculation on the meaning of every up and down blip in the bond market, periodically crystallize the broader dynamic at work. Occasionally, he even manages to blow us away, as he did with "Which Market Is Wrong," 1-6, a 10 Best selection which appeared nine months before Europe's currency crisis and offered a stunningly prescient analysis of the "conflicts between domestic and international demands on monetary policy" that would play out across the Continent. After such insight, reports such as "Does the Future Belong to the Kiwis or Finns?" 9-14, confuse us. Though he concedes that the Finnish devaluation route isn't the way to go, he holds up New Zealand's austerity programs as a model for Europe: "Kiwis endured 20%-plus interest rates . . . through the 'Eighties. As a result, inflation has plunged from 12% five years ago to 1% this year. . . . Interest rates are now down in the 6% area. . . . Does Europe have the will to stay that course?" It's interesting that he concludes "Lack of growth, more than anything else, is hampering the greenback." Doesn't that hold for European currencies too? Furthermore, Forsyth doesn't mention New Zealand's paltry average GDP over the past 10 years, which was in the 1.4% range. Debunking the fears of the cash-flow crowd in "Some Capital Ideas," 3-23, he looks at demand for foreign capital and its positive effect on the dollar and bond markets, even raising the striking possibility that if Japan falls into recession, U.S. bonds may rally as Japanese savings are invested overseas. He's too focused on M2 in "Politics to the Fore," 6-1, harping on an indicator that Fed members have publicly stated may be misleading. He also continues to predict an equity market meltdown in light of Bush's political uncertainty. A possibility, but he ignores other forces at play in the debt and equity markets.

Milt Freudenheim
The New York Times
★★

"Business and Health" columnist. This precise, no-nonsense columnist provides an important window on health care as the issue rises to the top of the nation's political agenda. Careful not to take sides in this contentious national debate, Freudenheim serves as a font of unique and balanced information on this complex topic. We found "States Press U.S. on Insurance Plan," 3-31, to be highly-informative on the roadblocks posed by the Employee Retirement Income Security Act (Erisa) to state governments that are trying to institute health care reform. He gives us the facts straight up for "Companies' Costs:

How Much Is Fair," 1-7, an educational report packed with valuable info and diverse opinions on which sector is paying the most for health care—the government, business or patients. With the IRS scrutinizing the tax exempt status of non-profit hospitals, especially their executive pay arrangements, Freudenheim pens "I.R.S. Studies Pay of Hospital Chiefs," 4-14, a quick, but telling survey of the way different hospitals deal with CEO pay. In "Trying to Curb Prices of Drugs," 6-9, he examines efforts by Sen. Dave H. Pryor (D-AR) to deny tax credits to drug makers that raise prices faster than general inflation. Pryor's primary target is an exemption for products made in Puerto Rico: "The credits enabled 26 drug companies to slice at least $8.5 billion from their Federal and local taxes in the 1980's . . . " But, Freudenheim is careful to note the impressive number of jobs the exemption has created. We read with great interest his front-page article "Rochester Serves as Model in Controlling Health Cost," 8-25, an in-depth look at this city's efficient, unified regional insurance program which is characterized by cooperation between business and health care providers and the practice of community rating, which groups everyone together to spread out the risks. In "Companies Acting to Trim Benefits Promised Retirees," 12-24, he alerts that 23 large companies have terminated health benefits to retired employees before new accounting rules go into effect January 1.

Jonathan Fuerbringer
The New York Times
★

New York. Fuerbringer relies heavily on handy technical explanations for the ups and downs of the credit and currency markets, rarely venturing a serious analysis of the larger dynamic at work. And while he manages to stumble upon an interesting fact or two, he seldom displays enough curiosity to capitalize on its value. Typical of his work is "Yield on 30-Year U.S. Bond at Lowest Level in 5 ½ Years," 8-11, a compilation of standard remarks on the reasons for the bond rally: " . . . slow growth . . . good data on inflation. . . . " He completely misses the opportunity to analyze the deeper monetary forces at work, and shows no recognition of the interplay between the market for bonds and the market for goods. It's worth noting that on the day this story was prepared, gold closed at $350.40. His "Bonds Rally on Buying by the Fed," 9-2, is more of the same. The subhead reads "Decline of the Dollar Ignored by Traders," yet Fuerbringer makes only the shallowest attempt to explain why, neglecting commodity prices which indicate the DM, not the dollar, is out of whack. Similarly, "Post-Election, Bonds Remain Vulnerable," 11-9, provides only superficial analysis. One source suggests "the Veterans Day holiday . . . could hurt [the Treasury Auction] by interrupting whatever momentum might develop." The only thing that redeems Fuerbringer's market reports is that occasional, useful tidbit we find, as in "Gold Loses Its Appeal as a Haven," 5-20: "Watch the Chinese. At the current rates China should soon overtake the United States as the world's largest gold market." Unfortunately, Fuerbringer doesn't seem to recognize the significance of this news taken from a report. His "In Tokyo's Decline, a Glint of Silver," 3-22, is little more than a handy technical guide for new players in the Nikkei. Fuerbringer does manage respectable work on market regulation, where there are fewer variables to juggle. "Treasury Market Study Said to Seek New Policy," 1-21, for example, is an important alert on the Treasury's proposal to intervene by selling more securities if a squeeze is perceived.

George Gilder
Forbes
★★★½

Contributing editor. Gilder is truly in a class by himself. A remarkable futurist, he is one of the nation's leading thinkers on telecommunications trends, as evinced in "Cable's Secret Weapon," *Forbes* 4-13, an amazing essay about which technologies are best positioned for the exponential growth of information technology: "The telephone companies' existing narrowband copper wire links

... can normally hold only voice and data. But CATV's coaxial broadband links ... can act as conduits for billions of bits of full-motion digital video, high resolution medical images, vivid educational simulations and lifelike videoconferences. Comparing the two wires is like comparing a five-car ferry with an eight-lane bridge." Serialized from his book *Telecosm*, "Into the Fibersphere," *ASAP* 12-7, offers another window on the breathtaking challenges ahead. He offers an excellent assessment of why U.S. capital isn't flowing to high tech anymore in "The Outsider Trading Scandal," *The Wall Street Journal* 7-29, walking us through a series of government policy mistakes that has encouraged the smart money to seek less risk. Gilder is passionate about his economics, for instance in his tribute to the "Inc. 500" entrepreneurs, "The Enigma of Entrepreneurial Wealth," *Inc.* 10-1, he goes to extremes to make the case that efforts to paint "capitalism as a Faustian pact by which we trade greed for wealth is simple hogwash." And he absolutely gushes over Francis Fukuyama's book, *The End of History and the Last Man*, in "Four Cheers for Liberal Democracy," *Washington Post Book World* 1-12, praising the work as "a counterculture blitzkrieg."

Howard Gleckman
BusinessWeek
★★½

Gleckman has improved markedly by focusing his energies more toward problem-solving, less toward ideological battles. Throwing plenty of muscular, non-partisan punches at the political establishment in numerous commentaries, he admonishes economic policymakers and offers numerous creative solutions of his own. His stinging critique of President Bush's January growth package, "Why Bush's Budget-Shuffling Doesn't Add Up to Growth," 2-17, exposes the President's contradictions: "Bush is trumpeting his support for families.... But by subsidizing the cost of children without ending the tax penalty on married couples, the 'profamily' President sends a mixed message." Though we think he dismisses the flat tax proposal too quickly, in "'Jerry's Tax': Wrong Answer, Right Questions," 4-13, we appreciate his earnest evaluation of the serious economic questions raised by Jerry Brown. His criticism is direct in "Why a Tax Break for Developers Wouldn't Be Constructive," 7-20: "The bill ... would be a windfall for real estate pros. But it will do nothing for outside investors. And, most important, there is no evidence that the bailout will generate any new construction or create jobs." Pre-election, he disappoints with "Dear Bill: Steer Clear of the Short-Term Fix," 11-2, a conventional plea for would-be President Clinton not to sink money into public works, Gleckman failing to explore creative alternatives that exist. Though better in the commentary format, Gleckman is also a good reporter, despite his tendency to insert opinion into news articles. For example, in the ashes of the defeat of the constitutional amendment requiring a balanced budget, he takes an original look at how Democratic conservatives, led by Rep. Charles W. Stenholm (D-TX), have left their mark on several crucial issues in "The Democrats' Agenda-Benders," 6-29: "The Stenholm coalition is of small use to Bush. Because he hasn't much of an agenda of his own, he can't emulate Reagan, who worked with Stenholm and other Democratic 'boll weevils' to build a working majority for his programs in 1981-82."

Steven Greenhouse
The New York Times
½★

Washington, economics. When we first heard of Greenhouse's return from Paris, we were genuinely excited. New blood, fresh ideas on this crucial beat, we thought. But after a steady diet of his tunnel-vision, we'd like to send him packing again. Greenhouse works as hard as anyone, but slaves away at the same tired, tapped-out sources. Some of his shoddiest analyses appeared amid the European currency crisis. His "European Unity? With Friends Like These..." 9-20, is an off-the-top-of-his-head assessment, which is agonizing to read: "The Italian Government lacked the courage to slash its astronomical budget debt, which made the lira's devaluation inevitable." And why didn't Britain's budget surplus save its currency? What about Germany's astronomical budget deficit? The lack of thought here is blatant. In "U.S. Also Guilty in Money Crisis, Europeans Say," 9-22, he allows panicked European central bankers to make a weak dollar their scapegoat and to pooh-pooh Bush's proposal to tie currencies to a basket of commodities: "'There are many disadvantages to such a currency construction,' said Helmut Schlesinger." We never learn what they are. On the domestic front, "Attention America! Snap Out of It," 2-9, is packed to the brim with vague, conventional ideas about how to increase the nation's global competitiveness: "Get companies to think long-term." Similarly, he turns an uncritical eye on Michel Camdessus and the IMF in "Point Man for the Rescue of the Century," 4-26. Greenhouse is nonchalant about the suffering the IMF's austerity plan will cause: "The fund has . . . called on Russia to lift its oil prices fifteenfold. . . . This would shock consumers and reduce consumption at home, but would enable Russia to increase exports and export revenues." It's obvious in "Ecology, the Economy and Bush," 6-14, that Greenhouse is eager to criticize the President for not signing the biodiversity treaty, and "A Clinton Win: Good for Stocks, Bad for Bonds?" 10-11, is an assemblage of quotes to support his thesis that Clinton's fiscal stimulus will spur equity markets and drive down the debt markets. This is as conventional as you can get in a two-dimensional Keynesian model that Lord Keynes would long ago have discarded.

John Greenwald
Time
★½

While Greenwald continues to be fond of a blurb approach to reporting that we find terribly uninformative, we do notice improvement in his work this year. He's probing deeper on business issues. His best piece of the year, "The Bankruptcy Game," 5-18, is a clear-eyed, well-informed critique of Chapter 11. With oodles of facts, studies, expert opinions and examples, he lays bare the distortions created by the provision: "A growing body of critics charge . . . companies in Chapter 11 can take advantage of the fact that they pay no interest on part of their debt by slashing prices and wreaking havoc on their competitors." Greenwald seems better suited for business than with broad economic articles such as "The Great American Layoffs," 7-20, a superficial skim that fails to ask "why?" Though "Why We're So Gloomy," 1-13, is a highly predictable assessment of why we feel so bad this recession, he's on to something: "People are smart enough to know when they are being squeezed. . . . Americans are unlikely to feel much better until they see that their well-founded concerns are at last being recognized and addressed." More blurb journalism turns us off in "May the Best Plan Win," 3-23, which skips quickly from topic to topic, a mere laundry list that tells us next to nothing about the issues: "income taxes," "capital gains," "competitiveness," etc. In "Baby Steps," 9-28, Greenwald, through his sources from a "*Time* . . . panel of leading economists and marketplace experts," accuses Bush and Clinton of taking baby steps on the economy when something more dramatic is needed. But, Greenwald's blurb-happy analysis only takes baby steps in assessing the problem, with no hard questioning of the panel, no creative thinking. On the other hand, his post-election analysis of Clinton's economic proposals, "How Much Can He Do?" 11-23, is worthwhile reading, though it is peppered with a noticeable bias toward austerity programs: "Now is precisely the time to talk of sacrifice."

Lisa Gubernick
Forbes
★★

Senior editor. Gubernick can be counted on to unearth unique stories from the world of entertainment. She's a colorful writer with good business sense, although we'd like to see her dig even deeper for the specific financial and management concerns that propel this mega-bucks industry. Gubernick's fluid writing style whisks us through "Know Thy Limitations," 1-20, a people piece about how talent agent Marvin Josephson of ICM fell on his face when he tried to run a conglomerate, but is riding high again now that he's back in familiar territory. Joined by Peter Newcomb for "The Wal-Mart School of Music," 3-2, the duo provides a delightfully enthusiastic piece about the rise of country music. With plenty of facts and insightful analysis, Gubernick and Newcomb make clear that Garth Brooks is no aberration: "Ten years ago there were 1,800 country radio stations. Now there are more than 2,500. And the listeners aren't just people driving beat-up pick-up trucks and swilling from six-packs. According to a study by Simmons Research, more people with household incomes of $40,000 or above listen to country music radio than any other format." "Money Talks," co-written by Amy Feldman 6-8, examines the enormous potential for pay-per-view TV. We're alerted to the fact that pay-per-view has even run its first movie *before* its appearance in the theater, suggesting a possible industry realignment down the road. She's not as hard-hitting as usual for "Butterless Popcorn," 7-20, dabbling in too many mini-stories about Cineplex Odeon that she never fully pulls together. On the other hand, "Dollar House Mitchell," 10-12, is a pithy business profile of Lee Roy Mitchell whose low overhead, inexpensive tickets, and junk bond-financed Cinemark theaters are making money while other chains suffer.

Udayan Gupta
The Wall Street Journal
★★★

Venture capital and small business. Gupta is a unique source of information on the financial ebb and flow of the entrepreneurial sector. An excellent intelligence gatherer, he is constantly wildcatting for the next financial gusher for credit-hungry small businesses, be it in banking, the markets, venture capital sector or elsewhere. "Venture-Capital Funding Falls, but 'Incubators' Thrive," 2-11, is the type of work that attracts us to his byline. There's plenty of fresh info here and a nifty segment on the enormous growth of "incubators, which provide low-cost space and shared services to fledgling business..." Joined by co-writer Brent Bowers for "IPO Slump Is Stalling Expansion of Small Businesses," 7-2, the duo reveals how unsteady the macroeconomic environment is for non-bank financing: "Proceeds from new offerings have plummeted from a record $4.28 billion in March to little more than half that in June." Always scanning the horizon, he notices an upswing in venture capital, which he reports with co-writer Jeffrey Tannenbaum in "Venture Funds Regain Appetite for Start-Ups," 9-21: "Behind the renewed interest ...is mostly the growing pile of money.... Venture funds in the first half of 1992 raised a total of $1.2 billion, compared with $418 million in the year-earlier period." "Minority Businesses to Get Capital From Pension Fund," 11-20, provides news we didn't see elsewhere: "The Small Business Equity Enhancement Act of 1992...may attract as much as $550 million over the next five years to funds that invest in minority-owned businesses..." There were a few mild disappointments in Gupta's portfolio, among them "Disabilities Act Isn't as Burdensome as Many Feared," 4-20, in which Gupta relies heavily on anecdotal evidence to assert small businesses aren't finding compliance with the Disabilities Act as difficult as expected. And his "Small Business Is Getting Big Loan Relief," 5-6, fails to provide national stats on the percentage of small businesses benefitting from banking's renewed interest.

Lawrence J. Haas
National Journal
★½

Budget and taxes. We turn to Haas on numerous economic policymaking issues, fully confident that we will find competent reporting and analysis. However, when it comes to discussing the deficit, Haas is paralyzed by conventional wisdom. After consuming over a page to make the point that voters are dubious about Washington's financial wisdom, Haas, in "Confronting a Double Bind: Debt and Doubt," 3-14, concludes that in order to tax our way out of the deficit, the government needs to regain credibility. Amazingly, growth is assumed to be exogenously determined throughout, and Washington's corpulence is negative to the extent it presents a hurdle to wheedling a tax increase out of the public. Similarly, we found the title of "Deficit Dynamics," 4-4, somewhat ironic in light of the fact that Haas displays much more knowledge of the static here. He argues that holding down entitlements and keeping up the "fire walls" erected in 1990 will help, but spends no time assessing how higher growth rates could lower deficits in relation to GDP. He reveals why traditional resistance to VAT taxes may be breaking down, and provides a sturdy analysis of the particulars, in "Bubbling VAT," 6-6, one of the more complete assessments we've seen recently on the issue. "Corporate Do-Gooders," 8-1, is worthwhile reading on what Haas sees as corporate America's new interest in shaping public policy. To crystallize the trend, he zeros in on the Businesses for Social Responsibility, which "wants to turn corporate thinking on its head. Its members say, for example, that environmental protection is neither costly nor unprofitable. Ditto for family support programs for employees.... The group views itself as a counterweight to the White House Competitiveness Council that Vice President Dan Quayle, its chairman, has turned into a major policy tool."

Kathleen Hays
Investor's Business Daily
★

New York bureau chief. Hays holds a key position at this increasingly important daily, yet she is clearly not among the best on its masthead. Her consistent and extremely heavy-handed criticism of the Federal Reserve's monetary policy confounds us. She falls back on M2 figures to nudge the Fed toward easing in "Fed Ponders Another Rate Cut," 2-4, revealing she's behind the curve as the Fed has indicated M2 might be misleading. Similarly, her statement that some economists "worry that the Fed is repeating the same mistake it made last year" reveals that she hasn't done her homework, as it was the press that labeled the Fed's handling of monetary policy a mistake, not the markets. Fed critics run wild in "America's Money Supply Woes," 8-14, another misleading, one-sided harangue against Fed policies. Also off base is "Fed Fiddles as Economy Burns," 9-14, in which she accuses the Fed of a destructive policy of gradualism to reduce inflation. She turns to monetary history for support, but conveniently fails to mention that the yield curve was inverted in the '82 recession, but is not today. In one of her best efforts of the year, "Wall St. Eyes Balanced Budget," 6-9, she conveys skepticism about the purported merits of a balanced-budget amendment: "Instead of disappearing, the budget deficit has grown bigger than it was in 1986, the first year after the original Gramm-Rudman law passed." She gathers a surprisingly diverse selection of material for "Currencies in Chaos as British Rates Soar," 9-17, offering key facts we didn't see elsewhere: "Several economists pointed out that the U.K. pound is probably close to what would be considered purchasing power parity against the mark, adding that its rate of inflation is actually running below that of Germany's." This was also the only place in which we saw a reference to Helmut Schlesinger's quote in *Handlesblatt* "that one or more European currencies might face realignment before the vote on the French referendum." Her subject steals the show in "Economist Lawrence Kudlow," 11-4, a fascinating profile of Lawrence Kudlow and his reasons for supporting supply-side economic policies.

Diana B. Henriques
The New York Times
★★★

Her Sunday "Wall Street" column is a virtual treasure chest of insights into the deals and trends nestled in the nooks and crannies of Wall Street. She's a dynamite reporter, extremely perceptive and straightforward. Most of all, she's more open to new information than a majority of her peers. A perfect example of her inquisitive nature is found in "Debunking the Junk 'Bomb' Theory," 3-22: "Any discussion of the behavior of junk bonds, of course, usually deteriorates into a hot-worded debate on the behavior of the people who promoted, packaged, sold and bought them. That's too bad, since the name-calling may deter researchers from continuing to explore this quirky class of assets." What she discovers by being open minded is that recent studies dispel the "time bomb" default theory. She takes us on a fascinating peek behind the scenes of a joint shareholders meeting of Fidelity Investments in "Testy Questions for Fidelity," 2-23, delving into the complex power issues that heated up a relatively ordinary meeting. Handling front-page news reporting with complete competence in "S.E.C. Asks for Sweeping Changes in Rules Governing Mutual Funds," 5-22, she gets right to the meat of the proposals. She's also very focused in "Delayed Financial Reports Show a Company in Trouble," 8-17, an in-depth report on how omissions in SEC filings and bogus annual reports left many brokers red-faced over their investments in Met Capital Corp. Her follow-up, "Falsifying Corporate Data Becomes Fraud of the 90's," 9-21, fingers a disturbing new trend: "a growing parade of companies have been sent to the regulatory woodshed in the '90s in what some securities lawyers and regulators say is a sharp resurgence of fraud rooted in the way public companies are managed, not in the way their stocks are traded..."

Tom Herman
The Wall Street Journal
★★½

"Your Money Matters" columnist. For investors trying to learn the complex ins and outs of Wall Street's investment products, Herman is an invaluable source of critical information. He carefully weighs issues of yield, taxation and risk. It is when Herman embarks on broader economic issues that he reveals the limits of his expertise. Typical of his direct, instructional style is "Tax Fears Shouldn't Dictate Choosing Single-State vs. National Tax-Free Fund," 4-15, which challenges our customary investment assertions: "Buying a single-state fund isn't always the smartest move, even for investors in... high-tax states.... At current interest rates, many upper-income taxpayers could probably do even better by investing in a national tax-free bond fund." The explanation of municipal bond credit ratings found in "Muni Investors Should Peer Beyond the Market's ABCs," 5-18, is very instructive: "Significantly, at a time when many municipal bond investors' three biggest concerns are yield, yield and yield, similarly rated bonds can sometimes offer quite different yields." "Building a Bond Ladder Is Safe Way to Increase Yields," 9-1, offers a lucid and educational explanation of the promise and pitfalls of "laddering," buying a group of bonds that represent different rungs on the investment maturity ladder. Herman's work isn't quite as incisive when he ventures out of the "Your Money Matters" genre. Though he gives equal time to the bulls and the bears in his survey of economists' predictions, "Economists Predict Bleak Winter, Then Mild Recovery," 1-2, there's nothing here that surprises us. "Bond Gloom Is Starting to Clear Up," 3-2, offers a useful compilation of insights from sources who say lower inflation and an expected upturn in the economy will create a bullish environment for bonds. Though not especially sophisticated, the analysis here rang true.

Robert D. Hershey, Jr.
The New York Times
★½

As the plethora of statistical blips cross the nation's economic screen, Hershey is there to tell us which indicators are up and which are down. But much like a market analyst who tries to explain yesterday's five-point move, Hershey has only limited success. "Why Economists Fear the Deficit," 5-26, is full of contradictions, opening with highly alarmist statistics, yet saying later that "Few economists regard the debt buildup as having reached crisis proportions." A comparison of his analysis in other articles leads us to believe that Hershey merely rolls with the punches, instead of digging for broader economic trends at work. For example, "Housing and Output on the Rise, Spurring Talk of Recession's End," 3-18, and "Good Riddance to Recession?" 6-18, are typical of Hershey's data-heavy, analysis-light reporting style. In the latter, he assures us that "Statistical and anecdotal evidence is mounting almost daily that the recovery is gathering momentum..." Yet, a few months later as factory employment skids, Hershey, in "167,000 Jobs Lost by U.S. Businesses; Fed Cuts Interest," 9-5, is just as confident that we're headed for another downturn. There's too much puff in "The Experts Talk But Who Listens?" 1-15, a quirky look at how "the economics fraternity has suffered from the perversity by which the Government both overpraises and ignores it and in doing so often creates policies that are wasteful and counterproductive." Failing to lay the groundwork before an important Fed Open Market Committee meeting, Hershey serves up nothing more than a formulaic skim of the issues in "Fed Isn't Expected to Trim Rates," 8-17. After surprising news that GDP grew 2.7% for the third quarter, he adequately reports on the Commerce Department's efforts to fend off criticism that it cooked the data for President Bush's political gain in "U.S. Officials Defend Their Economic Data," 11-19.

John Holusha
The New York Times
★★½

Technology. A veteran of the automotive beat, Holusha is in the unique and important position of regularly examining how changes in technology and environmental regulation affect business. He reliably provides fresh perspectives on the business-environment axis. He examines how changes in both consumer awareness and legislation are changing packaging in "Learning to Wrap Products in Less—Or Nothing at All," 1-19, a meaty and enjoyable Sunday business read. He briefly sketches the alternatives available to businesses trying to phase out CFCs in "Ozone Laws Worry Appliance Trade," 2-10. Holusha critiques Appliance Recycling Centers of America Inc. in "Finding Money in Old Freezers," 3-4, a trim, cohesive assessment of the company that has "carved out a unique and profitable slice of the growing market for environmental services" by collecting old refrigerators and freezers and removing the CFCs. In "Plane Propellers Shed a Passé Image," 2-23, he probes the reasons for a return to the propeller, a taut feature that showcases his pithy writing: "Far from fading away, propellers are making something of a comeback on new generations of large commuter aircraft because they are more fuel-efficient than pure jets and recent developments have increased their performance to near-jet range." He is equally cogent in "Needed by Space Plane: Space-Age Composites," 7-1, a thorough examination of how the National Aero-Space Plane project has sent companies scrambling to create new alloys that will survive the use of the plane. He explores the possibilities of turning table scraps into compost, in "Two Towns Experiment With the Alchemy of Trash," 8-9, a realistic and smart perspective in which he concludes it's not yet really feasible. And "Japan Is Tough, But Xerox Prevails," 9-3, is all business on the battle of the copiers, taking us step-by-step to show how Xerox "beat the Japanese at their own game."

Bruce Horovitz
Los Angeles Times
★★½

Marketing. A perceptive reporter with a nose for trends and an eye for key details, Horovitz brings style and enthusiasm to his beat. His "Advocacy Is New Trend at Ad Agencies," 1-5, is a fascinating examination of cause-related advertising, which industry executives say "could become one of the ad world's most lucrative growth areas in the 1990s. While spending in almost all ad categories has been decreasing for the past two years, advocacy ad spending nearly doubled between 1988 and 1990..." He fully explores the implications of this interesting trend. R. J. Reynold's troubles with its highly successful "Old Joe" cartoon campaign is big ad news, and Horovitz weighs in on the story with "Cigarette Ads Under Fire," 3-10, a sturdy report which assesses the larger implications of the surgeon general's pressure to end the campaign: "The surgeon general does not have the authority to make companies change their advertising. But marketing experts point out that, with a minority of Americans now smoking—and that number continuing to decline—it has become more politically acceptable to publicly criticize tobacco firms." He puts an interesting story spin on the L.A. riots in "Riots Lay Waste to L.A.'s Fun and Sun Facade," 5-5, exploring how the city has lost much of its luster for advertisers. In "Nike Does It Again," 8-25, he takes what might have been merely a story about Nike's new controversial ad about two black inner city youths, and turns it into a lively discussion of advertisers' attempts to become more relevant and real to their ethnic customers. The practice of circulating two covers for the same magazine issue is the subject of "Double-Takes," 9-22, and though we've seen the story elsewhere, Horovitz adds new information. In "When X Equals $," 11-3, he broadens coverage of the marketing of one of "the most recognized film logos of all time," the "X" in Spike Lee's new film "Malcolm X," and reveals how Warner Bros. has attempted to attract older people and white viewers by portraying Malcolm X as a moderate.

Bruce Ingersoll
The Wall Street Journal
★★★½

Washington, agriculture and food issues. Ingersoll, a consummate beat reporter, is the journalist of record on the FDA and USDA. He is constantly probing policy issues and assessing the efficiency of the two agencies. On the silicone breast implant story, he remained professionally detached in such reports as "Doctors' Cases on Implants Get Review by FDA," 1-20, which reviews evidence of problems caused by implant ruptures, and "Implant Makers Predict Skewed FDA Hearings," 2-18, in which Ingersoll gives fair time to breast implant producers as they prepare for a hearing that they feel will be stacked against them. Although he raises evidence to confirm their fears, he does not play an industry advocate here. He expands on the breast implant crisis in "Amid Lax Regulation, Medical Devices Flood a Vulnerable Market," 3-24, which was part of a two-article series called "Who's Checking?" His contribution is a carefully-researched investigation of the FDA's approval methods for medical devices: "Of 60,000 devices on the market today, from breast implants to lasers, the vast majority received the same cursory review as the innocuous tongue depressor, according to government auditors." Careful not to come down on either side of the issue, he later reports on industry charges of FDA paralysis, in a balanced and informative "FDA Attacked for Holding Up Medical Devices," 9-9. We truly enjoyed "Your Tax Dollars Help the Horsy Set Dispose of Manure," 4-8, the tale of the Agricultural Stabilization and Conservation Service's desperate attempts to subsidize someone so that they're not closed down. Ingersoll explains that with fewer farmers, many ASCS offices spend more to administer subsidies than the actual value of the subsidy payment itself. He follows up the next day with "Agriculture Chief Promises to Trim Fat at His Agency," 4-9, as Agriculture Secretary Edward Madigan vows to clean up inefficiencies. The title of "Big Three Cars Get High Marks in Safety Study," 12-1, pretty much says it all, so Ingersoll keeps the writing tight, reporting only the most pertinent details.

Alex S. Jones
The New York Times
★★

Press. After spending the last seven years on the *Times*'s press beat, Jones announced his resignation in order to write a biography of the four generations of the Ochs-Sulzberger family which has presided over the *Times* for nearly 100 years. Only a few years ago, he and his wife co-authored a book on another journalism dynasty, the Bingham family of Louisville. He's certainly doing more novel writing than reporting these days. The announcement shed new light on the sweeping history of the family that Jones penned early in the year as the baton was passed at the paper, "Arthur Ochs Sulzberger Passes Times Publisher's Post to Son," 1-17. The book deal also made us question his neat little plug for the *Times*'s new "TimesCard" promotion, in "Papers Woo Long-Term Subscribers," 8-5. Overall, though, he had a solid last year, and we expect he'll be back at the *Times* once the book hits the shelves in 1996. His best work was on ethical questions confronted by the journalism community, the topic of "Weighing the Thorny Issue of Anonymous Charges," 3-3. This careful and thought-provoking examination looks at the controversy at *The Seattle Times*, which printed allegations from eight unidentified women who accused Senator Brock Adams of sexual misconduct. Also thoughtful is "Report of Ashe's Illness Raises an Old Issue for Editors," 4-10, on the heated debate over the *USA Today* report that tennis star Arthur Ashe has AIDS. Jones is careful not to make his own views known here, but collects a wide variety of opinions from within the editorial ranks of the nation's major newspapers. "Meet the Press: Dr. Jekyll and Mr. Hyde," 2-9, wasn't up to his usual standard, degenerating from an interesting discussion of press responsibility into a gossipy recounting of "A Current Affair's" exclusive interview with Gennifer Flowers. Jones is quite good on the ins and outs and ups and downs of the Big Apples' volatile newspaper wars. His coverage of Mortimer Zuckerman's purchase of the *Daily News* in such articles as "Zuckerman Seems Clear Choice to Buy Daily News," 9-18, was competent and complete in every way.

Bernice Kanner
New York
★★½

"On Madison Avenue" columnist. If you're in need of an ad agency, we recommend a look through Kanner's extensive portfolio for colorful and informative profiles of agencies big and small. While others track the latest Madison Avenue reshuffling, Kanner is busy scanning the country for up-and-comers, exploring what makes unique and successful agencies tick. She's clearly better at capturing an agency's creative soul, than scrutinizing its bottom line, however. "A New Breed of Ad Agency," 1-13, capitalizes on her wide range of contacts on and off Madison Avenue. Kanner takes us behind the scenes of Averett, Free & Ginsberg (AFG) to reveal that its image as a "dowdy... 'discounter'" is way off base. San Francisco-based Goodby, Berlin & Silverstein is the subject of "The Human Touch," 2-24, a candid, sweeping portrait of an agency that has ballooned "largely on the strength of its fresh, 'humanistic' creative. 'We're not into didactic arguments, in-your-face spikes, setting hot trends, or avant-garde esoterica,' says Goodby..." She's positive about the "quixotic counterculture" of Wieden & Kennedy in "Control Freaks," 3-16, but not oblivious to its shortcomings: "The 'magic' has attracted many prospects, but few stick around." Laying bare the "politics of self-congratulations" at the Andy Awards in her engaging "And the Winner Is..." 3-30, reminds Madison Avenue creatives not to take awards too seriously. Continuing her search for winners during the slump, she steers our attention toward the Deutsch agency in "The D-Team," 6-1. Here, she explores the synergy of the agency's new "stiff suit" president brought in to complement "wacky creative director Donny Deutsch." She delivers yet another fun and informative profile with "The Magic Touch," 8-31, on Richard Saunders International and its child-like approach to product development. Stepping away from the ad beat temporarily to indulge in her love of animals, she pens "A Dog's Life," 4-27, an emotional tour of an agency that serves as a safety net for man's best friend.

Peter T. Kilborn
The New York Times
★★

Washington, "Workplace" beat. Kilborn typically draws us into his reports with accounts of individuals. It's an effective writing technique, but all too often, Kilborn fails to follow through with information on the broader trend his anecdotes are supposed to represent. Thus, we are engaged, but ultimately not informed by much of his work. For example, Kilborn explains the success of a Boston youth program in "Inner-City Jobs Program Throws Young a Lifeline," 6-8, but fails to compare it to more established programs. Travelling to Pine Ridge, S.D., he provides a gripping chronicle of the Sioux Indians' economic and social plight, in "Sad Distinction for the Sioux: Homeland Is No. 1 in Poverty," 9-20. The stories of individual struggle and achievement draw us in, but once again we learn little about how the problems are being dealt with. Pulling together plenty of facts and observations for "The Middle Class Feels Betrayed, But Maybe Not Enough to Rebel," 1-12, he takes an early look at the middle class income issue, although he doesn't offer many conclusions except to say that there's an issue here for politicians to tap. His lopsided "Caterpillar's Trump Card," 4-16, on the Caterpillar strike, is written from a decidedly pro-labor perspective: "Half a century ago, under the leadership of Walter Reuther, the union vaulted the blue-collar work force into the middle class, forcing Henry Ford and the other sultans of Detroit to treat workers as something more than biceps and sweat. But the Caterpillar strike suggests that the Ford strain of American management is alive and well in Peoria . . ." He provides a window on the world of the growing number of "shift workers" in "Lives Upside Down to Help a World Go Round," 5-16. Kilborn strikes a chord as he describes the difficulties of their unconventional work hours and lives. In "Innovative Program in California Aids Those With Outdated Skills," 11-27, he makes clear he's a proponent of retraining, but this is still a balanced report, and more thorough on the big picture than most Kilborn articles.

Jerry Knight
The Washington Post
½★

Business columnist. Although Knight holds a key position on the *Post*'s business pages, he's far from impressive, as his work lacks diligence and enthusiasm, and continues to decline in quality. Two pieces epitomize this haphazard approach to his beat: "FDIC to Aid Bank for Second Time," 4-1, and "Bank Failures Could Cost Up to $95 Billion," 10-6. The former is a heavy-handed critique of the FDIC in which Knight reports that the FDIC has offered to bail out First City Bancorp for a second time. A "Correction," 4-3, ran two days later: "The FDIC has discussed the funding with First City and has said it will welcome proposals but has not yet formally committed funds." The latter report, on *Banking on the Brink*, a controversial book published by The Washington Post Co., that suggests hundreds of bank failures will occur after the election, caused quite a stir. But Knight downplays criticism of the author's methodology, not mentioning it until after the jump. A few weeks later he backtracks in "U.S. Regulators Don't Expect Explosion of Bank Failures," 10-27: "Federal bank regulators and some of their most outspoken critics agreed . . . that there will be no unexpected explosion of bank failures following the presidential election." Even when Knight gets the facts straight, he's still only a mediocre reporter. He fails to flesh out details on a very interesting Minnesota court decision in "Claims Court Says S&Ls Can Sue Government," 2-26, opting instead to take potshots at the "goodwill" accounting method in question, which he asserts was devised "as a way for the government to avoid paying for the losses of S&Ls that failed." "Hill to Get Plan for Bank Law Revision," 6-19, is merely a skim of the administration's plans for further bank de-regulation, and "Rate Cuts Boost Bank Profits, but Don't Spur Lending," 9-10, is a bland update on the banking industry.

Robert Kuttner
The New Republic
Washington Post Writers Group
BusinessWeek
★★½

Economics. Election year politics clearly invigorated this enterprising liberal commentator who is read by Bill Clinton. Though occasional flashes of knee-jerk Keynesianism led to contradictions during the campaign, his work for the most part was highly thought-provoking. Considering the deficit was a key Democratic weapon during the campaign, we were impressed by Kuttner's against-the-grain, "More Important Than the Deficit," *The Washington Post* 4-7, an earnest scrutiny: "The debt will be reduced relative to gross national product only when higher growth is restored." Similarly, he calls for a gradual and partial reduction of the deficit in "Don't Worry So Much About the Budget

Deficit," BusinessWeek 7-6, pondering why it has led "neither to economic stimulus, nor high interest rates, nor inflation?" He concludes that "$100 billion to $110 billion of the deficit is simply the result of recession. That leaves about $200 billion—almost exactly the annual interest on the accumulated public debt.... That also helps explain why there isn't much 'crowding out'; mostly, the interest paid on the public debt cycles right back into private capital markets." This last comment confused us, though, as he argued strenuously in "'Crowding Out' Has Business Up Against a Wall," *BW* 1-20, that banks were buying up Treasuries without making loans, thereby crowding out businesses in need of capital. With help from academia, he shatters another core assumption in "America Is Saving More Now, Not Less—If You Count it Right," *BW* 4-13, an expert critique of the way Commerce calculates savings: "If capital gains are counted, they more than double the official measure of savings." We wish his reporting on income distribution had been as rigorous in "The Slump That Broke the Public's Back," *BW* 2-17, in which he blames Reagan for alleged income distortions, even though his statistical evidence dates back to 1977.

Stephen Labaton
The New York Times
★★½

Washington, banking. With the troubled banking industry taking a back seat to election-year politics, Labaton continues to pursue the story with diligence. Though he has only followed banking for a few years, he has developed an impressive eye for detail, even on routine stories. We expect his work will continue to improve as he matures. His "Lower Interest Rates Revive Fears for Banks and S.& L.'s," 1-13, is an important alert on the significance of even-keel monetary policy to banks and S&Ls, which "by locking themselves into long-term mortgages at historically low rates, could be devastated if inflation accelerates..." There's plenty of pertinent information on the Treasury Secretary's latest about-face on banking legislation in "Brady Backs More Modest Banking Bills," 2-7, a cogent analysis with plenty of background. He scrutinizes the revised S&L figures in "Regulator Lowers Estimate of Cost of Savings Bailout," 5-17: "Some lawmakers and financial experts ...suggested that [RTC head] Mr. [Albert] Casey's numbers were...an effort to get a recalcitrant Congress to provide the additional $42 billion Mr. Casey has requested..." Plenty of attributed quotes support his raising of the issue. Carefully tracking legislation to tighten regulation of Treasury auctions, Labaton pens "Wall Street Opposing Bond Rules," 6-1, a solid overview of who supports the bill, who does not, and why. Out of character in "U.S. Bank Regulators Scale Back Rise in Fees for Deposit Insurance," 9-16, he shows surprising bias: "Bowing to political pressure, Federal regulators today cut in half a proposed increase in the insurance premiums that banks pay to the deposit insurance fund..." He doesn't fully consider the economic issues that played into the decision. On the other hand, his "$400 Million Bargain for Ernst," 11-25, is an impressive analysis of the government's settlement with Ernst & Young which regulators have "trumpeted" as a big win. Labaton proves through careful study that "In fact, the Government is getting only a fraction of what it says it was planning to seek..."

Jeffrey M. Laderman
BusinessWeek

Associate editor. Laderman understands the technical ins and outs of the mutual fund industry enough to introduce first-time investors to specific trends. He definitely doesn't display the sophistication necessary to appease the ravenous information appetites of seasoned market players. The majority of his work is unsatisfying and dry and he remains hopelessly trapped in a simplistic cash-flow model of the market mechanism. For instance, "Don't Let the Economy Scare You," 12/30/91-1/6/92, provides virtually no useful or fresh information. How's this for cutting-edge advice? "If you invest in stocks directly, check in with some of the pros and their model portfolios..." The same is true of "Suddenly the Password Is 'Value,'" 4-13, a general overview of the mutual-fund scene at the end of the first quarter. His conclusions here are especially generic: "High-growth has been giving way to value issues with rock-solid fundamentals." Equally undistinguished is "Midyear Investment Outlook: Where to Invest," with Mike McNamee and Howard Gleckman 6-22, a compilation of general observations on political and economic forces that could play on investments in the second half of the year. Other evaluations of European closed-end funds were much more sophisticated than Laderman's "Feeling Contrary? Check Out the Continent," 10-19, which is shaped by sources who don't take into account the deflationary forces at play in European markets. Even after conceding that the Swiss stock market is the only European bourse showing double-digit gains, one source says that France looks like a solid conservative buy "because inflation is down, wage growth is low, and France's budget deficit is under control." Laderman is much better when introducing novices to technical fundamentals, as in "This Time, it Pays to Be Nearsighted," 2-24, a quick trip down several investment routes, with Laderman pointing out the potholes. Also instructive is "Are Fund Managers Carving Themselves Too Fat a Slice?" 3-23, a detailed assessment of how creeping expense fees are more than nibbling away at shareholder profits.

Richard Lawrence
The Journal of Commerce
★★

"Trade Scene" columnist. Although Lawrence's column appears on the op-ed page, he usually does as much reporting as commentating. He's best when he sinks his teeth into one specific trade issue, as he does in "Big Steel Takes on the Imports," 5-14. Here, he provides an educational evaluation of the complex debate over anti-dumping duties on imported steel: "Most foreign suppliers, say steel savants, are selling more cheaply in the United States than in their home markets. Japanese price margins, they say, may be as high as 30% to 35%.... But... imports, say those who buy them, are not undercutting American mills, but priced only to meet depressed domestic prices." When Lawrence takes on broader subjects, the quality of the analysis is less consistent. His rebuke of Washington for not giving its due to the IMF, "Playing Politics With IMF Funds," 2-20, is only mildly effective: "U.S. lawmakers' overriding fear seems to be that in a recession-racked election year, opportunistic opponents would turn the $12 billion contribution into negative campaign ads." The most interesting suggestion in "Follow Russia's Bouncing Ball," 3-19, U.S.-financed "Enterprise Funds," is slipped into the conclusion, where it is unsatisfactorily explored. As the U.S. threatens "prohibitive" tariffs on EC products, Lawrence's sources predict U.S., not European, layoffs and bankruptcies, in "US, EC Brace for a Food Fight," 7-23. A near perfect balance of reporting and commentary shapes "Congress Botches Trade Policy," 10-15; in which he asserts that Congressional "procrastination and political pettifoggery" have stalled renewal of key programs such as the Export Administration Act, which expired two years ago. As a result, "the administration is compelled to keep imposing 'strategic' controls on U.S. exports under the guise of 'a national emergency.'" Evaluating Bill Clinton's ascension to the presidency in "Anything New Under the Sun?" 12-10, Lawrence, like many others, holds up the Carter years as an example of policies the new President should avoid.

Doron P. Levin
The New York Times
★★★

Detroit. The author of *Irreconcilable Differences*, considered by many the single best source on Ross Perot's clash with General Motors, surely enjoyed seeing his two subjects take center stage in this year of unique corporate and political uprisings. Levin is a keen observer of the increasingly global workings of the Big Three automakers. His "Parts Pact With Japan May Backfire," 2-3, is a very perceptive analysis of the recent pact: "...the uncertainty over how the agreement will play out speaks to the enormous cross-cultural misunderstanding that has grown up between the automotive industries of the two countries.... The Americans say they have been burned in the past when Japanese promises did not turn out as hoped. The Japanese feel stung too; they do not wish to be blamed for political tension between the countries, but they also resent having to alter their practices to accommodate less successful competitors." Covering the "shocking" changes in GM's executive suite in "President Is Demoted at G.M." 4-7, Levin gives us the inside track with the ease of a veteran: "The move sends a powerful signal of the activism of outside directors and suggests that G.M. must make major improvements or more changes will be coming, perhaps affecting [CEO Robert] Stempel as well." He takes us on a fascinating tour of Toyota's much raved about "lean production" methods in "Toyota Plant in Kentucky Is Font of Ideas for U.S." 5-5, and shines in his behind-the-scenes look at the scrambling over the terms of Lee Iacocca's retirement in "Why Iacocca Wants to Extend Role at Chrysler," 8-12: "... the board can compromise and grant Mr. Iacocca more time and authority as an honorary chief executive.... Or it can ... stick to its position on Mr. Iacocca's retirement. Chrysler's current top executives, though they dare not say so publicly, clearly are rooting for the second course." He's measured in assessing GM's "Grand Inquisitor," Mr. J. Ignacio Lopez de Arriortua, in "G.M. Ultimatum to Parts Makers Brings Showdown With Workers," 9-2: "The clear message to the auto workers' union is that the price cuts Mr. Lopez wants from G.M.'s parts operations could lead to plant shutdowns, divestitures and fewer union jobs."

Joshua Levine
Forbes
★★½

Senior editor. A perceptive reporter and stylish writer, Levine is well suited to cover the creative world of marketing. He's especially good at handling offbeat fads, as he does so well in "Dr. Pangloss, Meet Ingmar Bergman," 3-30, turning us on to the fact that these days death sells: "What's going on? Demographics. People born during the baby boom aren't getting younger, and they are coming to terms with the truth that no advertised product is potent enough to reverse the march of time." He provides numerous examples of the trend at work. He's savvy on Roberto Ruggeri's "ambition to be the Ray Kroc of snooty dining" in "Where the Maitre d' Outranks the Chef," 6-8, explaining how the restaurant owner is trying to turn his pricey Manhattan restaurant, Bice, into an international chain without diminishing its chic image. We're taken on a whimsical and informative tour of the International Advertising Film Festival in "Advertising's Summer Games," 8-3. Not only do we get a kick out of some of the ads, but we also learn about the ad world's changing tastes. One of his best pieces of the year, "Halloween Boo-quets, Anyone?" 10-26, examines a marketing trend we haven't read about elsewhere. A new breed of low-overhead flower retail outlets has reduced the retail florists' share of the $12.7 billion cut-flower market "from over 75% ten years ago to around 50% today." He examines how FTD is trying to save its member florists by coming out with new products and innovative ideas to draw back customers. More stylish writing and sharp reporting characterize "The Ivory Control Tower," 11-23, an informative analysis of how the profitable Gianni Versace markets his outrageous and expensive clothes by "enhancing his merchandise with the glow of music, theater and sex. 'I am like a *spugna*—a sponge,' Versace once told Donatella Girombelli, explaining how he soaks up all the celebrity pizzazz. 'I take it all in, and then I wring it out.'"

Marc Levinson
Newsweek
★★

The former editorial page editor at *The Journal of Commerce* has a tendency to editorialize in his news analyses, a characteristic we tolerate only because he brings to light so much new information amid the commentary. He gets right to the point in "Lay Off the Pricey CEOs," 2-10, remarking: "None of the purported ills of the U.S. economy ... has much to do with

MEDIAGUIDE 81

Paul Fireman's pay.... Congress has plenty of serious economic issues on its plate. This one is better left to shareholders." We were disappointed by the haphazardness of his analytics in "April 15 Could Be Worse," 4-13, in which he argues that U.S. taxes aren't that high when compared to other countries: "The purported relationship between taxes and growth doesn't exist. 'Growth rates in the '50s and '60s were higher than in the '70s and '80s, and marginal tax rates were higher,' recalls Herbert Stein, chief economic adviser in the Nixon administration." But Stein's comparison of the post- and pre-Bretton Woods eras ignores the impact that inflation had on a tax bracket and after-tax purchasing power. In "Let's Have No More Free-Trade Deals, Please," 8-17, he makes a cogent point about NAFTA's numerous provisions "favoring U.S. textile makers, Canadian farmers and Mexican banks," but his broader argument that free trade will grow with or without NAFTA fails to persuade us that the agreements don't speed the transition. Declinism is back in style, according to "The Hand Wringers," 10-26, an overview of the numerous doom and gloom books on the market. Plenty of interesting history on federal job-creation efforts is offered in "Bailing Out the Jobless," 11-16: "From Franklin Roosevelt to Jimmy Carter, the history of federal job-creation efforts is mixed at best." It was great to see Levinson policing his fellow journalists in "Banking on Scare Stories," 11-2. He does a fine job of explaining how a national banking crisis was reported by the press, even though there was scant evidence of its existence: "Banking, by and large, is a bore to the media.... Crisis, on the other hand, is hot stuff."

Larry Light
BusinessWeek
★★½

Corporate finance editor. It's very rare that you walk away from a report by Light without new information or perspective. He knows where to look for the potentials and hazards of a wide variety of financial deals and instruments, and his work on the beleaguered real-estate markets is always worth a look. "It Will Be a Bottoming-Out Year," 1-13, for instance, pulls together numerous mini-trends to give us a clear image of the big picture: "No matter how strong the recovery in housing... it won't counterbalance the shock waves from the collapse in commercial real estate.... Recession-racked lenders are reluctant to roll over many landlords' maturing loans. And tenants are getting rent cuts for lease renewals." Keeping his eye out for deals, Light reports a flurry of interest in the financial services company, Integrated Resources, in "Integrated's Latest Acquisitions: Two Big Bidders," 5-4: "The ultrarich Pritzker family of Chicago and Steinhardt Management Co., headed by Wall Street whiz Michael H. Steinhardt, are floating heavyweight bids..." He fully explores the allure and the downside of this bankrupt company. Providing a plethora of information for investors in "Another Black Eye for Cooper," 6-15, Light makes perfectly clear why the future of Cooper Co., a New York health care outfit specializing in contact lenses, is "extremely fuzzy." In a very professional manner, he takes us through the numerous allegations by "restive shareholders" and the SEC. In "How Much Prudence Is Good for Prudential?" 7-13, he applauds chairman Robert Winters for a successful turnaround, but cites employee frustration with Winters's "cautious thinking." By the end, we understand how Winters's go-slow tack could backfire as competitors like Met Life undertake risky, but lucrative acquisitions.

Joanne Lipman
The Wall Street Journal
★★½

"Advertising" columnist. A creative writer and level-headed analyst, Lipman rarely gets caught up in the hype surrounding the latest advertising fad. She is equally competent on both creative and financial trends in the industry. Her "'Terminator 2' Yields a Stylistic Overdose," 1-6, is useful on the ad world's overuse of "'morphing,' so named for its ability to metamorphose one object or person into another..." She notes it's likely to make a comeback as more sophisticated techniques give morphed products a unique identity. She explains ABC's "embarrassing retreat" from its "gutsy initiative" to ditch long-standing rules for advertisers in "ABC Retreats on Bid to Relax Ad Guidelines," 3-13: " . . . bowing to pressure from advertisers and some industry groups, ABC . . . quietly issued revised guidelines that are as strict as any of the old rules . . . Some advertisers howled that if ABC didn't regulate them, the government would do the job instead." With ad clutter on cable outranking network TV, Lipman pens "Commercials Are Cluttering Cable Shows," 4-29, a deft examination of how advertisers are factoring clutter into their price negotiations. While others predict an upturn in ad spending, Lipman provides a valuable reality check in "As Industry Feels Spring of Hope, a Forecaster Cools His Optimism," 6-3. She cites a "perennially overoptimistic" ad forecaster who has just "sliced his 1992 estimate for ad spending in the U.S. to 5% growth, from the 6.2% rate he forecast in December." Lipman typically explores her beat from unique angles and "The Making of a Best Seller Is a Might Serious Business," 7-21, is no exception. This is a enjoyable read which tells how "ads touting books as 'no.1' can be close to outright fiction," fleshing out humorous stretches, and explaining the serious implications. The latest fad is explored by Lipman's skeptical eye in "Interactive TV Entices Many Marketers, But So Far Hype Outpaces Technology," 8-25: " . . . an examination of the fledgling field lays bare a litany of broken promises."

Thomas W. Lippman
The Washington Post
★★★½

Energy. An extremely professional reporter, Lippman knows D.C. like the back of his hand. He walks us through the labyrinth that is Beltway policymaking, taking us behind-the-scenes, where we see the nation's power brokers jockeying for advantage in the latest legislative battle. What's more, we can trust him, as he doesn't use his reports to further anyone's politics, only our understanding. He turns what might have been mundane news conference coverage into "Energy Lobby Fights Unseen 'Killers,'" 4-1, a polished and informative tour of Big Business and Big Energy's joint effort to fight off hidden legislative proposals: "According to a March 30 draft obtained by *The Washington Post*, [a bill from George Miller (D-CA)] would put virtually all U.S. offshore waters off limits to new oil and gas drilling until 2002..." As the energy bill is pushed and pulled through the legislative process, he keeps a close watch in such articles as "Ambitious Energy Bill in a Precarious Stall," 7-27, an excellent clarification of the jumble of proposals. More than just a good reporter, Lippman is also an able feature writer. Through his profile of the Energy Department's chief historian, "Writer's Assignment: Synthesize Government's Energy History," 2-18, we learn "the gap between academic and government historians is disappearing." On his very informative trip to report on the Tennessee Valley Authority, in "TVA: New Deal for an Old Power," 3-29, he finds the institution much changed: "After half a century as the most durable monument of Franklin D. Roosevelt's New Deal, TVA is taking on a new image as a lean, business-oriented utility, and is causing a few political ripples in the process." During September, Lippman covered the emotionally-charged POW Congressional hearings with his usual professionalism, producing such balanced and informative reports as "Nixon Knew of POWs, Aides Say," 9-22, and "Kissinger Calls POWs Charge a 'Lie,'" 9-23. And travelling to Hanoi for a follow-up, "Hanoi Gives Personal Effects of GIs to Visiting U.S. Senate Delegation," 11-18, he describes how "Suddenly, information that could help close the books on the fate of 2,265 U.S. servicemen . . . is pouring out of Vietnam's long-secretive military establishment."

Steve Lohr
The New York Times

The quality of Lohr's work isn't as even this year. His stylish writing still draws us into the most mundane of business topics, but his analysis doesn't always carry us through. Based on his impressive performance last year, we're still willing to take the plunge when we see his byline. His profile of Aflac, Inc., "Under the Wing of Japan Inc., A Fledgling Enterprise Soared," 1-15, is the type of report we're used to from Lohr. It flies in the face of conventional wisdom, showing how an American insurance company has made it big in Japan. Thriving, "new-style sleuths" who investigate financial crimes are the subject of his enjoyable "A New Breed of Sam Spade Trails Crooks' Hidden Assets," 2-20: "Unlike the Sam Spades of the past, who relied on a .38, a hip flask and a hunch, today's private eyes use computers and data bases." His coverage of the turbulence at General Motors, "Shake-Up Is a Sign Rubber-Stamp Days Have Ended at G.M." 4-8, gave us the facts straight up, but we saw none of the cogent analysis or key detail offered by those who follow the Big Three more closely. For "Pulling One's Weight at the New I.B.M." 7-5, Lohr travels to an IBM branch and finds a leaner, more flexible sales and service team, but there's no surprising information here. On market economics Lohr comes up short, as with his mindless non sequitur, "Risky Stance on Dollar," 8-28: "The dollar has steadied in nervous trading... and the stock market has rallied somewhat in sympathy." Wall Street, sympathetic? Much more interesting is his talk with Harvard professor Michael E. Porter in "Fixing Corporate America's Short-Term Mind-Set," 9-2. After a two-year study of U.S. competitiveness, Porter wants to structure regulation to force long-term investment. Lohr covers Porter's arguments with clarity, challenging them in a professional manner. In "Signs of Thaw for Small Business," 11-4, Lohr's sources indicate it may be time to get positioned for the next big wave of entrepreneurial capitalism, and after reading through the supporting statistical and anecdotal evidence, we're hopeful.

Carol J. Loomis
Fortune
★★★½

Board of editors. Having successfully liberated her reports from heavy-handed commentary without sacrificing the muscle behind her trademark analytical punch, Loomis is now a lean, mean business writer who ranks among the best in the business. The only problem is we don't see enough of her name; she writes only four or five stories a year. When her byline is listed on the Table of Contents, though, we immediately turn to the article. Typical of her superior writing and reporting is "Victims of the Real Estate Crash," 5-18, in which she expertly tracks the reverberations of the real estate collapse which have shaken the banking and insurance industries and metropolitan communities. Packed with striking information and observations, she delineates the financial conundrum faced by appraisers and regulators as their various methods of valuation are rendered useless or highly controversial by a real estate market in flux. She covers all the bases in another top-notch financial evaluation, "A Whole New Way to Run a Bank," 9-7. Here, we learn all about the promise and pitfalls of maverick Bankers Trust's move away from holding loans into risky, but lucrative, new derivative funds: "Quips an institutional investor bemused by the figures: 'This isn't a bank. It's a hedge fund that's too big to fail.'" In a sidebar article, "How Bankers Trust Lied About $80 Million," 9-7, Loomis sheds new light on the bank's infamous Krieger affair. She does an impressive job of explaining how "draconian" new accounting laws will affect banks in "Banks May Face a Nervous New Year," 12-14, warning that "new pressures are bearing down on the banking industry.... One fallout...will surely be a pickup in the consolidation trend.... Even the new president of the American Bankers Association, William Brandon... claims to be contemplating escape from Washington's 'micromanagement.' Says he: 'A lot of bankers, like myself, are thinking it's a good time to sell out.'" And after reading *Wall Street Journal* reporter George Anders's new book on KKR, she offers a review with the same title, "Merchants of Debt," 7-27, a tentative endorsement of the book.

John Maggs
The Journal of Commerce
★★½

International economics. We were impressed by the first articles we saw from this precocious reporter, and we're even more impressed now. He is quickly becoming recommended reading. While most trade reporters follow only the broadest debates, Maggs is one of the few who scrutinizes the specifics of U.S. trade agreements. For instance, in "Computer Makers Hit Content Rules in Trade Proposal," 3-30, he carefully examines the arguments surrounding stiffer local content requirements under NAFTA: "For big computer makers like IBM, the change represents... hundreds of millions of dollars in lost revenue... On the other side is the American Display Manufacturers of America, which has argued that increasing the proportion of North American content in computers is essential to ensure that Japan does not use Mexico... to gain preferential access to U.S. markets." In "Pelosi Mulls New Tack on Trade With China," 6-1, he exposes a new approach by Rep. Nancy Pelosi (D-CA) "designed to gain veto-proof support in Congress for a bill to force human-rights reforms by China's Communist leaders." He's keen on the pre-election implications for Bush, if no trade agreement is reached with China, in "China Showdown to Test Bush Global Affairs Skill," 8-24. Post-election, Maggs prepares numerous instructive articles on the incoming administration's inclinations toward trade issues. Among the most notable are "Clinton Team May Seek to Slow GATT Agreement," 12-8, and "Clinton Seen Hesitant to Intervene in Trade Talks," 12-11. Maggs also writes a very informative "Memo to Bill Clinton on Trade," 11-12: "Why is the United States now limiting uranium shipments from Kazakhstan, where the mineral is one-fifth of that republic's exports? Why are there new quotas on apparel from Bulgaria? The United States certainly has an overwhelming interest in promoting trade with the former Soviet empire. The truth is that domestic industry will always have a powerful voice in foreign policy. The challenge for you is to make the right call each time."

Maggie Mahar
Barron's
★★★½

We never skip a Mahar byline, especially if the topic is Russia. For the past two years, she has been one of the few reporters actually pressing the margins on the economic deterioration occurring there, and she doesn't even write from Moscow. Two of her most unsettling articles this year are "Economic Miracle or Catastrophe?" 1-13, and "Wolf at the Door," 10-19. In the first article she peers into the future with the help of her ever increasing network of Russian experts. No government flacks, their vision verges on apocalyptic: "As Sergei Khrushchev points out, 'decisions about a market system are even more important than decisions about nuclear weapons.' The threat of what statesmen politely call a 'nuclear mishap' is remote. The danger of an economic apocalypse is imminent." She's not as tuned into the changes occurring in China, as is clear in her assessment of the Hong Kong market in "Skeleton at the Feast," 8-17: "The question mark of what happens in Beijing after Deng's death hangs over a market swollen by success to the point of complacency." The comment reveals she hasn't fully explored the ongoing institutionalization of Deng's reforms. On the domestic front, she pens "Under a Microscope," 3-2, an outstanding profile of FDA chief David Kessler: "When it comes to food labeling, the commissioner believes the FDA can be more than a censor, that it can actually create incentives for manufacturers to invent foods that are more healthful." This revealing profile was surely much discussed at food and drug companies. While Mahar doesn't fully convince us in "Blue Collar, White Collar," 5-11, that this recession is producing different, more permanent job losses, she does make a strong point that the costs of benefits is leading employers to hire fewer full-timers. Mahar turns to Wall Street analysts to look down the road at possible post-election scenarios in "Portfolio for All Presidents," 7-6, and "And the Winner Is...," 11-2, but most of this crystal-ball gazing is highly predictable.

Thomas McArdle
Investor's Business Daily
★★★

McArdle received a 10 Best citation last year for his work on tax policy. He is among the few journalists who get beyond the rhetoric and actually try to understand the economic dynamic of this controversial issue. On a wide variety of issues at the intersection of finance and economics, no one else scrutinizes the bottom line quite like McArdle. You rarely find such in-depth economic research by a daily reporter. Joined by co-writer John Merline for his most recent 10 Best selection, "Should Business Fear Clinton?" 7-16, we're offered an outstanding dissection of Clintonomics. There's enough valuable, fresh information here to permit us to formulate a solid opinion about the presidential nominee's approach to the nation's economic problems. The duo are back together for "How to Cut Taxes on Cap Gains," 8-26, providing one of the first and few follow-ups we saw on economist Paul Craig Roberts's provocative assertion that the President has the authority to index capital gains by decree. Studying the work of Lawrence Kudlow of Bear Stearns for "Not-So-Fine Print in Tax 'Cuts,'" 3-17, McArdle lays bare a costly exclusion hidden in Bush's proposal: "'In some cases the AMT provision would actually raise the marginal tax rate on capital gains to 30%,' [Kudlow] notes." We learn that what has been framed as a partisan debate is no such thing in "A Cap Gains Cut, Clinton-Style," 12-8: "The Clinton administration is widely expected to take away one of the Republicans' key weapons against the Democratic president: the capital gains issue." But, delving deeper into the specifics of Clinton's proposals, McArdle discovers strict limitations. Another outstanding example of what a little research can turn up is "New York: Closed for Business?" 5-14. Here, McArdle puts the numbers on the table and makes a convincing case that NYC is driving away business with one of the heaviest tax burdens in the country. Exploring the hot topic of industrial policy in "Does Gov't Always Know Best," 9-10, he evaluates the success story everyone loves to cite and asks: "Is government guidance the overwhelming reason for Japan's accomplishments as a high-tech exporter? The evidence suggests . . . no." And boy does he gather a lot of evidence to support this assertion: "One glaring illustration that MITI is no oracle of smart investment strategy is the fact that the government institution actually tried to keep Honda Motor Co. out of the automobile business."

Robert McGough
The Wall Street Journal
★★½

Financial World lost a savvy analyst when McGough headed over to the *Journal* mid-year. This high-energy reporter is sure to enhance the "Money & Investing" page with his sharp reporting skills. Joined by co-writer Alexandra Biesada for "A Game of Chicken," *FW* 2-18, we learn of the costly game of chicken being played by U.S. and European aluminum makers as prices hit historic lows: "The catalyst for this dangerous game is the former Soviet Union. To pay for desperately needed imports, Russia is flooding the West with metal at fire-sale prices . . . " "High Iron," 4-14, provides an instructive contrast of the divergent paths taken by two iron ore companies, one now successful, the other struggling. If you think U.S. airlines are a mess, read McGough's "Not Cleared for Landing," *FW* 6-23, and find out why the Europeans are threatened by U.S. expansion: "The answer is size: American Airlines had 622 aircraft at the end of 1991, versus 135 for Alitalia. Some Europeans believe that competing with these behemoths will require huge, cross-border mergers within Europe." Bounding onto the pages of the *Journal* with sharp financial analysis, he writes "Despite the Disorder in Europe, Analysts See Closed-End Stock Funds as a Bargain," *WSJ* 9-1, providing an informed buy recommendation on European closed stock funds: "It is the unusually large discounts in some European closed-end funds that attract some analysts today. When the markets turn around, the investor gets a double boost to his return. Not only does the fund's portfolio rise in value, but the discount to that portfolio shrinks." In the wake of the currency crisis in Europe, McGough pens "U.S. Investors in European Stock Funds Learn Big Lesson on Vulnerability in Currency Swings," *WSJ* 9-21, enlightening us on the impact currency swings can have on U.S. investors overseas. And his "Junk Funds Believe It's Time to Strike Back at 'Timers,'" *WSJ* 12-1, is an interesting exploration of the substantial outflow of money from junk funds in October.

Mike McNamee
BusinessWeek
★★

Washington. Though McNamee is competent on the political jockeying that goes on between the Federal Reserve and the administration, innocuous is how we would describe his analysis of monetary policy. He sees it in a vacuum, unaffected by fiscal or political forces. As a result, he can neither add much to our understanding of the monetary dynamic, nor cause any trouble, as policymakers know better. In his mediocre "What More Can Greenspan Do?" 2-24, with co-writer Alice Cuneo, we're told that "Until next November, Greenspan's best hope may [be] to keep long-term rates running flat." He's better in "Monday Morning Quarterbacking at the Fed," 3-30, but is still unsure of his footing when discussing the Fed's realization that their assumptions about M2 growth need to be revisited. McNamee certainly didn't prepare us for the currency crisis in Europe, but with 20/20 hindsight he skims the issues confidently, albeit superficially, in "Could the Plunge Have Been Prevented? Probably," co-written by William Glasgall 9-7. Assessing the Fed's price stability goals in "What Price Stability?" "Reinventing America" issue '92, McNamee packs the piece with generalizations: "After hearing economists talk for 30 years about the trade-off between inflation and unemployment, few policymakers want to enlist in an experiment to prove . . . that a credible central bank can cut inflation even in a growing economy." McNamee's simple deficit equations just don't hold water in "World's Biggest Credit Hog: Washington," 4-13: ". . . most pols seem interested only in economic growth. But without tough action on the deficit, high long-term rates may keep the pols' wish from coming true." The fact that long bond yields dropped this year, even as the deficit ballooned, suggests a more complex formula. His colorful profile of World Bank head Larry Summers, "The In-Your-Face Economist at the World Bank," 5-11, is mildly informative on Summers's "model of 'market-friendly' government." And his commentary, "Color Blind Credit: How the Banks Can Do Better," 6-29, advises that banks should self-regulate minority lending before the government steps in.

David Moberg
In These Times
★★★

Senior editor. We're increasingly turning to Moberg for important perspectives from the left. As a veteran on the labor beat he is one of best analysts of the repositioning of unions. On economic and political topics, he can be trusted to study problems long and hard, and with an open mind. He ably gives us the inside scoop on the Teamsters in "Can Teamsters Reformers Stop Old-Guard Retrenchment?" 12/25/91-1/14/92, skillfully profiling new Teamsters president Ron Carey, and giving us a crystal clear picture of the challenges he faces: "If Carey's reforms are going to take hold, the same rank-and-file democracy that brought him to power must sustain him in office." In his op-ed on the Caterpillar strike, "Local Strike, National Stake," *The New York Times* 4-10, Moberg asks government and U.S. corporations to start seeing workers "as an important part of the solution to our national woes —not as the problem." He uses statistical evidence effectively to make his case. There's no question where Moberg stands on free trade in "Sound Bites Without Teeth: Trade, Debt and Campaign '92," 7/22-8/4: "As a global leader, the United States must shift from blind advocacy of free trade to a more balanced policy that stresses debt relief and economic rejuvenation for the poorer countries... At the same time, the United States needs industrial policies that support innovation..." Though his conclusions are controversial, his arguments are well thought out and worth listening to. "A Star Is Born in Carol Moseley Braun," 9/30-10/13, provides excellent intelligence on the Democrat who later became the first black woman elected to the Senate: "[She supports] business incentives, such as investment tax credits and targeted capital gains. Braun calls herself a 'mature,' 'post-Roosevelt' liberal who believes 'government does not create jobs but creates a climate where job creation takes place in the private sector.'" His post-election follow-up, "Goodbye, Gridlock?" 11-11/29, notes: "It's possible that Clinton and Congress could diverge on several major issues." He capably outlines where the debates are likely to develop.

Gretchen Morgenson
Forbes

Senior editor. A spirited journalist who writes and reports with gusto, Morgenson is well versed on many topics. We were absolutely wowed by her shocking exposé "What Did Pop Expect to Happen When He Gave the Kid His Credit Card?" 9-28, a 10 Best selection, that makes clear that the FDIC is "a government agency utterly out of control, terrorizing innocent bystanders and frequently costing the taxpayers far more in legal fees than it is recovering." She has got plenty of evidence to back up this assertion. Morgenson's previous stints at both *Vogue* magazine and the stock brokerage firm Dean Witter, also make her perfectly suited to cover the business of retailing. One of her best reports of year, "The Feminization of Seventh Avenue," 5-11, is surely making waves: "Female designers have come out from behind their sketch pads and have built companies that are growing at 25% and more per year and outperforming the industry in profitability." She provides dozens of specific examples of female designers who are running extremely successful businesses, a fact that she says "*Vogue, WWD* and the fashion pages of the *New York Times* have paid scant attention to..." Morgenson carefully watches the changes forced upon retailing by discounters in "Business As Usual," 2-3, a pithy assessment of the May chain's strategy to preserve profits over market share during the recession. Her sources contend that while this strategy worked in the '80s, it might not work now: "[Retailing analyst Bernard] Sosnick points to Dayton Hudson, which has won traffic by discounting. Maintaining market share while times are tight is the only way a retailer can hope to profit when the consumer begins to spend again, says Sosnick." She zeroes in on discounting's impact on cosmetics in "Save $35 on Chanel," 3-16, revealing the shadowy world of "gray-market sales," in which major department stores sell cosmetics under the table to discounters in a process known as "diversion." In "The Foot's Friend," 4-13, she offers a smart, enjoyable read on innovator James Throneburg and his amazing success at building a brand image for Thor-Lo's "sport-specific socks." She scrutinizes Gitano's bottom line in "Greener Pastures?" 7-6, making worthwhile observations about the downside of the company's alliance with Wal-Mart, which contributes 26 percent of Gitano's revenues, but has been very tough on pricing. Her "Nose Under Tent?" 10-12, is an eye-opener on a provision in the proposed Revenue Act of 1992. Morgenson reporting that "If passed in its current form, the law would force Wall Street firms to pay taxes on unrealized gains in their securities trading positions."

Steven Mufson
The Washington Post
★½

Economics. Mufson is sinking his teeth into meatier economic subjects this year, but he's also imbibing in the ideological games that we thought were below him. It's too bad, because when he looks at the numbers straight-on, he usually provides useful analysis as he did with "In Budget, the Deficit Is a Victor," 1-31, effectively throwing the deficit figures in the administration's face: "For nearly every category of government spending, the 1990 budget agreement has succeeded in keeping expenditures in line.... However, the deficit has continued to climb, driven by lower-than-expected revenues from tax measures adopted in 1990..." This is an important observation, but one that he doesn't explore. In September, Mufson contributed to a three-part series on the national debt, "The Mortgage on America," 9-27/29. Not only is the information merely standard fare, but the timing, hyperbolic tone and questionable research make the piece look suspiciously political. For example, in the 9-28 report, Mufson piles on all the old "voodoo economics" jargon and blames today's deficits on Reagan and Bush's embrace of supply-side economics: "Despite the economy's vigorous 6.5 percent growth rate following the end of the recession in the last three months of 1982, individual income tax receipts actually fell slightly during 1983 because of the tax rate cuts. In 1984, as the economy continued to grow, tax receipts barely crept back to the levels of 1982." Had he scrutinized statistics from the actual boom years, he might have reached a different conclusion. The Mufson of years past takes control in "Treasury's Look at Income Mobility," 6-3, resisting the temptation to come down on either side of the politically-charged debate over income distribution. He even acknowledges "the study is sure to provide fodder for both sides of the debate over whether the United States is becoming a society rigidly divided by class." Though Mufson provides an adequate personal profile of Yegor Gaidar in "Charting Russia's Economic Course," 5-1, he asks no hard policy questions. Similarly, his profile of Robert Rubin, "Financier Rubin Faces a Different Set of Options," 12-13, is more detailed on the man than the future policymaker.

Alan Murray
The Wall Street Journal
★

Washington, deputy bureau chief. After nearly ten years on the economics beat, Murray continues to wear his Keynesian ideology on his sleeve. His close-mindedness to theories or data that do not fit his vision of economic correctness leads to some very skewed analysis. It's obvious in "Brown's Tax Plan Blurs the Distinction Between 'Conservative' and 'Liberal,'" 3-23, that Murray doesn't like the flat and VAT tax proposals: "The bottom line, according to Robert McIntyre of the labor-backed Citizens for Tax Justice, is that Mr. Brown's tax plan would triple taxes on the poor, raise taxes on middle-income families by 28%, and cut taxes on the nation's richest third." A week later, Alexander Cockburn, also a pro-labor leftist, and economist Robert Pollin, an informal advisor to Brown, laid bare in a 4-2 *Wall Street Journal* op-ed the errors in CTJ's calculations. In "Democrat Frontrunner Backs Industrial Policy With a Populist Twist," 4-23, Murray gushes over "Clintonomics." Critics can't get a word in edgewise as he lets Clinton's advisors go on and on about their candidate's innovative ideas. With the market uneasy about the election, Murray attempts to discern, in "What the Markets Say About the Campaign," 8-17, which economic platforms are influencing investment strategies, but his observations are just more of the same half-baked thinking we've seen elsewhere. "The Fiscal Proposals of Bush and Clinton Both Flunk Arithmetic," 9-15, is Murray at his worst—all accounting, no understanding. His assumption that all tax cuts and spending proposals are created equal guides this flat evaluation. We also found his addition here questionable, as Bush's deficit shortfall is bigger than Clinton's, because Bush's numbers represent five years while Clinton's represent only four. Also weak is his defense of the President's auto-parts agreement with Japan in "Managed Trade May Serve a Purpose," 1-20, Murray contending it was necessary because "the evidence shows clearly that the behavior of Japanese multinationals is an exception in world commerce."

Sylvia Nasar
The New York Times
★

For better or worse, Nasar is always in the middle of things. After reading her strong portfolio last year, we had high hopes for Nasar, who holds a

PhD in economics and an influential position at the *Times*. That's why her distortions and omissions in such stories as "Even Among the Well-Off, the Richest Get Richer," 3-5; "Fed Gives New Evidence of 80's Gains by Richest," 4-21; "However You Slice the Data the Richest Did Get Richer," 5-11; "Who Paid the Most Taxes in the 80s? The Superrich," 5-31; and "Is the Clinton Expansion Here? Rebound Seen, but a Slow One," 11-30, shocked us so much. In order to be able to say in the 3-5 report that the top one percent of the richest families received 60 percent of the gains in the '80s boom, Nasar cites CBO data for the years '77-'89, ignoring similar calculations in the same study for '80-'89, and '85-'89. The study points out that between '85-'89, the amount of income gains going to the bottom 80 percent were twice as great as the period '77-'89. Income distribution is roundly ignored in the 4-21 report, which deals instead with net worth. But the study she cites, the '89 Survey of Consumer Finances, is the most comprehensive source on family income available, and deals solely with the '82-'89 period. She blatantly ignores an opportunity to clarify the issues here. Also, she doesn't report that between '82-'89 the top one percent got 20 percent of the gains in family income, a dramatic reversal of the trends concentrating wealth on the ultra-rich during the late 1970s, and she makes no attempt to compare the implications of the drastic differences between the '77-'89 and '82-'89 studies. What's more, Nasar, in the 5-11 report, makes clear that she's thrilled that her distortions have helped Bill Clinton's cause, referring to the Democrat's reaction to her 3-5 report: "Governor Clinton... had been searching for months for facts to illustrate his claim that America's middle class benefited little from 12 years of Republican rule. The explosion of riches at the top struck him as a perfect vehicle." By her 5-31 article, she's reporting that "the top 1 percent of American families... reaped 70 percent of the growth in average family incomes..." After all this, we weren't surprised by her 11-30 post-election piece which opens: "A number of business executives say the Clinton expansion may have arrived even before the President-elect moves to the White House."

William Neikirk
Chicago Tribune
★★

Washington, senior writer. We read Neikirk primarily on the op-ed page of *The Journal of Commerce*. Though we're not always persuaded by his macroeconomic evaluations, he's a thoughtful analyst and a luminous wordsmith—a combination that makes for fruitful reading. He pokes fun at election-year policymaking in the delightful "The Scent of Freshly Cut Taxes," *JC* 2-3: "something odd happens at this time of year.... We actually entertain the idea that some of these new ideas, or warmed-over old ideas, might actually work." We also enjoy his thoughtful musings in "Mr. Bush's Policy-a-Week Plan," *JC* 4-24: "In this post-Cold War era... people are seeking... a president who can serve as their captain, not one of his staff aides. Perhaps out of this thicket of weekly messages, a clean, pure Bush administration theme will emerge. Right now, it looks like many themes, drawing from left, right and middle, all adding up to confusion." His message is much the same for "Tuning Out Political Cacophony," *JC* 6-15, though he's less poignant here. In "Flagging Confidence in the US," *JC* 8-31, be argues "When your currency falls like this... it means that we are letting our standard of living fall." He doesn't consider the idea that deflationary pressures might be pushing down *European* living standards, while in the U.S. the dollar remains stable against commodities. Playing on an old George Wallace adage in "Choosing an Economic Course," *JC* 9-11, Neikirk cuts through the political rhetoric to say "There's more than 10 cents' worth of difference between the two parties today. Billions would be more like it.... In contrast to Mr. Bush's idea of creating the conditions for new jobs, Mr. Clinton would try to spend them into existence." "Guarding a New World Order," *JC* 12-4, is a very impressive essay on the strategic and moral quandaries of sending troops to Somalia, but not Bosnia: "One feels a deep sense of anger that the United States and the rest of the world have allowed these situations to fester for so long. ...Little has been done to establish a new post-Cold War security structure to prevent future Bosnias and Somalias."

Peter Norman
Financial Times
★★½

Economics. The quality of work emanating from this intelligent analyst's pen lacks the steady insight to which we're accustomed, but then again this was no ordinary year in Europe. The intense political and financial forces that came to a head in the currency crisis overwhelmed even the most perceptive journalists. "Indigestion in the Body Politic," 6-17, is way below Norman's usually high-minded work. Rather than assess the German public's discontent with its government's economic policies, Norman latches onto national stereotypes: "so far there are only limited signs that the German public has the necessary patience to see the changes through." Discerning an important shift at the Bath meeting in "Bundesbank Allows Flicker of Hope," 9-7, he notes Helmut Schlesinger's agreement to a "no increase" statement: "...the UK chancellor, underlining it was 'the first time' the Bundesbank had committed itself 'openly and publicly' not to raise rates, said he regarded the promise as 'a significant outcome' of the talks." As the currencies tumbled, Norman's evaluations become more wobbly, as in "Impaled on a Sterling Skewer: a Primer," 9-17, and "US Puts Commodities Index at Centre-Stage," 9-22. In the latter, he's extremely suspicious of Bush's proposed commodity-basket-with-gold index: "There is also a suspicion that the US as a leading producer of primary commodities and gold would benefit from the scheme more than other industrial countries." Back in form for "Smiling, Not Drowning," 9-23, he interprets Norman Lamont's broad smile amid the chaos, explaining the chancellor is now freed of the constraints imposed by the Bundesbank on the struggling U.K. economy. Desperately searching for some kind of leadership in the aftermath of Black Wednesday, Norman finds none and says so in "Economic Policy in a Floating World," 10-5. And joined by co-writer Lionel Barber for "The Monetary Tragedy of Errors That Led to Currency Chaos," 12-11, we're served a grand and detailed behind-the-scenes portrait of the bureaucratic finagling that broke the camel's back: "Time and again, this autumn's crisis was bedeviled by both human failure and the weakness of European institutions."

Floyd Norris
The New York Times
★★½

"Market Place" columnist. Although we still regularly turn to Norris on Sunday for original insights on the week's market moves, we are more frequently feeling ourselves shortchanged by his analysis. He has been skittish about the investment environment for a long while, but increasingly he has a tendency to throw up his hands and cry "we've lost control!" Such is the case in "What a Show! But How Low Can the Fed Go?" 4-12: "Perhaps the wisest course is to stop trying to understand the markets, and just sit back and enjoy them." The same is true of "Why Currencies Move Faster Than Policies," 9-23, which quotes experts who don't know why the currency crisis occurred, but want to put in their two cents anyway: "'Governments have lost that power to control capital, and they probably have lost it forever,' said David C. Roche, Morgan Stanley's London-based global strategist." Taking a more serious look at the European horizon in "Less Flexibility in Europe's Rates," 5-7, Norris attributes the fall in the British bond market to Germany's inflation concerns. He cites comments by Helmut Schlesinger, the president of the Bundesbank, a day after the British easing that caused the bond market to fall after a long rally. Schlesinger "called [Germany's] current 4.5 percent annual inflation rate unacceptable, voiced concerns over monetary growth and said 'it would certainly be too early to sound the all-clear on monetary policy.'" It's this kind of sharp assessment that keeps us reading his columns. Also prescient in "A Danish Earthquake Shakes Europe," 6-7, he notes that if the momentum for Maastricht does not continue "there is a fair chance that Europe... could see a round of competitive currency devaluations." In "Waiting for the Capital Gains Shoe to Drop," 1-12, he assesses the impact of capgains news on the market: "If it becomes clear that capital gains taxes will not be cut, that fact could promote a sell-off. The October 13, 1989, mini-crash came in the same week it became clear that year's campaign to cut capital gains taxes... was doomed to fail." We always appreciate Norris's contributions to the debate on financial disclosure, as found in instructive articles such as "Nasdaq at Night: Risks in Trades in the Dark," 1-21, and "Swapping Woes: A Fed Official Sees Problems," 2-9.

Peter Nulty
Fortune
★★

Board of editors. We see further improvement from Nulty for the second year in a row. Increasingly, he's capitalizing on his talents as a writer and analyst, doing less cheerleading and more critical evaluation. Concise and information-rich, Nulty's "Lyondell Petrochemical: How to Live by Your Wits," 4-20, examines how one refinery has weathered volatile prices by being a low-cost producer that takes maximum advantage of its market: "Spending little money, Lyondell has tinkered its technology into unparalleled flexibility. Its refinery may be the only one anywhere that can process any crude in the world." "The Black Gold Rush in Russia," 6-15, is a strong report on the rush by global oil companies to position themselves to tap the amazing reserves of the former Soviet Union: "The huge western Siberian basin, which includes Samatlor, contains 16% of the world's discovered reserves, but less than a fifth of that is being produced. This turns the standard risk profile of the Western oil industry on its head. In the rest of the world, oil companies worry first about geological risk... and secondarily about political risk. On the new oil frontier, however, there is little danger of coming up dry, but when it comes to politics, no one knows what will happen next." Another invigorating read is "The Bounce Is Back at Goodyear," 9-7, on how new CEO Stanley Gault orchestrated an impressive turnaround at Goodyear Tire & Rubber Co., by making reduction of the company's debt load his number one priority: "With cost cutting, new stock, and asset sales, Gault reduced the debt from $3.6 billion to $2.6 billion in seven months, or as he quips with some exaggeration, 'We went down around a billion dollars in 80 days.'" In his savvy financial analysis "Pennzoil: How a Foxy Deal Became a Dog," 11-2, Nulty clues us into how Pennzoil founder and chairman Hugh Liedtke finagled a keen deal to avoid taxes, which is now being audited. He tells us Liedtke, whose "dealmaking is legendary," has one more trick up his sleeve, a deal with Chevron, but in the meantime Pennzoil shareholders are wondering if they "might be a lot better off today had Liedtke simply paid the taxes..."

Bridget O'Brian
The Wall Street Journal
★★★

Airlines. A fine reporter with excellent powers of evaluation, O'Brian covers the rough-and-tumble competition of the airline industry with impressive dexterity. Refreshingly, she eschews deregulation commentary, preferring instead to train her eyes on the latest developments and their impact on airline profits. Joined by co-writer Asra Q. Nomani for "Healthy Airlines Lash Out at Their Struggling Rivals," 3-17, the duo succinctly and equitably assesses the contentious debate over Chapter 11's impact on airline competition. Although we've read plenty on this issue, Nomani and O'Brian bring new insight to the dispute as American Airlines chairman Robert Crandall asks the government to consider yanking the certification rights of the airlines flying under Chapter 11. O'Brian sees the significance of American's price overhaul in "American to Simplify Fares, Shrink Price Range," 4-9: "If American is successful in lowering its unrestricted coach fare, it could also eliminate the need for corporate discounting.... That will certainly complicate matters for American's rivals, many of whom have negotiated long-term contracts to provide such corporate discounting." Following up with "Air Fare Wars Change Venue to the Courts," 6-10, she does a fine, balanced job of exploring the lawsuits that have emerged in the aftermath of the overhaul: "In its lawsuit, Continental contends American's pricing moves were part of a campaign to eliminate its weaker rivals 'by establishing industry price levels that would result in ruinous losses to weaken and destroy competitors.'" Her clear-eyed assessment of financially-troubled Delta Airlines, "Delta Air Makes Painful Cuts in Effort to Stem Red Ink," 9-10, provides a crisp overview of how the company is planning to tackle the major financial hurdles ahead. We really enjoyed her page-one "Southwest Airlines Is a Rare Air Carrier: It Still Makes Money," 11-26, a highly engaging and extremely revealing look at why Southwest remains profitable despite record losses in the industry. So effective are Southwest's procedures that "Robert Crandall...has ordered up studies on whether American should convert some flights to Southwest's bare-bones style."

Scot J. Paltrow
Los Angeles Times
★★½

New York. An outstanding year from Paltrow. Instead of the "grab-bag" portfolio we saw last year, Paltrow is focusing his energies and producing the kind of cutting-edge work we expect from the *LAT*'s primary news broker in the nation's financial capital. *Caveat emptor*, let the buyer beware, is the theme of his exhaustive investigation of securities brokers' dealings with their customers, "Investors at Risk: The Dark Side of the Brokerage Business," 7-1 through 7-5, a 10 Best selection. This is consumer/watchdog journalism at its finest. Paltrow does an enormous amount of research for this eye-opening five-part series, uncovering indicting evidence of unethical, and even illegal behavior by members of some of the nation's most prestigious stock brokerage firms. More importantly, Paltrow, with surgeon-like precision, dissects the inefficiencies of the industry's self-regulatory policies. Confirming the impact of his effort, he follows up with "Probe Targets the Hiring of Problem Brokers," 12-22, noting: "The SEC began its wide-ranging review last July, demanding voluminous data from a dozen of Wall Street's top firms in response to a series of investigative stories in The Times.... The SEC staff is expected to formulate a general response to the inquiry early next year. Sources said it will include proposals for industry rule changes and may also include a wave of cases by the SEC's enforcement division." On daily beat reporting, his "Prudential Securities Must Pay $1.9 Million in Arbitration Case," 3-4, is typical of his competent, even-handed handling of such news. And dabbling outside the financial beat for "Peter Martins, Off Balance," 12-6, he pens a highly-engaging and very in-depth profile of the complex artistic director of the New York City Ballet.

Peter Passell
The New York Times
★½

"Economics Scene" columnist. It has been a quantity over quality year for Passell; painfully obvious that this intelligent journalist with a PhD in economics isn't pushing himself on the issues. His work on the currency crisis is thoroughly disappointing and most of his domestic economic coverage relies on the haggard "voodoo economics" mantra. In fact, throughout the year Passell inadvertently plays the apologist for George Bush in such articles as "Rudderless in the Recession," 6-25, and "George Bush's Sins of Omission," 8-20, calling the deficits created by Reaganomics the root cause of Bush's economic problems. But none of these articles ventures an examination of how Bush's policies could have exacerbated the deficit problem. In "What Counts Is Productivity and Productivity," 12-13, he provides muddled musings on how Clinton can get productivity growth moving again, even though the U.S. remains the most productive nation on Earth. On the other hand, his "Economic Myopia: Obvious Problem, Hidden Causes," 2-9 is an interesting assessment of the roots of this U.S. phenomenon. Passell contends that the trend leads to a lower savings rate: "Economic myopia, it seems, is a real problem. But it may have a lot less to do with a shortening of personal horizons than with the way markets and governments distort the view of collective needs." He provides a critical and useful survey of the election-year tax grab-bag in "The Great Search: A Perfect Tax," 4-1. We were surprised by Passell's lethargic analysis on the dollar's fall in "Bonn Punches, the Dollar Rolls," 8-27: "Just why the dollar chose this month to head south is anyone's guess." His coverage of the European currency crisis was mediocre at best, his passable primer on why exchange rates matter, "Why the Currency Crisis Erupted," 9-17, oversimplified for the ordinary reader. Conventional Keynesian analysis pervades "The Next Question: Should Europe Press Onward," 9-20, Passell blaming Germany for putting domestic needs ahead of its neighbors, but making no attempt to assess the damage the Bundesbank's deflation has done to its own economy.

Jonathan Peterson
Los Angeles Times
★★

Washington, business. Peterson is one of the freshest new faces we've seen out of the *LAT*'s D.C. bureau in some time. He's getting plenty of play on the front page, and it's well deserved, as his reports are typically energetic and original. His macroeconomic coverage remains the one area that needs substantial work. Peterson throws out the stereotypes and looks at the poor in the U.S. with a fresh pair of lenses in "Times Get Harder for the Poor," 3-16: "Contrary to stereotypes of welfare queens or urban hoodlums, the realities of poverty are varied and complex, encompassing the travails of unskilled laborers and laid-off supervisors, single mothers and displaced farm families, residents of rural trailer parks and Skid Row hotels." Though there are not many solutions proposed here, the report's surprising statistics wake us up to the complexity of the term "poverty." He's not as fresh in "Washing Our Hands of Politics," 5-20, a mildly interesting look at the roots of the angry-voter syndrome. Very conventional and shallow economic analyses are found in "Prospects for Rare, Triple-Dip Recession Seen," 7-3, Peterson unconvincing on the possibility. In "Fed Cuts Back Amount Banks Need in Reserve," 2-19, he's balanced on the Fed's latest attempts to boost the economy. Joined by co-writer James Risen for "Best-Laid Money Plans May Go Astray, History Shows," 9-18, the duo provides a broad-stroke examination of attempts to manage international exchange rates despite the divergent political and economic paths of the world's nations. They conclude rather obviously that responsible policymaking is the key. His "For Many, Retraining Is a Myth," 10-22, is a clear-eyed assessment of the benefits and limitations of the current political touchstone, worker retraining. Peterson is a good writer who knows how to capitalize on an anecdote, but sometimes he relies too heavily on them, as in "Economics at Clinton's Hangout," 12-16, a trip to McDonald's where President-elect Clinton tries to understand the struggles of average Americans. It's an engaging journey, but there's nothing especially newsworthy here.

William Power
The Wall Street Journal
★★

Securities industry. A workmanlike reporter with a nose for news, Power reliably keeps us abreast of the latest trends at the exchanges, as well as key deals among the major Wall Street players. Joined by co-writer Randall Smith for "American Express Weighs Lehman Sale," 1-14, the duo spreads the news that American Express "is discussing selling a major stake in its Lehman Brothers investment bank in a deal that could return control to Lehman's management..." Power and co-writer Michael Siconolfi pen an enjoyable and informative look at how money has moved from Wall Street's wildcatting M&A crowd to the conservative IPO group in "Underwriting Boom Puts Tortoises Ahead of Wall Street's Hares,"

3-26, explaining why the sea change hasn't always been smooth sailing for Wall Street's dog-eat-dog culture. "Big Board, at Age 200, Scrambles to Protect Grip on Stock Market," 5-13, is a fitting anniversary tribute to the NYSE, but Power is careful to keep his eye on the Exchange's ever more competitive future. In "DaPuzzo, Settling Charges, Sits Again at OTC Tables," 6-25, we learn that after a "run-in with regulators, ace trader Peter DaPuzzo is back in the small-stock game." Power gathers oodles of tidbits for Streeters to chew on as DaPuzzo discusses the markets. A sturdy analysis of Mario Gabelli is found in "Gabelli Asks Investors for More, Again," 9-25, as his publicly traded Gabelli Equity Trust plans to launch another rights offering: "No holder should ignore the rights offering completely. To do so is to be guaranteed to lose money through dilution of your holdings." He gives us the lowdown on Peter Kellogg and his firm Spear, Leeds & Kellogg, in "Spear Leeds Breaks a Big Board 'Barrier,'" 10-2, as these specialists successfully breach "Big Board policy that has effectively barred any specialist from controlling 10% or more of exchange trading." "Peter Lynch's Advice to Small Investors: Don't Become Fixated on Mutual Funds," 12-3, is engaging coverage of the nation's most famous mutual fund manager and his improbable advice—invest in individual stocks.

Michael Prowse
Financial Times

"On America" columnist. Prowse could be a powerhouse, but he is hindered by the same problem as his predecessor in D.C., Anthony Harris. While we enjoy his political commentary, his saucy British wit can't compensate for his lack of inquisitiveness on economic issues. Chastising President Bush for his "free market" approach to health care in "Dr. Bush Makes a Faulty Diagnosis," 1-27, Prowse makes a passable case that tax incentives fall short, but his argument for socialized health insurance—hey, everyone is doing it—is very weak: "Mr Bush prides himself on being an internationalist. Why cannot he accept that on health care, it is the US, rather than the rest of the world, that is marching out of step?" "The Economics of a Democratic Victory," 3-9, is a weighty and even-handed evaluation of Clinton and Tsongas's economic proposals. In "Profitable Lessons for an Outdated School System," 6-4, he offers an enlightening profile of Christopher Whittle's Edison Project, exploring every dimension of this for-profit school project. The comments he solicits from Benno Schmidt, who resigned as president of Yale to join the Edison Project, are highly thought-provoking: "Support for a private college such as Stanford University, he says, does not constitute an attack on the University of California, a public-sector institu-

tion. In his view, American higher education flourishes because it is competitive and diverse; the same ought to be true of secondary education." Looking for a scapegoat amid European turmoil, he writes "The Fiscal Roots of Market Turmoil," 9-21, referring to the "pusillanimous G7 communique," and ranting that "Chronic US (and now German) deficits have greatly exacerbated a worldwide shortage of savings... and undermined global growth prospects." He provides no support for this assertion. He's well behind the curve in "The Risk of a Triple Dip," 10-5, citing "structural factors" as the U.S.'s problem, even though corporate and consumer debt have been greatly reduced. Equally conventional is "Recovery Is In Place, But Taking its Time," 12-9, which provides only the most vague counsel to Bill Clinton.

Jane Bryant Quinn
Newsweek

Personal investment columnist. Increasingly, Quinn is broadening her horizons. She still writes predominantly from the "news you can use" school of journalism, but more and more she's exploring broad financial and tax issues, as she does in "Tax Reform Takes a Step Back," *The Washington Post* 2-9, a historical discussion of tax reform. While we applaud her call for a simplified tax code, her contention that all tax incentives are created equal seems half-baked. Back to personal investment with "'Safe' Retirement Strategies May Suffer Most From Inflation," *WP* 3-29, Quinn provides a useful look at the effect inflation, "the retiree's most implacable enemy," can have on otherwise "safe" investments such as bank certificates of deposit, money market mutual funds, etc. Also helpful is "Clean-Hands Investing," 5-18, a primer on "Clean-hands mutual funds [which] lay out strict criteria—called social screens—through which every stock they buy has got to pass." Through effective use of examples, she makes clear that these funds do no better or worse because of their politically correct investment emphasis. Quinn's "Buyers Beware," 7-13, is a fine piece of consumer journalism, showing how some policyholders' cash-value insurance policies are coming up short without their knowledge, and how they can find out where their policy stands. She details precisely how aggressive agents may mislead: "What has lulled so many consumers is the computerized policy illustrations that agents may produce when they're persuading you to buy." "The New Rules for College Aid," 9-21, is a handy and eye-opening assessment of the changes ahead for student grant and aid programs to help with college tuition after Congress altered the rules. She provides an interesting collection of facts on the precarious job market in "The Good-Job Market: R.I.P." 11-30, outlining how professionals can prepare themselves for layoffs through offensive financial moves.

Michael Quint
The New York Times
★½

Though Quint provides the requisite facts and figures on the latest bank mergers and turnarounds, we rarely find any cutting-edge material in his reports. We had seen improvement in his work last year, but this year he doesn't seem to be digging for *the* stories. For example, his work on troubled Citicorp is serviceable at best. Such articles as "4th-Quarter Loss Seen by Citicorp," 1-14, adds little new detail on the bank's struggle through tough financial times, and his front-page "After Losing Ground in U.S. Citicorp Seeks Future Abroad," 1-20, is substantially late on an important story. In "Citicorp Criticized on Mortgages That Expose it to Too Much Risk," 9-3, he tries to make it seem as if he alone got his hands on a "highly unusual unauthorized release of a document that sums up a Federal examination of Citicorp's mortgage business..." The same report, though, appears elsewhere. Quint does make good use of the information, providing a level-headed account of Citicorp's over-exposure to shaky real-estate mortgages: "'An effective quality-control program is not yet in place,'... resulting in a delinquency rate on Citicorp mortgages that is four times the national average." While "Bank Directors Face Rising Risks," 3-26, is an interesting assessment of how bank directors are facing greater risk of fines and penalties due to a regulatory crackdown, "Mastercard and Visa in a Debit-Card Battle," 5-5, opens our eyes to the growing competition in the burgeoning debit card market: "Banks have already laid the groundwork for debit cards by issuing more than 191 million plastic cards for use at automated teller machines.... However, the banks are looking to Visa's Interlink debit card or Mastercard's Maestro card to handle transactions when customers are far from the banks' home markets." Though he raises numerous interesting questions about disclosure in "A Tough Call: What to Reveal on Sick Banks," 8-23, he leaves most of them unanswered. "A Bank That Lived to Tell the Tale," 11-1, is sturdier on Shawmut's turnaround, but Quint doesn't satisfy us on the bank's strategies for future growth.

James Risen
Los Angeles Times
★★

We see none of the missed opportunities that characterized Risen's portfolio last year. He is alert to the influence that election-year politics has on policymaking and fully capitalizes on the information his Beltway contacts provide. The beneficiary of several administration leaks, he pens the shocking "White House Pressure on Fed Chairman Told," 9-23. He handles the leak from "several high-ranking officials" professionally by landing on-the-record clarifications: "Greenspan, through a spokesman, acknowledged that he met privately with Treasury Secretary Nicholas F. Brady before his reappointment.... The spokesman said Brady urged the chairman to lower interest rates more aggressively . . . but characterized as 'nonsense' the notion that Greenspan would commit himself to specific economic growth targets." Having explained the situation, Risen perceptively questions the motivation for the leak. Another organized leak shapes "Bush Plan Said to Seek Tax-Exemption Boost," 1-17, where Risen carefully reports details of the "growth" package Bush plans to announce in his State of the Union speech. "Bush Tightens the Economic Noose on Teetering Castro," 4-19, is a tightly-written report in which Risen considers the political motivation behind Bush's efforts to "move the White House out in front" on the Cuba issue. Bringing together Bush and Clinton's economic proposals, Risen constructs a balanced and educational comparison in "Key Distinctions Separate Candidates' Economic Plans," 8-31: "'The critical difference between them,' said Robert Greenstein, director of the private Center on Budget and Policy Priorities in Washington, 'comes down to this question: Is the government an obstacle to economic growth, or an indispensable part of what is needed to obtain faster rates of growth?'" Risen rewrites history in the disappointing "History May Judge Reaganomics Very Harshly," 11-8: "Ultimately, Reaganomics was a failure . . . a governing philosophy based on a deeply flawed economic notion: that tax cuts . . . would not worsen the government's budget deficit. Ironically, it was the illogic of that theory that helped bring down President George Bush—even though it seems clear that Bush never fully believed in the theory himself." But, he fails to consider that Bush's rejection of Reaganomics might have been the true cause of his problems.

Robert A. Rosenblatt
Los Angeles Times
★½

Washington. Rosenblatt is a reliable, if unremarkable reporter who can be counted on to serve the facts straight-up—no more, no less. He takes few risks in his analysis, offering only the most general of observations. "What Will Be in the President's Budget Package: Businesses Hope to Make Gains in Several Key Areas," 1-26, reviews all the cogent proposals being circulated in advance of Bush's State of the Union address. Broad, but not deep, "Lincoln Savings' Law Firm to Pay U.S. $41 Million," 3-9, outlines the terms of what he describes as a "major victory for federal financial regulators in their aggressive campaign against lawyers and accountants involved with S&Ls that later collapsed into insolvency." He gets big play with "U.S. Calls for Duties on Subsidized Canada Lumber," 6-26, a solid reporting job on the latest salvos launched in the contentious lumber debate between the U.S. and Canada. Although the analysis here is fairly shallow, Rosenblatt does provide some worthwhile background. With the death of FDIC chairman William Taylor, Rosenblatt offers a tribute to the man's government service in "FDIC's Innovative Chairman Taylor Dies," 8-21, but he fails to fully explore the work of acting chairman, Andrew C. (Skip) Hove, Jr., or to capitalize on the opportunity to examine the FDIC's recent successes and failures. In one of his most impressive efforts of the year, "Footing the Bill for Our Future," 10-28, Rosenblatt successfully navigates the ideological potholes of the politicized Social Security debate to give us a competent analysis of the issues: "Social Security benefit payments are expected to total $301 billion during the fiscal year that began Oct. 1, surpassing defense outlays of $292 billion for the first time to become the government's biggest single expenditure." But he adds, "Without Social Security, a staggering 44% of the elderly population would live below the poverty line . . ." He provides professional and complete coverage of OTS director Timothy Ryan's resignation speech in "S&L Cleanup Chief to Quit Next Month," 11-9, peppering the report with Ryan's more poignant observations.

Hobart Rowen
The Washington Post
★½

Economics columnist. There aren't many fresh perspectives from this veteran political and economic watcher these days. Though he's one of the most experienced hands in D.C., he's getting quite curmudgeonly as he approaches his 75th birthday. In advance of Bush's State of the Union address, Rowen launches a frontal assault in "Voodoo Revisited," 1-23, accusing the President of preparing a message "redolent of snake oil." Just before Bush's Camp David meeting with Helmut Kohl Rowen, in "U.S. German Officials Need to GATT Together," 3-15, pressures the German leader to sway Francois Mitterrand on the farm subsidy issue so that "the tendentious GATT issue" can be put to rest. He's very good on the political posturing shaping the situation. After preaching about the evils of the deficit, Rowen weighs in with those who support a temporary "fiscal thrust" in "A Daring Plan for Recovery," 4-5: "We need a fiscal thrust—not via lower taxes that feed consumption, but from the expenditure side, feeding investment." Although we don't discover much new about Ross Perot the politician in "Looking for Clues About Perot," 6-7, we do get some interesting observations about what D.C. insiders think of the man: "'When I sit down with top officials in Washington, the degree of hostility to Perot is astounding,' [L. William] Seidman [former chairman of the FDIC and a 20-year friend of Perot] said. 'They call him a fascist pig and a militarist...'" Several pieces illustrate Rowen's clear support for Bill Clinton. The headline pretty much says it all for "Recovery May Come Too Late for Bush," 7-26, and in "... And Economic Scare Tactics," 9-24, he ignores Bush's speech to the Detroit Economic Club, trying instead to calm fears about the battle for Clinton's soul. Post-election, Rowen gushes about the Little Rock conference in "Breakthrough in Little Rock," 12-16, saying it "turned out to be an exciting and stimulating educational event." But he never tells us why, choosing instead to go on and on about how smart Clinton is to extend an ear to business.

Howard Rudnitsky
Forbes
★★

Senior editor. Company profiles geared toward the sophisticated investor are this veteran's forté, and this year they've been zestier and more incisive, a marked improvement. His sharpest profile of the year, "High Tech in the Cornfields," 11-23, is a top-notch look at Pioneer Hi-Bred International, which "produces hybrid seeds that are far hardier and more productive than varietal seeds." He explains that a USDA "set-aside" means farmers will be planting less acreage next spring and buying less Pioneer corn seed, but in the long run, Rudnitsky sees this as a good investment because genetics is the future and genetics is what Pioneer does so well. We're persuaded. "Battle of the Malls," 3-30, is savvy on how the shopping rages of the '80s are either transforming themselves into discount malls or losing business as shoppers of the '90s favor low prices over ambiance. Says John Mannix, who manages a converted mall that's now primarily discount: "The customers who visit the Galleria walk around, they ooh and aah, they have their Slurpee at the food court, and then they come to our mall to shop." Rudnitsky handily explains why there's "a lot of value in Forest City the stock market is not reflecting" in "Survivor," 6-8, and in "Halfway Home," 8-31, we learn that "Saul Steinberg, the takeover type who once terrorized the financial world, has been fighting for financial stability." Rudnitsky carefully analyzes the numbers and concludes Steinberg will weather this storm, but won't be the threat he once was. Scrutinizing the problems hanging over Catellus Development Co. in "Contrarians' Delight," 10-26, he advises: "In short, Catellus is a company for contrarians to start building a file on, while awaiting an opportunity to pounce." Back from bankruptcy, Lomas Financial Corp. is the subject of his upbeat "Reborn," 1-20, but Rudnitsky only gives us the bare minimum of facts, leaving us unpersuaded of a bright future for the company. This story reminds us of his unsatisfying coverage last year.

Kevin G. Salwen
The Wall Street Journal
★★★

Financial services, regulation and the SEC. Increasingly we turn to Salwen as *the* source on the SEC. A dogged fact-gatherer, Salwen keeps his ear to the ground alerting Wall Street to the implications of the Commission's latest regulatory proposals. "SEC to Push for Data on Pay of Executives," 1-21, for example, is a valuable alert on the SEC's attempts to require companies to use a specific method of valuing all stock options granted to senior officials, and "is designed to allow investors to compare executive pay plans from company to company." His "Big Business Is Big Winner Under Bush's Tax Proposals," 1-30, is the first place we saw in-depth coverage of proposed new taxes for Wall Street. Joined by co-writer Joann S. Lublin for a disappointing "Giant Investors Flex Their Muscles More at U.S. Corporations," 4-27, the duo squanders the opportunity to further a much discussed issue—the growing clout of institutional investors. On the other hand, "CFTC Rulings Draw Criticism From Dissident," 5-19, is highly informed on the irregularities of the CFTC's reversal of a previous ruling: "The subcommittee's decision to ask each commissioner to testify independently makes the hearing a rarity in Washington.... But subcommittee Chairman Glenn English (D-OK) is dissatisfied with the deregulatory policies of CFTC Chairman Wendy Gramm and has said he wants to find out why votes are occurring the way they are." Salwen handles the technicalities with expert ease in "SEC Proposes Rules Making it Easier for Large Companies to Raise Money," 7-17, fully explaining the latest SEC proposals designed "to scale back on regulatory areas that companies and large investors have argued are slowing the flow of capital." "Institutions Are Poised to Increase Clout in Boardroom," 9-21, is illuminating on proposals that will greatly empower shareholders, but could have "the effect of giving big institutional investors too much clout." An anonymous source gives Salwen an interesting update on the Paul Mozer case in "Mozer Is Said to Agree to Plead Guilty to Two Felony Counts in Treasury Case," 12-18.

Bill Saporito
Fortune
★★★

Board of editors. As in years past, Saporito is one of the best trend-spotters on the retail beat. It's only when he strays from this focus that the quality of his work is less predictable. Each year, he typically pens at least one definitive story. This year that story is "Why the Price Wars Never End," 3-23, a 10 Best selection, and a near flawless piece of business reporting. We walk away with a solid understanding of an entire financial phenomenon which is changing the way manufacturers, retailers, and even the service industries do business. By the end of the article, we know what's happening, why it's happening, and where it's likely to lead the marketplace. "Cutting Out the Middleman," 4-6, is a punchy profile of Leonardo Del Vecchio, head of Luxottica Group SpA of Italy, the world's biggest maker of eyeglass frames. We get a sense of how the man became a profit machine by doing just what the headline says. Of course, Wal-Mart is the quintessential retail success story these days, and Saporito continues to pursue the reasons why. He pens a lovely tribute to the late Sam Walton in "What Sam Walton Taught America," 5-4, obviously as impressed with the man as the merchant. Despite the Wal-Mart story having been told a thousand times, Saporito manages to add new dimensions in "A Week Aboard the Wal-Mart Express," 8-24. If he has a shortcoming, it is that he continues to tell these old stories instead of applying his estimable talents to new stories. The headline of "The Best Cities for Business," 11-2, should have been "The Best Cities for Global Competition," which is what the article examines. Though this is an enjoyable read, we're disappointed that the criteria doesn't place more emphasis on regulation and tax structure.

Laura Saunders
Forbes
★★½

Senior editor. Saunders is a very exact reporter covering a very exact science, that of paying the IRS exactly what you owe—no more, no less. For investors, searching for information on the tax implications of their latest purchase, she's a valuable source of information. Her "Taxable Munis," 2-3, is a very useful, technical discussion of "supposedly tax-exempt" municipal bond funds that may carry taxable bonds: "What gives? In 1986 Congress chipped away at the long-standing exemption for state and local government bonds by making some of them taxable to some people. The alternative tax... is levied at a flat 24% rate on a broader base of income than is used to figure regular taxes.... Included in the alternative tax's broad base is interest from 'private purpose' municipal bonds issued after 1986." In "Attention, Income Hiders," 3-2, Saunders alerts us to the "perverse" aspects of the current IRS procedures for distinguishing between an employee and independent contractor: "Apparently enough taxpayers have complained to their congressmen about IRS harassment on this issue that wheels are beginning to turn." More practical advice characterizes "Postmortem Wills," 7-20, a handy report on how to use disclaimers to avoid taxation if someone leaves a poorly planned will. The lead for "Commuter Tax," 8-3, gets right to the heart of the matter: "A little-noticed provision of a bill now making its way through Congress contains a big surprise for auto commuters: It makes free parking provided to employees a taxable perk." Saunders makes clear the provision is bound to cause administrative migraines. Not up to her usual standard for "Follow the Money," 10-26, Saunders shows her limitations as she delves into the macroeconomic taxation picture. Post-election, Saunders gives us sixteen sophisticated tips in "Tax Strategies for Clintonomics," 12-7: "Here's one certainty: The numbing complexity of the [tax] code will only get worse. Expect more phase-ins, phase-outs, ceilings, floors and the like, all of which will make tax planning at once more imperative and harder to do."

Michael Schrage
Los Angeles Times
★★★

"Innovation" columnist. A writer, consultant and research associate at MIT, Schrage is recommended reading for those who crave cutting-edge information on nascent technologies and technological policy issues. He delves into the debate over "ecological intervention" and "geo-engineering" for the fascinating "Tinkering With Environment Is Tempting," 1-16, and explains why these ideas are fast becoming part of the environmental policy lexicon. Examining Hitachi's controversial land-for-lab deal with UC Irvine in "Single-Company Deals Are No Way for Universities to Promote Research," *The Washington Post* 3-13, Schrage offers an intelligent, thought-provoking discussion: "The issue is just what forms of industrial cohabitation should a state-funded university permit." We can see how "A High-Tech Marriage That Computes," 6-11, might have started as a dinner discussion and blossomed into the suggestion that Hewlett-Packard make a friendly offer to Digital Equipment Corp. Tapping a wide variety of sources, he carefully ponders the pros and cons. "Paper Rises to the Fore in Clever New Xerox Software," 8-13, is highly illuminating on Xerox's PaperWorks, "that lets its users store, retrieve and distribute personal computer-based information by sending special 'forms' to their computers from any fax machine." Schrage's "Bush Unable to Capitalize on Science Record," 10-1, is one of the more thorough, election-year examinations of Bush's science and technology record. He explains that giving the "impression of an Administration that consider[s] government irrelevant to America's technological competitiveness... the Bush Administration has had a solid record of budgetary support for both science and technology."

Michael R. Sesit
The Wall Street Journal
★★

Sesit is at his best when he steps back to view the global

picture. A plain-speaking financial reporter, he takes us a level beyond humdrum technical market analysis by tapping into an impressive network of sources. Surveying how money managers are positioning themselves for the new year in "Global Money Managers Urge Caution," 1-3, Sesit finds that "defense may be the best offense," as his sources indicate that a falling dollar will benefit export-oriented investments. His "Another Hurdle in Europe? Devaluations," 4-2, is a savvy alert on the pressures building in Europe: "U.S. investors would get clipped by the currency devaluation." Though "Germany's Rate Decision May Determine Whether Dollar's Slide Will Continue," 7-16, isn't packed with sophisticated financial analysis, we appreciate Sesit's cognizance of the direct link between the German rates and the dollar's current value. Unlike many of his peers, he eschews the narrow-minded conclusion that structural decline is sinking the dollar. Though his heavy emphasis on the outcome of the French vote, in "Maastricht Is Haunting Europe's Stocks," 8-18, leads us to believe that he hasn't fully weighed Germany's deflationary pressures on European markets, his openness to well-informed sources compensates: "Regardless of what happens Sept. 20, some managers see reasons to be optimistic, mostly because they believe that slower German growth will eventually prompt the Bundesbank to ease monetary policy." We were disappointed by "Europe's Markets Are Seen Continuing to Surge, But Investors Should Keep an Eye on the Dollar," 9-15, Sesit falling back on conventional assumptions here, instead of looking at the situation through fresh lenses. Once again, though, his broad network of sources gives us interesting observations to contemplate. And in "Playing the U.S. Economic Upturn—Overseas," 12-22, he explains that it might be time to dabble in emerging foreign markets because "many export-oriented foreign countries stand to benefit from a pickup in U.S. growth." This a broad stroke assessment, but a worthwhile one.

Michael Siconolfi
The Wall Street Journal
★★

A key player for the *Journal*'s "Money & Investing" section, Siconolfi impresses us with his enthusiastic pursuit of the facts and his professional handling of the material he uncovers. We expect to see even more impressive work from this up-and-comer in the future. In his best effort of the year, "At Morgan Stanley, Analysts Were Urged to Soften Harsh Views," 7-14, Siconolfi provides a very in-depth and fair-minded investigation of tensions between research and investment bankers at Morgan Stanley, making the point that the situation "provides a case study in a fundamental conflict of interest on Wall Street. Investment banks routinely publish research advising investors which stocks to buy and sell. At the same time, the firms compete fiercely for assignments to sell new stock issues for corporate clients, which means drumming up demand for the stock among investors. And negative comments from their own analysts obviously don't help." He makes the important point in "Many Companies Sell Securities to Bolster Their Balance Sheets," 11-12, that "In the past two years, American companies' debt-to-capital ratio has fallen to 44.8% from 46.8%, according to the Federal Reserve Board." With most of the financial press overlooking this significant trend, we appreciated Siconolfi's sturdy analysis. He professionally handles a report on "an unusual arbitration case" in "Prudential Case Alleges Forced Political Gifts," 2-20, carefully reporting all sides of the story. Joined by co-writer William Power, we're offered an enjoyable and informative look at how money has moved from Wall Street's wildcatting M&A crowd to the conservative IPO group in "Underwriting Boom Puts Tortoises Ahead of Wall Street's Hares," 3-26, explaining why the sea change hasn't always been smooth sailing for Wall Street's dog-eat-dog culture. "Meet Jacques Coe: He Goes to Wall St. for a Wonderful Life," 5-15, is an engaging A-hed about "one of the world's oldest stockbrokers," who at 98 years of age "is one of the few Wall Street brokers to have been alive for nearly half the life of the Big Board."

Allan Sloan
New York Newsday
Los Angeles Times Syndicate
★★½

Sloan is a journalist who understands the art of the deal. Don't let his blunt, loose-lipped New York sarcasm fool you, he can dissect a complex financial arrangement with the accuracy of a diamond cutter. "Beauty and the Beasts: A True Tale of Two Different Investment Styles," *The Washington Post* 1-7, is quintessential Sloan—fancy wordsmithery and provocative analysis. Comparing the way long-term investor Warren Buffett and the Feshbachs, short-sellers, handled their Wells Fargo investments, he observes: "Buffett could hang in at Wells because he had staying power. Because of the way short-sellers borrow money, and because investors could take their money back, the Feshbachs lacked staying power..." Charles Hurwitz, whose Houston-based conglomerate has made a tentative deal to take over Continental Airlines after its bankruptcy, is the subject of "One Takeover Tycoon's Strange Love Affair With Big Government," *WP* 7-21: "Hurwitz is being sued by the Labor Department for allegedly illegal and unethical behavior at the same time another branch of the Labor Department is trying to cut a deal with Continental..." "In Search of Michael Milken," *Newsweek* 8-10, is more than just a review of Jesse Kornbluth's book, *Highly Confident*, which Sloan calls "the Milken crowd's answer to *Den of Thieves*." Sloan takes the opportunity to ponder the bigger picture: "The pro- and anti-Milken zealots have now been heard from, and still we're no closer to the truth. It would be nice if someone, someday, wrote an insightful, hard-hitting, down-the-middle book about Milken and the 1980s. Don't hold your breath." In "GI Joe Soldiers for Time Warner in an End Run Around the IRS," *WP* 12-15, Sloan offers an intriguing look at Time Warner's attempt to use a tax loophole or "what tax mavens call a 'bifurcated' security." Sloan says the "unusual feature... gives Time Warner $200 million of extra tax deductions. And these extra deductions don't lower the income that Time Warner reports to stockholders, even though they lower the income it reports to the IRS."

Randall Smith
The Wall Street Journal
★★

Smith just isn't as incisive as he has been in years past. We still find interesting detail on Wall Street trends under his byline, but his sharp analytical edge has dulled somewhat. Joined by co-writer William Power for "American Express Weighs Lehman Sale," 1-14, the duo spreads the news that American Express "is discussing selling a major stake in its Lehman Brothers investment bank in a deal that could return control to Lehman's management..." Smith brings good news on the debt front with "With Corporate Debt Hangover Easing, Leveraged Firms' Shares Are Taking Off," 4-28, talking to industry watchers in several sectors who say the corporate and private debt hangover is finally easing. He's careful to include comments from the skeptics and examples of companies and industries still suffering from over-leverage. Uncovering a "silent giant" in "Capital Group Isn't a Household Name, But Billions of Dollars Keep Pouring In," 7-9, Smith explains how this mutual fund's "conservative, defensive investing style" helps it maintain below-average risk and outperform the market during downturns. We get the trader's perspective on the currency chaos in Europe with "How Currency Traders Play for High Stakes Against Central Banks," 9-18, a long-winded primer that informs on some aspects of the crisis, but provides only a passing reference to macroeconomics and no discussion at all of currency sterilization, the process that invites so much volatility during assaults on central banks. He does small investors a service with "Futures Pools' Returns Are a Far Cry From Their Brochures and Prospectuses," 10-2, alerting that "Of the 10 largest pools sold, eight have returned less than 10% a year..." In "Commodities Corp. May Be Trading Away its Brilliance," 12-10, Smith offers an interesting profile of Commodities Corp., the one-time "power house," but we learn more about the company's illustrious history than about what's going wrong now.

Paul Starobin
National Journal
★★

Economics, financial institutions. A thorough, though sometimes long-winded journalist, Starobin reliably harvests the facts and satisfactorily analyzes them. His election-year portfolio is as full of political coverage as economic reports. In fact, some of his best work is from the campaign trail. Leading up to the New Hampshire primary, Starobin offers a narrative walk through New Hampshire politics in "Politics Lab," 2-8. He's a revealing storyteller, and leaves us convinced that despite what the politicians might believe "... attitudes among New Hampshirites are intriguingly complex." He could have made his point, though, in half the space. "Aspiring to Govern," 5-9, is a highly-enlightening investigation of Bill Clinton's advisors: "The candidate whose advertisements skewered Democratic rival Paul E. Tsongas as 'the best friend Wall Street ever had' is getting pointers from Robert E. Rubin, chairman of one of the Street's biggest firms..." He provides a very balanced analysis of Ross Perot in "President Perot?" 7-4, weaving all the known details into a huge tapestry of a complex man. He gives us the ups and downs, the good and bad, the praise and the criticism of the man, and then lets us make our own decision. Starobin tells us in "A Fed Robin Hood?" 3-7, how lower interest rates are moving wealth around, and causing political reverberations for Bush, especially among elderly voters whose interest income is being zapped: "Economist David Wyss of the Massachusetts-based consulting firm of DRI/McGraw Hill estimates that over the past two years, lower interest rates have reduced the incomes of people over the age of 55 by about $140 billion and have resulted in total gains to people under that age of about $70 billion." He takes us behind the fortress-like walls of the secretive Federal Reserve in "Wizards of Odds," 11-21, to introduce us to the staff aides who play an important role in monetary policy formation.

Richard L. Stern
Forbes
★★½

Senior editor. Stern is a muscular writer whose investigative research often delivers a knockout punch. But like others who throw themselves into their work so passionately, he sometimes goes overboard, as he does with co-writer Reed Abelson in the downright nasty "The Imperial Agees," 6-8, a profile of Bill Agee, "one of the best trend-surfers of our time." Most of the duo's legitimate gripes about Agee's management style are lost amid the cacophony of cheap personal shots: "People who should know say that when the couple travels on the company's new Falcon 900 business jet, [Mary Cunningham Agee] demands elaborate catered meals on fine china and Waterford crystal. Not so, says the company; Kentucky Fried Chicken provides the airborne meals. Pheasant under glass or Kentucky Fried Chicken, such tales, whether true, partly true or merely apocryphal, illustrate the damage an autocratic boss can do to the happiness of people he needs to help him through tricky times." These last comments do not suffice as a rationale for the report's gossipy tone. He is markedly more effective in the hard-hitting and professionally-toned "But Where Are the Cops?" co-written by Amy Feldman 10-26. Stern and Feldman do some fancy investigative footwork to expose stock promoter Robert Brennan's dubious schemes. With their credibility established, we listen closely when they explain that "...Operators like Brennan hide behind the vast array of securities laws designed to help young companies raise capital without excessive red tape." Joined by co-writer Tatiana Pouschine for "Junk Equity," 3-2, we're served up impressive, number-crunching analysis on reverse LBOs, and persuaded that it might be time to move out of this investment. In "The Graying Wild Ones," 1-6, Stern nails down a profitable new trend in the motorcycle industry: "... aging baby boomers buying big motorcycles to reclaim lost youth." We learn why he understands the syndrome so well in "Zell's Angels," 7-20, a bike tour through Europe in which we discover that Stern is a 50-year-old born-again biker.

Bruce Stokes
National Journal
★★½

International trade. Stokes is clearly honing his reporting and analytical skills. We notice his writing is crisper and his political evaluations are more incisive. Though his assessments of the economic dynamics that shape international trade are still far from sophisticated, we are turning to Stokes more often as a reputable source on the political forces at work. He's astute on how election-year politics are weighing on NAFTA in "On the Brink," 2-29, pointing out areas where Bush is likely to have to give and take, and laying out the behind-the-scenes maneuverings. Though he's apocalyptic about the fate of the U.S. auto industry in "Protection—for a Price," 4-4, he's perceptive on the politics of bailing out Detroit, noting that with 73 electoral votes from Indiana, Illinois, Michigan and Ohio, the issue is a political hot potato: "Many of the quid pro quos now under consideration are of questionable economic value. And fundamental change in Detroit's management practices, which most Wall Street analysts contend is essential, is clearly beyond Washington's reach." We found "Now, Who's This Perot?" 6-20, quite interesting on Japanese bewilderment at the Perot phenomenon, while his report on Japan's heightened interest in re-Asianization, "Tilting Toward Asia," 7-11, develops points we've read elsewhere. The big problem with this piece is that Stokes fails to factor China's emergence into the Japanese landscape. He fully compensates for this shortcoming in "Challenging China," 9-19, an intelligent examination of Washington's "new realism" as China's booming economy gives it new leverage: "In the long run, a successful U.S. policy may have to forgo bilateralism in favor of a policy embedded in a broader multilateral strategy in Asia." Though his analysis of the political jockeying occurring in the aftermath of Europe's currency crisis is informative in "Aftershocks," 10-10, his emphasis on a "two-track EC" reveals he hadn't fully considered the macroeconomic forces at work in Europe.

Stephanie Strom
The New York Times
★★

Retail. Reporting from the retail capital of the nation, the Big Apple, Strom takes over the beat that Isadore Barmash covered for 26 years. Although she's still finding her footing, it's clear that she has the potential to become an important player. She has already produced a few industry overviews, something we'd expect from a more-seasoned reporter. The best of this genre is "Department Stores' Fate," 2-3, in which she assesses whether department stores have a future. Her sources warn that big department stores must learn the efficiency lessons of smaller retailers if they don't want their market to erode. More alert reporting informs "Enlisting the Copyright Law in Battling the 'Gray Market,'" 7-21, in which we learn about the implications of a novel suit filed by Parfums Givenchy U.S.A.: "'This is a whole new approach in pursuit of the age-old problem of diversion,' said Robert L. Brady, president of the [U.S.] arm of the French cosmetics and fragrance company....' For what I think is the first time, a fragrance company is using the copyright laws instead of the trademark laws to protect the distribution of its products.'" Looking at the latest retail sales data for "Sales Gains Are Lackluster for Most Big U.S. Retailers," 9-4, she is careful not to make too much or too little of the unsurprising numbers. R. H. Macy & Co.'s financial troubles is one of the biggest stories of the year, and Strom provides reliable coverage of the events as they unfold. Just before the company's Chapter 11 filing, she ponders its financial woes in "Macy's Again Avoids the 'B' Word," 1-17, a well-sourced overview, and as the formal announcement occurs, she pens "Macy's Asks Court to Provide Shield Against Creditors," 1-28, adding the latest details and reviewing the events of recent weeks succinctly and professionally. In "Questions About Fees of Macy's Advisers," 12-5, Strom opens our eyes to the high fees being billed by legal, accounting and financial advisers to Macy's. She strikes a professional balance here, revealing the questionable bills while gathering rationales from those who submitted them.

James Tanner
The Wall Street Journal
★★★★

Oil industry. Tanner is *the* source on the political and economic considerations that guide OPEC and thus shape the international oil markets. There is no one else that even approaches his sagacity on this consequential beat. In "Saudis, in a Bid to Prop Up Oil Prices, Cut Output, Just Before OPEC Meeting," 1-22, he expertly discerns the political gesture behind the move. Joined by co-writer Allanna Sullivan for "Weary of 'Dry Holes' in U.S., Independents Search for Oil Abroad," 4-20, the duo explains precisely why independents are leaving the U.S. in droves. Says one source: "New discoveries are small, taxes and insurance are high, and there's ruinous litigation from any kind of environmental problem." "Saudi Minister Fails to Attend Key OPEC Parley," co-written by Bhushan Bahree 5-21, zeroes in on subtle, but telling details such as Saudi oil minister Hisham Nazer's no-show at a midyear conference due to illness: "There was speculation that Mr. Nazer's was a diplomatic illness and part of an enigmatic negotiating ploy." Even routine commodity updates such as "Oil Market Rally Continues as Confrontations Expand Between Iraq and the United Nations," 7-17, uncover important political developments. More expert coverage is found in "OPEC Aides Expected to Seek Price Rise to Compensate for Dollar's Weakness," co-written by Bhushan Bahree 9-15, in which the pair tells us of the quandary caused for OPEC as a result of the falling dollar. "OPEC Wants Flat Output; Ecuador Quits," co-written by Bhushan Bahree 9-18, and "OPEC Seems Shaken but Little Changed by Ecuador's Intent to Leave the Cartel," co-written by Bhushan Bahree 9-21, are both info-packed reports on the fallout from Ecuador's departure from the cartel. "Back in Business: Iran's Oil Production Is Soaring, With Help From American Firms," 11-25, provides excellent intelligence on the "boom-town mentality [that] has taken hold across southern Iran. Some 50 rigs are in action...up from eight just three years ago."

Alex Taylor III
Fortune
★★★½

Detroit. Clearly producing his best portfolio ever, Taylor jumps a full star and a half and becomes *the* standard on the automotive beat. Not only does his amazing network of sources enrich all articles with an insider's feel, but his stellar research and analysis also make each report a learning experience even for the CEOs at the Big Three. His outstanding "U.S. Cars Come Back," 11-16, a 10 Best selection, is likely to become *the* definitive press account of the auto industry in the '80s and early '90s. At the very least, this is the most ambitious analysis we've seen of this crucial industry's successes and failures. More accurately, it is a remarkable history of a remarkable industry, a book of knowledge condensed into an article: "Detroit's biggest collective failure has been its unwillingness to confront the threat from Japan. Instead, the industry has adopted a Maginot-line mentality." His work on GM is outstanding, beginning months before the first boardroom coup in April. We can imagine the outside directors stewing over the eye-opening information and suggestions offered in "Can GM Remodel Itself?" 1-13, a fine piece of analysis. After the first shake-up, his "The Road Ahead at General Motors," 5-4, explains that GM's "bureaucrats may have met their match—even their master. With the board behind him, [new president and CEO John F. 'Jack'] Smith has a clear mandate to accelerate GM's early retirement program and speed up job elimination." Packed with behind-the-scenes observations about Chrysler's new vice chairman and CEO Robert J. Eaton, "Iacocca's Last Stand at Chrysler," 4-20, has a very insider feel to it. In addition to assessing Iacocca's powerful and lingering role at the company, Taylor deftly pinpoints the problems Iacocca's successor will face as he takes the reins at a company that "has been running on empty." Assessing the skidding corporate performance of Nissan Motor Corp. U.S.A. in the quick, but highly informative "Driving for the Market's Heart," 6-15, Taylor crisply identifies the problems and delineates the company's plan of attack, evaluating the pros and cons of the plan along the way.

Paulette Thomas
The Wall Street Journal
★★★

Washington. Thomas shows true grit in her efforts to understand how complex financial issues impact communities. Her balanced and thoroughly-researched work on the dearth of minority lending displays an admirable balance of financial pragmatism and human compassion, as evinced in her lucid "Federal Data Detail Pervasive Racial Gap in Mortgage Lending," 3-31, an excellent dissection of the reasons for the shocking disparity between loans made to black vs. white borrowers: "Lenders contend the mortgage gap largely can be explained by factors other than bias. In the first place, they say, is the simple economic reality that median income for black households is roughly half that of white households." Also thought-provoking is "Small Businesses, Key to Urban Recovery, Are Starved for Capital," 6-11, a striking tale of the dry well that is inner city financing. "Bush's Plans to Relax Community Lending Law and Help Inner Cities Are on a Collision Course," 7-21, is an excellent analysis of the Community Reinvestment Act after the L.A. riots. Also excellent on the economic crisis of the nation's inner cities are "Weak Economy May Be Hurting Moves to Fight Mortgage Bias, Study Indicates," 10-28, and "Blacks Can Face a Host of Trying Conditions in Getting Mortgages," 11-30. In the latter, she recognizes the complexity of the issues surrounding mortgages to minorities and avoids jumping to shaky conclusions: "Some industry leaders now believe that... long-held industry standards concerning neighborhoods, employment records and financial practices may work unfairly against low-income people buying lower-priced homes, a disproportionate number of whom are minorities." Her work on the RTC's handling of the S&L crisis is as competent as ever. She gives us fine feel for the election-year toughness in Congress as the RTC asks for more money in "House Panel Rips Bush Plan to Save Thrifts," 2-26, a compact and informative report, and "Nearing Bottom of Asset Barrel, RTC Will Offer Junk Securities," 4-23, is a pithy evaluation of the RTC's "Multiple Investor Fund Program."

Rich Thomas
Newsweek
★★

Chief economics correspondent. Last year, we called him "the best economic writer at the newsweeklies," but his work just isn't as consistently fresh or edifying these days. We're surprised to find so much unoriginal thinking in his reports. "Why Japan Must Share the Blame," 2-3, is a general piece that adds little to our understanding of the U.S.-Japan trade imbalance. His update on the latest economic indicators, "The Recession's Over (Shhh!)" 3-16, is more conventional analysis —steady, but unspectacular growth is ahead. He hits below the belt in "Perot: The Handout Billionaire," 4-13, a harangue in which the genuine insights about the government financial assistance Perot has received are buried amid the mudslinging: "Nobody can recall a would-be presidential candidate who asked his country to do so much for him, upfront, before he does anything at all for his country." Just after the G7 summit in Munich, Thomas pens "Please, Don't Bother Me," 7-20, an interesting assessment of why world leaders are tolerating slow growth. Pre-election, he skims numerous long-term shifts affecting Bush's economic record, but delves into none of them deeply in "America, Stop Your Sobbing," 9-21. He's more thorough for "Marriages Made in Air," 11-23, a balanced examination of the debate over U.S.-foreign airline mergers. On one side, American Airlines CEO Robert Crandall "Argues that letting [British Airways] buy into the largest air market on earth without giving U.S. carriers the same opportunity abroad is 'the equivalent of unilateral economic disarmament.'" On the other, "Alfred Kahn, who launched airline deregulation...puts it: 'If we had only three or four domestic airlines, I'd be nervous. But I'd feel perfectly safe being supplied by seven or eight world-class companies. These foreign deals are great insurance...'"

Jeffrey A. Trachtenberg
The Wall Street Journal
★★½

New York, retail. Trachtenberg is a capable and perceptive reporter who really knows his beat. His ability to evaluate individual retailers, not only in the context of their specific management and financial situations, but also in the broader setting of a troubled economy, impresses us. The one viewpoint he has yet to master is that of the stock analyst. His best effort of the year, "How 4 Loyal Managers Invested in Macy—And Watched it Sink," 4-24, is a well-written record of Macy's downfall. Trachtenberg makes clear that more than heavy debt tumbled this retail giant, it was the abandonment of the enthusiastic and talented employees who had brought the chain so much success. All year, Trachtenberg kept a close eye on the Macy's story as in "Macy Files for Chapter 11, Listing Assets of $4.95 Billion, Liabilities of $5.32 Billion," co-written by George Anders 1-28, a highly thorough assessment of the store's mounting problems: "Macy Officials Preview Plan for Longer Than Expected Bankruptcy Protection," 8-31, is a brief, but important update on R.H. Macy & Co.'s continued financial deterioration. Trachtenberg reports that the latest business plan "suggests the retailer will be forced to operate under bankruptcy protection for longer than outsiders originally anticipated." He introduces us to Woolworth's latest chain, Northern Reflections, in the informative "Woolworth Hopes for a New Specialty-Store Winner," 7-2: "The rapid rollout here of the faux-country chain stocked with casual clothes underscores just how urgently Woolworth needs to make lightning strike again." One disappointment is "Limited's Stock, Out of Favor for a While, Could Be Ready to Bounce Back Into Style," 10-21, which isn't as savvy as most "Heard on the Street" columns. Trachtenberg doesn't provide enough analysis of the bottom line to convince us that Limited's stock is undervalued. He pursues an interesting angle of the HDTV story in "High-Definition TV Has Networks, Outlets Worried About Costs," 11-11, explaining that many stations won't be able to afford the $15 billion to $20 billion necessary to become HDTV capable.

James B. Treece
BusinessWeek
★★

Detroit, senior correspondent. Treece gives us a steady flow of reliable and insightful observations on the Big Three's ups and downs. In a year of unprecedented boardroom upheaval, he interpreted the implications of each new turn. With Chrysler Vice-Chairman Robert S. Miller's departure to Wall Street, Treece hedges his bets on Robert A. Lutz in "After Iacocca, Who?" 3-9: "Does that mean President Robert A. Lutz is the undisputed front-runner to replace Lee A. Iacocca as chairman? No way. Says Miller: 'The great management-succession race is still on.'" His view of the shake-up at GM, "The Board Revolt," 4-20, has an insider's feel to it, but doesn't match the depth of detail found in other reports on the event. There is, though, plenty of insightful analysis in the report: "In some ways, Stempel's relationship with [GM president Lloyd E.] Reuss may have been the most glaring symptom of the long, debilitating disease that has made GM the laughing stock of Corporate America. Without sufficient regard for merit, managers got ahead as their buddies got ahead." "It's Not All That Easy Having a Hit. Just Ask Caddy," 6-29, is a brief, but interesting look at how GM's Detroit-Hamtramck facility has struggled to keep up with the success of its Seville STS: "Part of the problem is that Cadillac misjudged the market. It thought 75% of Hamtramck's production would be the Seville's sister car, the two-door Eldorado, 15% would be the basic Seville, and only 10% would be the STS, which retails for $38,500. Instead, 58% of the output is the Seville, half of that the STS. Suppliers have struggled to keep up while quality glitches have slowed output." He provides powerful advice to GM's hard-nosed "purchasing czar" in his commentary, "The Lessons GM Could Learn for Its Supplier Shakeup," 8-31, recommending that J. Ignacio Lopez de Arriortua, who is souring the automaker's relations with parts suppliers in an effort to cut costs, emulate Toyota as an example of a carmaker with clout and good relations among suppliers.

Peter Truell
The Wall Street Journal
★★★½

Washington. The co-author of a new book on BCCI, *False Profits: The Inside Story of BCCI, the World's Most Corrupt Financial Empire*, Truell continues to probe the margins of this international financial scandal, even as others have lost interest. We do feel, though, that the BCCI affair has distracted Truell from his most important journalistic contributions, those on international economic coverage. Joined by co-writer Thomas Petzinger for "Biggest Saudi Bank Took Part in Effort to Hide Fraud at BCCI, Auditors Say," 2-19, the duo ferrets out information that Saudi Arabia's biggest bank, National Commercial Bank, has been identified by independent auditors "as a key participant in an effort to camouflage fraud at [BCCI]." Even more revealing is "New Records Indicate Sheik of Abu Dhabi Had Key Role at BCCI," co-written by Thomas Petzinger 3-11, a top-notch investigation which unearths highly-persuasive evidence that Sheik Zayed bin Sultan al-Nahyan, president of the UAE, is up to his neck in BCCI's shady affairs, even as he is the object of sympathy in D.C. and elsewhere in the wake of the bank's collapse. On another banking controversy, he professionally handles speculation that Congressional Democrats will call for a special counsel to investigate the Bush administration in "Democrats Are Expected to Seek Probe of White House Role in Iraq-BNL Affair," 7-8. Joined by co-writer John J. Fialka for "As 'Iraqgate' Unfolds, New Evidence Raises Questions of Cover-Up," 10-9, the pair provides a few new details on the BNL case, though Truell and company were not the pacesetters on this story. Just before the French referendum on Maastricht, Truell writes "European System Braces for French Vote; Major Nations to Urge German Rate Cut: Most G-7 Finance Chiefs See Growth Tied to Easing Credit, Calming Markets," 9-18, providing insightful reporting and useful comments from Truell's sources, who say that because of recent financial events, Maastricht has become an irrelevant sideshow.

Louis Uchitelle
The New York Times
★½

New York. Uchitelle dabbles in a multiplicity of subjects this year, an exercise which leads to work that runs the entire quality spectrum. Perhaps if he focuses on one area —the economics of the defense industry seems to be his strongest suit—then he'll excel. He spends the first part of the year writing about Russia, but his coverage in such stories as "Getting the Most From Each Ruble," 1-14, and "A Failed Cliché in Siberia: Rich in Oil, Not 'Oil Rich,'" 2-11, is much of the same standard fare we see everywhere. His work on Russia matured later, with such interesting reports as "The Russians Set Out Under Capitalists' Rules for Change," 5-3, one of the few places we find the IMF's policies challenged, and "Figuring Profits the Russian Way," 6-16, a fascinating discussion of how profitability is measured in Russia, Uchitelle explaining how old accounting standards, such as counting wages as "distributed profits," greatly distort profit/loss equations. Some of Uchitelle's best work is on the economics of the defense industry's restructuring, as he illustrates in "Weapons Makers Thinking Small," 8-11: "Most companies are focusing on the two or three weapons systems that they do best, and closing or selling off other operations." Also strong is "Guns or Butter? Labor Ambivalent," 10-6, an interesting assessment of the conflicting pressures bearing down on labor as it urges the military industrial complex to shift to non-military production, while encouraging the funding of defense contracts to maintain jobs. On other domestic economics topics, Uchitelle's portfolio is mixed. His "America Isn't Creating Enough Jobs and No One Seems to Know Why," 9-6, is a whining, unimaginative look at the recession's effect on labor. "Old Idea Gains New Respect: Spending Way Out of Slump," 10-8, is a thorough, even-handed exploration of how to get the economy moving. "Juggling Jobs and the Deficit: Executives Doubtful," 12-13, is just one more poll in which senior executives conclude that deficit reduction and job creation are mutually exclusive goals.

John W. Verity
BusinessWeek
★★★

Information processing editor. Verity's techno-business profiles are typically informative, high-energy assessments. We'd like to see him step back more often for the industry overview stories he handles so competently. His best piece of the year, "Deconstructing the Computer Industry," 11-23, is of this genre, well-informed, cutting-edge analysis of where the computer industry is going. We've seen aspects of this story before, but Verity brings them together quite well, providing important new specifics that add to our understanding of the issues: "The pattern for the industry's future structure has already been set—again, by the microprocessor revolution. In the past decade, the industry has splintered into an array of specialty companies. Each focuses on a different part of the value chain: chips, disks, distribution, data-base software, customer service, and so on. And, as a whole, they are proving more efficient than old-line, integrated makers." Joined by co-writer Peter Coy for "AT&T and NCR: So Far, A Sweet Duet," 1-20, the pair provides a sturdy primer on the promise and pitfalls of AT&T's expensive acquisition of NCR which is supposed to lead to "profitable synergies." After numerous high-level departures from IBM, Verity, in "Room at the Top," 3-9, offers a well-thought out report of who will succeed John Akers, running through the various possibilities proficiently. While many in the press are focused on IBM's financial contraction, Verity tells another, less reported story in "Call it Superbig Blue," with co-writer Julie Flinn 6-29, explaining how "quietly, [IBM] has become a major force in supercomputing." But he seems to back down from this judgement in "Twilight of the Mainframes," 8-17, a brief, but telling account of IBM's latest woes in which Verity notes that the company's biggest profit maker, the mainframe systems business, "still the source of about 60% of IBM's total profits, has peaked at last." Similarly, "It's PCs vs. Mainframes—Even at IBM," 9-21, is enlightening on how IBM is becoming more entrepreneurial, encouraging internal competition with its sacrosanct mainframe.

Kirk Victor
National Journal
★★½

Victor is at his best in the midst of stormy Congressional debates. He excels at chronicling the political rumbles which characterize the lively process of pounding out legislation. His coverage of the legislation itself, though, isn't always so thorough. With First Amendment and copyright concerns becoming ever more heated issues, Victor pens "Reluctant Dragons," 2-8, a highly informative look at the Association of American Publishers' efforts to increase lobbying efforts: "A recent example of enhanced activity by publishers on the lobbying front came late last year when Congress voted to spend $3 billion over five years to develop a nationwide, high-speed, supercomputer network to link federal research facilities with universities and businesses." He offers a measured assessment of Sen. John D. Rockefeller IV's (D-WV) plea that financial support be maintained for the health coverage of miners in "Who'll Pay to Do the Right Thing?" 3-7: "The problem...is that many of the retired miners... worked for companies that have gone belly-up...or otherwise stopped contributing to the funds.... A burden once shared by 80 per cent of the industry is now borne by less than 30 per cent.... Enter Rockefeller. His complex, 71-page bill would require companies to take care of their own retirees and would guarantee benefits...

by imposing an industry-wide tax to finance a government-administered health program." Plenty of behind-the-scenes detail make "Down to the Wire," 5-16, a rich read on the dispute over cable re-regulation. His study of how the debate became consumer oriented is excellent. Victor captures more Congressional bickering in "Sky Kings?" 7-25, examining whether American Airlines' hold over the Computer Reservation System has made the system anti-competitive. With franchise reform under consideration, Victor, in "Franchising Fracas," 9-26, expertly scrutinizes the relationship between franchiser and franchisee. This timely article informs on all sides of the debate. And "Cable Stakes Were as High as They Come," 10-10, is solid on the political and economic fallout after the override of President Bush's veto of the cable bill.

Matthew L. Wald
The New York Times
★★½

Energy. Wald continues to improve as a reporter and analyst. When he sets his sights on a story, the resulting reports are very high-impact. His most eye-opening investigations are of the nuclear industry. For example, his hard-hitting reporting and analysis in "Nuclear Fingerprints All Over but Try to Find the Hands," 6-7, informs us of the disturbing fact that despite evidence of terrible environmental horrors at the government's nuclear bomb production complex, there has been only one criminal conviction. Wald unravels the complexities of this outrage with expert ease. Also keen on nuclear inefficiencies "As Nuclear Plants Close, Costs Don't Shut Down," 9-20, in which he lands numerous good quotes from high-ups at the Rancho Seco Plant near Sacramento, which continues to cost millions to maintain even after voters shut it down. Although "To Fight Smog, 8 Northeast States Adopt New Curbs on Power Plants," 4-3, could have been much shorter, Wald does an impressive job of covering all the bases on the announcement of this unique pact. He is shrewd on the political maneuvering shaping the final drafts of the energy bill in "The Energy Strategy," 5-29: "Congress seriously considered drilling in the Arctic National Wildlife Refuge, requiring more fuel efficiency in cars and rapidly filling the Strategic Petroleum Reserve. But in the end, the House or Senate rejected all three. This was probably essential to the energy bill's survival, because opponents of either Arctic drilling or stricter gas-mileage requirements could probably have sunk the package; certainly they could have done so together." "Car Rentals Hide 'Welcome' Mat," 1-15, is instructive on how two car rental agencies with razor-thin profit margins, Alamo and Hertz, are creating policies intended "to steer to other companies the people who are deemed more likely to damage cars or hurt other people." Wald explains that the legalities of such policies have yet to be tested.

David Warsh
The Boston Globe
★★

"Economic Principles" columnist. Warsh is like an absent-minded professor—he's brilliant, but sometimes wanders off into never-never land at times. Indeed, when we read his columns, we're happy to settle for his plentiful, gem-like observations, well aware that waiting for him to string them all together is likely to prove unfruitful. His examination of the fundamentals that determine economic growth, "The Shouting in Congress Over Capital Gains Taxation Sounds So Trivial," *The Washington Post* 1-29, is erudite on the importance of education, R&D, etc. But by simply dismissing the importance of capital gains, Warsh trivializes the crucial role tax structure plays in capital formation. He covers a lot of territory in "It's Time for the U.S. to Weigh In on a Global Scale," *WP* 3-11, and though he doesn't bring the whole thing together, there are numerous valuable observations. Cerebral, but long-winded is how we'd describe "Economics, Ecology: Twin Sciences of the 21st Century," 5-24, an exhaustive discussion of what economics and ecology have in common. Disappointingly,

Warsh does virtually no original reporting for "President Perot? Record Suggests Some Big Risks," 7-12, opting to reiterate charges from *The New York Times*. Yet, Warsh feels comfortable concluding: "The likelihood is [Perot's] influence on the campaign will diminish as the impression grows of a man with a strong tendency to sidestep the democratic process." Though there's no evidence to support his statement that the German people want the Bundesbank to "keep...interest rates high," Warsh does provide a useful assessment of the way Maastricht has been pushed down Europe's throat in "Aprés le Deluge: Free to Be You and Me," 9-20: "But the Eurocrats . . . seem to have erred badly in estimating the readiness of governments to act against the interests of the voters who elect them." He conveys his disappointment with Clinton's Little Rock conference in "Start of a Long Four Years?" *The Journal of Commerce* 12-17, echoing the concerns of "technical, policy-oriented economists."

Rick Wartzman
The Wall Street Journal
★★

Economics. While it's clear Wartzman has a long way to advance up the learning curve on this new beat, his first-year portfolio indicates that he'll be an honest information broker in a reporting niche that invites ideological tinkering. "Daunting Implications of a Slow Recovery," 3-23, is a broad skim of the political and economic implications of a slow-growth economy which Wartzman calls "The economic equivalent of Purgatory," and "U.S. Economy Seems in a True Turnaround, Unlike Last Spring," 4-29, is rather predictable on the economy's slow forward movement. On the other hand, "Apprenticeship Plans Spring Up for Students Not Headed to College," 5-19, is a compelling portrait of a young student's experience with a creative new apprentice program that keeps him in regular high school classes. As Wartzman explains, kids opting out of a college education often fall between the cracks in vocational schools. Showing he doesn't carry the ideological baggage that others on this beat lug around, Wartzman renders a faithful telling of Alan Greenspan's Congressional testimony in "Fed Is Leaning Toward Cutting Money Target," 7-23, providing one of the more enlightening accounts we saw: "Lowering short-term interest rates...in the past would have been expected to spur M2 growth, Mr. Greenspan said. ...[but]... 'a couple of years ago, both of those relationships broke down.'" We also have to give credit to Wartzman for "Dollar's Fall Raises Broad Questions on Causes, Outlook for U.S. Markets," 8-26. He makes an earnest attempt to answer our questions about the swift decline of the dollar's value against the German mark. Joined by co-writer Dana Milbank for "Clinton's Strength With Business Leaders Is Rare for a Democrat," 9-24, we're served a purely anecdotal perspective of GOP defections in the business sector. And in "Clinton's Pledge to Trim Fat From Government May Fare No Better Than Diet Fads of the Past," 11-24, he offers a worthwhile study of the impediments Clinton will face as he tries to make the government more efficient.

Gary Weiss
BusinessWeek
★★

Markets and investment editor. Weiss is the type of journalist Wall Street technicians love. He grinds out the formulas and measures the markets ups and downs against them. If you're satisfied with this type of analysis, you'll appreciate the work Weiss does; if you're looking for information on how political and economic forces shape the markets, you'll have to look elsewhere. Weiss and co-writer David Greising examine why the "market wizards" ran so short on magic this year in "Poof! Wall Street's Sorcerers Lose Their Magic," 1-27, an engaging look at how the Street's most prominent names underperformed the S&P, while "faceless hordes of mutual-fund managers" beat the index. In "Are Stock Prices Too Stiff?" 3-2, Weiss bangs out all the valuation formulas to see if the market is overvalued: "Judged in isolation, this p-e spells trouble. But p-e ratios should not be judged in isolation. When compared with short term interest rates, the number appears far less threatening.... So long as interest rates stay low, they will continue to take the sting out of those nasty-looking p-e numbers." But if interest rates are so crucial then a look at the political pressures on them would have helped. He pens a fine study of the new breed of index arbitrage in "Program Traders: They're Back, Without the Bad Vibes," 5-18: "Index arbitrage has come into its own not as a stand-alone money-maker but rather as a hedging technique for sophisticated options and swap contracts." More technical advice pervades "A Second Wind for Small Companies?" 6-22, in which Weiss advises, incorrectly as it turns out, that small-cap stocks "on the whole, will be dogs for most of the remainder of the year. But don't despair. All of the fundamental factors that have sustained small-cap stocks remain intact." Commonsense analysis shapes "Sure, Profits Are on the Rise, But..." 7-13, a handy, but not especially instructive industry-by-industry breakdown. We thoroughly enjoyed "Chaos Hits Wall Street—the Theory, That Is," 11-2, an engaging report on how and why "Chaologists" are being taken more seriously.

David Wessel
The Wall Street Journal
★½

Washington. Though his feature work is often quite good, and his reporting is solid, Wessel's economic analysis remains a glaring weak spot. There are no signs that he does the hard thinking that leads to fresh insights. He's more comfortable latching on to the press pack's latest catch-phrase. For instance, we're disappointed by both "New Debt Phobia Is Slowing Economy," 8-10, an off-the-cuff assessment in which Wessel wonders when consumers will start buying big-ticket items again, and "World's Economies, Now Interdependent, All Suffer Together," 9-17, in which he and his sources rely on vague generalizations to confidently conclude: "The root causes of global economic stagnation are clear." In "White House Budget Proposal to Stretch Seams of 1990 Deficit-Reduction Law," 1-20, he comes down hard on the administration as news of Bush's budget leaks out: "Like a fat person trying to squeeze into last year's clothes, the Bush administration is stretching the seams of the 1990 law that was intended to reduce the deficit." We applaud Wessel for shedding light on the highly-politicized statistic that the richest one percent got 60 percent of the economic gains during the '80s boom in "The Wealthy Watch Gains of 1980s Become Political Liabilities," 4-8: "Mr. Clinton attributes the figure to a [CBO] report that doesn't exist.... In fact, it was calculated on the back of an envelope by Paul Krugman, a [MIT] economist, and is somewhat more complicated than Mr. Clinton suggests." Wessel's economic features, such as "Two Unusual Lenders Show How 'Bad Risks' Can Be Good Business," 6-23, showcase his strengths as a writer. Here he looks at the promising world of "micro-enterprises," which offers economic assistance and hope to inner-city dwellers who want to get off welfare. He speculates correctly that Lloyd Bentsen will be named to Treasury in "Clinton, Agent of Change, Looks for Candidates for His Team in All the Old, Familiar Places," 12-3: "'The appointment of a Bentsen,' says Charls Walker, a Washington lobbyist and former Treasury official, 'would be a strong signal to the political cognoscenti.'"

Joseph B. White
The Wall Street Journal
★★½

Detroit. The pivotal events occurring at the Big Three have definitely energized White. His reporting is decidedly more probing, and his evaluations of the sea change at General Motors contain the type of key information investors and industry watchers appreciate. He's observant for "GM Expects to Post a 1991 Loss of Nearly $6 Billion," 2-24, making key observations that gained currency as the year's events unfolded: "GM's non-employee directors are signaling deep dismay. They even held a meeting without Mr. Stempel in Detroit last month, despite Mr. Stempel's request that the meeting not take place."

With news of the boardroom shake-up at GM hitting the wires after the stock market closed, we're impressed that White and co-writer Paul Ingrassia are able to meet their editorial deadlines and bang out as sturdy an analysis as "Board Ousts Managers at GM, Takes Control of Crucial Committee," 4-7, which sheds light on a number of important aspects of the event. The pair is back together for "Behind Revolt at GM, Lawyer Ira Millstein Helped Call the Shots," 4-13, another top-notch beat report in which we peek behind closed-door meetings to discover a key player most reporters didn't notice—Ira M. Millstein: ". . . if Mr. [John G.] Smale was the leader of GM's board-room revolt, Mr. Millstein, the chief counsel to GM's outside directors for more than five years, was its ideologist." This is a fascinating, detailed portrait of what led up to the GM coup. As the GM story advances the duo keeps us up-to-date with very sharp analytical pieces such as "Determined to Change, General Motors Is Said to Pick New Chairman," 10-23, and "At Once-Stodgy GM, Management Change Is a Generational One," 11-3. The latter article, which reports on John F. Smith's appointment as CEO, is packed with insight: "The appointments are a stunning reversal of tradition. . . . The new generation's roots are in international operations and finance, areas where GM has had conspicuously greater success in recent years than it has in the U.S." In "Detroit Is Dealt a Big Blow in ITC Ruling on Minivans," 6-25, we hear mostly the Big Three's side of the story as the ITC rules that Japan is not dumping minivans.

Ford S. Worthy
Fortune
★★

Returning from a long tour in Asia, Worthy came back to the U.S. to cover finance, and then at the end of the year left the magazine to go to law school. His final months of work stateside are characterized by solid reporting and sound analysis. For example, in "Still Making Out on Wall Street," 4-6, he provides a strong examination of how Wall Street is trying to bring order into its unruly compensation process. Here, Worthy advises us to keep an eye on Salomon Brothers where Warren Buffett has been overhauling the way the firm pays its people. In "The Battle of the Bean Counters," 6-1, he provides a very complete discussion of the debate over GAAP versus marking assets to market, which critics say will lead to more volatility. While it is clear that Worthy favors some sort of market valuation to clarify financial institutions' stability, he provides a great deal of space to the opposition, recognizing their concerns and recommending a cautious approach to change. He deftly reviews the state of the financial markets post-1987 crash in "What We Learned From the '87 Crash," 10-5: "Most experts queried by *Fortune* believe the U.S. equities market in particular is a smoother-running, more resilient machine today precisely because Black Monday brought it near to collapse." Just before heading home he takes us on a whirlwind tour of the booming Guangdong province in "Where Capitalism Thrives in China," 3-9. It's an exciting read, but *very* late, as this same story was told elsewhere more than a year-and-a-half ago. In his last overseas dispatch, "Getting Ready to Get Into Vietnam," 4-6, Worthy gets ahead of a trend, as American companies are biting at the bit to get into Vietnam as soon as the embargo is lifted. He offers plenty of evidence that corporations and *Viet Kieu*, overseas Vietnamese, are positioning themselves for the growth period that is ahead for this country: "The parallels between China's gradual economic liberalization and Vietnam's are so close that many China hands have transformed themselves into Vietnam experts."

Robert Wrubel
Financial World
★★★½

Senior editor. We've long been impressed with the business profiles that appear under Wrubel's byline, and this year is no exception. His crisp writing and analytics continue to improve, and he's fast becoming one of the best business writers around. With the defense industry facing tough economic times, Wrubel gives us "The Cherry Pickers," 4-14, an instructive look at how well-capitalized contractors such as Martin Marietta and Lockheed, with their bid to acquire LTV's aerospace division, are cherry-picking "some of the industry's best assets and contracts at bargain prices." With most everyone concentrating on the management reshuffle at GM, Wrubel asks an important question in "Collision Course," 5-26: "What will Jack Smith, GM's newly anointed chief operating officer, do about the United Auto Workers union?" As Wrubel explains, UAW is in no mood for conciliatory action after its humiliation at Caterpillar. Smith's plans to slim the work force by some 60,000 will be a major challenge: "The big barrier to achieving these goals is the labor deal GM struck with the UAW back in 1990. That pact gave GM little work-rule flexibility and, even worse, guaranteed that laid-off UAW members would receive 95% of their full compensation and benefits for up to three years after losing their jobs. In theory, then, many of the 60,000 workers laid off in the next few years will be getting paid nearly in full . . . " "Rite of Passage," 6-9, is a keen survey of Ford Motors under Harold 'Red' Poling. Wrubel describes how Poling bet Ford's balance sheet to finance a costly product development effort, and won. Wrubel also looks toward problem spots in Ford's future. We found "The $6 Billion Opportunity," 10-13, to be an extremely enlightening assessment of the prospects that Japan's enormous investment in Liquid Crystal Displays might not pay off because "poor quality with expensive production and materials" has made their price non-competitive. Assigned to profile *FW*'s "Man of the Year," Boeing's Frank Shrontz, Wrubel pens "The Last Titan" 12-8, an excellent examination of the dramatic changes Shrontz has made over the years.

G. Pascal Zachary
The Wall Street Journal
★★★

San Francisco. Zachary has an eye for trends and a knack for turning orthodox thinking about Silicon Valley on its head. It's apparent that he begins each story with a clean slate, a fresh outlook. As a result, he uncovers unique and valuable stories on the high-tech beat. He challenges conventional wisdom in one of his best efforts of the year, "U.S. High-Tech Firms Have Begun Staging Little-Noticed Revival," 12-14, making clear that "those who speak of high-tech decline have missed a startling shift. Many U.S. companies that rely on technical and scientific research are stronger today than five years ago. . . . American high-tech has regained its lead in markets such as semiconductors and threatens to surpass the Japanese in high-definition TV, electronic books, wireless phones and other devices. U.S. pharmaceutical makers have seen a sharp rise in exports." We find more conventional wisdom bashing in the highly-instructive "High-Tech Firms Find It's Good to Line Up Outside Contractors," 7-29. In this article, Zachary explains that the use of outside suppliers and corporate alliances, a taboo in the high-tech industry, has led to success for some companies: "Today, Hewlett-Packard, with Canon's help, dominates the global laser-printer market. And its success suggests that high-tech companies that rely on others for crucial parts or manufacturing frequently rule fast-changing markets." Zachary lands a rare interview with the "reclusive programmer," John Walker of Autodesk, for "'Theocracy of Hackers' Rules Autodesk Inc., a Strangely Run Firm," 5-28, and in "Industries Find Growth of Digital Electronics Brings in Competitors," 2-18, provides a useful, broad-stroke overview of the changes that "Digital Revolution" will bring by blurring the lines between "the four huge industries: computers, consumer electronics, communications and entertainment." Venturing from his regular high-tech beat for "Many Journalists See a Growing Reluctance to Criticize Advertisers," 2-6, he plays the watchdog for his own industry, journalism. The report is an admirable examination of the growing pressure being placed on editors by advertisers trying to suppress negative reports.

★ COMMENTATORS ★

Ken Adelman
Tribune Media Services
★½

We respect Adelman's perspectives on security issues because of his résumé in the defense industry, his impeccable contacts within the strategic community and his trim and smart analysis. But when Adelman persists in examining topics apart from security, he lacks force and depth. For example, in "With a Winning Shove From the X Factor," *The Washington Times* 2-12, Adelman tries, unsuccessfully, to distill the essence of the so-called "X factor" that permits legends in sports to rise above their fellows. He offers only obvious advice to President-elect Clinton on the selection of advisors in "Tricky Transition Turnpike," *WT* 11-6, asserting superficially that "Appointees must also have stamina, as nearly three-fourths of top presidential appointees work more than 60 hours per week." "Failing Upward to Fame and Fortune," *WT* 5-1, is jumbled, comparing failed execs with outrageous pay to journalists whose predictions don't pan out. We don't get it. He is infinitely more effective when discussing global security topics, as in "Breathing New Life Into the U.N." *WT* 7-1, an excellent appraisal of the UN's potential for becoming the arbiter and negotiator of conflicts around the world. The article is packed with good

suggestions. In "Peace Initiatives Israel Could Take," *WT* 3-20, he offers an interesting, though impractical, proposal for Israel to participate in a confederation to govern the disputed territories while imposing no-weaponry conditions. Sensitive to the military hierarchy in "Brass Hats in Smallest Sizes," *WT* 9-23, he takes to task both Gen. Schwarzkopf and Adm. Crowe for effectively betraying, in print, their commander-in-chief, George Bush, strongly making his point that it only reflects back on the critics.

Russell Baker
The New York Times
★★★

"Observer" columnist. Baker's funny, poignant columns could never wear thin with us. He's less curmudgeonly now than ever, celebrating 30 years in print, and simply sparkling in '92 with his quick sense of humor and unerring common sense. "Six Mind Benders," 1-21, is a superb effort which punctures the hype of the major stories of the day, including the U.S. trade mission to Japan. He takes us on a madcap journey through the latest salvo in the tariff wars in "The White and the Red," 11-10, wittily but powerfully warning: "Why not Parma ham, Scotch whisky, Danish cheese, German farm machinery?" In "The Road to Coma," 2-4, Baker hilariously skewers the *Times*'s advice to consumers on health insurance, which includes calling state regulators: "Let's not even try to imagine the odds against getting through—on the telephone!—to a 'regulator' willing to give you a critique of the policy you're thinking of buying." "Monkey Business, Anyone?" 4-14, is vintage Baker, lampooning the notion of businessmen running the country, noting that if history is any guide, a business president would likely declare bankruptcy, sell the government's assets, and give himself a raise. Baker pokes fun at Bush's shock at Perot's alleged investigations in the wonderful satire, "Bush League Bogart," 6-30: "Isn't this the same George Bush, who, in one of his previous Government jobs, ran the C.I.A., America's multibillion-dollar snoop to the whole darn world?" Baker offers a moving tribute to

Eric Sevareid in "Against the Grain," 7-14, saluting the journalism he practiced. He hits the mark on the fallacy of Bush's Truman analogy with "Under Deep Cover," 9-1: During the '48 race, "Mrs. Truman said she had no use for men who lost their grip on their own identities every time a political campaign came along. 'If Harry's got to lose,' she told the First Ladies' Home Companion, 'he ought to have the gumption to lose as Harry Truman, not as Woodrow Wilson.'"

Fred Barnes
The New Republic
★★★

"White House Watch" columnist. While Barnes's columns, packed with insider information, remain must reading for Beltway inhabitants, we're used to Barnes setting the pace during a campaign season. This election year that simply didn't happen. Although replete with findings from the Bush camp, Barnes seems content to shoot the messenger in "Skinner Dipping," 1-20, placing the blame for the policy drift squarely on chief-of-staff Sam Skinner, rather than Bush. In another skimpy policy critique that's heavy with inside dirt, "Cry for Me," 2-10, Barnes conveys the fear in the Bush camp that the President's problems are the result of faulty public relations, not faulty policies. (Perversely, Skinner gets credit here "for creating a sense of urgency at the White House.") He spends most of "Loser," 5-4, detailing why, "absent a [White House] scandal or economic collapse, Clinton's a goner." We wondered why Barnes was writing off Clinton so early. He outlines, but does not see, the coming disaster as the Bush camp proposes to follow the Tories' example by emphasizing the negative, i.e., the draft and trust issues, in "Major Moment," 10-5. Here he argues unpersuasively that "Swing voters—Reagan Democrats, independents, non-liberal working women—have turned Bush off. They don't care about his [economic] plan." Barnes's strongest efforts came from outside the administration. "Beltway for Hire," 6-29, is juicy on how Ross Perot is unsettling "not only the two main political parties, but the business culture of Washington," as political consultants struggle with the decision of joining Perot. Barnes never considers the irony of the ultimate outsider shopping for a staff inside the Beltway. The best detail on Democratic disunion on abortion was provided in his insightful 10 Best selection, "No Womb for Debate," 7-27. He shows foresight in defining new factions within the GOP in "Kemp vs. Dole," 12-14, rounding out his portfolio for the year.

Michael Barone
U.S. News & World Report
★★½

Senior editor. Barone is the closest thing any of the newsweeklies have to a reporter-analyst who is comfortable in both roles. His reporting talents are considerable, and his analytics sturdy, buttressed by his vast knowledge of history. He's young, with ample time to mature into a pundit for the 21st century. Using history to his (and our) advantage in a debunking of "The American Isolationist Mirage," 2-3, he goes back to revolutionary days to define isolationism as unrealistic in terms of domestic policy. He also incorporates political history into his insightful advice to President-elect Clinton in "How to Do the Transition Right," 11-23. In "Old-Time Liberalism: The Sequel," 3-23, Barone makes a mildly persuasive case that Bill Clinton might be the one to transform liberalism from the ideology of entitlements to empowerment. "The New Face of American Politics," *National Review* 4-27, offers trenchant commentary early in the '92 campaign to which Bush and the GOP should have paid more attention: ". . . it should never be forgotten that both [the Dewey and Taft] forms of elitist Republicanism (elitism in the sense of trusting experts over the people . . .) were losers in the three general elections in the 1940s. It is the populist (trusting the people) conservatism of Ronald Reagan, borrowing the cheerfulness and optimism of Franklin D. Roosevelt, that won three general elections in the 1980s." Post-L.A. riots, Barone crafts a cohesive argument that the candidate who offers a better vision of stability will prosper in "A Common Interest in Civil Order," 5-18. Going against the pack, he asserts there were gains among the middle class during the '80s and puts the idea of redistribution on the margin for '92, in "The New 'Save Our Wealth' Voters," 6-22. And his "Litmus Tests for the Democrats," 9-14, is a powerful challenge for Clinton to seriously consider the meaning of the rule of law.

Robert L. Bartley
The Wall Street Journal
★★★

Editor. After years of penning tightly-knit editorials expounding the principles of supply-side economics, Bartley has turned his hand to column-writing. Bartley's principal utility this year was his defense of the economic policies of the '80s at a time when many others were distorting and denouncing Reaganomics for political gain. Although not as vigorous as supply-side commentator Paul Craig Roberts, his approach is well-reasoned. He traces the recession back to its roots in "OK, Family Values Score, Now Back to Economic Issue," 9-3, a defense of Reagan's economic policies. Bartley also uses his economic knowledge as a springboard to assess the political situation. In "Asia Trip May Yet Win New Verdict: Successful Debacle," 1-14, he shows his political acuity on Bush's junket to Japan, pointing out that this is the first questioning Bush has gotten on foreign, if foreign-economic, policy: "It will now be open season on the president's foreign record as well as his domestic one . . . it will be open season on his capacity for leadership." Persuasive in arguing that Perot isn't a true successor to Reagan's mantle in "Perot's Secret: Upstage Bush in Reagan Role," 6-4, he posits that Bush's best hope for re-election is "somehow to show that he, not Ross Perot, is Ronald Reagan's true heir." He attempts a rough draft of Bush's acceptance speech for the GOP nomination in "Define the Second Administration," 8-3, naming Jack Kemp Treasury Secretary and Vin Weber OMB director. These are provocative suggestions, but he fails to address the political infighting that would likely derail such choices. Bartley details the subtle shifting as some of Wall Street's "idealistic advocates of entrepreneurial capitalism" begin to consider a vote for Clinton with "Capitalists Seek Silver Lining in Clinton, Bush," 10-14. Post-election, he offers a superb appraisal of political history in "President Clinton Faces History, With Best Wishes," 12-10, positioning the President-elect as having an "enormous opportunity" to revitalize the country.

Tom Bethell
The American Spectator
★

"Capitol Ideas" columnist. While his efforts are still read in many conservative quarters, most of his reports are sourced from doings at Stanford's Hoover Institute, where Bethell has a fellowship. His work addressing Washington issues often seems uncritical and unoriginal. He was much sharper when located inside the Beltway a few years back. We get politics as sociology in "Doing the Right Thing," 1-92, as Bethell ties the failures of the Bush administration to the upbringing of elites who put a higher premium on good government than ideology and are thus susceptible to liberal entreaties to raise taxes. Bethell is dangerously misinformative in "Trojan Army," 4-92, and "Heretic," 5-92. In the former, he skirts why the gay rights group Queer Nation is distributing condoms at U. of San Francisco by raving about the "Sisters of Perpetual Indulgence." In the latter, Bethell sings the praises of scientist Peter Duesberg, as Duesberg lectures that HIV does not cause AIDS—drug abuse and AZT do. Bethell fails to examine the science of such a position. "Strange New Respect, 1992," 9-92, is a loose discourse on the judiciary, linking Supreme Court Justice Anthony Kennedy to Justice Roger Taney (*Dred Scott v. Sandford*), but the essay descends into the miasma of abortion and how the justices stack up. Bethell sees the end of the Bush reign and cheerleads for Clinton's failure in the unsportsmanlike "Silver Lining to a Clinton Presidency," *Los Angeles Times* 10-30. This short-sighted argument predicts conservatives will again have control of the GOP by '96 though Bethell provides no support. His best work of the year, "De Soto in Peru," 8-92, is an up-to-the-minute dispatch on what economist Hernando de Soto is doing to promote secure property rights in Peru. He extrapolates rich insights from this proposal, comprehending its positive implications for the political situation. Says de Soto: "Wherever we titled and registered, the Shining Path up and left."

Sidney Blumenthal
The New Yorker
★★★

Washington editor. This thinking man's liberal had an excellent year covering politics as a senior editor for *The New Republic*. Blumenthal's strength is his ability to provide fresh insights on the candidates, which makes him a must-read on the campaign trail. He will be an asset to *The New Yorker* which he joined in November. His first "Letter from Washington," 12-7, is solid, containing strong reporting on the "lend-lease of tactical advice" from the Tories to the Bush campaign. He offers a superb appraisal of the flaws of Bob Kerrey's candidacy and the Democrats in "The Politics of Self," *TNR* 1-20: "Kerrey's campaign is not about 'ideology'—it's about biography. . . . [He] lacks a theme except himself." Several illuminating essays on the eventual Democratic candidate, Bill Clinton, give us salient insider detail on his advisors, his philosophies, his place in politics, and his use of friendship and the party mechanisms to advance his political career: "The Anointed," *TNR* 2-3; "The Pol," *TNR* 4-6; and "The Reanointed," *TNR* 7-27. His work outside the Democratic party, though, did not produce equally consistent insight. Blumenthal describes well what he considers to be the wacky world of Ross Perot in "Perotnoia," *TNR* 6-15, adding to reports of Perot's 'fascination' with undercover ops. But he goes overboard on the Texan in "The Mission," *TNR* 7-6, alleging without solid, support that, "according to a reliable eyewitness," Perot had his children followed and their friends investigated. Similarly, Blumenthal crosses the line when he raises questions about Bush's military service in "War Story," *TNR* 10-12, asserting that the young Bush may have bailed out of his crashing plane prematurely, a story revealed four years ago during the debates, and dismissed by Michael Dukakis as inappropriate.

James Bovard
Freelance
★★

Bovard is a self-assigned watchdog on the international trade and subsidy beat, often focusing on agriculture—coincidentally the subject of his last book, *The Farm Fiasco*. His analysis provides a valuable service, bringing to our attention obscure but important trade beat issues frequently overlooked by others. He examines the various barriers Bush has erected during his presidency in "Bush Protection," *The New Republic* 1-20: "George Bush has been closing off American markets almost since his first week in office. In fact, by ceding to the demands of one domestic lobby after another, he may be the most protectionist president since Herbert Hoover." He doesn't however link this important observation to the current economic crisis. He updates the list of Bush protectionist moves in "'Truck' Tariff Traffic Troubles," *The Washington Times* 3-23, noting the potential for higher tariffs on foreign-made trucks, vans and jeeps, a move that would hit U.S. pocketbooks hard. This was a significant bit of reporting that wasn't highlighted anyplace else. He provides valuable information after the latest shot in the trade wars—the U.S. proposes to raise import tariffs on white wine—in "Free Trade, 1990s-Style, Is Anything But," *The Wall Street Journal* 11-10, offering precise detail on how we came to this point. Bovard makes a memorable, albeit heavy-handed, observation in closing: "Negotiating with the EC to achieve free trade is like trying to negotiate with prostitutes to achieve chastity." "Fair Trade Follies," *TNR* 5-11, is a listing of the different trade boondoggles pending in Congress. Bovard, though, keeps his criticism uncharacteristically general here, failing to examine the specific implications of this legislation. And "Bush's Wheat War Leaves Many Casualties," *WSJ* 9-8, suffers from esoteric writing. While the subject is important, Bovard fails to fully engage us.

David S. Broder
The Washington Post
★★★

Broder is the grand old man at *The Washington Post*, and is one of the most important political reporter-columnists in the world because of his post and his years of experience. He does his best work in presidential election years, slacking off during the Congressional campaign seasons. In the extensive dissection of the Veep, "Dan Quayle: The Premeditated Surprise," 1-5, 1-6, 1-7, 1-8, 1-9, 1-10, 1-12, a 10 Best selection, Broder and co-author Bob Woodward altered perceptions of many, inside and outside the Beltway. In "California Could Be Blank Slate for Brown," *Los Angeles Times* 4-1, he argues ineffectively that Brown might win California because so many voters have come of age since he was governor. He offers an appraisal of "Term Limits: The Movement Gathers Momentum," 7-29, concluding: "Those of us who think this remedy worse than the disease are going to have to crank up our arguments again," though he fails to explain those arguments. We did value his insights in such thought-provoking essays as the 10 Best selection "Odd Way to Choose a President," 1-28, a persuasive case for leaving the infidelity question out of the campaign. With "Urban Plan: From Back Burner to Hot Spot," 5-24, Broder puts Jack Kemp in the spotlight, including important reconnaissance as to why Kemp's plans were not acted upon early enough to impact inner-city economies before the L.A. riots. And "Clinton's Popgun Offensive," 9-11, is an excellent review of Clinton's campaign weaknesses. With his experience, it's Broder whom we turn to for an election wrap-up. He puts Clinton's 43% "mandate" in perspective with "Winning Is One Thing, Governing Is Something Else," *LAT* 11-18, and makes a compelling case for bipartisanship in "Please, Let Her Keep Her Job," 12-2, advising Clinton to allow Janet Steiger, head of the FTC, to continue in the post.

Richard Brookhiser
National Review
★★

We once thought Brookhiser was the heir apparent to William Buckley's editorship at *NR*. But after John O'Sullivan got the job, Brookhiser dropped out of sight until the beginning of this year. He's still the Buckleyite conservative he always was, and is best when not trying to emulate his largely inimitable former boss. "We Can All Share American Culture," *Time* 8-31, is an exposition on multiculturalism, in which his Buckleyish language obscures the thrust of his main point until the close: "If the toleration of differences is the be-all and end-all of America, then why not tolerate multiculturalism?" In "Hot for Teacher," 11-16, he ignores Camille Paglia's *Sex, Art and American Culture* by reviewing Paglia herself: "As with anyone who tries to explain everything, there are gaps, caused by the inevitable holes in an individual's knowledge or taste." He's much more palatable when exercising his reporting skills as in his surprisingly perceptive essay on the candidacy of Pat Buchanan, in "Waiting for Righty," 1-20. He culls from the candidate himself the best explanation for his running: "I'm challenging the President of my party because he's abandoned the principles of his party." His handicapping of the Democratic field for '92, "Democratic Disasters," 2-17, though not terribly deep, is memorable mostly for this ultimate assessment: "There is nothing, in short, that should worry Republicans [about the Democratic field]. But then, Republicans had not reckoned on George Bush." Brookhiser gives us a penetrating profile with "Clinton: The Roadside View," 3-30, offering the intuitive argument that one reason Clinton is doing so well is because he simply relishes campaigning, much as Harry S. Truman did. He also pegs the candidate as having an actual interest in ideas. Clinton "...has ideas in abundance; what he doesn't have is a compelling explanation of how they all fit together."

Art Buchwald
Los Angeles Times Syndicate
★★

Buchwald is as feisty as we've ever seen him, bringing chuckles all around. Perhaps invigorated by the rough-and-tumble games of election-year politics, Buchwald made the most of the material he had to work with in '92. He shows what might happen if Bush's flu attack were to undergo revisionism at the hands of such conspiracy-minded types as Oliver Stone in "Bugged: The Flu Conspiracy," *The Washington Post* 1-14: "He will show that the illness was caused by a cabal of the CIA, the military-industrial complex and leaders of the American automobile industry." "I Owe it All to Mr. Baker," *The New York Times* 7-17, is one of Buchwald's better efforts, a tribute to "The Grand Old Man of American Humor Columnists," Russell Baker, on the 30th anniversary of his first column. And in "Joblessness Begins at Home," *WP* 9-8, Buchwald makes direct jabs at Bush, as his fictional characters discuss the economy: "'If I were out of work, I wouldn't lay the blame on the White House. I would put it squarely where it belongs—on the cultural elite who make dirty films and hang nude pictures in art galleries. That's where unemployment starts.' Burlap was not persuaded. 'The President better face up to it. One jobless man means one Clinton vote. If we working stiffs have to take care of our unemployed relatives any longer, Bush and Quayle will be begging for their own food stamps in November.'" He's equally pointed in describing America's religious diversity with "A Nation on the Road to Salvation," *WP* 12-3, after Mississippi Gov. Kirk Fordyce caused an uproar by calling the U.S. a "Christian Nation." Says Buchwald: "Gov. Fordyce doesn't know what he's talking about, and each of us in our own way prayed for his soul." With many true, wacky examples of American goods made abroad, we're surprised he manufactures illustrations for "Don't Be So Sure About Origin of American Goods," *Los Angeles Times* 3-10. His fabricated examples don't stack up to reality.

William F. Buckley, Jr.
National Review
Universal Press Syndicate
★★

Buckley is the essence of all things intellectually conservative, and has been since the publication of *God and Man at Yale* more than thirty years ago. He has influenced all reflective conservatives in one way or another, even if his columns don't quite have the power of yesteryear. "Dear Ronald," 2-3, reviews correspondence between Gorbachev and Reagan. Buckley merely agrees with the pair's conclusion that they were responsible for ending the Cold War. With "Who Will Pay?" 8-3, Buckley reminds the Democrats of the logistical and economic problems of creating government-support programs for poor children. But since he never outlines what the Democrats might do, these qualifiers seem premature. He relates in some detail the pro-growth proposals of "Conservative Go-Goers," Kemp, Gingrich, *et al.*, in "The Other Republicans," 10-19, an important dispatch for conservatives. He pronounces "The Second Debate: Dull," 11-16, by arguing superficially that the format was wrong because it led the candidates to sing their own praises. He was very sharp on Jewish issues this year, as in "Rosenthal-Think," 4-13, where he superbly dismantles Abe Rosenthal's charges that Pat Buchanan is anti-Semitic: "There are cool thinkers in America who are on the alert to discourage anti-Semitism. Abe Rosenthal isn't one of them. His hotheadedness, his disposition to judge recklessly, sets his cause back. . . . To have said something anti-Semitic does not necessarily justify the assumption that the person who said it is anti-Semitic. Even as to say something stupid does not justify assuming that the person who said it is stupid." And "Is Baker Really Unfair to Israel?" *Los Angeles Times* 3-29, is an excellent defense of Jim Baker's withholding of loan guarantees until the peace process has run its course.

Mona Charen
Creators Syndicate
★★★

Charen's ability to report and analyze the issues of the day in a coherent, original and intelligent manner continues to impress us. She spares neither friend nor foe in her critiques, and yields not an inch of her conservative ideology to political or rhetorical expediency. Charen provides an excellent rebuttal to the growing isolationist sentiment in "Now's No Time to Disengage," *The Washington Times* 1-2: "The conservative isolationist case is based upon a false premise.... In the age of the fax machine, globalized industry and ballistic missiles, we cannot retire from the world." Looking homeward in "Between a Rock and the Right Stuff," *WT* 2-23, she smartly raps Bush and Buchanan on the knuckles for their failures, and is particularly trenchant on Bush. She does an exceptional job in "For Richer or for Poorer," *WT* 4-9, revealing that the CBO data, trumpeted by Sylvia Nasar at *The New York Times*, and Bill Clinton on the stump, are being skewed for political reasons, and she includes the evidence to back it up. Using polling data to buttress "A Dream, With a Bit of Vision," *WT* 7-13, Charen argues effectively that conservatism is rampant, and that a conservative should be running for president. "Keeping an Eye on Clinton's Record," *WT* 9-17, is a strong examination of Clinton's governorship: "Gov. Clinton's governing style has been a bureaucrat's delight. In 1988, for example, Bill Clinton said this about his 'Rural Development Action Program' to fight poverty in Arkansas, 'I believe it may wind up having an unbelievable impact.' Three years later, the program is dead, and poverty remains as intractable as ever. How was the money spent? According to the *Arkansas Democrat-Gazette*, most of the money in the program's budget was spent on salaries." Post-election, Charen mounts a call to arms for conservatives in "Premature Consignment to the Crypt," *WT* 11-8, arguing that Bush lost because he represented neither Reagan's legacy nor the GOP.

Alston Chase
Creators Syndicate
★½

Chase has a long way to go to fill the shoes of the late Warren Brookes, who was peerless in watchdogging environmental zealots. His value is in consistently providing information and perspectives on the environment that cut against the prevailing winds. But he does little to advance or enrich our understanding of these scientific debates. On pure political questions, Chase tries hard, but his views rarely rise above the conventional. A case in point is "Checking Into the Nanny Gap," *The Washington Times* 3-23, in which Chase meanders from Congress and check-kiting to nannies to Congressional pay cuts and term limits. He does some reporting for "Heart Bigger Than Our Brain," *WT* 1-5, an overview of new environmental developments such as the theory that the dinosaurs might have been done in by their own flatulence. Chase persuasively uses these wacky theorems to argue that mistakes in environmental policy can be costly and that "taken cumulatively, they can spell 'recession.'" He exposes the mismanagement of wildlife at Yellowstone in "Knavery in the Wolf War," *WT* 2-25, but proposes no real plan of his own, except to require honesty in managing the national parks system, which seems naive. He tries to incorporate history and politics to account for the poisoning of the Blue Danube in "Stealing the Danube as the World Watches," *The Indianapolis Star* 11-8, but he doesn't pull his information together cohesively. His prescription in "Perplexities of Park Service Reform," *WT* 7-2, is more focused, as he argues that education of rangers should be at the heart of any park reform. But doesn't really tell us how to achieve this. His "Grazing at the Fringes," *WT* 5-8, is an excellent debunking of the politically-correct anti-grazing movement: "The environmentalists' case is based on the notion that by grazing, wild creatures never, and domestic animals always, harm the range. According to this theory, deer and buffalo are good for grass, and sheep and cattle are bad."

Alexander Cockburn
The Nation
In These Times

Although he's fallen on hard times in recent years, Cockburn has retained his influence as one of the premier commentators of the Marxist left. With his wing of the Democratic Party shunted aside by moderates, Cockburn seemed even further out of the loop. In "All Prologue and No Real Program," *Los Angeles Times* 1-16, he is acutely perceptive on Clinton, critiquing his unwillingness to say anything substantive about programs during the primaries. He goes further with "More Shoes Are Dropping on Clinton," *LAT* 3-23, outlining potential problems with the governor, using his record as a yardstick. Joined by Andrew Kopkind, he makes a resounding call to "seize the initiative" with "The Democrats, Perot and the Left," *TN* 7-20/27, including a smart assessment of the Democratic failure to represent the far left. He strongly attacks the hypocrisy of the Jewish intelligensia, who deplore atrocities in former Yugoslavia while ignoring conditions in Israel, in his regular *Nation* column, "Beat the Devil," 8/31–9/7. Cockburn and Robert Pollin offer excellent reasons "Why the Left Should Support the Flat Tax," *The Wall Street Journal* 4-2, destroying Citizens for Tax Justice's "double counting" arguments: CTJ has "assumed, without a word of explanation, that businesses can raise prices a dollar for every dollar going to the payroll tax, but not pass along their corporate taxes. Of course, this ploy substantially strengthens charges of the regressivity . . . " But the remainder of Cockburn's work on economics was less explorative. From a liberal viewpoint in "The President's Pig-Out Manifesto," *LAT* 2-2, he cites the same old statistics against a capital gains tax cut. We'd hoped for at least a fresh approach to this issue. A Marxist evaluation would have been welcome. With "Beat the Devil," *TN* 11-9, all he does is inform us that he doesn't like any of the candidates.

Richard Cohen
The Washington Post
★

Cohen is still showing the residual effects of a midlife crisis that has been played out painfully and obviously in his columns. He evinces an irritating tendency to ramble about the obvious and is simply rabid on certain, closely-held issues, particularly anything concerning Israel, anti-Semitism, and/or Pat Buchanan. In "Buchanan's Beltway Buddies," 1-28, a paranoid Cohen accuses Michael Kinsley, Mark Shields, Albert Hunt and Morton Kondracke of being soft on Pat Buchanan because they are too interested in future talk show revenues that are, according to Cohen, tied to Buchanan's return to both "Crossfire" and "The Capitol Gang." He childishly hyperventilates that "Buchanan's a gay basher from way back and a bigot when it comes to Jews and blacks" without offering any substantive evidence. He weakly stresses that it is the fault of the Republicans that the candidates are not "Getting to the Issues," 4-16, as they have somehow managed to trick the voters into asking questions about Clinton's character. He's weaker still, musing on Clinton's lack of commitment to the liberal ideology, in "Political Muzak," 7-16. Cohen pins his hopes on Clinton's record, comparing the candidate's rhetoric so far to Muzak. He reprises this theme for the President-elect in "A Time to Be a Little Disagreeable," 11-6, in which he frets that Clinton will abandon liberalism to conform to the apparent will of the electorate on welfare. In "The Great Whiner," 9-10, Cohen whines that Bush whines. He offers little more than the standard pro-Israeli take that Bush wasn't supportive enough on loan guarantees and, predictably, he takes one last shot at Pat Buchanan. More restraint is shown in "Eye on Germany," 12-3, and the result is a carefully-crafted and well-reasoned argument in which Cohen places the political responsibility for neo-Nazi violence squarely on the shoulders of Chancellor Helmut Kohl.

Terry Eastland
The American Spectator
★★½

"Presswatch" columnist. With his sharp eye peeled for liberal bias, Eastland is one to watch for trenchant, conservative assessments of the media's performance. He provides an important service with "The Deep Six," 2-92, a list of '91 stories the press "underplayed, misplayed, curiously played, or [didn't] play at all." He includes re-regulation, race-norming, and evidence that acid rain, global warming, and dioxin may be less threatening than previously thought. Eastland offers an excellent reading of the press coverage of Justice Thomas's early work on the docket in "Doubting Thomas Again," 5-92. He captures legitimate nuances of Thomas's opinions, where the press seemed to be content merely to bash the newest justice and gloss over these important clues. In "Hill's Rats," 7-92, we join him for another visit to the Hill-Thomas case, with Eastland pointing out revealing details of the report by N.Y. lawyer Peter Fleming, Jr., who was asked by the Senate to find the source of the original Senate leak. His portraiture skills shine in a vivid "Rush Limbaugh: Talking Back," 9-92, with a succinct appraisal of this pundit's appeal: "What [Limbaugh] has done is fill a void created by the departure of Ronald Reagan, the last figure to speak unapologetically for American conservativism." He critiques effectively *Newsweek*'s lack of balance in its cover treatment of "Gays Under Fire," 9-14, in "*Newsweek* Acts Up," 11-92. Eastland rises above the conservative line to tell us where the magazine failed to accurately represent the issues at hand: "Throughout, the 'struggle for acceptance' was sanitized by *Newsweek*, with no mention of ACT-UP or Queer Nation or any other of the gay extremist groups." Eastland's trim, smart commentary also extends to the political. He echoes Pogo in "A Core of Convictions Needed," *The Washington Times* 2-21, as Eastland hits the primary trail: "Bush has met the enemy in New Hampshire and it is he."

Rowland Evans & Robert Novak
Creators Syndicate
★★★★

In 1986, we said that their brand of journalism was "based on relentless reporting, no sacred cows, access to everyone, intellectual honesty, integrity and fairness, steady travel outside the Beltway, a willingness to be ridiculed for unconventional attitudes and a determination to be the best." Seven years later, there is no reason to change that assessment. They have seen it all, compiling a record of scoops that any reporter would envy. The inside peek ahead of the curve is their specialty, and no one does it better. No one had as sturdy a handle on the party politics shaping the Democratic field as the duo did in their 10 Best selection "Clinton the Front-Runner," *WP* 1-3. The Bush camp's disarray is evident in the informative "White House Pandemonium," *WP* 7-24, in which the duo demonstrate how Bush refused to do anything about the economy. Insider information gives weight to their conclusion of the GOP homophobic view of gays in "Fear of the Homophobic Label," *WP* 12-4: "Instead of providing a reasoned alternative . . . Republicans are building themselves up for a furious and potentially bloody conflict over gay issues." But 1992 was most memorable for the duo's reporting on Israel and the subsequent column-by-column duel with *The New York Times*'s Abe Rosenthal. With the names, highly-placed sources and information presented in "Israel's New Ally," *WP* 3-16; "Whose Popeye Missile?" *WP* 3-25; and "Evans, Novak, Rosenthal and 'Pinocchio,'" *WP* 4-1, we come away persuaded that Israel may be courting China by supplying sensitive high technology.

Suzanne Fields
The Washington Times
Los Angeles Times Syndicate
★★★

As a former liberal turned conservative, Fields knows just where to find the Achilles heel in liberal social policy and theory. She also happens to be one of the mightiest warriors in the never-ending battle of the sexes. She turns the tables on Bill and Hillary Clinton by shrewdly observing in "Standing by His Wife," 3-19, that wives have always been targets on the campaign trail: "Hillary and Bill can't have it both ways. She can't come on as an independent professional woman and then hide behind her husband's outrage, real or theatrical." In a muscular critique of feminism, "Rebellion in the Sisterhood," 5-11, Fields socks it to NOW President Patricia Ireland for having a husband

and a female lover: "Criticism of Patricia Ireland is less homophobic than it is an acknowledgement of hypocrisy, less a single-issue condemnation than recognition of a double standard. If feminists attack adulterous men who make life miserable for their wives, how can they celebrate their leader who flaunts an affair? Is character an issue only for men?" She's astute on Madonna's book in "'Sex' and Blonde Ambition," 10-22: "'Sex' is actually the flip side of feminist puritanism, blatant indulgence of sexual desire without appeals to mystery, privacy, love or Eros." Fields doesn't articulate the premise of "A Lead for Ms. to Follow," 8-3, until the close, where we find D.C. Mayor Sharon Pratt Kelly as a feminist model for standing up to a crass Jack Kent Cooke. Her best for the year, "Birds, Bees and a Freeze," 9-17, is a bittersweet discussion of how the Politically Correct police are drawing the lines so severely that kids can't socialize. She asserts that "pocketbook issues drove the election for both men and women," but fails to relate it to her discussion of family values in "Romancing Realities," 11-5.

Thomas Fleming
Chronicles
★★

Editor. Although he is an intellectual paleocon, Fleming's work is difficult to categorize. As a rule, he thoughtfully discusses, in polished prose, themes and subjects out of the mainstream. Occasionally, though, he slips into a mechanical mode that doesn't suit him. Fleming fears the death of our civilization because of the way we conduct democracy in "Flies Trapped in Honey," 1-92. But we come away unconvinced by his sonorous lines: "The great success of American democracy is its ability to satisfy the most basic instincts of the human race while at the same time virtually eliminating its high qualities." He makes breathless, but irrelevant observations about both presidential candidates in "Leveraged Buyout," 6-92, pompously describing Clinton thusly: "'Governor Elvis,' as he is sometimes known in his home state, is too cute for words, the Peter Jennings of politics, an Al Gore with the common touch, a male model who knows how to flirt and leer at the audiences that even he must despise for their gullibility." "Voting Behind the Veil of Ignorance," 11-92, is an informative, obtusely civic-minded explanation of how we vote, with fascinating histories of the Electoral College and the Constitution. Fleming positions himself to the right in his superlative discussion of the culture and the penal system, "Law and/or Order," 5-92, persuading us that "in a very real sense we can define the qualities of a culture in terms of its punishments." Two essays examine the links between literature and politics, morality and behavior. "I Love to Tell the Story," 8-92, and "Literature and the Curriculum," 9-92, exemplify the type of esoteric philosophizing at which Fleming excels. He also makes astute observations on "Marriage—the Real Right to Privacy," 3-92, analyzing the institution from civil and religious perspectives: "In reconsidering marriage and divorce, our main objective as serious men and women, must be to teach ourselves, our children, and our friends, that these things are up to us, not government to decide."

Frank Gaffney
The Washington Times
★

The director of the Center for Security Policy and a former Reaganaut, Gaffney ably serves up the mechanics of policymaking. But when he attempts various "big think" efforts, he fails to reveal an appreciation of the intricacies of geopolitics. He delved into the latter quite often this year, with very limited success. In "Slow to Stand by Yeltsin's Efforts," 2-11, Gaffney offers a run-of-the-mill assessment of what the Bush administration ought to do to help Russia, complete with debt relief and forgiveness. He reprises this theme in "Aid to Russia: Is it Doable..." 3-17, and "Shortfall in the Aid Package," 4-6. But, even after three op-eds, we're still skeptical. Calling for a boycott of events honoring Gorbachev during his U.S. visit in "Gorbachev on the Comeback Circuit?" 5-6, Gaffney effectively outlines his case as to why the former Soviet leader doesn't deserve the effusive praise he receives. He caves in to conspiracy theories, though, when he asserts that Gorbachev is trying to stage a comeback. As the election draws near, Gaffney attempts to examine events in "Referendum for a Baker Regency?" 10-20, blaming the former Secretary of State for many international crises. But Gaffney mostly seems annoyed that "there has been no perceptible improvement in the president's standing" since Baker took over, and then goes on—coincidentally—to excoriate Baker on his record. He's stronger on more technical issues. In "Clouded Vision That Lingers Over the V-22," 7-8, Gaffney makes a good case for the V-22, the Osprey plane that takes off and lands like a helicopter and flies like a conventional aircraft, telling us the story of how the Bush administration mishandled the project's funding. With "A Big Hole in That Chemical Weapons Treaty," *WP* 9-8, Gaffney effectively refutes the *Post* editorial, "A Ban on Chemical Weapons," 8-26, poking holes in its assertions and offering his own persuasive evidence and assessment of the treaty's worth. His views are cogent in "High-Tech Transfer Trepidation," 12-2, as he outlines the dangers for President-elect Clinton of a burgeoning arms market.

Leslie H. Gelb
The New York Times
★

Although he has improved marginally after last year's abysmal performance, Gelb has yet to make his column required reading. He remains steadfastly mediocre as the *Times*'s "Foreign Affairs" columnist, rarely providing fresh information and frequently dispensing dubious analysis. His grasp of economic issues is painfully weak. He strains in drawing parallels between the elections of "1932 and 1992," 2-7, but manages to capture the country's current mood of uncertainty. In "Love Lombard Rates," 9-20, Gelb writes aggressively about Maastricht to conceal the fact he hasn't the slightest idea what is going on. He thinks it has to do with governments "running out of money." We get a lukewarm interview with a dynamic President in "Mexico's Economist Kings," 10-4, in which Gelb tells us Carlos Salinas is "bald on top." This column is barely salvaged when Gelb actually *comes to a conclusion*, albeit unoriginal, that Salinas is inching Mexico forward. After Gelb's close friendship with Clinton's foreign policy expert, Anthony Lake, was revealed by the *National Journal*, 5-9, we hoped Gelb might provide a glimpse into Clinton's world. With "A Mere 141 Words," 7-19, he fills an analytic vacuum by zeroing in on the near-total avoidance of foreign affairs by Clinton. Gelb warns that, despite the preoccupation with domestic issues, foreign policy will likely play a role in decision '92. He further defines potential Clinton foreign policy in "Get Cracking on Bosnia," 12-3, a well-reasoned essay outlining paths the Clinton and Bush might take during the transition. He paints a clear picture of the no-growth crowd behind the go-go campaign rhetoric by making predictions on "The Clinton Cabinet?" 8-30, a valuable column. Gelb further outlines this strategizing in "Who Gets What Jobs," 11-5, a useful effort that is hampered by an inane close: "May the force be with these two young knights [Clinton and Gore] of bright countenance on their journey."

David Gergen
U.S. News & World Report
★½

Gergen has moved to the front rank of political commentary on television, an important regular on "Mac-Neil/Lehrer NewsHour." But his writing, lacking spontaneity and imagination, remains second class. Gergen doesn't seriously examine the media's coverage of economic issues in "Is the Press to Blame?" 1-13, instead chooses to paraphrase the sociobabble of Richard Curtin, a consumer research director at the University of Michigan, who "suggests that the economy and media coverage of it reinforce one another." In "The Song of Tsongas," 2-24, Gergen bravely begs the press to consider Tsongas "a man of serious purpose, large vision and sparkling humor, challenging both parties to change course." Gergen doesn't quite tell us why he feels this way though, except for a vague appreciative outline of Tsongas's "Economic Call to Arms." He doesn't ask any tough questions of Lester Thurow in "Winning the World's Biggest Race," 4-6, a semi-review of Thurow's *Head to Head*. His lack of critical appraisal here short-circuits his assessment. He relates, again uncritically, the thoughts of "Nixon on the Final Chapter," 6-29, paying as much homage to RMN as to current players on the world political stage. Gergen waxes poetic on Clinton's election in "The People Have Great Expectations," 11-16, but concentrates on style rather than substance. On the other hand, he asks the right questions in "Ross Perot as Nation's Man on Horseback," *Los Angeles Times* 3-29, a smart evaluation of Perot's *potential*: "Can an outsider overhaul Washington? That's the toughest question of all because no outsider has ever tried and the problems here seem intractable. Jimmy Carter came as close as anyone to being an outsider—and no one has forgotten what happened." Gergen uses historical analogy in "Economy May Be Clinton's Vietnam," *LAT* 10-25, to smartly evaluate the "awful choices" Clinton will face on the economy.

Jack W. Germond & Jules Witcover
National Journal
★★

Like Evans & Novak, Germond & Witcover have been around for the last quarter-century, and are reliable handicappers of presidential races. Their sturdy appraisals are most useful during the primaries, but their overall body of work this election year lacks the incisive analysis of the other team. In an early assessment of why "Clinton Needs More Than an Early Win," 2-8, they aren't quite clear in analyzing the N.H. primary from the Democratic side. The team gives us useful comparisons between Clinton and Dukakis in "For Clinton, It's Time to Seize the Day," 4-25, including astute observations on Clinton and his turning the primaries into a "de facto first quarter of the general election campaign." We get a solid roundup of Clinton's prospects in the Golden State with "Are California's Voters Listening?" 5-23, a shrewd assessment of the difficulties Clinton is having in the wake of both the L.A. riots and Ross Perot. We appreciate their historic use of GOP campaigns, specifically Ford's '76 campaign, to illustrate the disarray in the Bush Camp after Mary Matalin's infamous memo on Clinton, in "Going Negative Can Be Risky Business," 8-8. What begins as a trim assessment of Bush's sudden retirement, "Life After Political Death for Bush," 11-14, fizzles as the duo begins to snipe at the retirement activities of other former presidents. They offer a smart, tough assessment of what Jim Baker brings to the campaign in "Baker to the Rescue: Is it Enough?" 7-25: "Baker's greatest value to the Bush campaign probably lies, however, simply in his relationship with the President. He is an old friend, a contemporary and a peer, not just a hired hand—suggesting that he might be able to persuade Bush to follow advice the President might resist if it came from others."

Georgie Anne Geyer
Universal Press Syndicate
★★

Either Geyer has the highest number of frequent flier miles of any working journalist or enormous phone bills, as she reports from everywhere on everything. She's a superlative reporter, providing important information on far-flung places, but she sometimes spreads herself too thin, ultimately productive but not always profound. "Salvador: Now the Crucifixion Is at an End," *The Washington Times* 1-6, is Geyer's overview of war and peace in El Salvador. Throughout the essay we feel her sorrow that peace did not come sooner and that it was bought at such a cost of lives and years. She's hopeful, though, that it will last, and builds a semi-convincing case that it just might. Intuitive in "Astray in a New World," *WT* 4-20, she outlines poetically how, in addition to the fight for military superiority and sovereignty, the Cold War was also about ideals, and as Geyer puts it, "men's souls." We find "The Hollow State: Venezuela's Democracy," *WT* 5-11, to be an excellent survey in which she defines the further problems of the government's experiment with a centrally-controlled democracy, but Geyer stops just short of suggesting proposals to move the country along further. On the homefront, we can't quite discern her ultimate point about the use of the legal system by feminists, in "The Very Public Face of Today's Feminist," *WT* 3-7, although her uncomplicated description of feminism is quite interesting: "women should be considered equals to men, whether they chose to stay at home and raise children, work in public service or (horrors, then!) actually work for money." From Tunisia, Geyer provides a quick snapshot of the foreign view of the U.S. election with "Looking Our Way From Afar," *WT* 11-7, arguing in passing that Clinton cannot possibly be only a domestic President. But this essay is nowhere near as comprehensive or in-depth as Jim Hoagland's treatment of the same theme the following day.

Paul Gigot
The Wall Street Journal
★★★½

The neoconservative Gigot's "Potomac Watch" column unquestionably is the first thing we read in the paper each Friday morning. He culls the most important economic and political information of the week from within the administration, drawing from an ever-widening network of key sources that no doubt emanate from his years at the Reagan Treasury. With "The Candidates' 'Middle Class' Confidence Game," 1-17, Gigot exposes the fallacy in the Bill Clinton-Robert Shapiro tax plan and finds that the fine print reveals that in reality top tax rates would simply be moved around with no real benefit to the middle class. His appraisal of Hillary Clinton, "Who's That Guy on the Ticket With Hillary?" 3-13, sparked the ongoing debate over her role. The muscular commentary revealed—some argued distorted—her strong liberal views on such issues as children's rights. Evenhanded in his powerful economic policy critique, "Bush and Clinton Vie for Economic Booby Prize," 6-26, he cuts to the heart of the problem of each candidate's announced economic program: "Mr. Bush seems to have settled on Nixonian Federal Reserve-bashing, circa 1971–72. Mr. Clinton is wandering in Mr. Carter's Neighborhood, circa 1978–79." Gigot echoes George Will in "One Term Is Enough," 8-3, crafting a strong case from a loyal conservative that Bush should step down from the ticket. With rumors of despair flying, Gigot offers "Quayle Fights, But Baker Goes AWOL," 10-16, an important political snapshot of how Jim Baker, Bush's right-hand man, seems to have given up in the campaign's closing moments. He expertly reveals the importance of the Federal Reserve to Clinton in "Clinton Will Find 'Angells' of Mercy at the Fed," 11-27, a 10 Best selection. Gigot rounds up the collective wisdom of foreign-affairs analysts to pen "Peace in Somalia May Require a New Colonialism," 12-4, an excellent review of the situation.

Ellen Goodman
The Boston Globe
Washington Post Writers Group
★★

Although often predictable, Goodman is always entertaining. This liberal commentator is most poignant when reflecting on the most emotional of social issues, such as abortion. For example, in "Away From Absolutism," *The Washington Post* 1-25, Goodman artfully captures the desire of many to finally put this divisive issue behind us: "Those of us who defend the right to choose do not comfortably endorse abortion as a first choice." Goodman finds a pro-lifer she respects in "One Man Who's Pro-Life and Pro-Choices," *Los Angeles Times* 9-18, a pithy profile of Jasper Wyman, head of the Christian Civic League in Augusta, Maine. She highlights Wyman's ideas lucidly. The best course, he says, "is [to] persuade women and men by offering better choices." With "The Right to Motherhood Is Limited by Affordability," *LAT* 4-17, Goodman aptly categorizes the basic incongruity of the current debate over welfare: "Working Americans do some cost-accounting as part of their family planning. Why not those on AFDC? On the other hand, we are properly queasy about punishing children for the behavior of their parents." Goodman intuitively and effectively links the sinking economy to the fraying social fabric after Bush's State of the Union address, in "Good Night, George-Boy," *WP* 2-1: "There is an intricate and daily interaction between losing your job and losing your self-respect, losing your mortgage and your temper and your marriage—ask anyone who has been sucked into this black hole." But her "So Far, the Campaign Buffet Barely Whets Appetites," *LAT* 6-12, is muddled on the candidates and their leadership qualities. And in "The Personal Really Has Become Political in '92," *LAT* 11-1, her strong windup celebrating a "bumper crop" of politically aware voters is hampered by her mushy discourse on how we got to this point in politics.

Paul Greenberg
Arkansas Democrat Gazette
Los Angeles Times Syndicate
★★

Editorial page editor. As a long-time resident and writer from Clinton's home state, Greenberg's observations on his governor carry added weight. What we saw from him was quite valuable. He exposes Clinton's "Gaps on the Home Front," *The Washington Times* 1-4, "Folks here in Arkansas will recognize the familiar Clinton Sidestep at work," then proceeds to list all the examples of the 'Sidestep' from New Hampshire and the early primary process. Similarly, in "Whiffs After the Clarifications," *WT* 4-4, he reveals Clinton's slips and flip-flops to date, but the candidate's policies aren't attacked here. He reprises these themes quite effectively in "Just Another Two-Day Clinton Story?" *WT* 9-5, providing a credible outline of the governor's pattern of denial and realignment: "Forget all that stuff about honor, truth, duty. They'll be replaced by Political Viability—Bill Clinton's phrase and I'm afraid, his essence. In the '90s, it won't matter what you do, or say, or believe. Only if you can explain it." In "Bracing for the Clintonized Culture," *WT* 8-3, Greenberg only addresses surface issues of the styles of Clinton, Kennedy and Bush, rather than their policies or politics. Greenberg gives a first-hand account of "A Very Big Night in Little Rock," *WT* 11-6, poetically written on Clinton's triumph on election night. But he doesn't tell us how he feels about his governor's ascension to the presidency. Greenberg toughly reveals the "Buildup on Ethics," *WT* 12-3, giving us the skinny on the "small print, the escape clauses, the explanations, [and] the slick underside" of Clinton's new code of ethics. On other issues we found Greenberg's brand of folksy conservatism refreshing but not always persuasive. With "No Pause in Talks," *WT* 2-29, he seems to inherently feel that the Middle East is inching towards peace, but doesn't fully explain why or how.

Meg Greenfield
Newsweek
The Washington Post
★★★

More intuitive and thoughtful this year, Greenfield's common-sense perspectives are finely crafted and tuned. She seems to be developing a directness that makes her work more accessible, without sacrificing any of her insights. "A New Year's Resolution," 1-6, is Greenfield's stunningly eloquent attempt to challenge the assumption that governments inherently stand for the people governed. This "slovenly mental habit contributed mightily to our slowness to perceive and credit what was going on in Eastern Europe and the Soviet Union." Greenfield pointedly jabs her fellows: "we read their press releases and believe we have seen the truth." She reprises a similar theme in "A Year of Surprises," 11-9, vigorously taking the media to task for not contemplating or analyzing events in the political realm effectively. Similarly, she clearly defines the symbiotic relationships between politicians, the voters and the press in "The Climate, Stupid," 12-7. An excellent contrast of the campaigns of today and yesteryear is offered in "Bam. Crash. Kersplat." 3-2: " . . . there is a true distinction to be made between candidates who fight for a cause and those who seek to inflict damage or pain for an advantage." She is equally tough on those politicians who expressed surprise at the L.A. riots, particularly Bush, in "The Great Scott Syndrome," 5-25: "What I cannot accept is that a man in the seventh decade of his life and the second decade of his time in the uppermost reaches of the national political system . . . looks at the state of American cities in the May of 1992 and says, in effect, 'Why, I had no idea,' or even 'Gee, we've got to do something about this.'" She then pens an even more in-depth review of "Bush's Problem," 8-3, a sharp roundup graced with style and substance. Off her feed with "Clinton's Danger Zone," 7-6, she posits that the convention and the transition from nominee to candidate is Clinton's true testing time. Unfortunately, there's nothing particularly groundbreaking here.

Richard Grenier
The Washington Times
★★★

The Marxist (that's Harpo, not Karl) Grenier is one of a new breed of cultural police. Not to be confused with the politically correct, he keeps watch on the National Endowment for the Arts and other artistic matters. His exceptional wit and authoritative commentary sting on both cultural and political fronts, and, in particular, where the two meet. In "Thinking Man's Attack Turtle?" 2-11, Grenier skewers the PBS-BBC series by Britain's Michael Wood, targeting the final episode, "Western Barbarians," in which Wood postulates that we're possessed by a "deep strain of violence" compared to the rest of the world. He has John Frohnmayer as a candidate for the looney bin after his whiny speech to the National Press Club in "Shrieking All the Way to the Departure Gate," 4-1. This is Grenier at his best, cutting the former head of the NEA to pieces, slowly but surely, and side-splittingly. In a follow-up, Grenier gives us a damaging critique of the NEA in "The Ecstasies of John Frohnmayer," *National Review* 8-3, as he posits that its problems are due to class as much as artistic considerations. He is hilarious on television environmentalism and other fashions in "Green in the Slob Mode," 9-17, as the Hollywood elite proclaim, "We're planetary thinkers out here! We're laboring day and night to save the planet! For the common man! Well, first we take lunch at the Polo Lounge. Then we save the planet for the common man." On a more serious note, Grenier's words are obviously heartfelt in "Honor for Heroes," 5-6, as he awards laurels to Greg Williams and other L.A. residents who came to the aid of people being beaten by rioters, and gives a Bronx cheer to various leaders such as Rep. Maxine Waters (D-CA), who "is making things worse" with her inflammatory rhetoric. He's pointed on democracy in lampooning the bureaucracy of voter registration in "Voter Turnout Handwringing," 11-4.

Nat Hentoff
The Village Voice
The Washington Post
★★½

"Sweet Land of Liberty" columnist at the *Post*. Now that *The Wall Street Journal's* L. Gordon Crovitz is in the Far East, the clever Hentoff is the legal columnist of record. We particularly appreciate his missionary-like dedication to the preservation and strict interpretation of the First Amendment. In "Squeeze on the First Amendment," *WP* 1-6, he intuitively defines the issues and the players in the fight over "hate speech" that is coming before the Supreme Court. His follow-up, "Looking Beyond a Burning Cross," *WP* 2-1, clarifies the ramifications of laws against "hate speech" with his usual finesse. As the question of abortion looms on the Supreme Court docket, Hentoff offers a set of *Village Voice* essays that take us through many of the forgotten legal points of the *Roe v. Wade* decision and the implications of future rulings. "The Perilous Journey of *Roe v. Wade*," *VV* 4-21, is a useful sketch of the legal history of the decision, and "The Freedom to Kill Act," *VV* 4-28, critiques the Freedom of Choice Act, concluding it is a scam because of its language. "Simple Justice—And How it Got Lost," *VV* 11-10, is a sophisticated discussion of integration, which Hentoff frames by journeying into the mind of Dr. Kenneth Clark, a figure from the original decision of *Brown v. Board of Education*. Uncharacteristic in "An

Ad That Offends," *The Progressive* 5-92, he fails to take a firm stand on Bradley Smith's advertisement in college papers alleging the Holocaust never took place. With "Not the Right Man for a Court of Last Resort," *WP* 8-29, Hentoff only presents circumstantial evidence against the confirmation of Ed Carnes to the 11th Circuit Court of Appeals. It's the same with "Thurgood Marshall Destroyed With Praise," *VV* 12-8, a not-quite-conclusive essay on how the Supreme Court justices venerate the former justice while dismantling his decisions on the docket.

Christopher Hitchens
The Nation
★

"Minority Report" columnist. The maniacal Hitchens is often rabid and sloppy in both his reporting and his evaluations. Although his columns shine with British spit-and-polish prose, we never know if we're in for a measure of substance or a bombardment of bombast. After covering the re-election of Syrian President Hafez al-Assad, what Hitchens finds is refreshingly pragmatic: "Co-religionists have made a wager in which Assad is, for the moment, the best imaginable leader of Syria. . . . But has a one-man regime that creates anxiety about its successor really brought stability?" He is relentless in trying to convince us of Clinton's opportunism in applying the death penalty in an Arkansas case, in "Minority Report," 3-2, smartly reviewing the sentence of Rickey Ray Rector who "had blown half his brain away after committing murder. . . . He was, by most standards, unfit to plead. . . . In no other 'civilized' country . . . could he have been condemned to death in the first place." His "Minority Report," 5-11, is a solid exposition of the U.K.'s Labor party loss. Like the Democrats, he says, they try to be all things to all people. Hitchens compares the situation in Bosnia to events in WWII with "Appointment in Sarajevo," 9-14, drawing parallels to "a Versailles mentality." His post-election overview, "Minority Report," 11-30, is haphazard, flitting from one thing to another. A "Minority Report," 2-3, rants and raves on the Kennedy assassination, outdoing even Oliver Stone: " . . . the fact that Kennedy was a howling little shit doesn't prove that there wasn't a plot to do him in." Hitchens endorses Jerry Brown, in "Minority Report," 4-13, but rather than telling us what he likes about the candidate, he goes ballistic on what he doesn't like, in particular Brown's association with Mother Teresa, who he calls a "dangerous, sinister person" who "prostituted herself for the worst of neocolonialism and the worst of communism."

Jim Hoagland
The Washington Post
★★★½

Hoagland has settled in nicely to the role of pundit and is far more preferable as a foreign affairs columnist than Leslie Gelb at *The New York Times*, probably his closest competitor. Maturing gracefully with ever-more refined prose and perspicuity, he's beginning to focus his estimable talents on the U.S. political scene. "Definitely Not Dukakis," 8-11, is a sharp evaluation of how Clinton is no Dukakis and how this is to his advantage. He offers an excellent appraisal of "Bush's Angry Constituency," 9-14, with a remarkably astute assessment of Bush following his Detroit Economic Club speech: "He is a conservative, status quo politician caught in a time of radical economic change." He fuses domestic and international politics in "The World: Range of Issues Expected to Pose Early Challenges," 11-8, a lucid and expansive overview of the world, what areas might mean trouble for the new President and what courses he might pursue. We get another useful overseas perspective earlier in "Dumbest American Export: Economic Advice," 4-30, penned after the Germans told Treasury's David Mulford to mind his own beeswax: "The Germans and others were telling Mulford last week that an American government cannot pretend to lead abroad if it does not show leadership at home." With "A Trip to Sarajevo," 6-30, it's praise all the way for French President Mitterrand's Sarajevo trip. Hoagland positions the journey as valuable if only to force "Europe to confront the divisions" causing the situation. He also gets an early bead on the administration's position here: "...the statements emitted by his spokeswoman, Margaret Tutwiler, suggest they see Yugoslavia more as a public relations problem to be managed rather than a threat to international peace to be resolved." Pertinent questions are also raised "On Somalia, a Mysterious Decision," 12-3. While conceding the need for action, he asks where the crisis fits into the larger, global context.

Molly Ivins
Fort Worth Star-Telegram
Creators Syndicate
★★½

Irreverent, sassy and smart, Ivins's columns are much the same as her personality. Her latest book is entitled *She Can't Say That Can She?* and we find ourselves asking the same question when reading her material. She can and she does, to the great benefit and amusement of her readers. Ivins turns her priceless wit to "Being an 'Arthur,'" *Mother Jones* 1/2-92, offering her own and others' stories from the book promotional front: "Myra MacPherson, author of *The Long Time Passing*, finally lost it upon arriving for some television show and finding the airhead hostess busy spraying her hair. 'I'll bet you haven't even read the dust jacket,' snarled MacPherson. 'What's a dust jacket?' inquired the airhead." Her quick, clever humor pulls us through the sad stories of the unemployment line in "Looking for Work," *The Progressive* 2-92, as Ivins joins the queue after the closing of her newspaper, *Dallas Times Herald*. She follows up with an eloquent obituary for the daily paper in "Deep in the Heart," *MJ* 3/4-92. "Read My Lipstick," *MJ* 5/6-92, is an excellent framing of the term 'populist,' in which Ivins argues skillfully that what passes for populism today isn't. She follows up with "Bubba's Billionaire," *MJ* 7/8-92, and endorses the idea of at least taking a look at the maverick, self-styled populist Ross Perot. Her snappy review of the Democratic National Convention, "Of Conventional Wisdom and Bliss," *TP* 9-92, ends with a revealing anecdote about how Clinton failed to appear at a reunion party for McGovern's '72 staff: "Of course, it would have been impolitic for Clinton, the moderate, to be publicly associated with old lefty McGovern. On the other hand, it was just the sort of thing that incurably decent and kind man, George McGovern, would have done had the roles been reversed." She provides the last word on the inanity of the campaign season in "Who Am I? What Am I Doing Here?" *TP* 12-92, using the title as a refrain throughout her recounting of events involving Dan Quayle's spelling and Gennifer Flowers improprieties.

John B. Judis
In These Times
★½

Washington correspondent. Judis's analytics and reporting seem less intellectually stimulating on the politics of the left. We're used to him consistently presenting a startling angle or some new tidbit of information; this year, such contributions are sporadic. He pans the American pavilion at the Seville '92 Exposition in "Show and Tell," *The New Republic* 1-20, saying the U.S. didn't spend enough money or pick the nicest design. In his lackluster "Forget About the American Century..." *The New York Times* 8-20, Judis argues lamely that the GOP isn't facing reality in positing that the best for America is yet to come because our difficulties require real problem-solving skills. He is sharper on very specific issues, as in "Statecraft and Scowcroft," *TNR* 2-24, which offers a detailed historical perspective on how the National Security Council's Brent Scowcroft has conducted foreign policy as a proponent of "realism" learned under Henry Kissinger. He reveals how Scowcroft is now stuck in his own model. Giving us a good sense of the economic views of "The Executive," *TNR* 6-15, he interviews Ross Perot. This useful clarification illustrates that Perot does have ideas. With "Clinton and the Lobbyists: Who is Paying the Bill?" 3-11/17, Judis raises pertinent questions, about the link between Clinton's fundraisers and what Judis feels are Clinton's flexible views. Similarly, "Clinton's Changing Bill of Health," 10/28–11/10, is a politically savvy evaluation of Clinton's smorgasbord on health care, ranging from play-or-pay proposals to managed care. "Administration Surrenders in the 'War on Poverty,'" 5-13/19, is a trenchant indictment of the Bush administration for failing to address the inner city problems until after the L.A. riots. He rages that there has never been a dialogue in the White House on the subject and, furthermore, "... once the smoke clears from Los Angeles, Bush will probably once again ignore these initiatives."

James J. Kilpatrick
Universal Press Syndicate
★

We now most often find Kilpo in *Human Events*, the conservative bastion of Capitol Hill, but there's evidence that his influence is waning as *The Washington Post* only infrequently runs his material. Even after 40 years of commentary, Kilpo still can come up with a fresh appraisal, a unique insight, a pointed one-liner, but now, they are less frequent. He gives a strong indictment of Congress for its inability to cut or even reevaluate favorite programs in "Congress That Can't Say No," *HE* 2-29, and offers a memorable, musical appraisal of the intractability of the problem: "Like Ol' Man River, [the programs] just keep rolling along." He sturdily defends the newest justice in "Justice Thomas Settling in Well at Supreme Court," *HE* 3-28, correctly and strenuously arguing that the debate over the docket is as important as the court's decisions.

With "Medals for a Few Old Sailors," *WP* 5-25, Kilpatrick gently salutes the heroic merchant marines of WWII, as they finally get their commendations, a moving, heartfelt tribute. He's feisty in critiquing the media and convention coverage in "He Can Win—Despite the Media Dirge," *WP* 8-23: "Instead of reporting the facts... the big media are feeding us facts as interpreted and analyzed by quasi-reporters who hunger for the pundit's role." But in the final lines, he goes overboard: "I want to see Dan Rather cry." He's adamant in "An Unconstitutional Abortion-on-Demand Bill," *HE* 9-12, calling the bill "Horsefeathers," though his argument is not as sophisticated as Nat Hentoff's treatise on the Freedom of Choice Act. The People for the American Way's cry for schoolbook censorship is in "PAW Report Cries 'Wolf,'" *HE* 11-14, when, really, the removal of books covering sexual or adult issues to higher grades is merely the exercise of parent-teacher democracy.

Michael Kinsley
The New Republic
United Features Syndicate
★★

Kinsley is one of the few journalists to consistently produce at least one column that changes the face of the American political debate each year. In '92, that column was his 10 Best selection, "Taxonomy," 8-31, a fine bit of reporting in which Kinsley reveals that the Republicans are having a hard time deciding precisely how many times Clinton raised taxes. Overall, though, Kinsley did not deliver the impeccable logic and reportage we've come to expect under his byline. Maybe he's too busy playing the pundit with John Sununu on "Crossfire" to pay much attention to his writing. More and more we find his commentary tends to echo rather than preordain the Beltway's liberal conventional wisdom. We thought Kinsley was taking a serious look at the controversial capital-gains tax cut proposal in "A Capital Gains Primer," 2-10, but it is really just another preprogrammed attempt to dismiss the issue: "Ideally, all taxes should be zero because all taxes discourage the activity being taxed." In "Oh, Grow Up," 4-6, Kinsley mildly critiques coverage of the House bank scandal, arguing that, as scandals go, it isn't really a big deal. "Ask a Silly Question," 7-6, is a more pungent contrast of journalists' versus voters' questions on call-in shows. It's clear, though, that Kinsley is wedded to the status quo: "...I do not subscribe to today's fashionable pseudo-populism, which holds that all wisdom lies with ordinary citizens, who are rightly outraged at all those out-of-touch, inside-the-Beltway cultural elitists..." We don't find out what Kinsley thinks in "Revisionist History," 10-5, as he relies too heavily on Michael Duffy and Dan Goodgame's *Marching in Place* in his assertion that Bush's comment about being forced into the budget deal is false. His *schadenfreude* poisons "Vindication," 11-23, but he does make one valuable observation: "The only debate will be over whether [Bush's] failure reflected the culmination of Reaganism or the betrayal of it."

Jeane Kirkpatrick
Los Angeles Times Syndicate
★½

Kirkpatrick still can't quite transmit all her widely-celebrated intellectual firepower to her column. Despite many years on the Beltway "expert" circuit, the former UN ambassador is only occasionally insightful. With "Germany's Independent Course," *The Washington Post* 1-13, she almost convinces us of the wisdom of Germany's recognition of Croatia as an independent state. Kirkpatrick carefully defines her theory that this is as much a political conflict as a nationalistic one. In "Sustainable Development for Whom?" *Los Angeles Times* 4-27, she pokes holes in the UN draft declaration for the Rio Summit, but offers no course to Bush other than to reject or support it, which seems obvious. Her critique of the document itself stings: "[It] reaffirms key elements of Third World ideology that has dominated 'North/South' negotiations for two decades. Its key concept is 'sustainable development,' which links a particular environmental doctrine to familiar schemes for redistribution of the world's wealth."

We see with "Europe Unites as Patriotism Is Redefined," *LAT* 5-26, that Kirkpatrick is enamored with a united Europe, overlooking the obstacles and glossing over the debates in this superficial assessment. In "The Failure Is in the Pursuit, Not the Goal," *LAT* 8-3, she points out glibly that the U.S. has failed to achieve world stability because it has not used the UN properly. Her advice is colored by a Cold Warrior view in "Open Letter to Bill Clinton: It's a Big World Out There," *New York Post* 11-9, but, nonetheless, it's worth considering: "...never forget that foreign policy is much more important to your political future than it appeared in this election...Make any significant misjudgment, and you will find out that foreign policy is only unimportant when there are no problems."

Morton Kondracke
Roll Call
United Media Syndicate
★★½

Senior editor. Kondracke moves to *Roll Call* from *The New Republic* and sends his column into syndication. But he remains best known as John McLaughlin's foil, "Mor-TON," on TV's "McLaughlin Group." He manages to balance television and print fairly well, probably because he does only a few tapings a week, as opposed to journalists who do five or six. His analyses are trim and his reporting informative. He is dogged in turning up examples of the dubious conduct of Sen. Bob Kerrey in "Careless Kerrey," *The New Republic* 1-20, going back to the candidate's alleged pocketing of $380 in profits from ads run by the student council in college. With "Greaseman," *TNR* 4-6, he finds that "close examination of Clinton statements before and during this campaign, and interviews with him and his advisers, suggest that Clinton has policy beliefs and priorities." Unfortunately, he gives us no sense of Clinton's long-term commitment to the ideas outlined here. Even Kondracke doesn't sound convinced by his own argument for the Clinton job training proposals in "Apprentices' Sorcerer," *TNR* 7-27. On the other hand, "None But Baker for the Job?" *The Washington Times* 8-3, is a trenchant assessment of George Bush's weaknesses, encapsulated in JBIII's having to take over the campaign: "Democrats are already accusing Mr. Bush of putting politics ahead of foreign policy by asking Mr. Baker to switch jobs, but Mr. Baker's triple role points up an even graver weakness in Mr. Bush's government: the paucity of talent he can call upon to do vital work." In "Missing the Mark on Values," *WT* 9-8, Kondracke talks common sense on the perversity of making family values a partisan issue. As did many others, he gave advice to the President-elect in "How Long Will the Mortar Hold? View From the Lawn," *WT* 11-7, but there was nothing startling here.

Michael Kramer
Time
★

"The Political Interest" columnist. Kramer is still trying to find his footing as a columnist. Maybe someone at *Time* told him column-writing is all punditry, because he still only shows the barest evidence of reporting to support the facile conclusions he often presents. Even so, Kramer marginally improved this year. We do find occasional evidence of legwork, but he's going to have to work much harder before fulfilling the promise he showed at *New York* several years ago. He doesn't tell us "Why Clinton Is Catching On," 1-20, except to list what's wrong with the other candidates. His sarcastic tone works against his premise that negative campaigning by the Bush campaign won't be condoned but will be conducted, in "It's Not Going to Be Pretty," 4-20. Kramer's simultaneous condemnation of Perot's drug sweep proposal and endorsement of Vince Lane's working drug sweep program in Chicago seems contradictory at best in "Perot's Smart Idea," 7-6. Apparently it's the way Perot presents his program that irks Kramer. He makes rather good suggestions to help keep crime and urban distress down in "What Can Be Done?" 5-11, providing viable suggestions, such as recruiting more cops from the demobilized armed forces. "Amateurs, But Playing Like Pros," 8-10, is a trim election update on how each side is positioning itself as the lesser of two evils. There's little that irritates us more than a columnist who tells us "Don't Waste Your Vote," 11-2, and Kramer, negative and supercilious, argues here against a protest vote for Perot.

Charles Krauthammer
Washington Post Writers Group
★★½

It was an erratic year for the brainy Krauthammer, a real disappointment after an exceptional 1991. While his writing style continues to engage, his delicious prose can't hide the dearth of truly provocative ideas in his columns. For example, he tries to equate efficiency with inanity after a trip to Disney World in "The Mouse That Roared Banality," *Los Angeles Times* 1-26, a strange essay in which he notes: "...one does tend to go a little insane at all the forced cheer. I had the momentary feeling of having wandered into a Chinese re-education camp where everyone, the guards included, was on Thorazine." In another silly, superficial column, "Little Lessons of the Campaign," *The Washington Post* 10-23, he argues as if Perot's campaign is based solely on his wealth and the will to promote mandated free advertising on radio and TV. On the other hand, Krauthammer's understated tone works in "The Pornography of Self-Revelation," *Time* 8-10, but he is still too judgmental on what he perceives to be the use of family tragedy for political gain as evinced during Bill Clinton and Al Gore's convention speeches: "This is not to say the feelings conjured up by Gore and Clinton were invented.... The cynicism lies not in counterfeiting a feeling but in packaging a genuine feeling into a neat anecdote contoured for political effect." Krauthammer is most effective in "Bush's Spent Presidency," *WP* 3-6, freezing Bush forever in our minds as having "a presidency, like Gerald Ford's, with a limited agenda that, when completed, lost its reason for being." He makes a smart delineation between the politics of abortion and fetal tissue research in "Hostage to Abortion Politics," *WP* 5-22: "Can you think of one person who would be influenced to have an abortion because of the research value of the tissue?" We also get an exceptional appraisal of the current politics of abortion in "Abortion: the Debate Is Over," 12-4, arguing vigorously here that an equilibrium has been reached after the Guam decision.

Irving Kristol
The Wall Street Journal
★★★

Kristol's ideas often quickly evolve into policy proposals, so respected is his sagacity on social issues. A shameless promoter of "family values," Kristol offers wise perspectives on tough questions. We may not always agree with him, but his erudite contemplations are always worth consideration. "Reflections on Love and Family," 1-7, is a perfect example, full of smart and witty observations on love, sex, the relations between men and women, and the family. He offers similar themes, but fresh perspectives in "Men, Women and Sex," 5-12, a learned compendium and evaluation of the changes that the sexual revolution has wrought. His rather obvious conclusion that the NEA needs new leadership, in "What Shall We Do With the NEA?" 3-16, is offset by his hard-hitting observations about its former director John Frohnmayer and Bush: "...it is reasonable to think that George Bush has the kind of negligent, deferential attitude toward 'culture' generally that members of his class and background display.... They 'go along' with the professionals who run these institutions, echo their opinions, and feel that one of their responsibilities is to shield the institutions from criticism, censure and controversy." In "AIDS and False Innocence," 8-6, Kristol places much of the blame for the spread of AIDS on liberal-progressive tolerance of promiscuity, and crafts a strong, common-sense argument for teaching abstinence instead of preaching "safe sex." He makes the definitive case that "family values" cannot be transformed into a political issue with "'Family Values'—Not a Political Issue," 12-7. He draws the line between the secular and the religious, and uses the quintessential conservative as his example: "If eight years of Ronald Reagan's presidency made so little difference to this issue, we have no right to entertain serious expectations from electing conservatives to office. They will always have more urgent and less controversial problems to cope with. So 'family values' is a do-it-yourself proposition."

Donald Lambro
The Washington Times
United Features Syndicate
★★

Chief political correspondent. Lambro is the *Times*'s answer to reporter-pundit David Broder, nearing year-by-year the standard set by the *Post* correspondent. He's an increasingly important player at the *Times* and his smart, conservative views of politics this election year were worthwhile despite occasional misfires on social issues. His best opinions are examinations of the political economy, where we nearly always find a tidbit to chew on. Although he's not specific about the tax incentives he'd recommend, Lambro, in "Business Starters Need a Spark," 1-6, shows an excellent intuitive understanding of entrepreneurial capitalism: "Entrepreneurs are a special brand of people.... Their leadership can inspire loyalty, ignite an explosion of inventiveness and motivate hard work and record-breaking productivity." Lambro's "Candidacies Stunted on Growth Ideas," 7-13, is a fine exposition of the policies that contributed to the recession and the lack of real growth proposals in all the candidates' platforms. In an important follow-up, "Clintonomics," 9-7, he supplies pertinent information and forward-looking analysis for those studying the candidate's proposals and record: "A National Federation of Independent Business survey of small business owners found that between 1 and 2 million jobs would be lost if Mr. Clinton's nationalized health care payroll tax plan became law." After the election, Lambro shrewdly waits to pen "Sorting Through the Rubble," 11-9, a smart essay in which he outlines the results of the election and offers a blueprint for the future, which includes support for entrepreneurial capitalism. And he celebrates the trend toward privatization in other countries in "Economic Gravity," 12-3, cogently linking this to the U.S.'s recent attraction to re-regulation.

John Leo
U.S. News & World Report
★★★

This "On Society" columnist really does make a concerted attempt to examine all aspects of modern life, and is becoming quite adept at crafting original, persuasive columns. Leo challenges our perspective on social issues, whether he's adding new insight to strengthen our opinion or making us the slightest bit unsure of our position. In "The Trouble With Feminism," 2-10, he alerts us early to the growing number of females who find the women's movement not answering their needs, but pandering to the radical left. "Sexism in the Schoolhouse," 3-9, exposes the flaws in a study, misrepresented by the press, about unfair treatment of female students. Leo makes himself the number one enemy of the Politically Correct police in "Fear and Loathing at Harvard," 5-11, a savage attack on the double standard of free speech at the university, where Leo alleges women may say whatever they like, but let a man make a questionable remark and he's accused of misogyny. He superbly defines the boundaries of "one skirmish in the cultural wars" over the grammar school curriculum additions of *Heather Has Two Mommies* in his 10 Best selection, "Heather Has a Message," 8-17: "The traditional civic virtue of tolerance (if gays want to live together, it's their own business) has been replaced with a new ethic requiring approval and endorsement." Leo becomes our barometer on educational issues with his follow-up, "Schools to Parents: Keep Out," 10-5, a trim examination of how parents are being "cut out of the loop." And he pointedly derides the culture of victimization by providing "A 'Victim' Census for Our Times," 11-23, calculating that, when all the categories of victims currently in vogue have been counted, "America's victims exceed 1.2 billion, not bad for a population of only 251 million."

Anthony Lewis
The New York Times
★★★

"Abroad at Home" columnist. Lewis is one of the most influential liberal commentators in the country, this year regaining his status as one of the best. Once again, Lewis uses more of the lawyerly logic of years gone by, when he was a must-read for liberals and conservatives alike. Relentless on Yugoslavia in "Yesterday's Man," 8-3, he pens a strong indictment of Bush's inaction on the civil war and atrocities in Bosnia. He echoes this theme in "Will Bush Act Now?" 8-7, and "Triumph and Tragedy," 9-28. Both are strenuous indictments of Bush that Lewis makes resonate. With "The Iceman Cometh," 3-22, he adds evidence of Jerry Brown's machinations, citing the candidate's misuse of a *Washington Post* story which Brown said reported "...Governor Clinton was 'funneling money to his wife's law firm as state business.' [Brown] said that was 'right on the front page of The Washington Post.' The statement was a lie. The Post story had made no such charge." A day after Ross Perot's re-entry into the race, Lewis asks "Why Perot?" 10-2, leading us through a thorough and insightful analysis that causes us to question a Perot presidency without dismissing the Texan's role as a catalyst for serious debate among the candidates. "Black and White," 6-18, is Lewis at his lawyerly best, indicting Clinton for using Jackson, Sister Souljah and the Rainbow Coalition to play *his* race card. He quietly culls information from various sources and we follow with admiration his intellectual progression as the episode becomes "a metaphor for the difficulty of politics in a divided country." Lewis recognizes and defines the "great change in the premises of international conduct" as Bush chooses a military option for Somalia, in "Changing the Rules," 12-4. He effectively broadens the essay to include another flashpoint: Bosnia.

Christopher Matthews
San Francisco Examiner
King Features Syndicate
★

As Washington bureau chief for the *Examiner*, Matthews holds an influential position, but his light commentary doesn't often stick with us after we put down the paper. For all his moaning and groaning, he doesn't say much. He echoes Japanese PM Kiichi Miyazawa's remarks that Americans aren't productive in "Miyazawa's Jibes... With a Ring of Unpleasant Truth," *The Washington Times* 2-7, but, rather than asserting we have no work ethic, Matthews argues arrogantly that we work for the wrong thing: money. His grotesque lead in "Practicing the Politics of Jonestown," *WT* 3-22, turns us off, as Matthews hyperbolically links the drinking of Kool-Aid at Jonestown to having to admit to bouncing a check at the House bank. He probes the meaning behind the bumper in "GOP Bumper Stickers Tell All: BUSH!/Quayle," *Los Angeles Times* 7-23, as the sticker screams BUSH and whispers

Quayle. Scrutinizing the broad implications of Bush's pre-election dole-out of state contracts for weapons to be sold overseas in " . . . And Bananas From Bush," *WT* 9-7, he contends that this early Christmas will worsen the international arms bazaar, while doing nothing to solve economic problems at home. He offers a hard-hitting rough draft in "A Script for Clinton's Acceptance," *WT* 7-11: "The choice in this election is between an American who knows this country as a land of special privilege and one who loves it as a country of open, indeed boundless, opportunity." What Matthews fails to tell us is how Clinton's liberal social and economic agenda will promote that vision. His discussion in "Record Turnout Fueled by Debates," *WT* 11-5, is an off-the-cuff evaluation of the link between presidential debates and voter turnout. Matthews concludes that they debate, therefore we vote.

Mary McGrory
The Washington Post
★½

After showing signs of improvement last year, we were once again dismayed by the mediocrity of Mother McGrory's efforts this year. She tries to tell us her opinion on everything in what becomes the muddle of a single column. McGrory is best when focused, as we see in the trim and taut "Bush's Muscular Message," 1-30, a review *cum* analysis of Bush's State of the Union address, in which Bush "said, in fact, little new. But he said it unusually well, with muscular verbs and sinewy sentences." Would that we could say the same for McGrory. She's unnecessarily vicious in "Thomas Walks in Scalia's Shoes," 2-27, on Supreme Court Justice Clarence Thomas and his concurring dissent with fellow Justice Antonin Scalia on *Hudson v. McMillan*. Uninterested in assessing the soundness of their legal interpretations of the Eighth Amendment, McGrory prefers to play politics here. McGrory zooms wildly from Quayle's "potatoe" mishap to Bush's performance in Rio and the White House in "Bush's 35 Percent Solution," 6-21. Although she tries to use the chaos as proof of Bush's disorientation in seeking a solid constituency, there's too little holding this slapdash column together. She meanders to no conclusion in "The Lingering Quayle Question," 7-30, an ineffectual overview of the campaign and the question of replacing Quayle. Though she makes a strong case for Bush to go to Vietnam after the shouting exchanges with the families of POWs/MIAs, this intriguing idea isn't fully developed in "Missing the MIA Action," 8-2. Her "Democracy Is the Winner," 11-5, praises Clinton "for ending the estrangement of young voters" by being open to the advice of youth. But we only see enough of his young staff to whet our appetite on this trend.

Edward Mortimer
Financial Times
★★★

"Foreign Affairs" columnist. Mortimer is not quite as quick as he has been the past several years. Rather than concentrating on foreign affairs, his forté, he has been dealing more with social issues, where he's simply not as perceptive. For instance, with "Islam and Integration," 4-1, Mortimer ponders the question of Muslim assimilation into European, and particularly British, cultures, a mildly interesting discourse that offers no real conclusions. We are still faithful and appreciative readers of his geopolitical appraisals. In "All Atlanticists Now," 2-12, he cuts through the headlines to announce that NATO's obituary is premature. In fact, Mortimer goes on to incorporate the idea of a positive Franco-German contribution to the alliance, seen by some experts as a threat to NATO: "Where they are wrong is in failing to understand and support the efforts of the Germans, and more generally of France's European partners, to wean France away from [its] anachronistic attitude and engage it in building Europe on the only realistic basis, which is that of a close, even if more equally balanced, alliance and partnership with the US." Mortimer was on the mark with "Bosnia's Tragic Example," 5-27, jarringly accurate on ethnic cleansing in Bosnia. Further addressing post-Cold War flare-ups in "How to Contain Conflict,"

8-5, his razor-sharp mind takes us through the process as few others have. In "The Dangers of Disorder," 9-9, Mortimer provides an excellent outline of why a European union is imperative, without overlooking the flaws of the Maastricht treaty. He offers advice to President-elect Clinton with "Dear Mr. President..." 11-4, his counsel here both learned and practical on the international front.

Michael Novak
Forbes
★★

"The Larger Context" columnist. Musing on world events from the perspective of a learned conservative Catholic theologian, Novak does make a concerted attempt to place events in a larger context. But this social philosopher's jabs at liberal ideology are rarely knockout punches. In "Middle-Class 'Meltdown'?" 1-20, Novak strenuously defends the conservative thesis that real incomes for every class of Americans went up during the '80s. He presents plenty of hard, inflation-adjusted statistics to make his point credible. He follows up with "Dead but Fair," 3-16, reviling the media myth of the '80s and effectively linking this mode of redistributionist thinking to the debate over national health care, a smart, intuitive evaluation. In "Seize the Moment," 4-13, he warns cogently that we must look closely at the Russian situation, and act with the utmost care: "East and West should deepen every possible link—like a gigantic blood transfusion." He reminds us that the U.S. can still lose all the gains of "winning" the Cold War. Novak says little new in "The Long-time-Democrat Blues," *National Review* 7-20, plaintively attributing the Democrats' troubles to their being the party of a diverse collection of bureaucrats and various special interests with no common thread that binds. Addressing the question of intervention in Bosnia, his "The Call to Arms Is All-American," *Los Angeles Times* 8-11, is thoughtful on how America views itself as a moral force. Rather than advising a ground war, in addition to bombing depots and supply lines, Novak comes up with an original, albeit limited proposal: "Their leader should be declared a war criminal. A bounty should be put on his head, payable to anyone bringing him to trial." He takes a good first step toward deeper truths in "Judicial Tyranny," 10-26, ultimately blaming the judiciary and the cultural elite for a fraying social fabric.

Thomas Oliphant
The Boston Globe
★★½

For the first time, the *Globe*'s Oliphant comes under our purview. His blunt, forthright opinions and uncluttered writing bring to mind a tough Boston pol who has seen much and is fooled by little. As such, Oliphant's arguments have a muscular impact. He provides a business blueprint for the Bush campaign in "A N.H. Company With a Success Formula for Bush," 1-15, an insight-packed talk with the founders of Cabletron System: "[T]heir views on trade are tough, but Bush will be making a huge mistake if he interprets their insistence on reciprocity as a call for protectionism." He gives us a hard-nosed comparison of "Clinton and Tsongas: Actions That Speak Louder Than Words," 2-12, replete with candid observations: "The only thing blocking a Clinton discussion of America's problems and Clinton's ideas is Clinton's preoccupation with Clinton." Taking on his peers in "A Challenge to Journalism to Get Its Act Together," 6-7, he pens a rigorous examination that concludes: "We have gotten too big for our britches, and our kind of pride usually precedes a serious fall." Oliphant touches a nerve with "Still No Economic Message," 8-23, an uncompromising essay on the failure of both candidates to produce a viable economic plan. Oliphant's observations on the economy are sharp in "Charting the Right Economic Course," 12-6: "A re-elected President Bush might have been satisfied with the third-quarter news, but a freshly elected Bill Clinton can't afford to be." But he can tend to the obvious, as we see with "For Clinton, the Climb Now Gets Tougher," 3-22, in which he states what's manifest for the front-runner: it gets harder. He says little new in "Bush's Capitol Gridlock Issue Has Backfired," 9-20, using events in West Coast Congressional races ineffectively in attempting to illustrate his point that Bush's run against Congress will prove a losing strategy.

P. J. O'Rourke
The American Spectator
Rolling Stone
★★½

Editorial board member at *The American Spectator* and foreign desk at *Rolling Stone*. Releasing yet another book this year, *Give War a Chance*, the prolific, right-wing political essayist and humorist gave us another enjoyable year of searing wit. While his pen is often caustic, O'Rourke can cut to the heart of an issue with the precision of a diamond cutter. He does just that in "The Fifty-First State," *RS* 7-9/23, a vivid account of today's Vietnam where the underground capitalist economy continues to come out of the closet: "Never has there been such pure, unconcealed all-hogs-to-the-trough capitalism among the citizens of a supposedly collectivist milieu." Going too far with "Liberals: A Tribute," *TAS* 4-92, an article adapted from one of his books, he pays tribute to liberals the way Little Big Horn was an Indian tribute to General Custer: "Liberalism is a philosophy of sniveling brats." Also cutting, but much more enlightening, is his "Going for the Green in Rio—Greenbacks, That Is," *RS* 8-20, a hilarious journey through the Earth Summit. The essay is riddled with standard O'Rourke diatribes that sting with a kernel of truth: "The people who came to the Earth Summit cheered the likes of Fidel Castro. Then they wondered why we won't give them money." Following Bill Clinton's interview with *RS*, O'Rourke pens "Pulling the Donkey Lever," *RS* 7-17, a sarcastic but instructive musing on what he considers Bill Clinton's overly structured policies: "Bill Clinton should remember that America wasn't founded so that we could all be better. America was founded so we could all be anything we damn well pleased." Nary a liberal is left unscathed in the cover story "1992 New Enemies List Third Annual Readers' Update," *TAS* 11-92. This compendium of readers' submissions looks like a Christmas list of people and organizations conservatives wish they could send to another planet.

Clarence Page
Chicago Tribune
Tribune Media Services
★★

In this year of racial turmoil, Page offers plenty of worthwhile food for thought, but rarely pushes the boundaries. The social concerns of America are compelling and require rigorous study and innovative thinking. We find evidence of both in his material, but not enough to move policy or change significantly the tenor of the debate. He trenchantly points out that most rappers preaching ghetto angst are from middle class suburbs in "Public Enemy Descends on Arizona," *Los Angeles Times* 1-17, but disappointingly stops short of exposing the double standard of these groups which are advocating violence in the ghettos. In "Sifting Through the Ashes for Answers," *The Washington Times* 5-4, somehow Page finds hope that resonates, perceiving the L.A. riots as the genesis of some good, much as the '65 Watts riots inspired the War on Poverty. His "The Fault Line Is Words vs. Deeds," *LAT* 8-4, is an excellent appraisal of African American-Jewish relations, as Jesse Jackson goes to speak to the World Jewish Conference: "I have no delusions about how much easier it is for 'courageous' black writers to denounce someone like Farrakhan in mainstream newspapers that are easily ignored by the isolated and marginalized grass-roots blacks we most want to reach than it is for Jackson and other black leaders to reach them without turning them off." He indicts The President's urban policy powerfully by citing Bush's plan to veto an urban aid bill in "Belated Discovery by Bush?" *WT* 10-17: "I would have appreciated Mr. Bush's words more had they been accompanied by deeds instead of indifference." Page less vigorously indicts television for children in "TV's Education Plan," *WT* 12-3, via the arguments of Peggy Charren, founder of Action for Children's Television.

Virginia I. Postrel
Reason
★★★

Editor. Postrel applies creative approaches with a libertarian bent to the issues and questions of the day. She has a rare gift for language and organization that, coupled with innovative ideas and lawyerly logic, make her work very persuasive. Constructing a smart examination of how the politics of resentment have become the politics of Pat Buchanan's neo-isolationism, in "New Bedfellows," 2-92, she powerfully outlines the dangers therein. A Los Angeles native, Postrel's essay on the riots rose well above the ordinary. In her 10 Best selection, "The Real Story Goes Beyond Black and White," *Los Angeles Times* 5-8, she argues convincingly that the true message of the riots has been obscured by rhetoric: "... the riots were multiracial—television viewers could see plenty of whites among the rioters smashing downtown, and Latinos among those hauling away furniture, food and other loot from ravaged stores. The victims, too, came in all colors, as did the cleaning crews. To suggest otherwise is not only to grossly distort the truth but to further the fear and bigotry that led to the beating of Rodney King, to the verdicts and the riots." She's perceptive on unions in "Unions Forever?" 6-92, offering creative suggestions on how they might be more constructive by "adopt[ing] an entrepreneurial vision. Instead of treating workers as factory drones, they can offer them skills that will command both respect and high wages. That means getting into the training business..." Similarly, her "Trade Wins," 10-92, contains solid, original arguments for the free trade agreement, in which she uses the economics of Arkansas as a parallel to Mexico. She provides a smart delineation of how the election is really a choice between the static and the dynamic in "Dynamic Tension," 11-92. Postrel, of course, advocates dynamism, but proffers only standard libertarian arguments.

Wesley Pruden
The Washington Times
★★½

Editor-in-Chief. Pruden is an excellent writer, though a bit too caustic for some tastes. His sharp wit and defense of the daily he heads make for a powerful combination in dissecting the politics, the players and the papers in D.C. His detailed look at Paul Tsongas, "The Cold Shower for the Liberals," 2-17, is executed without his customary nastiness, and is much more effective than usual. He takes a hard—and, for Pruden, detached—look at Tsongas's economic proposals. In "Wrapping It Up for Slick Willie," 3-20, he urges Bush to take the gloves off with Clinton, as the governor's wife "took a $2,000-a-month retainer from the savings and loan in which the Clintons had more than a passing interest and which was having a spot of trouble with the state agency regulating the state's banks." In "Rough and Randy Ships Out to Sea," 7-8, Pruden questions retired officers on the Tailhook incident, zeroing in on the military's insensitivity to women's issues. Says one male officer, "I wish someone would set me straight. Getting raped and violated as a prisoner, to [Rep.] Patsy [Schroeder], is no big deal. But let someone pinch a bottom or squeeze a breast and the world comes apart." Pruden picks Clinton apart on his response to the latest allegations of draft dodging in "When a Tantrum Is Not an Answer," 9-4. His subdued tone here works well, but his analogy of a bad cow and a frustrated farmer wastes a third of the column. He's better on the non-existence of a Clinton coalition, in "The Grand Coalition of the 43 Percent," 11-6, advising that the crowing in the Clinton camp about a "mandate" from voters should be avoided. Unfortunately, he doesn't fully assess the meaning of the popular vote. With so much advice for Clinton floating around, Pruden offers his two-cents on the NEA in "Seeking the Spigot for the Arts," 12-2, but his counsel here is conventionally conservative.

Anna Quindlen
The New York Times
★½

"Public & Private" columnist. Though Quindlen was awarded a 1992 Pulitzer for commentary, her sentimentality is appropriate for only a portion of the questions she addresses in her columns. Now entering her third year on the op-ed page, she is beginning to discern which issues require emotional treatment and which demand a more detached approach. She admirably balances both in "Somalia's Plagues," 8-12, quietly and strenuously making a case for intervention in the African nation "living through—and dying of—a lethal combination of clan warfare, drought and famine that has wrought what one U.S. official called the worst humanitarian crisis in the world right now." With "The Right Call," 3-4, Quindlen superficially, though soberly addresses the printing of sexual harassment allegations against Sen. Brock Adams (D-WA). "Hearts and Minds," 4-22, is beautifully written on the chasm between the two sides in the abortion debate, but Quindlen says little that's new. In the wake of the L.A. riots, she adds her voice to clamor over Bush's lack of social policy in "No There There," 5-6, an effective reversal of an old saw: "It is the opposite of the emperor's new clothes. There are clothes, all right, but nothing inside the empty suit." Reminiscent of her days penning the "Life in the 30s" column, "Abhors a Vacuum," 9-9, provides a funny, biting examination of the dichotomy of how "When men do dishes, it is called helping. When women do dishes it is called life." She stops short of helping to define Hillary Clinton's role in "The (New) Hillary Problem," 11-8, a pensive discussion of her potential: "This is a woman who lives and breathes social welfare policy, who has a résumé that would have put her on transition team lists had Bill Bradley just been elected President." But Quindlen still can serve up pap like "A Team Dream," 7-8, a pedantic daydream in which she expresses her wish to be part of Barcelona's "Dream Team."

William Raspberry
The Washington Post
★★★½

This year, Raspberry is the preeminent columnist when it comes to social issues. His incisive intellect and his authoritative command of the language consistently broaden policy debates. In "Health Care Giveaway," 1-15, Raspberry serves up the intriguing proposals of Pat Rooney, who suggests that businesses give their employees an allowance for medical care once a year and then let them keep what's left. Raspberry insightfully advises that the NAACP "needs to find a new direction" in his 10 Best selection "NAACP: Time for a Change," 2-19: "The big threat to our progress—to our *survival*—is now more internal than external, and mostly beyond the reach of legislation and court decrees." He takes on the cause of Haiti in "Haiti: Hell in the Heart of Paradise," *New York Daily News* 9-8, reporting on the UN letter which lists further human rights abuses. He explains lucidly why he is optimistic about the prospects of healing racial wounds during a Clinton administration in "Let's Fix It Together," 11-7, and "Change Is Up to Us," 12-4. The latter is a populist call to arms: "Leadership to be effective needs the rest of us. Clinton may be what we need to address our problems, but it won't matter unless we are willing to address them." Raspberry asks the unanswerable in "Where's the Outrage From White America?" 5-1, a stunning indictment of the Rodney King verdict that rises above bitterness. He powerfully and persuasively offers the solution as jobs in "Change One Tax," 5-6, and "Healing the Cities," 5-18. His other 10 Best selection, "When People Feel They Don't Matter," 5-4, was an exceptional dissection of the psychology of anger that led to "...a rampage by a berserk man whose rage is triggered by his having been reminded, once again, that he doesn't matter." His quiet yet muscular prose helps all of us *understand*.

Paul Craig Roberts
The Washington Times
★★★★

Undoubtedly one of the most influential journalists on economic policy this year, his work on the indexation of capital gains prompted a legal policy review at the highest levels of government. Roberts set the tone for the debate that raged throughout the election over "the tax thing" by crafting airtight arguments that persuaded. His first bombshell hit with "Instant Way to Cut Capital Gains Tax," 1-22, a 10 Best selection alerting Bush to the fact that he might have the power to index capital gains without Congressional authority: "If Mr. Bush consulted his lawyers, he would find that the word 'cost' in calculating capital gains at the Internal Revenue Service is not defined by statute, but by regulation. The president can cut the capital gains tax rate simply by exercising his authority to change the regulatory definition to index capital gains for inflation." He reinforces this argument in "A Way Bush Could Cut Capital Gains Taxes Today," *Insight* 2-17, citing *precedents* for changing definitions in order to change policy. Exceptionally acute on what's wrong with the balanced budget amendment in "Budget Control: The Amendment Can Go Wrong," *The Wall Street Journal* 6-10, he argues convincingly that the bill's emphasis is wrong. Balancing the budget, rather than restraining spending, is what he sees as the real problem. In "The Tax Heave," 8-5, Roberts turns Lloyd Bentsen's tax bill effectively on its head: "The high tax rates are anti-growth, but even worse they assault equality before the law in the name of 'fairness.'" He crafts three sophisticated scenarios for "Clinton as President: Consider the Possibilities," *BusinessWeek* 10-5, only one of which is positive for economic life under President Clinton. And Roberts serves up the familiar theme of Bush as Dukakis in "More of the Same?" 11-6, arguing post-election that the real change occurred four years ago when Reagan handed a growing economy over to George Bush.

A. M. Rosenthal
The New York Times
★★

"On My Mind" columnist. Rosenthal performs an invaluable public service as the paper's unofficial human rights advocate, keeping these issues in the public consciousness. He is at his best in this realm, crafting powerful commentary that would merit a three-star rating were he to limit himself to this topic. He provides compelling views of the labor camps in China, with "Prisoners of China," 2-4, and "China's Black Book," 7-7. The most potent selection, "Sixteen Million Slaves," 6-19, is a traumatic look at *Laogai: The Chinese Gulag* by Hongda Harry Wu, who "slaved in a vineyard where prisoners were tied to posts and left to the sun and black clouds of mosquitoes. They screamed, beyond agony to madness." Somberly, he outlines the ethnic hatreds that are the root cause of "The European Danger," 9-4, reprising themes powerfully. He turns his emotionally-charged experiences at Manjaca Prison for Bosnian Muslims into a ringing call for a "new U.N. protection system," with "In a Serbian Prison," 12-4. But it seems as though there are two Rosenthals. Israeli-Jewish issues are too close to home for him to maintain a logical progression in his impassioned columns. He is unhinged on Pat Buchanan, as we saw with "In Search of Buckley," 1-21, and "Victory for Buchanan," 2-14, in which he ineffectively indicts the press for allegedly protecting Pat. He was wild over reports that Israel might be selling sensitive technology to China in "The Hard Corps," 3-17, later excoriating Evans & Novak for publishing "leaks." Rosenthal's treatment was characterized by attacks: He calls Evans & Novak "biased," "receptive" pawns of the "anti-Israeli hard corps," in "Evans-Novak & Popeye," 3-20. He accuses them of using intelligence "to dovetail for an attack against a common enemy," in "Popeye's Revenge," 3-27. And in "Missile-Mongering," 4-10, he's simply virulent on "journalists who spread cockamamie stories that divert attention from the real dangers" of the arms bazaar and "make wars more likely."

Mike Royko
Chicago Tribune
Tribune Media Services
★★½

Royko's pointed social commentary makes him more than a humorist. Unlike other columnists who hide behind their wit, Royko uses his barbed humor as a weapon to shake up the perceptions of his readers. As such, he always gives us something to think about. He takes no prisoners in a critique of the Democratic leadership, in "Non-Candidate Still Leads the Pack," *The Washington Times* 1-6: "It now appears that Mr. [DNC Chairman Ron] Brown has been telling political insiders that he had nothing to do with Mr. Cuomo's decision to withdraw. If that's the case, it's all the more reason for him to find another line of work. As party chairman, he should have dragged Mr. Cuomo into New Hampshire. What does a party chairman do? Just sit in a chair?" Tackling reverse discrimination effectively with "Acute Rash Over Diaper Duo," *WT* 3-28, he exposes the Japanese fear that Konishiki, an American, may win the sumo wrestling championship and achieve the highest sumo rank: *yokozuna*. In "Daring to Be Vague," *WT* 5-2, the Chicago columnist makes a superbly funny case for the damned-if-you-do, damned-if-you-don't theory of politics: "A candidate used to be able to say 'A chicken in every pot,' and people were happy. Now you have animal rights groups demanding to know how you can let all those chickens suffer." We loved "No Love Lost on Terminated Relationship," *New York Daily News* 9-8, in which Royko makes short work of the trendy terms of amour by plopping them down into the appropriate places in timeless love songs. And in "Hey Bill! You Could Make Ross the Boss of..." *NYDN* 11-9, Royko goofily suggests that President-elect Clinton make Ross Perot "chief night watchman at the White House," a critique that fails to tickle our funny bone.

William Safire
The New York Times
★★★★

"Essay" columnist. The former Nixon speechwriter scores again with relentless reporting on the connections between the Bush administration and Iraq prior to the Persian Gulf War. As with last year's high-impact work on John Sununu, Safire's dogged reporting on the U.S.-Iraq relationship was in no small measure responsible for Congressional calls for a special investigation of possible administration wrongdoing. In "Bush's Lavoro Scandal," 4-27, he's strong on Henry Gonzalez's subpoena of classified material on the bank and the administration. He receives a 10 Best citation for his body of work on "Iraqgate," beginning with "Baker's Guilty Knowledge," 6-22. Safire sounds the alarm loudly on the administration's ties to Iraq by uncovering a 10-13-89 memo by State Dept. officer Frank Lemay that warned Saddam Hussein might be diverting agriculture subsidies and credits to acquire nuclear technology. Safire discovers that the Lemay memo was marked "'Not in the System,'" 6-25, which restricted its distribution. He puts together the first pieces of "a mosaic of cover-up: first, in State's perverting the use of Agriculture's farm-export guarantees; second, in Commerce doctoring documents to mislead Congress; finally, in the Department of Justice delaying prosecution of a huge Iraqi fraud." In "Digging Deeper in Iraqgate," 7-6, Safire crafts a strong rebuttal to Bush's denial of knowledge of the Lemay memo. He shares more new evidence of possible administration complicity in Saddam's war buildup in "A Smoking Gun?" 9-10, rounding out this body of work. Safire ends the story with a strenuous indictment of the investigation in "Iraqgate Whitewash," 12-10, reprising powerfully familiar themes of "power abusive arrogance" in government. Safire turned in fine work on other topics as well. Two weeks before the election, Safire explores Bush's political inclination to cull support from the far right in "Bush's Gamble," *Magazine* 10-18, exceptionally describing GOP despair regarding the President at a critical juncture in yet another 10 Best selection. Simply a stellar year for Safire.

Robert J. Samuelson
Newsweek
Washington Post Writers Group
★

His light commentary rarely breaks new ground, although we were very impressed by one of his early efforts this year. "The Twisted Politics of Trade," *The Washington Post* 1-22, is a terrific blast against protectionism and "managed trade" in which Samuelson makes the important point that our export position has

MEDIAGUIDE 143

been getting stronger and we must work to correct the myths about the trade deficit and American "uncompetitiveness." More often during the year, though, he mushed around as a conventional Beltway commentator. He takes an awfully long time to tell us that things aren't so bad and that prosperity can't cure everything anyway in the goofy *Newsweek* cover "How Our American Dream Unraveled," 3-2: "Every age has its illusions. Ours has been this fervent belief in the power of prosperity. Our pillars of faith are now crashing about us.... The result is a deep crisis of spirit that fuels Americans' growing self-doubts, cynicism with politics and confusion about our global role." Yet, he adds, "...most Americans remain *personally* content," and "our idea has, despite glaring shortcomings, worked splendidly for most Americans." In "The Dilemma of Democracy," 4-13, Samuelson takes an elitist view, concluding that government by a smart few people is really what's needed. Scoring some points in "Technology in Reverse," 7-20, he explores how some technology doesn't improve the quality of life, calling it "retarded technology." While Samuelson is provocative in his political evaluation of the situation in Europe, his discussion of the economics of East vs. West is puffy in "The Dangerous Power Vacuum," 8-17. Samuelson explores the ideas of economist best known for "creative destruction," in "Schumpeter: The Prophet," 11-9. And he reviews the state of the economy for Clinton in "Is This Summit Necessary?" 12-7, but provides no substantive policy suggestions.

William Schneider
National Journal
Los Angeles Times Syndicate
★★

CNN's public opinion analyst just hasn't produced anything special this year, certainly nothing remotely resembling his 10 Best reporting in '87. He produces respectable, solid material, always with one or two new morsels to chew on, but he only rarely startles us. He moves ponderously from one subject to another in "Democrats Have Campaign Strategy, Just Need Candidate," *Los Angeles Times* 1-26, but is so heavy-handed here that his points are obscured. He doesn't convince us that "Right now, Clinton is like Ronald Reagan was in 1980" in "It's Now Clinton vs. Clinton and Bush vs. Bush," *LAT* 3-22, although he does provide an apt description of the presidential race: "Each candidate is trying to overcome his own negatives." "Bush's and Clinton's Missed Opportunities," *LAT* 5-31, posits that people "will settle for the most plausible alternative." In "For Democrats, No News Is Good News," 7-25, he downplays the role of Ross Perot's withdrawal in Clinton's post-convention upswing, decreeing that Democratic unity and Bush-bashing did the trick. Schneider is also too narrow in assessing the foreign policy gap between the candidates in "Clinton: Me, Too; Bush: No Thanks," 8-8. He focuses on the Middle East and Iraq, ignoring other hot spots. Back to domestic politics, he sharply assesses Bush's failings in "The Opposition: Bush Picks His Shots," *LAT* 2-2: "The Republicans have lost their advantage as the party that can do a better job of managing the economy. The State of the Union speech was supposed to turn that image around. Instead, the President tried to beat the Democrats at their own game." He is thoughtful in examining the unique characteristics of politics this election year, pondering "The Questions Left Unanswered," *LAT* 11-1. Despite his attempts, though, he provides few definitive answers.

Daniel Seligman
Fortune
★★★

"Keeping Up" columnist. Seligman sturdily defends the free-market practice of business in his witty, fact-packed columns. He keeps us up-to-date on a multitude of eclectic topics, covering three or four separate issues each column, skimping on none. In his "Keeping Up," 3-23, Seligman critiques Paul Tsongas's economic proposals, revealing how "Paul's vaunted pro-businessness comes with a familiar liberal spin on it. He wants American companies to think of government 'as a full partner.' He wants an industrial policy.... Why would anybody in his right mind expect politicians to make better investment decisions than private-sectorites with their own money on the line?" He reprises this theme by vigorously defining industrial policy in "Keeping Up," 5-4: "Sometimes it refers to *any* government programs that affect the economy. People using the term in this sense almost invariably proceed to argue that since we already have an industrial policy, why not make it explicit? That sounds reasonable enough, except that the explicit version they have in mind usually turns out to be synonymous with 'government economic planning.'" In "Keeping Up," 7-13, he lists his concerns that banks may be forced to make uneconomic loans to inner-city businesses as government agencies talk tough about bringing economic life to affected areas after the L.A. riots. He captures the mood of many voters when he asks "which candidate has the least god-awful plan for national health insurance?" in "Keeping Up," 9-7, and unlike many of his peers actually has an answer: Pat Buchanan—who modeled his idea on that of John Goodman, *Fortune*'s "own favorite authority figure." Seligman buttresses his assessment with appropriate details on Goodman's ideas. And with "Keeping Up," 11-2, Seligman reveals that among the problems of reregulation during the past two administrations is the IRA withdrawal rules for women which are based on men's life expectancy.

Mark Shields
Associated Features
★★½

One of the primary reasons we turn on "MacNeil/Lehrer NewsHour" is to watch this insightful populist spar with David Gergen over politics and policy. Shields moves from his long-time berth at *The Washington Post* into syndication this year, with only a bump or two. In "Two of a Kind," *WP* 2-18, Shields effectively parallels the roles of Tsongas and Buchanan as candidates who could shake up the Beltway establishment. He predicts presciently that both would do better than expected in the N.H. primary. Shields compliments Kerrey for "A Becoming Exit," *WP* 3-10, smartly noting that "It is a tribute to Bill Clinton's political skills, and an indictment of Bob Kerrey's lack thereof, that the Arkansas governor, the overwhelming favorite of the Washington political and press establishment, could position himself as a genuine outsider." He makes a cogent assertion about the waning influence unions have with the Democrats in "Played Out in Peoria," *WP* 4-21: "This will inevitably mean a Democratic Party less concerned with economic dinner-table issues and more absorbed with social coffee-table causes. A Democratic Party whose voice grows quieter about college opportunity and louder about abortion availability has become more culturally elitist and less economically populist." With "After Houston, The Politics of Resentment," *NYP* 8-25, Shields provides strong criticism of Bush and the GOP: "The GOP campaign (remember, the convention was Jim Baker's 1992 debut) will be Us against Them with precious little about what together We might be able to do beginning next January." His post-election critique of the GOP stings in "Four Inevitable Stages of Republican Despair," *NYP* 11-10, as Shields points out the pitfalls of self-deception that the GOP may use to avoid changing.

Hugh Sidey
Time
★½

"Hugh Sidey's America" and "The Presidency" columnist. The best thing about Sidey and his columns is his prose. What his columns lack in news or information is partially compensated for by lyricism and feeling. His stylish descriptions of Americana are always quietly accessible. The words of this old hand echo a simpler time. Sidey and Bush look back on the year that was in "'Twas a Famous Victory," 1-6, particularly with regard to Bush's greatest triumph, the Persian Gulf War. "Blasts From the Past," 3-23, is less about what kind of impact ex-Presidents are having on world events than merely what they are doing and saying. We miss Sidey's usual intimate touch here. He appears haphazard in "Time for Some Decorum," 2-17, a call for restoration of the grandeur of the presidency, which he virtually reneges on in "Hail to the Prisoner," 8-31, an argument for simplifying the office of the President, rather than maintaining it as the big, oversized production number it has become. With the unveiling of his new column, "You Can Go Home Again," 9-7, we find pure Americana. In this atmospheric look at Sidey's last high school reunion in the old school building, he takes the best of the stories and plumbs them into one page—sweet, but easily forgotten. He celebrates the 200th anniversary of the White House in "Two Centuries and Counting," 10-19, peppering this account with colorful anecdotes about ghosts in the Lincoln bedroom. Sidey offers a memorable, bittersweet tribute to Dorothy Walker Bush, and to her son who faces a major life transition, in "Tidings of Sadness and Loss," 11-30.

Joseph Sobran
National Review
Universal Press Syndicate
★★

Sobran does a superlative job of defining conservative positions on the issues of the day. He can come on strong, even ruffian-like, although it's plain he does so not for showmanship but because of commitment to his convictions. Although we've heard the theme before of how "a vote [in 1988] for George Bush turned out to be a vote for Mike Dukakis," Sobran, in "Revenge of Mike Dukakis," *The Washington Times* 2-17, makes it pungent by asking point-blank if Bush should get another term. He is uncommonly smart on Bush, "whose strategy is to lose slowly even when he's winning," in "The Appeasement Thing," *WT* 3-9, effectively arguing for the flat tax: "In the right hands it could produce another Republican landslide. Not only would it be fairer and more intelligible than the current tangled code, it would give the taxpayers a unified interest against the government. That's why the government is unlikely to enact it. And Mr. Bush is too unimaginative even to ponder it." In "Riots and Wrongs," *WT* 5-2, he has no empathy for the rioters and is tougher still on Jesse Jackson for his views on the explosion in L.A. His zealous response seems typically conservative. Similarly, he overstates his disapproval of Bobby Fischer in "Back Like a Breath of Fresh Halitosis," *WT* 9-7, while failing to tell us why he doesn't like him. On the artistic front, Sobran serves up an excellent review of actor Sir Ian McKellan and "Richard III" which comes with politically correct "allusions to fascism, such as military uniforms with armbands bearing sinister insignia" in "Brutalizing the Bard With Fascist Fantasy," *WT* 7-10. He's equally quick-witted on Clinton's career of pulling strings in "Making Connections," *WT* 10-24, a well-phrased, though familiar, discourse. Sobran takes too long to discuss Packwood and Kennedy peccadillos before concluding term limits might minimize abuse of Congressional power in "National Moral Pothole?" *WT* 12-3.

Thomas Sowell
Forbes
Scripps-Howard News Service
★★★

"Observations" columnist for *Forbes*, columnist for Scripps-Howard. Sowell is that rarity of journalistic combinations, a conservative economist and philosopher. He *explores* positions rather than merely taking them, and his thoughtful, learned examinations help to define the conservative agenda as much as anyone's. From his perch at the Hoover Institution at Stanford, Sowell informs us that the battle over political correctness is at a critical point, in "Academia's Herd at a Crossroads," *The Washington Times* 2-8: "If the new leadership no longer tolerates barbarian behavior from anyone, and no longer promotes ideological indoctrination in the dormitories or the classrooms, then the long and dishonest nightmare of 'political correctness' may begin to dissipate." He makes a strong call for turning out the incumbents in "Scandal Scenario," *WT* 3-25, and with "... And Lesser Evils," *WT* 4-7, Sowell offers a precise evaluation of the candidates and the election. Sowell's columns for *Forbes* are also consistently challenging. His observations about race are intelligent in "Free Markets vs. Discrimination," 7-6, but Sowell hasn't quite prepared the ground for his conclusion that "discrimination has always been most prevalent... in government employment, in regulated utilities, or in non-profit organizations." In "Verbal Fraud," 9-14, he blasts politicians for impeding progress by obfuscating over the word "access," disassembling the semantic arguments of the politicos. We get Sowell's perspectives on the anti-family propaganda being distributed by both parties in "The New Conformity," 1-20, revealing important statistical data concerning the conflicting definitions of family that are helping to shape the terms of debate over family values. Discussing the GOP's future post-election, he makes a provocative suggestion for the GOP nominee in '96, in "Surveying the Wreckage," 12-7: Rep. Richard K. Armey of Texas. As always, we come away challenged by his views.

Col. H. G. Summers, Jr. (Harry)
Los Angeles Times Syndicate
★★½

We thought that Summers's utility would diminish along with the size of the military. Not so. He has remained a player in strategic discussions by using his vast knowledge of military history to give context to the high-stakes debate over military downsizing. His value as a resource is particularly evident in "A New Path on Preparedness?" *The Washington Times* 1-2, where Summers uses quotes from such diverse sources as Robert Frost and Gen. George C. Marshall to strenuously warn that complete demobilization may be dangerous.

He effectively reprises this theme in "Risky Reserve Retreat," *WT* 4-2, by detailing the dangers of proposed cuts in the reserves and National Guard, using warfare history for support. Offering cogent dos-and-don'ts for the military, "Safeguarding Our Internal Security," *WT* 5-7, he persuades us with a short history of the use of federal forces to quell internal unrest, provided after the L.A. riots. Similarly, in his "Military Miscast on Drug Frontier?" *WT* 9-17, Summers uses history to craft a solid argument that the military ought to get out of the drug wars in South America because the U.S. military can be ineffective in implementing the policies of other governments over the long term. He warns again of the danger of using military troops to quell domestic discontent in "To Insure Domestic Tranquility," *WT* 11-5, effectively linking such action to the rise of fascism in Nazi Germany and the police state. Just when everyone was deriding Bush for not removing Saddam Hussein, Summers comes to his rescue with "When Victory Is Less Than a Total Triumph," *Los Angeles Times* 7-9: "War, [Americans] believe, should be a fight to the finish. ... The problem with that paradigm of war, soul-satisfying as it may be, is that it is out of touch with reality. In the history of warfare, World War II was an anomaly. Almost all wars have been limited wars. And the Persian Gulf War was no exception."

Strobe Talbott
Time
★★

"America Abroad" columnist. This year Talbott has managed to avoid the knee-jerk liberalism that we've come to expect from him. He surprises us by getting beyond the conventional wisdom, doing his own legwork and on occasion advancing our understanding of the issues. In "Post-Victory Blues," *Foreign Affairs America and the World 1991/92*, Talbott constructs a well-argued case that the country's disillusionment with the Gulf War's outcome can be traced to Bush's desire to preserve the status quo, which led him to pursue aims that would end Saddam's ability to threaten his neighbors while leaving his sovereignty intact. He crafts an excellent argument that Russia needs a stable currency in "Underwriting Peace in Russia," 3-23, but disappointingly ends by endorsing the IMF proposals, without giving them any real critical scrutiny. His more in-depth examination of Russia's difficulties, "A Miracle Wrapped in Danger," 12-7, is well reported and written, but contains little in the way of creative proposals. Talbott gives some of the 600-year history of ethnic conflict in "The Serbian Death Wish," 6-1, broadening our understanding of the problem in Yugoslavia. "And Now for Some Good News," 8-31, outlines the unlikely circumstances that have brought the possibility of peace to Cyprus. Talbott does some good reporting here; we'd not seen this issue widely covered. He provides an early warning that Greece may be adding to the problems in Yugoslavia by holding onto claims of the name Macedonia, in "Greece's Defense Seems Just Silly," 10-12. Talbott takes apart Greece's defense and recasts it in the light of their blockade of fuel shipments, potentially sowing the seeds of upheaval through economic deprivation. For the record, he offers his own view on "Clinton and the Draft: A Personal Testimony," 4-6. Talbott was Clinton's roommate at Oxford and tells it the way he remembers it.

Cal Thomas
Los Angeles Times Syndicate
★★

Thomas helped set the tone of the "Family Values" debate, which was so primary to the energy of the Bush-Quayle campaign. No other columnist examines the issues surrounding family values with more finesse and sensitivity. Despite his born-again Christian perspective, Thomas does not praise or damn. He simply analyzes issues unapologetically through this prism. We laugh at his memorable lead in "Flash Flood of Sex," *The Washington Times* 2-16: "I'm tired of sex." But then he persuades us that we probably are too, at least of the pervasiveness of sex on TV and in the news: "Part of the joy of sex used to be its unfolding mysteries. Like the preparation of fine foods, sex was something one approached slowly and tenderly, adding new ingredients as the process continued....Now it seems we approach sex, and nearly everything else, as we do microwave dinners—quick and pretty tasteless." Thomas crafts a strong argument for establishing standards for the Corporation for Public Broadcasting in "A Familiar Game at Public Broadcasting," *WT* 3-12. We admire him for remaining logical and detached throughout. Post-L.A. riots, Thomas warns, in "Spending Stampede," *WT* 5-6, that racial issues must be discussed in the proper context, but he does little to establish such a context. Thomas's point that AIDS is largely spread due to avoidable behaviors is well taken in "Politicizing AIDS—The Price We Pay," *New York Daily News* 8-27. But he is torn between treating this as a moral or as a medical issue, and as such, misses its application to family values. His "A Presentation Better Left to Phil and Oprah," *WT* 10-18, is an ineffective critique of the second debate that was done in talk-show format. And his "Press 'Bias' and the Beholder's Eye," *WT* 12-3 is merely conservative commentary about liberals in print and on the airwaves.

R. Emmett Tyrrell, Jr.
The American Spectator Creators Syndicate
★

Editor-in-chief of *The American Spectator* and columnist for Creators Syndicate. The creative and sometimes witty wordsmithery of this smart provocateur can't disguise the shallowness of his analysis. We are asked to agree with Tyrrell because he says so, evidently. We get a rote attack from the right on "The Brady Bunch," *TAS* 1-92, mere blathering on Nicholas Brady, Richard Darman, taxes, Democrats, etc. Tyrrell launches lunatic attack on Gloria Steinem and her new book, but his missiles in "Laureate of Literary Losers," *The Washington Times* 2-23, don't quite reach the target, as it's a personal, not professional strike: "Miss Steinem has been at war with normal life for more than two decades, much as a brat teenager is at war with normal life for, perhaps, half a decade. Yet the teenager grows up or goes insane. Miss Steinem has merely gone to a shrink and discovered she suffers a malady common to the middle-aged battle-ax: 'low self-esteem.'" Tyrrell offers support for Nixon's ideas to help Russia, but as there's little critical analysis here, we can't be persuaded by "The Nixon Doctrine," *TAS* 5-92. In "Unheavenly Cities," *TAS* 7-92, he supports HUD Sec. Jack Kemp's plans for inner cities, recommending Clinton take a look, but he includes too few specifics to convince. Tyrrell serves up the goofy idea that Republicans, who "do not have the guile for masks," should become more adept at crafting different images in "Dramatic Democrats," *TAS* 9-92. We're asked to take on faith his assertions that Clinton lies in "Dread October," *TAS* 11-92.

Tyrrell pompously predicts Clinton "will issue his equivalent of 'I am not a crook,' and by November he will be a goner." He offers a Bush farewell, apparently written prior to the election, with "The Lost Gentleman," *TAS* 12-92. Here Tyrrell is surprisingly logical on how Bush's capitulation to the "*Kultursmog*," the prevailing wisdom on the failure of Reaganomics, may doom him.

Ben Wattenberg
Newspaper Enterprise Association
★★½

This neocon Democrat sometimes tries to cover too much in too short a column space. Consequently, his interesting perspective sometimes gets lost in the shuffle. For instance, in "Taking a Longer View of the Race," *The Washington Times* 3-25, Wattenberg touches on many salient issues, such as Clinton's potential break with the civil rights lobby, but because he lists so many items, there's no room for in-depth thinking on any of them. When Wattenberg gets organized and thinks through his subjects, though, he can be quite perceptive. In "Hidden Fungus Among Us," *WT* 4-8, he reveals early what he believes to be the socialist intentions of the UN Rio Earth Summit: redistribution of the world's wealth to "be centrally regulated by U.N. bureaucrats." Wattenberg was also insightful on Clinton. With "Starting to Get it Right," *WT* 7-1, he alerts us to the fact that within the Democratic platform there is an implicit admission that policy hasn't worked, as the platform apparently rejects some traditional party notions: "Welfare should be a second chance, not a way of life . . . no one who is able to work can stay on welfare forever." But Wattenberg doesn't tell us whether he thinks Clinton will—or can—implement these policy changes. In "One Nervous Vote for Clinton," *New York Post* 10-20, he argues persuasively "I'm voting for Bill Clinton for two reasons: George Bush and Bill Clinton. Bush won't attack liberalism. Clinton made a break with liberalism." His "Will He Govern as He Ran?" *WT* 11-5, is very smart on Clinton: "Clinton, like Mr. Bush, is also of two traditions. There is the anti-war Bill Clinton . . . and there is Bill Clinton who worked tirelessly with moderate Democrats. . . . How will Mr. Clinton govern? As a liberal? As a moderate? As a synthesizer, which could risk a Bush-style split vision?"

Lally Weymouth
The Washington Post
★★

A unique part of the *Post* dynasty of Grahams (she's Katharine's daughter and a conservative), Weymouth shows a particularly strong talent for interviews, on which she bases many of her columns. She allows her subjects to speak their minds to us, and for that alone we appreciate her material. Weymouth relates the views of King Hassan II of Morocco on the situation in the Middle East in "'We Must Make Peace,'" 2-7: "Today Hassan remains firmly committed to a regional settlement: 'It is a requirement. . . . We must make peace.' And he is willing to make the startling prediction that Syria's Assad would be willing to sign an actual peace treaty with Israel, and to extend to the Israelis appropriate security guarantees, if Israel were to return the Golan. Under such conditions, ' . . . there would be no obstacle for Syria to sign a peace treaty with Israel,' says Hassan." She also provides an excellent reconnaissance of Iran's quiet rearming in "Iran Resurgent," 4-10, cogently warning in the conclusion that Bush and Baker must not permit the country to go the way of Iraq. Weymouth puts the challenge of "Choosing a New Israel," 6-21, in context with a minute dissection and trim definition of the importance of the Israeli elections. With "In Israel, a New View of Syria," 7-6, she pins much of the hope for peace in the Middle East on the behavior of Syria and Hafez al-Assad. Weymouth also can be good on domestic politics. "The World Through Weld's Eyes," 8-31, is a mini-profile of Massachusetts Governor William Weld as a possible GOP up-and-comer, an informative view for those outside of Boston. But we found "The Lessons Daryl Gates Learned," 5-27, merely an apologia for the former Los Angeles police chief and his department in the wake of stern criticism after the riots. She avoids the tough questions here, permitting Gates to gloss over his controversial behavior. And "A Crime in Brooklyn," 12-4, lacks her usual depth in telling the story of Hasidic-black tensions in Crown Heights, Brooklyn.

Roger Wilkins
Mother Jones
★★½

"Uncommon Ground" columnist. An eloquent social philosopher, Wilkins offers grounded, intelligent, left-of-center perspectives on racial concerns. He makes an important contribution to the debate over race by stressing job creation in the inner city to the thinkers of the left. Challenging the wisdom of the liberal establishment in "Today's Lessons From King's Leadership," *The Washington Post* 1-20, Wilkins brings to bear his years of involvement in the civil rights movement, advising what is needed: a self-help mentality and some federal aid for those utterly at the bottom. It's plain he feels for the residents of Los Angeles in "L.A.: Images in the Flames," *WP* 5-3, poetically defining the vicious circle: "Black male unemployment is a devastating blow to the men themselves and heaps a crushing burden on the women they might otherwise marry. It sears the children they father and destroys the families they might otherwise strengthen." Wilkins again draws movingly on his experience for "Without Jobs, Human Virtue Cannot Flourish," *LAT* 5-15, offering the prescription of jobs, but pushing industrial policy. With "Don't Blame the Great Society," *The Progressive* 7-92, Wilkins persuades again that jobs are the answer to many of the social ills being debated. He adds that social problems are not unique to any single race, a fact that some tend to overlook: "In every recession, we begin to see rising alcoholism and drug addiction among people who have lost their jobs. . . . The black ghettos have been in *depression* for almost twenty years." He insightfully finds an important component of racism in "White Out," 11/12-92: the power "to define reality where blacks are concerned and to manage perceptions and therefore arrange politics and culture to reinforce those definitions." But again, he relies singularly on the idea of industrial policy to help create jobs for the poor.

George F. Will
Newsweek
Washington Post Writers Group
★★½

We are beginning to sense a new maturity in some of Will's political assessments, but we continue to be concerned that he's spreading himself too thin. He has the advantage of reputation and nationwide exposure, and uses both to the utmost. But the rigors of his appearance-packed schedule sometimes show in his columns. Will did score one breakthrough column that changed the tone of debate on op-ed pages around the country. "A Figure of Genuine Pathos," *The Washington Post* 7-29, a 10 Best selection, was the first, and the strongest call we read for Bush to step down: "If he runs he almost certainly will lose, perhaps in a landslide that does considerable damage to his party. If he wins, his second term almost certainly will be even worse than most second terms, worse even than his first." Though it did not have the impact of the preceding citation, Will offers a provocative listing of tough questions for both candidates in "Some Answers, Please," *WP* 9-9. In "Twilight Along the Potomac?" 10-19, he provides a devastating assessment of Bush's position: "Democrats understood what Bush still does not: They can win the 1990s by discrediting the 1980s." In "Vacuum vs. Resentment," 3-9, Will argues that neither Bush nor Buchanan represent the true conservative or his or her ideals, but he fails to define what he considers to be the beliefs of a true conservative. Will reverts to name-calling and overgeneralization in the hyperbolic "Who Would Kill Big Bird?" *WP* 4-23: "Public television is a paradigm of America's welfare state gone awry. It is another middle-class—actually, upper-middle-class—entitlement." And his "Here Come the Eager Beavers," 11-16, is an unfocused discussion of the liberal illusion that government can cure anything.

★ FOREIGN ★

David Asman
The Wall Street Journal
★★½

Editor of the "Americas" column. At a time when revolutionaries in the region are not storming plantations but privatizing them, Asman's free market, pro-growth analytical framework provides a reliable and, at times, profound understanding of regional trends. Occasionally he suffers from predictability, as in "Semper Fidelis: Yanqui Supporters Rally for Castro," 2-3, where he pokes obvious fun at unreconstructed U.S. leftists. An informative overview of the reorientation to growth in Latin America, "Wealth of Naciones," appears in *Policy Review*, Spring. The players and policies that Asman sharply identifies here prove that individuals, like ideas, do matter. He sheds light on the shadowy Vladimiro Montesinos, special advisor to President Alberto Fujimori, in "Peru's Man Behind the Throne Gets Unwelcome Limelight," 5-8, positioning Montesinos as a potential threat to Fujimori. Incumbency problems of a different sort are addressed in the thought-provoking "Anti-Incumbency, Latin Style," 6-11, where Asman alertly draws a connection between the discontent in the U.S. and upheaval in Peru and Venezuela. In "Cleansing the New Russia of Old Privileges," 7-9, he pens an impressionistic report on how entrepreneurs are being strangled by oppressive taxes and regulation. He slams U.S. aid programs to Nicaragua in "Is U.S. Aid to Nicaragua a Sandinista Windfall?" 9-18, condemning "handing over so much money to a country that continues to sacrifice growth in order to support a money-losing clientele of Sandinista thugs and layabouts." However, he doesn't consider that the U.S., having financed the Contra war, may now have a responsibility to help Nicaragua get back on its feet. He delivers a well-reasoned critique of the Mexican government's policy of choking economic growth in order to fight inflation in "Let Mexico Grow," 12-10: "One would expect such restraint more from the Bundesbank than from a Latin government."

P. T. Bangsberg
The Journal of Commerce
★★

Hong Kong. As the region becomes the economic tugboat pulling China toward entrepreneurial capitalism, Bangsberg consistently provides details on the pushing and shoving. This year, though, his analytics were not always up to telling us where the great ship was going, and why. In "Vague Scheme for 'Greater China' Gets a Decidedly Mixed Reception," 1-23, he writes on the growing economic integration among China, Taiwan, Hong Kong and Macao. He delivers one insightful comment: "If [China] could lower its profile by nestling among the others, some of the sniping from Washington might be less intense." We receive a somewhat inaccurate look at the political and economic situation in Thailand in "Investors Keeping Eye on Military as Thais Prepare to Go to the Polls," 3-20, Bangsberg labeling Thailand a "stable" country, good for business. At times he can be incisive, as in "US Must Make Significant Changes to Recover Market Share in Asia," 4-16, a hard-hitting look at how U.S. manufacturers are "missing the boat" on opportunities in Asian markets, especially the so-called "Four Dragons," Bangsberg contending that Americans have no one to blame but themselves. In "China's US Trade Status Worries Hong Kong," 6-8, he provides a good sense of the growing fears of Hong Kong's business community that a U.S. Congress, motivated by election-year emotions, may kill China's MFN status. But analyzing the new Hong Kong Governor, Chris Patten, and his confrontation with the Chinese regarding the costs of the new airport, in "New Chief, New Style, Old Woes," 8-26, he leaves us wondering what the Chinese are really after and what type of administrator—and diplomat—Patten will turn out to be. In "E. Asia Textile Fraud Is 'One Long Chase,'" 11-2, he marshals facts and figures to outline the murky world of illegal textile transshipments through Hong Kong, which are used "as an unwitting cat's-paw" by producers in China, Thailand and the Philippines.

Lionel Barber
Financial Times
★★½

Brussels bureau chief. Barber seems to have made a fairly smooth transition from covering the political volatility of the U.S. 1992 presidential campaign, to covering the political volatility of Western Europe's road to integration. For him to really shine on this new beat, though, he's going to have to improve his handle on macroeconomics. Assuming the Brussels beat in early autumn, in the comprehensive analytic "Europe's Tactical Time-Out," 9-22, he expertly outlines the challenges to European unity posed by the British decision to drop out of ERM and the French referendum on Maastricht: "How to bring the EC closer to the European citizen is one of the most urgent tasks of the next few months." Similarly, in "Bad Blood in Brussels," 11-9, he thoroughly crystallizes the difficult choices facing Europe's leaders as they struggle to save European unity in the face of political and economic turmoil they helped create. The dissatisfaction of voters with their political leaders was one theme of his U.S. political coverage early in the year, in "America Wakes Up to a Stricken Commander," 1-9. Here Barber draws an alert parallel between the President's health and his political problems, noting that his penchant for turning to activity in both fields may be backfiring on him. His analysis of the political landscape following the New Hampshire primary, "Battle for the Soul," 2-20, is astute on the realignment taking place in U.S. politics, but oversimplified on the economics: "The president is a hostage of the ballooning deficit of the 1980s, in which he, as vice-president, played a significant role." Touring the wreckage in Los Angeles in "Signs of Hope Amid the Ashes of Destruction," 5-5, he respectfully warns that U.S. society must still come to grips with the social and economic crisis afflicting its inner cities: "Failure would raise the spectre of a society hopelessly divided on class, race and ethnic lines, a glimpse of which millions of Americans caught on their television screens in the last few days."

Bruce Barnard
The Journal of Commerce
★★

Brussels. While a valuable insight can still be gleaned from Barnard's reports on European integration, increasingly we find him simply echoing what we are reading and hearing elsewhere. In one of his more astute "Europe View" columns, "Recoiling From EC Leadership," 1-21, he observes that for the criticism Germany is receiving for taking a leadership position, other EC members have done more to "rock the boat": "The nub of the problem isn't that Bonn is throwing its weight around, but that it is still recoiling from leadership." He showcases his knowledge of the inner workings and squabblings of the EC in such reports as "EC Industry Criticizes Environment Initiative," 3-10, which looks at the ins and outs of a European environmental policy, and "Return of Europe's 'Dirigistes,'" 8-4, which covers the blurred line between EC free-market aspirations and the interventionist impulses of member governments. "EC Faces Uphill Battle in Wake of Summit," 6-30, observes that, irony of ironies, the Community is looking to eternal dissident Great Britain to bring Denmark back into the fold and rescue European integration: "The acid test will be whether Britain's subsidiarity campaign can win over the doubting Danes." In one of his best reports all year, "Bracing for a Single EC Market," 7-14, he provides a comprehensive look at the shakedown currently underway in European businesses as they prepare for a single market and position themselves for full-blown global competition, Barnard writing that the two questions now are "Will the single market live up to its name, and will U.S. and Japanese companies skim off the benefits?" His ability to deliver the inside scoop on the EC is demonstrated in "An EC Showdown Over GATT," 11-17, a revealing look at how France was outmaneuvered in its showdown with Washington by other EC members.

Henrik Bering-Jensen
Insight
★★

Writer. Readers looking for European news filtered through an anti-Maastricht, anti-welfare state perspective may get the most out of Bering-Jensen's reports. At times he is authoritative and original, and at others he rehashes material found elsewhere. In "Germany Resurgent," 3-23, he is crisp on the reasons behind growing German assertiveness and its potential implications: "For those favoring a less centralized, less Delorsian EC," he writes, "this may not be such bad news." In a follow-up, "The New East Germany Has an Old West Feel," 3-30, he artfully captures the economic devastation and psychological malaise afflicting eastern Germany as it struggles to achieve some sort of parity with the west. He is prescient on how Labour leader Neil Kinnock may prove to be his own worst enemy in "Tough Times, Tough Vote for Britain," 4-20: "Despite all his efforts to moderate his style, Kinnock still comes across to many voters as an old-fashioned Labour politician." "Crushed Velvet," 6-1, is comprehensive on the problems facing Czechoslovakia three years into its post-communist era, but uncharacteristically the prose here lacks Bering-Jensen's usual finesse. In "Islamic States of Siege," 7-20, an atmospheric report on the battle between Muslim fundamentalists and the Algerian military, Bering-Jensen postulates insightfully that for Islam and democracy to be compatible, a stable middle class will be needed. We were less impressed by "Maastricht Teeters on the Edge," 10-19, which is over-long on the obstacles facing European integration, and makes no mention of the ongoing debate between "deepening" or "widening" the Community or of the concept of "subsidiarity," one of the key European developments this year. "Prosperity Taxes Swedes," 12-7, is detailed and thorough on the failures of the Swedish welfare state.

Lisa Beyer
Time
★½

Jerusalem bureau chief. Now based in the region, this resourceful reporter offers strong coverage of Israeli religious issues and the Palestinian equation of the Israeli-Arab conflict. Her reports on major political stories, though, usually don't press the margins. Beyer's expertise on the Israeli religious community is demonstrated in "Expecting the Messiah," 3-23, a nuanced look at the schisms being created in Judaism by the claims of Rabbi Menachem Mendel Schneerson's followers that he is the Messiah. A report on Israel's ultra-Orthodox community following its setback at the polls, "Getting Too Much, Giving Too Little," 7-13, deftly sketches the shifting relationship between the ultra-Orthodox, who have been a major force in Israeli politics despite their small numbers, and secular Israeli society: "Now many secular Israelis hope for a reckoning." She was also a reliable source on developments within the Arab community. In "The Enemy Within," 4-13, she is thorough on the rising tide of nationalism and Islamic extremism among Israeli Arabs, observing that "the blatant discrimination Arabs suffer in Israeli society makes the community fertile ground for radicalism." "The Wet Clay Protest," 10-12, is detailed on the renewed threat to the peace talks with Israel posed by Palestinian rejectionists, Beyer reporting that the opposition is strengthening as the talks begin to deal with autonomy: "Hard-liners fear that if the Palestinians agree to limited self-rule, even as a temporary measure, the world will forget their cause and they will never achieve their ambition of creating a Palestinian state." "Hold the Euphoria," 7-6, echoes the conventional wisdom that, while he is no dove, newly-elected prime minister Yitzhak Rabin may be able to strike a deal with the Arabs. She works more shades of gray into her report on the controversial use of undercover Israeli commandoes in the occupied territories in "Deadly Force," 8-31.

Carroll Bogert
Newsweek
★★

Moscow. Bogert provides what we look for from newsweekly foreign correspondents; well-written, succinct reports that keep us up-to-date on developments overseas with a maximum of detail and a minimum of opinion. In "The Battle Against the Bottlenecks," 1-27, she effectively conveys the messy fallout from the Yeltsin government's decision to free prices but not privatize distribution: skyrocketing prices, empty shelves and trade officials sparring with each other over distribution. She provides an illuminating look at the current wave of Westernmania sweeping through Russia accompanied by feelings of shame and disgrace toward the motherland, in "The West Is Best," 3-16. She warns that while anti-Western sentiments exist only on the far-right so far, a backlash could occur if Western experts and ideas fail to restore the economy. Her depiction of the mood in Russia one year after the coup attempt, "They Beat the Coup —So Why the Gloom?" 8-31, vividly captures the malaise now afflicting the Russian psyche and the historical changes which the former U.S.S.R. has undergone. But the analytics here are surprisingly one-dimensional, Bogert warning direly of the possibility of another hardline coup, never considering that a quieter coup may have already occurred within the government by former party officials and officials in the military-industrial complex. In the richly-detailed "Nothing Personal," 10-19, she deftly captures the ongoing personal feud between Boris Yeltsin and Mikhail Gorbachev, being played out against a backdrop of increased legal actions against former high party officials. "Get Out the Geiger Counters," 11-2, is a chilling look at the catastrophic legacy of the ex-Soviet Union's nuclear weaponry and nuclear power programs: "Cleaning up this horrifying mess will take more money, time and brains than fighting the cold war did. And the Russians lost the cold war."

Celestine Bohlen
The New York Times
★★½

Moscow. A skilled journalist with the touch of a novelist, Bohlen specializes in revealing the human dimension of the revolutionary developments in the former Soviet Union. Her reports are often salutary reminders that high-level policy debates over geopolitical concerns, or economic reforms, impact real human lives, often tragically. She provides a vivid symptom of the "growing panic" Russians are feeling about the shrinking value of the ruble in "Russians Take a Flier on Oil in Capitalism for the Masses," 1-19, a poignant report on Russians investing hard-earned savings in a shadowy organization. She provided several vivid ground-level reports on the birth pangs of the C.I.S., including "In Russia-Ukraine Fight Over Navy, Crimea Lies at Heart of the Struggle," 3-31, a flavorful report from the Crimean naval town at the center of the nationalist tug-of-war between Ukraine and the C.I.S.; and "Re-enter Shevardnadze, the Phoenix of Georgia," 4-20. In this important update, we get a feel for the Herculean task ahead for Eduard Shevardnadze. Her talent for writing features that humanize the forces of history shines in "For Lost Comrades and Old Causes, Vodka Helps," 8-3, a profile of the young veterans who fought the last battles of the Red Army, from Kabul to Vilnius. She provides a thorough report, imaginatively written, on the Russian government's "next economic gamble" in its drive toward creating a capitalist economy, in "Citizens of Russia to Be Given Share of State's Wealth," 10-1, comparing the reform to "something akin to a vast Monopoly game." Capturing dramatically Boris Yeltsin's fall from political grace in "A Wounded Yeltsin," 12-13, she writes: "Like Mr. Gorbachev before him, Mr. Yeltsin seems to be the victim of a self-serving cycle of disinformation, a politician taken to re-reading his own favorable press clippings."

Leyla Boulton
Financial Times
★★

Moscow. Boulton displayed a greater degree of resourcefulness this year in searching out unique angles to the ongoing story of Russia, but she still needs to hone her interpretive skills. Profiling Yegor Gaidar in "Courage of a Russian Reformer," 1-20, she deftly imparts some sense of this young man and his huge responsibility. But she seems to offer unqualified support for the reforms being implemented, labeling his opponents "thuggish" old men trapped in the past. She provides a first-rate survey of the prospects and potential pitfalls awaiting outside investors in the oil fields of the former Soviet Union in "The Lure of Oil's Final Frontier," 3-6. On Moscow's decision to bow to the inevitable and remove the Red Army from the centralized command of the C.I.S. in "New Marching Orders for Red Army," 5-28, she fully examines and smartly outlines the challenges ahead: "'They can't simply abandon troops outside Russia. They've got enough armed orphans running around the country as it is,' said [one] military attache." We find a revealing, ground-level look at privatization, as Western experts prepare to auction off hundreds of shops, restaurants and services in Volgograd, in "Stalingrad Falls to Onward March of Capitalism," 7-31. She gets a handle, somewhat, on Russia's continuing slide into policy chaos in "Yeltsin Warned to Ease Up on Reform," 9-12/13, writing that even the "constructive opposition" is divided over whether or not hyperinflation should be avoided. But more analysis was needed here. In one of her best efforts of the year, "A Risky Farewell to the Nanny State," 11-11, she provides a comprehensive look at the cumbersome process of privatization now underway, in the face of such obstacles as the lack of a market infrastructure: "The closest thing to a securities market in Murmansk is a sullen, undernourished teenager sitting in a supermarket with a sign saying 'I buy vouchers' pinned to his chest."

Rose Brady
BusinessWeek
★½

Moscow bureau chief. We find reams of data but little illuminating analysis in Brady's reports. She doesn't seem to be sure if Boris Yeltsin has tossed the Russian people to the wolves with his reforms, or is the hunter with the wolf in his sights. In "The Latest Russian Expatriate: Hard Cash," co-written by William Glasgall, with Mike McNamee and Igor Reichlin, 2-10, she provides a good sense of the ruble's growing irrelevance: "One Russian entrepreneur estimates his circle of friends has bought $50 million worth of foreign currency." Monitoring the economy in "After Yeltsin's Strong Medicine, a Few Twitches of Life," 3-2, she draws on the strengthening ruble as a sign that the government has turned the corner. However, by late spring, she is back in the gloom-and-doom school. She reports from the Ural mountains to convey the grim condition of Russian industry in the wishy-washy "The Great Russian Depression of 1992?" 4-20, explaining weakly how it may affect Moscow's policy debate: "Yeltsin and his youthful team of reformers may have to give some ground [to the industrialists], but if they surrender too much, they'll hurt prospects for the $24 billion in aid pledged by Western nations." She covered the policy debate through the prism of the Western aid package and the IMF reform plan, echoing conventional wisdom in such reports as "Will Yeltsin Get Thrown From the Train?" with Karen Pennar and Brian Bremner and Amy Borrus, 6-22, and "Yeltsin Discovers the Tricky Side to Democracy: Compromise," 7-20. She concludes that "Yeltsin will have to persuade the West that a distinctly Russian go-slow approach is better than the sudden and dramatic changes being urged upon him." "Yeltsin's Economic Shock Trooper," 2-24, gives us a good sense of Economics Minister Yegor Gaidar, and "Bob Strauss Learns How to Say 'Rolodex' in Russian," 8-3, is a revealing look at how Texas-style lobbying can work just as well in the Kremlin as on Capitol Hill. Joined by Roma Ihnatowycz for the detailed "Ukraine: Breadbasket or Basket Case?" 10-5, the duo comes down on the side of basket case, laying the blame on President Leonid Kravchuk for "playing fast and loose with the International Monetary Fund." She provides a prescient scene-setter for the next big showdown, in "For Yeltsin's Foes, It's Now or Never,'" 11-9.

William Branigin
The Washington Post
★½

Manila bureau chief. A battle-hardened veteran willing to go after a story, Branigin continues to keep abreast of developments in southeast Asia. But he has yet to duplicate the vigor which marked his Central American coverage of the mid-'80s, the rigors of covering this vast region may be taking their toll. Early in the year he provided several vivid glimpses of combat, Third World style, in the taut "Burmese Rebel Prospects Rest on Sleeping Dog Hill," 2-12, and in "Philippine Rebels Show Signs of Life," 2-26. In the latter report, he expertly places the incident in the larger context of the Philippine political economy, which is keeping the communist rebellion alive. Analyzing Cory Aquino's six years in office in "Departing Aquino Bequeaths Philippines a Mixed Legacy," 6-29, he agrees with a diplomat's assessment of her greatest accomplishment: "She survived."

Yet, he fails to probe any deeper than to enumerate her failures. His best report on the regional economy all year was "Effort Planned to Boost American Trade in Asia," 3-20. Here, he details the efforts of U.S. diplomats to attract U.S. corporations to invest in the region. We get a clear sense of the new role for diplomats in the post-Cold War world. In September, Branigin anchored a *WP* series entitled "The U.N. Empire," providing reports that were highly detailed but lacking in impact, perhaps due to their excessive length. "As U.N. Expands, So Do Its Problems," 9-19, is thorough to an extreme on how mismanagement, corruption and bloated bureaucracy are choking the UN's peace-keeping efforts. He provides a case study of this in "Missteps on the Path to Peace," 9-22, a comprehensive but unengaging look at how the UN has been worse than a plague of locusts on Phnom Penh. An anecdotal report on the economic transformation under way in Vietnam, "In Vietnam, 'Hyper-Capitalism' Reigns," 12-5, only skims the surface of this fascinating subject.

Ethan Bronner
The Boston Globe
★★★

Middle East. Dividing his time and attention almost equally between the Israeli and Arab worlds, Bronner excels at capturing the pressures and promises of a region just a stone's throw away from an historic breakthrough—or catastrophic upheaval. A skilled reader of political and cultural tea leaves, Bronner, in "In War's Aftermath, Saudis See Small Changes," 8-9, penetrates the official veil of Saudi society to see nascent stirrings of change, from the top down. The opening of "On Syria's Margins, Dissent," 10-12, typifies Bronner's ability to capture a country with just the right brush strokes, as he conveys signs of cautious dissent in Syria's political and artistic communities: "The talk of Damascus these days—which means no official has mentioned it publicly and newspapers and television have been utterly silent on it—is the return from exile of [Hafez] Assad's younger brother, Rifaat." Bronner's Israeli coverage featured outstanding work on the settlement issue. With "In Occupied Lands, Jewish Settlers Toil for Vision of Empire," 1-26, he superbly details efforts by West Bank settlers to "Judaize" the land they occupy before it is negotiated away. Bronner explores this theme further in the 10 Best selection "The Battle for the West Bank," *Magazine* 4-5, where he documents with nuance and expertise how the new settlers have "claimed—with surprising success—the mantle of the prestate Zionist pioneers revered throughout Israel." He pens a poignant look at Israel trying to come to grips with the fact that it convicted the wrong man as Treblinka's death camp guard "Ivan the Terrible," in "As Israel Looks for 'Ivan,' Serene

Demjanjuk Looks On," 6-14. And in "Religious Schism Perils Rabin Coalition," 11-2, Bronner takes an ironic look at how Yitzhak Rabin's first major political crisis concerns religion.

James Brooke
The New York Times
★★½

Rio de Janeiro bureau chief. Brooke displayed more flashes of the kind of reporting that earned him four stars back in his Africa days. His literate reports placed day-to-day developments in full historical and social context, helping us understand how events might play out in the future. He still needs to pay more attention, though, to the role economic forces play in these developments. In the prescient "Venezuela's Two-Faced Boom: Riches and Riots," 1-21, he draws an illuminating sketch of rising popular discontent in Venezuela, preparing us fully for the February coup attempt and its high degree of popular support. We find an in-depth look at Peru's counter-insurgency efforts against the Shining Path in "A Lethal Army of Insurgents Lima Could Not Stamp Out," 4-7: "At stake is an ancient nation with such a deep tradition of mismanagement that a 19th century Peruvian geographer called it 'a beggar sitting on a beach of gold.'" Brooke often delivered a sure touch to his coverage of the Shining Path. "Roadblock on the Shining Path: Angry Peasants," 5-26, fills us in fully on the creation of village defense militias in rural Peru. We were also impressed by his coverage of the capture of Shining Path leader Abimael Guzman Reynoso in "The Snaring of Guzman: 'Bingo—We Got Him!'" 9-15, providing good details on the painstaking police work which led to the arrest. In the inspired "Where Shining Path Took Root, the Seed of Hope," 9-17, he travels to the small rural town that is "the cradle of Peru's Maoist revolt," and finds that the Shining Path still casts a shadow. We can find a detailed update on the tense political situation in Caracas, in "Venezuela Still Edgy: Will There Be Coup No. 3?" 12-3, with key economic data folded in.

David Buchan
Financial Times
★★½

Paris bureau chief. While it would be going too far to say that Buchan went "native" his final year in Brussels, his commentary did seem to reflect the increasingly outspoken assumption of the Eurocrats that political and economic unity was a done deal. Although his move to Paris in September may not have shaken this outlook, we continue to refer to him for details on EC policy, as he is usually ahead of the pack. Profiling European Parliament President Egon Klepsch and the institution he now leads in "Master Fixer," 1-22, Buchan colorfully explains why the "Daleyesque" Klepsch just might be the right man at the right time. He turns to the European Court of Justice to examine the ramifications of the growing policy of "subsidiarity" in the insightful "Judges Sent Into Battle to Hold Maastricht Line," 2-20. Charting the treacherous waters the Maastricht Treaty must navigate in "Final Uphill Push for the Treaty," 4-23, he is incisive on the details, but surprisingly predicts clear sailing in the end, "if only because no country will want to risk incurring the wrath of its 11 EC partners by bringing down the whole temple." He has to have a better handle on things in "Maastricht Back on Track," 6-20/21, asserting that while the process will go forward following the vote in Ireland, the reverberations of the Danish rejection continue to be felt. Providing a timely look at Jacques Delors's state of mind in "Delors Seething at 'Power-Mad' Jibes," 7-4/5, he sympathetically portrays a man "seething about the role of power-grabber which he feels some people have cast him." Taking over the Paris bureau just as France takes the fate of Maastricht into its hands, he pens "Wrong End of the Maastricht Stick," 9-3, an expert deconstruction of the misrepresentations on both sides of the debate. And in "Agricultural Superpower Throws Weight Into War," 11-6, he lays out with imagination and precision how Paris has essentially carjacked the EC's position at the GATT talks, for purely domestic political reasons.

John F. Burns
The New York Times
★★★½

Toronto bureau chief. Over the past decade, Burns has easily been one of the finest foreign correspondent in the U.S. press. Perhaps believing the old saying that "only odd-numbered world wars begin in Sarajevo," the *NYT* had Burns spend the year there working under fire. He covered the civil war in Bosnia and Herzegovina in richly evocative dispatches that brought the war home daily, while also achieving a powerful cumulative impact. He artfully draws a nuanced picture of Russian peace-keepers, many of them Afghan veterans, arriving in Croatia in "Russians March Into Croatia Armed With Promise of Peace," 3-17. On occasion, Burns steps back and presents a masterful overview of the big picture, as in his 10 Best selection "New, Virulent Strains of Hatred in the Balkans and Beyond," 5-3, in which he brilliantly ties together recent events from around the globe to portray a modern world still haunted by the ghosts of history. In the elegantly written "A People Under Artillery Fire Manage to Retain Humanity," 6-8, he pens an "Elegy for Sarajevo," documenting that while the city may be dying, the human spirit persists. His psychologically astute "Getting By in Sarajevo: Villains Even Get Rich," 8-6, provides key details on the economic impact of the siege. Just as we thought we could no longer feel moved by stories on "the miserable realities of ethnic cleansing," Burns proves us wrong with the haunting "500 Muslims Driven by Serbs Through a Gantlet of Terror," 10-2. Interviewing a captured Serb militiaman in "A Serbian Fighter's Trail of Brutality," 11-27, Burns places a very human face on the mass murder that is the Bosnian conflict, withholding judgment as he lets this self-confessed war criminal speak for himself.

Hugh Carnegy
Financial Times
★★

Jerusalem bureau chief. A Mideast correspondent with a keen sense of history, Carnegy's acute awareness of the dramatic changes now possible in the region was not always matched by a corresponding alertness to shifts in domestic Israeli politics. In "Israel Embarrassed by Corruption Probe Into How It Spends US Aid," 1-31, he provides a straightforward, detailed account of growing evidence of corruption by Israeli military procurement officials. While a solid rundown of party leadership votes is found in "Reshuffle of Israel's Old Guard May Unlock Peace Process," 2-19, Carnegy provides some uncommonly weak analysis, falling back on the assumption that the upcoming general election is certain to produce another coalition government featuring Likud, despite the party's botch-up of the economy. He pens a multidimensional report on Israeli settlements in "All for One Glass, and One Glass for All," 3-10, hinting that, at some point in the future, Jewish settlements may be under some sort of Palestinian authority. He is forceful, direct and persuasive on the stagnation prevalent throughout Israel's political economy on the eve of elections in "Loss of Direction at the Crossroads," 6-22. Deftly documenting why incoming PM Yitzhak Rabin's reach may exceed his grasp as he announces plans to step up Israel's privatization policy in "Israeli Chorus for Privatisation Sets Labour's Agenda," 7-8, Carnegy mischievously observes that "at first sight it looks like a case of the cat being asked to hand over the cream." He is also insightful with "Second Fiddle's New Tune," 9-7, profiling new Israeli Foreign Minister Shimon Peres. Peres shares his vision of a Middle East at peace: "There is no answer to [Islamic] fundamentalism by writing a new Koran. You can do it by enabling people to read it differently." A thorough update on Jordan, "King Strikes Sombre Note," 11-12, reveals how King Hussein is beginning to distance himself from Saddam Hussein.

George J. Church
Time
★½

Senior writer. *Time* may have undergone its umpteenth renovation this year, but one thing remains the same—much of its foreign news is still written by writers and editors back in New York, who draw on news from reporters and stringers in the field. Church stands out as the best of this lot. He's learning to ease up on the editorializing, giving us more insight on events abroad, less opinion. He provides a respectable survey of the ravages of "shock therapy" in "Shock of Reform," 2-17, laying out how, and why, former communist countries "have received more pain than gain," and what this possibly portends for the former Soviet Union. Sharp writing characterizes "Growing Pains," 6-1, in which Church deftly captures the political and social forces leading up to the explosion in Thailand, and makes a strong case that the country's current system of government by corrupt generals and politicians is outmoded. His ability to mix reporting and analysis is displayed in "Saving Bosnia—At What Price?" 7-13, a knowledgeable summary of the unappealing options facing Western governments as public pressure mounts to intervene in the Bosnian civil war, but we must note the editorial overtones in this report: "There is still a moral basis for intervention, and the U.N. dare not flunk a test case of its ability to cope with the ethnic wars that increasingly loom as the greatest threat to world peace." In "Counterreformation," 9-28, he produces a wide-ranging look at how "diehards are rebelling against the rigors of converting state-run economies to free markets" in Russia and the former East Bloc, Church providing a good sense of how far along each state has come on the road to capitalist democracy. We were disappointed by "The Long Road," 11-2, a lengthy cover story on Bill Clinton's bid for the presidency. Church settles for a recap of the campaign up to the eve of the election, offering little in the way of fresh information or insight.

Roger Cohen
The New York Times
★½

Paris. As European economic correspondent, Cohen focuses on Germany and that country's high interest rates as the beast threatening economic recovery in Europe. This leads to some one-note coverage at times, with Cohen frequently searching out economists and officials who amplify his views, but do not challenge them. In "U.S. Unable to Lead Europe Out of a Slump," 4-7, he is detailed on how the European market remains strong for U.S. goods, but focuses mainly on how Germany is dragging down its neighbors. Setting the scene for the Munich Summit in "No. 1 on Agenda: The Limits to Promoting Growth," 7-6, he is sturdy on the global implications of the issues, but contends that "interest rates [offer] the leaders scant room for maneuver." In the thought-provoking "Germans Love the Mark More as United Europe Gets Closer," 8-17, he examines growing German uneasiness with the idea of exchanging the mark for the ECU, but is vague on what this reluctance portends. In "Out of Chaos, an Entrepreneur," 9-1, he draws an artful profile of Yugoslavian wheeler-dealer Jezdimir Vasiljevic as the embodiment of his country, as it "lurches toward a Lebanese approach to life in which the prevailing view is 'sauve qui peut,' or 'escape if you can.'" In the wrenching "Rumormongers in Calais Mirror a Demonic Time," 10-30, dogged reporting and detailed writing capture the racism and hysteria coursing through one depressed northern French town. "Spain's Progress Turns to Pain," 11-17, offers a detailed look at Spain's political economy. Earlier in the year this former business reporter turned in two lengthy reports on the shake-up at Time Warner, "A Divorce in the Executive Suite," 2-24, and "Steve Ross Defends His Paycheck," *Magazine* 3-22. Both were clearly based on the anti-Nicholas J. Nicholas, Jr. camp, which portrays Nicholas as a "secretive bean counter," according to Cohen in the 3-22 cover story. We get plenty of dirt, but other reports on this subject led us to believe there was another side to this major U.S. business story.

Steve Coll
The Washington Post
★★½

London bureau chief. It was shrewd of the *WP* to transfer this Pulitzer Prize winning former business reporter to London as European trade barriers are about to go the way of the Maginot Line. Bureau chief of New Delhi through the spring, Coll was especially strong on the end of the Afghan civil war. His 10 Best selection, "The Last Battleground," 4-26, presents the views of the losers of the Afghan war to memorably evoke the "Soviet generation's Spain." We find a thorough report on Najibullah's fall from power and effort to flee Kabul in "Afghan Leader Gives Up Power," 4-17. Coll moves the story forward, predicting imminent fighting between the country's two main guerrilla factions. He dramatically captures the "increasingly medieval health infrastructure" in Kabul in "Civilians, Children Bear Brunt of Kabul Battle," 4-30, while "Afghanistan's Fate: Healing or Disintegration?" 5-3, is observant on the strong desire to achieve some sort of reconciliation. An extensive two-part series on the CIA's covert support to the Afghan resistance movement during the 1980s, "Anatomy of a Victory: CIA's Covert Afghan War," 7-19, and "In CIA's Covert Afghan War, Where to Draw the Line Was Key," 7-20, was breathtaking in its scope and detail, but seemed padded, especially in part two. Tighter editing was needed here. Though we've only seen a few reports from his new post, we expect his business background will serve him well. In "South Asian Nations Scramble for Arms After Soviet Crackup," 1-5, he pens a knowledgeable report on India and Pakistan's efforts to find new arms suppliers: "The subcontinent is becoming an active if somewhat shabby arms bazaar, where merchants from around the world peddle Cold War leftovers, second-grade equipment and spare parts to buyers short on cash but eager to deal." His early reports out of London were specific on Iran's efforts to reestablish trade links with the West, such as "U.S. Firms Buying Oil From Iran; New Large Purchases Help Tehran to Fund Rebuilding Programs," 11-8.

Joseph Contreras
Newsweek
★★

Johannesburg bureau chief. Contreras was better at working shades of gray into his coverage of South African politics this year, and offered conscientious coverage of the on-again, off-again negotiations between the white government and the ANC. While his coverage of South Africa is far from comprehensive, he covers more ground than most newsweekly reporters. He is thorough on the pressures which led President F. W. de Klerk to call for a national referendum, and the divisions within the white community, in "The Gambling Man," 3-2. Similarly, "A New Day Dawns," 3-30, is a detailed snapshot of the South African political landscape following the referendum's passage by a wide margin: de Klerk is riding high, conservative whites have been marginalized, and the ANC is offering reassuring signals to whites about life under a black-ruled government. In "Can Reform Survive?" 7-6, and "The Fire in the Streets," 7-27, he sharply outlines the fissures in the ANC following the massacre in Boipatong township. He succinctly captures the dilemma of ANC officials: "For Mandela and other ANC leaders, the 'comrades' are a constituency too important to ignore, yet their excesses erode the wider public's confidence in the ANC to govern." Contreras draws on some first-hand evidence provided from a former South African army colonel to document how the government used state security forces to undermine the ANC, even after de Klerk legalized the organization, in "Secret War in South Africa," 9-14. He conveys the fury of the violence in the black "homeland" of Ciskei and the growing exasperation of many observers with South Africa's political scene in "Slaughter in South Africa," 9-21: "True to form, the government and the ANC at first blamed each other." He provides a colorful report on the "African klondike" being created in diamond-rich northeastern Angola, much to the consternation of de Beers, in "The Lure of Diamonds," 11-9.

A. E. Cullison
The Journal of Commerce
★★★

Tokyo, "Asia View" columnist. Cullison continues to be

one of the finest chroniclers of the *Noh* theater that is Japanese politics and foreign relations. However, at times this year, he failed to probe the depths as he more and more seems to be mirroring the growing cynicism of the Japanese electorate. He pens a masterful analytic on the state of U.S.-Japanese relations in "America in the Mind of Japan," 2-12, artfully capturing both the broad strokes and nuances of a relationship that is undergoing wrenching changes. Cullison took this same approach to nascent signs of reform in Japanese business and government in the cautious "Paying for Japan's Government," 3-25. He reports that a few "forward-looking business executives" are beginning to recognize that change is necessary in Japan's campaign finance laws. But he adds that the country's "politically immature" electorate is likely to stick with the status quo. Similarly, in "Asia View" columns such as "A Kinder and Gentler Japan?" 4-8, and "Learning to Act Like a Leader," 6-17, he writes at length on recent soundings that at least some elements of the Japanese elite are finally realizing that the time has come for the country to accept its role as a responsible economic partner in the world, while improving the quality of life for its citizens. In "Japan Fears Clinton Victory Will Raise Economic Tensions," 8-18, he provides a revealing look at how the U.S. election is playing in Japan, zeroing in on Tokyo's fears of a Clinton presidency. But Cullison fails to step back and offer an outside perspective. He is more critical in "Akatsuki Maru's Perilous Voyage," 10-21, weighing Japan's precautions as it faces international scrutiny for its attempts to transport more than a ton of extremely dangerous plutonium from France: "Widespread death and lasting destruction could be the result, if not from this trip then from some later voyage."

John-Thor Dahlburg
Los Angeles Times
★★

Moscow. Serving as acting bureau chief for much of the year, Dahlburg has begun to fulfill the potential on this beat that we noted several years ago. An intrepid reporter and imaginative writer, his interpretative skills still need some honing. He provided vivid, ground-level coverage of the ethnic violence flaring up on Russia's perimeter early in the year. "In Tbilisi, Victory Is Bittersweet," 1-7, captures the surrealism of the fighting in Georgia's capital, while "Old Struggle Flares Anew in Bitter Karabakh Battle," 2-23, effectively conveys the grim determination of the Armenians as they battle it out with the Azerbaijanis in Nagorno-Karabakh. Dahlburg also produced some key reports on the current state of the former Soviet scientific-industrial complex. He takes a detailed look at the run-down state of the Russian space program in "A Space Giant Out of Orbit," 3-26, and "The City That Led Russia Into Space Is in Retreat," 4-7. Artfully contrasting the hard times for the Russian space program today with the glorious Soviet years, when they beat the U.S. into orbit. We find a chilling look at the grim legacy of the Soviet nuclear power plant program in "Soviet Union Is Dead But Nuclear Program Has Dangerous Half-Life," 6-13. His ability to work a broad canvas is showcased in "Russia Sobers Up a Year After Freedom Binge," 8-16, a comprehensive survey of the malaise afflicting the Russian people, although Dahlburg seems a little uncertain of what lies ahead politically. An in-depth look at the debate being waged within Moscow's foreign policy community is provided in "Look Eastward, Russia: the New Asian Interest," 10-27, as Russia weighs how to harness the economic might of its Asian neighbors. But again Dahlburg draws no real conclusions here. Similarly, "Once-Skeptical Russia Warms Up to Clinton," 11-23, reflects the hopes in Moscow created by the new administration, without probing the underlying policy and personality clashes at work in Russia.

Damon Darlin
The Wall Street Journal
★★★

Seoul bureau chief. In a year when the biggest stories in Korea were what didn't happen—neither unification nor war over the North's nuclear weapons program—Darlin consistently produced dispatches distinguished by a strong feel for Korean politics and culture. In "Hyundai Owner Takes On Government," 3-3, he offers an illuminating report on the efforts of Hyundai founder Chung Ju Yung to challenge the ruling Democratic Liberal Party in upcoming elections. He expertly works background and context into "Migrants From China Go After Fortunes While Filling Labor Gap in South Korea," 4-22, turning the story of one worker into a forward-looking report on the South Korean political economy. Economical writing, vivid vignettes, and astute observations characterize Darlin's reports on a trip to the North, including "Pyongyang Lets Visitors Roam Free—Within Limits," 5-13, and "North Korea's Economy Staggers Along," 5-26. Darlin notes in the latter report that "Economic failure here could trigger political unrest and, if North Korea lashes out, destabilize Northeast Asia." He provides key details on the Tumen River project, "a grandiose plan to make the North Korean-Chinese-Russian border area into a booming free-trade zone, a kind of sub-Siberian Singapore," in "Free-Trade Zone May Appear in Far East," 6-10. A strong sense of irony matched by a strong grasp of the subject material makes "A War Breaks Out Among Followers of a Peacemaker," 8-5, a superb feature story on a battle over "money, power and sex" currently being waged by factions of an order of South Korean Buddhists. He is concise yet thorough on the costs and benefits of South Korea's growing commercial ties with China in "New Trade Relationship With China Is Changing South Korea's Economy," 11-17, reporting that not even South Korean "knee-jerk protectionism" can stop the flow of Chinese products.

Judy Dempsey
Financial Times
★★★★

Eastern Europe. Dempsey continues to be the best of the lot working the graveyard shift that is Yugoslavia, excelling at explaining which fires are burning where, who set them, and where the flames are threatening to spread. She expertly sets daily events against a backdrop of contemporary politics and backroom dealing, making clear the tragedy is not a force of nature but the work of man. In the superb "The Beginning of a Balkan Endgame," 1-13, she examines continued efforts to carve out a "Greater Serbia" by whatever means necessary, warning, prophetically, that "The current lull could still be the prelude to a final storm." In the well-organized "No Shelter From Bosnian Battle," 5-12, she blends in such developments as a purge in the Serb army and secret talks between Serb and Croat leaders on how to carve up Bosnia and Herzegovina. As the civil war in Bosnia worsened, Dempsey revealed that the republic's fate was sealed a year ago, when Croatian President Franjo Tudjman and Serbian President Milosevic secretly drafted plans to carve up Bosnia into ethnic enclaves in "Bosnian Carve-Up in the Making," 7-8. As debate grew in the West over military intervention, Dempsey, in the masterful "Balkan Minefield for the West," 8-8/9, makes a powerful argument for linking military action to political objectives, and the danger of not intervening at all: "The longer the West prevaricates, the greater the chance the war could spread to other parts of the Balkan peninsula." For all her command of the Big Picture, Dempsey never loses sight of the situation on the ground. "Serb Refugees Suffer From the Full Absurdities of Civil War," 9-23, is vivid on the human costs of becoming "pawns in the Serb policy of colonizing Serb-controlled regions of Croatia aimed at driving out non-Serbs." In "Cracks Behind the Unity," 11-16, she is comprehensive on the emotionally-charged debate within German political circles on the need to amend the country's law on asylum.

Michael Dobbs
The Washington Post
★★½

Moscow bureau chief. The veteran Dobbs continues to serve up revealing, detailed reports and informed analysis on Russia's long day's journey out of the communist night. The gap between the promise of 1991 and the reality of 1992 was a key theme in Dobbs's coverage. His superb report on the freeing of prices, "Officials, Not Market, Still Set Prices," 1-3, a 10 Best selection, offered information we did not see elsewhere on how Russian economic ministers still control the rudder through new regulations and red tape. Dobbs asks one grocery manager: "How do you set prices now that they have been 'freed' by the Russian government? 'The same way as before,' she replied. 'I pick up the phone and make a call.'" In the eyebrow-raising "Outlook" essay, "Russia Redux: What Yeltsin's Revolution Didn't Change," 6-14, we learn that in government offices, "it's the same old faces behind the same old desks," and in "A Year After Coup, Russia Is a Debating Society," 8-16, he adroitly conveys the apathy and despair now prevalent in Russia. Dobbs notes in the latter that while Yeltsin has an aura of democratic legitimacy, he still calls on security forces in a pinch. A keen observer of Yeltsin all year, in such pieces as "A Calmer, Subtler Yeltsin," 4-25, Dobbs builds a strong case that by moving away from the image of confrontational reformer to the more statesman-like role of president, Yeltsin may be preparing for a major social explosion just down the road. He capitalizes on recently declassified Kremlin documents for a fascinating two-part look at Moscow's Afghan intervention, in "Secret Memos Trace Kremlin's March to War," 11-15, and "Dramatic Politburo Meeting Led to End of War," 11-16. Not all of Dobbs's reports were of the caliber we expect from him. Such reports as "Russians Coveting Crimea's Riches," 4-12 and "Kazakh Leader Emerges as Key Ex-Soviet Figure," 5-18, serve up plenty of facts, but fail to probe.

Bob Drogin
Los Angeles Times
★★★

Manila bureau chief. Drogin is more than up to covering a part of the world that has the appearance of Eden and often the reality of Hell. He can conjure up images as colorful and revealing as a *National Geographic* photo spread, while keeping us fully abreast of political and economic developments in the region. In "'Anointed' by Aquino, He's Hardly a Shoo-In," 2-11, he provides a multidimensional profile of Fidel V. Ramos, enabling us to understand how this hardy survivor made the transition from Marcos to Aquino. Drogin then sets his sights on establishment-backed House Speaker Ramon Mitra, Jr., effectively contrasting Mitra's populist image with his reputation among Manila political circles as the "crony's crony." In "Philippine Rebels Down, But Not Out," 3-10, he provides vivid details on a New People's Army ambush of an army patrol, but fails to work in the country's devastated economy, which helps keep the communist insurrection alive. We get much better coverage of the Philippine economy at ground level in two reports centered around former U.S. military installations, "Hopeful Filipinos Foresee a Boom as U.S. Exits Subic Bay," 8-18, and "In Mt. Pinatubo's Wake, Buried Dreams and Lives," 10-18. The 10-18 report indelibly sketches the horrific living conditions surrounding abandoned, lava-covered Clark Air Field. In addition to the Philippines, Drogin's beat encompasses the entire region. "Losing Millions in Asia's Notorious 'Plastic Triangle,'" 6-23, is informative on the exponential growth of counterfeit credit cards in Southeast Asia, but the writing lacks his usual fine touch. On the other hand, "Fore! The Spears Are Incoming!" 7-29, is vintage Drogin, an in-depth, nearly anthropological look at Papua New Guinea. And he places us smack in the middle of the frightening violence surrounding the destruction of a Muslim mosque in India in "Scrambling for Safety Amid a Merciless Mob," 12-8.

Stephen Engelberg
The New York Times
★★½

Warsaw bureau chief. With a background in investigative reporting, the observant Engelberg can be counted on to cut through the sloganeering and get to the heart of a story. In eastern Europe in 1992, he found the story to be one of feuding politicians and outmoded institutions. In the satisfying "With Some Misgivings, East Europe Snaps Up German Money," 1-23, he provides plenty of data while evoking the historical baggage that accompanies German investment. He brings home the Poles' misery in "Polish Austerity Threatens Medical Care," 3-24, fully documenting how economic austerity is crippling one hospital, while IMF and World Bank officials continue to push their own brand of economic patent medicine. Analyzing the country's difficulties in "Poland: Practical Politics Vs. Economic Necessity," 5-17, he adroitly places much of the blame on structural impediments in the Polish government and personality-driven conflict, a theme he returns to in the elegiac "The Mood Turns Darker in East Europe's Drama," 6-14, where he also addresses the coming break-up of Czechoslovakia. In "Clearer Picture of Bosnia Camps: A Brutal Piece of a Larger Plan," with Chuck Sudetic, 8-16, he places the horrors glimpsed on our TV screens in full perspective, detailing the death camps' gruesome role in the Serbs' "ethnic cleansing." He is alert to the implications of the Polish government's hard-line handling of a recent auto factory strike, in "Poland Sets Rough Path in Market Restructuring," 9-6. In the graphic "Strange, Brutal Murders, and Everyone's Baffled," 11-14, he fully probes the murky questions raised by the killing of a former communist prime minister.

Steven Erlanger
The New York Times
★★

Moscow. Erlanger's first year in Russia was characterized by respectable coverage and distinguished by a strong feel for Russian society. He has the potential to become a major player on this beat if he can get a firm handle on the policy debates. He pens a stark depiction of the street-level alienation in the Russian capital in "Something There Is in Moscow Still That Doesn't Love a Crumbling Wall," 3-17. Also informative with "In St. Petersburg, a Fight Over Power and Property," 4-27, he draws a sharp picture of growing political tensions in St. Petersburg, hinting that Mayor Anatoly A. Sobchuk may be maneuvering to replace Yeltsin, should he fall. We came away from the well-rounded "An Islamic Awakening in Central Asian Lands," 6-9, feeling we had learned all we needed to know about Tajikistan, as that Central Asian republic begins the transition from a communist regime to a still undefined Islamic Republic. He is comprehensive on political developments as Western aid starts to trickle through, "In Russia, a Familiar Chill in the Political Air," 8-9. While some of the information here is old news, Erlanger does an estimable job of conveying the bleak mood and the pervading belief that the aid is too little, too late: "Russia was never there to be 'lost,' but it is heading in a direction the West may one day soon, in this fast-forward century, come to regret." He adopts a less apocalyptic tone in the personality-oriented "Economic Compromise Is in the Air as Russian Legislators Head to Moscow," 9-20, observing here that "Russia is . . . the country of the anticlimax and the messy compromise." And in "Compromise Empowers the People and, More Important, Yeltsin," 12-14, he expertly summarizes the parliamentary maneuvering at the "venomous" December session of the Congress of People's Deputies and positions the outcome for the near future: "the status quo . . . will essentially be restored."

Clyde H. Farnsworth
The New York Times
★★½

Toronto. Farnsworth capably held down the *Times*'s Canadian fort, producing a well-rounded portfolio of features, comprehensive Canadian business stories and political analysis. His coverage often reflected both his keen wit and his expertise in global trade. The biggest business story in Canada was the bankruptcy of Olympia & York Developments. In "Reichmann Troubles Roil Canada," 5-14, Farnsworth exhaustively probes the fallout in Canada's investment and business communities, while working in the family history of the Reichmanns. Another financially distressed family business is the subject of "The Bronfman's Leveraged Leviathan," 5-24, an expert study of the "other," non-Seagram side of the Bronfman family. As usual Farnsworth provides a good mixture of data in context, conveying a strong sense of how Canada's system of interlocking directorships at the top of the country's financial pyramid really works. The other big economic story, NAFTA, the Free Trade Pact, is examined fully in "U.S. Trade Pact a Spur to Canada," 7-22. In this lengthy but highly-readable report, Farnsworth is thorough and clear on the gap between the proven economic benefits of free trade and political opposition to it. He connects the low popularity of the Mulroney government to the defeat of the referendum to achieve a constitutional reconciliation with Quebec, in "The Canadian Impasse," 10-28, and smartly avoids an alarmist view of the secession question. He also offered insight on the darker side of Canadian society in his feature work. "The Day the Eskimos Were Cast Into Darkness," 4-10, sensitively evokes the plight of Inuits, while his report on one Northwest Territory town struggling to cope with a violent labor dispute, "Town's Neighborly Spirit Dies in Mine Explosion," 10-9, enables us to understand why the local publisher has likened it "to the tensions of the American Civil War." And his ability to convey all aspects of trade issues is showcased in the thorough "Next Trade War Target May Be Dogs," 12-2.

Mark Fineman
Los Angeles Times
★★★½

Nicosia bureau chief. Transferred to the Levant just as he was solidifying his stature as the best daily journalist out of the Asian subcontinent, Fineman immediately began illuminating the Middle Eastern political landscape. We gleaned from his resourceful coverage that the "New World Order" in this region may be a mirage. As tension mounted between the U.S. and Iraq in late July, Fineman, in "U.N. Inspectors' Work, Ties to U.S. Shrouded in Mystery," 8-3, provided an important dimension to the story—the close, if benign, ties between UN inspection teams and U.S. intelligence agencies. He masterfully weaves together history and contemporary geopolitical conditions in "Lines in the Sand Drawing Gulf Nations Into Disputes," 10-13, writing that "The sudden deluge of border bashing is largely coincidental, and each dispute is fueled by its own set of local political imperatives." On the U.S. elections, two reports "Kuwaiti Patriots See Stars and Stripes Forever," 8-11, and "Clinton Wows Angry Electorate—in Iraq, That Is," 11-2, are very observant on future U.S. relations. His geopolitical coverage of the subcontinent in the first half of the year was superb, although we would have liked to see more on Indian social and economic policy. "Sri Lanka's Bizarre Leader Confounds His Foes," 1-26, is a fascinating profile of Sri Lanka President Ranasinghe Premadasa, who Fineman expertly presents as a leader who "symbolizes a broader phenomenon, one in which less-developed nations are increasingly using democracy to elect authoritarian regimes." He dug deeper than many other reporters into the so-called "Islamic Belt" in Central Asia, in the three-dimensional "Pan-Islamic Movements Collide With Secular Policies in Broad Region of Asia," 3-7. "Weary Afghan Opponents Reunite in Zeal for Peace," 4-22, is an evocative report on how the combatants are trying to effect a reconciliation of sorts, while "Rebels Struggle to Rule a Divided Kabul," 5-5, is a superior depiction of the scramble to divide the spoils, with just the right combination of detail and analysis.

Marc Fisher
The Washington Post
★★½

Central Europe, based in Berlin. Fisher consistently probes the margins of a German society struggling to define itself. His work is characterized by strong insight on the human condition as it is being played out in Germany. He provides little, however, on day-to-day developments in the troubled German economy, which are exacerbating the country's social problems. He sensitively captures the poignance surrounding the opening of the Stasi files in "East Germans Face Pain of Redefining Pasts," 1-19. In the comprehensive "Eastern Europe Swept by German Influence," 2-16, he alerts us to Germany's tactic of the encouragement of German as a second language: "German executives say the connection between language study and economic influence is direct and immediate." "Improbable Leader, Skillful Navigator," 4-28, his profile of outgoing foreign minister Hans-Dietrich Genscher, provides a good sense of the man and his accomplishments. Fisher's strong grasp of the German business culture is showcased in "Deutsche Doze," 5-3, a skillfully written, highly knowledgeable "Outlook" essay exposing the high propensity for leisure among the highly efficient "German worker bee." His coverage of rising social tensions in Germany was very perceptive. In the chilling "Germany's New Generation of Neo-Nazis," 3-2, he incisively profiles neo-Nazi leader Ewald Athans, who tells Fisher: "We will not compromise... We'll wait for the people to come to us." As more people seemed to be coming to Athans's point of view, Fisher, in "Violence Against Foreign Refugees in Germany Shows No Sign of Abating," 9-15, and "900 Foreigners Swamp Town of 100," 9-26, presents the human face of Germany's xenophobia. The latter article effectively conveys the political, economic and cultural forces at work in a land where both factory workers and BMW owners are increasingly venting their fears of outsiders.

We find timely information on the economic impact of the rising anti-foreigner violence and corporate Germany's efforts to cope in "Violence Seen Hurting German Economy," 12-1.

Damien Fraser
Financial Times
★★★

Mexico City "superstringer." Fraser continues to be our journalist of choice on this important beat. He consistently packages reams of data and penetrating insight into reports that are economically written, embodying the concept of value-added reporting. We'd like to see more "big think" analytical pieces from him, however. He gives us a revealing look at how politics and bureaucracy are undermining Mexico City's attempt to rid itself of a reputation as "pollution capital of the world," in "Hasty Measures Fail to Lift Mexican Smog," 1-8. We receive an illuminating look at the close relationship between the Mexican government and the World Bank in "Like Minds Underpin Mexico-Bank Intimacy," 3-3. Fraser continues to be satisfying on *Salinastroika*. His "Salinas Sows Seeds for Economic Benefits," 3-6, expertly and effortlessly takes us through President Salinas's new agricultural reform program, while "Privatisation Pioneer Goes One Further," 5-20, is detailed and thorough on the Mexican government's efforts to privatize public services. In "Mexico Faces Hard Choice in Keeping Oil Out of Nafta," 6-11, he's forward-looking on the impact NAFTA will have on Pemex, the oil company which embodies Mexican nationalism. "Cuban Revolutionary in an Army Green Business Suit," 7-17, is incisive on Castro's attempt to bail out his floundering economy by appealing to foreign investors, while tightening the political screws at home. Covering the uproar created by new history books written by the Salinas Government for school children in "Bending Young Twigs in a Different Way," 9-11, he deftly contrasts the old official version of Mexico's revolutionary past with the Salinas version. In "Trial Shines Light Into Dark Mexican Corners," 12-15, he examines with care and insight "the greatest flaw in the Mexican state: corruption in the legal and political system—hardly touched by President Salinas's economic reforms."

Peter Fuhrman
Forbes
★★

Europe. Fuhrman has a talent for capturing and comparing the differences between U.S. and European financial environments, and draws up a business profile as well as anyone. But he has difficulty handling more abstract fare, at times falling back on oversimplification, such as labeling social democracy a "virus." In "The Sage of Fleet Street," 2-17, he pens a knowledgeable profile of Lord Rothermere, hinting that the British publishing baron's willingness to take on unions and modernize may hold the answer for struggling U.S. newspapers today. We receive a brief and interesting look at how bankruptcies are handled differently in the U.S. than Great Britain in "Blimey! CPAs!" 3-16. He throws out a lot of factoids for "The German Disease," 3-30. But, by not fully considering the country's macroeconomic picture, he fails to persuade that social democracy is the only ball and chain dragging down German competitiveness and productivity. The management side of economic integration is covered in "Getting in Bed Together," 5-11, one of Fuhrman's better efforts, as he details how leading European companies are constructing webs of cooperative deals in an apparent effort to forestall competition down the road: "And so everyone ends up related to everyone else, just as Britain's Hanoverian royals used to routinely marry their children to the heirs of Prussia's Hohenzollern line and the Romanov czars of Russia." His profile of RTZ head Sir Derek Birkin, "Sir Derek's Deal With Shareholders," 6-8, gives us a better sense of what it's like to run an international mining company, than a Birkin profile appearing roughly the same time in *FW*. He does a respectable job of leading us through the Byzantine maze of lawsuits, regulations and financial dealings surrounding British pharmaceutical company Wellcome's effort to sell 37% of the company to the public, in "Wellcome Worries," 8-3. In his best effort of the year, "Follow the Ancient Silk Road," 9-14, he provides an absorbing, data-filled report on the economic reawakening of former Soviet Central Asia. Back in Europe for "Jewelry for the Wrist," 11-23, he provides an absorbing update on the Swiss watch industry.

Edward A. Gargan
The New York Times
★★

New Delhi bureau chief. Gargan continues to flourish as a reliable chronicler of the everyday horrors and historical pressures on the subcontinent, though he's still weak on economic and other policy detail. His well-written, highly informative work leaves the impression that the region is a harbinger of the Third World's future in the post-Cold War era. We come away from "Diplomats Are Edgy as India Stubbornly Builds Its Nuclear Arsenal," 1-21, feeling fully informed on the state of relations between New Delhi and the outside world vis-a-vis nuclear weapons. In "Even Bleak Bangladesh Is a Haven to Muslims Fleeing the Burmese Army," 2-7, Gargan capably delivers a gut-wrenching report on another large-scale human tragedy in the making. Gargan's coverage of the end of Afghanistan's civil war was impressive in its scope. He provided vivid, on-the-scene reports and comprehensive analytics, fitting the story into a larger geopolitical framework. In the colorful report, "A Northern Afghan City Is Now a Power Center," 4-20, he positions the story of one former government officer who switched sides, as a paradigm of how the "bonds of shared ethnic identity" in the north are helping to forge alliances between the rebels and government officers. Gargan's understanding of the Indian culture was showcased in "Bound to Looms by Poverty and Fear, Boys in India Make a Few Men Rich," 7-9, a heartbreaking report about loom factories where young men are literally held in bondage. Several months after this report appeared, India toughened its child labor laws. In "India's Rush to a Free Market Economy Stumbles," 8-15, Gargan provides a serious look at the economic performance of the Rao Government on its first anniversary in office, but he clearly doesn't see the forces at work under the surface. He expertly pinpoints the political and historical pressures behind the growing militancy of the Hindus in "Peril to the Indian State: A Defiant Hindu Fervor," 12-8.

Francis Ghiles
Financial Times
★★½

North Africa, based in London. This talented reporter was on to the Algerian story as early as June 1991, when he wrote about how the IMF-backed austerity regime would fuel the growth of Islamic fundamentalism. He has continued to provide solid reporting and intelligent evaluations as the crisis deepens. In "Establishment Takes Fright at Algeria Election Results," 1-2, he conveys the growing concern in Algeria, North Africa and Paris that an Islamic Salvation Front government could lead to "what has historically often been feared —a fight to the finish among a group of Berbers." He artfully evokes the post-election malaise sweeping through Algerian society in "Algiers Starts to Play for Time," 1-6, noting that rumors of a coup attempt abound: "All of this looks like *hukkumat mikki* (Mickey Mouse government), the expression ordinary Algerians have come to use for those who govern them." In "France Divided on Arab Links," 3-17, he produces a superb, fully-informed report on France's tumultuous 132-year history with Algeria. He expertly delineates the current, painful reformulation of "what can only be described as the 'ball and chain' relationship [France] maintains with its former African colonies." Ghiles remained on top of Algeria's shaky process of reform, always keeping an eye out for trouble. In "Algeria Struggles to Find New Direction," 4-2, he provides a prescient look at how PM Sid Ahmed Ghozali is trying to effect reforms in the economic and political sector while facing opposition from both the military and the FIS. He also writes knowingly in "Algiers' Corruption Clean-Up Gamble," 6-17, assessing the risky decision by Algerian leaders to bring corruption charges against government officials. In "Algeria Takes Another Step in the Slide Toward Civil War," 9-4, he expertly captures the nuances of Algeria's fluid political situation, while in "Algeria Joins Egypt in War on Militants," 12-3, he is keen on the geopolitical implications of this development.

Tim Golden
The New York Times
★★

Mexico City bureau chief. The Mexican political economy is as big and varied as a Diego Rivera mural, but Golden too often focuses on one section of the picture. He continues to be better on culture and politics than economics. His analytics on regional stories, however, are always worth a look. In "Salvador Warily Prepares for War's Aftermath," 1-19, he produces a fine report on the El Salvador cease-fire accord, sharply outlining the economic and political problems ahead. His thought-provoking "Democracy Isn't Always Enough to Repel Attempted Coups," 2-9, confirms that he is alert to the threat posed to democracy by policies of fiscal austerity and inequitable distribution of wealth. Engaging but cynical on the Institutional Revolutionary Party's efforts to undermine the Democratic Revolutionary Party's electorial prospects in Michoacan Province, PRD's home base, Golden pens "Point of Attack for Mexico's Retooled Party Machine: The Leftist Stronghold," 7-12. In one of his best efforts of the year, "On the Mexican Market, Doubt Replaces Demand," 8-3, he takes an important look at economic, political and cultural factors behind the drop in the once-booming *Bolsa*. Covering the Mexican reaction to the signing of NAFTA in "An Outsider Nation at Last Arrived, Mexico Embraces the Trade Accord," 8-13, Golden emphasizes politics, not economics, contrasting opposition to the pact in Mexico to the government's all-out lobbying blitz to sell the accord in Washington—an interesting assessment, but a breakdown of the economic impact would have been appreciated. On the other hand, his expertise in Mexican culture and politics is exhibited in "Mexicans Look Askance at Textbooks' New Slant," 9-21, a nuanced look at controversy stirred up by newly issued school textbooks. He provides a thorough report on the still-unresolved question of how quietly El Salvador's officer corps will go off into the night with "In Salvador, Will Officers Now Salute Civilians?" 11-15.

Merrill Goozner
Chicago Tribune
★★

Tokyo bureau chief. An astute observer of the Japanese beat who steers clear of conjecture or knee-jerk Japan-bashing, Goozner kept *Trib* readers up-to-date on developments in Japan in tightly focused, highly informative reports. He produces an effective scene-setter for President Bush's trade mission to the region in "Bush Likely to Win Little From Japan," 1-3, clearly outlining why the visit is unlikely to produce much more than "omiyage, or parting gifts," for the President. He misfires with "Right Time, Wrong Place for Globex Start-up Announcement," 4-9, reporting erroneously that a 24-hour trading system set up by the Chicago futures exchange had been approved by the Japanese government for start-up in Tokyo in early 1993. The *Tribune* had to run the article again the next day, with a correction that the Japanese government had not yet approved use of the system. Other coverage was generally solid, as in "Perceptions Come to the Fore as Japan's Economy Stumbles," 3-30, and "For Japanese, Economic Misery a Relative Thing," 7-12, where he marshals the facts and figures to put the country's economic downturn in proper perspective. In "Japan Resisting Pull to 'Internationalize,'" 5-26, he is thorough on how Japanese firms are tightening their belts by cutting back on overseas operations. Reporting from Vladivostok in "City Basks in Freedom, but Must Find a Purpose," 8-18, he evokes the economic depression gripping the city now that the Russian Pacific Fleet is cutting back. We find a valuable report on the ramifications of Taiwanese investment on the mainland in "'Mainland Fever' Grips Taiwanese Investors," 10-21, Goozner writing that entrepreneurs are effecting a reunification of sorts beyond the control of political leaders. And in "Vietnamese Boat People Going Home to Rebuild Their Lives," 11-8, he depicts the grim conditions in Hong Kong refugee camps.

Peter Gumbel
The Wall Street Journal
★★

Paris bureau chief. Gumbel was alert all year to the ground-level rumblings of discontent with the process of political and economic unification in Europe, and seems to have a reliable, if conventional, fix on the Big Picture at the inter-governmental level. In "Noble Roquefort, The King of Cheese, Is Now Under Siege," 2-11, he delivers a engaging report on the uproar over a takeover battle between England's Nestle S.A. and Italy's Agnelli family: "They make saucepans on wheels," says one French critic. He hints that this battle of provincial pride over big business may be a metaphor for the new Europe. He does a superb job of showing us the face of French racism in "France First! Election Gives Voice to Far-Right Party," 3-23, evoking the chauvinistic far right which is winning increased support among French voters who are worried about unemployment and oncoming European unity. He travels to a site which has seen some of the worst of European history, the Alsace, for the inspired "They Speak German, Eat French Food, But Fear Maastricht," 6-26. He finds that citizens are open to the idea of a united Europe but feel that their political leaders are going about it the wrong way: "I say yes to Europe . . . But you can't make fools of the people." His roundup of the currency crisis and the French referendum on Maastricht, "French Vote Leaves Europeans Scrambling to Salvage Unity Plan," 9-21, is unremarkable, Gumbel focusing on how western Europe appears to be moving toward two-tier economic integration, centered around the German mark, a subject he returns to in the serviceable update, "European Countries Put On Show of Unity," 10-1. In the absorbing "A Swiss Bank Squirms as Official It's Suing Tells of Sleazy Deals," 12-11, he penetrates the veil of secrecy surrounding one of Europe's most powerful institutions, the Rothschild banking firm.

Clyde Haberman
The New York Times
★★½

Jerusalem bureau chief. Thomas Friedman has written on the power held by the occupant of this post, and it is power Haberman generally exercises wisely. His coverage of Israeli society remains impressive, but he offers little on the Israeli political economy, a particularly acute shortcoming in a year when economics helped bring down the Likud government. He provides a sensitive survey of the psychological scars one year after the Gulf War in "Scuds Are Gone, But the Israelis' Fears Linger," 1-21, and in "Killings of Palestinian Suspects Raise Questions About Israeli Army Agents," 4-12, he examines all sides of the issues raised by undercover killings of wanted Palestinian activists. In "Israelis Worry if World's New Epoch Will Find Them Shunted Aside by U.S." 8-3, he offers a detailed summary of the continuing strains on U.S.-Israeli relations. He positions Yitzhak Rabin as the man of the moment in "Battle-Scarred Warrior," 6-25, while in the post-election analytic "Israel's Vote Shows It Has Tired of Ideology," 6-28, he packages Rabin's victory as the triumph of pragmatism on the part of Israeli voters, revealing his personal preferences a bit too clearly. He fully examines the yawning gap between the expectations raised by Rabin's victory and the awesome problems confronting the country in "Israel's New Broom: How Much Time to Sweep?" 7-15: "The challenge for Mr. Rabin will be to keep the various hopes from sagging, and right now there are many questions in key areas." When the Rabin government faced its first crisis over attacks from Lebanon, Haberman deftly notes how Rabin's campaign promise to provide security is coming back to haunt him in "Early Test for Rabin: A Rise in Attacks on Israel," 10-29. We learn that Iran's nuclear weapons program may be behind the worsening diplomatic atmospherics between Jerusalem and Tehran in "Israel Focuses on the Threat Beyond the Arabs—in Iran," 11-8.

Blaine Harden
The Washington Post
★★★½

Warsaw bureau chief. Eastern Europe's news was a vast canvas this year, but the indefatigable Harden covered it all with the precision of a pointillist. Harden is a talented on-the-spot reporter who effortlessly works the bigger picture into his stories through his keen observations and informed judgments, masterfully mapped out the story of eastern Europe. He artfully presented the Polish political economy as a paradigm for "shock therapy," as Russia prepared to take the plunge. In "Poles Sour on Capitalism," 2-5, he evokes the "high costs, jerky pace and inequitable benefits of post-Communist reform," and in "Poland Changing Fiscal Policy to Meet West's Demands," 3-15, he provides plenty of data on how Poland is struggling to split the difference between meeting IMF economic guidelines and cushioning the transition as much as possible for Poles. Harden devoted the bulk of the year to diligently covering the ravages of ancient hatred in former Yugoslavia. "In Bosnia, 'It Is Very Ugly, Very Sad What Is Happening,'" 4-13, is grim and thorough on the growing refugee crisis. "Bosnia's Capital Reels Under Serbs' Onslaught," 5-3, lays out with precision how Bosnians are increasingly at the mercy of Serb forces, with little in the way of internal or external military power to stop them: "'Basically, it is a Serbian land grab,' said a Western diplomat in Belgrade." The inability of outside powers to stop the horror is examined in detail in such conscience-pricking analytics as "West Sends in Cavalry, But After Bosnia Is Gone," 7-11, and "Sarajevo's Fortunes This Winter Hinge on Serbs' Mood," 9-27. And human face of the crisis is revealed in such haunting reports as "Under Siege in Sarajevo—32 Days of Mounting Gloom," 6-2, and "'Juka's Wolves' Prowl Sarajevo Streets for Serbs, Untended Merchandise," 9-18. "'Winter Is Here and Hope Is Lost,'" 11-23, graphically reveals why "Sarajevo is more concentration camp than European capital."

Joel Havemann
Los Angeles Times
★★½

Brussels bureau chief. As the business of Europe increasingly becomes big business, Havemann provides comprehensive coverage of the ins-and-outs of European economic integration and continental business developments. He goes beyond number-crunching or trend-spotting to work in the larger political and historical forces at play. His ability to find "microcosms" of larger European stories is aptly demonstrated in "Banks, Business Find Bigger Is Much Better," 2-4, an in-depth case study of how one German tire manufacturer fought off a hostile takeover bid by Pirelli with the aid of a German-owned London bank. Havemann positions this as an anecdote for Europe as national trade barriers come down. We find a multidimensional look at western Europe's extensive social welfare programs as contrasted with those in the U.S. in "A Safety Net Snags on Its Cost," 4-21. He thoroughly documents why something is going to give, soon. His expertise at sketching European markets and the potential opportunities and pitfalls for U.S. businesses is showcased in "European Car Market Hits the Road in Fits and Starts," 5-5, and "U.S. Phone Companies Lay Stakes in New European Frontier," 5-31. The latter report is an especially fascinating look at why "Europe has become the Wild West of the telecommunications industry," with regional U.S. phone companies "among the Daniel Boones and the Davy Crocketts who have flocked here." He travels to a Polish farming community to provide a valuable ground-level look at the inability of eastern European countries to crack the western European market in "Decay Behind a 'Silver Curtain,'" 8-11. His coverage of the currency crisis was solid and alert to the potential impact on the U.S. economy, as in "Europe Currency Markets in Chaos," 9-17, a blow-by-blow account of the turbulence. And we receive a salutary reminder of the need to keep GATT talks on track in "Dear Mr. President," 11-3.

Chris Hedges
The New York Times
★½

Cairo bureau chief. From the marshes of Kurdish Iraq to the slums of Cairo, Hedges goes where the stories are. While we appreciate his resourcefulness, he often spreads himself too thin, blunting his analytical edge. His coverage of Libya, as it confronted the UN over the Lockerbie bombing, was mixed. In "Outlook in Libya: Adapt, Improvise," 4-17, he reports from Malta on how Libyans are fatalistically preparing to cope. In June, however, he travels to Tripoli and finds a society on the brink of revolution in such reports as "Libyans' Patience With Qaddafi Ebbs," 6-24, and "Libyan Doubts About Qaddafi Are Growing," 6-28. Both reports provide some revealing details, but neither is clear about where Libya and Qaddafi are headed. In "Kurds' Dream of Freedom Slipping Away," 2-6, he skillfully evokes the growing deterioration of conditions in the Kurdish zone in northern Iraq. These conditions, he concludes, have led to near-anarchy and the end of any hope for a Kurdish state. He provides a vivid ground-level report in "Kurds Creating a Country on the Hostile Soil of Iraq," 8-12, enabling us to understand the determined spirit of the Kurds in the face of nearly insurmountable odds and the vagaries of international power politics. As the U.S. enforced a no-fly zone in Iraq, south of the 32nd parallel, Hedges, in "At 140 [Degrees] Below Decks, You Might Say War Is Hell," 9-15, makes us feel the heat, tension and boredom of pseudo-combat duty in the Gulf. He provides key details on how the Muslim Brotherhood is winning support in Cairo's slums by filling a humanitarian void following a natural disaster, in "After the Earthquake, a Rumbling of Discontent," 10-21. He reveals how relief operations, many backed by the Saudi government, are funneling weapons and fighters to Bosnia's Muslims in "Muslims From Afar Joining 'Holy War' in Bosnia," 12-5, but the article is somewhat scattered in its presentation of facts.

Fred Hiatt
The Washington Post
★★½

Moscow. As communism and the Soviet Union melted away like spring snow in Moscow, the imaginative and resourceful Hiatt excelled at portraying the people and institutions left behind, struggling to find their way in a not-so-brave new world. If one theme ran through his coverage, it was the smoldering resentment of the people. As in late 1991, when he started on this beat, his coverage of the post-Soviet military was especially strong. In "Russian Nuclear Scientists Seek Business, Food," 1-18, he provides one of the best reports we saw on this troubling topic, searching out officials and scientists who tell of financial hardships. One tells him they have already been approached by the Libyans. He travels above the Arctic Circle for "Russian Test Site Displays Pride, Perils of a Superpower," 10-18, a revealing look at how some officials want to keep Russia's nuclear weapons program going, if for no other reason than "atomic might . . . is all that separates this struggling nation from being relegated to Third World status." We get a full sense of the wounded pride of the Northern Fleet as U.S. vessels steam into port bearing toys and medicine in "Russian Navy's Mood as Gloomy as Its Port," 7-5. All year he probed the margins of the economic dynamics of the Soviet collapse. In "Resentment of West Rising to Surface in Russian Congress," 4-9, he is precise on the growing disenchantment with Western financial aid packages and the accompanying economic advice. While other Russian correspondents were viewing the industrial complex as resistant to reforms, Hiatt, in "Closed Russian City Opens Door to Reform," 3-16, takes us to the formerly closed city of Gorky to document how capitalists and managers in their 30s and 40s are making the transition to a market economy. And "Russians Apathetic About Congress as Life Spins Out of Control," 12-6, dramatically captures the growing "disintegration" of day-to-day life in Russia.

Murray Hiebert
Far Eastern Economic Review
★★½

Hanoi bureau chief. As Vietnam slowly opens up to the world, we appreciate Hiebert's ability to see the country as it is today in all its complexities. Hiebert is chasing an exciting story, the creation of a new political economy in an ancient civilization. In "Woes of Ownership," 4-16, he provides an absorbing and revealing report on efforts of party officials to reverse a 1983 anti-capitalist campaign, placing a human face on the arbitrary twists and turns of one-party rule. We find a multidimensional report on the plight of Vietnamese minorities in "Dynamics of Despair," 4-23. Hiebert writes that the party's pro-market reformers want to integrate the highland minorities into the national economy while developing their resource-rich lands, but obstacles remain. His comprehension of Vietnam's cultural scene is displayed in the fascinating "Playing for Keeps," 5-7, an account of how one daring producer was able to mount a production of a play which deals with some of the hottest issues in Vietnam today. His revealing look at rising corruption in the North, "No Dong, No Deal," 6-25, expertly documents how "Party officials appear gradually to have lost much of their revolutionary discipline and become more interested in personal profit." He goes back a millennium to explore the cultural differences between North and South in "Vietnam's Dichotomy," 10-15, expanding our understanding of why the South is leading the drive toward economic modernization: "'Northerners are like the British,'" explains one overseas Vietnamese businessman, "'while southerners are like Australians.'" And in "New Landed Gentry," 12-3, he provides a comprehensive report on Vietnam's recent real estate boom, deftly folding in economic and cultural factors.

Michael A. Hiltzik
Los Angeles Times
★★★

Nairobi bureau chief. Having an outstanding year, Hiltzik, in his luminously written, in-depth reports, allows us to observe the crisis in Somalia firsthand, and enables us to understand the man-made causes that produce the pictures of starving children that fill our TV screens. We share fully the plight of international relief officials striving to bring aid to a lawless country, in "A War Within a War in Somalia," 8-18. Here Hiltzik starkly documents Western officials withdrawing into a "form of the 'Stockholm syndrome,' in which people who feel trapped by the intransigence of the culture they are trying to assist, respond by finding some primitive virtue in behavior they otherwise consider egregious." We find the real story of the crisis in his 10 Best selection "Somalia—Anatomy of a Famine," 9-24. Here, Hiltzik does a masterful job of deconstructing the political and economic forces which, like starvation in the human body, made the Somalian political economy break down and begin feeding upon itself. In "Hanging by a Thread," 12-1, Hiltzik soberly outlines the pros and cons of intervening for humanitarian reasons in strife-torn African nations such as Somalia, providing a salutary reminder that there are no easy solutions. Hiltzik also produced some impressive material on Ethiopia. In "Ethnic Pride Gets a Test in Africa," 2-11, he is detailed and thorough on the provisional government's program of promoting, not suppressing, tribal and ethnic differences, while in "Ethiopia Fears New Civil War, Loss of Its Aid," 4-15, he is observant on growing tensions between the two largest ethnic factions in the country. He gets an early start on what may be one of the biggest African business stories of the decade, the integration of South Africa's business community into the continent's economic structure, in the vivid "They're Set to Wheel and Deal," 7-8.

David Hoffman
The Washington Post
★½

Jerusalem. Replacing Jackson Diehl, Hoffman's early material out of Israel, which concentrated on strategic issues, hints of the solid, insightful reporting we associate with his White House years, not the uninspired coverage that characterizes his State Department posting in the first half of the year. He sketches a brief, but revealing portrait, of the evolving strategic relationship between Washington and Jerusalem in "New Era Forces U.S., Israel to Redefine Alliance," 7-28, where we learn how and why Israel hopes to become "the biggest carrier in the Mediterranean," in the words of one senior Israeli official. His report on the increasing violence associated with undercover Israeli agents in the occupied territories, "Israeli Undercover Units Targeting 'Hard-Core' Palestinian Cells," 8-24, is thorough on both the tactical reasoning and the human costs, but appears months after other dispatches on the subject. Fully examining one of the biggest issues separating Israel and Syria, the Golan Heights, in "Israeli Hopes, Fears Clash Over Return of Golan," 9-28, he presents a clear picture of the strategic pros and cons of a withdrawal. A two-part series marking the fifth anniversary of the start of the *Intifada*, "The Intifada's 'Lost Generation,'" 12-7, and "'There's No Black and White,'" 12-8, dramatically captures the psychological toll the uprising has taken on both Palestinian children and young Israeli soldiers. His State Department coverage early in the year, was serviceable at best. "Major Powers Differ on Ways to Aid Ex-Soviet States," 1-23, is straightforward on an international conference to discuss aid to the former Soviet Union, while in "Power Competition in Central Asia," 2-14, we receive the State Department view on the current situation in that region. Similarly, a survey of the mood of the country's foreign policy establishment, "Americans' Mood Limits Foreign Aid," 3-10, offers little insight, as Hoffman and the experts label the national mood isolationist, with Patrick Buchanan as its embodiment.

David Holley
Los Angeles Times
★★★

Beijing bureau chief. As capitalism asserted itself as the real last emperor of China, the observant Holley was one of the best daily journalists on the scene. Cognizant to both the ideological and institutional shifts underway, and alert to both the irony and the importance of the telling incongruities, Holley kept readers abreast of the China story. He expertly deciphers a directive against excessive "leftism" in "China Signals an Easing of Ideological Controls," 3-13, and reveals how Chinese leaders, under the guise of building "socialism," have decided to go all out for economic reform: "While such semantic maneuverings may seem abstruse, they can have profound effects." We find an expert look at the fault lines running through the Chinese political economy in "Beijing Wants Open Market But Closed Society," 5-19, Holley marshalling facts to show that, while the opposition is "being inexorably swept aside," most observers do not expect the changes to solidify until the octogenarians running the show are gone. Similarly, "China's Reformers Are Back on the Offensive," 7-18, is a superb update on the roller coaster progress of Deng's reform efforts, Holley reporting how and why "rhetoric has changed more than reality." Analyzing the Communist Party Congress in "China Congress a Pep Rally for Party Line," 10-15, Holley subtly, yet knowingly, plays up the party's decision to introduce a new way of thinking on the part of the people, and using the old ways to do it: "It seems that the party wants this new, more accurate thinking to be accepted more or less unanimously." "In Russia's Far East, Chinese Are Building on Cooperation," 11-24, he provides details and context on the growing use of Chinese labor in the Russian Far East.

Tony Horwitz
The Wall Street Journal
★★

London. Horwitz's reports reflect a keen wit, razor sharp powers of observation and, when the story calls for it, physical courage. He has the makings of a fine correspondent, although he needs to step back more often and place his anecdotal stories in a broader context. He tackles a story of Dickens-like proportions in "Working Class Culture Erodes Britain's Rank in a Unified Europe," 2-11, and artfully evokes class differences and lowered expectations which have become as solid as bedrock in England. But Horwitz never really addresses how this will affect Britain's competitiveness in the new Europe, only pointing out the obvious: "This may bode further decline as Europe's economy integrates and becomes more complex." Writing from Northern Ireland, he brings just the right touch to "Dear Mom and Dad, Having Fun, So Glad You're Not Here," 7-28, gently playing up the irony and the surrealism as the site of some of Europe's worst sectarian violence becomes a tourist stop on the Grand Tour. As the crisis in Bosnia heats up, Horwitz provides a rare look at the war from the Serbian side of the lines in "Ringing Sarajevo, Serbian Snipers Fire at Muslim Neighbors," 9-16, and "Life in Pale, Serb Headquarters, as Winter Nears," 9-23. Horwitz humanizes the Serb irregulars in the latter dispatch: "Young, cheerful and clad in a medley of civilian and paramilitary garb, they resemble rowdy college kids at the tail end of spring break." He also crystallizes the dehumanizing effects of war: "It is just like killing rabbits" says one Serbian gunner in the 9-16 article. We also get a sense of what motivates these irregulars—bravado, brandy, and fear. He captures with great sensitivity the poignancy—and irony—of true believers keeping the faith in the middle of Bosnia's "satanic" civil war in "Forward Into Battle? Not Here, Where the Virgin Reigns," 11-9.

Tom Hundley
Chicago Tribune
★★

Middle East. Hundley's reports on Middle Eastern politics often have the epic scope and penetrating detail of a David Lean movie. However, he needs to integrate the economic dynamics of the region into his coverage more often. His ability to work on a broad canvas is demonstrated in "Water May Be Next Flashpoint in Mideast," 2-2, a comprehensive look at the geopolitical implications of this precious resource. Also, "Islam Surges as Communism Recedes," 3-1, is quite good on the nascent Islamic movement in former Soviet Central Asia. He was keen all year to the shifting political sands in the region as they increasingly blew in the direction of democracy. "In the Arab World, Democracy Is a Foreign Concept," 6-7, provides background material as the region enters an age when "CNN has turned the world into a glass house," but falls into a pat psychology, blaming lack of Arab political progress on historical feelings of "humiliation." Much better are two reports on Arab democracy in action, "With Guns in Hand, Yemenis Test Democracy," 7-12, and "In Kuwait, Democracy Is Selective," 10-4, both multidimensional reports on the politics of two Arab countries which have just been through massive upheavals. He provided some of the best details we saw on the growing anti-Coptic violence in Egypt, "Sectarian Violence in Villages Reverberates in Far-Off Cairo," 9-27, reporting from Sanabu: "When an unfamiliar car churns slowly down the mud-rutted streets of this wretchedly poor village deep in the Nile Valley, mothers gather up their barefoot children and watch nervously from behind bolted doors." He artfully contrasts the Israeli military's declining prestige with the continuing desire of young males to enlist in the elite units in "Israeli Military Gradually Losing Its Allure," 11-29.

Youssef M. Ibrahim
The New York Times
★★★

Paris. Ibrahim continues to be one of the most knowledgeable and observant analysts of the Middle Eastern scene. His thoughtful reports are sensitive to the weaknesses and failings of the region's regimes and the yearnings of the populace in increasingly turbulent times. In "Algerians, Angry With the Past, Divide Over Their Future," 1-19, he expertly delineates how the country's "once-revolutionary leadership" lost touch with the masses, creating a "dispossessed majority" for the Islamic Salvation Front. In "A Peace That Still Can't Recover From the War," 5-6, Ibrahim is thorough on the post-occupation "malaise" afflicting Kuwait, while "Still Reeling From Gulf War, Jordanians Harden Attitudes," 6-14, is revealing on how the anti-Western mood in Jordan has solidified one year after Desert Storm. Ibrahim excels at conveying how the Arabs and the West view each other in the post-Cold War world, in "The Arabs Find a World in Which They Count Less," 4-5. Here he draws on officials from both the region and Washington to document how the U.S. now deals with each country individually, no longer concerned about an "Arab nation." In "Europe Looks at Iraq and Shrugs," 8-9, he artfully conveys the mixture of apathy and cynicism with which Europe is treating Washington's latest confrontation with Iraq. Like Washington, Ibrahim reports, the Europeans are now moving on to other concerns. In "The Middle East Lets Itself Consider Peace," 9-27, he provides an expert read on the changing atmosphere of Middle Eastern geopolitics, brought about by the end of the Cold War and growing fears of a militarily resurgent Iran. He is keen to the geopolitical implications of King Hussein's apparent distancing of himself from Saddam Hussein's regime in "Jordan's King Urges Iraqis Put an End to the Hussein Era," 11-8.

Adi Ignatius
The Wall Street Journal
★★½

Moscow bureau chief. In his first year on this beat, Ignatius excels at capturing the human face of the momentous changes underway. In a land where sometimes everyone seems unhappy, Ignatius enables us to understand how everyone is unhappy in their own way, and what this portends for the country as a whole. He was one of the first to report on how the growing Russia-Ukraine tensions were affecting military personnel, in the enterprising "Black Sea Fleet Stranded in Tug-of-War," 1-17, conveying a sense that ethnic conflict may be forthcoming. He aptly tracks the roller-coaster process of reforms in such dispatches as "Russians Endure a Winter of High Prices but Face More Economic Shocks on Spring," 3-10, "Economic Pain Set to Intensify in Russia," 4-20, and "Russia Isn't Shifting Direction on Reform," 8-10. He reports in the later dispatch that while the Yeltsin government evidently believes it can't go back, it is no longer moving ahead like a locomotive either: "Indeed, a new pragmatic line has made its way into official thinking: There is no point pursuing radical reform if the economy collapses in the process." His sketch of the growing unemployment problem, "Russians Face New Threat: the Pink Slip," 6-8, is well rounded but seems to accept the constriction as an inevitable by-product of the end of communism, with no possible alternatives. An existentialist note is sounded in "Disarray in Russian Army Leaves Its Officers Wondering if Government Really Wants Them," 9-8, Ignatius finding in the fears and complaints of the officers a potential powder keg. He quotes one officer:

"If the coup last year had succeeded, the army would have gone right along. We follow a winner." Expertly setting the scene for a key session in "Russia's Congress, Opening Today, To Test Yeltsin's Political Prowess," 12-1, he foresees plenty of hard political bargaining, with Yeltsin and his reforms surviving relatively intact.

Jim Impoco
U.S. News & World Report
★½

Tokyo bureau chief. Impoco has a flair for imaginative analogies and metaphors which add a dash of color to his writings on the Japanese political economy, but this inventiveness isn't often reflected in his reporting or analysis. As a result, his wordsmithery is only mildly effective. Commenting on President Bush's upcoming "trade mission" to Japan in "Uneasy Riders in Tokyo," 1-13, he is thorough on the political pressures and economic factors weighing on the minds of both Bush and Japanese PM Kiichi Miyazawa. He concentrated much of the year on the efforts of Japanese businesses and industries to cope with recessionary times. "Hitachi Tries to Dig Out Profits," 5-11, is detailed on how the electronic giant, which "sprinted full tilt on something like corporate steroids during the easy-money '80s," is retrenching. Similarly, "Watching the Roof Cave In," 8-17, competently conveys the near-depression in which Japanese securities firms are finding themselves, after expanding during the '80s "when the Nikkei stock index was levitating like a Sufi mystic." We find a brief yet informative look at the Japanese aerospace industry and how it is thriving as a parts supplier to U.S. firms in "How to Succeed Without Really Flying," 6-8, Impoco noting that some observers are concerned about the off-shore selling of U.S. technology in one of the few remaining high-tech sectors that the U.S. still leads. A broad overview of the Japanese economic downturn, "Tokyo in a Tailspin," 10-5, adequately reveals why the Japanese government's recent economic stimulus package is unlikely to turn things around: "Despite the potent fiscal injection, consumers are still retrenching; corporations are cutting investment as profits fall and inventories rise, and the financial sector still has a Leaning Tower of Pisa look."

Canute James
Financial Times
★★½

Caribbean bureau chief. James continues to be a singular source on the political economy of the region, providing details and insights we do not find elsewhere. He is comprehensive and thorough on the political and economic questions raised by the defeat of a referendum backed by Governor Rafael Hernandez Colon guaranteeing "democratic rights" for islanders regardless of future relations with the U.S., in "Puerto Ricans Ponder Future," 1-7. Commenting on the Dominican Republic's efforts to both cash in on and celebrate the 500th anniversary of Christopher Columbus's landing, in "Columbus Fever Runs High," 2-27, he strikes just the right note of wryness: "Cynics and the political *cognoscenti* concur that 500 years after he arrived, Columbus still has a profound effect on contemporary Dominican politics." He provides a crisp update on the Haitian political situation in "Haiti: A Theatre of the Absurd," 3-10. And in "Caribbean Feels Cold Winds Blow," 4-16/17, he is concise on the woes facing the region's crucial tourist industry, while in the highly informative "Political Bridge," 9-22, he is comprehensive on Belize's hopes to use its strategically placed position between the rest of Central America and the Caribbean to become a political and economic *entrepot* between the two regions now that its territorial dispute with Guatemala appears to be nearing a settlement. James places this development in full regional, historical and economic perspective. He forcefully reveals why the deteriorating diplomatic and economic situation regarding Haiti will likely push that nation to the front-burner of the incoming administration in "Haiti Set to Hold Clinton's Attention," 12-10, observing that "The overthrow of former president Mr. Jean Bertrand Aristide...has left the Organization of American States and the US embarrassed by their seeming impotence to restore the president."

Sam Jameson
Los Angeles Times
★★★

Tokyo bureau chief. A sure grasp of the subtleties of the Japanese way of life and this Asian country's unique perspective of looking at the world underlies Jameson's coverage of the Japanese political economy. With more than three decades on this beat, he has accumulated a vast database of knowledge and insight which frequently gives his work a three-dimensional edge. In a year when Japan and the U.S. has had more than their share of disagreements, Jameson's comprehensive "The Practical Side of Japan Wins Out," 8-4, is especially valuable. Here Jameson draws on his deep understanding of Japanese culture to thoroughly document how and why the Japanese view the world through the prism of pragmatism, not principle: "Precise rules . . . however, are precisely what Japanese wish most to avoid." He provides concise, informed reports on this pragmatism in action in foreign affairs with "Japan Aide Rips China 'Fussing,'" 9-8, and "Akhito's China Visit Won't Focus on 'Unfortunate' Past," 10-16. In the intriguing "Japan in Search of Its Heart," 2-22, he delivers a sensitive report on the growing debate in Japan over the medical and religious question of when death occurs. The article does seem a little stretched out, however. No report we saw in 1992 gave us as much illumination on Japanese society as "Does Japan Ever Really Change?" 12-9, Jameson providing the complex answer. We were impressed by Jameson's regional coverage in 1992. "Inflation Shakes Up S. Korea," 3-23, is an informative snapshot of the current state of South Korea's political economy as viewed by everyone from housewives to business leaders. In his best effort all year, "Freer Than Ever, Asia Goes Its Own Way," 5-19, he provides a breathtaking look at the Asian political economy and geopolitical situation at this pivotal moment in history, drawing on a vast network of contacts and his own encyclopedic knowledge of the region.

Henry Kamm
The New York Times
★★★

Geneva bureau chief. From the parks of the Crimea where Marxist idols still stand, to the neon-lit streets of Ho Chi Minh City, Kamm sorts out the debris left in communism's wake, while also monitoring nascent societies. His masterfully detailed reports move the story of communism's demise forward with fresh information, leaving indelible images on our minds. Kamm takes us into the Donets Basin mines in "Struggling Ukrainian Miners Are Put Off by Diet of Nationalism," 2-16, providing a firsthand look at miners upset that their leaders put nationalism ahead of economics. Adroitly working in everything from the ghosts of history to the material discomfort of the average citizen in "Picture Lenin and the Czar, Commuting by the Sea," 3-10, he offers a colorful dispatch from Yalta. His next stop on the ex-communist tour was Albania where he deftly contrasts the pro-democracy protestations of President Ramiz Alia with his Stalinist background in "Still in Power but a Convert, Albanian Says," 3-16. His observations on Thailand's near-chokehold on the Laotian economy in "Vietnam, Now Master of Its Own House, Mends Fences in its Own Neighborhood," 6-19, where he finds Vietnamese officials worried that Bangkok "wants to achieve through trade and investment what Vietnam failed to gain through military and political might," namely, regional hegemony. The 6-19 report, along with "As Marxism Fails, Ho Chi Minh City Becomes More Like a Saigon Redux," 5-31, and "Talking in Vietnam, Few Now Use the Party Line," 6-8, brilliantly depicts life in a land where non-believers in and out of government are ruled by priests worshiping a god that has failed. In "Nation Split, Havel Aspires to a New Political Life," 9-30, has Kamm wisely stepping back and letting the articulate Vaclav Havel speak for himself, while "Romania's Monuments Make Strange Bedfellows," 12-15, graphically captures the political and economic malaise gripping that country three years after the overthrow of Nicolae Ceausescu.

Thomas Kamm
The Wall Street Journal
★½

Rio de Janeiro bureau chief. As a reporter, Kamm has a talent for evoking time and place, but he can still stumble when it comes to offering the larger perspective, a particularly noticeable shortcoming in a region with several of the largest political economies in the world. In "Urban Problems Yield to Innovative Spirit of a City in Brazil," 1-10, he effectively captures a local mayor's efforts to turn his city into "something of a Mecca for urban planners and environmentalists," but provides little on the economic impact of all this. He conveys the mood of the army and the peasantry in Peru's Ene River valley in "Valley in Peru May Show a Glimpse of Things to Come," 4-8, but fails to move forward the story of President Alberto Fujimori's anti-insurgency efforts. Some of his best work was on the Rio Summit. "Some Big Problems Await World Leaders at the Earth Summit," 5-29, is a well-written, three-dimensional scene-setter, Kamm keen on both the ironies surrounding the summit and the serious conflict between the developed and underdeveloped worlds: "It will be Bretton Woods by way of Woodstock." "'Snow' as Rio Swelters at 100 Degrees Is Apt Metaphor for the Earth Summit," 6-8, artfully conveys the artificiality pervading the conference. On the other hand, he provides only a scattered overview of Latin America's political economy after the formal end of the '80s debt crisis in "Brazilian Accord Puts End to Debt Crisis in Region, But Not Economic Woes," 7-10. His "Talk of Buenos Aires Is That Latest Revival Is for Real," 9-11, is a more organized and comprehensive look at the "Argentine Miracle" wrought by President Carlos Menem and economy minister Domingo Cavallo. He provides a good sense of the mood of uneasiness surrounding the Brazilian political economy as President Itamar Franco settles into office in "Brazil's Enigmatic Franco Breeds Uncertainty," 11-5.

Gregory Katz
The Dallas Morning News
★½

Mexico City bureau chief. An enterprising reporter with a strong grasp of Mexican history and culture, Katz is a dependable source of engaging, informative reports on the Mexican scene. More than many reporters, he incorporates the voices of Mexicans into his reports. Katz makes little effort, though, to dig into the workings of Mexico's expanding economy. He captures the improvements U.S. franchisers are making in the lives of average Mexicans, by both offering popular goods and services and making Mexican businesses more competitive, in "Prosperity Gives Mexico a Taste for U.S. Goods," 1-27. Journeying to the Mexican southwest to expose the continuing fault lines running through the Mexican justice system in "Bitter Struggle Over Forest Land Tests Power of the Law in Mexico," 2-2, he offers an important look at the ability of elected officials to enforce environmental laws as NAFTA looms. Some of his strongest coverage of the year was of the tragic gas explosion in Guadalajara. In the detailed "Oil Factory Denies it Is to Blame," 4-24, he searches out the owners and workers of the family-run cooking oil factory, initially blamed by Pemex for the tragedy, making it evident that the factory is being set up as a scapegoat. As the facts emerged in "Mexican Groups Hope to Prevent More Environmental Disasters," 5-2, Katz crisply details the political fallout both locally and nationally, writing that the country's "rising environmental consciousness" is likely to get a boost. He provides a well-rounded report on Mexico's reaction to NAFTA's signing in "Salinas Tells Mexicans Treaty Will Bring Better Jobs," 8-13, presenting the views of both government supporters and treaty opponents and noting that many are nervous over the "legal drafting" of the future treaty. In "A Radical Change . . . Among Many in Mexico," 12-6, he artfully captures the fears of many Mexicans that the upcoming currency shift to "new pesos" will translate into higher inflation, despite government protestations to the contrary.

Jonathan Kaufman
The Boston Globe
★★

Berlin. Kaufman excelled at tracking the ghosts of political extremism and the upheaval which haunted Europe in 1992. He zeroed in early on Germany's internal angst and growing external might and stayed on top of the story. But, he fails to explore any connection between Germany's political and social strife and its slowing domestic economy. In "As the Continent Tilts Toward Germany," 1-5, he provides an interesting, albeit slightly slanted perspective on Germany's growing regional clout: "The German model of a social-market economy—capitalism with a human face—is far more attractive, [than the U.S. model] especially to countries used to cradle-to-grave services." We get good details on the development of eastern Europe as a sphere of German economic interest, even at the expense of the U.S., in "Anguish in Adaption," 2-23, and "The Battle for Foreign Business Becomes a Battle for Future US Economic Growth and Political Influence," 2-24. Driving home the human face of the anti-foreigner violence in Germany was the gist of such detailed reports as "Germany Hastens Exit of Gypsies," 11-1, and "The Issue of Identity That Underlines Germany's Violence," 8-31. In the latter, he takes us beyond the barricades, expertly explaining why the phenomenon is "rooted in the way Germans define their identity, combined with missteps and political maneuvering by the German government." However, "New Wall of Hate Tilts Germany to Right," 11-15, is over-alarmist, Kaufman seeing a tidal wave of neo-Nazism rolling over Europe if economic conditions do not improve. His coverage of the German economy was centered around its role as an "overloaded caboose slowing Europe to a crawl," as he puts it in "Rise of German Mark Tips Balance in Europe," 9-3. But he doesn't correctly assess the fiscal/monetary equation creating this situation.

Lincoln Kaye
Far Eastern Economic Review
★★★

Beijing bureau chief. A deeply knowledgeable observer of the Asian scene, Kaye specializes in smart, sophisticated reporting and analysis in prose that is usually a literary step above what we generally find in *FEER*. In "Deng Speaks Out," 2-13, he provides an expert summation of recent signals that Deng and his allies are intending to lock in place the shift of large sectors of the economy from public to private. We get a rich, comprehensive report on Mongolia as it teeters on falling back into China's sphere of influence in "Faltering Steppes," 4-9. Here Kaye effortlessly links Mongolia's ethnic ties and historical points of conflict with its neighbor to the south. Kaye uses the occasion, May Day, to provide a valuable look at the labor side of Chinese economic reforms in "Mayday May Day," 5-7, writing that top labor officials believe "Rising output, rather than independent labour advocacy, is the key to conflict management in the work place." We find a clever distillation of the changing mood in China as Kaye observes the new McDonald's in Tiananmen Square, directly across from the Chinese leadership compound, in "Traveller's Tales," 6-11: "Judging from the number of family snapshots posed in front of the two doorways on the Sunday before 4 June, McDonald's has far more fans than Zhongnanhai." In "Waiting for Godot," 7-16, and "Out of the Loop," 7-16, he produces two fine, brief pieces on burgeoning stock markets in Shanghai and the outer regions. He offers a wealth of details on the back-room politicking behind the public reshuffling at the 14th Party Congress in "Uncertain Patrimony," 10-29, and "Deng by a Whisker," 11-12. Kaye draws on unnamed diplomats, Chinese observers, and his own reading of the Chinese scene to warn that the real message of the Congress is that the hardliners are standing by if the reformers come a cropper.

Bill Keller
The New York Times
★★★½

Johannesburg bureau chief. Keller's South African coverage displays the same sophisticated analysis and inspired, ground-level reporting that characterized his excellent work out of Moscow. A talented wordsmith, his prose illuminates the South African political landscape. Finding himself covering a massacre for his first major story, "South African Massacre: Fingers Point at the Police," 6-20, he adroitly conveys the murky relationship between the police and *Inkatha*, played out against the grimy despair of worker hostels and squatter camps. He also provided incisive and imaginative analysis of the political climate, as in "A Fitful Pas de Deux," 7-10, observing in the 7-10 report that both sides are now participating in "news-conference diplomacy," which "seems to have brought the adversaries closer to an agreement than they were when talks deadlocked in May." He deftly documents the ambivalence of middle- and lower-class blacks toward an ANC-sponsored two-day strike with "In a South African Township, 2 Views of a Strike," 8-5. In the superb "Democracy vs. Dictator in Apartheid's 'Homeland,'" 9-10, he profiles the "make-believe country of Ciskei," in the aftermath of a massacre. The tale enables us to understand why such a tragedy was inevitable, due to the intractable nature of South African racial politics and the psychological makeup of Ciskei's ruler, Brigadier General Oupa J. Gqozo. In the forward-looking analytic "South Africa's Peril," 10-1, he examines the potential peril Zulu leader Mangosuthu G. Buthelezi poses to any power-sharing agreement between the government and the ANC, warning that if Buthelezi allies himself with other homeland leaders and conservative whites, a possible Yugoslavia could result as the country fractures. His stellar writing skills are richly displayed in "For Rich Tourists (and Not Too African)," 12-3, a memorable look at a new resort, brimming with African *kitsch*.

Frederick Kempe
The Wall Street Journal
★★

Brussels bureau chief. Kempe's final year in Bonn was marked by a tendency to put Germans, and Germany, on the couch. At times we found this approach imaginative and observant; other times we thought it contrived and narrow. In the timely update, "Germany Is Seeking to Ease Concerns in U.S. Over Its Reliability as an Ally," 2-4, Kempe reveals that the Kohl Government has decided to do what it can to aid Bush this election year, even if it puts relations with other European governments at risk: "Underlying the German approach…is a belief that Washington will increasingly be the only consistent friend on which a more influential Germany can rely." Addressing Chancellor Kohl's political difficulties in "Rightists' Success in Germany Reflects Voter Anger Over Foreign Obligations," 4-10, he astutely observes that, like Bush, Kohl must be seen paying attention to domestic economic issues at a time events warrant a greater international role. The emphasis is on the psychological as much as the political in "Germany's Huge Bill for Bailing Out East Is Riling its Workers," 5-15, as Kempe profiles the west German work force at a time of great uncertainty. He takes an imaginative look at Germany's efforts to forge a new foreign policy as Washington and Paris offer different visions of post-Cold War security arrangements in "Europe's Awkward Love Triangle," 6-17. Kempe forces the analogy that, like an independent lover, Bonn is coyly leading both on while preparing to go its own way. He offers an anecdotal report on symptoms of creeping optimism in east Germany in "After Two Hard Years, East Germans Believe Worst Is Finally Over," 8-28. No mention is made, though, of the ongoing anti-immigration unrest, which suggests things are not quite as placid as Kempe depicts. In "Berlin Flourishes Again as Newcomers Pour In, But Difficulties Arise," 11-4, he artfully captures the social dislocation and artistic ferment in reunified Berlin.

Stephen Kinzer
The New York Times

Bonn bureau chief. The German story for Kinzer this year was a country uneasily trying to come to terms with its past. Usually, he offered revealing snapshots of a troubled society, but sometimes he simply recycled material seen elsewhere. In the appropriately somber "Germany Marks Place Where Horror Began," 1-20, he examines a contemporary Germany still struggling with the nightmares of the Nazi era, as he reports on the opening of a Holocaust memorial in the Wannsee Villa. He is detailed and thorough on the difficulties created by Bonn's policy of "return, no compensation," for private dwellings seized by the communists in "Anguish of East Germans Grows With Property Claims by Former Owners," 6-5, but doesn't fully address the larger policy issues. He sensitively profiles a quietly remarkable man, Joachim Lehmann, in "Living, and Living With Oneself, In the Grip of East Germany," 5-3, the story of an east German clergyman and artist who was able to balance dissidence with survival during the communist years, and who is confident about the new Germany. However, by the time Kinzer profiles Barbel Bohley, "Mother of the Revolution," for "One More Wall to Smash: Arrogance in the West," 8-12, the story of former East German dissident leaders, disillusioned by the course of events, was becoming cold. His ability to vividly depict the rising alienation of east German youth cut off from the security of a system they despised is showcased in "Youths Adrift in a New Germany Turn to Neo-Nazis," 9-28. One chilling quote from a young tough says it all: "Something is very wrong in Germany. We're going to fix it." In the richly illuminating "History Is Another Recruit in the Balkan War," 11-15, he artfully conveys the historical factors motivating the Serbs without condoning the atrocities they are committing in history's name.

Robin Knight
U.S.News & World Report
★

European senior editor. While Knight can work a great deal of information into his reports, his analysis is usually too general to further our understanding of a story. Characterizing the Russian people as "always fatalistic" in "New Year, Old Fears," with Julie Corwin 1-13, he provides a comprehensive look at the economic and political forces tearing away at the newly-formed Commonwealth of Independent States and Boris Yeltsin's new government. An evocative report on the economic devastation the communists left behind in Siberia, "Northern Exposure," 3-30, gives us a good idea of how the economic reforms are playing "out in the sticks," where former *apparatchiks* still have a choke-hold on power and many "stoic" Russians are living lives of deprivation. Reporting on Scottish nationalism in "The Ghost of Robert Bruce Stirs Again," 2-24, Knight gives the impression that independence for the highlands is just around the corner—"a tide of discontent every bit as revolutionary as the one that brought independence to the Baltic States is now flowing through Scotland." Yet, a few months later the Scottish National Party was swamped in the April elections. He has a better grasp of the political aspects of the British election in "Britain Springs a Major Surprise," 4-20, but has little evidence to back up his assertions about the British economy: "With Britain on the verge of economic recovery and locked into the inflation-busting European exchange-rate mechanism, the Tories are set to preside over a period of stable prices, moderate taxation and steady expansion." His best report all year, "Serbia's Hollow Victory," 9-14, provides some of the key details we were looking for on the current political and economic picture in Belgrade.

Scott Kraft
Los Angeles Times

Johannesburg bureau chief. Although his South Africa coverage lacks the authoritative touch of a Patti Waldmeir or a Bill Keller, Kraft is still a reliable source of news and analysis on South African political developments, often capturing the nuances of its fractured racial divisions. We would like to see more, though, on the South African economy, especially as it impacts, and is impacted by, political events. He insightfully places in context F. W. de Klerk's decision to hold a nationwide referendum for whites only on negotiations for multiracial rule in "De Klerk's Question for Whites: 'Do You Support Reform?'" 2-25. His usual subtle touch is missing from "Anti-Apartheid Vote Inspires Optimism," 3-20, an overly-broad survey of South Africa's mood the day after the referendum passed. Kraft writes here of "warm feelings [spreading] across the land...creating an atmosphere of racial harmony never before seen in South Africa's long history of conflict and bloodshed." The spine of the South African story through the winter and early spring was the on-again, off-again negotiations between the ANC and the government in the face of violent flare-ups, and Kraft provided several superb analytics along the way. Detailed for "On the Brink," 6-30, he thoroughly assesses how the Boipatong massacre has ended the de Klerk government's hopes of maintaining support among the "silent majority" of black South Africans, a key detail we did not see elsewhere. Analyzing the political scene in the aftermath of the Ciskei massacre, in "Killing of 28 Underlines Need for S. Africa Talks," 9-9, he draws on pro-government newspaper editorials and statements of black leaders to buttress his contention that negotiations are the only way out. He sketches a three-dimensional portrait of UNITA leader Jonas Savimbi following his defeat at the Angolan polls, in "Savimbi: A Rebel Discredited," 11-10.

Nicholas D. Kristof
The New York Times
★★

Beijing bureau chief. We were heartened to see Kristof expanding his coverage of the Chinese economic picture, but in a year when the big story in Beijing was the massive institutional changes underway, he had a tendency to focus on personalities. In "Chinese Wait for Deaths of Their Leaders, Who Just Get Older," 1-24, he gives us a bemused survey of rumors and speculation as the aging communist leadership pushes the edge of the actuarial envelope. A profile of PM Li Peng, "the most hated man in China," in "Who's Wounded Now? It's the Tiger of Tiananmen," 3-25, typifies Kristof's personality-oriented approach toward Chinese politics. Throughout the year, NYT foreign correspondents contributed to a special series, "After the Cold War." While most were content to simply recycle existing material, Kristof, in his installment, "As China Looks at New World Order, It Detects New Struggles Emerging," 4-21, went out and dug, coming up with evidence of increased Chinese military spending and a secret government document showing China positioning itself as a superpower. A flavorful report on Chairman Mao's grip on the populace 16 years after his death, "China's Newest God: The Godless Mao," 6-2, is late on the subject. In "After Riots, Will Beijing Sell Reform Short?" 8-16, he provides a thoughtful look at the riots surrounding a stock offering in Shenzhen: "The Shenzhen riots suggest the difficulties with pursuing a free market in which citizens are free to buy shares but not to protest corruption." He gives a good read on the mood in the Chinese capital toward the U.S. presidential election in "China Worried By Clinton's Linking of Trade to Human Rights," 10-9. In "Old Animosity in Hong Kong," 12-3, he places the escalating dispute between Governor Chris Patten and Beijing in historical perspective, but fails to work in exactly what Great Britain and China agreed to in the 1984 treaty at the heart of the dispute.

Christina Lamb
Financial Times
★★★

Rio de Janeiro bureau chief. Lamb's coverage of the southern cone is consistently characterized by political and economic savvy, healthy skepticism, and an expert ability to pull together many facets of a complex story, without resorting to oversimplification. We usually finish her stories feeling others have said far less in twice the space. She is thorough on the "question marks" still hanging over the Brazilian economy, despite evident signs of improvement in recent months in "Brazil's Turnaround Is All in the Mind," 1-31. She provides a lucid assessment of the economic reforms being implemented by the Collor regime in "On the Road to Righteousness," 3-16, observing presciently that "The big question is whether, having introduced a market model for the economy, Mr Collor can go on to stabilise it." Of all the reports we read on the eve of the Earth Summit, Lamb provided some of the most thought-provoking, as with "Fragile Frontline of the Forest," 5-30/31. Here she makes clear that, while a way needs to be found to promote "sustainable development," there are no easy answers. She also produced some superb reports on President Collor's political decline and fall. "Political Resentment Thrives in a Country Divided," 9-29, places the crisis in the context of north/south tensions, while "Collor Scandal Has Put Brazil's Economic Reforms on Ice," 9-4, is detailed on the economic impact. She also produced an article on "Collorgate" for *The Spectator* of London, "An Awful Lot of Trouble in Brazil," 9-12, imaginatively summing up the story in all its elements, from class tensions to soap opera. "Brazil Remains Mystified by Its 'Ordinary' Man," 11-12, effectively conveys the questions surrounding Collor's successor, Itamar Franco, who has espoused a more populist approach in both style and policy.

Flora Lewis
The New York Times
★½

Senior editor. A thought-provoking nugget or two can usually be gleaned from Lewis's columns, but often her work lacks fresh insight and reporting. It is clear she wishes to use her position to push the world toward greater political and economic integration, but sharper debating skills would help. In the wide-ranging essay, "The 'G-7 ½' Directorate," *Foreign Policy* Winter 1991-92, she fleshes out an argument advanced by *The Economist* nearly a year earlier, contending that the G-7 ½ (the current G-7 and Russia) are the best positioned actors on the current world stage to deal with challenges presented by the new world order: " . . . the G-7 ½ has both the supple informality and the continuity to give some cohesion to the attempt to keep the world from mindlessly stumbling along." Keeping the world from "mindlessly stumbling along" comprised much of her work this year. In "Europe's Last-Minute Jitters," 4-24, she provides a salutary reminder that, despite recent domestic political hitches, European economic unity has taken on near-irreversible momentum. But, she needed more evidence to support her case. In "The End of Sovereignty," 5-23, she advances the provocative notion that democracy becomes incompatible with a free-market economy when economic decisions can be made outside the hands of accountable elected officials. But no matter what, she writes, "This is the way the world is going." In one of her best efforts all year, "Would Rabin Go to Damascus?" 7-7, she talks to both Palestinian and Israeli officials to buttress her argument that a historical breakthrough may occur if newly-elected Israeli PM Yitzhak Rabin is ready to take a high-risk gambit for peace. And in the compelling "Save Lives in Bosnia," 11-9, she calls on the world Jewish community to take the lead in rescuing the Muslim inmates of Serbian concentration camps: "The moral duty is general, but refusal to shirk it and to be indifferent is especially appropriate from the representatives of Jews."

John Lloyd
Financial Times
★★½

Moscow bureau chief. Increasingly, Lloyd offers an apocalyptic vision of the former Soviet Union, portraying a vast region on the brink of civil war and economic meltdown. How much of this is based on his own observation, and how much is the perspective of his sources, is open to question. Overall though, his perspicacity is commendable. He is quick to write an RIP for the new C.I.S. in "C.I.S.O.S." *The New Republic* 1-6/13, and for Boris Yeltsin's economic reforms in "Yeltsin's Perilous Balancing Act," 2-5. He warns in the latter, that the last-ditch solution appears to be large-scale financial support from the West: "It is the Demand —some would say the Hold-Up—of the Century: the plea for huge sums, or the consequences will be disintegration, conflict, a huge Yugoslavia." Lloyd can still step back and offer superior analytical efforts, as in "Fault-Lines Spread From Without to Within," 3-23, and "The Cauldron in the Caucasus," 5-26. Both are three-dimensional looks at the fires flaring up on Russia's perimeters. In "Painful Legacy of an Empire," 7-9, he alertly picks up early signals of Moscow's growing hard-line attitude toward the former republics. The Russian economy was Lloyd's other main focus this year. In the masterful "The Quagmire of Russian Reform," 8-5, he persuades that the experiment is not likely to end with a bang but a thousand whimpers from an impoverished population and a polarized government: "The Gaidar team has not run into a wall, but it appears to have waded into a marsh, which grows steadily deeper and stickier the more it attempts to plough on." He provides an incisive scene-setter for the reconvening of the Russian parliament, against a backdrop of economic decline and political maneuvering on all sides, in "Carrots and Sticks," 9-22. In "The Winter of Discontent," 11-19, he produces an authoritative summation of the Baltic political economies.

Mark Magnier
The Journal of Commerce
★★½

Southeast Asia bureau chief, Singapore. After a transitional year, Magnier has come into his own. His work is now exhibiting both a keen understanding of the complexities of the region and a return to the engaging writing style that marked his West Coast bureau days. In "Executives Kick Tires of Car Deal, Frown," 1-10, he offers a concise yet revealing summation of views from both Japanese and U.S. automakers, enabling us to understand why neither side came away from Bush's trip to Tokyo particularly happy. His equally shrewd follow-up, "Japan-Based US Executives Assess Bush Trip as Naive, Ineffectual," 1-13, articulates the poor impression the President made. He provides a superb report on an evident breakthrough in negotiations between the U.S. and Asian nations over the protection of property rights in "US Gains in Effort to Protect Intellectual Property in Asia," 2-3. This report is especially lucid on why "getting the laws on the books is only the first battle in this war over protection of ideas..." A visit to Vietnam produced several valuable reports on that country's efforts to emerge from the deep freeze. "Prison Guards Are Reluctant Guides for US Group in Vietnam," 4-30, offers an artful metaphor for U.S.-Vietnamese dealings. The superior "Vietnam Trade Growth Vested in Garments," 6-11, offers both a look at one Vietnamese entrepreneur taking advantage of a changing political climate and a revealing glimpse at how Vietnam is working its way back into the world economic community. He takes an amusing look at Lee Kuan Yew's efforts to make Singaporeans more polite and courteous in "Singapore Government Wants Citizens on Their Best Behavior," 7-13. "Singapore Bars Evangelist From Conducting 'Miracle' Services," 11-3, deftly conveys the uneasy relationship between Western religions and Singapore authorities in the city-state.

Victor Mallet
Financial Times
★★★

Bangkok bureau chief. There were some fascinating stories in his region this year and they were artfully told by Mallet, whose keen eye and journalistic instincts remain as sharp as ever. This is a journalist who can put his finger on the exact point at which the diverse aspects of a story converge. In "Asia Greets Burma Human Rights Abuses With Deafening Silence," 2-25, he probes the reasons behind the official silence with which ASEAN nations are treating mounting atrocities in Myanmar, contending that commercial, not cultural, factors are behind the decision. He also takes a picaresque look at the Thai political scene as that nation heads into elections. His "Thai Election Raises the Price of Corruption," 3-11, effectively contrasts the bribery and horse trading against the backdrop of a military regime that has found its handpicked civilian government to be both disobedient and "one of the most competent the country has known." During the political unrest in Bangkok in the spring, he offered perceptive analytics that examined all the implications for the country and the region, as with "Thai Political Failures Reach Economy," 5-29. Here he notes that some are seeing a silver lining: "Many economists and bankers, however, dismiss fears of a balance of payments crisis, saying that the violence has simply aided the necessary process of slowing down an overheated economy." An update on the Thai political situation, "Putting the Generals Out of Business," 7-14, is thorough and compelling on how deeply interwoven the Thai military and the country's political economy have become. And in the engaging "Enterprise Brews in Cambodia," 8-5, we learn of efforts by foreign investors to restore an abandoned Cambodian brewery. He incisively reveals that the Burmese military regime's commitment to reform is essentially camouflage for continued control in "Burmese Junta Sports Reformist Robes," 11-12.

John Marks
U.S. News & World Report
★★½

Berlin bureau chief. While many newsweekly foreign correspondents offer quick once-overs of the week's events, the observant Marks often weaves German history and culture into his reports, which are usually substantive and literate to an uncommon degree. References to Immanuel Kant elevate "New Life for a Ghost Town," 1-13, a vivid report evoking the grim, post-industrial air of Kaliningrad, formerly Konigsburg, a city with "all the charm of a bivouac in an abandoned graveyard." Moscow hopes to turn the port into a Hong Kong of sorts. He puts the expected escape from justice of former East German *Stasi* chief Erich Mielke in full historical and moral perspective in "An Old Account," 2-17: "The 19th-century German playwright Georg Buchner wrote: 'The Revolution is like Saturn—it eats its own children.' With Erich Mielke, it sleeps on a full stomach." In "A Fond Farewell to Former Conquerors," 4-6, he artfully captures the departure of the U.S. 2nd Armored Cavalry Regiment from Amberg, where it had been stationed for 47 years. In "The Shadow of Their Swastika," 6-15, he memorably profiles neo-Nazi leader Thomas Kreyssler, incisively revealing how historical forces, along with a talent for self-promotion, have made this 22-year-old more than "just another self-absorbed post-adolescent rebelling against his parents, his school or his lot in life." He thoroughly probes the reasons why German Chancellor Helmut Kohl appears to be losing his "Faustian bargain" of delivering German unification on the political and economic cheap and what this portends for Germany and Europe in "The Devil and Helmut Kohl," 10-5.

David Marsh
Financial Times
★★★½

Deputy foreign editor. Able to pick and choose stories to which he can apply his formidable talents, Marsh takes on topics as familiar as the refugee crisis and as obscure as the debate over the European Central Bank. With this broad scope, Marsh tells us the story of Europe in 1992, usually with more understanding and comprehension than anyone else. In "Right-Wing Parties Plan Push for Power," 1-20, he expertly positions what a resurgence of far right parties portends for a unified Europe, noting that an anti-EC "backlash" is most prominent in France and Germany, the "traditional... sponsors of European integration." He pens a beautifully-written report from border towns and refugee camps, recording the growing hostility in "civilized" Europe toward uprooted immigrants from eastern Europe and the Third World in "No Hiding Place for Europe's Fugitives," 5-9/10. Marsh, in his understated but devastating way, brings home the growing dimensions of this human tragedy. He takes an astute look at the political and PR battle being waged over the site of the European Central Bank in "No Place for Bank to Call Home," 7-14, providing good details on the behind-the-scenes disputes over the ECB's independence. In "A Hard Act to Follow," 9-23, he produces a highly readable, knowledgeable history of Germany's Bundesbank as England debates whether it should move toward a politically independent Bank of England geared toward price stability. Marsh makes it abundantly clear that unique political and historical forces have made the Bundesbank what it is today: "Venerated for its orthodoxy, vilified for its obstinacy, the Bundesbank is deity and demon combined." Marsh also produced a book on this subject in 1992, *The Bundesbank: The Bank That Rules Europe*. His breadth of knowledge of the inner workings of the Bundesbank and the policy goals of its president, Helmut Schlesinger, give added value to "After-Shocks Shatter Currency Union Illusion," 11-23.

Gary Marx
Chicago Tribune
★★

Latin America correspondent. Asked to cover a huge and diverse territory, Marx has proven himself a reliable, even occasionally provocative, source of fresh, critical details on South America's political economy. In "Latin America's Reforms Begin to Bear Fruit," 1-19, he provides a thorough roundup of the formal and informal economies of South American nations, noting that "public opposition [to juntas] could weaken if the current leaders falter and countries become paralyzed by strikes and political unrest." He provided nuanced coverage of Peru this momentous year, often focusing on peasants and slum dwellers caught in the middle, in such reports as "'Campaign of Terror,' Strangling Peruvians," 3-22. A journey into Peru's upper Huallaga Valley for "Flighty General Takes a Powder," 8-28, effectively conveys the gap between official pronouncements on successes in the drug war and the reality on the ground. He is detailed and thought-provoking on the Peruvian government's efforts to "demystify" captured Shining Path leader Abimael Guzman in "Peru Tries to Demythologize Rebel Leader," 9-18. Writing from Rio's largest slum, Rocinha, in "In Rio Slums, Saving Earth Is a Luxury," 6-7, he reports that "Just over the hill from Rocinha, wealthy Brazilians are cutting the forest to build swimming pools and tennis courts. Why, [a slum dweller] asks, don't politicians complain about that?" Writing on the coming impeachment of Brazilian President Fernando Collor de Mello in "Brazil Move Aids Democracy—But Is it Enough?" 10-4, he pungently argues that democracy will remain fragile in Latin America while power remains in the hands of elites and economic growth benefits the few, not the many. He expertly positions the economic impact of Collor's replacement and the new economic team in "Uncertain Course for Brazil," 10-11, while "Paraguay Democracy Strains for Credibility," 11-8, is thorough on Paraguay's political and economic history.

Hamish McDonald
Far Eastern Economic Review
★★½

New Delhi bureau chief. McDonald is a steady and reliable source of information and insight on the subcontinent's political economy and the security concerns of the region. Highly illuminating in "Wind of Change," 3-12, he assesses Finance Minister Manmohan Singh's overhaul of India's trading policies. Also excellent is "The Toll of Terror," 4-9, an educational portrait of India's efforts to address human rights concerns amid ethnic separatist violence and terrorism. McDonald contrasts one view from street level, where nervous young soldiers face hostile crowds and provocations "day in and day out, with the safety catches off," and another view from New Delhi, where government leaders struggle with external criticism and fears of hurting military morale. In "Destroyer of Worlds," 4-30, we find an incisive look at how New Delhi and Islamabad are increasingly, hinting that they hold nuclear weapons. McDonald deftly probes the ambiguity surrounding India's handling of outside diplomatic efforts to end the regional arms race: "India appears to be playing for time because it has not yet worked out whether the new international setting, and relations with Pakistan, require policy changes." "Round One to Reforms," 7-23, is an authoritative look at the progress PM P. V. Narasimha Rao has made in his attempt to transform socialist India into a free-market capitalist country. We find out where Rao has backtracked, and where progress has been made. His expertise on the Indian military is demonstrated in "Arms Squeeze," 10-15, a thorough investigation of the problems posed to India's arsenal by Moscow's economic difficulties. Joined by co-writer Rita Manchanda for "Shattered Covenant," 12-17, the team effectively conveys the communal violence in December and the political fallout: "The Ayodhya crisis could...mark a shift in India's political culture, away from secular institutions supported since independence, towards Hindu chauvinism."

James McGregor
The Wall Street Journal
★★

Beijing bureau chief. In a year when China underwent revolutionary political movement toward entrepreneurial capitalism, McGregor seemed overwhelmed like much of the press corps. While he continues to produce illuminating snapshots, the big picture with its important global implications often eludes him. He strikes a Malthusian tone in "A Dash of Capitalism Just Might Help China Control Its Population," 1-2, on UN efforts to bring birth control to rural Chinese peasantry. The report abounds with euphemisms. He refers to state-enforced abortions as "strong-armed" tactics or "heavy handed policies." Presenting both sides of the equation for U.S. firms trying to crack the Chinese market in "U.S. Companies in China Find Patience, Persistence and Salesmanship Pay Off," 4-3, he draws on company histories to reveal the long, difficult road to success. "China's Modernization Draws Pioneers," 5-20, explains why U.S. firms face a disadvantage: "Unlike nearly all other industrialized nations, the U.S. doesn't offer 'soft,' or concessionary, loans. And U.S. businesses often don't operate in unified groups, as do many of their European and Japanese competitors." Able to penetrate China's secretive Fujian Province, in the resourceful "Overseas Chinese Quietly Invest at Home," 6-16, he documents how this province is prospering, thanks to investments from highly successful ethnic Chinese. In "Chinese Dissident Who Returned to Lion's Den Pays the Price for Taunting the Beijing Regime," 9-15, McGregor gives us a rich portrait of this courageous, if foolhardy, young man and a revealing glimpse of dissidence in the media age. He resourcefully portrays the city of Shekou as a paradigm of how "the socialist market economy" may work, in "Chinese City Has One Ideology: Profit," 12-10.

George Melloan
The Wall Street Journal
★★

"Global View" columnist and editorial page editor of *The Wall Street Journal Europe*. While Melloan was quick to observe that the end of the Cold War would mean as much adjustment for the West as for the East, his analytics declined appreciably this year, frequently coming across as one-dimensional, knee-jerk, or stale. It's a pity, as we used to turn to him regularly for unique insights, which are all too rare in his columns these days. He serves up froth in "When Will the Next Hostage-Takings Come?" 1-6, offering strident commentary on Islam and the Islamic world. We find nothing new on western European discontent in "Not Only East Europe Is Coming Unglued," 3-30. Surveying the "hypocritical" European reaction to the L.A. riots, in "Getting the Wrong Slant on L.A.'s Crisis," 5-4, he settles into predictable bashing of the Great Society. He raises some provocative questions in "How About Some Concern Over Ecojournalism?" 6-22, but fails to address them. We appreciate his blunt, but effective, note of caution on the rush to intervene militarily in Bosnia in "Peace Enforcement? Choose Your Weapons," 6-29. His forays into economics often prove troublesome, as in "Major Is Right to Resist the Coin Clippers," 7-27, in which he praises British PM John Major's decision to peg the pound to the DM, oblivious to the currency troubles ahead. The column drew a sharp response from former Thatcher economics adviser Alan Walters, who argued that "Pegged exchange rates promote perverse monetary policies." Responding, Melloan writes in "Monetary Jitters: Deja Vu All Over Again," 8-31: "The intended point of my July column was that the pound is now pegged to produce a low rate of inflation and to force British industry to become more efficient." As the currencies tumbled in Europe a few weeks later, Melloan compares Britain and Italy's departure from the ERM to the breakdown of Bretton Woods, in "Europe's Money Rift Won't Be Easy to Mend," 9-21. To our astonishment, he writes that the Federal Reserve took "interest rates down to near rock bottom.... But that brought no economic recovery, only a slump in the value of the dollar and a financial earthquake in Europe." After citing Bretton Woods, we would think Melloan would take a look at gold, which indicates that his arguments are ill-conceived.

Matt Moffett
The Wall Street Journal
★½

Mexico City bureau chief. Moffett tuned down the cynicism, which we found so distracting last year, and turned up the volume on the economic impact of *Salinastroika*. But, while things weren't as bad as he pictured them in '91, they weren't always as upbeat as he portrayed them in '92. We hope that in '93, he'll finally strike the right balance. Bullish on Mexican economic reforms as exemplified by the modernization and privatization of the Mexican phone company Telmex in "Telefonos de Mexico Makes Promising Start on a Daunting Task," 2-19, he fully documents why "For investors, Telmex is a play on a country that's coming on strong." The report provides a good comparison of Mexican business culture before and after *Salinastroika*. In the thought-provoking "White-Collar Migrants Head Into Mexico," 3-27, Moffett details how U.S. corporate executives are fleeing a depressed job market for a booming Mexican one. He seems amused by the Mexican *Bolsa* as it tries to absorb such shocks as Ross Perot, uncertainty about NAFTA, and U.S. investors suffering "dizzy spells" as if they've begun inhaling Mexico City's high altitude air in "Mexican Stock Market Deserts Investors Who Had Grown to Love It," 6-25, but a more in-depth analysis of the Mexican government's economic policies would have been more fruitful. In "Old Habits of Mexico's Ruling Party Imperil Goals of Reform-Minded Salinas," 7-9, he draws a brief, yet knowledgeable sketch of the Mexican political scene on the eve of two crucial provincial elections. He effectively conveys the benefits and losses of trade with Mexico through real-life case studies in "U.S. Manufacturers Already Are Adapting to Mexican Free Trade," 10-29, while "Mexico Gets Over Fears of Clinton Presidency as Analysts Cheer Statements on Trade Pact," 11-9, concisely summarizes the advantages Mexicans are already foreseeing in a Clinton administration.

Ray Moseley
Chicago Tribune
★★½

Chief European correspondent. A steadfast observer of Europe, east and west, Moseley keeps readers one step ahead of key stories and developing trends on the continent. With immigration an important European theme all year, Moseley, in "Spared Immigrant Tide, Europe Remains Wary," 2-16, provides some valuable perspective, observing that alarmist scenarios have thus far failed to materialize. He was quick to sight the potholes on the road to European unity, in "With Treaties Signed and Unity in Sight, Europeans Develop Cold Feet," 4-19. And in "European Leaders, Unity Hurt by Vote," 9-22, he imaginatively compares Europe's political landscape after the French vote on Maastricht to a plane crash: "There is a lot of wreckage scattered about, and a search is on for survivors." "On the Brink of Unity, Europe Rifts Widening," 11-29, zeroes in on the economic reasons behind the Community's difficulties, while "Left Out," 4-26, is insightful on the decline of socialism in Europe, which Moseley ties to the rise of the service economy. He gamely tries to get to the bottom of the role Pope John Paul II played in bringing down communism in eastern Europe in "The Pope Triumphant," 7-26, suggesting that a recent *Time* story on the subject exaggerated the Pope's role. But, even after his report, the real story remains murky. We get a clear picture of why British PM John Major was able to pull out a victory in "British Boom Town Feels Recession as Election

Nears," 4-6, Moseley finding hard-hit voters blaming global forces, not any individual politician. His Yugoslavian coverage often conveyed the complexity of the situation while holding political leaders, both inside and outside the former country, accountable for the spiralling disaster in such reports as "Be it Murder or Suicide, Yugoslavia Is Shadow of its Former Self," 5-3, and "Bosnian Crisis Too Deep for Quick, Tidy Solutions," 8-30.

Caryle Murphy
The Washington Post
★★½

Cairo bureau chief. While the Middle East saw nothing as dramatic as a war in 1992, readers came away from Murphy's coverage with an understanding that it was an important year all the same. She provided several incisive assessments of the regional geopolitical picture, such as "Iraq, Region Still Await Full Impact of Gulf War's Outcome," 1-17. Her history-rich "Shifting Sand: Rethinking the Changed 'Middle East,'" 9-6, in particular, expertly summed up the changes underway in the region and moved the story forward. She kept us fully updated on Saudi Arabia in "'Glass Ceiling' in House of Saud," 3-15, producing good details on the generational and familial fissures developing in the royal family. In "Saudi Wealth Stirs Discontent," 3-27, she draws a revealing sketch of growing displeasure on the part of both Islamic fundamentalists and the professional class. Covering a great deal of ground in a three-part series in April, "Islam: Politics and Piety," she successfully conveys plenty of useful data but fails to put it into the context of the big picture, except in the most general terms. In "A Battle for Egyptian Souls," 4-26, she is thorough on the continuing battle of wills between the Egyptian government and the Muslim Brotherhood, while in "Fundamentalists Take Power, Action in Jordanian Policy-Making," 4-27, she alertly draws on Jordan's recent experiences to illustrate how Islam and politics can co-exist, albeit uneasily. However, "Iran: Reconciling Ideology and a Modern State," 4-28, offers little fresh information or analysis on Iran. She did provide strong coverage of the U.S.-Iraqi confrontation, as in "Saddam: Rehabilitation by Willpower," 7-28, and the compelling "On 24-Hour Watch in the Gulf," 8-30, in which she provides a firsthand look at U.S. naval pilots coping with both boredom and fear. And we find an evocative look at the precarious existence of a semi-independent Kurdistan in "With West's Protection, Kurds Realize a Precarious Dream," 11-9.

Kim Murphy
Los Angeles Times
★★½

Cairo bureau chief. Murphy's coverage of the Middle East continues to expand in scope and insight. She views the region like a mobile by Alexander Calder—when any point is struck, she looks for the entire structure to vibrate. Providing strong coverage of Algeria early on in such stories as "Algeria Vote Canceled as Crisis Grows," 1-13, she gives us an informative and balanced report on the developing crisis. In the evocative "Revolution Again Echoes Through the Casbah," 3-15, she takes the reader directly into the winding, twisting alleyways, where fundamentalists are waging guerrilla warfare against the military regime, similar to the uprising against the French colonialists 30 years earlier. She also kept readers well abreast of developments in countries throughout the region. In "Voting Is Over, but Not Iran's Revolution," 4-16, she provides a comprehensive analysis of Iran after the parliamentary vote, presciently noting that Iran may once again become a major geopolitical player in the region. A report on Yemen, "Arabia Watches Warily as Yemen Marches Toward Democracy," 6-1, expertly positions that country's move toward democracy in both a national and regional context. The vivid "Gunfire in the Garden of Eden," 10-3, reveals that Saddam Hussein may be engaged in the same sort of scorched-earth campaign against southern Iraq that marked his departure from Kuwait. "Gulf Dilemma Is Born Again: Who Is Watching the Store?" 9-4, is a timely, informed update on the inter-Arab security alliance, or lack thereof, in the Gulf. Murphy also provided the best report we saw anywhere on the reaction in the Muslim world to the fighting in Bosnia in "Islamic World Galvanized by Reported Killing of Bosnia's Muslims, Deplores Inaction by U.N." 8-14. She poignantly captures the mounting pressures on Yasir Arafat in "PLO's Aging Warriors Use Politics, Position Papers to Fight Latest Battles," 11-22.

Nathaniel C. Nash
The New York Times
★★½

Buenos Aires bureau chief. While still an important voice from south of the border, Nash disappointed us somewhat this year, diverting his estimable talents away from the region's political economy, concentrating instead on features and security stories. Nash still uncovers a scoop from time to time. In one of his smarter efforts, "Chile's Army Stands Tall, and Casts a Shadow," 1-26, he analyzes the power Gen. Augusto Pinochet retains as army commander-in-chief, expertly placing the Chilean military in regional and cultural perspective. On the issue of Alberto Fujimori's "presidential coup," he shines through with several important insights. For example, in "Peru's Basic Problems Won't Be Ordered Away," 4-12, he offers a superior summation on the historical precedents and contemporary social and economic ills which laid the groundwork for Fujimori's action. He scores an interview with former President Alan Garcia, now hiding out from federal troops, in "Peru's Fugitive Ex-President Tells of Escape From Troops," 4-24. Doing what he does best, Nash captures the drama of the moment and conveys Garcia's impression that "the economic austerity measures encouraged by Washington and required by the International Monetary Fund from Peru and other poor Latin countries would only lead to more autocratic seizures of power." In "Latin American Indians: Old Ills, New Politics," 8-24, Nash skims the surface of an old story. Back in form for "Blow to Rebels in Peru: An Elusive Aura Is Lost," 9-14, Nash provides a well-rounded sense of the mysterious Shining Path leader, Abimael Guzman Reynoso, following his capture by Peruvian authorities. He expertly provides the full financial context of Argentina's final agreement with its creditor banks in "Argentina Signs Debt Accord With Banks," 12-7.

Robert Neff
BusinessWeek
★★

Tokyo bureau manager. Neff continues to be a reliable source of straightforward information on the always-intriguing world of Japan's business. He has a talent for capturing the nuances of Japanese business culture, with less editorializing in his news reports this year. He delivers a timely, fascinating report on the huge discrepancies in compensation between Japanese and U.S. corporate bosses in "How Much Japanese CEOs Really Make," with Joyce Barnathan 1-27, placing the comparison in full cultural perspective. He reveals that Japan's current soul-searching is likely to produce a nation that promotes its unique brand of "neocapitalism" much more aggressively in the well-researched "Japan Takes a Good, Hard Look at Itself," 2-17. A profile of the new president and CEO of Mitsubishi Corp., "The Harvard Man in Mitsubishi's Corner Office," with William J. Holstein 3-23, is a textbook example of a well-crafted business profile. Here, Neff gives us a full sense of the man and what his promotion portends for Japanese business and U.S.-Japanese relations. Similarly, "The Man Who Said 'The Bubble Has Burst!'" 4-27, is an informative sketch of bearish Tokyo economist Tetsuo Tsukimura of Smith Barney. Neff also produced several impressive reports on key aspects of the Japanese economy. In "Japan Opens the Export Spigot," with Paul Magnusson 6-29, he is detailed on why Japanese exports to the U.S. are once again on the rise—and why there has been no backlash, so far, in the U.S. And in "For Bankrupt Companies, Happiness Is a Warm *Keiretsu*," 10-26, he expertly draws on real-life examples to reveal how Japan's famous system of interlocking conglomerates operates in practice: "Of course, the problem with this safety net is that it only works for Japan's largest companies."

Colin Nickerson
The Boston Globe
★★½

Tokyo bureau chief. A knowledgeable observer of the Asian scene and a clever writer, Nickerson covers Asia with a knowing subtlety, which enables him to lift the veils surrounding a story and provide the reader with fresh insight and data. He adroitly marshals the facts and figures to demolish the myth that Japan is a "protectionist enclave" in his impressive "Many Firms in Japan Prove Trade Barriers a Myth," 1-9. Following up several weeks later with a well-told success story of particular interest to New Englanders, "For L.L. Bean, Japan 'Easy Street,'" 3-9, he documents why "the opening of the first L.L. Bean store in Tokyo seems less a gamble than a bet that the sun tomorrow will rise in the East." He authoritatively contrasts the "almost-medieval squalor and misery" prevalent in North Korea with the extravagant celebrations of Kim Il Sung's birthday in "A Party Amid the Poverty," 5-8. Similarly, in "Nation's Farewell to Aquino Tinged With Bitterness," 5-10, he offers a detailed survey of the wrecked economy Corazon Aquino is leaving behind. He provides a historically-informed look at the haunting legacy of Japan's role in WWII in "Neighbors Fear a Japan Militarily Resurgent," 6-28, observing that "Japan has expended nearly as much energy seeking to suppress information about its bellicose past as it has spent building a mighty economy to ensure a powerful and prosperous future." Dispatched to Sarajevo in the summer, his "Rage Rises, Hope Wanes in Sarajevo," 7-7, dramatically depicts life during urban warfare, while in "At Sarajevo Holiday Inn, a Few Surprises," 8-3, he conveys the gallows humor which enables journalists to maintain their sanity under hellish circumstances. He sensitively probes several of the darker corners of Japanese society with "In Japan, Safe Streets but Hard Life for Accused," 10-11, and "For Japanese, Foreigners Are Suspects," 11-3.

Andres Oppenheimer
The Miami Herald
★★★

Latin America. A Pulitzer Prize winner for his coverage of Iran-Contra in the late 1980s, Oppenheimer has a reputation as one of the best journalists covering Latin America. Drawing on an extensive network of contacts from his listening post in Miami and his frequent trips into the field, Oppenheimer offers a steady source of data and insight on how countries ranging from Cuba to Argentina are being affected by the winds of change buffeting the region. One story he kept his eye on all year was the ebb and flow of democracy in the region. In "Many Aren't Set to Accept Army Cutbacks," 3-23, he draws on the recent coup attempt in Venezuela and reduced military spending throughout the region to warn that there may be increased restlessness in the barracks. Returning on the eve of another coup attempt "Discontent Still Brews in Venezuela," 11-22, he expertly summarizes the alienation prevailing in the country. Traveling to Caracas for "Army Becomes More Political in Wake of Coup," 4-6, he scores an interview with Defense Minister Gen. Fernando Ochoa Antich, whose vague answers raise Oppenheimer's antenna. He produced a critically acclaimed book on Cuba in 1992, *Castro's Final Hour*, and he was a singular source on developments there. In "Tourism Alone Can't Rehabilitate Cuba's Economy," 8-3, he marshals the figures to prove that Castro's hopes of compensating for the collapse of the Soviet trading bloc with the tourist trade is doomed. We find a revealing look at Cuba's dissident movement in "Some Castro Critics Harassed, Some Tolerated," 8-17, learning that the regime will allow individual protests, but never any organized dissent. Oppenheimer's expertise on the Cuban government is showcased in "Don't Be Fooled by 'New Cuba,'" 6-29. He leaves no doubt that while Castro remains in power, any attempt at reform will be strictly cosmetic.

Julian Ozanne
Financial Times
★★★

Nairobi bureau chief. A remarkable reporter, Ozanne has seen the worst that turbulence on the African continent can inflict, without becoming hardened. He can effectively convey the horror he witnesses without losing critical detachment. Ozanne draws on his wide breadth of knowledge of sub-Saharan Africa to give us both the story, and the story behind the story. In "Unity Hangs on People's Will," 2-6, he is forceful and knowledgeable on how the Ethiopian interim government's lack of economic reforms and policy of "ethnic federalism" is a recipe for disaster. He works plenty of details into "Khartoum Presses Its Offensive Against the South," 4-23, but writes twice that the Sudanese military is receiving support from Iran, including Iranian military advisors, without citing any source for this important kernel of news. He draws an incisive portrait of Nigeria, on the eve of parliamentary elections designed to end military rule, in "Few Bets Placed in Nigeria for a Certain Future," 7-3, deftly evoking the political and economic turmoil threatening to destroy the nascent move toward democracy. Taking a concise yet comprehensive look at the factors behind the complete breakdown of civil authority in Somalia in "Old Clan Rivalries Fuel Bloodshed in Somalia," 8-8/9, Ozanne spreads the blame equally between Somalians and Cold War superpowers alike. He turns in a superior report on UN humanitarian efforts in the cauldron of Somalia's civil war in "Somalia Provides Key Test of UN Resolve," 9-2, insightfully outlining how the operation may be a preview of the UN's role on the continent in the decade ahead. In "US Marines Make First Easy Inroads in Somalia," 12-10, he effectively conveys the confusion surrounding the Marine landing while sounding a sober note: "The experience of the marines in Lebanon a decade ago ought to provide a cautionary tale."

Michael Parks
Los Angeles Times
★★

Jerusalem bureau chief. Parks replaced Daniel Williams here in late summer. Consequently, we're withholding judgment on his Mideast coverage until we've seen a greater body of work. Several early reports, "Freed Palestinians Count Blessings, Tribulations," 9-6, and "Prisoners' Strike Puts West Bank, Gaza on Edge," 10-4, effectively convey the mood of the Palestinian community toward the Rabin government, indicating that Parks intends to produce well-rounded coverage of the Israeli-Palestinian story. Similarly, "Palestinians Can See a Future—And It Is Theirs," 11-24, is comprehensive on Palestinian preparations for possible self-rule, Parks making it clear that civil servants and technicians, not rock-throwers, will be running things. As Moscow bureau chief before the move to Jerusalem, Parks captured the dramatic changes being wrought in Russia, but his analysis seemed to be keyed to Boris Yeltsin. In "Russia Taking Painful Steps to a Free Market," 1-2, he dramatically depicts the enormity of the leap into the unknown that Boris Yeltsin and his team are making. In "Yeltsin Shows He's Almost Indispensable," 4-14, he positions Yeltsin as a "great, even heroic, figure," documenting how the Russian leader dominated a showdown between his cabinet and the Congress of People's Deputies, by failing to show up. However, two months later, in "Yeltsin, No Longer a Hero, Under Fire From All Sides," 6-16, he sees the "indispensable" Yeltsin as a leader besieged because of his inability to get a firm handle on Russia's economic crisis. Thus, things have reached the point where he is "bringing back some managers of the old Soviet planned economy, particularly its military-industrial complex, for their hands-on experience." We find a primer on the perils of conducting business with Russia and the newly-independent republics in "Doing Business," 7-21.

Quentin Peel
Financial Times
★★½

Bonn bureau chief. Peel has yet to recover the form which earned him our highest rating in Moscow. While his coverage of German politics generally holds up well, he hasn't yet developed that breathtaking feel for the margins of the German political economy that we expect from him. He provides a balanced analysis of Germany's growing new identity on the world stage in "Damned If it Does— And If it Doesn't," 1-18/19, enabling us to understand the view from Bonn. Peel's dry wit enlivens "King Kohl Comes Off His Throne to Kiss a Princess," 3-26, a revealing sketch of how the immigration issue and the extreme right are becoming increasingly important players on the German political scene. He had a tendency to connect all of Germany's problems to that now-reliable standby, "reunification hangover," as in "Squalls Around the Ship of State," 4-28, and "Tough Choices Now Kitty Is Bare," 5-9. In "Revolt of Germany's Low-Paid," 5-15, he provides a good sense of the shock waves generated by rejection of a 5.4% pay raise by striking public workers, Peel placing the event in the context of increasing worker anger over the costs of reunification: "The feeling is ever more widespread that 'it would have been better if the Wall had been left where it was.'" In one of his best reports all year, "Mixed Feelings in Bonn on Result," 9-22, he fully captures the crosscurrent of emotions in Bonn, following the French vote on Maastricht, documenting why "On Maastricht, the German body politic seems to want to eat its cake and have it…" In the impressively detailed "Forced to Find Common Ground," 12-8, he examines Kohl's efforts to fashion a "solidarity pact" with the opposition and trade unions to finance reunification.

Jane Perlez
The New York Times
★★

Nairobi bureau chief. Other than one major misstep early in the year, Perlez delivered solid coverage of the often hellish events which transpired in East Africa. She was usually able to maintain a grip on her material and objectivity while tugging at our consciences. Reporting from Khartoum, she conveys the growing concerns of Western diplomats in "Sudan Is Seen as Safe Base for Mideast Terror Groups," 1-26, but Perlez makes a big deal of this story with little hard data about the terrorist groups or what they might be up to. The story was later debunked by Raymond Bonner, in "Letter From Sudan," *The New Yorker* 7-13, who reported that accounts of Sudan becoming a bastion of terrorist activity "have been exaggerated." We receive an important update from post–civil war Ethiopia in "Can a New Ethiopia One Day Feed Itself?" 2-24, which is thorough on that country's efforts to become agriculturally self-sufficient in ten years. She is also keen on the tribal nuances influencing a growing tragedy in "Kenya, a Land That Thrived, Is Now Caught Up in Fear of Ethnic Civil War," 5-3. Providing a stark depiction of the post-war wasteland that is Mozambique, in "A Mozambique Formally at Peace Is Bled by Hunger and Brutality," 10-13, she places most of the onus on the rebel group Renamo. Her coverage of Somalia was the most notable in her portfolio. In the outstanding "Food Relief Grows but So Do Somalia's Dead," 7-19, she vividly portrays the growing famine, crisis and anarchy which have prevailed since President Mohammed Siad Barre's overthrow. Her well-organized "Somali Warlord Agrees to Allow U.N. to Protect Its Relief Efforts," 8-13, clearly outlines the details of the agreement and the logistical and security problems which remain. As the U.S. prepared to intervene militarily, Perlez, in "Expectations in Somalia," 12-4, provides a revealing look at the high hopes many Somalis have for the operation.

Andrew Pollack
The New York Times

Tokyo. Like one of the computers he writes about, Pollack is able to parallel process numerous aspects of complex stories. His coverage of technological breakthroughs, for example, integrates both the scientific elements and the commercial feasibility, along with the political implications where they occur. Transferring from San Francisco to Tokyo in the spring, he immediately set his sights on the Japanese electronics political-industrial complex at a critical time in its development. He provides the full scoop on the end of the Ministry of International Trade and Industry's ten-year dream of creating computers with reasoning abilities in "'Fifth Generation' Became Japan's Lost Generation," 6-5, incisively noting that the venture "is a reminder that even Japan's highly regarded [Miti] can make mistakes in predicting which technologies will be important in the future." He fully follows up on this key story with "Japan Plans Computer to Mimic Human Brain," 8-25, deftly sketching out how Miti's latest scheme is seen by many as an act of self-preservation, because "Japan's electronics companies are now so big and strong they can do their own development." "Japan Lures Auto Workers With 'Dream' Factories," 7-20, imaginatively documents how the Japanese auto industry is attempting to make assembly-line work more appealing to employees. His "Japanese Fight Back as U.S. Companies Press Patent Claims," 9-5, is detailed on the rising patent war being fought in U.S. courtrooms, Pollack finding the Japanese are getting better at fighting back. In the fascinating "Cold Fusion, Derided in U.S., Is Hot in Japan," 11-17, he captures both the scientific aspects and cultural context of Japan's decision to fund cold fusion research. His last reports from the states, "Commercial Test of Gene Therapy," 2-14, and "Drug Industry Going Back to Nature," 3-5, are textbook examples of business reporting; sharply detailed, forward-looking, and engaging.

Victoria Pope
U.S. News & World Report
★★

Moscow. When we see work from Pope, which is all too rare, we are impressed by her talent for producing well-written, balanced and illuminating features that often expand our understanding of the former Soviet Union. Her work is both compact and comprehensive. In "Descendants of Genghis Khan Are Marching," 2-24, she artfully conveys the hopes and dreams of Tatarstan nationalists as they threaten to break away from Russia. We come away with a full appreciation of both the political and spiritual questions raised by the liberation of the Russian Orthodox Church in the lustrous "God and Man in Russia," 3-2: "In the scramble for post-communist power, both democrats and autocrats are trying to cultivate the church." She graphically evokes the environmental destruction of the Volga River during 70 years of communist rule in "Poisoning Russia's River of Plenty," 4-13: "Waste water flowing into the ponds has been treated, but not well: The water is so laden with chemicals that the ponds don't ripple in the wind, nor do they ever freeze." "Unquiet on the Baltic Front," 8-24, presents the perspective from both sides on the growing tensions between Estonians and ethnic Russians living in the newly-independent Baltic state. Pope reports the tensions have deep roots and threaten to escalate into a serious military conflict. Her ability to glimpse the Russian soul is showcased in "Russia's Beacons in the Darkness," 12-7, a report which fully captures the sights and sounds of everyday life in Russian villages, illuminating why "Rural life in Russia has outlasted Lenin's revolution, Stalin's persecution and the ill-starred reforms of Nikita Khrushchev and Mikhail Gorbachev."

Janet Porter
The Journal of Commerce
★½

Chief European correspondent. Porter can pack a lot of information into her reports on Europe's shipping industry or a country's political economy, but her analytic efforts can sometimes fail to leave the dock. She displays little fresh thinking in "Jawboning Britain's Economy," 1-7, arguing that the hands of PM John Major and Chancellor of the Exchequer Norman Lamont are tied by fears of stimulating inflation and British participation within the EMS. While a Porter report is usually well organized, "Sale of Ports Raises Questions," 2-4, is surprisingly scattered on the difficulties encountered by the British government as it goes about privatizing the country's public-sector ports. Porter touches on many topics but fails to bring the article together. She is much more focused in "British Coal Fights for Survival," 3-17, a thorough update on the beleaguered British coal industry, in which she foresees the massive closings announced later in the year. In "An Enviable Stability in Britain," 5-19, she provides a good sense of where Great Britain stands economically and politically *vis-á-vis* western Europe in the wake of Major's re-election and the first faint signs of an end to the recession. Her ability to cover a lot of ground in a short article is exhibited in "The Travails of Greek Shipping," 6-16, a three-dimensional look at a storied industry now at a historic crossroads. Back to probing the obvious, not the margins, in "Euro-Currency's Costs for Britain," 7-21, she looks at the growing pressure on John Major to ease up on interest rates and jump-start the economy. She is thorough on the state of the Swedish economy following Stockholm's all-out defense of its currency in "Stockholm's Bid to Join the EC," 11-10. Although interest rates shot up to 500%, we learn that "The country is now firmly set on a new course that should see it fully integrated into the EC within three or four years."

Bill Powell
Newsweek
★½

Tokyo bureau chief. Powell's reports can suffer from such frequent newsweekly maladies as taking an overly broad approach or penning prose that's been through a blender. Occasionally, though, he works in a fresh bit of intelligence or a perspective that transcends the generic; this makes his work worth scanning. For instance, a contrarian viewpoint surfaces in his thought-provoking "The Good News in Bush's Trip," 1-20. Powell perceptively contends that Bush's visit, while a PR disaster, accomplished much. The Americans having won some important concessions and, more importantly, having served notice to Tokyo that economic competition, not international security threats, will now be the basis of official U.S.-Japanese relations. He produces a broad, knowledgeable overview of the "Nikkei's nose dive" and its possible implications for Japanese business and society in "And After the Fall?" 4-20. He raises the possibility that the Japanese business culture may become more like the U.S., with an emphasis on short-term gains and higher returns on dividends. "Down, but Not Out," 5-18, draws on Japan's remarkable history of strong resilience, warning that reports of the country's demise as an economic powerhouse may be exaggerated: "The easiest way to fall behind five years from now is to underestimate the Japanese today." In "Scenes From a Bust," co-written by Hideko Takayama 7-13, he makes good use of details to reveal that individual investors and workers have been victimized by the current recession in Japan. "Japan: The Fall of 'The Don,'" 10-26, is thorough on the scandal which brought down LDP *shogun* Shin Kanemaru: "The saga illuminates the murky world of Japanese politics . . . a system that, far more than most in the developed world, is greased by large sums of money."

Carla Rapoport
Fortune
★★½

London. Rapoport appears with less frequency than during her Tokyo days, and her reports lack the four-star verve that we found in her Japanese coverage. While her reports are well written and thorough, we often feel we could have found the information elsewhere. We expect, however, that once she settles into her new beat, the talented Rapoport will once again provide the cutting-edge material we expect from her. In "The Rights and Wrongs of *Rising Sun*," 3-23, she delivers an incisive, non-hysterical review of Michael Crichton's controversial thriller, drawing on her own first-hand experiences covering Japanese business and culture to observe that "Crichton's basic depiction of what U.S. business is up against in its battles at home and abroad with Japanese competitors is basically correct." Profiling workaholic Percy Barnevik, "Europe's leading hatchet man" and head of a highly successful Swiss-based electrical equipment concern ABB, in "A Tough Swede Invades the U.S." 6-29, she artfully documents how "Barnevik's global experiment is a compelling managerial case study" in how to succeed in the new international business environment. In the concise "Euroflop?" 6-29, she reports that the glass of European integration is half filled —open borders and free trade are on the way, but the political and economic unity promised in the Maastricht Treaty may be defeated by "voters' anxieties." We find a flash of the old Rapoport in "Why Germany Will Lead Europe," 9-21, as she marshals facts and statistics to argue powerfully that reports that Germany is on the ropes are "mostly sauerkraut." But she ignores the political equation here, and the potential threat to German stability posed by rising far-right violence. She writes on the rising xenophobic tide in western Europe in the face of swelling immigration from the east and south in "Them," 7-13, and while the report is well written, she comes to the topic late and with little new information.

T. R. Reid
The Washington Post
★½

Northeast Asia bureau chief, based in Tokyo. The potential we saw in Reid's coverage last year was less evident this time around, as a perfunctory tone has crept into his work. He is failing to produce substantial coverage of the Japanese political economy during this crucial juncture in U.S.-Japan relations. He probes the causes of the rampant corruption prevalent in the Japanese political system in "Japan's Culture of Corruption," 9-6, but offers little that we hadn't seen elsewhere. The details provided by Reid make "The Company Wedding," 4-2, absorbing reading, as Reid takes us through the traditional rite of the "Entering-the-Company Ceremony" at Nippon Electric Corp. But we need more than features on Japanese business. He pens a sturdy analysis of the latest developments in the Strategic Impediments Initiative talks in "Unique U.S. Approach to Japan Trade Talks Raises Questions," 8-3, quoting one U.S. electronics industry representative: "The basic problem with the SII talks is that they focus exclusively on some professor's idea of how the Japanese economy works." He perceptively notes in "Tokyo Fears Repeat of Gulf Outcry," 12-5, that Japan's reaction to the intervention in Somalia is a virtual replay of its reaction to the Persian Gulf crisis, when it sent money and no men or equipment. Reid's best work this year was on North Korea. In "Tourists in North Korea: Strangers in Strange Land," 5-4, he pens a brief but evocative sketch of the grim conditions in that country today as it emerges from the deep freeze. One quote from the deputy prime minister for economic affairs says it all: "We never beg, but we just want [foreign countries] to be generous." While in Pyongyang, Reid and two other journalists wandered into a neighborhood "that the government did not want foreigners to see," and were detained for several hours.

Sharon Reier
Financial World
★★½

Europe, based in Amsterdam. Reier has a gift for conveying how businesspeople translate their visions into successful enterprises. She's quite good at using these individual stories to exemplify the effects policy has on different companies and industries, but occasionally she gets bogged down in tedious number crunching. We find out all we need to know about why western European computer companies are struggling to cope with shrinking, nervous markets in, "People Ask for Cathedrals," 1-21. Addressing rising anti-immigration sentiment in Europe in "Xenophobia," 3-3, she expertly places what has been labeled a cultural phenomenon in the context of economics and trade policy. As usual, Reier's forté is the business profile. In the compact "Weather Eyes," 3-31, we learn how Vaerner of Norway turned around a slump in the shipbuilding industry largely because its CEO, Erik Tonseth, foresaw a day when the world's aging fleet would have to be replaced. The informative "Testing the Mettle," 5-26, is also well done, enabling us to understand how RTZ, the world's largest mining combine, has prospered in a notoriously cyclical business under the leadership of Sir Derek Birkin. A profile of the CEO of Dutch insurer Aegon, "Marathon Man," 9-1, drowns in insurance industry jargon and technicalities right from the start. More productive use of details adds value to "Freedom's Ring," 9-15, a report on the potential bonanza presented to Western companies by Russia's efforts to bring its telecommunications system out of the Age of the Tsars. Similarly, in "Waltzing Rosinka," 11-10, she artfully conveys the construction boom in Moscow, "a city that hasn't seen a major building boom since the days of Joseph Stalin."

Keith B. Richburg
The Washington Post
★★★

Nairobi bureau chief. Not content to simply document the plight of Africa, Richburg, fresh from an academic sabbatical, continually seeks out the reasons behind the continent's political turbulence and stunted economic growth. The result is coverage that reveals the yawning chasm between the rulers and the ruled. As the Somalian story went from civil war to humanitarian crisis, Richburg took us to the scene, painting a stark landscape in "Solutions for Somalia Complicated by Chaos," 8-30. He sketches relief officials in action, deliberately avoiding extremely chaotic areas, despite the food needs there. In "In Somali Town, A Warlord Rules Over the Starving," 9-3, and "Aideed: Warlord in a Famished Land," 9-8, he profiles the warlord mostly responsible for his country's desperate plight, skillfully detailing Aideed's material comfort and complete lack of regard for his countrymen.

Richburg excelled at multidimensional surveys of African political economies in absorbing, data-filled reports such as "Tanzanian Reforms Opening Up Socialist, One-Party System," 3-24; "In 'Stable' Malawi, Government by Illusion," 5-5; and a two-part series on Zaire, "Economic Collapse Withers African Eden," 3-31, and "Mobutu's Yacht Is Refuge From Unrest," 4-1. Richburg draws on his experience in Asia for the hardhitting "Asia and Africa: The Roots of Success and Despair," 7-12, a comprehensive look at why Asia has prospered in the post-colonial age and Africa has not. He lays the blame at the feet of Africa's elite: "The single feature of African autocracies seems to be their inability to impose their will on their populations." He perceptively analyzes the hard questions raised by the U.S. intervention in Somalia in the thought-provoking "Liberians Ask Why U.S. Avoided Their War," 12-4, questioning Washington's responsibility to other African nations.

Alan Riding
The New York Times
★½

Paris bureau chief. Riding seems to be recapturing some of the form which characterized his Latin American tour of duty. He is a reliable observer of the French political landscape and his forays into the crises affecting European unification are usually solid and straightforward. But Riding's work is rarely cutting edge. He is thorough on French President Francois Mitterrand's efforts to weather the latest political storm, in "How France Is Sliding From Mitterrand's Grip," 2-9, hinting that he may not serve out the full length of his second term. Like other observers of the French elections, he detected disenchantment with both the mainstream left and right. In "Political Doubt in France: Challenges to the Status Quo," 3-24, he zeroes in on one reason—all major parties have virtually identical economic policies: "steady growth accompanied by tight control over inflation and wages and an acceptable unemployment level of around 10 percent." We were disappointed by "Only the French Elite Scorn Mickey's Debut," 4-13, Riding rehashing the debate among intellectuals over whether the Disney park is a "Cultural Chernobyl." In "Yugoslav Strife: Challenge for Europe," 5-26, he effectively conveys the cynicism in some circles that greeted Secretary of State James Baker's call for greater action on the crisis. Detailed and complete on the challenges facing Spain as it prepares to meet the rigorous requirements for economic unity, he pens "Spain Aims for a Competitive Edge in a Unified Europe," 6-14, an effective contrast of the government's EC-backed austerity program and increasing public opposition. He produces an accurate and balanced assessment of the political and economic factors behind the currency crisis in "The High Cost of Unity," 9-17. And "French Politicians Sound Like Farmers (i.e. Angry)," 11-26, vividly captures both the drama and the international issues at stake as the French government attempts to protect both French farmers and its own precarious political position.

Eugene Robinson
The Washington Post
★★

London. A rising star among the *WP*'s foreign staff, Robinson transferred from Buenos Aires to London and hit the ground running, handling with aplomb major European stories such as the currency crisis and Yugoslavia. A lack of focus on the region's political economy was the biggest drawback of his Latin America coverage, but he shows signs of rectifying this problem in his early coverage of Europe. His first major work out of London, "Communal Violence Likely to Endure in Post-Cold War Era," 8-18, is quite good. Robinson provides a comprehensive survey of experts and academics, deftly making the causes and possible remedies for nationalist violence understandable to a U.S. audience. In the brief, but well-rounded, "British Prime Minister Major Faces Critical Political Test," 9-18, he covers the domestic political fallout over the decision to float the pound. He takes us into the trenches for "Trading Room Frenzy," 9-19, a revealing glimpse at the trading floor of a major London bank where men and women in their twenties feverishly react to the latest price quotes, moving millions in currency per minute. "Elizabeth II Offers to Pay Taxes," 11-27, is a biting, yet informative look at the monarchy's difficulties. As we said, his Latin American coverage early in the year was strong on politics, uneven on economics. "Optimism Spreads as Inflation Falls in Latin America," 1-13, exemplifies this weakness. This report superficially surveys improved economic prospects as regional governments shift from "state-dominated economies" to free markets, Robinson contending that public opinion is willing to tolerate "short-term pain" in exchange for competitiveness. He is more illuminating on the Chilean political economy in "Chile's Poor Await Benefits of Nation's Economic Turnaround," 2-18, missing out only on how IMF and World Bank policies played a role in creating deepening poverty in the region. In "Peru's Takeover: Boost to Rebels?" 4-12, he provides insight into the early popular support for Alberto Fujimori's "presidential coup."

Keith M. Rockwell
The Journal of Commerce
★★½

Chief of European bureaus, London. Rockwell continues to provide vigorous coverage of the increasingly important intersection of trade and politics in Europe. Few reporters are better at taking readers through the ins-and-outs of European economic disputes or at exposing politics masquerading as policy. In "'Trustbusters' Play Influential Role in EC," 1-6, he provides a revealing look at internal politics as he profiles EC Competition Commissioner Leon Brittan. Analyzing the latest U.S.-French tensions in "French Play Down Talk of Rift With U.S." 3-2, he alertly zeroes in on French concerns that Washington is allowing the relationship to be soured by differences over agricultural subsidies. He draws a knowledgeable comparison of outgoing French PM Edith Cresson and incoming PM Pierre Beregovoy in "France Likely to Retain Rigid Farm Stance Under New Prime Minister," 4-3, astutely observing that while the diplomatic Beregovoy may improve the atmospherics in trade relations, a politically beleaguered President François Mitterrand still calls the shots. In June, he penned several thoughtful but unconvincing defenses of besieged EC President Jacques Delors such as "Delors' Future Clouded by Danish Vote," 6-15, and "Sacking Delors Won't Help EC," 6-23. Surveying the difficulties surrounding the British economy in "Mr. Major's Very Rocky Road," 8-18, he is thorough on the facts, but not as astute as usual, writing from the it's-all-up-to-the-Bundesbank-school: "Until German interest rates fall, British recovery is little more than a gleam in John Major's eye..." There is more to this complex story. He pulls no punches in "Tilting the Vote on Maastricht," 9-8, lambasting Mitterrand, "a tired old man desperately out of touch with his own people," for his cynical attempt to stage a referendum on European unity for his own domestic political reasons, and consequently stirring up anti-German passions and putting the whole European Community at risk. In "Route to Trade War Marked by Mistrust, Misunderstanding," 11-10, he forcefully lays bare the political calculations and miscalculations, largely in Europe, which have brought the world to "the precipice of a trade war."

David E. Sanger
The New York Times
★★★½

Tokyo bureau chief. A talented wordsmith and resourceful journalist, Sanger provides superlative coverage of Japan's efforts to define its place in the New World Order while coping with the same old political order at home. As talk of a trade war grew, Sanger, in "As Ugly Feelings Grow, It's Hard to Separate Fact and Friction," 1-26, masterfully probes the margins of the U.S.-Japan dispute. He deconstructs some myths on both sides, such as declining U.S. productivity and Japanese efficiency. Occasionally Sanger disappoints, as in "Tokyo in the New Epoch: Heady Future, With Fear," 5-5, an installment in the *NYT*'s series "After the Cold War." Sanger's contribution is extremely well written, but fails to break any new conceptual ground. At times, Sanger reports from elsewhere in the region. "Her Term About to End, Aquino 'Hasn't Made Much Difference' to the Poor," 6-8, is balanced on the failures of the Aquino administration to improve the Philippine economy and alleviate the plight of the poor. His expertise on Japan's geopolitical affairs is showcased in "Recriminations Fly in Japan on Collapse of Yeltsin Visit," 9-11, where Sanger superbly documents how nationalist interests and emotions can cloud "the apparently seamless way that [Japan] merges business and Government interests." His expert grasp of Japanese domestic politics is demonstrated in "Japan's New Scandal: The More Things Change . . . ," 10-2, in which he probes the reaction of the Japanese electorate to yet another money scandal involving the LDP. "Japan (Bush Backer) Tiptoes Around Clinton," 11-29, is thorough on the circumspect attitude Tokyo is trying to take toward the change in U.S. administrations: "In a country perpetually in policy overdrive, restraint is not easy."

Jacob M. Schlesinger
The Wall Street Journal
★★★

Tokyo bureau chief. High definition reporting characterizes Schlesinger's coverage of the Japanese political-industrial complex. Whether the subject is high tech or the environment, he produces a clearer picture than most working this reporting niche. He is perceptive on efforts by Japanese business and government to improve their environmental standing in "Japan Cultivates an Environmental Image," 2-27, shrewdly observing that ulterior motives may be involved: "Government officials confess that their behavior marks less a conversion than a campaign by a country increasingly worried about being an international outcast." His commanding expertise of the Japanese electronics field is displayed in "Electronics Industry in Japan Hits Limits After Spectacular Rise," 4-28, offering vivid details on the "pack mentality" inherent in that field. He incisively delineates where Japanese industry and government have made an actual contribution to environmental efficiency, and where it has fallen short, in "In Japan, Environment Means an Opportunity for New Technologies," 6-3. He's also effectively skeptical in "Japan's Ruling Party Makes a Comeback," 7-27, alertly tying the LDP's electoral success to growing uncertainty about the economy and events abroad, noting that voters are looking for security, despite unhappiness with LDP corruption. He fully captures the atmospherics surrounding Tokyo-Moscow relations in "Japan-Russia Relations Grow More Rancorous," 9-14, reporting that the recent cancellation of Boris Yeltsin's visit because of the Kurile Islands dispute "spurred some Japanese to criticize their government for insisting that politics and economics are 'inseparable.'" In "Japan's Military Stirs Just

Enough to Worry Citizens and Neighbors," 12-1, he provides a well-rounded look at Japan's apparent military re-awakening, knowledgeably probing both the psychological and geopolitical factors involved.

Serge Schmemann
The New York Times
★★★

Moscow bureau chief. Schmemann concentrated less on day-to-day developments and more on the broad changes, being wrought by the end of communism and the Soviet Union. He often deepens our understanding of Russia, and his historically informed, sharply observant reports never fail to hold our interest. Artfully personalizing the disorienting aspects of Russia's new freedoms, in "A Gulag Breeds Rage, Yes, but Also Serenity," 2-12, he interviews newly released prisoners convicted of treason under the communists. He incisively documents how strains between Ukraine and Russia over military hardware are based as much on commercial interests as nationalist pride in "Friction Rises as Ukraine and Russia Clash Over Ex-Soviet Armed Forces," 3-5. In "Mr. Gaidar Goes to Moscow (and Yeltsin Listens)," 6-2, he succeeds in offering a penetrating report on the Yegor Gaidar-Grigory Yavlinksy struggle for power. Traveling to Yerevan, Armenia for "In the Caucasus, Ancient Blood Feuds Threaten to Engulf 2 New Republics," 7-8, he shows us how this centuries-old conflict is being observed through the eyes of contemporary Armenians, deftly contrasting their passions with the harsh realities of ethnic war. Analyzing Boris Yeltsin's decision to cancel an upcoming summit with Tokyo over the Kurile Islands in "Little Isles, A Big Fight," 9-11, he effectively drives home the point that the decision is a victory for "the right," but he's a little vague on what may lie ahead. Displaying his encyclopedic knowledge of the subject in "Free-Market Ideas Grow on Russian Farms," 10-6, he conveys how the adjustment to a capitalist economy is just one more transitional phase in the long, long history of Russian agriculture. Similarly, he insightfully places the political chaos surrounding the December session of the Congress of Peoples' Deputies in full historical perspective in "Russia's Parliament Hesitates Between Law and Power," 12-13.

Uli Schmetzer
Chicago Tribune
★★½

Beijing bureau chief. Schmetzer provides sophisticated coverage of China's Not-So-Long-March to the free market this year, capturing the full smorgasbord of a society where Red Guards, Cantonese entrepreneurs, corrupt government officials and get-rich-quick artists all compete for bigger slices of an expanding pie. He captures some of the overnight changes in China, brought about by the move away from communist dogma in "China Using Capitalism to 'Save' Socialism," 3-13: the planes are on time, sales clerks are courteous, and indoctrination classes have ceased at universities. The downside of China's move toward capitalism is explored in "After Palace Coup, 'Gang of 3' Takes Over in Beijing Hotel," 9-1, which chillingly details how government officials are employing Cultural Revolution tactics to take over commercial enterprises for themselves, and "China's Stock Debacle Deflates Capitalist Dreams," 11-2, on the collapse of the Shanghai stock exchange. Schmetzer opines here that Shanghai is finally realizing that "hard work is more conducive to wealth than conjuring up stock-market castles in the sky." In "Nixon Trip 20 Years Ago Opened China to Change," 2-22, he credits the former President's visit with having "presaged an infusion of values and ideas that his hosts have been trying to control or expunge ever since." He produced two of the best reports we saw all year on the Australian economy, "Australia's 'No Worries' View Creates a Few," 4-26, and "Australia's Sunshine State on the Rise," 4-27, both detailed and thorough on that country's near-depression. Assigned to Sarajevo during the summer, he memorably documents the horrors and heartbreak surrounding the conflict as seen through the eyes of the participants in "Sarajevan Takes a Bride, and Then an Assault Rifle," 7-6, and "Hate's

Wartime Toll: A Close-Knit Town Unravels," 7-19.

Philip Shenon
The New York Times
★★

Bangkok bureau chief. Shenon's beat encompasses a vast geographic region. At times the stretch to cover it all takes a toll on his work. While his more substantial efforts are generally first-rate country studies, his day-to-day coverage can be spotty. He shares the disbelief of government officials and diplomats over support for Ferdinand Marcos's widow in "Wow, It's 'Eee-mel-da!' Now Shopping for Votes," 1-17, but fails to talk to voters themselves, leaving us wondering what did account for Mrs. Marcos's appeal. His talents as both reporter and writer are fully showcased in "Cambodia, Bleak and Fearful, Yearns for U.N. Peacekeepers," 3-5. In this compelling special report, he evokes the wrenching poverty prevalent in both Phnom Penh and the provincial countryside, as that star-crossed country prepares for economic rehabilitation under the shadow of the Khmer Rouge. In "Mobile Phones Primed, Affluent Thais Join Fray," 5-20, he artfully depicts how middle- and upper-class Thais are participating in the "cellular phone revolution." Profiling PM Anand Panyarachun's efforts to calm Thailand's troubled political waters, in "A Tall Order: To March the Soldiers Out of Politics," 7-10, Shenon hints that the task may be beyond the PM, but provides few details. Shenon has a talent for capturing the human dimensions of ethnic and political strife, as displayed in the moving "Age-Old Hatreds Haunt Vietnamese in Cambodia," 8-21, a vivid depiction of how individuals are bearing the brunt of ancient hatreds fanned by the Khmer Rouge. In "Rearranging the Population: Indonesia Weighs the Pluses and Minuses," 10-8, he produces a balanced, comprehensive report on Indonesia's policy of resettling volunteers on the nation's less-populated islands. A rich sense of history informs "U.S. Team in Hanoi Studies Relics of the Missing," 11-15, a poignant report on Pentagon investigators cataloguing U.S. military artifacts in a Hanoi museum.

Nathaniel Sheppard, Jr.
Chicago Tribune
★★★

Latin America. Courageous in going after a story and sufficiently skeptical of those who wield power, Sheppard brings alive the region's political economy. We come away from his absorbing, highly-detailed reports well aware of the human costs of political and economic mismanagement being played out in the region. His Haitian coverage, without being editorial, was a devastating critique of Washington's policy toward that beleaguered country. In the hair-raising 10 Best selection, "Army Uses Terror to Widen Grip Over Haiti," 2-16, Sheppard ventures out into the restless Haitian countryside to provide firsthand details contradicting Washington's assertion that Haitian refugees "stopped at sea and forcibly returned home do not face repression." Similarly, in "Embargo Bleeding Poorest of Haitians," 2-23, he documents how the embargo has resulted in a nation where "youngsters with swollen bellies and rust-colored hair ... [roam] the streets, [where] the generals [dine] on French champagne and imported delicacies." Updating us on the Haitian situation with "In Haiti, Debate Over Aristide Is Class Fight," 7-26, and "The 'Politics of Empty Chairs,' Brings Haiti's Staggering Government to Halt," 8-2, he masterfully delineates the fault lines running through Haitian society, precluding any agreement to bring deposed President Jean-Bertrand Aristide home. A colorful report on a lush Olympian-sized tourist attraction, "Turmoil, Old and New, Stalks Columbus Monument," 4-24, becomes a revealing look at the Dominican economy: "In a nation where electricity is rationed and unemployment tops 30 percent, El Faro a Colon (the Columbus Lighthouse) is especially unpopular among those of its neighbors whose homes lack running water." His skills at covering regional trends is showcased in "Spain Once More Sees Economic Promise in New World," 9-15, an insightful look at Madrid's growing interest in Latin America.

Elizabeth Shogren
Los Angeles Times
★★★

Moscow. An observant reporter who usually wields her pen with the precision of a scalpel, Shogren broadens a reader's understanding of developments in Russia. Whatever the topic, she digs deeper for the key details and adds an extra layer of historical perspective, enabling us to understand how a development came about, and what it portends for the future. Reporting on Russian Vice President Alexander Rutskoi's denunciation of Boris Yeltsin's policies as "economic genocide" in "Russia's VP Slams Yeltsin's Economic Policy," 2-9, she artfully captures the flavor of the Congress of Civic and Patriotic Forces where Rutskoi spoke, making it clear that other than resurrecting some form of Russian patriotism, Yeltsin's critics on the right have no real idea of where to take the country. In the timely "Wounded Nuclear 'Heroes,'" 3-24, she produces an informative profile of Russia's nuclear scientists. We find an insightful effort at putting the turbulent relations between Moscow and Kiev in historic perspective "In the Shadow of 'Big Brother,'" 5-1, adding to our comprehension of Kiev's antipathy toward Moscow. In "Georgian Comes Home to Trouble," 6-23, she pens an incisive profile of Eduard A. Shevardnadze and the problems he's inheriting as he assumes political leadership in Georgia. She provides one of the best reports we saw all year on Russia's class of industrial managers and their growing influence within the government in "Next Step: Russia Mixing Business With Politics," 9-29, Shogren writing that these managers can evidently count on the support of the people who work in their factories, shop in factory-owned stores, and live in factory-owned apartments: "'The government should do what the directors say,' says one worker, 'because they are close to the workers.'" The colorful "Traders' Tiny Kiosks Hold Big Dreams," 11-20, is yet one more report on the hopes of Moscow's street-level entrepreneurs and the difficulties they have to contend with.

John Simpson
The Spectator
★★½

Contributing editor. We always find the thoughts and observations of the foreign affairs editor of the BBC worth reading, and though we do not always agree with his sometimes hyperbolic views, we appreciate his unique vision of world affairs. In November he received the 1992 Magazine Publishing Award in Great Britain as the Best Regular Commentator for his *Spectator* contributions. Simpson's penchant for overstatement is showcased in "The Closing of the American Media," 7-18, an otherwise powerful indictment of the paucity of foreign coverage in U.S. TV newscasts and newspapers. We agree there should be more foreign coverage, but disagree that "the freest society in the world has achieved the kind of news blackout which totalitarian regimes can only dream about." He calls for massive Western aid in the apocalyptic "What Is to Be Done in Russia?" 1-4, foreseeing deep trouble ahead if hyperinflation and instability continue to worsen and frighten the large Russian middle class. Even John le Carré may have learned something about the restructuring of spy agencies, east and west, from the breathtaking "The New Espionage," 2-22. A deft use of anecdotes strengthens "For a Few Dollars More," 3-7, a revealing look at how the collapse of the Russian economy has brought into the open a never-ending chase after the U.S. dollar by officials and functionaries with a secret or service to sell. Wry humor underlines "Swallowed by the Amazon," 5-30, in which Simpson recounts how he wound up stranded overnight in the rain forest. In this single report, he gives the reader a better sense than a thousand communiques of what's at stake at the upcoming Rio Summit. In the delightful "The Irish Empire," 11-21, he takes an admiring if irreverent look at politics Irish style, and its impact in democracies throughout the world.

Daniel Singer
The Nation
★½

Europe. Though an unreconstructed class warrior and proud of it, Singer resists the temptation to fall back on sloganeering, often providing solid reporting along with his opinions. For readers searching for an alternative perspective on developments in Europe, east and west, he is worth a look. One subject which drove him to the barricades all year was European integration, which he deconstructed as an attempt by the continent's managerial class to codify the interests of capital above the interests of the workers. In "Germany Muscles In," 2-3, he alertly zeroes in on the Maastricht Treaty's key weakness: "The striking feature of the European construction is that it is being carried out entirely from above, with no participation of the people." Following the Treaty's narrow victory in France, Singer in "Buba Knows Best," 10-12, cogently positions the opposition as a "a new political force [that] depends on those who oppose the Europe of big business without the slightest concession to the growing nationalism." This "growing nationalism" was also a chief target in Singer's cross hairs this year. In "The Ghosts of Nationalism," 3-23, he makes a game attempt to place the rise of European xenophobia in an ideological and economic context, usefully pointing out that proportionately the number of immigrants in Europe today is the same as it was twenty years ago. The difference between now and then, Singer explains, is the collapse of socialism and the economic slowdown of the early '90s. "Hate in a Warm Climate," 4-20, vividly evokes the rise of the National Front in Nice and Marseilles. Drawn by Italy's historically large Communist Party and affinity for the Left, Singer provided several in-depth reports on that nation's political scene, including "Italy's Summer of Discontent," 8/31-9/7. And he was alert to the dangers posed by the International Monetary Fund to the former Soviet Bloc in such reports as "Boris the Brief?" 1-20.

Douglas Stanglin
U.S. News & World Report
★★

Moscow bureau chief. An economic reporter who avoids rhetorical flourishes or oversweeping analysis, Stanglin kept us up-to-date on developments in Russia with straightforward coverage that often had an insider's feel when it came to Boris Yeltsin and his administration. He provides a concise summary of Boris Yeltsin's political troubles as the Russian president implements market reforms with "In Russia, Economic Reform Collides With Democracy," 1-27, writing that "opponents charge that Yeltsin, who has never been known as a detail man, has grown ever more dependent on his advisers and on economists who have no practical experience." In "Yeltsin at the Crossroads," 6-22, Stanglin connects Yeltsin's and, by extension, Russia's difficulties to Yeltsin's management style: "Yeltsin, as president, is eager to please, often dependent on old party cronies and easily swayed by the last adviser to get his ear." Stanglin digs a bit deeper into the Russia story in "A Victory Gone Sour," with Victoria Pope, Pat Szymczak, John Marks and Julie Corwin, 8-24, documenting how, in the words of Yeltsin's former press secretary: "Communism is not an ideology, but it is a system of relations, a system of making decisions, and the system remained intact. Actually, there was no victory." In "Half-Baked Reforms," 2-3, he imaginatively reports on one day in the life of a Moscow baker to illustrate the horrendous obstacles confronting any would-be Russian entrepreneur. Readers can taste and smell the polluted air of the industrial city of Magnitogorsk in "Breathing Sulfur and Eating Lead," 4-13: "The parks and sidewalks are a blur of gunmetal gray. At night, the taste of sulfur settles thickly on the tongue." He effectively draws on the lot of one steelworker to convey the dark days ahead for Russia's dying manufacturing base in the detailed "As the Fires Dim," 12-7.

James Sterngold
The New York Times
★★

Tokyo. Sterngold continues to provide sturdy, if unspectacular coverage of the ups-and-downs of the Japanese investment community, though he is better at compiling data than fitting it into a cohesive whole. At times he can be astute, as in "Japan Seeks Ways to Tame Stock Market," 1-23, where he steps back from examining efforts to stabilize the Japanese stock market to wonder if the Japanese can successfully "turn back the clock" in this high tech era of capital flows. He tracked the story of declining Japanese foreign investment all year in reports such as "Japanese Shifting Their Investments Back Toward Home," 3-23, and "Losses Force Japan's Banks to Halt Expansion Overseas," 6-2, but offered scant information on how Japanese tax policies contributed to the crunch. Similarly, his coverage of the troubled Japanese stock market in such reports as "Japan Faces a Crisis of Confidence," 4-6, and "Wake-Up Call in Tokyo," 8-20, usually settled for rounding up the usual suspects who blame the "bubble economy." He still produces knowledgeable reports on Japanese business culture, such as "A Rare Airing of Japan's Corporate Dirty Laundry," 7-22, an expert sketch of a "bitter palace revolt" at media conglomerate Sankei Shimbun. "For Tokyo Brokers, Time of Pain," 10-7, is nuanced and comprehensive on how Japanese stock brokerage firms are having to scale back their operations and their ambitions. His coverage of Japanese politics is also fairly strong. In "Another Scandal in Japan, This Time Involving Billions," 2-23, he seamlessly ties together myriad details and allegations to document how a trucking company, politicians, the Yakuza and the banks may be involved in a scandal of massive proportions. In "Koreans in Watershed Vote: Is the New Democracy Real?" 12-14, he is thorough on the economic and political changes in South Korea since the last presidential election in 1987.

Richard W. Stevenson
The New York Times
★★

London. Stevenson found himself covering many of the biggest stories of '92, from the Los Angeles riots to the European currency crisis. Based on the quality of his domestic business coverage from L.A. in recent years, he has the potential to develop nicely in his new European assignment, but he still needs to get his bearings. Arriving in London just as the currency crisis was getting underway, his "Europeans' Currency System Shaken as Britain Cuts Free," 9-17, lays out the circumstances surrounding Britain's decision to temporarily drop out of the ERM and its implications for European unity. But, the report fails to capture the drama of the moment, nor does it push beyond conventional conceptual frameworks, Stevenson failing to question Bundesbank policy toward the German economy. His analytics on the crisis were mixed. In "Europe's Mixed-Up Money: Economists Foresee a Transition," 9-19, he never goes beyond sketching out the concept of a "two-speed Europe" centered around currencies pegged to the mark. However, in "Big Stakes in Europe," 9-24, he aptly documents how Bonn and Paris are preparing to go to war with currency speculators to preserve European economic unity, giving a sense of how big a role politics plays in economic decision making. In "A Unifying Europe Tries to Dot Its 'I's,'" 11-16, he details how "new regulations that strike many Europeans as invasive, arbitrary, or just plain silly," conflict with the promise of free trade. Before heading to London, he provided strong coverage of the L.A. riots, both as a breaking story and as a continuing economic crisis. "Toll Is 38 in Los Angeles Riots but Violence Seems to Abate; Bush Dispatches Force of 5,000," 5-2, "A Stumbling Economy Absorbs Another Blow," 5-4, and "Patching Up L.A.—A Corporate Blueprint," 8-9, were all fine reports. In the authoritative "Will Aerospace Be the Next Casualty?" 3-15, he knowingly lays out the problems confronting Boeing and McDonnell Douglas, and the pros and cons of greater government intervention.

Lena H. Sun
The Washington Post
★★½

Beijing bureau chief. No reporter likes to become the story they are covering, but unfortunately that is what happened to Sun this year when Chinese authorities harassed her in May. A true professional, Sun persevered and provided sharp, balanced coverage of the political and economic dynamics at work in the country. She provides a chilling account of the Big Brother tactics used by Chinese authorities to control foreign correspondents including herself in "Foreign Press Pressed by Chinese System," 3-22, and "Beijing Authorities Harass Reporter," 5-18. She notes in the latter report: "The episode comes at a time when Western journalists have been under increasing harassment even as officials are trumpeting a new era of reform and opening to the outside world." In "China's Economic Reformers Get Big Boost," 2-21, she provides a thorough look at recent indications that pro-market reforms and reformers are making a political comeback. Comprehensive on Guangdong late in the year, with "South China Drives Boom Region," 12-2, she captures the flavor of the opportunities presented by the "Greater China triangle." Sun's contrast of the economic boom in the southeast versus other regions provided a useful window on the varied pace of reform throughout this vast country. "China Slogs to Market," 7-3, makes clear why reformers in Beijing may find it difficult to break the three "irons" which have a grip on the country's heavily industrialized northeast. Here she tells us conditions resemble Russia's hidebound industrial complex rather than China's southeast, where entrepreneurs and investors are able to literally build from the ground up. "Crowded Shanghai Tries to Catch Up With Booming Economic Free Zones," 9-24, fully captures Shanghai's precarious position as it fears both being left behind economically and running afoul of government hard-liners, many of whom retain residences in the city.

William C. Symonds
BusinessWeek
★★

Toronto bureau manager. Symonds is better on the economics than the politics of Canada's political economy. He has as firm a handle on the NAFTA story as any U.S. print reporter north of the border, but his coverage of such topics as the Quebec separatist movement can be overly alarmist. In "Canada's Choice May Be Free Trade or Free Health Care," 1-27, he provides a smart rundown of how Canada's depressed economy may be eating away at the country's extensive social welfare programs, and the dangers posed to NAFTA by PM Brian Mulroney's declining political fortunes. This topic is updated for "In Canada, the Free-Trade Deal Is Hardly Home Free," with Paul Magnusson 9-7, where he expertly places NAFTA's troubles in full political and economic context: "To many observers, Canadians seem on the verge of shooting themselves in the foot." His business profiles are well-crafted reports on Canadian corporate strategies. "There's More Than Beer in Molson's Mug," 2-10, is thorough on Molson's decision to expand into chemicals and a chain of do-it-yourself stores, while "When the TV Lights Start to Dim," 3-16, resourcefully uses the Montreal Canadians as a case study of how professional sports franchises are trying to cope with declining TV revenue. His Quebec coverage was strong on economics, but weak on politics and culture. In "Quebec: What Price Freedom?" 3-23, he knowledgeably details the economic pluses and minuses of an independent Quebec, but writes ominously that "if Quebec secedes, the rest of Canada could come unglued." An alarmist tone prevails in such updates on Quebec as "Canada's Future Hangs on a *Oui* or *Non*," 9-21, and "Quebec Strides Toward Schism," 10-12. He correctly sees the voter rejection of the constitutional referendum granting more autonomy toward Quebec as "a stunning rebuke to Canada's ruling elite" in "Northern Disorder," 11-9. But while he details the immediate economic fallout here, the political outlook is less nuanced.

Andrew Tanzer
Forbes
★★★

Pacific bureau manager. Tanzer is a businessman's foreign correspondent, a thorough, no-nonsense reporter and a concise writer. He is an especially strong profile writer, as evinced in his fascinating "The Birdman of Bangkok," 4-13, better known as Dhanin Chearavanont, "an entrepreneur who's rapidly changing the diet of a billion Asians," from traditional fare to Western-style food. In the compact and informative "Sharing," 1-20, we learn how Sony Corp. suffered a humiliating defeat to Matsushita in the VHS market because it was so concerned with the technological propriety. His coverage of Japan's software wars, "Software on Black Ships," 12-21, makes mincemeat out of conventional ideas about prospects for business ventures in Japan: "Foreign —mostly U.S.—vendors control about 50% of Japan's $1 billion (wholesale) market for packaged software for business use." Tanzer's forays into larger subjects, such as Asian politics and economics, are also strong. His pithy financial analysis of the robust economy of the "three Chinas," China, Hong Kong and Taiwan, "The Three Chinas Boom," 7-6, was surely read by many eager investors. Says one of Tanzer's sources: "Getting into China now could be the same as buying Tokyo in 1950 . . . " While most of the press corps looked backward at the Chinese story, unable to see past China's human rights record, Tanzer dared to offer a dispassionate perspective on the country's bold moves toward entrepreneurial capitalism in "The Chinese Way," 9-28: "Calculating that the way to his countrymen's hearts was through their stomachs, Deng [Xiaoping]'s first reforms were targeted at agriculture. Up went food production, up went food supply. China's peasants, who numbered 80% of the work force, responded instantly to the incentive-based system launched in 1979: Real farm incomes quadrupled in eight years." But we cringe a little when Tanzer refers to Tiananmen Square as merely a "terrible blemish."

Paul Taylor
The Washington Post
★★½

Johannesburg bureau chief. Taylor's early work from South Africa exhibited some of the sophistication which we associated with his previous coverage of U.S. politics. A skilled reporter and thoughtful writer, he appreciates the nuances of the South Africa story at this passage in history. Taylor underwent a baptism of fire, receiving a gunshot wound early in his tour of duty. Recounting the violent incident for "In S. Africa, a Life Not Lost," 8-10, he displays a cool head, on the incident to convey a larger message about the changing nature of violence in South Africa: "The scary thing about the attack on us isn't that it was political; it was that it *wasn't* political." Covering the country at the time of the referendum on negotiations toward a multiracial government in "Keepers of Afrikaner Flame Scorn de Klerk," 3-16, he deftly evokes the ambivalent mood of Afrikaners as the vote approaches. He attributes the resounding victory to the political cunning of F. W. de Klerk in "South Africa's Morning After: Now for the Hard Part," 3-29, a serviceable summary of South Africa's mood in the immediate aftermath of the vote. In "South Africa's Bitter Loss of Hope," 9-4, he draws on a wide range of sources to convey the sour mood gripping the country. He expertly examines the issues raised by an armed attack at a country club in "Killings Send Chill Through White South Africa," 12-1, hinting it may be an omen of more violence to come. His domestic U.S. coverage earlier in the year was mixed. He takes a touchy-feely approach to the issue of health insurance in "Health Coverage Worries Intruding Into More of Life's Choices," 1-26, while "Campaign '92: Thrills and Spills and . . . Substance," 2-16, presciently foresees the campaign producing a substantive debate on the nation's future.

Michael Vatikiotis
Far Eastern Economic Review
★★★½

Kuala Lumpur bureau chief. An outstanding journalist and writer, Vatikiotis provides richly-textured coverage of the country which may represent Asia's future. A reader usually comes away from a Vatikiotis article feeling like he's spent time with an expert, and a raconteur. In "Traveler's Tales," 4-9, he brilliantly dissects Malaysia's almost blind faith in the powers of modernization: "That many Malaysians no longer vote for political ideals, take holidays abroad, forget their mother tongue and aspire to own a suburban house and two cars, may worry those who consider being exotic the essence of the region; but they are looking at its future norms." One of the biggest Malaysian political stories all year was the growing support for the Islamic Party, or *Pas*. In "Battle for the Margins," 5-7, Vatikiotis offers a revealing snapshot of how the ruling United Malays National Organization (UMNO) was able to prevail by the skin of its teeth in one local election. He also conveys a good sense of day-to-day campaigning in rural Malaysia. His expertise at capturing the confluence of ethnic concerns and politics is also showcased in "State of Siege," 6-18. Here Vatikiotis incisively reports on UMNO's efforts to rattle the provincial government of Chief Minister Datuk Joseph Pairin in the state of Sabah for having committed the unpardonable sin of creating a regional party which stretches across ethnic lines and dislodges a Muslim-led coalition. He is thorough for "In God's Name," 9-3, assessing how *Pas* is concerned that the efforts to install the Islamic criminal code in one province will scare off mainstream voters nationwide. In the picaresque "Pole Position Ploys," 11-19, he produces a revealing look at the battle underway within the UMNO party to succeed PM Datuk Seri Mahathir: Mohamad. "Money and character assassination are the two weapons of choice in this campaign."

Stefan Wagstyl
Financial Times
★★★

New Delhi bureau chief. Wagstyl's final year in Japan was marked by astute readings of the political scene and comprehensive reports on the structural changes now underway in the Japanese economy. He makes clear that changes there will be gradual, if not glacial; that the reorienting of Japan, Inc. is the equivalent of turning a nuclear aircraft carrier around. In the superb "On the Campaign Trail—in Japan," 1-7, he expertly offers the perspective from Tokyo on how domestic political considerations are overriding geopolitical issues and long-term economic concerns, during President Bush's trip to Japan. Summarizing PM Kiichi Miyazawa's political fortunes following the loss of a parliamentary election in "Japanese Voters Turn Up the Heat on Miyazawa," 2-11, he is thorough on the "international implications" of Miyazawa's descending star. In the wide-ranging "The Big Squeeze in Japan," 4-27, he documents how major Japanese companies, spurred on by the rising cost of capital and the recession, are slowly readjusting their strategy of placing market share ahead of profits. Wagstyl also offers perceptive coverage of Japan's efforts to redefine its role in the international order. In "Public's Distrust of Militarism Is Rekindled," 6-17, he provides a good sense of the national debate surrounding controversial legislation, enabling the Japanese military forces to participate in UN peacekeeping forces under limited circumstances. This is a story he fully follows up in "Voters Likely to Give Miyazawa a Rough Passage," 7-9, commenting that: "Japan appears to be equally divided between those who support the law for its effort to increase Japan's role in international affairs, and those who are opposed because it might revive the role of the Japanese military." Assuming his New Delhi post late in the year, he pens "A Country Split Along Its Deepest Fault Line," 12-8, deftly outlining the political origins of the current unrest following the destruction of a Muslim mosque.

Peter Waldman
The Wall Street Journal
★★

Jerusalem bureau chief. Waldman's coverage is certainly imaginative. He excels at probing the margins of the Middle East's cultural dynamics and finding individual stories which illuminate larger forces at work in the region. He needs, though, to step back more often and give us the bigger picture. In "Conflict in Algeria Over Islamic Militancy Pits Father Against Son," 1-23, he draws on the family of the leader of the Islamic Salvation Front to illustrate the generational split exposed by the rise of Islamic fundamentalism in Algeria. He is part movie critic, part social commentator in "'Burning Bed' Meets 'Thelma and Louise' in Egyptian Movies," 3-19, writing on the recent success of Egyptian films in which women turn the tables on their male abusers. He captures our interest here, but leaves us wondering what this portends for Egyptian society as a whole. In one of his best reports all year, "Mullahs Keep Control of Iranian Economy With an Iron Hand," 5-5, he is thorough and detailed on the choke hold the clergy has on the Iranian economy thanks to the *bunyods*, huge foundations created with assets confiscated after the revolution. An intriguing lead, "From Ahmad Ali's front porch, it's easy to see what peace might look like in a place called Palestine," starts off "Arab Collaborators With Israel Find Refuge in Fakhme," 7-8, a colorful account of a highly-protected enclave on the occupied West Bank where Arab collaborators and their families dwell. The emphasis here is on Mr. Ali, and we are asked to make our own assumption about what one man's situation suggests for Israeli-Palestinian relations. In "A Fortune Disappears in Demise of Holdings Kuwait Had in Spain," 11-24, he and co-writer Carla Vitzhum, produce a textbook example of financial investigative reporting.

Patti Waldmeir
Financial Times
★★★★

Johannesburg bureau chief. Sensitive to nuance and never losing sight of the Big Picture, Waldmeir continues to be the best source of news and analysis on a society precariously balanced between evolution and revolution. Only rarely did she allow the onrush of events to cloud her lucid judgment. In "S Africa's Whites Look to a Future Past," 2-3, she provides expert analysis of white efforts to retain as much power as possible in a post-apartheid regime and the dilemma this poses for the ANC. We find a clear-eyed assessment of a non-sentimental man in "Political Gambler Raises the Stakes," 2-22/23, Waldmeir positioning F. W. de Klerk's "gamble" on an upcoming referendum as an attempt to avoid a race war, plain and simple. "White South Africa Faces Its Last Trek," 3-14/15, offers a brilliant distillation of the mood of rural Afrikaners in the *platteland* on the eve of the referendum vote, beautifully documenting how and why these besieged and bewildered people feel highly threatened by the new course their country is taking. She explores the economy in great detail in the masterful "Battle to End the Economic Civil War," 6-5. In the sophisticated analytic "High-Stakes Power Play in the Homelands," 9-9, Waldmeir expertly places the Ciskei massacre in the context of how the struggle over the role of the government-created black homelands will play in a future multiracial South Africa. She zeroes in on de Klerk as the only man who can lead South Africa out of its current political malaise in the thought-provoking "Long Trek Ahead for S Africa on the Road From Apartheid," 11-18. She openly wonders if he is up to the job, noting that, like Mikhail Gorbachev, he must reform his state without destroying it: "The next few months will tell whether Mr de Klerk can succeed where Mr Gorbachev so tragically failed."

Tony Walker
Financial Times
★★

Cairo bureau chief. Walker provides reliable coverage of Egypt and the Middle East. Often, he weaves the mood of Cairo's intellectual community into his thorough stories on Egyptian politics and culture. He conveys the uneasiness in Arab moderate circles as the first anniversary of the Gulf War arrives with Saddam Hussein still in power, in "Vengeful Saddam Keeps Arab Opponents on Edge," 1-16. Smartly skeptical over Syria's efforts to present a "moderate" image to the outside world, Walker pens "No Queues Form Outside Syria's Newly Opened Door," 3-18. His understanding of the Palestinian community is exhibited in "Relieved PLO Celebrates Arafat's Survival," 4-9, Walker artfully placing Arafat's disappearance and subsequent re-emergence in full personal and political context. He produced one of the most illuminating reports we saw all year on Islamic fundamentalism in Egypt in "Islamic Extremism Haunts Egypt's Elite,"

5-6. He eschews the impulse to over-dramatize the problem, choosing instead to talk to experts and intellectuals who feel that the government's "carrot-and-stick" approach—encouraging official Islam, while cracking down on the extremists—will not work, especially, cautions one intellectual source, "at a time when International Monetary Fund inspired price increases are causing widespread hardship." Examining Iran's efforts to extend its influence in Central Asia in the thoughtful "Iran Seeks Silken Ties With Its Central Asian Neighbours," 6-23, Walker reports that while Tehran has toned down its religious fervor, at least for now, "it would be naive to believe that the country's theocratic leadership does not harbour ambitions to use religion as a means of enhancing Iran's regional role." He fully illuminates the plight of the Egyptian government as it is pressured to both reform and retrench in "Cairo Struggles to Deal With Islamic Zealots," 10-23: "Inertia is not likely to solve Egypt's internal problems—or make life any safer for visitors."

Charles P. Wallace
Los Angeles Times
★★

Bangkok bureau chief. Wallace is an observant reporter and imaginative writer with a strong feel for Asian culture. But we saw less from him this year on the economic dynamics of the region. He also came late to several major stories on Asian society, such as AIDS and the advent of cable TV. He takes us into refugee camp Site Two in Thailand in "Putting Cambodia Together Again," 3-3, a valuable firsthand look at the mind-boggling human and logistical problems confronting UN authorities as they prepare to repatriate 360,000 Cambodians. His colorful account of the transformation of Phnom Penh into a boomtown of sorts, "War Over, Out Comes the Pate," 4-15, is competitive with similar reports we saw on this story. We came away from "Infantry Assault Routs Protesters in Bangkok," 5-19, with a good sense of the anarchy prevailing on the streets of Bangkok. However, a broader overview of an important regional trend of which the Thai violence was a symptom, "Rising Middle Class Finds Political Voice," 5-19, was somewhat anecdotal in tone, Wallace waiting until the last third of the article to work in the political dynamics of this volatile economic and cultural phenomenon. Wallace produced the best report we saw all year on former Burma, "Myanmar Awakens to Kinder, Gentler Military," 10-27. Reporting from the capital of Yangon, he resourcefully documented how, "Like a tortoise tentatively poking its head out of a shell after a long hibernation," the military regime is apparently moving to end its diplomatic isolation and modify its totalitarian ways. His "AIDS Fuse Is Lit in Asia," 1-7, conveys a good sense of the numbers afflicted and the myriad problems confronting health organizations, but we had already read this story elsewhere. However, "Asians Say: Pardon Me, Your English Is Showing," 11-10, a report on the intersection of language and culture, showcases Wallace's feel for Asian society.

Teresa Watanabe
Los Angeles Times
★★½

Tokyo. The versatile Watanabe produced an impressive portfolio of important stories on regional security concerns and fascinating peeks into the darker corners of Japanese society. Her reports fully immerse us in Japanese culture, the topic she covers best. For example, "Global High-Roller's Trail Ends in a Mystery," 2-8, is a picaresque profile of the shadowy Akio Kashiwagi, who worked his way up from humble beginnings to a fortune in Japanese real estate, before dying violently and deeply in debt. We learn how Tokyo is planning to use its leading role in rebuilding Cambodia as a means of establishing itself as a diplomatic superpower in "Putting Cambodia Together Again," 3-3, an important piece of intelligence. In "N. Korea Trolling for Dollars," 5-8, she masterfully puts the North's effort to open up in full historical, economical, and geopolitical perspective. Her feature work was illuminating on Japanese societal shifts. Detailed and thorough for "In Japan, a 'Goat Man' or No Man," 1-6, she explores how a growing number of Japanese women are becoming economically empowered and showing more independence in selecting, and then living with, a mate: "Yet, despite the media hoopla, the changes have not seemed to penetrate the male psyche, those on both sides of the issue say." Reminiscent of her excellent series on Japanese education a few years back, "A Lesson for Japan's Kids: Play!" 9-14, vividly captures the toll that Japan's emphasis on highly pressurized education at an early age is taking on Japan's children, who are literally pulling their hair out and turning into *otakuzoku*, or "socially inept, nihilistic computer whiz kids who manipulate machines brilliantly but lack skills to deal with other humans." In "A Bean Grows in Tokyo," 11-24, she expertly places the opening of a L.L. Bean store in the context of Japan's move toward more leisure time.

Craig R. Whitney
The New York Times
★★

London bureau chief. Whitney can be counted on to keep readers up-to-date on political developments in Great Britain and on the continent, but rarely to take them beyond the curve. We often come away from his work knowing how a particular politician or country came to a present pass, but wondering where they are headed. His coverage of the British elections was conventional, focusing on public discontent with the Tories over the poor economy, while noting doubts remained about Neil Kinnock. In "Kinnock Alters Course, Raising Question: Where's He Now?" 3-13, he is detailed on the Labour Party leader's move toward the political center. Surveying signs of public discontent in "In British Campaign, Too, Many Voters Ask: Why Don't Things Get Better?" 4-6, he zeroes in on personal income tax as the only major difference between the parties, ignoring their stands on taxation of capital. In his survey of the international reaction to the Los Angeles riots, "Europe Is Aghast, Fearing Unrest There; Japan Takes Moral High Ground," 5-3, Whitney penetrates the veil of moral smugness and finds that the violence has tapped into some of Europe's worst fears. His essay on how domestic political difficulties of Western leaders are leading to a lack of resolve on the international scene, "Irresolute Meetings Chip Away at Summitry's Stature," 7-12, is enlivened by Whitney's perceptive prose: "President Saddam Hussein of Iraq could have told them that the illusion of resolve is never as persuasive as resolve itself." His acute sense of European history enriches "Europe: Muted Joy, and Many Misgivings," 9-21, as he analyzes the close passage of the Maastricht referendum in France. And in "Europe's Doldrums," 12-3, he provides a thorough summation of the political, economic and security tensions eroding the drive toward European integration.

Carol J. Williams
Los Angeles Times
★★★½

Vienna bureau chief. Williams continues to supply impeccable coverage of developments in Eastern Europe. A lyrical writer with a sense of history, she skillfully weaves in the economic, political and cultural facets of this complex region. For example, "Skilled Workers Suffer as Bulgaria Steps Back in Time," 1-14, is a masterfully drawn portrait of a nation undergoing a massive shift away from central planning and industrialization. Her Yugoslavian coverage is consistently excellent. "No Solutions in View, Serbs Cling to Status Quo," 3-11, is a concise analytic on how the democratic opposition has been unable to mount any serious opposition to Serbian President Slobodan Milosevic's rule, because of its inability to offer any viable hope of economic recovery. We come away from "A 'New Yugoslavia,' but Old Problems Remain," 5-10, fully understanding how Milosevic has managed to avoid international isolation, despite determined efforts by the West to accomplish just that. Reporting from Belgrade for in "Unruly Troops Threatening Serbian War Efforts," 7-5, she writes that the Serb forces are descending into a "useless rabble" bent on drinking and looting, along with more horrifying actions: "Morale is very low," one military analyst tells her. "You can't carry out massacres of civilians without having an effect on the morale of your troops." She delivers an important update on the meltdown of the Serbian economy in "Fascism Stirs Amid the Ruins of War in Serbia," 8-25, evoking a society rapidly heading toward Weimar Republic-type conditions. Once again ahead of the curve, she alerts us to another potential flashpoint in the chilling "Tempers Flaring in Transylvanian City," 10-27.

Howard Witt
Chicago Tribune
★★½

Moscow. With his unerring eye for detail and sharp interpretative skills, Witt makes the ethnic violence, political turbulence, and the economic collapse in the former Soviet Union seem as stark as a solitary birch tree in the foreground of an autumn sky. He deftly covered the conflict in Nagorno-Karabakh at a critical turning point in the late spring, when the tide of battle turned in the Armenians' favor. In "War's Ebb and Flow a Cycle of Revenge," 5-27, "Besieged Armenians Live in Daze," 5-31, and "Two Wars, in Mirror Images," 6-18, he fully updates us on the tactical situation on the ground. We find a clear picture of the conflict's impact on the Azerbaijani economy in "Oil Firms Find New Wild West, in Azerbaijan," 6-21, an intriguing report on Western speculators hoping to tap into the oil fields in the region. In the valuable "Ethnic Pride, Bias Fuel Moldovan War," 8-2, he conveys the simmering nationalist passions threatening to boil over in Moldova, as Russia's 14th Army hovers in the background. Witt excelled at working in the ground-level impact of the economic policy debate at the national level. In "Russian Plants Grinding to Halt," 7-12, he is concise and complete on how the economic reforms as implemented "have so far brought only disaster" to Russia's industrial base, while in the memorable "Muscovites Waiting for Oil-Price Reform," 9-13, he takes us along a sprawling gas line where "booksellers, comic-book vendors, spare-parts hawkers, Hare Krishnas and other impromptu entrepreneurs" hustle their wares. We find a chilling hint of the potential political impact of the deteriorating situation in Russian society in "Russian's Extremists Feed on Nation's Pain," 10-11. And "In Russia, Rule by Law Is Often Like Roulette," 11-29, artfully conveys the "Potemkin Village" nature of Russia's democratic institutions.

★ NATIONAL SECURITY ★

James R. Asker
Aviation Week & Space Technology
★★½

Space technology editor. A conscientious reporter and analyst, Asker demonstrates a commendable understanding of both the technical and Congressional engineering that go into the development of space systems and anti-missile defense hardware. His solid, forward-looking "31% Increase Proposed for Anti-missile Efforts," 2-3, explores the President's proposal to increase the budget for SDI by 31%, in order to fund both ground- and space-based interceptor systems. Continuing this theme in "ABM Enthusiasm Wanes in Congress, Sets Stage for New SDI Funding Fight," 3-16, he cleverly juxtaposes the deterioration of Congressional support for SDI funding after the Patriot missile's Gulf War track record was revised and the President's popularity began to wane. His "Purchase of Russian Space Hardware Signals Shift in U.S. Trade Policy," 4-6, is an excellent analysis of Soviet space technology: "Ironically, it is a Pentagon program that once was one of the chief irritants of the Soviet Union—the Strategic Defense Initiative—that will benefit most from the initial deals." Careful and detailed in "House Kills Proposal to Cancel Space Station," 5-4, he recounts the Congressional vote to reject an amendment to halt the development of the NASA space station. Citing both critics and proponents, one source argues that "NASA without the station would be left with a hollow space program, leading, if anything, to more [program] cancellations." His "Atlantis to Evaluate Characteristics of Tethered Satellite," 7-20, is an interesting, albeit highly technical description of some of the difficulties that faced scientists deploying NASA's Tethered Satellite System. Asker offers a telling glimpse into the controversy over NASA's price hike for cargo space in the space shuttles in "NASA Hikes Price for 'GAS' Payloads," 10-26. In the brief "Space Telescope Shows Details of 'Black Hole,'" 11-23, he vividly describes of the Hubble Space Telescope's discovery of what could be a black hole.

John M. Broder
Los Angeles Times
★½

Washington, national security. Rather than addressing the tough questions that face the national security community, Broder pens mostly anecdotal articles on peripheral topics. He simply doesn't provide ahead-of-the-curve information or evaluations. In one of his stronger efforts, "Mysteries & Secrets," *Magazine* 4-19, he thoughtfully examines the changes being proposed at the CIA by Director Robert M. Gates. Best here is Broder's discussion of how "ambivalence is the stuff of spying these days in Washington," as the agency confronts a different world and begins to redefine its utility. Broder and co-writer Robin Wright dutifully file "CIA Authorized to Target Hussein," 2-8, but there's so little substantiated here that by the close, we're left with as many questions as when we started on this investigation of U.S.-Iraqi cat-and-mouse games. Perhaps because of the election, Broder was assigned to numerous stories outside the National Security community. Addressing crime, Broder conducts interviews in Omaha, the city closest to the national averages on crime, income, etc., in "A Search for Crime Suspects," 6-26, unsuccessfully attempting to apply his anecdotal evidence to the national level. He gives us some history on the Perot campaign as the Texan bows out in "The Runner Stumbles: Perot and the Gauntlet of Politics," 7-24, but we first have to slog through lines such as "Like Shakespeare's Caesar, ambition was Perot's grievous fault, and grievously has he answered it." In a scattershot follow-up, "Perot Expected to Re-Enter Race on Monday," 9-25, Broder and co-writer Ronald Brownstein provide only vague generalizations: "Both sides acknowledge that Perot's precise impact is virtually impossible to predict." Though unnecessary, Broder's tongue-in-cheek "An Earful of Arkanspeak: Like Chasin' Whiffle-Bird," 11-10, delightfully delivers some of Clinton's home-state aphorisms: "*Seeing double and feeling single.*"

Craig Covault
Aviation Week & Space Technology
★★½

Paris. After his "remarkable portfolio" on the Gulf War, Covault underwent a transition this year that slowed his pace temporarily. Shifting from senior space technology editor to Paris bureau chief, Covault gave us excellent coverage of the problems and promise of the C.I.S.'s post-U.S.S.R. space program. His work on U.S. space technology, though less definitive, was also satisfying. A strong example of his work on Russian technology was "Rocket-Launched Engines Sharpen Hypersonic Face-off," 2-3.

Here Covault describes the Russian Ramjet/Scramjet test program which is spurring Western interest in an acquisition: "[The tests] represent progress in an internationally competitive 'new space revolution' aimed at developing a space transport that can fly into orbit from a runway take-off." Alerting us to possible trouble within the C.I.S. space program in "Russians Perform Complex EVA's; Ukraine Disrupts Radio Link," 10-12, he uncovers news that the Russians were performing maneuvers outside the Mir space station when Ukraine cut off radio contact with the Russian flight control center. Much better in the gripping "Intelsat Rescue, Space Station EVAs Set for First Endeavor Flight Test," 5-4, where he graphically describes the difficulties overcome by precision piloting as the shuttle crew made a third and final attempt to rescue the satellite. "USAF Urges Greater Use of Spot Based on Gulf War Experience" 7-13, is an excellent account of the success of satellite reconnaissance during the Gulf War. Covault relates several fascinating uses of SPOT satellite photos, including an attack that successfully targeted the meeting of several Iraqi generals in a house in Kuwait. In "Russian Instability Draws Nato's Attention," 11-23, Covault once again delivers excellent insights into the "New World Order." He accurately contrasts the cooperation between NATO and the Hungarian military with the recent harder line being taken by the Russian military.

Giovanni de Briganti
Defense News
★★★

European defense reporter. Excellent on a broad range of European defense issues and even better on U.S.-Europe defense trade, de Briganti is among the most important sources of information for the defense community. His command of the political, economic and strategic issues that weigh on the global defense market is impressive. A useful illustration of de Briganti's scope is his "France, Germany to Develop ANS," 1-6, a very competent summary of the political initiative to move ahead cautiously with the development and production of two joint Franco-German defense programs. His lively account of frictions between the U.S. and its NATO allies over reciprocal trade in defense materials, "U.S. Trade Stance Irks Europeans," 6-13, is balanced fairly between the contrasting European and U.S. views. He pens a well-balanced comparison between the two anti-missile missiles under consideration by the German defense ministry, "Bonn to Pick Corpsam or FSAF," 2-3: "Most government and industry officials say Germany will confirm its original intent to join the FSAF [European] program, although it was suggested that the delay in tactical air-defense funding makes [the U.S. program] Corpsam a viable alternative." In his forward-looking "Europe Firms Report Profits Despite Cuts in Defense," 5-18/24, he cautions that defense profits won't last for long, as European integration will lead to future defense purchasing being made by a Euro-agency. The consolidations, he reports, will reduce "defense procurement costs by 20 percent to 30 percent, according to the preliminary conclusions of an EC study..." He's brief but illuminating on Dutch Ministry of Defense plans to buy Boeing CH-47 Chinook heavy-lift helicopters in "Dutch to Buy as Many as 35 Lift Copters for Brigade," 11-2/8. And in "Scheme for European Arms Agency Falters," 10-12/18, he handily and thoroughly examines a setback that could delay plans to establish a European armaments agency.

Michael A. Dornheim
Aviation Week & Space Technology
★★

Engineering editor, Los Angeles. A nuts-and-bolts reporter, Dornheim delights in technical detail and brings to life topics that the rest of us might dismiss as dull, such as noise abatement and control systems. Though rarely the one we turn to for "big picture" air transport industry overviews, he does a fine job of zeroing in on specific aspects of this industry. At his best for "Veteran Designer Offers Reconfigurable Alternative to NASA Space Station," 1-13, he offers a very interesting account of criticism leveled at the NASA space station program by former Rockwell engineer Oliver Harwood: "Industry has abandoned its professional obligation to tell the customer when he is wrong..." Taking an informative look at small, but rapidly expanding America West Airlines in "America West Recovery Plans Focus on New Hub at Columbus," 3-2, he thoroughly chronicles the carrier's fight out of bankruptcy. In "John Wayne Airport Suspends Noise Rules to Test Draft Procedures," 4-27, Dornheim clearly and simply explains the tradeoff between safety and thrust cutback. His excellent forecast of the future aspirations of the Japanese aerospace industry, "Japan Monitors High Speed Civil Transport Market," 8-17, alerts us to government support for a consortium of Japanese aerospace companies: "Japan does not expect to play a primary role in supersonic transport, and instead is looking down the road at a hypersonic transport." Assessing the ramifications of a fly-by-wire flight control system failure during a C-17 transport test in "C-17 Pilots Report Flight Control Problem," 10-12, he observes somewhat pessimistically: "Solutions to some problems that were noted by the end of 1991 will not be available on the aircraft until a year later, and it is not clear that the fixes will work..." In "NTSB Recommends Changes to 737 Rudder Actuator," 11-23, he describes in great technical detail the changes recommended for the Boeing 737 rudder actuator, which has been cited as the possible cause in two recent crashes.

John J. Fialka
The Wall Street Journal
★★

Military. While there are more incisive journalists tracking the nation's military bureaucracy, Fialka continues to impress us with his well-scripted articles, culled from an impressive variety of sources. From farm procedures to high-speed fighter jets, he gives us a steady stream of informative, engaging material. Fialka recounts Russians comparing agricultural notes with Westerners for "In Canada, Ukrainians Discover the 'Lost' Art of Modern Farming," 1-24, but by overstressing the failure of the collective farms, he misses an opportunity to explore the virtues of Canada's free-market model. His ear-to-the-ground "C.I.S. Admirals Lobby U.S. for Help in Scrapping Part of Nuclear Fleet," 3-27, provides plenty of worthwhile intelligence on military downsizing in the former Soviet Union. Showcasing a witty style, he subdues for his more critical Pentagon reports, Fialka penning an enjoyable A-hed on a weed that can absorb toxic waste, "Salute the Jimson! The Noxious Weed Could Be a Boon," 6-18. Back to more serious topics with "Bush Ignored Data on Iraq, Gonzalez Says," 7-22, he constructs an all-too-short report on allegations that President Bush knowingly supplied Iraq with warfare technology. Fialka fails to shed light on the background of these allegations, or give us a time-frame when these events occurred. This was an issue that was much more thoroughly handled by reporters at *The New York Times*. Playing the armchair enthusiast for "Russian MiGs Now Are All the Rage in Friendly Skies," 8-3, he pens a highly readable feature on U.S. pilots who are purchasing attack planes from the former enemy. Continuing his reports on the sale of ex-U.S.S.R. craft, Fialka offers the highly-readable "Iran's New Submarine, Built by Russia, Stirs Concern in U.S. Navy," 11-16. Though not quite Tom Clancy, we get a good idea of the sub's questionable reliability, but not its effect on the Gulf.

Philip Finnegan
Defense News
★½

Defense. An impressive fact-gatherer, Finnegan has proved a reliable chronicler of the turbulence in an economically retrenching defense industry. But times of great fluctuation call for lucid analysis, and this, unfortunately, we often do not get in satisfactory doses. For instance, landing an interview with the powerful House Budget Committee Chairman, Leon Panetta, in "Panetta Pans Precipitous Defense Cuts," 1-13, Finnegan squanders an opportunity to ask some tough questions. We get Panetta's virtually unedited version of why his proposal to spread budget cuts over a five- to ten-year period makes sense. Without the appropriate economic or strategic analysis here, Finnegan shows no savvy on the politics behind Panetta's proposal. His "DoD Request Awaits Trial by Fire," 2-3, is a vivid portrait of feverish Congressional pork-barrelling in hard economic times. In the same vein, Finnegan thoughtfully analyzes proposals by House Democrats to create an industrial conversion plan for defense contractors in opposition to the Bush administration's free-market approach, in "House Democrats Eye Plan to Help Industry Diversify," 5-18/24. Cost-cutting issues also dominate "Defense Bill Provisions May Draw Bush Veto," 6-8/14, a pithy analysis of the House's proposal to reduce defense spending through increased burden-sharing with U.S. allies and increased withdrawal of U.S. troops from Europe. Showing his strong deadline-reporting skills in the solid "New Thomson Bid for LTV Would Face Obstacles," 7-13/19, he provides plenty of juicy tidbits on how Paris-based Thomson-CSF is finagling to overcome the "formidable hurdles" it faces in its bid for the U.S.-based LTV missile division. The very critical debate is more fully explored in "Congress May Curb Foreign Buyers," 10-5. Here, he keeps us abreast of Congress's latest attempts to ban foreign acquisitions of U.S. defense contractors. In Finnegan's "U.S. Girds for Waves of Mergers," 11/30–12/6, he predicts that the pace of defense industry mergers will continue to increase.

Thomas L. Friedman
The New York Times
★★★

State Department. A consummate insider and expert analyst, Friedman continues to impress us with precise coverage of global diplomacy from a U.S. perspective. Unlike many journalists, his passage to the post-Cold War world has been relatively smooth; his intellectual flexibility enables him to see global relations clearly, in the context of a changing world. Detailing a 47-nation decision to help the C.I.S. get its feet on the ground in "Ex-Soviet Lands to Get Swift Aid," 1-24, he cautiously notes: "... it is still unclear how many of these new initiatives will become reality." He embarks on a valuable reconnaissance into the mechanism that might shape foreign policy during a Clinton presidency in "Clinton Uses Loose Circle of Advisers," 3-28. In "Baker on Hill, Passes Hat for Russia," 5-1, Friedman gets a clear, if brief reading of Capitol Hill's reaction to the "$24 billion international aid plan for the former Soviet republics..." The report's brevity hampers its scope, but we get an adequate view of the opposition the aid package faces. His high-level sources prove valuable after the Labor Party victory in Israel in "U.S. Aides Say Real Winners Are Peace-Talk Negotiators," 6-24. Along with news of the administration's subdued congratulations, we get the enthusiastic scuttlebutt. He sketches a rare bird's-eye-view of Secretary of State James Baker's security shield for "In a Bulletproof Motorcade, Baker Whips Into Lebanon," 7-24: "Two Silverado vans, with machine-gun turrets planted on their roofs, sandwiched Mr. Baker's Cadillac ...ready to pounce upon any suspicious movement." More important, the article outlines Baker's strategy to bring about a Syrian withdrawal from Beirut. His post-election "Clinton Warns U.S. Foes and Reassures Its Friends," 11-5, displays Friedman's intuitive understanding of international concern and reaction: "The Europeans have always been more comfortable with Mr. Bush's unsentimental realpolitik view of the world, than traditional liberal democratic instincts."

David A. Fulghum
Aviation Week & Space Technology
★★½

Washington military editor. With over ten years of experience on defense and aerospace issues, Fulghum is one of the most seasoned veterans on this beat. He is a conscientious reporter and a pragmatic analyst, viewing new defense technology through the useful prism of post-Cold War applications. Concise and clear on this restructuring of the nation's strategic nuclear forces in "Manned Bomber Force Accelerates Shift From Nuclear to Conventional Roles," 4-6, he fully assesses the reasons for a more coordinated command structure and development of a conventional/nuclear mission plan. With the Soviet Union gone, he observes, "The number of possible conventional targets for U.S. bombers is skyrocketing." In a related article, "Study Details New Conventional Role for B-2 Stealth Bomber," 6-8, he follows the evolution of the B-2 from a deep penetration nuclear bomber to one using conventional ordnance: "The Stealth bombers would open gaps for the B-1s which then would act as 'bomb trucks' to strike ground forces with their massive payloads . . ." Showcasing his technical acumen in "Navy to Test Fluidic Backup as Defense Against Electromagnetic Disturbances," 2-3, he examines development of a new fluid hydraulic backup system that would "give pilots enough control to conduct aerial refueling and land on board an aircraft carrier even with damaged or inoperable electronic flight controls." In his informative "F-16 Mid-Life Update Wins Favorable European Response," 10-19, Fulghum fully details new practical technologies that are available to Europeans in an F-16 Mid-Life Upgrade (MLU) kit. And his "Defense Conversion Plans Full of Flaws," 11-16, is an excellent, well-rounded discussion of the issues faced by government and industry in defense conversion.

Barton Gellman
The Washington Post
★★

Gellman's fine coverage of U.S.-Israel post-Cold War relations proves he has the potential to cogently assess broad, complex issues. But all too often, he trades analytical depth for the party-line cant of military brass and congressmen. Joined by co-writer David Hoffman for "U.S., Israel Reassess Relations in Painful Time of Adjustment," 3-23, we're served a generous overview of the post-Cold War re-alignments that find the U.S. broadening its relations beyond Israel in the Middle East. Gellman scripts a lively report on possible war scenarios drawn up by congressmen to gauge cuts in the military in "Debate Over Military's Future Escalates Into a War of Scenarios," 2-26. While the analysis here is limited, this loose compilation of Congressional opinions does offer an informative smattering of rationales for budget cuts. On the other hand, Gellman provides little more than a bulletin on the Senate Appropriations Subcommittee on Defense in "Senate Panel Cuts B-2 to Fund Seawolf," 5-1. He skirts over the issues behind this partisan fight for projects, mentioning, but not evaluating, " . . . a nearly party-line 19 to 9 split . . ." According to other news accounts, the problem of sexual harassment in the military goes deeper than Gellman admits in his tilted "Tailhook Group Seeks to Polish Image," 8-8. Here, high-ranking naval personnel are given plenty of space to present their side of this case of "drunken debauchery," but little room is made for other points of view. In "Security Issues Loom on the Horizon," 11-7, Gellman presciently examines issues that could sidetrack Clinton from his economic agenda.

Bill Gertz
The Washington Times
★★½

Impressively well-connected within intelligence and specific policymaking circles, Gertz delivers a plethora of telling tidbits on national security issues. He is a perceptive analyst and a dogged fact gatherer. His extensive network of sources proves profitable as he scripts a fast-paced report on the intelligence gathered from reconnaissance photographs in "North Korea Digs Tunnels for Nuclear Arms," 2-21. Not as explicit, though, is "Gates Warns of Nuclear 'Brain Drain,'" 1-16, in which Gertz offers only a serviceable recap of CIA Director Robert Gates's testimony on the dangers posed by an idled Russian scientific community's willingness to sell its knowledge to other countries. Gertz evinces a dogged determination to keep on top of the ex-Soviet Union's compliance with international military treaties, a valuable service in light of the growing unrest in the region. Examples of his substantial contribution in this area are "Radar of Ex-Soviet Violates ABM Treaty," 4-10, a succinct elucidation of a Congressional report on C.I.S. non-compliance with a radar treaty, and "Russians Can Foil START Curbs," 7-24, a valuable read with Gertz's well-placed Congressional sources providing a lucid explanation of the technicalities. In the same vein, his detailed analysis and solid Russian contacts bring an added dimension to his gripping "U.S. Missed Soviet Nuke Alert in Coup," 5-12, an in-depth review of the U.S. failure to detect a Soviet nuclear alert during the 1991 coup attempt. Gertz revisits a mystery in "Pilots Knew KAL Flight Was Civilian," 8-15. This above-par dispatch clears up numerous misconceptions about the downing of a Korean airliner by Russian aircraft in 1983. His intelligence sources serve him well in "India, Pakistan Cited in Spread of Nuclear Arms," 10-31. Though not as detailed as we would like, Gertz gives a dramatic reading of the 1990 border conflict that could have triggered a nuclear confrontation between these two nations.

Michael R. Gordon
The New York Times
★★

Washington. A capable journalist, Gordon details the post-Cold War's international conflicts and arms reductions with a steady hand and a sharp eye. Overall, though, his body of work this year did not match the outstanding coverage we saw from him throughout the Persian Gulf War. His "Pentagon Study Cites Problems With Gulf Effort," 2-23, is a direct and informative presentation of a DoD report on contradictions in air target sites during the Persian Gulf War. Equipping us with the necessary background on SDI for "'Star Wars' X-Ray Laser Weapon Dies as Its Final Test Is Canceled," 7-21, we are able to absorb a great deal of information about this latest termination. Unfortunately, Gordon doesn't include reaction from SDI proponents, who might have shed light on the virtues of this scrapped project. He supplies a detailed re-examination of U.S. air patrols over southern Iraq in "A New Resolve on Iraq," 8-20, Gordon's sources serving him well here, though most of the information appears to be a well-strategized leak: "Administration officials conceded privately that Washington knew little about the Shiites when the Gulf War ended, failed to anticipate their uprising and tended, wrongly, to lump them with the Iranians." Looking toward the situation in Bosnia, Gordon does a fine job explicating the U.S.'s quandary in "Bush Backs Ban on Jets Over Bosnia," 10-2: "The Pentagon has been wary, fearing that it would be the first step toward deeper military involvement and that it could lead to retaliation... against the United Nations relief effort." Gordon provides a decisive roundup of international concern over a UN agreement in "Negotiators

Agree on Accord to Ban Chemical Weapons," 9-2. His "U.S. Force Must Meet Its Every Need by Itself," 12-8, is a satisfactory detailing of the extensive operations being coordinated in Somalia.

Melissa Healy
Los Angeles Times
★★½

Washington. Healy came into her own this year with detached, professional coverage of the Navy's Tailhook scandal, keeping us up-to-date on the emotionally-charged subject of sexual harassment in the armed forces without being shrill or judgmental. Healy gets a hearing with Adm. Frank Kelso, chief of naval operations, in "Top Admiral Seeks to End Navy Sex Abuse," 6-6, rounding this out with background from the Tailhook incident and internal reports that show harassment may be widespread. She continues to keep us well informed of developments surrounding Tailhook in such illuminating reports as "Navy Leader Says Officers Assisting Tailhook Probe," 8-12; "Pentagon's Tailhook Report Expected to Detail Obstruction, Cover-Up," 9-16, a fine preview of the report and potential repercussions; and "New Plans Offered to Fight Sexual Harassment in the Navy," 9-18, a solid overview of O'Keefe's ideas to curb harassment. She provided substantial coverage of crime and punishment following the fiasco in "Pentagon Blasts Tailhook Investigation," 9-25, an in-depth examination of the release of the Pentagon report on Tailhook which found the Navy investigation to be "halfhearted" and "hobbled by bad planning." Healy was exceptionally detached on the politics of defense as well, using salient detail and telling quotes to craft her stories. She gives us a sturdy overview of the history of the B-2 bomber in "U.S. to Halt B-2 Program at 20 Planes," 1-8, outlining what the production shutdown of the bomber will mean to the defense industry in California. In "Guard, Reserves to Lose 234,000 in Cheney Plan," 3-27, she thoroughly reviews Defense Secretary Dick Cheney's plans to cut spending. And her forward-looking essay, "New Set of Marching Orders," 11-2, fully examines the changes ahead in the wake of Tailhook and in the face of continued downsizing.

Breck W. Henderson
Aviation Week & Space Technology
★★½

Military electronics editor. Henderson's rich, forward-looking assessments of advanced power systems with military and avionic applications are always recommended reading for those who track these technologies. Occasionally, though, his articles are weighed down by too much techno-babble. In his excellent "Pressure Mounts on Defense Dept. to Approve Purchase of Russian Topaz 2," 3-30, he analyzes pressure on the DoD from other government agencies to approve the purchase and importation of the Russian Topaz 2 space nuclear power system: "Nuclear scientists in the U.S. want the opportunity to study Topaz 2 because it is an operational, flight-tested thermionic nuclear power supply, something the U.S. does not have." In another enlightening article on the Russian Topaz system, "SDIO Planning Mission With Russian Topaz 2 Reactor," 6-29, he reports that not only is the U.S. going to buy the Topaz system, but it may also invite Russian scientists to assist. He offers keen analysis on competing proposals for new Japanese AWAC planes in "U.S. Offers Japan Proposals for Early Warning Aircraft," 2-10, explaining why an untried design, based on the Boeing 767, might have certain advantages over a less expensive Grumman/Lockheed offering. Unfortunately, his insights get buried under too much technical jargon in "U.S. Industry Close to Producing Long-Life Space Cooling System," 4-6, a long and somewhat tedious explanation of technologies that will be employed to cool sensors on NASA and SDI satellites. He thoroughly explores future uses for superconducting materials in defense systems in "Superconducting Modules to Find Application in Future EW Systems," 10-19. And in the perceptive "Ames Labeled 'High Risk' to Hostile Intelligence," 11-23, Henderson reports that attention is turning to economic espionage as an emerging threat, and aerospace technology "is likely a prime target."

Theresa Hitchens
Defense News
★★½

Brussels bureau chief. Delving deeper into defense issues each year, Hitchens offers unique and increasingly detailed perspectives on how post-Cold War budget cuts and the move toward European integration are impacting the entire European military-industrial complex. In "Sweden, Norway to Ease Export Rules," 1-27, she reveals why Scandinavian countries are shooting themselves in the foot through strict arms export control. A penetrating look into the mind of angst-ridden EC technology planners, "EC Launches Research Plan," 5-18/24, provides a thorough discussion of the Community's plans to expand spending on research and development, particularly in high tech. Her "Military Leaders Stir Over Belgian Plan to Flatten Budget," 7-13/19, is an interesting examination of opposition to Belgium's defense budget cuts: "The new plan raises doubts about Belgium's ability to command, as it has promised, one of the three multi-national ground corps envisioned by NATO to make up its main defense forces." She rambles a bit in "Yugoslav Dispute Disrupts CSCE Summit," 7-13/19, but ultimately shines through with a sharp juxtaposition of the disorder in Yugoslavia, the re-ordering of European security, and the disruption of a meeting of the Conference on Security and Cooperation in Europe "designed to lay the foundations of a new European security order." She discerns the reasons eastern Europe is trying to increase its arms exports in her perceptive "East Europeans Accelerate Export Push," 10-5/11: "Converting military production to civil production is especially hard in the former East Bloc because of a general lack of a solid civilian manufacturing sector, especially high technology." Hitchens succinctly delivers the goods in "WEU Ponders Merger of European Reserves," 11/30-12/6, a report by the Western European Union which was "Prompted by concern over the lack of attention to reserve requirements as Europe's defense ministries attempt to cut costs."

Robert Holzer
Defense News
★★½

Naval affairs, helicopters. Holzer's well-placed naval contacts and appreciation of technological wizardry make him a valuable resource for those tracking the U.S. Navy's reconfiguration. His thoroughly-researched, highly-focused reports continue to catch our eye. He keeps us abreast of the financial details of the controversial tilt-rotor aircraft program in "Panel to Prepare Osprey Development, Financial Strategy," 1-6, but uncharacteristically, he fails to fully examine Defense Secretary Dick Cheney's opposition to the program. Holzer adds dimension to the latest checklist of cancelled programs in "U.S. Navy Submarine Programs Take Direct Hit," 2-3: "In the wake of Seawolf's cancellation, the Navy is seeking $50 million to evaluate concepts under the more affordable Centurion follow-on submarine project..." His comprehensive "U.S. Services Eye $1 Billion Buy of SSF Prototype," 5-25/31, showcases Holzer the reporter and analyst at his best. By examining an illuminating combination of military intelligence, private technological research and a government proposal to include European allies in the venture, he clearly defines the objectives of this project and lays out its future. Once again it's Holzer's focus and clarity that define "U.S. Navy Shifts ASW Priorities to New Technology," 6-8/14, an informative analysis of how and why the Navy is "shifting its efforts in antisubmarine warfare (ASW) toward advanced research and development..." He gathers the inside scuttlebutt in "U.S. Navy Continues to Tinker With AX Role," 9-14/20: "Current debate within the Navy's aviation and acquisition communities is focusing on how much more capability the AX [attack aircraft] should possess beyond the current 30-year-old A-6 Intruder..." Once again he peers into the future with a plausible assessment of how Russia could distribute its nuclear weapons and the U.S.'s response in "Weapons Accords Expand Mission for ASW," 12-21/27.

David Hughes
Aviation Week & Space Technology
★★

Northeast bureau chief. Although Hughes occasionally gets mired in technical non-essentials and overlooks the broader context of a technology's practical applications, he more often than not delivers the goods on a wide array of defense systems and issues. He starts the year with one of his best articles, "Regional Nuclear Powers Pose New Risks to U.S. Military," 1-13, an excellent primer on Third World nuclear proliferation and the challenge it poses for U.S. defense strategists. In a disappointing "Digital Automates F-22 Software Development With Comprehensive Computerized Network," 2-10, Hughes gets lost in a bunch of technological minutia without ever thoroughly explaining the point of Digital's software development effort. "Joint-STARS Officials Provide Data for Missile Defense Plan Analyses," 4-27, represents an improved attempt by Hughes to explain experimental technology. Very upbeat about the capabilities of the J-STARS program, he writes that planners were "surprised at how many individual targets presented opportunities for a direct link to fighters in the air." He hits his stride with a fascinating walk through the world of futuristic armaments in "Army Antitank Weapon Test Shows Sensor Fuzed Technology Is Maturing," 6-29. This sweeping examination of sensor fuzed mines explains how they can be used to attack tanks and even helicopters using "smart" components: "The mines could form a defensive barrier at a disputed border with another country, only to be activated if needed." In "Lockheed, GE Plan to Deliver First F-22 EW Units in 1995," 10-19, Hughes again delves into technical detail surrounding the electronic warfare (EW) unit being developed by Lockheed and GE. And in "Boeing, United Pursue Major Cockpit Advance," 11-23, he cleverly explains new technology being developed by United Airlines and Boeing to improve collision avoidance systems.

Clifford Krauss
The New York Times
★½

State Department. We find Krauss's work somewhat muted this year, his writing less lively than usual, his examinations less probing. The eclectic mix of non-State Department assignments he receives seem to distract him. While Krauss provides a colorful snapshot of the factional Democratic infighting over a package which might include a capital gains tax break in "Democrats Act to Keep Ranks Tight on Taxes," 2-19, he fails to get beyond the politics for a proper assessment of the proposals being weighed. Doing little more than repeating what has been said by the State Department, on the Haitian refugee problem in "To Stem Exodus, U.S. Won't Pick Up All Haiti Refugees," 5-22, he tells only part of the story of this emotional and political trauma. His report on the Senate's proposal to extend jobless benefits, "Senate Votes to Extend Jobless Aid, Creating Another Bush Veto Threat," 6-20, is serviceable at best, only skimming the economic and social implications of the plan. In "Envoy to Moscow Presses Congress for Russian Aid," 7-24, Krauss depends too heavily on Capitol Hill aides for his report on the U.S. ambassador to Moscow, Robert S. Strauss. His lack of high-level sources leaves the article one-dimensional. His best of the year was the prescient "Late Surge by Republicans Dims Democrats' Hope for Senate Gains," 11-1, a pithy assessment of the volatility in the Senate races where Republican incumbents, written off only weeks before, were suddenly running even with their Democratic challengers: "Some Republican strategists said they believed that Democratic Senate candidates shot to a big lead in the aftermath of the Republican National Convention, because the inflammatory appeals of Patrick F. Buchanan and a few other speakers turned off most independents and even some Republicans. Now, they say, the voters are finally focusing on the Senate races and the party's candidates."

John Lancaster
The Washington Post
★½

Military. Lancaster has fared well in his move from the environmental thicket of the Department of Interior to the technical jungle of the military beat. While he has yet to develop the high-level sources that many of his counterparts tap into, we think his purposeful research style makes him worth keeping an eye on. He notes the problems the Navy is having placing pilots in squadrons because of military downsizing in "Newly Minted Pilots in Holding Pattern at Desks," 3-28. The information here is timely, and the sense of frustration conveyed by the pilots is acute. He enters a sterling report on redundant programs between military services in "Hill Takes Aim on Duplication in Military Services," 8-8. Among the big-ticket items, he finds a "separate chaplain corps, medical corps, dental corps, nursing corps, legal corps and...separate fleets of executive-style aircraft." We get a solid update on the stealth bomber in "B-2 Bomber May Never Meet Requirements, Air Force Concedes," 5-22: "That even a truncated version of the [B-2] program had managed to stay alive despite the Soviet collapse speaks volumes about the task faced by Congress as it seeks to tailor the nation's defenses to the post-Cold War era." Outside the military budget debate Lancaster is less effective. "Possibly 80 Vietnam POWs Left Behind, Kerry Says," 6-25, finds him providing a workman-like, but lifeless report on Sen. Kerry's heated allegation. On Tailhook, the now infamous military sexual harassment case, he weighs in with a dutifully accurate, but detail-sparse "Tailhook Prober Ousted After Harassment Complaint," 7-9. And in "General Bars Disarming Somali Clans," 12-15, he gathers the scuttlebutt around the Pentagon on questions arising from U.S. intervention in Somalia, but fails to provide any cogent analysis.

Jeffrey M. Lenorovitz
Aviation Week & Space Technology
★★½

Senior international editor, Washington. After filing rather routine dispatches during the Persian Gulf War, Lenorovitz has returned to familiar territory and the useful reporting more characteristic of his journalism. In "French Investigators Seek Cause of Rapid Descent," 1-27, he gives a lucid, technical account of the investigation into possible causes of the A320 Airbus crash outside Strasbourg, France. In his impressive follow-through, "French Government Seeks A320 Changes Following Air Inter Crash Report," 3-2, he details telling tensions between Airbus designers and government investigators: "French Transport Minister Paul Quiles [ordered] Airbus Industrie to furnish within one month 'a precise program of studies and application of an ergonomic modification to the aircraft-crew interface linked to the vertical guidance modes and their utilization procedures.' Airbus managers questioned the tone of Quiles's order, which could be interpreted as making changes a foregone conclusion before the study work is completed by the aircraft manufacturer." He draws an effective contrast between the successful French SPOT imaging satellite program and the troubled U.S. Landsat program in "Spot Image Plans Better Resolution on Next Generation of Satellites," 6-15. He pens a revealing report on the struggle to overcome extremely tough economic times at Energia, the Russian space agency, in "Russia to Upgrade Mir 1 Space Station, Prepares for New Orbital Facility," 5-4. The article is peppered with observant reporting and comments from key sources. In "Congress Cancels NLS Launcher Family," 10-12, he cites credible reasons for cancellation of the National Launch System (NLS) program including cost, delays and insufficient power: "Critics [argued] . . . that other launch vehicles now in service or under consideration could fulfill NLS mission goals." Lenorovitz gives us a timely update on the ongoing consolidation of the defense industry in "GE Aerospace to Merge Into Martin Marietta," 11-30.

George Leopold
Defense News
★★★

Staff writer. Broadening his scope each year, Leopold continues to refine his reporting, writing and analytical skills. He is most impressive when painting the big picture on shifting military-political alliances in today's swiftly changing world. A careful observer of the global arms control environment, Leopold's "Study: Arms Controllers Must Stress Strike Aircraft," 1-13, is a pleasure to read. This look at a Stanford University study urging arms controllers to change their focus from missiles to one that encompasses the threat from strike aircraft is most illuminating. In "Kazakhstan Resists U.S. on Nukes," 5-18/24, Leopold provides a very perceptive account of the situation between the Kazakh president, Nursultan Nazarbeyev, and U.S. officials who are trying to get him to surrender his control over nuclear weapons that are stored in his country. Leopold unsnarls the confusing numbers involved in assessing warhead counts for the START treaty in "Multiple Warheads Snarl U.S.-Russia Summit," 6-15/21, expertly dissecting the constraints it imposes on both sides. "Ruehe Acts to Ease U.S. Concerns Over New Franco-German Corps," 7-6/12, is another superior effort. Here, he explores U.S. concerns that new Franco-German cooperation will pull Germany away from NATO: "The formation of a Franco-German corps has raised concerns in the United States about its relation to NATO's command structure and whether it would be subordinated to alliance commanders in a crisis." In "Japanese Accord Raises Transfer Issues," 10-5/11, he gives an interesting report on how export controls and national sensitivities are slowing progress on a U.S.-Japanese agreement to develop new propulsion technology. And in "Industry Awaits Clinton's Action on Dual-Use Technology," 11/30-12/6, Leopold is insightful on the future of defense conversion under the Clinton administration, which plans to shift defense-related research work toward civilian projects.

Paul Lewis
The New York Times
★★★

United Nations. Often, a report by Lewis can be crucial to our understanding of the UN's role in a changing world. A veteran on this beat, he is well respected by the diplomatic community for his balance and accuracy. His work abroad, such as his reports from Rio and Iraq, skillfully illustrates the dynamic at work in the ever-shifting sands of international relations. Thoroughly and accurately detailing Iraq's refusal to come up with a plan to destroy UN-targeted military equipment in "U.N., Hinting at Force, Gives Iraq a Week to Scuttle Arms," 3-18, Lewis captures the mounting tension of the diplomatic standoff: "It is unclear whether the allies, for political reasons, would seek a new Security Council endorsement of [a possible] military action or whether they would operate on the basis that since Iraq refuses to comply with the cease-fire terms, that truce is no longer in effect and they are free to attack again." Continuing his coverage of Iraq's belligerence toward the UN with "Iraq, Assets at Risk, Asks to Reopen U.N. Oil Talks," 9-29, he deftly characterizes the give-and-take between the two bodies. He paints a near-complete picture of reluctance on the part of some countries to back the agenda at the Rio Earth Summit in "Some Gains Seen in Environmental Talks, but Big Divisions Remain," 3-29. The article is forceful because it delineates the financial burden the industrialized world will have to bear for environmentally-correct technology. He resumes his Rio Summit reporting with "Pact on Environment Near, but Hurdles on Aid Remain," 6-12, noting that "the continuing standoff over money has contributed to the stalemate between North and South over steps to preserve the world's forests." His illuminating "Under Shadow, Serb Culture Blooms," 11-17, fills in a number of questions as to why the culture-clash in Yugoslavia has caused so much upheaval.

Christopher Madison
National Journal

★★

Foreign policy. A capable generalist, Madison occasionally dazzles, though overall, his work remains painfully inconsistent. His best piece of the year is his stunning expose on the "October Surprise" investigation, "There Was a January Surprise, Too," 2-15, which takes us behind the scenes to witness an abortive attempt by House Foreign Affairs Committee Counsel R. Spencer Oliver to negotiate for information from a convicted arms smuggler: "The real smoking gun, as far as the House is concerned, may be Oliver himself. Long known among fellow staff members as a 'loose cannon' with a conspiratorial bent, he may have turned a somewhat partisan investigation into one that will be completely partisan." His "Mixed Signals on the Middle East," 3-14, is a solid review of the administration's increased pressure on Israel: "It is Baker's good fortune that pro-Israel sentiment in Congress has waned, partly from an aversion to foreign aid in general and also from a belief that with the demise of the Soviet Union, Israel is less important strategically in the Middle East." Exploring the reasons for improved relations between the U.S. and Latin America in "U.S.-Latin Tango," 6-13, he keenly observes that improved relations are based on a new spirit of cooperation based on "renewed emphasis on economics rather than ideology." His revealing, albeit overly forgiving profile of Deputy Secretary of State Lawrence Eagleburger, "Super Deputy," 7-11, came to mind later in the year as Eagleburger took over as acting Secretary of State: "A key to Eagleburger's success is that he appears to have few identifiable enemies." Madison offers mostly vague generalization in his "Internationalist Clinton," 10-17: "Clinton's election might signal that Americans want their President to concentrate on domestic affairs, not diplomacy." "Readying the Deck on the Ship of State," 12-12, delivers a well-written essay on the Clinton transition team at the State Department and the man leading the process, J. Brian Atwood.

Jim Mann
Los Angeles Times
★★½

Washington, national security. We've come to appreciate Mann's distinctive combination of experience in Asia, as the former Beijing bureau chief, and considerable knowledge of strategic issues. His specialization in U.S. national security concerns in Asia perfectly maximizes his talents. We get an early bead on the souring relations between the U.S. and the countries of Asia, in "America's Dwindling List of Good Friends in Asia," 1-19, in which Mann notes, for the first time, that the U.S. will have no real ally in either Japan or China because of economic and political pressures here and in those countries. He compiles different quotes and insinuations to put together the first hints of a completed puzzle of Iran's nuclear armaments program in "Iran Determined to Get A-Bomb, U.S. Believes," 3-17: "From Feb. 7 to 12, four inspectors of the IAEA [International Atomic Energy Agency] toured six Iranian nuclear facilities... The IAEA report noted that its conclusion that Iran's purposes are peaceful was limited to the sites visited by the team and only for the specific six-day period of the inspectors' visit. U.S. officials said the agency's report was very carefully worded and does not contradict their view that Iran has embarked on a plan to develop nuclear weapons." He follows up with further evidence in "China Reported Seeking Missile Deal With Iran," 4-3, advancing the case that China might be selling sensitive technology to the Iranians. Mann and co-writer Sam Jameson give us Japan's reassessment of its forces in "Japan May Shift its Forces to Western Flank," 9-26, the duo asserting that as the Cold War winds down, the threat from China and North Korea is greater than from the former Soviet Union. Mann switches gears and pens "As Presidents Cross Paths, Interval Is Often Awkward," 11-7, an engaging history of presidents welcoming their successors to the office. More feature than story, Mann's grasp of history is evident in this interesting report.

Robert Mauthner
Financial Times
★★½

Diplomatic editor. An intuitive sense of how historical forces play on current events enhances almost all Mauthner's work. His professional detachment and rigorous intellect have made him a key journalist to watch for critical, illuminating assessments of Europe's subtly shifting alliances. Mauthner's expert probe of the UN Security Council's changing role in a changing world, "Suitable Subjects for Reform," 1-8, pegs the institution's role in the post-Cold War era "as a peace-maker and peace-keeper to the civil and ethnic conflicts which are likely to dominate the world scene until the turn of the century." His brief, but telling account of British Foreign Secretary Douglas Hurd's attempts to assure his nation that the European Monetary Unit is in the U.K.'s best interest, "Hurd Says Nation State in Good Shape," 2-5, came to mind later in the year when Britain had to bow out of the European Exchange Rate Mechanism. After the spring elections in England, Mauthner usefully detailed the Major government's EC policy in "EC Hopes for a More Positive Major," 4-11/12. At his best for "Turkey Strides Confidently Onto a New Political Stage," 5-12, he finds the tea leaves of Turkey's economic future very favorable, in light of the collapse of the U.S.S.R. and despite being denied entrance to the EC. Uncharacteristically, he adds little to Hurd's recent speech at the Conference on Security and Co-operation in Europe in "UK Supports Wider Area for NATO," 6-3. This surprisingly stark report merely skims the pros and cons of using NATO as a peace keeping force. Joined by co-writer William Dawkins for "French Interest Groups Lend Support to Yes Campaign," 9-9, the duo relies too heavily on poll data to illustrate the reservations Europeans have about the Maastricht treaty. We missed Mauthner's historical perspective in this uncommonly one-dimensional assessment. He also doesn't bring much perspective to news that France is seeking another international conference regarding the crisis in Bosnia and Herzegovina, in "France Seeks New Bosnia Conference," 11-19.

Doyle McManus
Los Angeles Times
★½

National security. McManus seemed to be coasting this year, rarely pushing at the edges of policy or advancing the debate over strategic issues. More disappointing, though, was his frequent failure to provide subtle details or in-depth analysis. He rehashes the Secretary of Defense's remarks on Boris Yeltsin's arms reduction proposal on CNN's "Newsmaker Sunday" in "Cheney Rejects Yeltsin Plan for Big Arms Cuts," 2-3, but there's little evidence here that McManus did more than turn on his TV for this report. He is sparse on the details for "Baker on Tour to Sell Public on Aid to Russians," 4-22, a cursory recounting of the Secretary of State's attempt to replicate the Marshall Plan with "an unusual barnstorming tour" to promote aid to the Russians. In "Kazakhstan to Get Rid of A-Arms," 5-20, he quickly outlines the agreement to confine nuclear weapons to Russia to accommodate the START treaty, but McManus neglects to assess the geopolitical implications in this light report. "U.S. Production of Nuclear Explosives Formally Halted," 7-14, brings us up-to-date adequately: "... officials said that the Administration move is important diplomatically because it turns the existing halt in production into a long-term policy." With "U.S. Aid Agency Helps to Move Jobs Overseas," 9-28, he vigorously takes the Agency for International Development to task. He devotes considerable time to the critics and only vaguely lists AID's denials of allegations that they are actively trying to replace U.S. workers with cheaper labor overseas. Post-election McManus is entirely out of his element as he describes "a roughly 30-year cycle in American history that has brought reformers to power..." in "Vote Marks Turn in Nation's Direction—and Consciousness," 11-6.

Michael Mecham
Aviation Week & Space Technology
★★

Bonn bureau chief. Though Mecham's recent work doesn't match the quality of his definitive 1991 coverage of NATO's post-Cold War security concerns, we still rely on him for dependable perspectives on a wide range of issues, including military planning and aerospace technology. In "Belgium Gains Anti-tank Capability With Agusta A-109CM Helicopters," 1-20, he provides useful intelligence on Belgium's advanced helicopters which "are adding vitality to the air mobility forces that the country can contribute to NATO's new rapid-reaction corps." We have new respect for the training U.S. military transport pilots receive after reading "U.S. Mercy Missions to CIS Show Technology No Substitute for Airmanship," 3-9, an upbeat report on how piloting skills enabled crews to cope with extremely rudimentary navigation guidance. Attending the first aerospace exhibition in Berlin since before WWII, he pens "Unified Germany Brings ILA Exhibition Home to Berlin," 6-15, efficiently highlighting the new products to be rolled out at the show. In his engaging "Europeans Prepare to Build on Early ERS Satellite Success," 7-13, he assesses plans for the launch of a second earth monitoring satellite. The first satellite, he reports, put the European Space Agency (ESA) "at the forefront of meteorology and climatology research, especially in polar- and ocean-based investigations." In "Gulfstream 5 Launch Includes BR 710 Engine," 9-14, Mecham capably reports on Gulfstream's entry into the long-distance business jet market. And in "U.N. Recognizes Need for Halons," 11-23, he sharply reports that the UN has granted an exemption to halon, an ozone depleting chemical, for use in aircraft: "The exemption recognizes that no effective substitutes yet exist for halons in critical fire control systems used for aircraft, ACT and defense."

David C. Morrison
National Journal
★★½

Defense. Morrison gives us a rich and comprehensive accounting of the perils and hard-earned progress that characterize U.S. security planning in an election-year. Perceptive on the political pressures coming to bear in "Saudi F-15 Sale: Jobs, Jobs and Jobs?" 4-18, he explains that even the powerful Israeli lobby is having difficulty convincing congressmen that Israeli security is more important than U.S. jobs: "Never mind that the vast bulk of the F-15 work is done in five states; a roster of communities listed in the [pro-sale] ad reads like a paean to small-town America..." He's also astute in "Missile Defenses: More Debate," 2-8, explaining that the essence of the debate over missile defense is whether or not deployment violates the Antiballistic Missile Treaty of 1972. Also impressive is "Changing Speed," 3-7, a thorough examination of the sea change in defense procurement. In "ASAT's Orbit Has Gotten Much Lower," 5-2, he tracks the declining fortunes of the DoD's anti-satellite program from its heyday to its near demise. As the apparent need for ASAT diminishes, he tells us: "Termination appears a lot likelier than full deployment." A glib title, "Too Many Birds?" 7-4, belies the very serious nature of Morrison's thorough and highly useful examination of the future of U.S. tactical aircraft: "The dogfight over aircraft will determine not only the new hardware that the Air Force and Navy will operate, but also their roles and missions in the 21st century." Though not as comprehensive in his report on military downsizing, "Veterans for Hire," 10-17, Morrison does offer some compelling stats: "...today's army accepts only 31 per cent of applicants—compared with the University of California acceptance rate of 47 per cent." And in "At NASA, Goldin Is in His Own Orbit," 12-5, he pens a strong article on the changes at NASA since Daniel Goldin took over, and the possibility that Goldin may continue on into the next administration.

John D. Morrocco
Aviation Week & Space Technology
★★★★

Washington senior military editor. Though Morrocco will have trouble matching his near perfect coverage of the Gulf War, this talented reporter and analyst is still one of the best, providing some of the most penetrating work on post-Cold War defense planning and procurement anywhere. In his excellent editorial, "U.S. Must Redefine Threat, Needs in Post-Soviet Era," 1-13, he warns that current procurement plans will waste billions. He suggests that "flexibility will be the new watchword." He passes on insights from an interview with Marshal Yevgeny

Shaposhnikov, the former Soviet defense minister, in "CIS Armed Forces Seeking Order From Chaos in Revamping Soviet Military R&D Plans," 2-10, and discovers that Russian "procurement is being cut in order to shift more funds into military personnel accounts." In his critique of DoD's acquisition process, "Dangers Cited in Implementing New Pentagon Acquisition Strategy," 3-9, he cuts right to the chase: "Developing new technologies and putting them on the shelf could be prohibitively costly and erode not only the defense industrial base but the nation's science and technology base as well . . ." In "House Panel Backs 20 B-2 Force, Faster AX Program and Delaying MRF," 5-18, he thoroughly canvasses the House Armed Services Committee budget proposal and the winners and losers in the Navy and Air Force aircraft procurement plans. In "Cheney Urges Senate to Preserve Funding for F-22, C-17 Programs," 7-20, he faithfully details Secretary of Defense Richard Cheney's plea to Congress to restore full funding to several programs the Pentagon deems essential. In "Congress Defers Tough Choices on Weapons Spending Plans," 10-12, he details cuts in the '93 defense appropriations bill, observing that "Lawmakers sidestepped hard decisions on weapons programs they have criticized as unaffordable . . ." Morrocco ably wraps up the final stages of planning for relief efforts in "U.S. to Spearhead Somalia Relief Force," 12-7.

Neil Munro
Defense News
★★½

Staff writer. Munro continues to demonstrate a very sturdy grasp of defense technology and communications issues. We've noticed his inquiries are more in-depth, his evaluations more precise. For example, he takes a fascinating look into inter-service infighting over long-range anti-aircraft and anti-missile weapons in "U.S. Army Resists Move by Air Force on Air Defense," 9-14/20: "The proposal calls for the Army to hand over its . . . Patriot and the older Hawk air defense missiles . . . and other Army-managed antimissile development programs to Air Force planners . . ." He efficiently outlines some of the dilemmas facing defense planners, as they battle a dramatic constriction of the military industrial base, in "Army Program Setbacks Fuel Industrial Base Concerns," 2-3. "U.S. Army Wants More Bradleys," 6-15/21, nicely juxtaposes the argument for more Bradley Fighting Vehicles against the planned shrinkage in the number of Army divisions: "The Army may not even need the new Bradleys if the number of Army divisions is reduced in forced cuts, said one industry official." "U.S. Army Adapts EW to Shield its Tanks," 8-3/9, has Munro offering some nice tidbits of intelligence on the Army's efforts to increase the survivability of their tanks: "Adapting electronic warfare technology developed to protect fighter aircraft, the U.S. Army is attempting to give tanks more protection against missiles without adding bulky armor." In "U.S. Navy May Urge Cooperative ID System for Aircraft," 10-5/11, he concisely reports on the Navy's call for an aircraft ID system for its planes: "The focus on battlefield identification systems was precipitated by events in the Gulf War, where U.S. weapons were fired at U.S. and allied troops . . ." Munro provides an adequate review of new accounting and management procedures designed to save billions in "DoD Management Reform Aims to Save Up to $35 Billion," 11/30-12/6.

Bruce D. Nordwall
Aviation Week & Space Technology
★★½

Avionics editor. We complimented Nordwall last year for his detailed reports on the use of avionic technology during the Gulf War. This year, he shows his versatility as he trains his eye on commercial aviation, delivering punchy articles steeped in facts and valuable insights. In "FAA Says GPS Lacks Accuracy Needed for Precision Approaches," 1-20, Nordwall gives us the nuts-and-bolts of the Global Positioning System instrumentation being implemented to aid aircraft navigation. He offers a nice roundup of the international avionic manufacturers' debate over the future of the worldwide market for commercial air transport in "Avionics Firms Focus on Core Businesses," 3-16. His "Poor Radome Maintenance Degrades Performance of Aircraft Radars," 5-11, on the problems some airborne weather radar systems have been having, is for techno-wonks only. Nordwall does an impressive job with "United Engineering Groups to Develop Smaller, Lighter, Cheaper, RWR," 7-27, relating to the layman how a universal radar warning receiver will improve identification of unknown threats during wartime: "One big advantage of a system that does not rely on a threat library is that it can characterize threats encountered for the first time as well as known threats. That capability could be crucial in combat." He shows off his avionics knowledge in a sprightly "FAA Speeds GPS Approval, 1993 Operations Planned," 10-19, expertly detailing how a satellite-based navigation system will improve the airline industry. His "Hand-Held Passenger Device Provides Rapid Feedback," 11-2, fully explains the latest commercial airline gizmo—a small computer used to gauge air passenger's satisfaction.

Don Oberdorfer
The Washington Post
★★

Foreign policy. A conscientious, but sometimes long-winded veteran reporter, Oberdorfer's occasional verbosity can be overlooked due to the harvest of information we take from many of his articles. At his best for "N. Korea Seen Closer to A-Bomb," 2-23, he crafts a finely-researched and well-organized report tracing the beginning of N. Korea's quest for nuclear weapons. Oberdorfer's scope here is impressive: "The acquisition of nuclear weapons by North Korea...might prompt South Korea, and even Japan to reconsider its non-nuclear weapons stance." In "Top Cambodian Official Sees U.N. Mission as Key to Survival," 3-25, he doesn't allow himself enough exposition to properly build a framework to set the proper scale of the troubles blighting the Cambodia peace process. His in-depth look at Secretary of State James Baker's "intense diplomatic struggle to maintain control over the world's largest...array of long-range nuclear weapons," "3 Ex-Soviet States to Give Up A-Arms," 5-24, highlights Oberdorfer's fact-gathering skills and acumen. Joined by co-writer Marc Fisher for "Bush Turns Aside Bosnian Plea for Military Intervention," 7-10, the pair scripts a detailed, though verbose, examination of the U.S. and UN response, or lack thereof, to the president of Bosnia's plea for help against the Serbs. He provides the latest graphic statistic on starvation in Africa in the brief "Bush Orders Food Airlift to Combat Somali Famine," 8-15: "The U.S. Agency for International Development, says as many as one in every four Somali children under the age of five has already perished." Oberdorfer's report on reaction to Japan's violation of a U.S. embargo, "Japan to Resume Aid to Vietnam," 10-28, is nicely nuanced: "A State Department official who declined to discuss details of the Japanese plan said 'no country in the world has been more cooperative than Japan' with U.S. policies toward Vietnam. His remarks suggested that the U.S. reaction to the expected Japanese announcement will be muted."

Barbara Opall
Defense News
★★★

Staff writer. An excellent writer, a well-informed reporter and a highly-perceptive analyst, Opall can be relied upon to articulate the implications of the latest aircraft and missile technology developments. A perfect example of her ability is her impressively discerning "U.S. Air Force Seeks to Shift SDIO Funding," 10-12/18, in which she clarifies the significance of the shift by some Air Force planners to theater missile defense, which involves attacking missiles in their launchers rather than the terminal phase: "Inherent in the Air Force Plan is a challenge to SDIO spending strategy..." In "U.S., Germans Plan Research on Fighter Jets," 1-27, she provides an insightful and well-written examination of the logic behind U.S./German cooperation on jet fighter upgrades, focusing largely on vectored thrust: "By harnessing the power of multidirectional engine thrust and combining it with advanced aerodynamic controls, aircraft of the future might not need conventional external control surfaces." Her "Air Force Pursues Variant of HARM," 2-3, analyzes the Air Force's needs as it ponders a follow-up to its very successful anti-radiation (radar) missile program. Precise and detailed in "Air Force Impels GD to Correct F-16 Flaws," 5-18/24, she explains how many defense procurement screw-ups are inflating costs and may push the F-16 out of consideration for the new Multi-Role Fighter (MRF) program. Similarly, in "USAF, Congress Duel Over Cruise Missile," 7-6/12, she expertly uncovers yet another GD program foul-up, creating cost overruns that endanger full deployment of a new generation of cruise missiles. And in "U.S. Eyes Looser Controls on Israel Tech Use," 11/30-12/6, Opall reports on attempts to repair the rifts created between the U.S. and Israel over the issue of military technology transfer. She insightfully reports that "U.S. officials must still be convinced that Israel has departed from its past practices of selling sensitive and unauthorized technology to China, South Africa, and a number of South and Central American countries."

Andy Pasztor
The Wall Street Journal
★★★

Pentagon. Pasztor's reports are never flashy, but they are certainly substantial. We were drawn to his coverage of the defense procurement investigation, "Operation Ill Wind," and the political squabbling over military downsizing. He was consistently one step ahead of the pack. Unfortunately, he relies heavily on anonymous sources, a trait we forgive only because his stories and his sources usually end up providing accurate and important information that stands the test of time. In "Cheney Tells Navy to Halt Seawolf Plans," 1-7, Pasztor differentiates the latest budget slash with some helpful background information. Thoroughly examining the political fallout after Cheney proposed reserve troop cuts, Pasztor pens "Pentagon Set to Unveil Plan on Reserve Cuts," 3-26, capturing the feverish struggle by congressmen to preserve jobs for their constituents. When Pasztor attends Congressional hearings, as he did for "Pentagon Says Air Force Gave McDonnell Aid," 5-14, he details the interactions and nuances of the testimony so thoroughly that we feel we've attended. Uncovering rumors that "Federal prosecutors have recommended seeking criminal charges against Grumman Corp. and its former chairman," Pasztor pens "Charges Against Grumman Said to Be Urged in Inquiry," 6-18. Although based almost completely on anonymous sources, his report does provide useful analysis on what might be ahead for the company: "A comprehensive settlement probably would enable Grumman to avoid losing its eligibility to receive new government contracts." And "Grumman Corp. Ex-Chairman Pleads Guilty," 11-19, is a lean follow-up to Pasztor's in-depth coverage of the operation. Showcasing his political acumen in "Senate Defense Spending Bill Criticizes Cheney's Efforts to 'Reform' Programs," 8-7, he usefully describes in the political posturing taking place as a result of Cheney's austere defense spending bill: "The one thing [Cheney and Gen. Powell] have balked at doing...is knocking enough heads together inside the Pentagon to force admirals and generals to share weapons with their sister services."

Robert Pear
The New York Times
★★½

Defense. This distinguished reporter's domestic policy beat forces him to juggle a mélange of issues—some he handles expertly, others he handles less confidently. His finest work tackles the ideologically-charged health care debate, a topic he handles with admirable objectivity and clarity, as in his highly-instructive "Health Care Policy: How Bush and Clinton Differ," 8-12. Here, Pear does his readers an important service, by allowing both Clinton and Bush equal opportunity to expound upon their health care proposals. Playing the watchdog in "Many on Medicare Illegally Forced to Pay Deposit to Nursing Homes," 7-6, he fills in all the sordid details to lay bare yet another Medicare scam. Outside the health care issue, the quality of Pear's reporting is less consistent. Careful and precise in "President Offers Cautious Changes in Spending Plan," 1-30, he pours over the numbers trying to figure out where domestic spending is flowing. In "Clinton, in Attack on President, Ties Riots to 'Neglect,'" 5-6, Pear smartly points out that Clinton's ideas on social policy are remarkably similar to those of Jack Kemp and Jim Pinkerton. He casts a shadow over Ross Perot's "can-do" spirit in "Audits of Federal Contracts Indicate Major Failures by Perot Companies," 6-24, detailing how the presidential nominee overlooked errors in some jobs his company performed for the government. But unlike many of the attacks on Perot, this one had facts and figures to back it up. In "Top Bush Aide Denies Approving State Dept. Search of Clinton File," 11-15, he's disorganized in investigating whether a State Department employee dug up Bill Clinton's files with or without orders.

Paul Proctor
Aviation Week & Space Technology
★★★

Hong Kong bureau chief. Proctor possesses a rare combination of technological, political and marketplace savvy that makes his coverage of the Far East aviation scene some of the best anywhere. Typical of Proctor's insightful reporting is "Air China Upgrades Fleet to Vie With International Mega-Carriers," 7-6, in which he explores China's push to duplicate Western-style airline services. So detailed is his reporting that he can even cite how the Chinese airlines handle specific lightly travelled routes: Two Russian Antonov An-24s "are assigned to the small, unprofitable regional hub in Hohhot, Mongolia." Proctor takes a poke at the future of air travel in his entertaining "Airline Passengers of Future to Bathe in Technology-Driven Luxury," 1-13, examining research done by a Japanese firm that suggests fictional whimsy might just become technological reality. Offering a liberal overview of New Zealand's new corporate air traffic control system in his highly proficient "For-Profit New Zealand ATC System Cuts Costs and Increases Efficiency," 4-27, he showcases his deft understanding of the commercial market dynamic. He isn't his thorough self for "Rescue Spurs Fleet Expansion for China Ocean Helicopter," 5-11, reporting on a "fleet expansion" for CHOC(orp.), but failing to assess competing models. Proctor probes another burgeoning market in "Pakistani Factory Seeks Share of World Market," 9-14, a perfect example of Proctor's technological and business smarts. His business acumen shows through as well in "Hong Kong Airport Work Resumes Despite Financing Plan Dispute," 12-7, as he traces the terms, agreements and financial backing necessary for a new airport in Hong Kong.

Elaine Sciolino
The New York Times
★★★

Washington. Sciolino's careful, yet riveting coverage of the subplots of what became known as "Iraqgate" sheds much light on the government in-fighting that is usually kept under wraps. Her most important work of the year comes in the fall, as she doggedly tracks down leads on allegations that the CIA and Justice Department were involved in duping Atlanta Federal prosecutors working on the Banca Nazionale del Lavoro case. She lands a bold front-page headline with "Justice Dept. Role Cited in Deception on Iraq Loan Data," 10-10, dropping this bombshell: "[CIA] officials have told Congress that, at the urging of the Justice Department, they deliberately withheld information from Federal prosecutors in Atlanta about a multi-billion dollar bank fraud involving Iraq. . . . The disclosure contrasts with statements made . . . by the C.I.A.'s chief lawyer, who said the misinformation was an honest error. But in a highly charged, closed hearing before the Senate Intelligence committee on Thursday, agency lawyers changed their account." Sciolino's work on the CIA's adaptation to a post-Cold War world was quite respectable, as exhibited in "Panel From C.I.A. Urges Curtailing of

Agency Secrecy," 1-12, and "Lawmakers Unveil Spy Agency Plan," 2-6, a look at a proposal to diminish the agency's power. She takes a very enterprising look at Iran's attempts to become part of the global market in "Iran Struggles to Attract Investors," 4-30, providing plenty of background on the country's volatile political and financial history. Sciolino's "U.S. Is Said to Withhold Evidence of War Crimes Committed by Iraq," 7-6, is a serviceable report on the political and diplomatic reasons the administration has not brought charges against Saddam Hussein. And she pens a tidy report on acting Secretary of State Eagleburger's pronouncement that certain Serbs might be war criminals, in "U.S. Names Figures to Be Prosecuted Over War Crimes," 12-17, dutifully noting UN reaction.

William B. Scott
Aviation Week & Space Technology
★★

Senior engineering editor. Scott is a reporter who understands the link between capital investment and innovation. He also has a tremendous grasp of the technology he covers, so much so, that he often loses us on its finer points. His thought-provoking "Killing the Spark of Risk Douses the Fires of Aerospace Innovation," 1-13, places some blame on the media for inhibiting risk and thus innovation: "Bad press, ostensibly broadcast in the name of protecting the taxpayers' dollar, unwittingly may cost millions when it generates and then reinforces incorrect perceptions." In "Several Western U.S. States Drawing High-Tech Business From Traditional Sites," 2-10, he provides an informative and readable report on the effectiveness of business incentives offered by Colorado, specifically to high-technology industries. Thorough and precise for "Brilliant Pebbles Development to Change Building of Spacecraft," 5-4, he admirably lays out the details on this space-based interceptor missile, but the report becomes mired in too much techno shoptalk. Riding on a B-1B bomber for a simulated bombing mission in "B-1B Crews Adapt Readily to New, Conventional Role," 7-27, he captures the complexity of the aircraft, but a plethora of technical jargon flies over our head. He uses "Large Market Predicted for Hawk 1 Gyroplane," 9-14, as a well-detailed billboard for this up-and-coming mini-helicopter, and though it may cost about $150,000 ($230,000 fully equipped), Scott senses a large demand by law enforcement applications. Heavy techno-lingo weighs down "Airborne IR/EO Technology Applied to Surface Vehicles," 10-19, an otherwise solid recounting of efforts by research firms to develop a jamming device for tanks. His "NASA-Led Team to Study Supersonic Laminar Flow," 11-2, is more accessible on research work to improve wing shapes.

Gerald F. Seib
The Wall Street Journal
★★½

Diplomacy and foreign policy. Seib's analysis isn't as thought-provoking as we've seen in years past. He seems to be distancing himself from hard-news stories and writing more features. Nonetheless, his work from Russia and eastern Europe was quite interesting. His "A Defector Describes a James Bond Life Inside the Soviet KGB," 2-12, entertains in its glimpses behind the KGB's veil. Much of the information from the defector sounds dated, but Seib includes enough cloak-and-dagger intrigue to make it worthwhile. He again focuses on the breakdown of the U.S.S.R. in "A Private U.S. Group Finds Aiding Hospitals in Ukraine Isn't Easy," 3-31. This heartwarming story captures the state of deprivation and desperation in which Ukraine has been left. Seib dutifully reports Rep. Henry Gonzalez's accusations that the White House knowingly supplied aid to Iraq before it invaded Kuwait in "Congressman Questions Actions of Bush Adviser," 4-29, but he does little original research here. He quotes a plethora of experts to refute Ross Perot's assertion that our allies should be made to shoulder the cost of our military presence abroad in "Perot's Plan to Charge Allies for Their Defense Is Fuzzy on the Facts, but Politically on Target," 6-16. Joined by co-writer James M. Perry for "Clinton Cruises to Victory at Democratic Convention," 7-16, the pair files a balanced report on the previous week's events at the Democratic Convention. In "Many Americans Choose East Europe but Few Renounce Their Citizenship," 8-24, Seib uses the story of a Latvian-American's return home as a diplomat, to discuss how more Americans with dual citizenship are trying to work for foreign governments while retaining their U.S. citizenship. His "Clinton Could Get Tough With China Without Hurting Ties, Analysts Say," 11-17, takes an intelligent look at the fine line President-elect Clinton will have to walk on relations with China.

David Silverberg
Defense News
★★★

International marketing. An unparalleled knowledge of practically every dimension of the international defense trade makes Silverberg a primary source on such issues as international arms proliferation and military hardware markets. "McDonnell Douglas Gives Saudi Sale Uncharacteristic Push," 1-13, catches the story at its inception, as Silverberg presciently notes the extent McDonnell Douglas plans to throw its lobbying weight behind the sale. His ahead-of-the-curve "Bush May Announce F-15 Sale to Saudis Next Month," 8-17/23, accurately predicts: "Congress is likely to be notified of the administration's intention to sell 72 F-15s to Saudi Arabia when it reconvenes in September." Arduously tracing critical weapons parts to foreign firms in "Study Says U.S. Suppliers Can Fill Most Weapon Needs," 5-18/24, he effectively underlines the perilous nature of international weapons production. Silverberg does an admirable job of tracking down Congressional Armed Services Committee members for "Congress Awaits New Defense Players," 7-20/26, a worthy attempt to gauge the shape of this committee once new members come on board. Silverberg accurately describes the issue and its conclusions in "DoD Eyes Restrictions on Foreign Ownership: Draft Guidelines Limit Investment Efforts by Non-U.S. Firms," 9-21/27. His impressive knowledge of the international defense trade adds an analytical dimension to the report. His international defense acumen shapes "Russians Pursue U.K. Copter Deal," 12-14/20, updating us on competition between U.S. and Russian aircraft dealers trying to sell their combat helicopters to Britain.

R. Jeffrey Smith
The Washington Post
★★

National security. Smith's vision narrowed this year, tending almost exclusively to defense reports and Iraq's noncompliance with UN demands. He provides a detailed listing of weapons on the chopping block in the first major U.S. arms reduction plan in the post-Cold War world in "Bush Plans Steeper Arms Cuts," 1-24, but his sources contribute little to the piece: "The U.S. officials... said Bush's new actions are intended to reshape the U.S. strategic deterrent into a smaller force..." With "White House Prepares to Step Up Pressure on Iraq," 2-9, Smith comprehensively details the options open to the U.S. with regard to Saddam Hussein. His "U.S. Tolerated Arms Sales to Iraq After Iran War," 6-11, is a one-note report on House Foreign Affairs subcommittee chairman Sam Gejdenson's revelation of a declassified document revealing the U.S.'s toleration of weapon sales to Iraq. Smith fleshes out the President's warning to Iraq to comply with inspections in "Bush Warns Baghdad on Inspections; President Vows to Aid U.N.," 8-7. His grasp of technology and the ability to assess defense reports prove valuable in "SDI Success Said to Be Overstated; Four 'Star Wars' Tests Fell Short, GAO Finds," 9-16. And in "CIA Found Rome Tie to BNL Case; Analyst Concluded Loan Involvement Went Beyond Atlanta," 11-3, Smith fully probes the allegations made by the CIA and Rep. Henry Gonzalez that "Iraqi purchases of food and military equipment was not limited to bank officials in Atlanta but also... headquarters in Rome."

Barbara Starr
Jane's Defence Weekly
★★★½

International security affairs. This diligent, multi-faceted journalist constructs expert reports and analyses. Competence and credibility give her access to key sources, and a no-nonsense style enables her to pack more insight into a few columns than most do in several pages. Her "Calmer Waters Force Changes," 2-15, is an outstanding discussion of the U.S. Navy's attempts to refashion itself from a big-war footing in a bi-polar world, to a down-sized, more agile force, capable of responding to the diverse challenges of the new world order. She allows her well-placed sources to do the explaining: "Navy Secretary H. Lawrence Garrett III has called for a re-assessment of navy missions, including deep strike, continuous presences and over-the-horizon assault. The aim is to see if doctrine can be changed to save money." After the U.S. Air Force threatened to withhold F-16 progress payments, Starr provided a pithy assessment of how General Dynamics deals with non-conformances in "USAF Warns GD Over F-16 Quality," 5-23. She's also extremely detailed and informative in "NATO Harbours Doubts Over Franco-German Corps," 6-6: "At the heart of the matter is the 'double hatting' proposal raised by the UK . . . " She showcases her political savvy in "Make or Break for SDI as ABM Doubts Surface," 7-4, a well-sourced, behind-the-scenes look at the pivotal dispute between Sam Nunn, chairman of the Senate Armed Services Committee, and SDI Origination Director Henry Cooper. Her financial acumen is revealed in "Make or Break for GD," 8-29, a superbly specific and balanced analysis of the strengths and weaknesses of the restructuring at the troubled General Dynamics. "Soviet Production Continues to Fall," 9-26, provides previously undisclosed DoD statistics which show "significant production declines in virtually all areas." Starr's "US Army Rethinks ATCCS," 11-14, is a finely-tuned article, which transfers a tremendous amount of relevant information on the $20 billion Army Tactical Command and Control System which is being rethought to contend with possible conflicts arising in southeast Asia.

Patrick E. Tyler
The New York Times
★★★½

Pentagon. A wonderful year for Tyler. The brass at *The Washington Post* have to be gnashing their teeth at the loss of his masterful reporter and analyst. We hope to see him continue his exemplary work as he transfers to an overseas' desk in '93. His probing on the Pentagon's post-Cold War intentions produces a veritable cornucopia of electrifying front-page scoops. First, he creates a stir by getting his hands on classified documents for "Pentagon Imagines New Enemies to Fight in Post-Cold-War Era," 2-17, in which he observes that the DoD instructed military chiefs "to request forces and weapons sufficient to fight at least two large regional wars simultaneously . . . while also being ready to conduct a major military campaign in Europe to prevent a resurgent Russia from pursuing expansionist aims." In his follow-up the next day, "War in 1990's? Doubt on Hill," 2-18, he gathers skeptical reactions to the Pentagon's intentions in the leaked documents, but these two reports were only the tip of the iceberg. With his 10 Best selection "U.S. Strategy Plan Calls for Insuring No Rivals Develop," 3-8, Tyler shocks the nation by disclosing more classified draft documents that reveal a broad and highly controversial new policy statement: "the Defense Department asserts that America's political and military mission in the post-cold-war era will be to insure that no rival superpower is allowed to emerge in Western Europe, Asia or the territory of the former Soviet Union." So contentious is the nature of Tyler's disclosures that by May, the Pentagon has revised the documents, an event Tyler depicts in another 10 Best selection, "Pentagon Drops Goal of Blocking New Superpowers," 5-24. Tyler provides an uncharacteristically muddled and inconclusive "No Evidence Found of Patriot Sales by Israel to China," 4-3. Belying the headline, Tyler describes no vindication for Israel, only how the State Department abruptly closed the investigation. On the more mundane duties of day-to-day reporting, Tyler also fares well with such informative pieces as "Bush Is Asking Allies to Support Air Action to Protect Iraq Shiites," 8-17, a thoroughly nuanced article.

Ralph Vartabedian
Los Angeles Times
★★

Defense and aerospace. Vartabedian specializes in the business of defense as it impacts Southern California. He provides solid overviews of contract negotiations and company developments. With the industry in turmoil, his perspectives are valuable, though not always as comprehensive as we'd like. He gets an excellent snapshot of the new CEO of Hughes Aircraft, C. Michael Armstrong, in "Hughes Picks IBM Executive as CEO," 2-20, noting the telling detail that Armstrong's not the scientist traditionally chosen for the job. He and co-author Bruce Einhorn cull excellent detail from the business side as Taiwan Aerospace Corp. lowers a bid to buy 40% of McDonnell Douglas's commercial airline business, instead offering to buy a 5-10% share, in "Bid Dropped for Stake in McDonnell Aerospace," 5-19. We find in this crisp snapshot that McDonnell needs the cash to finance production of a new generation of commercial craft. Vartabedian crisply addresses industry changes in "Defense Profits Up as Spending Falls," 7-16. But he doesn't ignore the severe problems the industry still faces: "At the current rate of defense spending cuts, the industry will be left with an estimated 750,000 jobs [from a peak of 1.3 million] nationwide by 1994. What happens after that depends on the next step in the national defense debate and on the future of commercial aircraft orders." He follows this up with an examination of an engineer shortage, in "Southland Aerospace Firms Suddenly Lack Engineers," 8-22, but he only sounds an early warning, failing to examine the root causes. "Air Force's Spy Unit Leaving State," 10-16, fully examines the implications of news that the Air Force is moving its HQ for designing secret spy satellites from El Segundo to D.C. Vartabedian does a top-notch job of highlighting several emerging California aerospace companies despite the gnawing recession in "Flying in the Face of Turbulence," 12-4.

David White
Financial Times
★★½

Defense. We found White's reports a bit less explorative than last year, but nonetheless he continues to cram in intelligence on EC and NATO defense issues. His competent coverage of British Aerospace is certainly scanned by industry executives. Such reports as "BAe Announces Further Job Cuts at Guided Weapons Plants," 2-7, in which he announces numerous layoffs at the company, is handily reported with satisfying detail. Also sharp is his "BAe and Hughes Win 570m Pound Missile Order," 3-4, an illuminating appraisal of the contractors besting of the competition to supply RAF air combat missiles. On the broader European defense and NATO issues, White also fares well. European defense is the focus, with co-writer Robert Mauthner, in "Germany Warned Not to Quit Euro Fighter Project," 6-11, an enlightening interview with Mr. Malcolm Rifkind, Britain's Defence Secretary, who criticizes Germany for wanting to withdraw from a joint Euro-defense project. He broadens this theme with "Plan to Save 20bn Pound Eurofighter," 9-7, proficiently outlining the connection of the fighter to several countries in Europe. In "Cheney Fears Nuclear Technology Will Spread," 1-10, he voices the Defense Secretary's concern that "…it might be impossible to prevent new nuclear-armed states emerging as a result of the break-up of the U.S.S.R.," but more analysis of where the hot spots might be would have been helpful. His "NATO Fails to Resolve Ex-Soviet Missile Row," 4-2, is a brief, serviceable account of Cheney's meetings in former Warsaw Pact countries. And "Ceasefire Brings Relief to Sarajevo," 11-13, delivers a brief glimpse of relief efforts undertaken during a ceasefire in Bosnia: "UN plans for escorting relief convoys in Bosnia risk being seriously set back by delays in deploying Canadian troops to the Serb stronghold of Banja Luka. It is feared that because of difficulties with local authorities, deployment may not be possible until February."

★ SCIENCE/HEALTH/ENVIRONMENT ★

Rudy Abramson
Los Angeles Times
★

Although technically assigned to the environment beat, Abramson devoted the latter part of the year to the doings at NASA. His work on space and NASA is refreshingly dependable and thoughtful, whereas on the environment he tends to offer alarmist perspectives. He verges on misinformation in "Potential New Ozone Hole Alarms U.S. Science Team," 2-4, only *quietly* noting that the study in question is still in progress. "U.S. Says It Can Cut Output of Carbon Dioxide Further," 4-25, is a barely acceptable rewrite of press releases on negotiations over CO_2 emissions prior to the Rio summit. His coverage of the Rio summit was among the poorest of any we saw. Four examples are typically green: "Expectations for Summit Come Down to Earth," co-written by Maura Dolan 6-1; "Bush Defends U.S. Policy at Summit," co-written by Douglas Jehl 6-13; "Bush Sees Role on Environment as Political Plus," 6-14; and "Earth Summit Ends on Note of Hope, Not Achievement," co-written by Maura Dolan 6-14. Abramson presents the greenhouse theory as fact throughout, and his distaste for Bush is plain. He also fails to investigate Bush's environmental record. He is more balanced in "Ice Cores May Hold Clues to Weather 200,000 Years Ago," 12-2, noting appropriately that "the ability to study climatic patterns has been critical to the debate over the phenomenon called 'global warming.'" Abramson is best at covering outer space. He captures the drama of space flight *and* handles the technical aspects well in "Atlantis Blasts Into Orbit With Space Lab, Satellite," 8-1, and "Glitch in Communications Delays Shuttle's Launch of Space Laboratory," 8-2. His "Satellite to Track Shifts in Earth's Surface," 10-21, is vivid on the laser geodynamics satellite (LAGEOS II) that will examine plate movements, detect gravitational changes and "record the way the planet's crust rebounds after the withdrawal of glaciers" from space.

Lawrence K. Altman, M.D.
The New York Times
★★½

"Doctor's World" columnist. Altman carefully avoids penning a "news you can use" column. He covers health *news*, specializing in new developments on the health scene, and with his M.D., he has a special air of authority in his professional diagnoses. Altman was also the journalist to whom we turned for the final evaluations on Paul Tsongas's cancer. Cautionary but authoritative in "Doctors Say Cancer Therapy Has Tsongas in Good Health," 3-5, he notes that Tsongas's prognosis is favorable, but adds that this particular type of lymphoma has been known to recur unexpectedly. Altman reveals, "after further inquiries by The New York Times," that "Doctors Now Say That Tsongas Had Cancer Recurrence," 4-22, a readable evaluation that caused quite a stir. He continued to provide valuable updates on Tsongas's condition with "Tsongas Has Abdominal Surgery to Determine if Cancer Recurred," 11-24, and "Preliminary Results of Biopsy Point to Return of Cancer in Tsongas," 11-26. But Altman softpedals Tsongas's bitter criticism of the press in "Tsongas Says He Mishandled Issue of His Cancer," 12-1, downplaying the issue so much he is almost misrepresentative. Altman includes all the pertinent information in a graphic account of how a "Terminally Ill Man Gets Baboon's Liver in Untried Operation," 6-29. We almost feel like a member of the patient's family, so complete is his description. He follows up with a detailed post-op roundup in "First Human to Get Baboon Liver Is Said to Be Alert and Doing Well," 6-30. We get a clinician's view of the discovery of the AIDS-like illness that occurs without the presence of HIV in such competent reports as "'AIDS' Without Trace of H.I.V.: Talks in Amsterdam on 5 Cases," 7-22; "New Virus Said to Cause a Condition Like AIDS," 7-23; "AIDS-Like Illness: More Study Vowed," 7-24; "U.S. Is Tracking AIDS-Like Illness," 8-7; and "Working in Public to Explain AIDS-Like Ills," 8-18. In each, Altman quietly and carefully examines the epidemiological evidence to dissect the preliminary reports in a manner that informs.

Natalie Angier
The New York Times
★★★½

"Science Times." We approach Angier's material with the eagerness of a student heading for a favorite science class. We always *learn* from her dispatches, as she oozes excitement about her topics, bringing them to life through her animated prose. Angier even makes the arcane world of genetics accessible. "A Clue to Longevity Found at Chromosome Tip," 6-9, is fascinating on the discovery of telomeres: "Some researchers suspect that there is a strong correlation between telomere length and the aging of the entire human being." Angier takes us all the way through the research and we come away enriched. She doesn't quite grab us at first with "A First Step in Putting Genes into Action: Bend the DNA," 8-4, but as we push forward we find that this discovery, whereby proteins temporarily bend DNA to make the cells perform a certain task, is quite important. She makes this kind of material, once relegated to the most technical of medical and chemical journals, accessible to the layman. There is a similar payoff with "U.S. Permits Use of Genes in Treating Cystic Fibrosis," 12-4, with Angier balancing well the scientific and political aspects of this experimental research. And then, of course, there is her work on animal behavior, for which she was awarded her 1990 Pulitzer. "Dolphin Courtship: Brutal, Cunning and Complex," 2-18, a 10 Best selection, is delightful on the habits and socialization of dolphins. She offers a fascinating look at hyenas and research which may enhance scientists' understanding of human and animal behavior, in "Hyenas' Hormone Flow Puts Females in Charge," 9-1. Her "Cheetahs Appear Vigorous Despite Inbreeding," 11-6, is a superlative description of this "magnificent cat," from its genetic problems to its eating habits: "The cheetah hunts not by stalking prey, but by bolting at its quarry in an explosion of energy so exhausting the cat has to wait 15 to 20 minutes, panting, before it can eat."

Jerry Bishop
The Wall Street Journal
★★

Bishop has been the paper's science and health reporter since 1960. He keeps a steady eye on developments and is consistently readable and reliable. He seemed particularly attuned this year to developments on diabetes, updating us on the latest research in "Cell Advance Holds Promise for Diabetics," 1-15, a clear and concise account of insulin-making cells that help to fight the disease. He details how "Future Diabetes Tests May Use a Flash of Light," 6-19, to replace needle pricks. Bishop asserts that, should this new, invisible infrared light method be developed into a practical system, diabetics might be more diligent in tracking their glucose levels. But he doesn't assess the potential for such a system's development. Bishop adequately defines the results of a study published in *The New England Journal of Medicine* in "Researchers Suggest Cow's Milk Triggers Diabetes in Some," 7-30, but we get little beyond the basics. We have to read his "Scientist Mounts Malaria Counteroffensive," 11-10, twice to fully understand this report and profile of how Dr. Andrew F. G. Slater has made advances in dealing with the parasite that causes malaria. He's unusually disorganized here. Getting the scoop on the new procedure of "stereotactic automated large-core biopsy" in "New Biopsy Technique for Breast Lumps Is Called Quicker, Cheaper, Less Painful," 2-5, he describes a breakthrough method for early breast cancer detection. While enthusiastic that the procedure takes less time and money than a surgical breast biopsy, he's careful to convey the doctors' concerns about a "false negative" from the needle missing the dangerous cells. In his best of the year, "New Generation of Electric-Car Batteries to Be Unveiled," 5-15, Bishop takes us through all of the testing of these different batteries and is frank on the bottom line: "Although all three big auto companies have announced plans for limited production of electric vehicles, none of the vehicles is expected to be an economic alternative to the gasoline-fueled auto."

William J. Broad
The New York Times
★★

Science. Broad is at his best when he deals with space, crafting vivid and detailed dispatches. On other subjects, though, he's informative but unenthusiastic, providing expansive outlines of stories that don't quite satisfy. We get a solid roundup of the internal controversy over the feasibility of early SDI deployment in "Pentagon Analyst Questions Plan for Early 'Star Wars' Deployment," 6-2, but Broad comes up short on costs, a flaw in an era of concern about deficits. Broad gets a scoop with "Russia Offering Nuclear Arms Fuel for U.S. Reactors," 7-22, but he's somewhat premature on the Russians selling uranium for hard currency, as there are many bureaucratic hurdles to be overcome. Broad manages to keep a straight face for "After '10,000 Mistakes,' Biosphere Is in Hot Pursuit of Credibility," 9-22, detailing some of the errors made by participants in the Biosphere project. Broad gives these folks the benefit of the doubt in this even-handed effort. Profiling physicist Harold M. Agnew in "Present Since Atom Was Split, Physicist Reflects on Turbulent Era," 12-1, he offers a soaring, vivid portrait: "Dr. Harold M. Agnew has been active, sometimes even radioactive, at nearly every juncture since man first kindled a sustained nuclear reaction. While no titan of discovery or invention, he has long wielded power and influence, sometimes as a Presidential advisor and always as a gregarious hawk, as restless and unpredictable as the era he helped to define." When in orbit, however, it's plain he's enjoying himself. Broad entertains with a different "Recipe for Love: A Boy, A Girl, A Spacecraft," 2-11, a peek into one of NASA's "most delicate and secret topics... sex in space." He provides an informative follow-up to his 10 Best selection of 1991 with "Asteroid Defense: 'Risk Is Real,' Planners Say," 4-7, which is meticulous in giving voice to the critics of NASA's plan to develop an early warning system, while not stinting on the science itself.

Malcolm W. Browne
The New York Times
★★

Science. After seven years at the "Science Times," Browne seems to have lost some of his ardor, providing less salient detail in his reports. We're reading him less thoroughly now, whereas we used to savor every word. Browne relates all the pros and cons of new cooling systems not requiring CFCs in "Cooling With Sound: An Effort to Save Ozone Shield," 2-25, an acceptable but uninspired effort. He takes us for an unimaginative ride on the train that would float on "invisible magnetic cushions" in "New Funds Fuel Magnet Power for Trains," 3-3, getting bogged down in tedious details, and failing to thoroughly evaluate the cost effectiveness of a project that could cost anywhere from $8 to $63 million *per mile* of track. His esoteric "Despite New Data, Mysteries of Creation Persist," 5-12, on microwaves and their role in the Big Bang, loses us in the third paragraph, so obtuse is his writing. On the other hand, "40-Million Year Old Bee Yields Oldest Genetic Material," 9-23, is vividly written, though taken mostly from *Science*, on how scientists have extracted DNA from amber-encased insects. Browne even ventures into the sci-fi possibility of grafting paleolithic DNA to living DNA to create new animals. "On July 4, Chemistry Will Paint the Night With Fire," 6-30, was the best effort we saw this year from Browne. His writing is invigorated with the excitement of a child at Christmas as he describes the shapes and colors of fireworks and how they are made. The article is packed with readable detail on the chemical reactions required to light up the sky: "The leading pyrotechnicians agree that the real artistry of fireworks is not in making the big bangs but in painting pictures in fire." At year's end, he was covering technological developments abroad, as seen with "Bulgaria Must Fix Run-Down A-Plant," 12-8. We hope the change of scenery refreshes him.

Gene Bylinsky
Fortune
★★½

Bylinsky is probably the best of all the periodical science reporters, as would befit one of the originators of this beat in the periodical press 30 years ago. He closely tracks technological developments and business opportunities in the science and technology fields, always adding to our knowledge. Bylinsky intrigues with the story of Alza Corp. in "Got a Good Idea? Stick With It," 2-24. This company was responsible for the development of such products as the nicotine skin patch. We appreciate the businesslike approach Bylinsky takes, as he adds his comments on stock values to round out his assessment. "A U.S. Comeback in Electronics," 4-20, is excellently written on DSP (digital signal processing), as he outlines possible industrial and lifestyle applications. He seems positively, almost inappropriately, gleeful though, "that DSP isn't a fairly simple technology like the one that underlies DRAMs (dynamic random access memories), which the Japanese picked up, copied, and ran away with. DSP technology is considerably more complex, which makes it far tougher for the Japanese to appropriate." Bylinsky provides a superlative handling of "The Race for a Rare Cancer Drug," 7-13, examining how Taxol, derived from yew trees, is used in treating cancer patients, and how Bristol-Myers Squibb is getting close to synthesizing the drug. Bylinsky pens a quick sidebar update on the progress made in isolating possible neurological factors in the inherited form of the disease in "Finally, Hope for Curing Alzheimer's," 9-7, but he provides little on the implications. He's marvelously straightfaced on ScrubMate in "High-Tech Help for the Housekeeper," 11-9, describing the computerized robot that will clean toilets and bathrooms, but he's long on the gee-whiz and short on the R&D that Transitions Research Corp. put into development of the contraption.

Marilyn Chase
The Wall Street Journal
★★

San Francisco, health and medicine. Chase flavors her dispatches with healthy doses of information on the business aspects of the drug industry. Her specialty is the R&D of treatments and we appreciate her diligent coverage of this issue. As a rule, Chase is stalwartly detached and professional. She intrigues us with "Gilead Sciences Poised to Begin Clinical Tests," 3-19, as the company files an FDA application for a new AIDS drug and plans to file a second application for yet another AIDS drug in the fall. She provides a sharp snapshot of the business issues here, but could have been more thorough on the science. In "FDA Panel Backs Roche's AIDS Drug, DDC, but Only When Used With AZT," 4-22, Chase skillfully assesses the overall situation on the availability and development of AIDS drugs. For "Men in Study of AIDS Cases Outlive Women," 6-19, Chase gets her information from *Science*, and makes the most of it, smartly interpreting the data as an argument for the inclusion of women in clinical trials because their AIDS ailments often differ from those which occur in men. With "AIDS Gender Gap Narrows World-Wide as Women Continue to

Be Highest at Risk," 7-21, Chase updates us with a trim dispatch that should have been fleshed out into a leder, as she provides startling statistics on AIDS transmission: "Worldwide, over 70% of infections are estimated to occur through heterosexual relations, according to Anke Erhardt of the Columbia School of Medicine." Outside the world of drugs and AIDS, she and co-author Carrie Dolan describe, in the sweeping overview "California's Beacon to Newcomers Dims as Services Face Cuts," 9-1, the paradox of California—a traditional haven for immigrants that is being severely tested as budgetary factors force the state to start curbing social services. And we appreciate her precise snapshot, "Federal Scientists Expand Tests of Two Vaccines Against AIDS," 12-2, as she includes pertinent information on the chemical trials and the drugs.

Marlene Cimons
Los Angeles Times
★

Health, Washington. Cimons rarely provides research beyond the Washington press release, often failing to ask the tough questions or provide the in-depth information that is so critical to her work. Consequently, we seldom come away enriched. While Cimons isn't exactly a shill for the AIDS lobby in "Bush's AIDS Funding Plan Is Called Decrease," 1-26, she does seem to belabor the flashpoints of the administration's funding. She tries to present the need for more funds on a scientific basis, but there aren't enough specifics to make the case. In the disappointing "Magic Johnson, in Rebuke to Bush, Quits AIDS Panel," 9-26, Cimons fails to evaluate Bush's record, which Magic is protesting, and neglects to tell us that Johnson only attended one panel meeting. "House OKs Fetal Tissue Research," 5-29, is long on the political battle over fetal tissue research and short on the science, relegating the debate to three paragraphs in this P.1 article. We get a reasonably good overview at the close of the case of Dr. Cecil Jacobson in "Infertility Doctor Is Found Guilty of Fraud, Perjury," 3-5. Cimons is sensitive in describing the different issues involved, such as patient-doctor trust. Her work on R&D for AIDS drugs is satisfactory and a bit more detailed. She provides information on the major studies on DDC in "3rd Major Drug for AIDS May Win Early OK," 4-21, following up with "FDA Approves AIDS Drug for Use With AZT," 6-23. The latter is a good roundup of the approval of DDC, with information on how DDC and AZT work together to prevent the infection of T-cells. She comes up short of the expertise we found elsewhere in "AIDS-Like Mystery Virus Isolated by UCI Scientists," 7-23, a lightly-detailed overview. She reminds us that the "U.S. Needs More Family Doctors, Study Warns," 11-9, but provides little beyond the political aspects of this development.

Philip Elmer-DeWitt
Time
★

Although *Time* has gone ballistic on science coverage, Elmer-DeWitt is more subdued. He's clearly trying to craft his dispatches professionally, and in some detail, but has met with only limited success. "How Do You Patch a Hole in the Sky That Could Be as Big as Alaska?" 2-17, is an efficient endnote on the science of replacing CFCs. It follows Michael Lemonick's awful cover story on the greenhouse effect, "The Ozone Vanishes," in the same issue. In "Depression: The Growing Role of Drug Therapies," 7-6, he informs on the impact different drugs can have on this condition, although he's supercilious in spots: "...some scientists wonder how a single neurotransmitter could trigger the disruptions ... that characterize a typical depressive episode. The nerve endings responsible for these functions, after all, are located in totally different regions of the brain." "Dream Machines," Fall '92, is an intriguing discussion of 21st-century technology, though his lead puts us off: "Try this sexual fantasy on for size: author Howard Rheingold, who writes about the you-are-there technology known as virtual reality, predicts that consenting adults in the not too distant future will be able to enjoy sex over the telephone." "Catching a Bad

Gene in the Tiniest of Embryos," 10-5, is a sturdy discussion of the ethics and technology of genetic screening. Not completely detached in "Rich vs. Poor," 6-1, he can't decide if Rio will be "bigger than the momentous meetings at Versailles, Yalta, and Potsdam" or if "the outlook . . . is far from certain." He preaches sustainable development here without examining what it means. "Oregon's Bitter Medicine," 8-17, is editorial on Oregon's health care plan. After Bush sent the plan back, Elmer-DeWitt decides that "the action not only undermined one state's initiative, it raised broader questions about whether the U.S. will ever muster the political courage to replace today's patchwork medical-insurance systems with one that provides for all citizens."

Malcolm Gladwell
The Washington Post
★★½

AIDS and science. After several years on this beat, Gladwell has an impressive collection of relevant information stored in his head; as such, he knows what questions to ask and to whom to address them. He gets the scoop in "Dow Corning to Quit Silicone Breast-Implant Business," 3-19, a well-rounded overview with good background on the controversy and the company. Staying on the story, he produces "FDA Will Allow Limited Use of Silicone-Gel Breast Implants," 4-17, in which he offers background material on the FDA's role. He provides a trimly-rounded overview of Congressional approval of the FDA plan to charge user fees to drug companies for hiring more personnel to speed drug approval, with "Congress Acts to Speed Drug Review," 10-8. Gladwell gives us an important update in "'Safe Sex' Campaign Said to Be Missing the Mark," 5-16. He carefully examines many of the factors involved, from teenage embarrassment at buying condoms to a lack of interpersonal skills in discussing their use. Gladwell is almost plaintive in an overview of what scientists don't know about the AIDS virus and how this impedes progress in "Meeting Shows Wide Gap in Knowledge About AIDS," 7-26, an impressive gathering of expert views. Fuzzy in "Reports of AIDS-Like Illness Inconclusive," 8-25, he fails to provide the clear reporting necessary for this complex issue, attempting, instead, to list various theories of researchers. His skills are shown to best advantage in his profile of NIH director Bernadine Healy, "The Healy Experiment," *Magazine* 6-21. In this engaging portrait, he sketches a backdrop and fills in the foreground with insightful quotes, crafting a colorful and well-drawn picture. Though not as well-rounded, his examination of the controversy surrounding AIDS researcher Mika Popovic, "Science Friction," 12-6, also impresses us, as Gladwell clears up many of the questions of this case. He moves to New York as bureau chief as 1993 begins.

Philip J. Hilts
The New York Times
★

Health, Washington. Hilts, a one-time *Washington Post* science scribe, rarely breaks new ground these days. He never quite gets to the bottom of things and sometimes it seems he's not even trying. In "Senate Backs Faster Protection of Ozone Layer as Bush Relents," 2-7, he doesn't go much beyond the press release he was handed, and then only tells us that his impression is that the change is due to the departure of the environmentalists' foe, John Sununu. He also skimps in "Federal Agency Announces Start of Human Tests of AIDS Vaccines," 12-2, only presenting the most basic information in this dispatch. Similarly, he skims the surface of an FDA decision in "F.D.A. Restricts Use of Implants Pending Studies," 4-17. In "U.S. Agency Is Criticized for Dropping AIDS Ads," 7-1, he doesn't quite get to the heart of the criticism, the lobby, or the excuses of the Center for Disease Control for not getting some of these PSAs on the air. He fails to examine the finer points inherent in a new FDA "Plan to Speed Approval of Drugs: Makers Would Pay Fees to U.S." 8-11, a proposal by which the FDA would hire, through fees from drug companies, extra examiners to get the paperwork and tests completed more expeditiously. Hilts doesn't address the potential conflict of interest here. On the other hand, he penned one of the more complete overviews on this subject with "Senate Passes Bill to Charge Makers for Drug Approval," 10-8, offering good detail from both Congress and the FDA on Senate passage of an FDA plan to charge drug companies user fees. His features are much more analytically satisfying. We get a pithy, detailed overview of the case of David Baltimore, who was accused of knowing a study conducted on his watch contained false data, in "The Science Mob," *The New Republic* 5-18. Here Hilts briefly examines the broader implications for the scientific community and how "collegial protection" works against the ideas and ideals of science itself.

Gina Kolata
The New York Times
★★

Science and medicine. Once the daily source on AIDS news, Kolata barely covers the subject now, forcing us to turn to other, less informative sources for the latest dispatches. Kolata has to be content with covering spot news science stories which don't fully employ her considerable talents. She trimly updates us on Halcion, as the FDA begins an investigation of Upjohn, in "Maker of Sleeping Pill Hid Data on Side Effects, Researchers Say," 1-20. Kolata and the *Times* end up with egg on their faces with "U.S. Panel Backs Restriction on Use of DNA in Courts," 4-14, a P.1 report that had to be retracted the next day in "Chief Says Panel Backs Courts' Use of a Genetic Test," 4-15. She handles the retraction professionally: "'We based our interpretation of the report on the views of legal experts,' said Nicholas Wade, science editor of the *Times*, 'but erred in saying that the panel called directly for a moratorium on the use of DNA typing.'" On the other hand, Kolata does scoop the competition on fetal tissue research in "Evidence Is Found That Fetal Tissue Transplants Can Ease a Brain Disease," 5-7, emphasizing that this data is preliminary, but promising. She compellingly outlines the difficulties of using high technology medical tests in "When Doctors Say Yes and Insurers Say No," 8-16, an important addition to our portfolio of essays on national health care: "The problem, many experts say, is that in the name of cost containment Americans may be showing progress toward medical advances—even ones that might ultimately save on health costs by detecting disease at an early stage, curing it at a lower cost or preventing it." With her 10 Best selection, "Support Grows for Vitamins as Roadblocks to Heart Disease," 9-22, Kolata precisely explains how vitamins may help prevent heart disease. And in "New Views on Life Spans Alter Forecasts on Elderly," 11-16, she outlines the latest debate on aging, as scientists argue that there may be no biological limit to age.

Julie Kosterlitz
National Journal
★½

Health, welfare, pensions, environment and energy. Kosterlitz is adept at providing views of the politics and policymaking on her beat. She reports in some detail on policy and always provides the names of the players, though she only infrequently pulls these aspects together into a cohesive analytic overview. In "A Sick System," 2-15, Kosterlitz begins with a political history of health care, but doesn't really address the viability of any of the proposals she mentions. She covers the debates on the Hill over pension legislation well in "Pension Zigzag," 3-21. As legal changes move forward, her report provides a good definition of the law as well as the proposals. She doesn't, however, look into what effect these changes might have on the economy. In "Pension Penury," 8-1, Kosterlitz takes too long to get to her main point that Notch Babies, "people born from 1917–21, who narrowly missed out on a social security windfall enjoyed by retirees born from 1910–16," aren't being treated fairly. She's also too editorial here, including phrases like "it's a shame" and "it's a travesty." "AIDS Wars," 7-25, is an in-depth political portrait of how the Center for Disease Control and its current head, William Roper, are fighting AIDS. Despite the title, the

CDC is the real subject here and this well-rounded look informs. She offers another satisfying snapshot of the Health Insurance Association of America in "Shaky Times for Insurers," 11-21, putting the issues in big-picture context. Her best of the year, "Wanted: GPs," 9-5, is exceptionally mind-broadening on the debate over health care at the most primary level: "Overhauling the way the nation delivers health care may be the biggest sleeper issue in the increasingly raucous debate over health care reform." She also covers why doctors don't want to be GPs, even though the need for family care is increasing.

Margaret E. Kriz
National Journal
★½

Energy and communications. Kriz is providing well-shaped overviews more often these days. She has always collected relevant data and key quotations, but this year she is starting to develop style in assembling them. There's evidence of solid reporting in "Born Again," 7-4, as Kriz effectively relates that "reports of the impending death of nuclear power were greatly exaggerated." She assembles good detail and we come away informed on a subject often overlooked by other news outlets. Her trim overview of the energy bill debate gives ample time to both sides on Capitol Hill and the energy companies, in "Power Politics and the Energy Bill," 3-28, but she provides little depth on the scientific arguments. In "Fuels Errand?" 10-17, she outlines the identity crisis at the Department of Energy, explaining it is not only the Defense Dept. which is affected by the end of the Cold War: "Everything from the high-cost military weapons production facilities to the more modest domestic energy programs is coming under the microscope. The outcome could be a dramatic reconfiguration—or even elimination—of the Energy Department." With her treatment of the greenhouse effect, "Warm-Button Issue," 2-8, Kriz is meticulously balanced on the sidebar, "The Basics of Global Warming," in which she makes much of the fact that "the scientific community can't agree on how carbon dioxide, methane and other chemicals affect the earth's complex weather systems…Global warming continues to be a theory not a fact." Similarly, "Global Warming Causes Political Heat," 4-11, is a balanced view of the different political sides in the global warming debate. Disappointingly, she skips any discourse of the scientific validity of the greenhouse theory in an otherwise acceptable examination of European legislation to curb CO_2 emissions, with "Europe's Cooldown," 11-28.

Thomas H. Maugh II
Los Angeles Times
★★

Science. A long-time science journalist, Maugh has a BS from MIT and a PhD from the University of California at Santa Monica. We've been watching him for several years and are as impressed by his writing as by his credentials. Maugh has the enthusiasm of a cub reporter, and, though he sometimes comes up short on details, we relish his colorful reports. Maugh entertains with his colorful account "Ubar, Fabled Lost City, Found by L.A. Team," 2-5, though he fails to provide hard-core data on how the team found the city. His marvelous dispatch, "Research Supports Bible's Account of Red Sea Parting," 3-14, describes in vivid detail how a computer model has discovered that winds surrounding the Red Sea could have caused it to part "precisely as the Bible describes it." His "Researchers Inject Genes in 2 Fights Against Disease," 6-10, is exceptionally readable on gene therapy studies at the University of Michigan. Maugh is completely professional in reporting the procedure, the dangers and the potential for success in treating both cancer and cholesterol-related problems. Conversely, he's skimpy on the actual mechanisms of the test in "Scientists Detail New Early Test for Alzheimer's," 8-22, an overview of a study in *The Lancet*, which details the test that can identify the gene and thus help in diagnosing the disease. He's more satisfyingly detailed in recounting study results from the *Journal of the AMA* on tacrine, an Alzheimer's drug, in "Study Finds Drug Helps Some Alzheimer's Patients,"

11-11. Maugh professionally describes the findings of biochemist Gary Evans, of Minnesota's Bemidji State University, in "Longer Life Span in Rats Linked to Chromium," 10-20. Evans's studies indicate that ingestion of the chemical chromium picolinate increases the lifespan of rats, a phenomenon he says may be applicable to humans. Maugh carefully describes the results as "potentially...a major finding."

Spencer Rich
The Washington Post
★

Health. A veteran reporter on this beat, Rich seems to spend most of his time at the Department of Health and Human Services waiting for the next press briefing. He doesn't push his sources or offer his own analysis, a disappointment in a year when the debate raged over health care. He gives us adequate information in "Details of Health Care Plan Filter Out," 1-30, but never identifies his "administration sources," though he does make clear that this is only "the basic shape of President Bush's still unreleased plan to solve the nation's health care crisis." He's off-center in reporting Sen. George Mitchell's charge of Bush administration "cynicism," in "Bush Accused of Health Care 'Cynicism,'" 4-6. This partisan point/counterpoint report doesn't aid our understanding of the situation. Rich merely offers an uncritical list of who's proposing what in "Democrats Struggle With Health Care Overhaul," 6-14, but doesn't examine why. In "Ranks of Poverty Swell by 2 Million," 9-4, Rich defines and catalogues the Census data well, but neither assesses its accuracy nor puts this into a contextual picture of the overall economy. He's at his best when laying out the big picture, as with "High-Tech Advances Offer Troubling Prognosis for Curbing Health Costs," 7-12, a good overview of the problems confronting those who want to reform the health care system to cut costs. In "Rochester's Revolution in 'Universal' Care," 11-8, Rich doesn't quite get at the specifics, or offer firm estimates of how much costs were cut. Overall, though, this enterprising overview of the Rochester plan, which Clinton cites frequently as a model, is appreciated. He's more thorough in "Cost Cutting in Maryland Paves the Way," 12-8, looking at the state's Health Services Cost Review Commission. Though he admits the program is not applicable on a national level, he's plainly enthusiastic.

Kathy Sawyer
The Washington Post
★★★

Space and developments at NASA. Sawyer is adept at assessing developments on both the scientific and political side, though it's plain her forté is the science of space, and space flight. She pens a useful primer for those of us not quite familiar with astronomical terms, in "Peering Into the Violent Mysteries Inside Distant Frothy Clouds," 1-20, an eminently readable article. In "Mikulski Backs Shifting Defense Research to the Environment," 4-10, she serves up a taut dispatch relating Sen. Barbara Mikulski's (D-MD) proposal, buttressed with various statistics provided by the senator. There's little, though, that goes beyond the press briefing. Engaging detail is provided after the satellite recovery in her "Second Female Spacewalker Takes on Construction Tasks," 5-15: "The crew of seven, after Wednesday's triumphant satellite rescue, was awakened this morning by the funky sound of Boxcar Willie singing 'I Wake Up Every Morning With a Smile on My Face.'" "NASA Prepares Craft for a Deep Encounter of the Martian Kind," 9-21, is a finely crafted dispatch on the Mars *Observer*. Instead of concentrating on minute technical detail, Sawyer does a comparison-contrast of Mars and the Earth. And "Searching for Intelligent Life Forms Outside the Solar System," 10-5, is a cogent, examination of the Search for Extraterrestrial Intelligence. Sawyer's writing here brings the issue to life: "There will be no blastoff, just the clank and rumble of huge radio telescope dishes in motion. At 3 p.m. Eastern Daylight Time next Monday—exactly 500 years after Columbus reached the New World—scientists in Puerto Rico and California will push buttons simultaneously to launch their own new era of exploration." And she professionally details the concerns for future American-Russian cooperation as "U.S. Scientists Protest Pentagon Plan to Orbit Russian Reactor," 12-6, Sawyer remaining appropriately detached throughout.

Keith Schneider
The New York Times
(—)

Washington, agriculture and energy. Schneider is an advocate who doesn't hesitate to skew his dispatches so that we know where he stands on everything he covers. His position gives him such extraordinary exposure to the movers and shakers, though, that we are compelled to review him, as his biased analysis may affect policy. Rather than address the legitimate claims by landowners against the government for passing environmental restrictions on the use of their land, Schneider derides their case in "Environment Laws Face a Stiff Test From Landowners," 1-20: "... environmental lawyers say such a legal strategy has been used before in efforts to thwart social changes. Southern slave owners in the 19th century argued, for example, that the Fifth Amendment protected them from demands to free their slaves." Schneider may be correct in positioning "Environment Laws Are Eased by Bush as Election Nears," 5-20, as pure politics, but he doesn't prove a "pattern of altering environmental laws" or examine the economic consequences of the loosening of these laws in a recession. His green philosophy crosses party lines as he takes Clinton to task in "Pollution in Arkansas Area May Be Key Campaign Issue," 4-21, detailing the White River pollution. He then outlines the dispute over toxic waste at the Vertac Chemical pesticide plant with "In Arkansas Toxic Waste Cleanup, Highlights of New Environmental Debate," 11-2. Schneider makes little effort here to evaluate Clinton's overall environmental record. He gushes over the environmentally friendly William Reilly in "U.S. Environment Negotiator in Rio Walks a Tightrope in Administration," 6-2, describing the EPA head as "tall and slim, with sandy hair and green eyes." And in "U.S. Set to Open National Forests for Strip Mining," 9-28, he tries, but can't hide his outrage as this change becomes a possibility.

William K. Stevens
The New York Times
(—)

Stevens is the primary shill for those who position the greenhouse effect as fact, not theory. His scientific articles on the subject are always heavily colored by politics, completely obscuring the science. Instead of discussing the scientific import of CO_2 controls, and the UN meeting addressing that subject, in "Washington, Odd Man Out, May Shift on Climate," 2-18, Stevens sticks to the political aspects of the U.S.'s refusal to bow to environmentalists on global warming. He offers a long prelude to the Rio summit, "Humanity Confronts Its Handiwork: An Altered Planet," 5-5, in which he proceeds to outline every alarmist view known to man, plus a few new ones. In "Earth Summit Finds the Years of Optimism Are a Fading Memory," 6-9, Stevens seems baffled by the fact that the differing needs of various countries are causing havoc over declarations of principles at Rio. He lists the problems and squabbling well enough, but seems to think, naively, they are a public relations problem, rather than symptoms of a divided scientific and world community. In "A Strategy to Survey the Vast Unknowns of Life on the Earth," 9-22, Stevens operates on the assumption that species are being destroyed by the millisecond as development occurs, but he does not take into account Darwin's theory of survival of the fittest. In "With Cold War Over, Scientists Are Turning to 'Greener' Pastures," 10-27, he recounts how former SDI and weapons scientists are now concentrating on better forecasting for the greenhouse effect. But he doesn't give us a great deal of information on how either the scientists or the labs might better predict this alleged phenomenon. His material on other topics is more balanced. He reveals the slaughter of the much-maligned shark population in "Terror of Deep Faces Harsher Predator," 12-8, providing enough interesting information to engage us in the shark's plight, without seeming knee-jerk or politically correct.

David Stipp
The Wall Street Journal
★★

Boston. Reliable and forward-looking, Stipp provides useful dispatches linking technology and business applications, one of the few reporters to do so from a Wall Street perspective. His business expertise shows in "Northeast Utilities Says Agency Clears Its Acquisition of PS New Hampshire," 1-30. Stipp is careful here to note that "Northeast said the federal Nuclear Regulatory Commission also must approve the acquisition." Similarly, in "Genzyme Counters Criticism Over High Cost of Drug," 6-23, he insightfully reviews the potential of Genzyme, one of the few biotech firms to be profitable. The company faces criticism over its drug for Gaucher's disease, Ceredase, which has "become a lightning rod for resentment against the pharmaceutical industry—and biotechnology in particular—over skyrocketing health care costs." He then reports on a potential replacement for the drug in "'Gene Therapy' for Gaucher's Disease Shows Promising Results in Tests on Mice," 12-3, a professional dispatch. His best work comes on scientific topics which he really sinks his teeth into, as we see with two P.1 leders. "The Insanity Defense in Violent-Crime Cases Gets High-Tech Help," 3-4, is an excellent overview of what Stipp calls "the neurological defense," which was used by convicted killer Robert Alton Harris and his legal counsel in a last-ditch attempt to avoid execution: "[His lawyers] say neurological tests administered during the past two years suggest that his brain is damaged so as to impair his judgment and cause impulsive, violent behavior." We come away enlightened. And in his 10 Best selection, "Heart Attack Study Adds to the Cautions About Iron in the Diet," 9-8, Stipp tells us nearly everything we've ever wanted to know about iron but were afraid to ask, concurrent with the publication of this information in *Circulation*, the American Heart Association periodical.

Michael Waldholz
The Wall Street Journal
★★

Medicine and drugs. Waldholz has quietly shifted the focus of his beat from the industry doings of the pharmaceutical world to the medical aspects of different drugs, their effectiveness and their competition. His perspectives are always useful, though not always conclusive. Waldholz apprises us of the growing problem of the high cost of AIDS drugs, but we get bogged down in all the statistics in "Astra Faces Fight Over Cost of AIDS Drug," 1-21. The ultimate question of how to keep costs down is left unresolved. In a sidebar to Ron Winslow's leder on managed care, Waldholz outlines only the surface issues of Medicaid regulation in "Specter of Regulation Sets Off Price War," 9-25. He is best on the scientific aspects of reporting. Joined by co-writer Hillary Stout to examine the debate over gene patents as the head of the genome project, Dr. James D. Watson, resigns, they pen "A New Debate Rages Over the Patenting of Gene Discoveries," 4-17: "How much of the unfolding 'secret of life' should be left in the public domain and how much should be locked up in private hands with patents?" Waldholz provides important news on the search for AIDS treatments in "New Discoveries Dim Drug Makers' Hopes for Quick AIDS Cure," 5-26, calmly informing us of the dire nature of the situation, as "some drug company executives are so frustrated they're privately considering a desperate move: asking competitors, for the first time since the development of penicillin, to pool research." He also informs with the important "Gene Raising Melanoma Risk Is Pursued," 11-13. Here he assesses progress in the search for a gene which may predispose an individual to melanoma, the most lethal type of skin cancer. He comes close to relating this to the greenhouse effect/theory, as sun exposure may only be a factor: "researchers at the University of Utah in Salt Lake City had been gathering families in which the cancer had struck through numerous generations in patterns that looked as if susceptibility to the disease was being inherited." He offers similar information on breast cancer in "Stalking a Killer," 12-11, informing us in this valuable article that "about 5% of breast cancers are inherited, but researchers suspect that when the gene itself is found, it may also turn out to be the long-sought biological master switch that can trigger the more common, non-inherited form of breast cancer."

Michael Weisskopf
The Washington Post
★

EPA and environment. We get a good taste of the policy-making bureaucracy in Weisskopf's dispatches. Unfortunately, in most reports he bypasses the scientific issues, and when he does include them, he tends toward a pro-environment bent. But our loudest complaint is that Weisskopf adds little to our understanding of the ongoing policy debates at EPA. For instance, he asserts in his lead for "Regulatory Freeze Impact Is Assessed," 1-23, that "President Bush's plan for a 90-day freeze on new federal regulations will delay and possibly weaken some rules governing U.S. business, but it is unlikely to produce substantial savings for the economy, administration officials and outside experts said yesterday." He never names the "senior" officials, and tells us little about which rules Bush is talking about. "Global Warming Pact Talks to Resume," 2-18, is okay on the policy developments, meetings and mechanics, but Weisskopf never examines the economic impact of the proposed rules. It's the same story with a follow-up on the UN talks held in preparation for the Rio summit in "U.S. Unlikely to Budge at U.N. Global Warming Talks," 4-12. He reviews William Reilly's Rio summit performance in "'Outsider' EPA Chief Being Tested," 6-8, but it's rather misleading for Weisskopf to call Reilly an outsider, as he has been part of the environmental policy apparatus for years. With "EPA Won't Tighten Urban Ozone Standard," 8-4, he offers an acceptable overview of EPA's refusal to tighten the smog parts-per-million standard. He's satisfactorily detached here, including views from both the EPA and environmentalists. He finished out the year covering the Clinton campaign with dispatches such as "Clinton to Curb Aides' Future Lobbying," 11-11. Here, Weisskopf is premature in calling the guidelines "a sharp break from business-as-usual and a commitment to the highest standards of official behavior," as the specific rules are yet to be determined.

John Noble Wilford
The New York Times
★★★

Science. Wilford is back in fine form, having finally adapted to covering the earth instead of outer space. He's also beginning to find enthusiasm for past civilizations, perhaps likening them to the potential for civilizations we might someday find on other planets. It's clear he relishes his beat now, and we read him with pleasure. We're fascinated by his vivid and engrossing tale of how ancient maps and detailed satellite photographs led archaeologists to discover a lost city, in "On the Trail From the Sky: Roads Point to a Lost City," 2-5. The city may be "Ubar, the fabled entrepot of the rich frankincense trade thousands of years ago." Wilford stays on this story and offers an update with "The Frankincense Route Emerges From the Desert," 4-21, a breathless account of the discovery of an ancient trading center for frankincense, Saffara Metropolis. He is so excited we have trouble following him in the first few paragraphs. Wilford captures our imagination with a well-written, info-rich dispatch on the Norse of North America in "Norsemen in America Flourished, Then Faded," 7-7. He recounts evidence that they were there long before Columbus, and then just disappeared. "Philistines Were Cultured After All, Say Archaeologists," 9-29, is atmospheric and readable on the excavation of Ashkelon, a Philistine port, dating from around 1000 B.C. He casts this dig in the light of biblical history to add interest and context. In "Astronomers Open New Search for Alien

Life," 10-6, we get infectious enthusiasm as NASA begins a search for alien radio signals. And he tells the story of the research spacecraft *Galileo* vividly and delightfully in "Planetary 'Slingshot' Aims Craft at Rendezvous With Jupiter," 12-8.

Ron Winslow
The Wall Street Journal
★★

Health care. With an impressive nose for facts and figures, Winslow always manages to provide new information. Yet, his dispatches often lack verve and we sometimes lose interest before he comes to a conclusion. A new study shows a 17% decline over three years in adult smokers in California due to an "ambitious" PR campaign funded by a cigarette sales tax. He gets in all the facts and figures on the triumph in "California Push to Cut Smoking Seen as Success," 1-15, but fails to examine the program's potential for success on a large scale. "Colon Cancer Test Cuts Chance of Dying From the Disease Up to 70%, Study Says," 3-5, is a nicely rounded dispatch on the *New England Journal of Medicine* study of the statistics on colon cancer and a new test for the disease. Similarly, in "Test Changes Prostate Cancer Treatment," 4-22, an informative account of a blood test called PSA (prostate-specific antigen) for diagnosing prostate cancer early. He doesn't flinch from the clinical aspects of the story, remaining characteristically detached. He widens the debate beyond Medicare in "Medicare Tries to Save With One-Fee Billing For Some Operations," 6-10, an examination of "bundling" where a patient gets one bill, rather than dozens. Winslow provides more satisfying detail on health care reform in "Coalition Set Up to Lower Costs of Health Care," 7-1: "Fourteen Minneapolis companies said they will combine their purchasing muscle to induce local doctors, hospitals and clinics to cut health-care costs by changing medical and administrative practices. The plan represents one of the most ambitious efforts yet by U.S. business to rein in health costs—now equal to nearly half of corporate profits—by rewarding quality of care. Cost savings are expected to follow." A slow start mars "Prescribing Decisions Increasingly Are Made by the Cost-Conscious," 9-25, an otherwise excellent leder on how "managed care is changing the [pharmaceutical] industry," with Winslow adding a trim business perspective. Winslow capably defines the difficulties of establishing guidelines for mental-health care from a business-insurance point of view in "Experts Try to Gauge Mental-Health Care," 12-1, noting importantly that "Prospects for changes in national health care add urgency to the effort."

★ SOCIETY & POLITICS ★

Jill Abramson
The Wall Street Journal
★★

Washington, lobbying and campaign finance. Abramson's beat takes on extra importance during national elections, placing this precise reporter at the heart of the campaign action. Such circumstances have shaken more than one good reporter from their moorings, but Abramson stayed the course, rising above the fray and gaining our respect. We believe she's capable of even better work. In "Women's Anger About Hill-Thomas Hearing Has Brought Cash Into Female Political Causes," 1-6, she provides a detailed overview of how the Anita Hill–Clarence Thomas fiasco has energized fundraising efforts and activism for women's political groups. She continues the presidential fund-raising theme, this time with the powerful Clinton campaign machine, in "How 'Outsider' Clinton Built a Potent Network of Insider Contacts," 3-12. Doing a much better job of getting her foot in the door here, she gives us a solid feel for how the candidate has cultivated a growing circle of contacts since his school days, and how he now puts this influential clique to use. Abramson sets her sights on a financial web that the Democratic National Committee chairman may be spinning in "Brown Juggles Roles as Party Leader and Washington Lawyer With Agility," 7-9. The topic certainly sparked our interest, but there is little follow-through and her insinuations ultimately lack punch. Her "Top Republicans Found Many Ways to Avoid Vietnam," 9-10, provides a list of GOPers who circumvented the draft, but her attempts to make parallels to Clinton fall short. Post-election, she offers a serviceable thumbnail sketch of Clinton administration wannabes, including the "Anglers," the "'New' Democrats," the "Overeager," and the "Booted," in "Opportunists Knock at Clinton's Door, Seeking Posts in New Administration," 11-9.

Henry Allen
The Washington Post
★★

"Style." Covering everything from sports talk to politics, Allen gives us more than we bargained for in this year's eclectic collection of essays—surprising us with lucid insights in one piece, boring us with verbosity in the next. We miss the old Allen and his steady stream of well-crafted reminiscences. He gripes in "Super Bowl Notebook: In Minnesota, Little Blimps and an Absence of Big Guys," 1-25, that the game "is being turned into a theme park, a museum here in the Minneapolis Convention Center..." Taking on political analysis this election year, he pens a somewhat wishy-washy profile of a presidential hopeful in "The Hard Right of Pat Buchanan," 2-17. The author finds himself caught awkwardly between humoring the Republican candidate and wondering what makes him tick: "In the world of the Scots-Irish outsider, where loyalty is paramount, betrayal always lurks." Allen clearly enjoys himself in "What's Up With Sex? Not Much, It Seems," 4-26, a witty muse over the portrayal of male sexuality in today's women's magazines. His "Getting to the Heart of a Whore," 5-17, is a *tour de force* through the lurid mind of filmmaker Dennis O'Rourke, who spent "part of his $100,000 Australian government grant on sex with a variety of Patpong women..." to research his film. Back to politics for "Perot Doesn't Pity You," 6-28, he takes an interesting, semi-serious glimpse at the spunky Texan, an enjoyable read. He stumbles, with "The Democrats, Waiting to Serve," 8-7, dragging us through a rambling essay on Democrats who are biting at the bit to get back into service. Unfortunately, Allen slings more inside-the-Beltway lingo here than the average reader is willing to tolerate. He isn't able to pull off his profile of William Kristol, "Dan Quayle's Gray Matter," 10-21. This feature on the Vice President's chief-of-staff leaves us wondering what motivates him. His "The Muffled Gray of Overcoated Winter," 12-11, is a failed attempt at humor: "Dwight D. Eisenhower had overcoatedness...John F. Kennedy did not . . . Mia had overcoatedness, Woody does not."

Jonathan Alter
Newsweek
★½

Senior editor. A stylish writer, Alter always engages us in his political and press critiques, but increasingly, he equates cynicism with criticism. His seemingly unshakable acrimony overshadows his splendid ability to crystallize the issues. In one of his better articles this year, Alter captures the media's pack mentality during the New Hampshire presidential primary in "The Beast Is Always Hungry," 2-17, delivering a pithy assessment in the vernacular: "Then there's the Dan Quayle pattern—if we decked him, we have to deck Clinton." After charging Democratic candidate Jerry Brown with cynicism, Alter weighs in with his own in "Jerry's Date With History," 4-13: "He certainly won't fight at the convention for his silly flat tax." Such off-the-cuff dismissals of important issues leave us unimpressed. In his report following the L.A. riots, "TV and the 'Firebell,'" 5-11, he tries to assess how visual images impact events, vigorously scolding local L.A. stations for fanning the flames of violence. Picking up on the "New News" theme that Jon Katz addressed so thoroughly in *Rolling Stone*, Alter pens "How Phil Donahue Came to Manage the '92 Campaign," *The Washington Monthly* 6-92, a perceptive follow-through on the topic: "At their best, Phil, Larry [King] and Brian Lamb's C-Span interviews are as democratic as American media politics gets." He casts his skeptical eye on President Bush's depiction of himself as Harry Truman, in "Truman and the Man in the Mirror," 9-21, pulling out enough historical data to support his suspicion that Bush is no Truman. In "How He Would Govern," 10-26, he turns his incredulous pen on Clinton, trying to read tea leaves on the legislative agenda that would emerge from a Clinton administration. Alter's cynicism toward lobbyists is obvious, but effective in "Clinton's Challenge," 11-30: "No one expects his new ethics rules to transform Sodom into some New Jerusalem. But to accomplish anything, Clinton needs to chart a course through the sludge."

R.W. Apple, Jr.
The New York Times
★★½

Washington bureau chief. The *Times*'s preeminent political pundit skips a beat this year, perhaps distracted by his promotion to bureau head. He still captivates with penetrating insights, but such efforts are less frequent than last year. There are times, late in the political season, when Apple seems partisan. For instance, in a review of the final presidential debate, "Bush's Hopes to Alter Campaign's Flow," 10-20, he credits Bush for his performance, but notes this achievement isn't likely to reverse his slide. Then he goes overboard in praising Clinton's "commanding lead," and his "calm, well-organized and direct" demeanor. He uses history well to explore the beltway's post-Cold War realignment, in "White House Is Recast: No Kremlin to Run Against," 2-6. Although he names no sources in "Perot and Riots Redraw Bush Campaign Plans," 5-12, Apple provides inside information that stands up throughout the race on the divisiveness within the Bush camp over strategy and personnel. At the GOP convention, Apple encapsulates the divisions between the politics of deficit-cutting, via Sen. Phil Gramm, and the politics of growth, via Jack Kemp, in "G.O.P. Is Flirting With the Dangers of Negativism," 8-19. In two "Political Pulse" selections, "Missouri's Word of Advice to Bush: Jobs, Jobs, Jobs," 9-29, and "Bush Surges in Ohio, His Big Battleground State," 11-2, Apple provides solid campaign roundups. In the first report, this old campaign hand culls a prescient observation from former Missouri Senator Thomas Eagleton, one-time McGovern running mate: "'The Republicans down the ticket are running away from Bush the way the Democrats used to run from McGovern and later from Mondale,' he said. 'It's a sure sign the national platform is out of touch with local ideas.'"

Peter Applebome
The New York Times
★½

National correspondent. The presidential campaign failed to stir Applebome from his malaise. Last year we blamed his decline on the drab subject matter he was obliged to cover; this year we realize the problem is Applebome. Trying to stretch a story that isn't with "In Alabama, Blacks Battle for the Authority to Govern," 1-31, he pens a foggy report on a Supreme Court review of two black commissioners' complaints that procedural changes have diminished their power. Applebome does little to conceal his support in "Bill Clinton's Uncertain Journey," *Magazine* 3-8: "Still, for someone often accused of being too slick, it's remarkable how much Clinton's campaign has touched the cultural and generational fault lines of American life." In "Condemned Man in Virginia Fails Polygraph Test," 5-21, he recounts the futile attempt made to save the rapist and murderer, Roger Coleman. The reporting here is only adequate, and the writing nondescript. His report on the colorful Edwin Edwards, "On Louisiana's Future, Governor Deals From Past," 7-12, is livelier than most of Applebome's profiles, but he still fails to capture the true flavor of Edwards's surprising political resurrection. His coverage of the ebb and flow of anti-incumbency fever, "Prospects Looking Up for 7 Southern Senators," 9-27, is little more than a laundry list from candidates who hope to ride Clinton's coattails. Applebome doesn't properly define the subtle issues at hand in "From Carter to Clinton, a South in Transition," 11-10. His highly romanticized portrayal of the South leads him to a murky conclusion: "Like the dusty Carter Administration souvenirs and painfully out-of-fashion, segregation-era memorabilia at the antique shop . . . Plains is a reminder that the South's economic progress has largely bypassed the places that are most distinctly 'Southern.'"

George Archibald
The Washington Times
★★

Congressional investigative reporter. The scandal-tainted House keeps Archibald's byline on the front page, but too often we find that, despite burning plenty of shoe leather to get the facts, he fails to inject much analysis into his stories. His House coverage begins with "House Advised: Cut Patronage in Postal Unit," 2-9, where he sufficiently details the House's post office troubles and the prevalence of patronage in the institution. We enjoy reading the platitudes of House members fingered for bad checks, in "303 Named in Rubbergate," 4-17, but we're not sure that providing such a forum, without scrutiny or evaluation, is good journalism. Keeping an eye on the changes at the controversial National Endowment for the Arts in "New Leader Sees NEA Near Abyss," 5-4, we're offered a knee-deep look at new director Anne-Imelda Radice, whose views differ from those of her predecessor, John Frohnmayer. Post-Democratic convention, he reviews Bill Clinton's tenure as Governor of Arkansas in "The Clinton Record," 7-26, seeing the candidate's campaign promises as half empty rather than half full: "Mr. Clinton promised in his acceptance speech 'an America in which middle-class incomes, not middle-class taxes, are going up.' . . . State government spending and taxation both almost doubled in Arkansas during the Clinton years." His overview of the highs and lows of the Bush years, "The Bush Record," 9-13, is quintessential Archibald—detailed, but unenlightening: "Mr. Bush made the tax issue a defining difference between himself and . . . Michael Dukakis." We remember, but Archibald doesn't explain how this well-known fact has impacted the President's re-election efforts. And in "Political Right Warned to Look to Grass Roots," 11-25, he provides an unenlightening report on the conservative Heritage Foundation's new tack as Clinton comes to Washington.

Terry Atlas
Chicago Tribune
★★

Washington. Although Atlas rarely breaks new ground in his reports, he is skilled at bringing the pieces of complex stories together in a clear, logical progression. He captures in a nutshell the immense political capital squandered by President Bush following the Persian Gulf War, in "One Year Later, Desert Storm a Gray Memory," 1-17. Playing devil's advocate here, he scrutinizes the long-term accomplishments of the war, strategically and politically, for the administration and the nation. Atlas gets the facts, figures, recommendations and bipartisan Congressional reactions to aid for the C.I.S. in "Bush Ready to Help Ex-Soviets," 3-23, a comprehensive and useful overview of the political climate in which the aid package is being proposed. "Baker Reluctant to Return to Campaign Arena," 8-9, is a measured report on Secretary of State James Baker's successes and failures in foreign relations as he leaves office to run Bush's campaign: "... Baker has made little effort to disguise his reluctance to return to the thrust-and-parry of domestic politics." Straightforward on a controversial topic for "Note Suggests Bush OK for Iran Arms Swap," with Timothy J. McNulty and Mitchell Locin 10-31, he offers just-the-facts-ma'am as to new allegations that Bush was "in the loop" as Vice President, during the Iran-Contra scandal. He is fair in reporting Bush's defense on all points: "[Bush] also has said that . . . he approved of what he thought was a diplomatic overture to 'moderates' in Tehran." He provides a serviceable report on the President-elect's low profile immediately after the campaign in "Rested Clinton Starts Detailed Work on Transition," 11-10: "For now, Clinton is trying to resist the pressure to rush...decisions by lowering his visibility."

B. Drummond Ayres, Jr.
The New York Times
★★

Washington. Ayres is a veteran political storyteller, with the impressive ability to remain objective even in an election year. Although he often relies more on style than content, we applaud him for being one of the few voices at the *Times* willing to carefully scrutinize the paper's apparent candidate of choice, Bill Clinton. With reams of information, he effectively sheds light on Clinton's school refurbishment record in "Despite Improvements, the Schools in Arkansas Are Still Among the Worst," 4-1. This telling exposé of the governor's questionable education track record even implicates Hillary: "Many [of the programs] were first suggested by an education study committee that he appointed his wife, Hillary, to head." His analysis is general, but effective in "Clinton Unveils a Plan for the Economy," 6-22: "The Governor is a moderate who has spent much of the 1992 campaign condemning big government spending . . . but today...Mr. Clinton offered some big spending proposals of his own." His flattering look at Ron Brown, "Man Behind Convention Emerges as Major Force," 7-20, presents the Democratic party chairman as a genius who can charm diverse factions into compromise, but there's little on Brown's weaknesses. He spent a generous amount of time chronicling the oddities of the presidential race in his "Campaign Trail" series. Such pieces as "Now Bush Is in Trouble in His 2nd Home," 10-7, give us a sense of the type of quirky information these reports impart: "There's been another creature sighting out on the trail. First there were protestors dressed as Bush and Clinton chickens... Now, from Daytona Beach comes a report of a duck waddling in." His "Shadow of Pessimism Eclipses a Dream," 2-9, is a hard-hitting, human-interest examination of a U.S. population increasingly disillusioned with politics and the state of the union. "Robb Is Expecting Federal Indictment Over Eavesdropping," 12-18, though, is only a cursory examination of the feud between Sen. Charles Robb and Gov. L. Douglas Wilder.

Charles R. Babcock
The Washington Post
★★

Investigations. The *Post*'s head sleuth hasn't shaken up the Beltway as he did last year with his exposés on John Sununu. His best work this year deals with party fund-raising. Such articles as "Regulators Probing GOP Campaign Donor," co-written by Ann Devroy 4-24, succeed in casting light on contributors, in this case the misdeeds of James Elliott. The convicted felon, according to the duo, acted as a co-chairman at a Republican party fund-raiser, raising numerous questions. "Parties Rack Up 6-Figure Gifts of 'Soft Money,'" 9-28, delineates "soft money" donations which help "the candidates via state party advertising, local television ads and voter registration drives." Joined by Kenneth J. Cooper for "House Postmaster Resigns," 3-20, the pair reiterates, rather than investigates, the controversy surrounding the House post office. This tale of lax rules and privileges offers few insights, and mostly rehashes what we read elsewhere. With "Skinner Repays Government $3,275 for Questionable Travel Expenses," 5-14, he attempts to land another travel misuse story equal to his hard-hitting coverage of John Sununu's junkettes, but he doesn't quite hook White House chief-of-staff Samuel K. Skinner. Babcock makes sure the figures add up in "Clinton's Very 'Sensitive' to Conflicts of Interest," 8-1, reviewing allegations of questionable investments by Bill and Hillary Clinton. After scrutinizing the facts, he concludes there was no wrong done. In "Hefty Pensions Ease Departure Pains," 11-10, Babcock completely details how federal pensions are devised, especially for past presidents and congressmen.

Dan Balz
The Washington Post
★

Politics. Balz's direct reports provide adequate snapshots of the day's political events, but rarely display the type of politically sophisticated analysis necessary to shade in the picture. He also tends to react to events, rather than clarify them. He gives a straightforward view of the Democratic party's discontent over the crop of presidential candidates in "Activists Find Democratic Field Less Than Inspiring," 1-27. Just before Super Tuesday, Balz offers a fairly informative report on how the Democratic presidential candidates will be playing the field, and managing their money, in "Next 16 Days to Test Candidates' Strategy," 2-23. He centers on the mad rush for electoral votes in "For Democrats, Florida Looms as Key Test on Super Tuesday," 3-9: "A Tsongas victory here, however, could dampen Clinton's celebration and give Tsongas a big boost for the potentially crucial contests on March 17." In "Democratic Convention Opens Today," 7-13, Balz provides a serviceable overview of the New York convention and does a competent job of articulating the conflicts in the liberal wing, especially the concerns of Jesse Jackson and Mario Cuomo. His coverage of the Republican convention also focused on party divides. For instance, in "GOP Convenes, Opens Fire on Democrats," 8-18, we read: "But Buchanan said little about the economy or Bush's broken no-new-taxes pledge . . . and he gave his former boss Reagan, not Bush, the credit for winning the Cold War." Post-election, Balz offers a bloated report on the ripples Clinton's campaign manager Mickey Kantor has caused among the staff, in "Clinton Sidestepped Advisers in Choice of Team Leaders," 11-8, getting long winded on their insistence that he not head the transition team.

James A. Barnes
National Journal
★½

As chief political correspondent for one of the most expensive periodicals in America, we expect a lot from Barnes. But, all too often he buys into the quantity-is-quality theory, repackaging the season's political news in lengthy, inefficient word-fests that fail to further the discussion at hand. One report that didn't fall prey to needless verbosity was "Unions Poised to Abandon the Sidelines," 2-15. In a tidy one-and-a-half pages, we learn where the trade unions are throwing their support in the

Democratic primaries and why. More important, Barnes explains what this portends in terms of money and delegate power. Back to wasting words, and our time, in "Clinton's Slow Roll," 3-28, he spews out polls and quotes, page after page, without ever placing them in context. Rather than simply recapitulating the past, he should use his articles to position the reader to understand the future. Faring a bit better with fewer words in "When a Pledge Isn't Really a Pledge," 4-4, Barnes addresses a clause in the Democratic National Convention's bylaws that allows delegates to change allegiance. The chances of a major shift just before the convention are improbable, he notes, but we find his observations worthwhile. In "The Big Bounce," 7-25, he spews out little more than conventional wisdom on how the Democrats will lose some of their verve in the polls after the convention. With populism a hot topic, Barnes highlights an under-explored trend, low voter turnout for the primaries, in "Voter Turnoff," 8-15, but there's little probing into the reasons for this occurrence. His half-hearted "President Bush's 'Clintonesia' Gambit," 10-10, doesn't further our understanding of presidential campaign strategies in the final weeks before the big vote. Barnes uses polls to his advantage after the Clinton win to script a better-than-average piece about the fragility of the "New Democrat" block, in "Tainted Triumph?" 11-7.

Barbara Benham
Investor's Business Daily
★★½

National issues, Washington. Reporting for a Wall Street audience, Benham focuses on the symbiotic relationship between societal and economic issues. Her examinations, steeped in information, prove consistently instructive and intellectually engrossing. She weighs Japan's charge that U.S. workers are less productive than their foreign counterparts, in "Are U.S. Workers Getting Lazy?" 2-18, addressing this heated debate with professional balance and using statistics to prove that U.S. workers are indeed more productive than either the Japanese or Germans. Her clear-eyed analysis brightens another report on U.S. productivity, "America's Productivity Puzzle," 4-14: "Economists are in broad agreement that one thing in particular drives productivity growth: Investment, especially in equipment . . . Smarter 'tools' yield more efficient workers." She backs up her somewhat alarming look at the Pension Benefit Guaranty Corp., "Is Pension Agency Next Bailout?" 3-6, with a generous amount of research. Her detailed fact gathering reveals that this federal agency, which insures the pension plans of some 40 million Americans, "concedes that its program is not based on sound insurance principles." Also potent and eye-opening is her assessment of the alienation of Americans who are "Young, Male, Black, Troubled," 7-24, in which she notes that "alarming numbers suggest that the very institutions that make up society—family, schools and government—are failing a generation of young men." Pulling together the myriad aspects of this disturbing social trend, she drives home the essence of the problem with particular force. Uncharacteristically, her "MTV Generation Gets an Issue," 9-4, suffers from an ill-focused framework. She too quickly jumps from 20-year-olds angry about the deficit, to the future high costs of Medicare, to baby boomers inheriting Social Security problems, losing the point of her article along the way. Her post-election evaluation "How New Is the New Congress?" 11-20, is more focused, neatly meshing together the societal and economic challenges ahead.

Richard L. Berke
The New York Times
★½

Washington. An efficient and workmanlike reporter, Berke spent the year writing features on the contradictions and peculiarities of the presidential campaign. But when it comes to serious election-year analytics, he often comes up short. In one of his few in-depth evaluations, "Seeking Super Tuesday Votes, 2 Campaigns Turn Deficiencies Into a Virtue: Tsongas Plays Role of David Opposing a Goliath, Clinton," 3-10, Berke presciently writes off Tsongas due to lack of organization, especially in the South: " . . . it is with envy and fear that

Tsongas aides describe the Clinton organization." Off kilter in "Brown Renews His Battle Against the Moonbeam," 4-12, Berke has a good old time with Jerry Brown's eccentricities, childishly trumpeting the "moonbeam" moniker in nearly every paragraph. On the other hand, he skillfully sums up the mood of the campaign in "White House Race at Emotional Peak Many Weeks Early," 6-21, weaving together a variety of anecdotes for a revealing behind-the-scenes tapestry. His witty "Democrats Use TV to Ride Momentum," 7-23, pokes fun at the contrived atmosphere of the Clinton bus tour: "The bus tour has been like a rolling advertisement, with the networks cooperating all the way." Berke really puts the screws to the Republicans for using the Willie Horton ad campaign last election, with "In 1992, Willie Horton Is Democrats' Weapon," 8-25, then he adds as barely a footnote: "... The man who helped discover [Willie Horton], Senator Al Gore of Tennessee." His "Insider Paving Way for an Outsider," 11-13, on the chairman of Clinton's transition team, Vernon Jordan, is mere fluff, telling us little other than what and where he likes to eat.

Jeffrey H. Birnbaum
The Wall Street Journal
★★

Congress. Birnbaum's ability to gauge the Congressional climate has steadily improved in recent years. His fact-gathering is more thorough and he continues to expand his network of sources, adding depth and credibility to his reports. He launches the opening salvos of what was to become a painful thorn in Bill Clinton's side in "Clinton, Like Others, Missed the Vietnam Draft; Accounts Now Differ as to What Happened Then," 2-6. In "Sen. Specter's Tough Stance Against Anita Hill Haunts Him as Women's Groups Vent Anger," 4-22, Birnbaum and co-writer David Shribman give us a good taste of the uphill battle the senator from Pennsylvania faces in his re-election bid. Without passing judgement, they convincingly demonstrate that the Senator's controversial tactics during the highly-charged Hill/Thomas hearings, continue to taint his political career. We were impressed by his even-handed reporting on a politically-charged story in "House Rejects Bid to Require Balanced Budget," 6-12. He takes us on a tour down both sides of the aisle, revealing feverish lobbying efforts both for and against a constitutional amendment requiring a balanced budget: "In the days leading up to the vote, Speaker Foley and Majority Leader Richard Gephardt...raised an unspoken warning that members who voted for the amendment would be hurting their chances of moving up the Democratic leadership ranks." Birnbaum isn't able to sufficiently distance himself from his subject, Clinton's campaign Manager James Carville, providing a wishy-washy profile in "Top Clinton Aide Shows Effective Jab, but Critics Wonder if He Has a Punch," 9-23. As President-elect Clinton holds his first meeting with Congressional leaders, Birnbaum offers a deft reading of how the new leader might conduct policymaking, in "Clinton Bends Under Pressure From Congress," 11-17: "Mr. Clinton demonstrated an inclination to compromise with rather than confront friendly lawmakers on some of the most contentious issues..."

Katharine Boo
The Washington Post
★

Assistant editor of "Outlook." Boo left for the *Post* late in the year following her tenure at *The Washington Monthly*. But since the majority of her work appeared in *WM*, where she was also an editor, it is on this that we base our assessment. We're used to editors at the *Monthly* challenging the status quo of liberalism and watchdogging the excesses of government, but Boo often fails on both counts. She attempts to map out a new capitalism that would fuse the best of Karl Marx with the best of Adam Smith in "Why We Need a New Marx," 3-92, but she comes up with alphabet soup. Her simplistic analysis here recommends nothing new: government spending and higher wages. Boo seems disoriented in "Grow Up Twenty-Somethings, You *Can* Go Home Again," 4-92, as she undertakes an examination of a growing trend: young people ages 18-34 living with their parents. Her heavy reliance on literary analogies to make her point tells us next to nothing about life in the '90s. Offering a frivolous examination of how fashion is finding the blue-collar suddenly chic, in "Wolves in Cheap Clothing," 7/8-92, she tries to create a class issue to give the essay depth, but it simply doesn't work. Finally producing the type of work we expect from a *Monthly* editor, Boo offers an insightful comparison of Paula Coughlin, the Naval officer who blew the whistle on the Tailhook convention, and Anita Hill, in "Universal Soldier," 9-92: "... [Hill's] choice of silence has been so energetically defended it now seems to rank among the unassailable feminine prerogatives.... Yet it is precisely for those who argue that Anita Hill had no other choice that Paula Coughlin's story is a countermyth of crucial importance, one that cries to be rescued from the brig of military lore." And Boo provides a powerful critique of *New York Times* reporter Maureen Dowd and her signature style in "The New Writers' Bloc," 11-92: "The democratic process is reduced to Pirandello, to theater of the absurd. Trouble is, this audience can't get up and leave."

Gloria Borger
U.S. News & World Report
★½

Capitol Hill. Borger's work can best be described as uneven. While she tracks important issues, her appraisals of them are often scattered and disorganized. Though informative on the man, her portrait of Democratic primary candidate Paul Tsongas suffers greatly from this problem. "The Democrats' Castor-Oil Candidate," 2-24, offers such lines as "Tsongas as Tsinderella," and reveals a confused Borger unable to decide which Democrat he reminds her of most: "He could be the frustrated Eugene McCarthy of 1968; the idealistic nominees, like George McGovern of 1972; or the blazing comet, like Gary Hart, burning out early. And maybe he's like Jimmy Carter, the outsider who taps a national mood that carries him right into the White House." She relates divisions in the conservative movement over Pat Buchanan's candidacy, but her dispatch "Standing Pat? Civil War on the Right," 3-16, is as disorganized as the mess she describes. She is much more focused and effective in "The Reform War," 8/31-9/7, positioning D.C.'s bureaucracy as a barrier to change: "The 1990 Clean Air Act, for example, went through no fewer than seven House committees.... 'The way it now works,' says House Democrat David Obey of Wisconsin, 'there is no accountability.'" Her report on Geraldine Ferraro, "The Child Star's New Role," 9-14, merely updates us, providing no new insights into Ferraro's role as a Senate candidate in the N.Y. primary during the "year of the woman." She provides few insights on how Clinton will deal with Congress in "How Would Clinton Manage Congress?" 11-2. Scenarios are discussed here, but not fleshed out. And with "Clinton Breaks Out," 7-27, she hits the same nail on the same head, noting, like others that the state of the economy will dictate the election's outcome.

Ronald Brownstein
Los Angeles Times
★★★

After being out of the loop his first few years with the *Times*, Brownstein finally is recovering that muscular journalistic voice we so admired when he was at the *National Journal*. He wryly notes the unorthodox style of a Jerry Brown fund-raiser in "Brown Presses His 'Guerrilla' Approach," 2-8, where "...actor Martin Sheen introduced Brown by asking the audience to hold hands so he could lead them in prayer..." Also capturing our attention in "Early Primaries Feature Candidate Role Reversals," 3-5, he takes a rather uninspiring theme and turns it into a well-defined discussion of demographics and the presidential race: "... Sen. Paul E. Tsongas' striking success in attracting suburbanites has forced Clinton to remake himself into the choice of the party's traditional constituencies..." He genuinely admires the Clinton camp's effectiveness in "Clinton Uses Team Tactics to Plot a Daily Battle Plan," 4-20. He avoids political favoritism by making clear that his respect is for the exemplary organization of the campaign without commenting on its ideals. Using Perot as a touchstone for "Business Executive as Populist," 6-13, Brownstein examines why more businessmen are running for office, and by the end of the article, we know why national office is no longer restricted to political careerists. In "Another 1988? Democrats Are Counting on the Differences," 7-30, he expertly gathers all the negatives plaguing the Bush campaign, leading us to join him in questioning the assertion that a sitting president is unbeatable. His 11-4 post-election report, "Economic Concerns Fueled Clinton's Drive to Victory," merely translates polls, but "Clinton's Efforts May Redefine Party's Appeal," 11-5, casts a slight pall over Clinton's victory: "Unlike 1980, when Ronald Reagan's victory over a discredited incumbent swept in dozens of Republican Congressional candidates, Clinton had no apparent coattails."

Jackie Calmes
The Wall Street Journal

Congress and taxes. This bright young reporter does a commendable job of tracking key economic proposals as they navigate their way through the policymaking labyrinth of Congress. But, we can't help but note that her appraisals would be even more satisfying if her grasp of economics matched her political shrewdness. A strong example of her political acumen is showcased in "Bentsen Vows to Oppose Efforts to Pare Provisions From Pending Tax Measure," 9-16. While Calmes doesn't detail the tax bill, she accurately depicts the political reaction: "Some Republicans fear...[the] Arkansas governor now opens the president to attack if he signs a bill with a number of tax increases." She provides a smart assessment of the upcoming battle over the budget, in "The Budgeteers: Beware a Bidding War as Bush and Democrats Compete on Tax Cuts," 1-30. Her analysis is insightful and refreshingly free of bias: "A real danger is that a partisan bidding war could cause that tax cut to grow into a budget-busting fiasco." Although she faithfully reports the conclusions of The Joint Committee on Taxation in "Bush Tax Plan Favors the Rich, Analysis Shows," 2-6, Calmes doesn't have a strong enough understanding of the tax plan in question to scrutinize the committee's conclusions. She files a serviceable report on Congressional doubts over the balanced-budget amendment in "Proposal for Balanced-Budget Amendment Moves to Front Burner as Lawmakers Hunt for an Issue," 5-13. Calmes highlights the cantankerous partisan feelings an enterprise zone package has caused in "House Panel Passes Package on Urban Zones," 6-25. This lean report sticks to the facts and not Congressional infighting. Joined by David Rogers for the bloated "Shake-Up of Congress Yields Coalition of Women, Minorities," 11-5, the duo attempts to rush through virtually every idea of every new congressperson, leaving the article garbled and inconclusive.

John Canham-Clyne
In These Times

Washington correspondent. We turn to Canham-Clyne for informative polemics left of center. A freelancer for the trim tabloid, we hope to see more of this smart journalist as *ITT* converts to a biweekly magazine format. He is heavy-handed but perceptive in a critique of former Gov. Jerry Brown's candidacy, "Brown's So Sick of Politics He Wants to Be President," 1/29-2/4: "He has seized a powerful message, but unfortunately only barely understands it himself.... Indeed, Brown seems only dimly aware of the often-subtle link between the campaign finance system and substantive issues." We get a sharp profile of Paul Tsongas in "Tsongas Takes The Road Less Traveled," 2-19/25, as he examines the Democrat's substance, using "An Economic Call to Arms" as his guide. It's plain that he's intrigued by Tsongas's perspectives, and by the end, we are too. Canham-Clyne provides an excellent interview with Haiti's ambassador to the U.S., Jean Casimir, in "Haiti After the Coup," *World Policy Journal* Spring 1992, an in-depth examination of the situation in the island country. Most compelling is Casimir's criticism of U.S. policy: "For most people in the Western hemisphere, Haiti is a land of the 'savage imagination,' of voodoo, of poverty and illiteracy. They cannot fathom how this land of illiterates can think politically, can control state power, can elaborate survival strategies." He follows up with "U.S. Policy Supports Haitian Coup," 5-6/12, hinting that U.S. policy ambiguity is part of the problem. In discussing the budget in "Black and Progressive Caucuses Trying to Change Political Debate," 6/24-7/7, Canham-Clyne makes some useful observations about the value of the grassroots movements, but neglects to explore what either group would do specifically in their proposed alternate budget. With "The Mistrial and Tribulations of a CIA Officer," 9-16/29, he offers another version of the Clair E. George trial, but his tone is rather sarcastic, and not much pertinent information comes through as a result.

Lou Cannon
The Washington Post
★★

Los Angeles. Though the best reporting on the riots and California's budget crisis came from local reporters at the *Los Angeles Times*, Cannon provided satisfactory, if not entirely satisfying dispatches on both issues for folks back in the Beltway. He seems more willing now to be a reporter as well as an analyst, and his dispatches are richer for his trouble. Cannon offers insider detail on how the infamous videotape was used by both the prosecution and the defense teams in the trial of four L.A. police officers accused of beating Rodney Glen King, in "At L.A. Beating Trial, Officer Accuses Colleague," 3-6, a vivid, evocative update, which briefly skims the legal issues. He sounds an important early warning in "Bradley, Black Leaders Try to Head Off Violence," 4-28, noting that black leaders in Los Angeles were asking blacks not to riot should the jury come back with an acquittal. A promising lead opens "L.A.'s Civil Disturbance Singes Political Landscape Nationwide," 5-4: "The riots that ravaged this city have also rearranged the political landscape, raising long-neglected issues in national and state campaigns and placing in doubt the future of police overhaul in the nation's second most populous city." Unfortunately, after the lead, Cannon descends into a rather conventional overview of finger-pointing and who-said-what. His "Economic Ills Turn California Dream Into a Nightmare," 8-3, even-handedly examines California's budget and economics from a political perspective, specifically that of the legislature. Cannon does quite a bit of digging here. As California's insurance commissioner suggests a $34 billion plan to provide health insurance that eliminates double coverage, Cannon, in "California Official Offers Health Plan," 2-13, cites quite a few folks, but provides too few specifics to get excited. The day after the election, Cannon covers the West Coast angle of the "Year of the Woman" in "In California, Women Triumphed at Many Levels," 11-5. He brings little analysis to the story, relying instead on cliches: "Beyond their numbers, women provided a spark..."

Margaret Carlson
Time
½★

Deputy Washington bureau chief. Carlson's witless prose and strident advocacy journalism load down her features to the point that reading them can be a real turnoff. In an election year full of partisan bickering, she merely added to the din instead of rising above it. Gloria Steinem becomes Joan of Arc in "Even Feminists Get the Blues," 1-20, with Carlson's unadulterated hero worship badly marring the profile: "At times it seemed as if she had taken personal responsibility for every oppressed woman in America." Another example of her grating presentation appears in "Why Jerry Keeps Running," 3-23, on Jerry Brown's presidential campaign: "That Brown is still around to pick up this support confounds the experts who pronounced his candidacy dead on arrival due to terminal flightiness." She weighs in on the Dan Quayle/Murphy Brown brouhaha with a confusing "Why Quayle Has

Half a Point," 6-1. Hillary Clinton becomes the vehicle for Carlson to vent her views on a woman's place in society, and Hillary's as First Lady, in the biased and snooty "All Eyes on Hillary," 9-14: "Ask a stay-at-home mother at a cocktail party what she does, and she looks at you as if you just asked if you could have one of her fingers as an hors d'oeuvre." She practically deifies key Clinton campaign player George Stephanopoulos in "Altar Boy at the Power Center," 11-30: "His power whisper makes people lean into him, like plants reaching toward the sun." In one of her few worthwhile efforts of the year, "Perot and His Presidents," 5-25, she pens a fairly competent report on presidential candidate Ross Perot's longstanding D.C. connection. Carlson's footwork on the story provokes important questions about Perot's rhetoric that his campaign will not be about "politics as usual."

William Claiborne
The Washington Post
★½

Urban affairs. Claiborne returns to the U.S. after having spent fifteen years in various assignments with the *Post*'s foreign service, most recently in Toronto. At home and abroad, Claiborne specializes in clear snapshots of the landscape. He reliably informs, but rarely plumbs the depths of policy questions or advances debate on issues. For example, his "Loophole Could Let English Back Into Quebec Ads," 1-9, is a clear, compact roundup of the ongoing fight in the courts over Quebec's French-only signs in public places. But the report adds little new to our understanding of the broader issues involved. Claiborne informs on the procedures and the debate over the constitution in Canada with "Canadian Reform Process Hits New Snags," 2-13, a solid overview of the complications of Native American demands to be recognized as a sovereign, separate and distinct society in the same way as Quebec. He and co-writer Kathleen Day provide trim insider detail on the Reichmanns, such as the fact that they run Olympia & York according to strictly Orthodox Jewish practices, in "A Dynasty of Control," 4-26, but the team fails to give us enough detail on the business end of the financially troubled empire. Providing little more than a superficial overview in "Canada Grants Further Financial Aid to Russia," 6-20, he examines PM Brian Mulroney's decision to lend more money to Russia by quadrupling technical assistance to $100 million and providing $200 million in guarantees to Canadian businesses which invest there. Back in the States for "Health Costs Squeeze State Budgets," 10-29, he simply recapitulates information from two reports which state that revenues aren't keeping pace with medicaid increases and are causing problems for state and local budgets. Claiborne offers a coherent article on U.S. forces securing an ex-Soviet air base in Somalia in "U.S. Opens Base in Famine Zone," 12-14.

Eleanor Clift
Newsweek
½★

Washington. This "McLaughlin Group" regular will be best remembered this year for her on-air assessment of the Clinton-Gore pairing as "the all-Beefcake ticket," 7-12. The clever, pithy phrases Clift employs on the program don't work in her dispatches, as they reveal her strong pro-Beefcake tilt—necessary for a TV pundit, unacceptable in a newsweekly reporter. Clift first reveals her bias while investigating Gennifer Flowers in "Character Questions," 2-10: "Truth is, the press is willing to cut Clinton some slack because they like him—and what he has to say. He is a policy wonk in tune with a younger generation of Democrats eager to take the party beyond the liberal stereotype." After this, we discounted almost everything she wrote. She proclaims in "Testing Ground," 3-30, nearly four months before the convention, that "Today Clinton is poised to win the Democratic nomination for president of the United States. His return from near-oblivion is a tale of personal fortitude and shrewd strategy." Clift and co-writer Michael Meyer examine the relationship between Bill and Roger Clinton in "His Brother's Keeper," 5-4, in which we hear stories about the difficult childhood both endured, and the happy ending. Clift is slightly less revealing in "Hillary Clinton's Not-So-Hidden Agenda," 9-21. While she asserts that "a careful reading of Hillary Clinton's 27-page treatise [on children's rights] leaves a different impression than the one created by her husband's political opponents," she doesn't cite anything from the document itself. In a look at '96 GOP contenders, "Eyes on the Prize," 8-31, she posits "If Quayle is the dauphin, Baker is Cardinal Richelieu." Her "Facing the Powers That Be: With Friends Like These," 11-30, delivers an unsatisfying glimpse at liberal constituents looking for their pound of Clinton's flesh. And in the superficial "Perot: Pulling the Race Out of the Mud," with Ginny Carroll 10-26, she proclaims: "Though he inched up in NEWSWEEK's Poll, he had about as much chance of being elected the next president as Madonna."

Adam Clymer
The New York Times
★½

Chief Congressional correspondent. Clymer kept us adequately appraised of dealings within Congress, from the tax proposals being batted around at the beginning of the year to the growing anti-incumbency mood which haunted representatives in the fall. But, we didn't feel he had the same consistent flow of insights we saw from others on this important beat. His "Democrats See Support for Capital Gains Tax Cut," 1-27, is a quick, but interesting read on Senate majority leader George J. Mitchell agreeing with minority leader Bob Dole, to some kind of capital gains tax cut, but Clymer's failure to place this shift in the context of traditional Democratic opposition to this measure limits the piece. Insightful for "To Republicans' Ire, Bush's Package Advances in House," 2-13, he colorfully characterizes the latest political posturing on election year-tax proposals as having "a schoolroom atmosphere... where the object is to make the other guys sound as if they support the recession or like the rich." Clymer's "Just Imagine: It's January 1993 and Ross Perot Is the President," 4-26, hints at Perot's probable problems with Congress, but this scenario had already been dissected from every angle. His "In Congress, Gore Has a Reputation of Taking the Long View," 7-12, verges on sloganeering for Vice Presidential candidate Al Gore. Not only does Clymer gush over Gore throughout the piece, but he also fails to challenge his flip-flop on federal funding of abortion, a move Clymer depicts as positive, not political. Despite the provocative title, "After the Election, a Certain Revolution in Congress," 9-28, he meanders through what amounts to a laundry list of changes, never fully delineating the "revolution" he purports in the title. He fares better for "Campaign Spending in House Contests Soars to New High," 10-29, providing pertinent information on incumbents' and challengers' campaign spending.

Richard E. Cohen
National Journal
★★

Congress. We've always appreciated Cohen's frank reporting style, but we're afraid the quality of his work continues to be surprisingly inconsistent. Pondering the lack of Congressional support for any of the Democratic candidates in "Democrats Wary About Top of Ticket," 2-8, Cohen does what he does best—gathers the Hill scuttlebutt and plies it into a coherent form. In "Keeping Their Distance," 4-11, he showcases his fluid style, constructing an enjoyable, leisurely read on whether it pays to have Congressional backing in this year's presidential race. Cohen's "Hill Upheaval," 5-23, is exceedingly long for anyone, other than fellow Hill members interested in the platitudes of their colleagues. Also lackluster is "Clinton Keeps Congress at Arm's Length," 7-25, in which he rehashes news of the uneasy partnership between Clinton and the Democrat-controlled Congress. The reliance on anonymous sources is also annoying. His candor and straightforward approach light up "Look Out, Congress," 8-1, a pithy examination of the possibility of changing Congressional players in 1993. Cohen does his investigative legwork and ultimately presents a level-headed assessment. His report on Sen.

John B. Breaux (D-LA), "the first Senator this year to win a new term," highlights the impending change in the air at the Capitol, in "Playing It Safe at the Right of Center," 10-10. He pens a muddied and confusing report comparing ex-Senator Russell B. Long of Louisiana, chairman of the Senate Finance Committee, with Lloyd Bentsen, the chairman, with regard to their dealings with southern presidents, in "A History Lesson for Bentsen, Clinton," 11-28. The comparisons here are stretched too far for the article to be instructive.

Steve Daley
Chicago Tribune
★½

Washington. As a D.C. correspondent for one of the nation's largest circulation newspapers, Daley's reports on the election inform a large population of voters. Although his journeyman articles are solid, they tend to be summaries more than explications. His "Democrats Use Debate to Show Voters Who's Who," 1-20, is able reportage discussing how uncommitted most of New Hampshire is to a single candidate, as the primary date nears. Daley delivers the latest poll results here and a recap of the debate in which the candidates tried to distinguish themselves. Little fresh information was offered in "Perot's Challenge Faces Daunting Odds," 3-29, as he rehashes the Texan's history: "Ten years later, Perot again showed his flair for the dramatic, organizing a commando operation inside Iran to rescue four of his employees from captivity. The story was later made into a movie." We must have read this same observation a million times. Daley's "Clinton-Jackson Jousts Have Democrats on Edge," 6-24, is a reasonable recounting of bubbling friction between two of the nation's most prominent Democrats. His assessment of what it would take for Clinton to win without the black vote is helpful. His "Bush, Clinton Focus on Key Electoral States," 8-23, is another mere summation of the major candidates' prospects after the GOP convention. And his post-election "Season of Change," 11-8, is a thumbnail sketch of what the future portends for the Republican party. His assessment, though not overly probing, was helpful immediately after Clinton's electoral triumph: "While politicos such as Vice President Dan Quayle, Housing Secretary Jack Kemp and Sen. Phil Gramm of Texas auditioned for the 1996 presidential nomination, the party will continue to debate some of the most explosive issues of the era: abortion, tax policy and the role of religion in political life."

Ann Devroy
The Washington Post
★★½

White House. Advancing up the learning curve with striking speed, Devroy, now on this important beat for three years, impresses us with her increasingly sophisticated political analysis. Although her "New Hampshire Awaits Latest Edition of Candidate Bush," 1-15, was a bit too caustic for a straight news story, her detailing of the President's chameleon-like positioning on the issues did strike a chord. She allows Republicans caught in the House check-kiting scandal to air their excuses in "3 Cabinet Members Admit Writing Bad Checks in House," 3-18, noting the hypocrisy, though she's a shade too easy on them. Making waves in "White House Said to Be in Gridlock," 4-4, Devroy interviews more than a dozen officials, finding "a consensus that [chief-of-staff] Skinner has constructed a mini-bureaucracy top heavy with officials inexperienced in White House operations who fail to follow things through." Her "How the Perot Factor Is Altering Campaign," with Dan Balz 5-27, details how Ross Perot's campaign has muddled the comparative simplicity of a two-way race. Her excellent organization and fluid style make for a sleek article on how each camp is handling the would-be intruder. In "Malek Target of Worried Republicans," 7-30, Devroy captures the frustrations of fretting Congressional Republicans toward GOP campaign manager Frederic V. Malek, and reveals how their concerns are being played out in Texas. Devroy provides a faithful detailing of a desperate memo sent to the President in "Conservatives Pressure Bush for Tax-Cutting Economic Plan," 8-9. But while she carefully enunciates the conservatives' concerns, she doesn't seem to grasp how the proposals in the memo could impact Bush's campaign and the economy. In her post-election coverage, Devroy notes that there's enough fault to go around in GOP circles after the election in "...And the Losers; Bush Defeat Blamed on Bad Campaign and Bad Economy," 11-5. She commendably stresses mistakes made during the Bush tenure, not the past 12 years, as some reporters have.

Helen Dewar
The Washington Post
★★½

Senate. As election-year politics heated up the Hill, we increasingly appreciate Dewar's muscular reporting and pithy sketches of Congressional in-fighting. But her partiality toward the Democratic party, kept under control in recent years, did pop up noticeably a few times this year. Her "Senate Passes College Aid Expansion," 2-22, is typical of her inquisitive reporting style, digging up all the pertinent information a reader could hope for on this issue. In "Democrats Attack Bush for Regretting Tax Boost," with Kenneth J. Cooper 3-5, she examines why Congress believes Bush is trying to appease Pat Buchanan with his renouncement of the 1990 tax hike. Unfortunately, despite the division in the Republican party over this issue, she quotes only Democrats here, turning the story into a partisan affair. Dewar does a commendable job of recounting the Senate's attempts to uncover the leaks that led to the Clarence Thomas/Anita Hill fiasco, in "Senate Probe Fails to Identify Leakers," 5-6. We wish, though, she had further developed her intriguing observation that "Many senators said they had no stomach for a constitutional confrontation with the news media." In top form for "In a System Divided, Partisan Politics Has Stranglehold on Progress," 8-3, Dewar delves into Congressional battles that amount "to a legislative version of trench warfare..." She gathers the evidence and slams both the White House and Congress for the partisan bickering that has mired the two branches in inaction. Post-election, we find Dewar cautioning the overly optimistic about the impact of having both Congress and the White House under Democratic control, in "Next President's Diplomatic Skill to Be Put to Test," 11-5: "[Clinton] will find neither the intense political gridlock ... nor a compliant legislature ready to respond to his every command."

Edwin Diamond
New York

"Media" columnist. A primary source of analysis on Big Apple media issues, Diamond broadened his scope this year to enhance our understanding of the so-called "New News" and its impact on the political process. In "Pop Politics: The New Word Order," 4-20, Diamond charts how the media has transformed the campaign game. He raises some good points and furthers the argument made in *Rolling Stone* by former CBS News producer Jon Katz, who explains that "New News" is here to stay because "the line between journalism and entertainment is blurred." He chronicles the rise of broadcast news sources, beyond the big three networks in "Primary Source," 3-9, making cognizant points about the increasing authority of CNN and local broadcasts. His "Riot Act," 5-18, fairly coherently describes how N.Y.C. local news kept its head while L.A. burned during the riots. His "Garden Variety: Covering the Convention," 7-13, surely provoked discussion in several newsrooms: "New media and old media have achieved an implicit division of labor. The candidates make policy or announce campaign moves on the talk circuit. The traditional mainstream hard-news purveyors pick up on these developments and relay them in the familiar news-story formats." Diamond continues his exploration of the changing media, this time on the campaign trail, in "Getting It Right," 11-2. Though far from definitive on the media's coverage of this year's presidential race, Diamond's analysis does offer some telling observations: "This year, the newsweeklies read more like the opinion magazines and the essay-minded monthlies in their campaign coverage."

E. J. Dionne, Jr.
The Washington Post
★★

What has happened to E. J. Dionne? Since first spotting Dionne's byline in *The New York Times* when he was stationed in Rome, we have found him to be consistently insightful. His work this election year, though, is steadfastly mediocre, devoid of the perspicacity we found so delightful in earlier years. He only addresses the GOP manipulation of statistics to answer the question "are you better off than you were four years ago?" in "Speeches, Statistics and Some Unsettling Facts About America's Changed Prospects," 1-26, failing to note that the Democrats and other factions of various parties are also guilty. He reviews the Pennsylvania primary perfunctorily in "Bush, Clinton and Yeakel Win Pennsylvania Primaries," 4-29, listing the winners and losers, but putting little of this in big-picture context. In fact, he came up short on analysis throughout the year. With "Abortion Joins GOP 'Values' Debate," 5-27, he only adequately encapsulates party divisions over abortion, while in his overview of Democratic finagling, "Democratic Platform Reflects Clinton Goals," 6-28, he fails to assess critically what Al From, president of the centrist Democratic Leadership Council, asserts is "a fundamental change in the direction of the party." Dionne offers an industrious argument in "Guess Who Lost Bush's Agenda?" 8-2, but doesn't tell us how or why Bush lost his way, only that Clinton will capitalize on it. He turns "As an Issue, the Deficit Doesn't Play in Peoria, Political Pros Warn," 9-29, into a catalogue of polling data, failing to flesh out the important issues he touches upon. Dionne, in "Forum With Voters Steers Clear of Invective," 10-16, only addresses surface issues of style in this review of the second debate. He asserts that "the next era will be shaped in part by arguments over what the old order was about, and what it achieved," in "After 12 Years of Conservatism, a New Era Emerges," 11-4. But his contention that Clinton's ascension is the death of conservatism is not credibly supported. At the beginning of the new year, Dionne became an editorial writer for the *Post*.

Cathryn Donohoe
The Washington Times
★★

"Life!" writer. The talented Donohoe remains the premier scribe in the section, but slipped a bit this year, failing to deliver the provocative political and cultural portraits we've come to expect. Instead, she turned out mildly interesting reviews and updates that only shadowed her earlier gems. Perhaps because of the cautiousness of the leaders of Operation Rescue, Donohoe never gets beneath the surface in the quick superficial update, "Operation Rescue Fights to Save the Country, Too," 1-20, penned just as the movement was beginning to go underground. For "Got a Spare Femtoseconds Clock Into Timely Exhibit?" 3-16, a review of the National Geographic's exhibit "It's a Matter of Time" in D.C., she does little more than interview schoolchildren, leaving us with only the sparsest sense of the exhibit and its purpose. More accomplished in portraiture, she allows her subject to come through in "William Kennedy Rails Them Bones," 5-19, an in-depth profile-review of William Kennedy and his novel *Very Old Bones*. In "The Outsider," 8-31, Donohoe follows Fred Barnes's lead of a month earlier to profile pro-life Democrat, Pennsylvania Gov. Bob Casey. But, unfortunately, she limits herself to providing mostly a political profile, rather than painting the entire picture. "Snips and Snaps: A Personal Archive," 11-7, is a reasonable, though lightweight, profile of George Tames, the first photographer to be presented with the National Press Club's Fourth Estate Award. We only get a taste of the stories he must have experienced while photographing presidents from FDR to Bush. Her best for the year, "US + THEM = WE," 9-14, is an engaging exploration of the Hearst-Izvestia project to produce the journal *We/My*: "With a stateside press run of 50,000 and a 350,000 circulation in Russia (and seven other republics), with mixed Russian/American editorial staffs in both Washington and Moscow... its editors crow that the newspaper is not just one more American product translated and shipped overseas."

Maureen Dowd
The New York Times
★★½

White House. With her feisty, no-holds-barred style, Dowd was clearly among the best reporters covering this year's chaotic campaign struggle. Despite occasional excesses and creeping self-importance, she more often than not penned key stories on the defining moments of the race. In fact, her controversial, shoot-from-the-hip style is being called a new journalistic genre and has been the subject of several analyses this year. Her sharp-eyed profile of Senator Bob Kerrey effectively conveys the "Theater of the Absurd" atmosphere engulfing his run for the White House in "Sensing an Opening, Kerrey Tries to Reinvigorate and Focus His Campaign," 1-27. The delightful "The Night of a Lifetime as Brown Meets Match," 4-22, on Jerry Brown's efforts to get a good night's sleep, is typical of Dowd's irreverent campaign insights. She doesn't seem to want to point out Mrs. Clinton's seams in "Hillary Clinton as Aspiring First Lady: Role Model, or a 'Hall Monitor' Type?" 5-18, her sympathies a bit too obvious here: "Mrs. Clinton may have far more integrity than Bush and Quayle." Written in Texanese, "Bush and Perot Battle to Be Truer Texan," 6-8, is harmless fun on the upcoming war between the "Dallas computer puncher and the Kennebunkport cowboy." "Weary and Feeling the Presidency's Weight," 8-16, is Dowd's overly-disparaging account of Bush's political troubles as he prepares for the most combative stage of the campaign. She does a tremendous job of adding up the negatives that contributed to the Bush defeat in "Bush: As the Loss Sinks In, Some Begin Pointing Fingers," 11-5. Though the paucity of named sources slightly weakens the piece, Dowd's barometer is right-on: "...Mr. Bush is a politician, with a politician's ego, and he grew complacent, freezing out old friends and advisers who long ago tried to sound the alarm..."

Elizabeth Drew
The New Yorker
★½

It has been a rough couple of years for this veteran political reporter. After 19 years, she announced that she'd be giving up her "Letter from Washington" column. We wondered if at least part of her chronic staleness was due to the atmosphere at the magazine where she worked. We hope to see her byline rejuvenated after she moves on. Her best "Letter" of the year, 9-7, provided an exceptionally sharp account of the Houston GOP convention. The shadings and subtleties that color the piece, confirm the touch of an experienced political observer. She observes that former President Reagan's speech was like a "balm...after so much harsh rhetoric." But her skimpy 2-17 letter exemplifies the rut she has been in for the past few years. It's a typical Beltway perspective of the current crop of Democratic presidential hopefuls, with a rather bland account of what Republican Pat Buchanan portends for the White House and his party. Her 3-30 letter is less generic, but takes an overly acerbic view of recent political affairs such as the growing nervousness in Democratic circles over Clinton heading the ticket, and the demonstrated lack of ability on the part of Bush to grasp the domestic concerns unsettling the electorate. She flashes her potential again in her 4-20 letter, delivering some astute observations on the Clinton campaign: "The Clintons tend to think that what has worked for them in the past will work in a Presidential campaign—and that's where they can get into trouble." Back to mediocrity in her 7-6 interview with Brent Scowcroft, as she blandly questions the NSC advisor about ethnic warfare in eastern Europe and the former Soviet Union. Drew offers a level-headed appraisal of Clinton's successes and Bush's failures in "Change," 11-16. Though she doesn't cull any exceptional insights from the race, her frankness is admirable: "We'll never know whether Bush had lost the election before the campaign began..."

Gregg Easterbrook
Newsweek
The Atlantic
★★★

Contributing editor. An agile journalist, able to carry off serious analysis on numerous topics, such as defense and the environment, Easterbrook impresses us with his cool, logical assessments. On defense issues, he is quite observant, as in "Stealth-Creators," *The New Republic* 1-6/13, in which he scripts an intelligent assessment of the next generation of stealth fighters, the F-22, which he asserts is cheaper, more efficient and stealthier than the B-1 or B-2 bomber. Also strong on environmental issues, Easterbrook is one of the few newsweekly reporters to actually explore the issues and question the facts from both sides of the debate. In his Rio Summit piece, "Why Rio Will Make History," *Newsweek* 6-15, he provides a valuable counterpoint to knee-jerk factions of the right wing, observing that "Some people like to think that sustainable development means no growth. It does not and should not: it means growth we can live with." He questions the "Green Cassandras," *TNR* 7-6, challenging "the sky is falling" mentality of some environmental activists in this detailed, informative article. There's plenty of guesswork involved in his dissection of what scientists believe may cause the next ice age in his engaging "Return of the Glaciers," *Newsweek* 11-23: "If scientists have been perplexed by the genesis of ice ages, figuring out why they stop—why the glaciers start to roll back—has been even more difficult." He ponders which candidate has the better environmental record, Clinton or Bush, in "Who Would Be Cleaner?" *Newsweek* 10-19, a fair and enlightening assessment of both of their records. On the art world, he's perceptive in "Risque? No! Some Art Is Just Lousy," *Los Angeles Times* 4-5: "The existence of bad art is a natural and even healthy sign of a vibrant, risk-taking cultural scene. The problem is the NEA has enormous difficulty coming to grips with this harmless fact."

Thomas B. Edsall
The Washington Post
★½

Politics. Occasionally fresh, but typically too unfocused to crystallize important trends, Edsall was more apt this year to slap coarse strokes on the canvas than to fill in the compelling details. It's unfortunate, since in years past we have relied on his political acumen. He's sketchy at best in "Clinton Wins Applause From Rainbow Coalition," 1-26, bouncing around too many mini-topics concerning the Clinton campaign. Infidelity, racial implications in the term "middle class" and the execution of a black man in Clinton's state are all poorly juggled in this overly ambitious report. His "Trouble for Bush in the Cradle of Reagan Democrats," 3-16, is an eye-opener from Roseville, Michigan, where working class "Reagan Democrats" are increasingly saying they'll return to their party, due to Bush's mishandling of the economy. In the toothless "The 'Values' Debate: Us vs. Them?" 7-31, Edsall verges on editorializing, giving Clinton complete credit for shanghaiing the issues of values and family: "Clinton has gained the initial advantage in this battle to appear representative of commonly shared values." He fails to convince us that a group of ethnic Catholics will vote as a Democratic bloc in "In a Tense Philadelphia Neighborhood, Ethnic Catholics Talk of Change," 8-8. Rather than capturing the subtle conflicts that always accompany change, Edsall tries to force the issue, making us wary of his intentions. His "Democrats Make Gains in Voter Registration, Especially Out West," 10-23, is a serviceable compendium of data from around the country indicating the upswing in Democratic registration. Once again, he glosses over the details here, notably the reasons why such gains were made. Edsall does an effective job of highlighting the different factions of the Democratic party in "Clinton's Task: Contain Intraparty Tensions," 11-5, but doesn't effectively pit them against each other as they'll surely vie for Clinton's time.

Timothy Egan
The New York Times

Western correspondent. Egan now keeps a firm check on the environmental bias we noted in his work several years back, crafting solid, serviceable overviews that inform without being judgmental. With "Trees That Yield a Drug for Cancer Are Wasted," 1-29, Egan reveals mismanagement of yew trees by the forestry service, which researchers use to make Taxol, a drug vital to the treatment of ovarian cancer. He's evocative in describing the National Forestry Service campground for the homeless in Oregon's Umpqua National Park, in "A Shelter for Rural Homeless: Trees and Sky," 5-11. He balances "Space Photos Show Forests in Pacific Northwest Are in Peril, Scientists Say," 6-11, by citing specifics from both NASA and forestry officials who "say it is misleading to make judgments about forest practices based on pictures from space. Almost all the cut-over Forest Service land has been replanted with new trees, they say, but this is not shown in the pictures from space because newly planted plots look the same as bald, deforested areas until the trees are about 10 years old." The only time we saw a hint of his green side was in "A Final Clear-Cut and Goodbye to Logging," 3-30, a P. 1 dispatch in which Egan portrays loggers as backwoods hicks who are doing a dirty job. Although "Eskimos Learn They've Been Living Amid Secret Pits of Radioactive Soil," 12-6, makes a good story on Eskimos who claim to have a high rate of cancer, Egan doesn't flesh out the facts, leaving the Eskimos' claims uncorroborated. We get an adequate read on the folks supporting Ross Perot, as Egan conducts follow-up interviews to a NYT/CBS News poll for "Perot's Support Is Often Found in Those Who Think They Read His Mind," 4-26. "Anti-Gay Backlashes Are on 3 States' Ballots," 10-4, is a sensitive, anecdotal treatment of a thorny topic.

Howard Fineman
Newsweek
★

Washington. Derisive as ever this election year, Fineman continues to undermine his genuine insights with heavy-handed sarcasm that we find rather distasteful. It is hard to get through Fineman's material without feeling that he is a bit trigger-happy. He feigns familiarity in his profile of Jerry Brown's insurgent presidential campaign in "The Method in His Madness," 3-23: "He may sound like Savonarola (and dress like Giorgio Armani), but in his heart Brown is closer to the original Mayor Daley." In "Leadership? Don't Ask Us," 4-11, he takes the presidential candidates to task for not being quicker to respond after the L.A. riots. His criticism is valid, but his sneering tone detracts from the report. Fineman's "Sixties: Coming of Age," 7-20, is a thinly-veiled Clinton campaign flyer masquerading as journalism. Reminiscent of William Manchester's version of JFK, Fineman unabashedly gushes over the presidential candidate, describing his life and work in only the most glowing terms. He also gives a pro-Clinton spin to "Keeping the Big Mo Rolling," 8-3: "He isn't eating pork rinds yet, as Bush did in 1988 on his own bus trips through the Heartland. But give Clinton time. It's still only July." His "What Does He Want?" 9-28, is a respectable report on the presidential campaign now that Perot has re-entered the fray, with little of Fineman's characteristic snideness arising in this detail-packed update. We are served another highly-flattering portrait of Clinton, post-election, for "The Torch Passes," special issue 11/12-92: "Like Kennedy, he offered himself as a new kind of youthful, centrist Democrat. Like his hero, he sought an elemental mandate for change…"

Sara Fritz
Los Angeles Times
★★½

Washington. Fritz is a valuable asset on the *Times*'s campaign team, always ferreting out the salient detail and providing a framework for digesting it. She gives us a smart assessment of how Clinton's attempt to mend the "traditional Democratic coalition of blacks and blue-collar whites" ripped apart by Reagan will play into his strategy to win the nomination in "Clinton Is Preaching Racial Harmony," 3-14. For "Bush Kin: Trading on the Name?" 5-10, she gathers much evidence of the Bush family's apparent conflicts of interest, centering on his sons, George

Jr., Jeb and Neil. She avoids partisanship by allowing those concerned to speak for themselves. Thoughtfully examining the reverberations of America's most infamous scandal in "Watergate: Lessons of a Scandal," 6-16, she insightfully reviews Watergate itself, what happened to the Watergate babies and reforms enacted in the scandal's wake. She pens a revealing political profile of the Gores with "Some See Expediency Not Principle as Gore's Guide," 7-15, using his stand on explicit music lyrics as a case in point: " . . . Gore received generous contributions from the recording studios during his 1990 Senate campaign, and his wife has helped the industry defeat music censorship legislation in several state legislatures. To critics of the soon-to-be Democratic vice presidential nominee, Gore's little-known rapprochement with the record industry is evidence of what they see as his habit of presenting himself as a man of principle, while at the same time trimming his views to conform with political expediency." She dutifully conveys Clinton's "trickle down" speech at the University of Connecticut, in "Clinton Rejects Bush's Charges He Is Tax-and-Spend Democrat," 9-26, but there's little analysis here. Though slightly wordy, Fritz's "Big Insurers Cast Wary Eye on Clinton's Health Plans," 12-7, explores challenges the Clinton administration will have to address as it molds a health insurance plan.

Michael Fumento
Investor's Business Daily

National issues, Los Angeles. Like most *IBD* articles, Fumento's dispatches are content-rich and compactly composed. He is a persuasive and thought-provoking analyst who always does his homework, but on social concerns there's no hiding his conservative bias. He monitors the debate between deregulation and environmental concerns in the penetrating and fact-filled "The Hidden Cost of Regulation," 3-9, but with characteristic Fumento partiality, he allows the deregulationists to wrap up each argument. Scripting a report tailor-made for this anti-incumbent election year, "Is Congress Too Inexperienced?" 4-6, he notes that 40% of the nation's congressmen are lawyers with no practical business background. To drive home the import of this statistic, he reviews these legislators' poor business voting record. It's the type of report sure to be talked about at the office, but never to be seen in the *Congressional Record*. He's sure to please anti-regulationists with "Global Warming or Hot Air?" 6-2, weighing in heavily against the green movement's efforts to regulate greenhouse gases in this provocative report. Fumento offers an insightful and entertaining bio of "Editor Andrew Sullivan: Leading *The New Republic* in Era of 'Blurring Ideologies,'" 9-24, discussing the right-to-center shift *TNR* is taking under the direction of its new "Catholic, Tory and gay" editor. His portrait of Bill Clinton's wife isn't quite so delightful. In "Hillary—the Other Clinton," 10-14, he gathers the anti-Hillary forces and lambastes her for her liberal, legal and political activism. It's hard not to wince at such an onslaught. He continues his scrutiny of legal activism in "Is the ABA a Captive of Politics?" 12-7. The article raises a number of questions about the American Bar Association's support of abortion rights, but Fumento's bias against the liberal agenda dulls the piece.

Christopher Georges
The Washington Monthly

Editor. A former investigative reporter for CNN, Georges brings his experience to bear on the pages of the *Monthly*. We suspect he needed minimal training from editor-in-chief Charles Peters. He is skilled at digging up the relevant details on the institutions that the *Monthly* loves to expose, pulling his information together so well that there's rarely a word wasted in his essays. Georges gives us a vigorous assessment of how the Office of Thrift Supervision is performing in "Egads! The S&L Scandal Lives!" 1/2-92, providing the particulars on how the bureaucracy and its rules are allowing some bankers to suck up the taxpayers' S&L bailout money. He uses his experience at CNN to take his colleagues to task in "Confessions of an

Investigative Reporter," 3-92, a 10 Best selection on the dearth of real investigative reporting in the media: "By launching our own independent investigations of large institutions, we have the opportunity not just to reveal problems within the system, but to help *fix* them before the bailout bill reaches $500 billion or the *Challenger* explodes." In "Is the President a Plagiarist?" 4-92, he gets an early bead on George Bush's lack of commitment to his own platform. Georges gets the goods by citing Bush's actual words and tracing them back to their original—and *Democratic*—authors. Although he fails to deliver a knockout punch to the American Association of Retired Persons (AARP) in "Old Money," 6-92, Georges digs up enough information, on the way the group operates, to make us suspicious of its highly-publicized, government-subsidized, non-profit status as the voice of senior citizens around the country. In "Power Play," 9-92, Georges alerts us to the Nuclear Regulatory Commission's rule changes that will make it harder for citizens to voice their concerns over nuclear plants. For example, on the NRC's new license renewal regulations, a utility inspects its own plants "for any safety or age-related problems and passes its report onto the NRC. The commission then gives thumbs up or thumbs down. No NRC inspection or public hearing on safety is required" He closes the year with a headshaking exposé on why Washington is unable to clean up its 13-year taxi scandal in "Checkered Past," 12-92, a well-researched chronology of the scandal.

James Gerstenzang
Los Angeles Times
★

White House. Unfortunately, Gerstenzang continues to be one of the least effective reporters on this important beat, frequently failing to flesh out the necessary details. At his best he dutifully gathers quotes from the appropriate parties on the issues of the day. For instance, "Bush Vows Fight on Hard Times: He Calls for Tax Changes to Spur the Economy," 1-29, is a detached report on the President's State of the Union address, with reactions from both Republicans and Democrats. Gerstenzang and co-writer Cathleen Decker offer a satisfactory skim of the issues during the primaries with "Toward a New Hampshire Decision: Republicans," 2-16, scanning the latest from Bush, Buchanan and the voters. He trimly defines the post-L.A. riot finger-pointing in "White House Blames 'Liberal Programs' for Riots," 5-5, a reasonable roundup of the press briefing in which White House spokesman Marlin Fitzwater first blamed liberal programs for inner-city strife. Adding his voice to the din over family values in "Quayle Attacks 'Cultural Elite' on Moral Values," 6-10, he only probes a bit deeper than the text of Quayle's talk, offering a cursory examination of the strategy behind such speeches. In "Early Praise for Skinner Tempered by Complaints," 4-12, he never names a source for the praise or complaints, and annoyingly skips back and forth between the two. His scattershot presentation here leaves us wondering what all the fuss is about. He and co-writer Doyle McManus talk to the historians for a fine discussion of how "Candidates Conjure Up Heroes Past," 9-21, but this selection appeared after other, similar dispatches elsewhere. He gives a serviceable reading of how the Bush administration might act on sensitive policies before leaving office in "White House Debates Its Next Moves," 11-8: "Bush is unlikely to go so far as to establish full diplomatic relations with Vietnam."

Linda Greenhouse
The New York Times
★★½

Supreme Court. With the abortion issue constantly bubbling to the surface of the national campaign, this experienced hand's understanding of where politics and constitutional law meet makes her an important resource. Although she occasionally flashes her personal prejudices, we admire her deliberate effort to tell the highly-charged abortion story as it presents itself. Heavy-handed, but effective, in "Justice Thomas Hits the Ground Running," 3-1, she paints a vivid portrait of judicial activism, asserting that the newest Court appointee may be writing concurring opinions designed for other purposes than helping decide the question before the Court: "Opinions like these serve as messages, tracer bullets streaking across an otherwise placid legal sky to announce that a doctrine that might appear to be settled is in fact open to challenge." Covering the closely-watched Pennsylvania abortion case in "Court Gets Stark Arguments on Abortion," 4-23, Greenhouse showcases a highly impressive comprehension of the legal and political stakes. Not only does she expertly capture the mood of the Court as it delves into this contentious national debate, but she obliges us to understand the philosophical, legal and political approaches being taken by both sides. Her "High Court, 5-4, Affirms Right to Abortion but Allows Most of Pennsylvania's Limits," 6-30, isn't nearly as compelling, and we don't get the full impact of what appeared to be a murky victory/loss situation for both anti- and pro-abortion camps. Slipping temporarily from her role as impartial observer in "Revealing View of Court," 7-1, Greenhouse takes unwarranted liberties in discussing what she calls "The hard-edged, take-no-prisoners, stance by the Justices..." on abortion. Her "At the Supreme Court, a Pendulum Stops," 11-8, discusses the tenure of the individual members solely with regard to abortion.

Lloyd Grove
The Washington Post
★

"Style." Last year, Grove received a *MediaGuide* 10 Best for his profile on the inner-workings of the American Israel Public Affairs Committee (AIPAC), "The Israel Lobby, on the March," 6-13-91 and "The Men With the Muscle," 6-14-91. Nothing we saw from Grove this year matched the quality of reporting, writing or analysis of those dispatches. We also saw an unattractive bias in his work. In the unfunny "George of the Jungle?" 1-28, Grove makes the absurd, discombobulated and insulting comparison of the President of the United States to a primate, with regard to his speech mannerisms. Although we do get a rather thorough profile of Mrs. Clinton in "Hillary Clinton, Trying to Have it All," 3-10, Grove seems quite enamored of the lady: "If Bill Clinton is a 'gray-haired, middle-aged fat guy,' as he described himself... she is a svelte vision of feminist influence." While Grove's sarcastic style entertains in "The Campaign Crush," 2-18, his anecdotes from the campaign trail are simply superficial, providing little that sticks to our ribs. He reports that the GOP is outlawing homemade, or unapproved signs at the convention in "The GOP, Squelching Signs of Trouble," 8-10, nastily positing that delegates are "getting the message that someone, somewhere wants them to sit down and shut up." His best for the year was an early, energetic profile of Clinton campaign strategist, James Carville, "The Double-Fidget Campaign Whiz," 1-23, in which we learn among other things that he doesn't change his underwear in the last week of a campaign for fear of disturbing the candidate's momentum. He provides a bio on Bush campaign chairman Robert Teeter by way of a multitude of strung together quotes in "The Handler, Hanging Tough," 10-29. Grove seems intent on depicting him as a nice guy, unfit for the shark's cage of politics. He is particularly snide in describing Jeane Kirkpatrick and Jack Kemp as "has-beens and wannabes" at a dinner party for *The American Spectator*, in "Spectator, Preparing for Battle," 12-4.

Ralph Z. Hallow
The Washington Times
½★

National politics. The "wise-guy conservative" title we pinned on him last year still says it all. While his loyalties sometimes give him insider access on one side of the aisle, he's much more effective as a mouthpiece than a reporter. His "GOP Takes Bush Foe Seriously," 2-27, on Republican challenger Pat Buchanan, doesn't fully define Bush's conservative opponent, but does capture the conservative wing's nervousness about the incumbent. In "GOP Lawmakers Push 'Tough Love' Welfare Plan," 4-29, Hallow is more concerned with conservative congressmen's reaction to Rep. Vin Weber and Newt Gingrich's welfare/work proposal than the plan's details or likely impact. His "Rollins' Independence Riles GOP Believers," 6-5, gives a nice smattering of views on former Reagan White House political director Ed Rollins's defection to the Perot campaign. Hallow offers an interesting take on the anti-incumbency mood of the nation by focusing on House Minority Whip Newt Gingrich in "Gingrich Faces Possible Upset," 7-13. Due to redistricting in Georgia and his House bank overdrafts, he tells us, this "conservative icon" could face a tough race. His disjointed "Baker Accepts Controls of Bush Campaign," 8-14, presents predictable conservative enthusiasm over James Baker's appointment to Bush's re-election campaign: "...Jack Kemp, a former professional football quarterback, said: '... He's a quarterback. He's going to go into the huddle and he's going to call plays.'" He doesn't disguise his dislike for Ross Perot, labeling him "the decade's most famous quitter," in "Did 'Psychodrama' Dupe President?" 9-29. His conservative loyalties glare in this report on the Democratic and Republican delegations sent to meet with the Texan just before he formally entered the race. Hallow views Clinton's win with his own interpretive slant in "Economic Woes Drive Mandate for Change," 11-4: "So the governor of a small state ran on what was in many ways a conservative platform...He mastered Mr. Reagan's secret of success..."

Richard Harwood
The Washington Post
★★★

Columnist. One of this group of media watchers' favorite media watchers, Harwood, with almost three decades of experience, is able to give us the long view on media trends. An easy, conversational style steadies the rigorous standards he applies to the reports he reviews. His articles are always recommended reading for news junkies. "To Choose a President," 5-3, a look at the negativity and bias that surfaces in the press during elections, reminds us why we appreciate Harwood so much: "This looks to be one of those years... in which editorial neutrality goes out of fashion." In "Long Lunch in January," 2-9, Harwood is taken aback by the "apathy or mental exhaustion" that seems to have overtaken the nation: "...the newspaper performs a therapeutic function similar to that of the dogs we kick as surrogates for whatever irks us. It was a universal sport 20 or so years ago. ...The 1990s, by comparison, are placid. The counterculturalists have become middle-aged, middle-class establishmentarians." Witty and authoritative in "Media Wilt," 6-26, Harwood sheds light on the candidates' attempts to press the media out of the loop by courting talk show audiences. His "Snaps at the Heels of the Press," 8-8, is an expansive assessment of curtailing of press freedoms, but the piece is ultimately ineffectual, failing to foster a strong emotional or intellectual response. He provides us with a lively jaunt through the editorial pages of major newspapers during presidential endorsement time, in "The Final Score," 10-7. Harwood knowingly questions the need for endorsements, in light of today's corporate ownership of papers: "These executives are not political brawlers.... In partisan terms, they tend to be eunuchs, unlike the colorful and passionate newspaper entrepreneurs of the 19th century..." He takes on such sacred cows as "60 Minutes" for its deceptive practices in getting news in "Knights of the Fourth Estate," 12-5.

Michael Hedges
The Washington Times
★½

Investigative reporter. A middling to off year for Hedges, who failed to rock the Beltway with any of his probes. Nonetheless, he delivered workman-like reports that occasionally added a new dimension to our understanding of an issue. His overseas reports early in the year on post-war Iraq were quite impressive. Hedges delivers a short, but effective article on the Iraqi population's reaction to their somewhat humbled leader, Saddam Hussein, in "Mr. Yes Doesn't Agree With All," 3-30. His generous use of quotes here relays a good snapshot of the Iraqi peoples' frustrations and hopes. His point/counterpoint style for "He's Not Saying Much, but Voters Like What They Hear," 5-8, results in sophomoric back and forth shots from the trenches, adding nothing to our understanding of the Ross Perot phenomenon: "Mr. Perot has criticized President Bush for backing . . . dictators. . . . Mr. Perot also has been criticized for his forays into maverick, extra-governmental foreign policy." Hedges goes digging and comes up with a faux diamond for "Clintons Profited From S. African Investments," 7-9, finding that as Governor of Arkansas, Bill Clinton invested in DeBeers Consolidated Mines Ltd. But the report failed to make waves. In "Andrew Devastates South Florida," 8-25, Hedges ably bangs out a deadline story on the horrors inflicted on Florida by Hurricane Andrew, but without quotes or anecdotes, the article lacks feeling. Also cursory was "D.C. Fines Iran-Contra Prosecutor Over Taxes," 9-23, a follow-up to news reported elsewhere of special prosecutor Lawrence Walsh allegedly failing to pay D.C. income taxes. Hedges challenges the notion that Sen. Al Gore is an expert on the environment in "Gore's Ideas Wilt in Science's Light," 10-11, gathering opinions from numerous environmentalists, but only touching on the scientific arguments against Gore's assertions. He relies disproportionately on wire service reports in his initial dispatch on the U.S. landing in Somalia in "Media Spotlight Predawn Landing," 12-9.

Steven A. Holmes
The New York Times
★½

Politics, Washington. Holmes concentrated on the renegade presidential campaigns of Pat Buchanan and Ross Perot this year. His fact-finding abilities are strong, but his analytical skills still need honing. His coverage of Ross Perot made no attempt to nail down the candidate's stands on the issues, but rather focused on trying to demystify the Texan, sometimes to the point of rebuking him. In a front-page special report, Holmes ponders the maverick's special appeal in "A Man Who Says He Wants to Be Savior, if He's Asked," with Doron P. Levin 4-13. Though this is an in-depth exploration of the candidate, the authors seem intent on casting the man as a shadowy figure: "The unusual method of dipping one toe into the presidential creek is vintage Perot . . ." He continues his research into Perot's background with "Notes Say Perot Was Allied With the Nixon White House," 5-8, painting him as the ultimate Washington insider, with surreptitious dealings to benefit his business. In "Bold Perot Plan to Attack Deficit Thrusts Issue at Bush and Clinton," 9-28, Holmes presents Perot's economic plan in a forthright manner, unfortunately he doesn't scrutinize the merits or weaknesses of its proposals. He ably captures the dilemma confronting conservatives frustrated by President Bush in "As Buchanan Runs, the Right Fragments," 2-4: "By espousing positions . . . tinged with a kind of isolationism and protectionism that are anathema to many free-market and globalist conservatives, Mr. Buchanan is seen by some as an imperfect spear with which to impale the President. . . . For some conservatives, supporting Mr. Buchanan therefore seems like a Faustian bargain." In his day-on-the-campaign-trail report, "Rats! We Certainly Didn't Expect That," 8-15, he compiles some of the little unexpected occurrences that have mildly ruffled the campaign. Post-election, Holmes writes a balanced profile of Vice President-elect Al Gore, "A Focused Leader on an Uneven Climb," 11-4: "When the subject of Al Gore Jr. is raised, inevitably the phrase 'born to lead'—spoken with either admiration or sarcasm —somehow seeps into the conversation."

Gwen Ifill
The New York Times
★★

Politics, Washington. Now settled in nicely at the *Times*, after leaving *The Washington Post* in 1991, Ifill penned spirited pieces from the nooks and crannies of the presidential campaign. In the years to come, we foresee even bigger and better reporting from her, although she'll have to learn to hold the reins a bit tighter on her ideological prejudices. For instance, she loses her objectivity in "The Clinton Team's 'Utility Infielder' Is Becoming a Major-League Hitter," 9-1, giving campaign staffers too much room to gush over campaign communications director George Stephanopoulos: "...Mr. Carville called this reporter to volunteer an observation: 'If George's I.Q. could be converted to Fahrenheit, that boy could boil water.'" Uncharacteristically listless in "Mining Unhappiness in a Changed New Hampshire," 1-12, she gives editorial weight to trivial asides: " . . . campaigning in New Hampshire, it is no longer enough to politely introduce themselves to voters at house parties and coffee shops." Aiding the Democrats with damage control in "Clinton Admits Experiment With Marijuana in 1960's," 3-30, she observes: "Polls show that most Americans say smoking marijuana in college should not disqualify a person from becoming President . . . " In "Clinton Plan Offers National Education," 5-15, Ifill faithfully recounts the Clinton speech, capably shading in useful background material. Funny and illuminating, her "Clinton Finds Time to Take on G.O.P." 7-20, exposes the Clinton/Gore cross-country bus trek: "Dressed in polo shirts, both men ran and tossed the ball for several minutes while staff members on the sidelines took pains to tell watching reporters how spontaneous it was." Slightly cursory in her report on Clinton's plans to hold an economic summit, "Clinton to Summon Economic Leaders to Set Priorities," 11-9, Ifill provides little beyond the "when" and "where" of the announcement.

Michael Isikoff
The Washington Post
★½

Drugs, justice. Typically a wooden, press-release slave, Isikoff seems to be addressing a few more "whys" and "hows" in his articles these days. Drug enforcement and prevention have been political touchstones for the Bush administration, and Isikoff occasionally tunes us into the bureaucratic posturing behind the latest battle of the "war on drugs." Unfortunately, his work remains distressingly inconsistent. His "New Drug Strategy Targets Alcohol Use by Minors," 1-26, is a serviceable update on the latest phase in the administration's drug war, which is now targeting alcohol and treatment. As for the politics behind this strategy, Isikoff points out that "Administration officials acknowledge that the anti-alcohol efforts are largely symbolic and unlikely to stir opposition from alcohol industry groups." Adequately nuancing the cold shoulder Drug Czar Bob Martinez is getting from the administration in "Martinez Suffers Setbacks as Drug Control Director," 2-24, Isikoff gives us an adequate feel for the rift, but he barely skims the drug-abuse figures under Martinez's tenure. He doesn't deliver the big-picture scenario of the Bush administration's "weed and seed" drug program in "Critics Question Bush's Urban Bottom Line," 5-21. His focus on the program's impact in Kansas City, Mo., which hasn't received its full funding, diminishes the credibility of his report. One of his best pieces investigated Ross Perot's drug enforcement interdiction in Texas, "Perot Championed Unorthodox War on Drugs," 6-10: "Perot helped pave the way by instituting a rigorous urinalysis-testing program at EDS." Back to wire-service quality with "Bush Camp Distributes Memo in Effort to Keep the Clinton Draft Issue," 9-18, she offers little beyond the headlines. Also cursory is "Drug Survey Shows Rise in Use Among Students; White House Aide Reportedly Opposed Release," 10-19, in which Isikoff simply recapitulates the findings of this report, adding virtually no fresh information or insight to the issue.

Douglas Jehl
Los Angeles Times
★★

White House. We had heard from various sources last year that Jehl would join *The New York Times*. Fortunately for the *Los Angeles Times*, he remained in the Washington bureau, turning out solid work from both 1600 Pennsylvania Avenue and the campaign trail. While he does not set the pace for White House reportage, he provides sharp snapshots of the day's events. He highlights middle-class discontent with Bush's State of the Union address, putting this phenomenon down as too little, too late in "Middle-Class Americans May View the President's Proposals Too Modest," 1-29. He and co-writer James Gerstenzang bring out early signs of dissatisfaction in "Bush's New Team Struggles With Campaign," 2-10: "Still, the mood among those closest to Bush —while insistently optimistic about eventual victory—is surprisingly unsettled." With "Clinton Takes a Grilling in N.Y. and Gains an Audience," 4-2, he provides an excellent look at the "Donahue" show, as Phil is chastised by an audience member for grilling Clinton about his sex life once too often. He dutifully reports administration retorts to European nations trying to pressure Bush into signing the global warming and biodiversity treaties in Rio in "U.S. Assails its Critics at Summit," 6-10, but he fails to question the validity of either side's position seriously. As did much of the press, Jehl virtually ignores the Vice President's message in "Quayle Deplores Eroding Values, Cites TV Show," 5-20, highlighting the Murphy Brown sound bite. He details Bush's strategy to hit hard at voter uncertainty about Clinton, but his lead seems overstated in "Bush Takes Aim at Clinton Draft Status, Economic Plan," 9-18, pegging the strategy as "a calculated one-two assault . . . [that] used language laden with images of duplicity and the welfare state in an intensified bid to convince Americans that they can neither trust nor afford to put Bill Clinton in the White House." Jehl does offer some prescient insights in "Christopher, Jordan to Plan Clinton Transition," 11-7: "It nevertheless remained evident that his choice of the well-respected duo meant he had chosen to postpone what may be his most difficult personnel decision: the selection of a top deputy to serve as White House chief of staff."

David Johnston
The New York Times
★

Justice. Johnston's work seemed limp again this year, lacking the narrative punch to deliver a story and the research to flesh it out. His bare-bones presentation fails to shed new light on the important innerworkings of the Justice Department. In "Border Crossings Near Old Record; U.S. to Crack Down," 2-9, Johnston updates data on Mexicans crossing into the U.S. and law enforcement's attempts to ebb the flow, but he doesn't bring any fresh insight into this oft-told story. His "Inquiry on House Bank Case May Focus on Use of Money," 4-8, recounts the direction former Federal judge Malcolm R. Wilkey plans to take as special counsel. Johnston does no digging on his own, leaving the story one-dimensional. He reports on the Attorney General's discovery of two criminal laws that may be used to prosecute the four L.A. policemen accused of beating Rodney King in "U.S. May Use 1870 Statutes to Revive Case of 4 Officers," 5-1. While Johnston thoroughly outlines the laws, he fails to fully explain how the judge will apply them to the King case in this all-too-brief article. In "Aide to H.U.D. Secretary Under Reagan Is Indicted," 7-8, Johnston again relies solely on information supplied by the Federal government, never shaping the report with his own information or analysis. His "Ex-Senator Says Panel Was Misled on Iran-Contra," 8-8, fails to flesh out allegations by former Senator Thomas Eagleton, that CIA member Clair George misled the committee. He provides a cursory report on accusations that FBI Director William Sessions is using air trips for personal use. And "'New' F.B.I. Still Shackled by Past," 10-30, suffers from the same lethargy as the rest of Johnston's FBI reportage, his lack of perspective and quotes minimizing the article's readability and impact. Johnston's "Investigator Finds Evidence of Crimes in House Bank Use," 12-17, dutifully reports on the Justice's initial inquiries into Congressional improprieties, but he fails to inject any analysis or reaction into the story.

Joe Klein
Newsweek
★★

Once one of our favorite writers, Klein is able to pack more flavor and information into the turn of a phrase than most can in an entire column. This year, though, Klein turns his estimable talents into a political stiletto, attempting to shape and/or destroy candidates with the flick of his pen. He dismisses most of the Democratic field in January, opting instead to provide the Democrats with a definitive reading of the strengths and weaknesses of the man he considers the front-runner, Bill Clinton. And for Republicans, he offered only disdain. Klein comes off as a concerned team player in "Bill Clinton: Who Is This Guy?" *New York* 1-20, gushing about Clinton's dynamism and masterful control of the issues. But, Klein takes off the kid gloves for President Bush in "Bush Back in Tension City," *Newsweek* 7-20: "The real problem [with the Bush campaign] is the lack of an agenda, or even a rationale, for a second term." His heavy-handed sarcasm here undermines his genuine insights. The same is true of "'Message: I Care,'" *NY* 1-27, in which Klein holds the President up to the light and discovers he looks anemic after his disastrous trip to Japan; again, his worthwhile insights are lost beneath jabs and punches. He is back to pouring over Clinton's inner being in "What Clinton Must Do," *NY* 4-20, and finds himself a bit befuddled by the candidate—on one hand, impressed with Clinton's leadership on the Phil Donahue show, on the other shocked by Clinton's latest military draft fiasco. Klein's "The Year of Living Seriously," *Newsweek* 10-12, only confirms our diagnosis of blatant prejudice: "Clinton has experienced the anguish [of the electorate],

but doesn't seem to understand what's expected of him ...George Bush remains clueless on all counts." He colors in the details of Clinton's election promise to create a "Domestic Peace Corps," noting that the President-elect appears to be keeping the issue on the front burner, in "Copping a Domestic Agenda," *Newsweek* 12-7.

Howard Kurtz
The Washington Post
★★

Media. Although his work is decidedly less notable than last year, Kurtz still manages to file a number of worthwhile reports in this, his second full year on the beat. He might not be the reporter who crystallizes a new trend, but he's usually among the ones to track it carefully. "In Quadrennial Rite, Press Bestows Front-Runner Status: It's Clinton," 1-12, takes a few friendly swipes at those peers who have signed onto the pack mentality, bestowing the coveted title of front-runner on a candidate before he has earned it. In the informative "Young Media Trio Behind Bush Ads," 2-9, Kurtz focuses on the men behind Bush's television commercials. Regrettably, Kurtz dwells on the negative ads they've done for campaigns of yore rather than assessing their '92 campaign work. At his best in "Questions of Privacy," 4-23, written in the wake of the press leak on Arthur Ashe's battle with AIDS, he provides a superb survey of the ethical and professional questions con-

fronting editors and journalists in our increasingly voyeuristic society. In "Garry Trudeau's Cartoon Beat," 5-30, Kurtz turns a surprisingly uncritical eye on the controversial work of cartoonist Trudeau: "Trudeau...is squarely in the tradition of Thomas Nast and Pat Oliphant, who use humor to deflate the official gasbags of their day." He provides only a serviceable reading of how the networks plan to cover the Democratic convention in "Brush Fires in the Forest of Newsmakers," 7-14. Putting Marlin Fitzwater in the limelight for "Attack of the President's Flack," 8-1, he provides a partial picture of the White House press secretary's daily trek in front of the press corps' firing line, where he attempts to shape coverage of the president. Kurtz takes a novel approach to article writing in "The Press's Difficult Transition," 11-12, offering a look at the problems that could develop for Clinton during the transition period before inauguration: "The Clinton team... may have miscalculated by allowing a news vacuum to develop."

Neil A. Lewis
The New York Times
★½

Legal affairs. With Vice President Dan Quayle bringing legal issues to the fore of the campaign, Lewis's beat took on new import this election. But, Lewis failed to catch the wave, having another lackluster year, characterized by unenterprising reports. His "U.N., Hinting at Force, Gives

Iraq a Week to Scuttle Arms," 3-18, is a flat report on a deadline issued by the Security Council. "Lobbyists Favor Senator by Financing Son's Race," 5-25, is an interesting take on campaign financing. Sen. J. Bennett Johnston's son, an environmental advocate, is running for election, while pipeline and energy groups donate to his retiring father for influence. His brief "Wider C.I.A. Role Seen in Nicaragua," 7-18, doesn't expand on recently released documents at the Iran-Contra trial of former CIA official Clair George. Lewis provides no comprehensive background to place the latest round of accusations in context, weakening the article. Lewis's penchant for using the minimum amount of quotes mars "Judge's Delay May Mean Clifford Will Never Face Trial," 9-11, but he does offer several impressive insights on the possible trial of former presidential adviser Clark Clifford and his law partner over their role in the BCCI scandal: "If Mr. Clifford is not brought to trial . . . [Mr. Altman] would have to face charges without his mentor, a figure generating admiration and enormous sympathy, at his side." Lewis takes the questionable stance of the *NYT* with regard to Anita Hill's redemption in the public eye, a year after her sexual harassment allegations against Clarence Thomas, in "Anita Hill Says She Is Skeptical About Specter," 10-7. In "Issues of Race and Home Rule Confound Death Penalty Vote in Washington," 11-1, he fails to focus on the larger issue of the unique relationship Congress and D.C. have with each other, with regard to laws enacted.

Charles M. Madigan
Chicago Tribune
★½

Washington. Although his articles sew together a respectable number of facts, Madigan doesn't consistently capitalize on their full significance. He is characteristically a reliable reporter, yet toward the end of the election, a creeping bias often soured his reports. When he's straightforward, he's quite good, as in "New Hampshire on Center Stage," 2-16, a healthy fleshing out of poll statistics from the first primary of the season. Madigan offers a very positive look at the so-called "Year of the Woman" in politics in "Anger Over Hill Flames Up at Polls," 4-30. Yet he isn't able to distinguish between this "anger" and possible career opportunists exploiting it. Madigan leaves "Clinton Seeks a 'New Covenant,'" 7-17, sorely empty, without any scrutiny of Clinton's acceptance speech at the Democratic National Convention which he describes as the "crowning moment of Clinton's quest." In "GOP Yearns for Reagan, Glory Days," 8-23, Madigan takes nearly every opportunity to downplay Bush at the Republican National Convention and contrast the event unfavorably with the Democratic convention: "The Republicans left Houston in the wake of a week of messages aimed mostly at a very narrow and very conservative audience . . . quite a contrast to the inclusion-fest staged by the loud, jubilant Democrats in Manhattan in July." He twists election results to an extreme in "Season of Change," 11-8: "Although Clinton failed to win a majority of the votes last Tuesday, there is still a broad mandate for a return to federal activism because both Clinton and independent Ross Perot proposed creation of a government that works to solve problems, and together, they collected more than 60 percent of the vote."

Susan Mandel
Investor's Business Daily
★½

National issues and politics. Though Mandel's articles often lack precise analysis, we appreciate her information-packed delivery. But this profusion of data is rarely processed, leaving her articles bloated. Mandel nicely weighs both sides in the debate over campaign financing reform in "Is Campaign Reform Possible?" 1-22. She centers on Congressional inability to propose legislation, critiquing their at-odds proposals. She goes overboard in "Bush's Banking Deregulation," 4-27, seeming to list every government regulation on which Bush has placed a moratorium. The examples where the deregulation had improved efficiency are welcome, but the article rambles after a while.

In "Can Perot Really Pull It Off?" 5-26, Mandel looks at the odds Ross Perot will get to the White House. Though not a must-read, it has its insights: "As is the case with most self-made tycoons, Perot isn't used to having his version of things questioned." In "America's Divided Government," 6-10, she ponders if our two-party government is the cause, or symptom, of policy-making paralysis. Some points are prescient, but Mandel spends too much time contrasting authors' opinions in a he-said/she-said approach. She gives us a smattering of ideas, offered by conservatives and moderates alike, on which Bush needs to focus at the Republican convention, in "Bush Seeking the 'Vision Thing,'" 8-17. Mandel seems intent on listing all points, deferring on analysis. She may not answer the question, "Is Family Values a Wedge Issue?" 9-1, but Mandel does manage to assess its impact coherently: "The Bush-Quayle campaign needs to neutralize voters' concerns about the economy first. But if it can do that, the family values theme could end up making a powerful difference for its side."

Ruth Marcus
The Washington Post
★½

White House. Marcus switched mid-year from the Supreme Court beat. Her coverage of the High Court in the first half of the year spent too much time restating the ideological predispositions of the justices. We'd have appreciated more dimension on the implications of the Court's decisions. Her campaign coverage during the second half of the year spent too little time fleshing out the behind-the-scenes political debate raging inside the White House. Her disjointed "High Court Eases Rules on Prisons," 1-16, makes a feeble attempt to say that the Court's decision to make "it easier for state and local officials to challenge court settlements" regarding prisons could infringe on prisoners' rights. On the other hand, she cleverly personalizes a legal conundrum in "Justices Weigh Louisiana's Criminal Sanity Law," 2-24, questioning whether a cured criminally insane man named Terry Foucha should be released, and leading us to ponder the subtleties of the issues before the Court. Covering one of the most watched legal battles of the year in "High Court at Abortion Juncture," 4-23, Marcus gives us a lengthy, faithful recounting of the Court's review of the Pennsylvania abortion ruling, but her report isn't nearly as compelling or perceptive as those filed by her counterparts at other papers, especially Linda Greenhouse of *The New York Times*. Following the campaign with fellow writer Edward Walsh for "Candidates Court Perot Supporters," 7-18, we get little more than a perfunctory recounting of the latest presidential campaign stump speeches. Back to the sensitive abortion issue in "Despite Shifts, Bush and Clinton at Sharp Odds on Rights, Limits," 8-16, Marcus takes a fairly balanced, but one-dimensional look at each candidate's stance. And Marcus does little to add to a recent news conference in "Clinton, Hill Leaders Hail New Teamwork," 11-17.

Michael Massing
Columbia Journalism Review
★★½

Contributing editor. As always, we sought out Massing's work in a broad array of publications this year. Having spent the year working on a book about the politics of the drug war, his articles on this subject were quite in-depth. Overall, though, Massing's offerings were not as provocative as in years past. In "What Ever Happened to the 'War on Drugs'?" *The New York Review of Books* 6-11, Massing explicates the current causes of, and government reaction to, drug use, giving us a sturdy sense of the problems, but leaving us with only a sketchy feel for solutions. He comes up with a solution for "The New Mafia," *TNYRB* 12-3, asserting that legalization of drugs would help curtail the drug trade, but he doesn't assess the lessons of other countries, such as Holland, that have legalized with mixed success. On the election, Massing's liberal leanings occasionally surfaced but, all in all, he offered insightful observations. He makes a very good connection between the media horde scrambling to cover

Clinton's supposed extramarital affairs and the necessity to get "nonconformist news and information..." in "With Clinton, Pack Journalism Strikes Again," *Newsday* 2-2. Massing's "Lending Weight to the Great Debates," *CJR* 7/8-92, is an interesting exercise, in which the author scripts detailed questions for the presidential candidates. His review of *The Tragedy of American Compassion*, by Marvin Olasky in *The Washington Monthly*, 9-92, displays his political leanings more than the strengths and weaknesses of the book. He mocks Olasky's conservative viewpoints, such as his distinction between "deserving" and "undeserving" poor, but his own arguments are little more than liberal boilerplate: "In today's America, though, the distinction is completely meaningless."

Jay Mathews
Newsweek
The Washington Post
★★★

New York. Mathews didn't miss a beat as he moved from the Golden Gate to the Empire State and took on added responsibility. Not only does he cover the Big Apple for *The Washington Post*, but he now watches it for the Washington Post Co.'s *Newsweek*, as well. Despite the heavy workload, he continues to burnish his own evocative brand of feature writing. We are struck, once again, by his near perfect balance of witty wordplay and heavyweight reportage. Giving us a view of his own life in "Transplanted Californian Finds There's No Cutting Corners in Manhattan," *WP* 2-26, Mathews wittily details the automotive withdrawals he has in going from one coast to another. In "Tall Tales & Presidential Timber," *WP* 3-8, he takes a tongue-in-cheek view of height's role in presidential elections. The author notes from his 5-foot 6-inch perch that, at 3-to-1 odds, the taller candidate is elected. Mathews offered a slightly different vantage point in his coverage following the L.A. riots. His "Playing Politics With Crime," *Newsweek* 5-11, notes that in Simi Valley where the King trial took place, "voting records show that the area differs little from other California suburbs, with residents who see police as a bulwark against chaos and crime." In "The Disabled Fight to Raise Their Children," *WP* 8-18, he paints a refreshingly balanced picture of a disabled couple fighting for the right to their child. It is a very well-researched report which is careful not to portray the state as villain, or the parents as saints. Mathews's "Consumer Confidence, Goods Orders Rise," *WP* 11-25, delivers an informative report on growing economic optimism after the Clinton victory: "A delayed cheer for Bill Clinton's victory rippled through the economy like a wave at a football stadium today, creating a surge in consumer confidence and giving a boost to the stock market." Though we may not fully understand "digital compression, high-definition, interactive and programming-on-demand television," Mathews's "Bethesda Firm Offers Cure for Cable Crush," *WP* 12-12, is still an interesting read on the emergence of 540-channel cable TV.

William McGurn
National Review
★★

We have the same complaint with McGurn that we had last year: his conservative bias drives rather than shapes his reporting. Yet, with the Republicans in turmoil this election year, McGurn's analysis of the party's problems was still worthwhile reading. His "Yankees Go Home," *The American Spectator* 1-92, is a patronizing report from Manila on the decision to close Clark Air Field and Subic Bay Naval Base. McGurn blames the decision on the "Jesse Jacksons" in the Philippine Senate who, he argues, are not representative of the entire country. His "Pat Buchanan and the Intellectuals," 2-17, is a revealing report on the John Randolph Club, which McGurn sees as the intellectual underpinning of the effort to take back the conservative movement from such moderates as Bill Buckley and Ronald Reagan. Though he is too partisan in "Rubber Congressmen," 4-13, he still offers an effective rebuke of those involved in the House bank check-kiting scandal by suggesting more productive uses for the wasted funds. He does his homework in "Throwing Stones," 5-11, investigating Ann Stone, who heads the Republicans for Choice and seems to profit handsomely from the organization's direct mail operation. Cutting through the glitz at the Democratic National Convention, to reveal what he considers a hypocrisy, McGurn bangs out a cutting critique, "The Democrats' Albatross," 8-3. He nails the pro-choice Democrats, especially party chairman Ron Brown, for not allowing pro-life Pennsylvania Governor Casey to speak. In his post-election "He Was Warned," 11-30, McGurn gave us one of the best summations we saw of Bush's political life: "...throughout his entire career George Bush has defined himself by what he was not: in this election he was not Bill Clinton; in the primaries he was not Pat Buchanan; in 1988 he was not Michael Dukakis;... he was not going to be Ronald Reagan II. And he was as good as his word."

Timothy J. McNulty
Chicago Tribune
★★½

White House. McNulty's four years at this post served him well as he followed the President on the campaign trail this year, his well-constructed and detailed reports displaying a confidence and objectivity we admired. He provides an accurate snapshot of Bush's trip to the Pacific Rim in "Bush Treks Foreign Roads Thinking Main St., U.S.A." 1-1: "Challenged by those on both his political right and left to focus more on the home front, Bush is trying to shape each speech and media event to appeal to America's domestic economy." Out on the primary campaign trail with the President, McNulty serves a detailed and highly-readable report on Bush's attempts to define himself against challenger Pat Buchanan in "Bush Campaign Offensive Is Sputtering," 3-5. With the advent of a third candidate into the presidential race, McNulty pens a fluid report on the mire in which the Bush campaign finds itself, in "Perot Forces Bush Team to Recalculate," 5-28: "Officials complain privately about each other's performance, and Bush's personal friends say he is getting conflicting and misguided advice." In "Bush Seeks Counterpunch," 7-22, he sees the President sinking even further as the "out-of-touch" moniker gains credence: "Bush lamented the country's anemic economic growth but told his Catholic audience: 'In my view, we are poised for a good recovery.'" His "Iraq Vows to Resist Order to Yield Southern Skies," 8-27, is a well-constructed piece on Bush's orders that allied warplanes "seize the skies over southern Iraq..." McNulty doesn't quite define the man and his presidency, in "Bush: Global Traveler Runs Aground at Home," 10-18, but this is a balanced report weighing Bush's résumé for the last four years. The article's breadth is impressive. He admirably catches the subtleties in Bush's actions, reviewing the last few days of the campaign as it begins to register that Bush will not win, in "Upbeat Bush Ends Race With Grace," 11-4.

Michel McQueen
The Wall Street Journal
★

The *Journal*'s White House correspondent left for ABC News just after the election. Distressed to see an abundance of multiple bylines in her portfolio early in the year, we didn't get a real sense of McQueen's work until the summer. Occasionally, she engages us, but all too often we find her reporting light, her analysis insubstantial. Perhaps she'll fare better on the airwaves than she did in print. Joined by co-writer Alan Murray for "Bad Trip: After Much Ballyhoo, Bush's Visit to Asia Appears to Fall Short," 1-9, the pair accurately assesses the President's trip to Japan, though there are numerous trivial asides that distract: "In Tokyo, he even played tennis with the emperor and the crown prince. He lost." In another shared byline, this time with James M. Perry, we get a well-drafted overview of the presidential race in "Bush Prevails, but Buchanan Makes Inroads," 3-4. Though not in-depth, the pair does capture the volatile nature of the campaign after the Georgia primary. McQueen doubles up for yet another report, "Clinton and Bush Stress Initiatives to Foster Traditional Family Values," co-written by John Harwood 5-22. This examination of the candidates doesn't rise above the perfunctory, recounting snippets of speeches by both campaigners in a lackluster manner. Her "Blacks at the Convention Are Divided About How Strongly to Back Clinton," 7-15, succeeds, to an extent, in crystallizing Clinton's relationship with black constituents through the eyes of two black men at the convention who view the candidate's position differently. In one of her best pieces of the year, McQueen uses the record of the first Bush term to blueprint what a second term might be like in the useful "Familiar Agenda: A Bush Second Term Would Probably Keep Foreign-Policy Focus," 8-19. Again looking into George Bush's future in "The Personal President," 9-21, McQueen focuses on the President's governing style and character traits, a story we'd seen many times.

John Merline
Investor's Business Daily
★★★

National issues, Washington. Merline impresses us with seasoned analysis and straightforward reportage. We get a whiff of conservative bias here and there, but his fact-gathering skills create a tapestry of information that is sure to intellectually engage readers of diverse ideologies. He presents a highly informative assessment of the International Monetary Fund in "IMF: A Banker to Basket Cases?" 4-30, in which he dissects the Fund's economic strategies and casts aspersions on its success rate. In "Time to Try Enterprise Zones," 5-28, he shows us, through numerous impressive examples, how such zones have helped small businesses create jobs in the nation's inner cities. Providing us with a well-constructed and balanced assessment of Bill Clinton's economic philosophy in "Clinton Economic Plan Gets Mixed Reviews," 6-23, we get a useful compilation of liberal and conservative economists' reactions and opinions. He's joined by co-writer Thomas McArdle for "Should Business Fear Clinton?" 7-16, a 10 Best selection that provides a serious, non-partisan and highly-informative analysis of the candidate's economic policies. Also powerful is his "The Forgotten Public at Large," 9-3, an unbiased eye-opener chock full of statistics and examples of how Americans' tax dollars are increasingly being spent on a minority of interest groups rather than the public at large. Merline challenges Bill Clinton's economic initiatives in "Clinton's Public 'Investments,'" 10-7, offering a level-headed assessment which provides evidence that contradicts Clinton's belief that increased public investments guarantees increased economic growth. He again plays the devil's advocate for Clinton's promised economic reforms in "Kick-Starting the Job Machine," 12-9. This sobering look at initiatives, such as regulations and increased spending on worker training, examines how they may hurt rather than help.

J. Jennings Moss
The Washington Times
★½

Congress. Moss's apparent inability to delve beneath the surface of an issue mars his otherwise respectable fact-gathering skills. His most prominent work this year dealt with the scandal-plagued Congress. Joined by Paul M. Rodriguez for "Grand Jury Looking Closely at Mrs. Foley," 3-26, the duo offers a worthwhile update on the House Post Office investigation, but this is really Rodriguez's story, as he filed the initial scoop on the Post Office intrigues and Heather Foley. Moss's brief "Democrats Buck Foley, Give In on Records," 4-30, continues to investigate the troubles on the Hill, this time on the debate to release Congressional bank records for criminal wrongdoing. He doesn't provide any prescient information or inside scuttlebutt in "'Jury Out' on How Defiance Will Affect Foley's Standing," 5-1, gathering reactions after Speaker Foley's weak attempt to fight a subpoena. From the campaign trail, Moss files "Clinton Chides Bush on Trust," 7-30, adding little to a recent Clinton speech deriding Bush for breaking his "no new taxes" pledge. Moss isn't able to expand upon Jesse Jackson and Bill Clinton's shaky relationship in "Jackson Shares Spotlight With Uneasy Clinton," 9-13. The article recounts an event the two attended to encourage voter registration, but little else. Also tepid was his report on the presidential debate, "'Oprah'-Style Debate Fails to Heat Up," 10-16. His lack of analysis here contributes to the mechanical he-said/she-said feel of the piece. In "House Likely to Gain More Than 120 New Faces," 11-4, he pens a fairly knowledgeable article on post-election victories and surprises on the Hill. Moss even manages a little flair in this well-researched piece: "House incumbents, once regarded as an endangered species, last night clung to early results..."

Frank J. Murray
The Washington Times
★

White House. Murray seemed trapped in the same malaise that, according to critics, permeated the White House this election year. While his dutiful fact-gathering was adequate, his pieces were usually devoid of insight or analysis, and rarely advanced our understanding of the players or the issues. His "Being There Is Biggest Perk," 3-31, is a no-show, with Murray merely recounting the benefits the President enjoys, such as "[Standing] in the Rose Garden with college football heroes, as Mr. Bush did last week." He also adds little to the President's speech on Congressional term limits in "Bush Asks Hill to Reform..." 4-4, injecting only one interesting aside: "Although Mr. Bush did not mention it, his White House staff rebelled last week against efforts by Congressional committees to investigate spending for entertainment, travel and staff at the presidential mansion." Joined by co-writer J. Jennings Moss for "Bush Compromises, Urban Aid Bill Passes," 6-19, the pair takes an uneven look at the recently approved aid bill for L.A. and Chicago. Murray does a credible job of outlining Bush's domestic policy proposals for a second term, including job training and spending cuts, in "Training Tops Bush Wish List," 8-25. While the article lacks indepth analysis, it stands as a convenient guidepost to Bush's political direction. Aboard the campaign train for "Bush Rides the Rails Through Rural Ohio," 9-27, Murray offers a brief report on the President's daily activities that gives us about the same amount of information as TV news sound-bites, without the colorful visuals. Tracking the President the night before the election in "Bush Says His Last Hurrah in Houston," 11-3, Murray effectively captures the bittersweet irony of Bush's remark that having finished his last campaign for the nation's highest office, this would be his last campaign speech.

Salim Muwakkil
In These Times
★★

Senior editor. Perfectly suited for this perceptive socialist tabloid, Muwakkil probes the underbelly of America's ethnic unease, but in a year in which festering racial tensions boiled over, he has not yet fully realized the promise we noted in his work last year. Voicing the black community's concerns in "With Jackson Out, Black Vote Uncertain," 2-19/25, Muwakkil gathers numerous credible sources to strengthen his argument that this large voting bloc is being ignored, due to Governor Wilder's departure from the race. Addressing the racial unrest following the L.A. riots with an examination of Chicago's poor blacks, "L.A. Lessons Go Unlearned as Despair Deepens in Nation's Ghetto," 5/27–6/9, Muwakkil attempts to use the poignant tale of an inner city drug dealer, "Slick," to capture the essence of the nation's woes. He ponders whether the hopes of black America will play a role in the new president's agenda in "Keeping Clinton's Feet to the Fire," 11-30: "For the first time in 12 long years, the Democrats will occupy the executive seat of power and set the political tone for the country. Let the fight begin." In "Can African-Americans Co-Opt the Blackest Insult?" 7-8/21, he takes on a virtually taboo question in the press—can the African-American community take back the racist term "nigga" in hip-hop vernacular? His answer is strangely muted, but his enunciation of the issue resonates. He's even more courageous in "Visible Man," 9-2/15, a provocative analysis of black scholar Henry Louis Gates, Jr.'s accusations in a *New York Times* article of creeping anti-Semitism in the black community. Muwakkil explains that Gates feels "that black intellectuals should more aggressively challenge the isolationists' arguments. By shunning confrontation with 'demagogues and pseudo-scholars,' Gates argued, responsible black theorists have allowed the debate to degenerate into the murky realms of genetic culpability and other forms of racist essentialism." This is the type of cutting-edge analysis we expect from the talented Muwakkil.

Seth Mydans
The New York Times

Los Angeles. A main player in the *Times* coverage of the Rodney King verdict and subsequent riots, Mydans conveyed many a powerful anecdotal tale of disillusionment after the violence. But he never fully articulated the forces that shaped the uprising or sufficiently explore the aftershocks that reverberated across the country's political landscape. Well before the riots, his front-page feature "Seeking Shelter in U.S. After the Soviet Storm," 1-25, chronicles numerous Russians taking up residence in the U.S. The overabundance of quotes and loose framework make the story disjointed and long-winded. Mydans presents a fairly straightforward report on the end of the Rodney King beating trial in "Los Angeles Policemen Acquitted in Taped Beating," 4-30, yet one of Mydan's observations seems out of place here: "In what seemed an effort to desensitize the jury to the violence, defense lawyers sometimes paced back and forth swinging a heavy metal police baton." In "Koreans Rethink Life in Los Angeles," 6-21, Mydans airs the feelings of betrayals among members of the Korean population who had participated in interracial activities before the violence. His "Quake Spares Buildings but Undermines Denials," 7-1, is one woman's take on the many problems of L.A., and how they have forced her to move back to Boston. He effectively captures the continuing tensions after the riots, as angry unemployed black construction workers watch their white counterparts land clean-up jobs, in "Blacks Complaining of Neglect as Los Angeles Is Rebuilt," 8-30. Confusing in "Friends Back Suspect in Beating of Trucker," 9-9, he allows one suspect's mother to lambaste the LAPD, even though her son was among the four blacks captured on-camera beating a white truck driver nearly to death. His special report "Separateness Grows in a Scarred Los Angeles," 11-15, thoroughly discusses the fact that half a year after the riots "Los Angeles seems to be a city coming apart rather than coming together."

Sonia L. Nazario
The Wall Street Journal

Social issues, health care and education. As we noted last year, her wide array of assignments tends to stretch her respectable talents, a limitation she overcomes with a vivid writing style that brings to life the hard-hitting social issues she covers. Though the work we assess here is from the *Journal*, Nazario moved to the *Los Angeles Times* at the beginning of 1993. Nazario graphically recounts the harrowing life of homeless children and their "grotesquely modern kind of family" in "Troubled Teen-Agers Create a Fragile Family Beneath a Busy Street," 1-21: "In return for his affection and discipline, the Trolls [30 or so teenagers] support Pops [the elder leader]—and themselves —by panhandling, prostitution and mugging." In "Schools Teach the Virtues of Virginity," 2-20, Nazario gets a good reading of sex education classes, bringing a level eye to the issue that pits supporters of explicit classes on AIDS prevention against those who favor a curriculum that favors abstinence. "Once again, this city has awakened to a nightmare," begins Nazario and co-writer Frederick Rose's powerful "Fury at Police Verdict Turns Los Angeles Into Scene of Mayhem," 5-1, a shocking portrait of the volcanic frustration that erupted into the anarchy that was the L.A. riots. Her "Church and State: Crusader Vows to Put God Back Into Schools Using Local Elections," 7-15, is a timely and valuable bio of Robert Simonds and his ultra-religious movement, the Citizens for Excellence in Education. The subject, and his extremist vision, are handled with appropriate professional detachment. Nazario poignantly brings to life the travails of the California school system and its disillusioned students in "Funding Cuts Take a Toll at University," 10-5. Her "National Medical to Sell Big Stake in Its U.K. Unit," 11-12, is a dry skim of the facts surrounding a public offering of "a U.K. chain of long-term care facilities."

Jack Nelson
Los Angeles Times
★½

Washington bureau chief. Nelson certainly made an attempt to be a player in election-year coverage, but he was only moderately successful. His best dispatches develop when he actually burns some shoe leather. Too often though, he just calls various analysts or relies on inside-the-Beltway players to fashion dispatches. Rather than compile information on the Buchanan candidacy and assess it independently for, "Buchanan's Real Threat to Bush Could Come on Election Day," 2-20, Nelson consults with all the standard talking heads—Kevin Phillips, Ed Rollins, and so forth—allowing *them* to evaluate Buchanan's threat to Bush. Similarly, he only offers views from unnamed "analysts" to round up the primary results on the GOP side in "Bush Gets Bittersweet Victories in Key Races," 3-4. A cub reporter could have made the phone calls to pen this dispatch. We know this 17-year Washington veteran has the potential to do better. Nelson delineates the players on each side in his useful insider look "Bush Reaction to Riots Splits Republicans," 5-8, but there's little holding this together, as we don't find out what a party schism might mean for Bush or the GOP. His most evocative dispatches emanated from the excitement of the convention floor. We can almost hear the cheering in the detail-laden "Democrats Nominate Clinton as 'New Voice for a New America,'" 7-16, as the Democrats nominate Bill Clinton for president. His "Bush, Quayle Renominated; President Lauded as a Battler," 8-20, is not quite as rousing, but is replete with relevant information. Post election, Nelson provides a serviceable report on what lies ahead for the President-elect, in "Clinton Plans Diverse Staff, New Jobs Package," 11-5.

Timothy Noah
The Wall Street Journal
★½

Housing, urban affairs and civil rights. While Noah's work is often worthwhile, it is rarely noteworthy. He's a who, what, when, where, reporter who often forgets the why and how of a story. In a year in which his beat became the center of a national debate following the L.A. riots, his ho-hum approach just didn't satisfy. He isn't able to enliven "Bush Pressured to Deepen Cut in Gains Taxes," 1-22, on conservative Republicans' attempts to influence the President on tax-cutting measures. Noah's style here is wooden, lacking panache and insight. He does deliver an eye-opening report, albeit on an old topic, the overcrowding of prisons, in "Prison Population Boom Sputters to Halt as States Lack Funds to House Criminals," 2-3: "...0.3% of the national population is behind bars, an incarceration rate that exceeds that of all other Western democracies." Showing more enthusiasm than usual for "What Do Ross Perot and the '29 LeMans Have in Common?" 4-30, Noah explores the entrepreneurial sector's support for a Perot presidency. We fail to get a balanced picture of Al Gore in "Gentleman Al Gore Shows a Knack for Fisticuffs, Taking Combative Stances in Democrats' Corner," 8-11. Instead, we're served a highly flattering tribute to the Democratic Veep candidate, with Noah barely touching on his more controversial stances on issues such as the environment. His "Term-Limit Measures Appear on Ballots in 14 States, but the Tax Front Is 'Quiet,'" 10-30, is a worthwhile wrap-up just before the election of the "mixed bag" of referenda voters face across the country: "Although no Proposition 13-style tax revolt has spread coast to coast, a few strong tax-limitation proposals did make it onto state ballots." Noah's haphazard "Clinton Aides Call for Boost in Gasoline Tax," 12-9, fails to satisfy in its exploration of certain appointees' calls for a gas and carbon tax.

Martin F. Nolan
The Boston Globe
★

National politics. Nolan's peculiar take on the political campaign earned him high marks for originality, but his witty reporting style quite often degenerates into partisan sarcasm. While this might fly on the op-ed page, it is unsuitable for the news pages. In "The Winner Keeps on Coming, the Party Keeps on Wondering," 4-8, he goes overboard in portraying Clinton's primary win in New York: "Clinton's winningugly triumph in the mean streets of New York evokes Poe's story, 'The Tell-Tale Heart.'" He allows the New York Governor an abundant amount of column space to proselytize in "Cuomo Says He's 'Nervous' About Nominating Speech," 7-13, a sloppy piece of journalism in which Nolan lost control of his own work. His "Abortion Ban Part of Platform Far to the Right," 8-18, is a remarkably biased and negative view of the Republican party platform. He harped extensively on the abortion issue, and said that "on more secular issues, the party avoids the president's 1988 pledge of 'Read my lips: no new taxes,' leaving it to Bush's Thursday night acceptance speech for possible reconsideration." He gets very close to psychoanalyzing Jerry Brown in "Brown's 2 Images: Prophet and Flake," 1-21, delivering a revealing look at the man and the presidential candidate through his history and current political objectives. He reduces much of the banter at one of the presidential primary debates to a he-said/she-said formula, failing to properly analyze the individual candidates' ideas, in "Memo to Spin Doctors, Little Change in Patients," 10-20. Nolan's knee-jerk boxing of the responses, as either winner or loser, grated when we were trying to view the debate as a whole. Also disjointed was his "Tide Shakes the Pillars of 2-Party System," 11-5, which intersperses historical trivia (" . . . the president-elect is from the smallest state since 1852 . . . ") with punchy one-liners: "If high voter turnout and partisan enthusiasm mean anything, the American electorate anticipates milk and honey out of both faucets."

Ronald J. Ostrow
Los Angeles Times
★½

Justice Department, FBI. An inconsistent reporter, Ostrow showed little of the enthusiasm that gave his material life last year, often failing to dig deeper than the report or indictment issued. He seemed lost in the legal, political and bureaucratic complexities that characterize this beat. It was difficult to follow his dissection of the federal bureaucracy in "Delay in Lifting Pot Ban to Aid Seriously Ill Is Assailed," 1-31, as doctors try to counteract the ill effects of chemotherapy with marijuana. While he informs as to how medical practitioners work the system to their advantage in "U.S. Targets Fraud in Health Care," 2-3, Ostrow is content to merely cite the report outlining the trend. He trimly describes the different agencies involved in Justice's review of police brutality in "Lawmaker Urges Release of Police Brutality Study," 3-4, but we find few new insights here. He gets a bit beneath the surface in "Bush Offered to Help With Arms Deal, Ex-Official Said," 9-26, probing the allegations of Howard Teicher, a "Middle East expert for the NSC during the Ronald Reagan Administration," who claims to have briefed Bush on the arms-for-hostages scheme and alleged "that Bush offered to get the stalled proposal moving again." Though detailed, Ostrow provides too little in the way of corroboration. We find some hard-core reporting as he and Douglas Franz uncover evidence that someone erased vital sentences in reports that would have tipped off the government to the fact that the U.S. was supplying sensitive technology to Saddam Hussein in "Iraqi Arms Sales Files Were Altered," 6-21.

James M. Perry
The Wall Street Journal
★★½

Washington. We're gaining new respect for this veteran reporter's work, and though partisan Beltway pressures occasionally influence Perry's perspectives, we are impressed by his ability to get to the heart of an issue. He's one of the slicker writers in the business, with an eye for both the unusual, the colorful and the ironic. Even his '88 campaign piece, "IMAGE PROBLEM: Bush Convention Task Will Be to Overcome Negative Perceptions," 8-15-88, which we criticized as a "stream of anti-Bush cliches," warranted a re-evaluation this election year as Bush once again fought the same battle. Writing with David Shribman for "Five Democrats Clash in Debate on Television," 1-20, the two give us a snapshot of the first debate of the campaign, but fail to fill in the picture with the detail and analysis we're used to from these veterans. After Clinton's New York primary win, Perry scripts possible strategies for the presidential contender's campaign to attract the necessary amount of delegates for the Democratic nomination in a thorough and well-sourced "Clinton Regains Footing, Wins Three Primaries," 4-8. He's too quick to generalize about the electorate's reaction to Ross Perot in "Meet Perot's Fans: They Crave Change, Not Specific Proposals," 6-17. While he effectively taps into the rage that drives the voter exodus from establishment candidates to the independent from Texas, we're not sure he proves that voters expect nothing specific from Perot. Perry presents a sophisticated analysis of what the Perot experiment might portend for the two-party system in "Win or Lose, Perot Proves One Can Run Without Major Parties," 7-14. By focusing on one state in "With Even Louisiana in Reach, Democrats Look to Break Republican Electoral Lock in the South," 10-6, Perry ably accentuates the indecision embracing an electorate that is questioning its traditional political allegiances. He pens an engrossing look at a worst-case scenario for Democrats who could lose seats in the Senate due to Clinton appointments, in "Partisan Arithmetic in the Senate Adds Up to Say Clinton Can't Afford to Subtract More Democrats," 12-10.

Art Pine
Los Angeles Times
★★

Congress. With more than 25 years experience in D.C., Pine knows where to find the Beltway's pulse. He has a sharp eye and a straightforward pen. But, Pine's respectable talents are often spread too thin, forcing him to skim issues he would otherwise cover in depth. His "U.S. to Stop Production of H-Bombs," 1-26, adequately outlines the history and implications of Bush's decision to halt production "of the W-88 hydrogen warhead, the last nuclear bomb the United States has in production..." Reminiscent of his strong work on the economic beat, Pine does a fine job of crystallizing the partisan fight over a Democratic tax initiative in "Tax Plan Barely Passes in House," 2-28: "The two sides are in a contest to see which will be able to use the tax-cut issue most effectively during the election campaign." His equally sturdy follow-up, "Bush Kills Democratic Tax-Cutting Measure," 3-21, outlines the President's reasons for a veto, and captures the partisan bickering that followed. Unfortunately, he provides little more than a blurb on Democratic presidential contender Jerry Brown's attacks on Clinton and Bush in "Clinton Votes Will Doom Democrats, Brown Charges," 4-25. The story had potential, but wasn't adequately developed. Joined by fellow writer David G. Savage for "Defense Can't Exclude Jurors Based on Race," 6-19, the pair properly defines the Supreme Court ruling, but doesn't adequately juxtapose the opposing arguments. A little more background would have fleshed out "Concessions Open Door in China to U.S. Exports," 10-11, an otherwise satisfying, point-by-point breakdown of the concessions. Joined by co-writer James Gerstenzang, the duo sketches an admirable portrait of U.S. objectives as President Bush announces the relief efforts for Somalia in "Bush Sending Troops to Help Somalia's Hungry Millions," 12-5.

Joyce Price
The Washington Times
★½

General assignment. Price seemed to be in a funk this year. Her articles remain compact and well organized, but she rarely fleshes out the events and poll data she covers. For instance, she does little to enhance the plethora of poll data in "Economy Ranks 1st With Women Among Worries, Abortion Is 6th," 9-4. "Trend Developing as Four States Vote Term Limits," 11-4, suffers the same fate. Here, she dutifully recounts the various state ballot initiatives, but fails to probe their implications. She paints a very brief, but informative picture of potential Democratic presidential candidate Lloyd Bentsen in "Bentsen Proved His Bonafides in 1988," 1-16: "One of the most overused adjectives to describe him has been 'patrician.' Other terms used to describe him: 'conciliatory,' 'reserved,' 'well-liked,' and 'powerful.'" Her "NEA Grant Rejection Hit From 2 Sides," 2-5, is limp on why chairman John Frohnmayer rejected two grants, though the NEA artist panel approved both of them. In "Leak Prober Seeks to Lean on Reporters," 3-25, Price fails to fully capture the frustration of the "special Senate counsel probing news leaks" as it threatened to subpoena reporters in order to compel them to reveal their sources. She provides an interesting story from the Rio Earth Summit in "Members, Wives Fly to Rio on the Cheap," 6-11, uncovering the expenditures the taxpayers footed for ten spouses of members of Congress to fly to the summit. Her cursory "Sergeant Charged in Sex Case as Military Scandals Unfold," 7-4, doesn't adequately fill in the details on allegations of rape made by a female soldier who served in the Gulf War.

Robert Reinhold
The New York Times
★★★

Los Angeles bureau chief. With the framework of California's fiscal and social structure shaken to the core, Reinhold once again has proven himself a sharp-eyed chronicler of the Golden State's contentious legislative debates. He knows the ins and outs of Sacramento's corridors of power, providing his East Coast audience with an insider's view of the state's political wrangling. In "Does 'Buy American' Mean Buying Trouble?" 1-27, Reinhold pegs the ethnocentricity of the 'Buy American' sentiment that surfaced after Bush's trip to Japan. He provides an interesting read on Brock Adams, the Washington U.S. Senator accused of sexual misconduct, in "Women on Senator's Staff Shocked by Accusations," 3-4. Obeying the "innocent-until-proven-guilty" mantra that is often overlooked in press reports, Reinhold explores the women's rights record of the Senator and presents quotes from befuddled staff members, who testify to his innocence. Uncharacteristically one-sided for "Who Is Jerry Brown? Voices From Past Show Why the Man Is an Enigma," 4-2, he pens a particularly vicious compilation of quotes on the presidential candidate, with nary a positive word. He's much more balanced and thorough in detailing California Governor Pete Wilson's troubles in "The Curse of the Statehouse," *Magazine* 5-3.

Reinhold's sturdy grasp of the subject matter molds this perceptive piece on the once popular, but now politically beleaguered Governor. In "Budget Fight Goes On in California," 9-1, he squarely captures the exasperation felt by Wilson and the teachers' union, as they both look a legislative deadlock straight in the eye. From Honolulu, he offers an interesting take on "the only indigenous people in America still not recognized by the Federal Government" in "A Century After Queen's Overthrow, Talk of Sovereignty Shakes Hawaii," 11-8. Though the information here is neither pressing nor explosive, it offers a peep into the ever-changing kaleidoscope of Americana.

Paul Richter
Los Angeles Times
★★

Washington. Richter switches from a business to political focus, showing a real knack for portraiture in his first try at this new beat. The political arena also gives him more of an opportunity to showcase his lively writing style. We're drawn in by the lead in "'St. Paul' Against the Odds," 2-20, an informative and timely profile of Paul Tsongas: "Nature didn't give him a pretty face or a stirring voice, but in 24 years of long-shot races Paul E. Tsongas has had one thing every politician needs: Luck." He then goes on to examine the combination of luck and determination that has led Tsongas to the presidential race. He delivers another satisfying political profile of the Vice President in "Quayle Tries to Shore Up Support, Build New Image," 8-18, a keen assessment of Quayle's endeavors to rally the troops round the ticket in the wake of a dump-Quayle movement and a post-convention Clinton surge. He makes a conscientious attempt to reassess Perot's sudden July withdrawal after the Texan's October accusation of GOP "dirty tricks" in "Perot Plays Hunches With Mixed Results," 10-30: "The billionaire Texan, they say, is a man who has forever ignored others' advice to follow his gut feelings—often to glory, sometimes to disaster. And he is a man who is always eager to convince the world—and perhaps himself—that he is following the best motives as he struggles in a glorious and dangerous cause." Early in the campaign, he and Virginia Ellis offer a close examination of Perot's 1980 EDS-Bradford National Corp. fight over the contract for Texas Medicaid, in "Contract Battle Showed Perot's Skill at Hardball," 5-25, but the team fails to directly relate this event to Perot's potential performance if elected President. Richter sufficiently chronicles Clinton's post-election excursion to California in the mildly entertaining, "Clinton, in Southland, Hangs Out at the Mall," 11-28.

Steven V. Roberts
U.S. News & World Report
★½

Senior writer. Not surprisingly, this former *New York Times* White House correspondent was assigned to the big-think beat this election year, away from the daily grind of the presidential campaign. If he broke away from his reliance on polls and press releases however, his analysis would be much more provocative. Despite heavy dependence on poll data, he is able to detail how the New Hampshire primary is distinguishing each of the candidates in "A Time of Fury and Despair," 2-17. Roberts ponders the much-discussed question of how much is too much in the media examination of a candidate's private life in "Defusing the Bombshell," 2-3. While we get a trim summation of Clinton's line of defense against Gennifer Flowers's accusations of infidelity, Roberts fails to truly scrutinize media accountability in this matter. With "Will 1992 Be the Year of the Woman?" 4-27, Roberts never progresses beyond pitting politicians against each other solely based on their gender. The issue is almost moot in this disappointing effort, and again, he crafts much of his analysis around various polls on how voters feel about female candidates in general. Roberts gets bonus points for his attempt to define swing voters, which he calls the "Squashed Generation," in "Anxious Swing Voters," 6-8: "It is better educated, more mobile, more securely middle class—and less loyal to a political party." He keeps his eye on these jittery, undecided voters as the election draws nearer in "The Moody Swings of Anxious Voters," 8-24. Though he cites the inevitable poll stats, Roberts describes the collapsing Reagan coalition well, and gives a balanced view of the electorate's apprehensiveness. Post-election, Roberts draws up a laundry list of political priorities that liberals are likely to push in "A Little Self-Restraint," 11-23, but he never moves beyond the obvious: "How Clinton performs in these early battles will provide important clues to his presidential character."

Paul M. Rodriguez
The Washington Times
★★½

Investigative, Congress. Rodriguez's tenacity proves profitable this year as he digs up and navigates through the muck and mire of Congressional scandals. His investigative work on the behind-the-scenes finagling at the House post office sped, if not triggered, the resignation of its Postmaster, Robert Rota. "Cocaine Sales in House Probed," 2-3, is *the* scoop on the initial travail befalling the House post office, and leads to his uncovering more suspect transactions in "Postmaster Accuses Mrs. Foley," 2-7. Here, Rodriguez dredges up heretofore unuttered whispers that Speaker Thomas Foley's wife, Heather, is one of the most powerful backstage players in the House. The article purports that Postmaster Rota accuses her of sidetracking a previous investigation of the House post office. Rodriguez's "Checking Scandal Spreads to Post Office," 3-19, was rumored to have caused the sacking of Rota by Speaker Thomas Foley the next day. The article details the illegal check cashing done by congressmen at the House post office. His commendable "GAO: Skies Friendly for Air Congress," 4-9, covers all the bases on the hefty bill inflicted on the taxpayer due to lavish Congressional travel. No one seemed to be digging as deep as Rodriguez, into Congressional perks this year. Rodriguez's "Democrats Seek Funds for 'Surprise,'" 10-2, briefly outlines a request by House Democrats for funds to more fully explore the accusation that the Reagan administration delayed the release of U.S. hostages from Iran. The article fails, though, to include Republican dissent to such a probe. He pens a judgmental article on liberties taken on Capitol Hill by D.C.'s "shadow" senator, Jesse Jackson, in "Jesse, Out of the 'Shadow,'" 12-3. The piece is hampered by its numerous unnamed sources who comment that Jackson "behaves as though his unofficial title carries the privileges afforded the official members from the 50 states..."

Larry Rohter
The New York Times
★★

Miami bureau chief. Finishing up his first complete year, in what proved to be the not-so-sunny Sunshine State, Rohter served as a reliable chronicler of Florida's troubles as its population battled Hurricane Andrew and weathered several social/political storms, such as the Haitian refugee crisis. We expect he'll be able to step back next year for those big picture stories that are so difficult to do when you're new to a beat. Usually balanced, he weighs in decidedly against forced repatriation in "Haven for Haitians Backed in Miami," 2-5, ignoring the many dimensions of the controversy. His "Arts and Leisure" interview of rock band U2, "A Chastened U2 Comes Down to Earth," 3-15, allows the multi-million-dollar Irish quartet ample room to expound on their social and political philosophies. On a more serious note, he tracks Gen. Manuel Noriega's trial with appropriate zeal, wrapping up with a comprehensive review of the three-year ordeal, in "U.S. Jury Convicts Noriega, Panama's Former Dictator, in Cocaine-Trafficking Case," 4-10. He covers another highly-charged court case just as commendably in "11-Year-Old Seeks Right to 'Divorce' Parents," 7-8. Rohter's methodical dissection of the positions of child-plaintiff Gregory K., and the numerous children's rights advocate groups on hand, made this a worthy report on a sensitive issue. His "Miami Cuban-Americans Accused of Resembling the Dictator They Loathe," 8-19, is a confusing presentation of dissension in Miami's Cuban community between anti-Castro organizations and those "who favor a softening of United States policies against Cuba." Rohter provided some of the best day-to-day coverage of events after Hurricane Andrew leveled parts of Florida. For example, in "As Army Gears Up, Floridians Rely on Private Relief," 8-30, he effectively captures the shock and emotion of the moment, the article's haphazard construction mirroring the chaos of the situation. His "A Hurricane's Longlasting Impact," 11-6, continues his reports from the ravaged Florida landscape. Though not as detailed as earlier dispatches, the article hits home with the long-term financial strain the hurricane has imposed.

David E. Rosenbaum
The New York Times
½★

Washington. There are reporters. There are commentators. And there is David Rosenbaum, the "reporter" who takes unprecedented poetic license with the term "news analysis" in his self-appointed role as economic policymaker. His flagrant promotion of what we call the "Rosenbaum Agenda" is an appalling abuse of his influential position at the *Times*. A perfect example is "Budget as Bush Campaign Manifesto," 1-30, a blatant work of anti-Bush propaganda in which Rosenbaum misses no opportunity to pervert the President's positions: "Mr. Bush relies in his budget proposals on fundamental Republican dogma... that low taxes for the wealthy lead to economic growth and therefore to jobs and prosperity for those less well off." Citing his favorite source, "many economists," in "Tsongas Is Quite Vague in Call for Self-Sacrifice," 2-24, he lambastes the Democratic presidential candidate's economic policies. Sure that there is no way to reduce the deficit without higher taxes (a supposition hotly debated between economic schools), Rosenbaum turns his own *theory* into *fact*, "reporting" that "...while [Tsongas] calls the large Federal budget deficit 'one of our most difficult and pressing problems,' he says he has no plans for an overall tax increase..." He's less lopsided in "Concern, Cash, but No Accord on Urban Woes," 5-10, conceding that solutions to inner-city problems are far from self-evident. In "Clinton and Tsongas Team Up to Keep Brown Issues Out of Play," 6-28, he fails to bring to life the behind-the-scenes horse trading over the Democratic Party platform, and he provides only a thumbnail sketch of what differentiates Clinton and Bush in "One Economy, 2 Visions," 8-23. Even here he slips in a distortion, asserting that "Mr. Bush believes that wealthy Americans are taxed too much." For "Bush's Double Bind," 9-11, Rosenbaum plays head critic, using vague generalizations and citations from "impartial economists" to make the President look confused: "...the President's basic goals...are often in conflict." Post election, he weighs in with "What Can Clinton Change, and When?" 11-8, but he doesn't press the President-elect on economic issues, saying Clinton's proposals will take time.

Thomas B. Rosenstiel
Los Angeles Times
★★

Media. Rosenstiel's fastidious evaluations were exceptionally informative in dissecting the complex relationship between the media and campaigns. He fails, though, to address the central question of how such interaction impacts the flow of information, and thereby, the vote. He precisely breaks down the story of Clinton's alleged affairs, in "Clinton Allegation Raises Questions on Media's Role," 1-29, giving us a clear sense of how the story unfolded. We get an exceptional inside look at how the media arrives at its political analysis in his entertaining "Primaries: a Cocktail Consensus," 2-18, describing vividly "the fragile game of setting expectations, then watching to see who exceeds or disappoints when the votes are counted. It is arrived at in barroom and street-corner colloquies among the press corps, the pollsters and campaign operatives who interpret what the results really meant, the voters' thoughts notwithstanding...." Dissecting Clinton ads in "Clinton Spots Aggressive, Misleading," 4-4, he offers a strong critique of the commercial attacking Jerry Brown. He also hits the nail on the head in "The Talk Is About New Media," 5-23, adding his two cents on the new synergy between the talk shows and the candidates. In both "Democrats Succeed in Getting Message Across," 7-17, and "In Politics, the Defense Never Rests," 8-7, he provides only a cursory view of how the increasingly savvy manipulation of the media by campaign strategists and candidates may cloud the meaning of the issues. He asks a perceptive question in "Did Gore or Quayle Win? It's Debatable," 10-15: "Who won the vice presidential debate Tuesday, or at least helped their side in the race for President? The answer depends on which media you rely on, as well as what criteria you care about."

Andrew Rosenthal
The New York Times

White House. With enough political acumen to cover the story but not the verve to write it, Rosenthal crept through the year in a malaise. He serviceably recounts the State of the Union address in "Bush Vows Economic Relief and Proposes Modest Steps in State of the Union Talk," 1-29, faithfully reviewing the main proposals. On the other hand, Rosenthal's "On Reflection, Bush and Clinton Have Likenesses," 3-24, is an interesting comparative piece, which reveals that both front-runners are apparent in their efforts to please everyone. His insubstantial human-interest piece "With Bloom Off, Bush Takes Time to Smell the Flowers,"

4-9, tells of Rosenthal's early morning walk among the cherry blossoms with the Bushes. Rosenthal catches the President casting out his fishing line at a media-op in "Bush Uses Fishing Demonstration to Speak About Urban Problems," 5-15. He sees only one side of the President's answer to the hypothetical question about his granddaughter wanting an abortion, in "Bush, Asked in Personal Context, Takes a Softer Stand on Abortion," 8-12, twisting Bush's response into a dubious cheerlead for pro-choicers. Dutifully tagging along with the President on the campaign trail, Rosenthal assiduously stresses the negative in "Bush Steps Up Attacks on Democrat's Character," 10-29: "Mr. Bush tried out a new closing line for his speech here, but was so excited that he could not seem to form the words."

Michael Ross
Los Angeles Times
★½

Capitol Hill. In his first full year on the political beat after some time abroad, Ross seems a bit undone by the rigors of the campaign season. While he crafts satisfactory snapshots, he rarely adds it all up to provide in-depth examinations of the big political picture. He simply hasn't found his footing on this beat yet. Ross takes the example of Jim Garrison, who runs the San Francisco-based relief effort Russian Winter Campaign, as a case in point for a pithy discussion, examining the difficulties of providing aid to the former Soviet Union in "Relief Agencies Swap Horror Stories on Aid," 1-23. Considering Special Counsel Malcolm R. Wilkey would not be interviewed, Ross makes the most of interim information in a solid roundup of the infighting between Wilkey and Rep. Tom Foley over the House bank records in "Call for House Bank Records Hints at Kiting," 4-28. He avoids the tough issues on the struggles in the House over the balanced-budget amendment with "Amendment: Tough Choice for Lawmakers," 6-12, only giving us anecdotal evidence of legislators' wrangling over the question. With "Dukakis Kept in Shadows as Party Tries to Forget Debate," 7-15, Ross offers an overview of how a nervous Democratic party is keeping Clinton away from his old friend, Michael Dukakis, to avoid linking them politically. With "Panel Grills Pentagon Over POWs," 8-5, he balances both sides of the aisle in a clear, detailed snapshot of the Senate committee hearing concerning allegations that POWs may have been left in Hanoi. Ross and co-writer William J. Eaton offer a sketchy portrait of how the new Congress may look after election day in "Mixed Expectations About Election's Impact on Capitol Hill," 10-23, a historical overview included in the article somewhat interesting, but there's little here we would actually consider newsworthy. He follows the Senate investigation into POWs, in such sturdy efforts as "POW Inquiry Ends, but Questions Don't," 12-5, dutifully reporting on the findings.

David G. Savage
Los Angeles Times
★

Supreme Court. After eking out a respectable '91, Savage is once again the least satisfying reporter on this beat in the major daily press. He shows an irritating tendency to divide the Court along ideological lines and views doings on the docket from a primarily political, rather than legal perspective. As the only Supreme Court reporter for the West Coast's premier daily, Savage must learn to better balance his dispatches between the questions of politics and those of law. Savage follows the pack in labeling Justice Clarence Thomas a hardline conservative jurist in "Thomas Shows Signs of Being a Hard-Liner," 1-18, employing Thomas's opinion on the use of witnesses and hearsay as an example. He includes little on the ruling upholding California's Proposition 140 in "State's Term Limit Initiative Upheld by U.S. High Court," 3-10, though he's thorough in outlining the state's battleground over term limits. He details well the particulars of *Jacobson v. U.S.* in "Sting Operation Limits Drawn by High Court," 4-7, but oversimplifies both the issues and players by dividing them ideologically. He draws comparable parameters for a broad discussion on abortion in "High Court Affirms

Right to Abortion but Allows Some Restrictions by States," 6-30, where he again lines up the justices according to what he feels are their ideological tendencies rather than their legal interpretations. We get little sense of the legalities over RU-486 in "Supreme Court Blocks Abortion Pill's Return," 7-18, though he does include a detailed review of the political infighting. In "Firms May Cut Ill Workers' Health Benefits, U.S. Argues," 10-17, he provides salient detail on a legal brief filed by the Justice Department which argues that "federal law permits employers to reduce insurance coverage sharply for workers with catastrophic diseases, such as AIDS or cancer." But he deals primarily with the political impact of the brief, not its legal implications. Savage adds little to our understanding of the important court ruling that struck down Guam's ban on abortion, in his cursory "Supreme Court Action Affirms Abortion Right," 12-1.

Jerry Seper
The Washington Times
★½

National desk. Seper moves from covering the Investigations and Justice Department beat to juggling an eclectic mix of topics that now pass through his PC at the national desk. Most of his work this year was solid and informative. His most noteworthy reports were on Bill Clinton's draft history, such as the eyebrow-raising and well-researched, "Clinton's ROTC Story Has Changed Since 1978," 9-4. He constructs another indicting review of Clinton's draft history in "Clinton Lied, Says ROTC Chief," 9-17, intelligently piecing together facts culled primarily from Lt. Col. Eugene Holmes's strongly-worded letter on the issue: "'I believe that he purposely deceived me, using the possibility of joining the ROTC as a ploy to work with the draft board to delay his induction and get a new draft classification,' Col Holmes said. 'These actions cause me to question both his patriotism and his integrity.'" He is appropriately skeptical of unsubstantiated election-year rumors being circulated by Rep. Steve Freind, Arlen Specter's Republican primary challenger, in "Specter Challenger Says Incumbent Has Mob Ties," 4-22, showing the type of professional restraint we respect. Seper goes sniffing for a scoop in "Justice: No Politics in King Investigation," 6-28, and lands a surprising, but unsubstantiated, quote with regard to a federal task force's investigation of the outcome of the Rodney King trial: "Defense attorneys and others suggested last week that the case had become a political liability and President Bush was pushing for indictments to help his re-election effort." Disappointing with "Carrier Missile Hits Ship," 10-2, he provides little more than a wire report version of the U.S.-Turkish naval mishap that occurred in the Mediterranean. He also fails to flesh out recent U.S. Immigration and Naturalization Service statistics indicating the stress a large number of immigrants may have on the country in coming years in "Amnesty Creates Record Immigration," 12-5.

Tom Shales
The Washington Post
★★½

Television. His witty and observant remarks reverberate as we scan less edifying reports by others on the same beat. Yet all too often this year, Shales hasn't lived up to his own high standards. His dry wit still engages, but he is less consistently probing. One of his best pieces of the year, "Campaign '92: The Muck Starts Here," 1-28, strikes that near perfect blend of humor and insight we've come to expect from Shales. This commentary, on TV's scandalous coverage of the alleged Bill Clinton-Gennifer Flowers affair, makes clear that the media's hunger for hype ends any hope that this campaign might take place on a higher plane. In "It Turned the World on With its Smile," 3-23, Shales pens a quaint tribute to the "Mary Tyler Moore Show" after the cast stages a reunion. But he veers into schmaltz when he overpraises the show. Shales takes aim at the "MTV Generation" in "'Real World': MTV's Ego Trap," 5-28, an eye-opening analysis of some of the unsettling social messages endorsed by the station: "And to think Dan Quayle is worried about the values endorsed by 'Murphy Brown.'" Wearing his disillusionment on his sleeve for "Goodbye to the Thrilling Games of Summer," 8-10, Shales tells of a graceful swimmer who "could walk right into a job as a TV sports commentator. But perhaps he aims higher." A perplexed Shales tries to figure out Perot's TV appeal in "Uncanned Ham: Perot's Shows," 10-27: "What's confounding the skeptics is trying to figure out if Perot is cunning in his approach, in his attempt not to seem canned and packaged, or whether this really is a Frank Capraesque case of a politician absolutely and unaffectedly being himself." He shows no mercy as he trashes a *Spy* magazine television show, never relenting in heaping abuse on what he calls "antitainment," in "Spy, 'Hit List' It Was a Very Bad Year," 12-2.

Walter Shapiro
Time
★★

Senior writer. A colorful essayist, Shapiro handily profiled the campaign players. He knows how to use his political connections to open doors and capture the behind-the-scenes mood at campaign headquarters, especially at the Clinton-Gore camp. While he remains a muscular writer, we fortunately saw only flashes of his shrill tone of years past. His "Japan Bashing on the Campaign Trail," 2-10, is an adequate reading of the presidential candidates' various views on Japan's trade policies and the effect they have on the U.S. economy: "The debate over economic relations with Japan represents the first campaign issue of post-cold war politics." In "Perot's Army," 4-20, he captures the flavor of the Perot for president phenomenon: "The Perot petition coalition fuses spare-no-expense business sophistication with a giddy volunteer enthusiasm." Reverting to his stridency of years past in "Lessons of Los Angeles," 5-18, Shapiro has LAPD chief Daryl Gates in his sights from word one. Without objectivity, Shapiro allows the article to sour into a tirade, and while such hostility may be expected from Gates's critics, it is not appropriate from journalists. Shapiro's "Gore: A Hard-Won Sense of Ease," 7-20, too vocally stresses the character issue, while almost entirely side-stepping the vice-presidential candidate's policies. A look at how Gore's views have changed since his failed run for the presidency in '88 was in order. He regains his footing in "So Happy Together," 9-7, exploring the synergy between one-time political rivals, Clinton and Gore. This engaging article offers a very solid sense of how the two candidates' "inseparable campaigning" has helped with "damage control" when critics charged Clinton with inexperience in foreign affairs or over-experience with women. "Worst-Kept Secrets," 12-21, reports more on the press corps' guessing game with regard to Clinton's cabinet appointees, than it does on the administration's direction.

David Shaw
Los Angeles Times
★★★

Media. We first recognized Shaw in the *MediaGuide* two years ago for his January 1990 series on the media coverage of the McMartin Preschool child molestation case, awarding him a 10 Best citation. This year he penned *two* ground-breaking series, "The Media & LAPD: From Coziness to Conflict," 5-24/28, which has been selected as a 10 Best this year, and "Media Impact: Why Some Stories Have It—And Others Don't," 10-24/27. Shaw's astute, insightful commentary is buttressed by exhaustive research and braced by colorful wordsmithery. In the first installment of "The Media & LAPD," he goes back to L.A.'s early days to provide a vibrant history that examines how connections between the two were cemented in "Onetime Allies: Press and LAPD," 5-24. He continues this history in "Chief Parker Molded LAPD Image—Then Came the '60s," 5-25, as the relationship begins to change after the Watts riots and the upheaval that followed. "Media Failed to Examine Alleged LAPD Abuses," 5-26, is a sterling example of what Shaw does best, a tough examination of his own newspaper's record in reporting racial incidents involving police abuse, sharply evaluating coverage on a case-by-case basis, both in the *Times* and other area publications.

In "Story of King Beating Put L.A. Media in Spotlight," 5-27, Shaw wraps up his assessment of local coverage well. To finish, he insightfully critiques the coverage of the riots and police response in "Gates Hammered by Media Over LAPD Riot Response," 5-28. Though shorter, his "Media Impact" series is also relevant on the press and what makes it tick. In "News With Impact? It's Simple," 10-25, he trimly conceptualizes what gives news impact: "The presence (or absence) of heroes, villains and other recognizable characters in the story. The presence (or absence) of personal resonance with readers and viewers." We get a fascinating comparison of stories in "Media Set Agenda but Often Misjudge Public's Interests," 10-26, his treatment smart on the mechanisms of setting the agenda from *within*. But it is "Iraqgate—A Case Study of a Big Story With Little Impact," 10-27, a definitive study of press coverage of Iraqgate, that has power as a case in point.

Robert Shogan
Los Angeles Times
★★

Political writer. An old hand on this beat, Shogan has been plumbing the depths of politics for the *Times* for more than 20 years. He was valuable in dissecting the strategies of the campaigns, viewing clearly the risks and benefits of each. Shogan evaluates Bush's tactic of highlighting his foreign policy accomplishments early in "Bush Seeks Home Market for His Diplomatic Skills," 1-19, carefully documenting that the real concern for voters is no longer nuclear holocaust, but the economy. He and co-author Douglas Jehl further refine their definition and critique of the GOP approach with "GOP Seeks to Link Gains in Foreign Policy to Economy," 8-18, as Bush argues that ending the Cold War "was a necessary first step toward action on pressing domestic problems." The team also culls a prescient quote from an unnamed senior official that categorizes the difficulty in executing this plan: "We sort of said, 'Containing communism means American jobs,' but we haven't been any good at explaining the steps in between." He updates us on GOP strategy in "GOP Weighs Options, Finds 1 Left: Massive Attack on Clinton," 9-17, a good overview on both the line of attack and defense. On the Democratic side, he outlines Clinton's strategy to address the issue and attack Bush for the N.Y. primary, in "Clinton Plans a Double-Barreled Attack," 4-2, incorporating polls and other data to gauge the plan's potential for success. He reveals how Clinton strategists are calculating victory, by concentrating on the electoral college in the insightful "Win the West by Moonlight, and Other Clinton Strategies," 7-16. Shogan is heavy on the anecdotes, and light on the strategy and the analysis, in a preview of the final debate in "It's High Noon as Bush Loads Up for Debate," 10-19. And in "GOP's Comeback Trail Looms as Long, Bumpy," 11-15, he takes a balanced, though shallow look at how Republicans are positioning themselves for the next presidential election.

David Shribman
The Wall Street Journal
★★

Special projects, politics. Shribman's coverage of the campaign this year proved inconsistent. Though politically adept, his forceful leads occasionally gave way to pedestrian analysis. At his best during the New Hampshire primaries for "Democrats' Task in New Hampshire Is to Emerge From the Pack as a Plausible Challenger to Bush," 1-16, he provides a cogent analysis of the strengths and weaknesses of each candidate as a leader and campaigner. We were impressed by the number of significant observations he was able to extract from key players in his highly informative "As Clinton Reshapes His Image, He Often Befuddles Democrats," 3-19. Shribman is as stumped as the rest of us for "In a Three-Way Presidential Race, the Old Rules of Campaigning Suddenly Have Become Obsolete," 5-27. Unable to figure out the long-term impact of the Perot factor despite studying numerous polls and pundits, he offers a generic conclusion that, if nothing else, Perot's presence forces tactical changes. Lending too much weight to the abortion issue's role in an Iowa Congressional race in "As High Court's Abortion Decision Reverberates Across U.S., an Already Hot Iowa Race Heats Up," 6-30, Shribman scuttles what could have been a much more multidimensional article. In "Catholic Voters, Core of the 'Reagan Democrats,' Returning to Their Party Amid Economic Fears," 9-14, he expertly nails down the possible consequences of one demographic group's discontent with the status quo: "Draw them back into the Democratic fold with promises of a brighter economy, and Gov. Bill Clinton will be impossible to stop..." Joined by co-writer Jeffrey H. Birnbaum for "Clinton Still Must Win the Faith of Markets, Leaders of Nations," 11-5, the duo offers an involved piece on Clinton's economic projections, but their analysis is shallow: "Having made 'trickle-down economics' the villain in campaign [appearances] ... Mr. Clinton must find a way to stimulate the economy without favoring the rich."

Ronald Smothers
The New York Times
★½

General interest, southeastern U.S. Smothers has yet to develop the juggling skills necessary to adequately handle the plethora of subjects he is asked to cover. His articles typically skim the surface of an issue, leaving us to look elsewhere for definitive facts and more rigorous examinations. He is more detailed than usual for "Birmingham Mayor Says New Attack Points to Racism," 1-20, but this report on Mayor Arrington, who is under investigation by a Federal grand jury for corruption, meanders. We were impressed with Smothers's objective presentation here, looking at both sides equitably. His cursory review of a day-care center abuse trial occurring in North Carolina, "Defense Lawyer Blames Town in Sex-Abuse Case," 3-25, fails to adequately examine the history of the case, leaving us unprepared to assess the fairness of its conclusion. He doesn't give us quite enough perspective on Jimmy Carter's plans to bolster the poor in "Carter's Civic Crusade Tries to Meld Two Atlantas," 4-11. While we're introduced to the goals and the fundraising efforts, we're not told how he'll proceed, nor is Carter's track record on such efforts evaluated. Abrupt in "Doctor's Act on Embryos Sends Case Back to Court," 6-4, he tells us of a divorced couple's fight over their frozen fertilized eggs. Though he mentions that "The case has attracted the interest of... abortion rights groups," he fails to explore their concerns. Smothers' blanket approach to information in "Plan to Desegregate Universities in Mississippi Is Met With Anger," 10-23, detracts from the article's readability. The finer points of the plan and its implications are discussed, but the piece is decidedly overextended. Smothers does little to enrich the story of a clothing manufacturer which is retraining its workers to switch quickly from making McDonald's outfits to military uniforms in "A Winner in the War of Attrition for Pentagon Suppliers," 12-1.

Rochelle L. Stanfield
National Journal
★★½

Demographics, education and immigration. Finishing up her first full year on this expansive beat, Stanfield has settled into her position nicely, addressing some of the more involved aspects in a controlled, forthright manner, never losing her precision or readability. Her scholarly accounting of the immigrant population's financial impact on the U.S., "Melting Pot Economics," 2-22, is too long. Still, her message is unique and relevant in light of the global population shifts brought about by the end of communism. She embarks on a lively and informative foray into the world of national testing for elementary and secondary school students in "Testing Frenzy," 3-7, where we get a snapshot of educational erosion: "Once a controversial pedagogical topic, testing has become the latest knee-jerk, flag-waving education improvement steamroller." In "Black Frustration," 5-16, she does a service to those seriously interested in the truth about economic disparity among blacks. Unlike so many on this subject, Stanfield refuses to bend the truth to fit either party's political message. Instead, we get straightforward reporting in which the facts tell a story of the "many nations of black America—poor, middle-class and rich; desperate, alienated and assimilated; striving and thriving." She is equally objective when analyzing the diversification of the family in "Valuing the Family," 7-4, a very well-researched report which offers several reasonable explanations not found elsewhere for the family's changing character. Stanfield provides a forum to proponents for allowing state governments, instead of the federal government, to assume more control of financial and domestic programs in "Rethinking Federalism," 10-3, and though she does little to enhance the discussion, its presentation is admirable. And with "Immovable Objects," 11-21, she pens an interesting article on the politics of getting funding for the Office of Educational Research and Improvement.

John Taylor
New York
★★

Political correspondent. In June, Taylor, a social issues reporter of estimable talent, steps confidently into the shoes of departing political correspondent Joe Klein. Upon assuming the new position, he told his editors, ". . . I've become more and more interested . . . in the anthropological aspect of human life, how people get together in groups and struggle for power." But, as election-year politics heat up, Taylor sometimes slips from dispassionate, anthropological observer to activist, becoming part of the power struggle. We forgive his obtrusive and unprofessional display of disdain toward Republicans at the conclusion of "It's Time for a Change," 7-27, only because this is one of the best pieces we've seen on the Democratic National Convention. The images created are so vivid, the analysis of the inner-party dynamic so crisp, that we're swept up. But, we can't look away when bias taints another otherwise solid report, "Pawning the Dirt," 8-17. Contrary to Taylor's partisan assertions here, negative campaigning is not a tactic exclusive to the Republican party, nor are Democrats defenseless victims. His heavy-handed criticism of Perot also leads him down the wrong path in "Diagnosing Perotphobia," 6-22. By wondering what the electorate could possibly see in this guy, Taylor misses an opportunity to enhance our understanding of this political phenomenon. His activist tendencies flare up in the one-sided "Sex Isn't the Issue," 11-30, as he wholeheartedly embraces with Clinton's proclamation that homosexuals should be allowed in the military. Abandoning his role as a journalist, he completely dismisses military opinion on the issue in favor of his own view as a civilian. Early in the year, Taylor delivers several colorful profiles such as "A Theory of the Case," 1-6, which offers an amazing amount of detail on the William Kennedy Smith trial, and "Mad Max," 2-10, a searing exposé of the life and death of publisher Robert Maxwell.

Ronald Taylor
The Washington Times
★

Domestic politics. A professional reporter who rarely surprises, Taylor moves from the environmental beat to the campaign trail this year. Covering the Democratic side, he provides cursory overviews that rarely add new information. We get lightweight accounts of the primaries with "Clinton, Bush Win Big in Pennsylvania Primary," 4-29, and "Clinton, Brown Tied in California," 5-29. In both he provides no information or analysis beyond the numbers. Turning to the head of Howard University's political science department, Ronald Walters, and Rep. Maxine Waters (D-CA), in "Clinton Campaign Not Aimed at Blacks," 6-29, he states that the Clinton campaign isn't directed toward black America, which is a major switch in the realm of Democratic party politics. But this interesting assertion isn't fully explored. "Democratic Camp Downplays Big Lead," 7-31, is solid on the worries of the Clinton campaign: "Political analysts outside the campaign say the current public embrace of the Clinton-Gore ticket masks weaknesses that the campaign must overcome to win in November. Privately, staffers involved in implementing campaign strategy agree, noting that they are still trying to solidify the core of what they see as the party's most reliable voter groups." He offers some information on Clinton's AIDS speech, but not much we couldn't find on the wires in "Confident Bush Bares His Knuckles: Clinton Talks About AIDS, Vaguely," 10-30. And "No Surprises, Clinton Tells World: Pledges Policy 'Continuity,'" 11-5, is a compact review of how Clinton will handle the transition.

Robin Toner
The New York Times

The animation of election year politics seems to have put a spring back in Toner's step after a lackluster 1991. Yet the quality of her work continues to swing wildly. She can be the bright spot on the *NYT*'s national page one day, and a robotic poll worshipper the next. Her "Slogans, Stories and Strategy: The Campaign on Television," 2-7, is a whimsical lark into the land of TV ads during the Democratic primaries. With a wink and a nod, she helps us read between the lines. "(Subtext: He is not another blue suit from inside the Capital Beltway, even if he did take the Senate raise.)" Slipping in "Clinton Dogged by Voter Doubt, Poll of U.S. Says," 4-1, she pens a drab front-page piece that regurgitates the latest polls *ad nauseam*. More typical of her day-to-day coverage was "Clinton, on Roads High and Low, Is Over Hump, Aides Say," 4-2, a knowledgeable, compact roundup of the day's events—Clinton denying character charges, and who has landed whose endorsement. Her "Anxious Days for Bush's Campaign as G.O.P. Heads Into a 3-Way Race," 5-21, is a revealing snapshot of a troubled Bush campaign, as the Perot factor continues to snowball and the President's poll ratings remain low: "Some analysts argue that Mr. Bush is buffeted by forces bigger than the business cycle —a sense of national drift, of a struggling middle class, of a government that does not work as it should." She is truly insightful for "While Others Shrank From Race, Clinton Clung to Dream of Presidency," 7-12, a commendable review of how Clinton progressed through the primary season to win the nomination. Back on automatic pilot for "Fractured G.O.P. Meets as Public Voices Disfavor," 8-17, she spews out the numbers and providing a perfect example of the poll-to-poll journalism we grew so tired of this year. Similarly, "At Dawn of New Politics, Challenges for Both Parties," 11-5, is more of a reiteration of previous political assumptions, than an analysis of the future party politics.

Edward Walsh
The Washington Post

Chicago. Still fairly new to the Midwest, Walsh impresses us with proficient reports on regional news events. His dispatches on the heartland's role in the national election, though, are sometimes surprisingly rote and unsophisticated. On the gruesome Jeffrey Dahmer case, Walsh does a fine job of distinguishing between the two phases of Wisconsin criminal insanity pleas in "Jury to Decide Dahmer's Culpability," 1-27. This effective dissection of the legal defense of a killer is highly instructive. His "South Dakota Becomes Political Battlefield," 2-21, is a failed attempt to give us a from-the-front-lines report on the campaign. He doesn't make clear why this state matters to the Democrats in the primaries or how the candidates are regionalizing their messages. He's much more insightful on a Minnesota plan to expand health insurance in "Filling Health Care Gaps," 4-18. Walsh presents the salient details of the plan, its opponents, its aims, what it will cost, and explores how such a system might be implemented nationwide. His "Rise of Casino Gambling on Indian Land Sparks Controversy," 6-16, sufficiently reports on a Kansas community which wants to legally place a casino on their reservation. Missing, though, is an analysis of the possible side effects, such as corruption. Walsh, along with co-writer Ruth Marcus, provides little more than a perfunctory recounting of the latest presidential campaign stump speeches in "Candidates Court Perot Supporters," 7-18. He's not much better in "As the Words Turn: Campaign Imitates Soaps," 8-13, a readable, but ultimately over-simplistic examination of the continuing spat between Bush and Clinton: "The presidential campaign is beginning to resemble a television soap opera about the troubles of a politically prominent family." "Clinton Victory Founded on Discipline, Energy, GOP Miscues," 11-5, offers the perfect opening line for a book on Clinton's victorious campaign: "Out on the campaign trail, Clinton and Gore were living embodiments of their message to the country."

Kenneth T. Walsh
U.S. News & World Report
★★

White House. Although we felt his work during the '88 campaign was tinted by an anti-GOP bias, Walsh has remained largely above the fray this election year. More and more, his lively and inviting writing style is complemented by balanced reporting and informative analysis. He takes a broad look at what Bush might do in a second term in "Blowin' in the Wind," 2-10, clearly presenting the goals (and legislation) within reach, should Bush be given four more years. He seems unduly tough on Bush, though, categorizing his term as "themeless, as if the president preferred dropping in and out of history rather than shaping it to his design." Walsh provides a good snapshot of how Beltway retrenching in the face of voter anger has reached the White House with "The Perk Wars," 4-13. The report is spiced with detail of the costs of White House perks to taxpayers. One of his more insightful ventures into Bush's psyche was "Bush's Watergate Lessons," 6-22. On the 20th anniversary of the scandal, Walsh recounts how, as GOP Chairman, Bush remained tenaciously loyal to Nixon during and after Watergate, revealing his political savvy and his complex attitudes towards duty: "...He refused to quit until Nixon had left office, telling friends his sense of responsibility required him to see it through. Above all, Bush tried to distance the Republican Party from the scandal, which he said was limited to a few individuals. Walsh and co-writer Matthew Cooper work the campaign trail, finding disarray in the Bush and Clinton camps, as the candidates struggle to be "All Things to All Voters," 9-14. And in his well-penned overview of Clinton's campaign, election and victory, "Thinking About Tomorrow," 11-16, he outlines future possibilities for the President-elect, capping a solid year for Walsh.

Laurel Shaper Walters
The Christian Science Monitor
★½

Winner of an Education Writers Association Travel Fellowship on National Standards and Vocational Education, Walters's fresh dispatches on the nation's school systems always catch our eye. She's especially good on the school choice debate, though we'd like to see her take more time to flesh out her interesting topics. Her "CEO-Run School Means Business," 1-21, details, in vivid color, the advantages of a school funded by over 60 Chicago-based corporations. Yet, contrary to the blurb beneath the title, Walters doesn't explore the "cost-effective results," or how the school may integrate with others in the region. In "'Breaking the Mold' of Education," 7-20, she reports that the New American Schools Development Corporation is awarding grants to implement changes in systems. But we never learn what the new program's goals will be. She doesn't stress forcefully enough the New York public school system's desperation with non-English-speaking students in "Immigrants Flood New York City Schools," 5-18, failing to fully explore the financial strain caused by the influx. Walters pens a good argument for school choice in the story of the Jenkins family who are charging the Chicago school system with inadequate education in "A Family Fights for School Choice," 9-14: "Out of desperation, the Jenkinses decided to use false documentation to enroll...at Ogden Elementary School on the affluent north side. 'I had no other choice,' says Mr. Jenkins." She continues this theme in "School-Choice Issue Fails to Reach Voters," 10-20, satisfactorily explaining the positions of both President Bush and Bill Clinton. Her "Students Sample Election Politics," 11-2, is an interesting piece on teenagers participating in mock presidential elections. But she never indicates why the project centers on education, women's issues and the environment, at the expense of other issues.

Daniel Wattenberg
The American Spectator
★★

Contributing editor. Wattenberg left *Insight* in September, scripting only one piece for *TAS* to date. He is poised to cover the Clinton White House in '93. If you can get past Wattenberg's less than subtle conservative slant, you may learn, as we have, to appreciate the verve and vigor of this capable reporter's journalism. Challenging the feminist credo of having it all in "The Parent Trap," *Insight* 3-2, he questions the dubious impact working mothers are having on the nation's children. His "Will the Real Elvis Please Stand Up?" *Insight* 3-23, is pure fluff on the Elvis stamp—a waste of our time. He's much more substantial reporting on Jerry Brown's walk on the supply side, in "Supply-side Brownnoser or Savior?" *Insight* 4-5, questioning the presidential candidate's rationale for his semi-embrace of this pro-growth school of economics. "Inner Vision for Our Cities," *Insight* 6-22, looks at the economic plight of the "underclass" from the author's decidedly right-wing perspective. He is unable to fully address the problem, skimming several philosophies, but never pulling the piece together. He certainly does his homework on Iran-Contra independent counsel Lawrence Walsh and his deputy Craig Gillen, who are being questioned by the General Accounting Office for unwarranted special privileges in "The Most Expensive Special Counsel," *Insight* 9-7. Though severely long-winded, and a bit too gleeful, Wattenberg effectively chronicles how these two controversial figures were caught with the goods. His tirade against Hillary Clinton, "The Lady Macbeth of Little Rock," *TAS* 8-92, paints the candidate's wife as an ultra-liberal lawyer, willing to bend her husband's ear for her own purposes. His personal assaults on Ms. Clinton undermine what might have been a legitimate examination of her professional writings and political associations: "Hillary Clinton . . . is going to cause her husband no end of political embarrassment . . ."

Isabel Wilkerson
The New York Times
★★½

National correspondent. From her Chicago perch, Wilkerson serves as a powerful and convincing chronicler of Middle America's mounting concerns about the nation. Her forceful, uncluttered dispatches add a man-on-the-street perspective to our understanding of the issues. She displays a commendable ability to let her sources provide the analysis in "Patch of Mid-America Not Impressed by Bush Talk," 1-30, conveying the disappointment felt by the residents of Oak Park, Ill. after Bush's State of the Union speech. She provides a very interesting read in "Fight for Airport Shows Chicago Mayor's Mettle," 2-12, on the battle to get a new airport built in Chicago instead of Gary, Ind. Uncharacteristically, she fails to include quotes from concerned citizens, which would have lent weight to the report. Sitting down in Rockford, Ill., a small factory town, she provides a forum for citizens to vent their anger at this year's presidential crop in "Here Come the Little Guys, and, Boy, Are They Fed Up With the System," 3-16: "These voters define themselves not by class or income but by how many times they have been kicked in the teeth by taxes, Medicare, Social Security, the economy . . . " As usual, Wilkerson is careful to let the people tell their story, a laudable trait in a year that produced so much journalistic manipulation. Evocative and compelling on the Nation's racial tensions in "Black Neighborhood Faces White World With Bitterness," 6-22, Wilkerson opens up a segregated community in Chicago and lets the reader peer inside. Wilkerson is unable to add fresh insight to questions of Medicaid fraud in the nationally-watched campaign of Carol Moseley Braun in "Senate Nominee Gets Caught Up in an Ethics Issue," 10-11, her presentation accurate, but lacking analysis. She offers a faithful retelling of James Porter's disturbing trial for sexual assault in "Ex-Priest Goes on Trial in Child-Molesting Case," 12-8.

Curtis Wilkie
The Boston Globe
★★½

National politics. Wilkie has an eye for key details that helps him craft prescient analysis on the campaign trail. His dispatches provide a fresh and accurate reading of the presidential race. Wilkie's best work of the year focused on Clinton's scrambling to stay alive during the New Hampshire primary. His 10 Best selection, "33 Days That Defined a Candidate," 7-12, is an extraordinarily detailed report on that frantic campaign manager accusations of adultery and draft-dodging. Wilkie's behind-the-scenes anecdotes and fluid writing make this one of the best political pieces of the year. His "Clinton to Confront Allegations, Aide Says," 1-25, carefully assesses the implications of Bill Clinton's remark that his marriage has had troubles. Wilkie doesn't side-step the question of infidelity and writes a detailed report as to how Clinton's staff is managing the flap. He succinctly addresses the winners and losers from the New Hampshire primary in "Victory Over Doubters and End to 'Phantom,'" 2-19, and in "Brown, New York Are the Wild Cards," 3-18, he provides an adequate forecast of the obstacles Clinton must face in N.Y.: "Local news there is not driven by the magisterial *New York Times*, but rather the racy tabloids..." He follows Jerry Brown to the end of his campaign line in California in the perfunctory, but still readable "Brown's Faded Campaign Limps Home for a Last Stand," 5-29. He provides a different take on the problems the President is having in "Bush's Year Reminiscent of Carter's in '80," 8-11, the comparisons interesting, but sometimes stretched too far: "While questions were raised about Carter's health after he aged visibly on the job and faltered in a long-distance foot race, nagging whispers about Bush's health persist." Wilkie gets a decent take on the ideology of Bill Clinton after the presidential election in "Shaping the Next Presidency," 11-9: "It seems fair to apply a term that was once used to describe Kennedy—'pragmatic liberal.'"

Juan Williams
The Washington Post
★★★½

Staff writer. The elegance of Williams's prose continues to shine in his erudite essays. His explosive coverage of the Clarence Thomas hearings in 1991 seems to have liberated both his reporting and writing style. His intuitive dissection of Democratic politics often casts events in a new light. He is nearly always ahead of the curve, as in "Liberation of the Black 'Bloc,'" 2-23, where he cuts against the grain, arguing that blacks will hold the Democratic nominees accountable for policy, rather than throwing emotional support to a black candidate, postulating further that this will increase the importance of the black vote. He updates this with "The New Black Powers: Younger Voters Lining Up With Clinton Have Clout but No Consensus," 11-1, an important snapshot of the established black leadership and the up-and-comers, and how they fit together in terms of Democratic and black politics. His exceptional lead for "D.C.: Dreaming of Statehood but Ignoring a Nightmare," 4-12, opens a thorough examination of the problems with D.C. statehood: "City Council Chairman John Wilson keeps having a politically incorrect reverie. Wilson dreams that Washington has become the 51st state, but not in its current tiny, 69-square-mile, poverty-ridden condition. Oh no. D.C. is joined by Fairfax, [the city of] Alexandria, Arlington, Montgomery and Prince George's counties. There is a solid tax base that includes not only the area's largest industries but also the white and black middle-class that has been leaving the city." We find further information on the decay of D.C. in "Mrs. Kelly's Neighborhoods: How Can the City Save Them?" 10-11, heart-wrenching and urgent on what must be done to preserve the integrity of Washington's small neighborhoods. And "The Continuing Education of Franklyn Jenifer," 9-20, is an exceptional portrait of the president of Howard University.

Bob Woodward
The Washington Post
★★★

Assistant managing editor for investigative news. The famed Watergate reporter tossed several boulders into the pond of Washington politics, the waves breaking throughout this election year. His consistent use of unnamed sources irks some of his colleagues, and sometimes bothers us, but it is a necessary evil for the high-level exposés which are his specialty. He scored with two series on the Bush administration. The first, "The President's Understudy," 1-5/10 and 1-12, is a 10 Best selection co-authored by David S. Broder. This extensive profile and political evaluation of Bush's vice president. changed perceptions inside and outside the Beltway, about Vice President, Dan Quayle. The series dispels many of the popular myths generated by the press. We came away with a real sense of Quayle: a savvy politician who may just be smarter than everyone thinks. Woodward had yet another 10 Best selection in this stellar year of reporting, "Making Choices: Bush's Economic Record," 10-4/7. While his sources here are generally not named, they seem to be high-ranking administration officials. What emerges here is a clearly drawn portrait of "bitter infighting [that] has hampered the administration's efforts to diagnose what is wrong with the American economy, explain its economic thinking to the public in a coherent way and then go about addressing the problems." Joined by co-author John Mintz for a bombshell on Ross Perot, "Perot Investigated Bush's Activities," 6-21, also has few named sources, hampering its credibility: "There is no evidence that Perot, Luce or any of their representatives broke any law or did anything improper in their inquiries about Bush. But what is striking about the undertakings is Perot's tenacity."

John E. Yang
The Washington Post
★★

Los Angeles. After cutting his teeth at *The Wall Street Journal*, Yang moved to the D.C. bureau of the *Post* where he quickly floated to the top and landed frequently on the front-page. Consequently, we were confused by Yang's reassignment to the West Coast. This move outside the Beltway has placed him in unfamiliar territory. Though the quality of his work has been somewhat inconsistent during the transition, his typically fine-tuned, elegantly-written essays continue to be worth a look. His "This Time, Budget Leaks Are 'Structured,'" co-written by Thomas W. Lippman 1-25, is a newsworthy glimpse of leaked news reports on Bush's upcoming State of the Union address. The duo conveys the appropriate amount of professional skepticism: "It is a coordinated strategy, pushed by Bush campaign chairman Robert M. Teeter...to generate positive news coverage for the president in the days leading up to his State of the Union address Tuesday and his budget submission the next day." Yang's "Line-Item Veto: Small Change, Big Politics," 2-26, is a strong report on what exactly the line-item veto would do for the President, but his humor undercuts the seriousness of the issue: "...the power to strike individual items in spending bills probably would be tantamount to dipping a teaspoon in the federal government's ocean of red ink." Faithfully transcribing Vice President Quayle's speech on family values in "Quayle Attributes Urban Problems to 'Poverty of Values,'" 5-20, he forgoes the editorial liberties taken by others. Looking beyond the Beltway, race and law meet in his "A Rallying Point for Blacks in Utah," 7-26, the story of a black man's conviction for manslaughter in a state that is less than one percent black. The emotive nature of the case makes for an engrossing read. His "Judge Sets Aside Retrial of L.A. Police Officer," 8-8, is little more than a cursory follow-up on the Rodney King case after the L.A. riots. As a footnote to the LAPD's response to the riots, Yang pens "L.A. Riot Inquiry Decries Lack of Planning by City, Police Officials," 10-22. He adds little analysis of his own to this report, a mere laundry list of the police department's woefully inefficient pre-riot planning. He and co-writer Steven Mufson pen a professional portrait of incoming Treasury Secretary Lloyd Bentsen in "Bentsen to Bring Pragmatism, Experience to Treasury," 12-6, coloring the article with anecdotes and sturdy analysis of what Bentsen brings to the new administration.

PUBLICATIONS AND SYNDICATES

Publications

The American Prospect
P.O. Box 7645
Princeton, NJ 08543-7645
(609) 497-2474 (Fax, no phone)

The American Spectator
2020 N. 14th Street
P.O. Box 549
Arlington, VA 22216
(703) 243-3733

The Atlantic
745 Boylston Street
Boston, MA 02116
(617) 536-9500

Aviation Week & Space Technology
1221 Avenue of the Americas
42nd Floor
New York, NY 10020
(212) 512-2000

Barron's
200 Liberty Street
New York, NY 10281
(212) 416-2700

The Boston Globe
135 Morrissey Boulevard
Boston, MA 02127
(617) 929-2000

BusinessWeek
1221 Avenue of the Americas
39th Floor
New York, NY 10021
(212) 512-2000

Chicago Tribune
435 N. Michigan Avenue
Chicago, IL 60611-4041
(312) 222-3232

The Christian Science Monitor
One Norway Street
Boston, MA 02115
(617) 450-2000

Chronicles
The Rockford Institute
934 N. Main Street
Rockford, IL 61103
(815) 964-5054

Commentary
165 East 56th Street
New York, NY 10022
(212) 751-4000

Defense News
6883 Commercial Drive
Springfield, VA 22159
(703) 642-7300

The Economist
25 St. James Street
London SW1A 1HG
United Kingdom
011-44-71-839-7000 (U.K.)
(212) 541-5730 (U.S.)

Far Eastern Economic Review
GPO Box 160
Hong Kong

Financial Times
Number One Southwark Bridge
London SE1 9HL
United Kingdom
011-44-71-873-3000 (U.K.)

Financial World
47 West 34th Street, 3rd Floor
New York, NY 10001
(212) 594-5030

Forbes
60 Fifth Avenue
New York, NY 10011
(212) 620-2200

Foreign Affairs
58 East 68th Street
New York, NY 10021
(212) 734-0400

Foreign Policy
2400 N Street, NW
Washington, DC 20037
(202) 862-7940

Fortune
Time-Life Building
Rockefeller Center
New York, NY 10020-1393
(212) 586-1212

Harper's
666 Broadway
New York, NY 10012
(212) 614-6508

Harvard Business Review
Harvard University
Boston, MA 02163
(617) 495-6182

Human Events
422 First Street, SE
Washington, DC 20003
(202) 546-0856

In These Times
2040 N. Milwaukee Avenue
Chicago, IL 60647
(312) 772-0100

Insight
3600 New York Avenue, NE
Washington, DC 20002
(202) 636-8800

Investor's Business Daily
12655 Beatrice Street
Los Angeles, CA 90066
(310) 448-6000

Jane's Defence Weekly
Jane's Information Group, Inc.
1340 Braddock Place, Suite 300
Alexandria, VA 22314-1651
(703) 683-3700

The Journal of Commerce
2 World Trade Center, 27th Floor
New York, NY 10048-0298
(212) 837-7000

Los Angeles Times
Times Mirror Square
Los Angeles, CA 90053
(213) 237-5000

The Miami Herald
1 Herald Plaza
Miami, FL 33132
(305) 350-2111

Mother Jones
1663 Mission Street, Suite 200
San Francisco, CA 94103
(415) 558-8881

The Nation
72 Fifth Avenue
New York, NY 10011
(212) 242-8400

The National Interest
1112 16th Street, NW
Suite 540
Washington, DC 20036
(202) 467-4884

National Journal
1730 M Street, NW
Suite 1100
Washington, DC 20036
(202) 857-1400

National Review
150 East 35th Street
New York, NY 10016
(212) 679-7330

New Perspectives Quarterly
10951 West Pico Boulevard
3rd Floor
Los Angeles, CA 90064
(310) 474-0011

The New Republic
1220 19th Street, NW
Suite 600
Washington, DC 20036
(202) 331-7494

New York
755 Second Avenue
New York, NY 10017
(212) 880-0700

The New York Review of Books
250 West 57th Street
Room 1321
New York, NY 10107
(212) 757-8070

The New York Times
229 West 43rd Street
New York, NY 10036
(212) 556-1234

The New Yorker
20 West 43rd Street
New York, NY 10036
(212) 840-3800

Newsweek
444 Madison Avenue
New York, NY 10022
(212) 350-4000

Policy Review
214 Massachusetts Avenue, NE
Washington, DC 20002
(202) 546-4400

The Progressive
409 East Main Street
Madison, WI 53703
(608) 257-4626

Reader's Digest
Pleasantville, NY 10570
(914) 238-8585

Reason
3415 S. Sepulveda Boulevard
Suite 400
Los Angeles, CA 90034
(310) 391-2245

Roll Call
900 2nd Street, NE
Washington, DC 20002
(202) 289-4900

The Spectator
56 Dougherty Street
London WC1N 2LL
United Kingdom
011-44-71-405-1706 (U.K.)

Time
Time-Life Building
Rockefeller Center
New York, NY 10020-1393
(212) 586-1212

USA Today
1000 Wilson Blvd.
Arlington, VA 22229
(703) 276-3400

U.S. News & World Report
2400 N Street, NW
Washington, DC 20037
(202) 955-2000

Utne Reader
1624 Harmon Place
Minneapolis, MN 55403
(612) 338-5040

The Wall Street Journal
200 Liberty Street
New York, NY 10281
(212) 416-2000

The Washington Monthly
1611 Connecticut Avenue, NW
Washington, DC 20009
(202) 462-0128

The Washington Post
1150 15th Street, NW
Washington, DC 20071
(202) 334-6000

The Washington Times
3600 New York Avenue, NE
Washington, DC 20002
(202) 636-3000

Syndicates

Associated Features, Inc.
P.O. Box 7099
Fairfax Station, VA 22039
(703) 764-0496

Creators Syndicate
5777 West Century Boulevard
Suite 700
Los Angeles, CA 90045
(310) 337-7003

King Features Syndicate, Inc.
235 East 45th Street
New York, NY 10017
(212) 455-4000
(800) 526-5464

Los Angeles Times Syndicate
Times Mirror Square
Los Angeles, CA 90053
(213) 237-7987

Newspaper Enterprise Association
200 Park Avenue
New York, NY 10166
(212) 692-3700
(800) 221-4816

Scripps-Howard News Service
1090 Vermont Avenue, NW
Suite 1000
Washington, DC 20005
(202) 408-1484

Tribune Media Services
Editorial & Customer Service
64 East Concord Street
Orlando, FL 32801
(407) 420-6200
(800) 322-3068

United Features Syndicate
200 Park Avenue
New York, NY 10166
(212) 692-3700
(800) 221-4816

Universal Press Syndicate
4900 Main Street
Kansas City, MO 64112
(816) 932-6600
(800) 255-6734

Washington Post Writers Group
1150 15th Street, NW
Washington, DC 20071
(202) 334-6375
(800) 879-9794

INDEX

A

ABC (American Broadcasting Corp.) 15, 37, 58, 83, 276
Abelson, Alan 50
Abelson, Reed 103
Abortion 31, 32, 116, 127, 129, 132, 134, 141, 238, 240, 258, 267, 274, 283, 287, 288, 291
Abramson, Jill 247
Abramson, Rudy 234
Adams, Brock 141
Adelman, Ken 115
Afghanistan, Democratic Republic of 33, 167
Aflac, Inc. 84
Africa 16, 197
African National Congress 160, 180, 182, 208
Agriculture, Department of 76, 98
AIDS 38, 40, 62, 77, 117, 135, 148, 209, 235, 237-240, 244, 272, 279, 288, 293
Air Force, U.S. 225, 227, 232, 233
Airline Industry 92, 214, 220, 221, 227, 233
al-Assad, Hafez 130, 149
Albania, People's Socialist Republic of 177
Algeria, Democratic and Popular Republic of 168, 175, 189
Allen, Henry 247
Alter, Jonathan 17, 24, **248**
Altman, Lawrence K., M.D. **234**
American Airlines 86, 92, 106
American Express 94
The American Prospect 78
The American Spectator 117, 122, 139, 148, 295
Anders, George **50**, 107
Andrews, Edmund L. **51**
Angell, Wayne 29
Angier, Natalie 37, **235**
Apple, R.W., Jr. **248**
Applebome, Peter **249**
Aquino, Corazon 156, 163, 199
Archibald, George **249**
Argentina (Argentine Republic) 191
Aristide, Jean-Bertrand 33, 201
Arkansas Democrat Gazette 128
Armey, Richard K. 147
Armstrong, C. Michael 233
Army, U.S. 220, 226, 232
Asia 151, 156, 161, 163, 165, 177, 184, 197, 209
Asker, James R. **212**
Asman, David **151**
Associated Features 145
AT&T 51, 53, 60, 66, 109
The Atlantic 263
Atlas, Terry **250**
Atwood, J. Brian 223
Auerbach, Stuart **51**
Australia, Commonwealth of 200
Automobile Industry 26, 63, 67, 104, 107, 112, 114, 120, 184, 190
Aviation Week & Space Technology 212-214, 216, 218, 220, 221, 224-226, 229, 230
Ayres, B. Drummond, Jr. **250**

B

Babcock, Charles R. **251**
Bacon, Kenneth H. **52**
Bahree, Bhushan 105
Baker, James A., III 29, 41, 42, 51, 120, 125-127, 133, 145, 149, 197, 216, 223, 224, 227, 250, 268
Baker, Russell **115**, 120
Balz, Dan **251**
Bangladesh, People's Republic of 167
Bangsberg, P. T. **151**
Banks, Howard **52**
Barber, Lionel 91, **152**
Barnard, Bruce **152**
Barnathan, Joyce 190
Barnes, Fred 31, **116**
Barnes, James A. **251**
Barone, Michael **116**
Barrett, Katherine 25
Barrett, William P. **53**
Barron's 27, 50, 63, 68, 85
Bartley, Robert L. **117**
BBC (British Broadcasting Corp.) 12, 129, 202
BCCI (Bank of Credit and Commerce International) 108, 273
Bearak, Barry 38
Belgium, Kingdom of 152, 157, 219, 225
Benham, Barbara **252**
Bentsen, Lloyd 67, 112, 142, 259, 283, 297
Beregovoy, Pierre 198
Bering-Jensen, Henrik **153**
Berke, Richard L. **252**
Bernstein, Aaron **53**
Bernstein, Harry **54**
Berry, John M. **54**
Berss, Marcia **55**
Bethell, Tom **117**
Beyer, Lisa **153**
Biesada, Alexandra 86
Birnbaum, Jeffrey H. **253**, 291
Bishop, Jerry **235**
Black & Decker 50
Bleiberg, Robert 63
Blinder, Alan S. **55**
Blumenthal, Sidney 24, **118**
Boeing, Inc. 53
Bogert, Carroll **154**
Bohlen, Celestine **154**
Boo, Katharine **253**
Borden, Inc. 28
Borger, Gloria **254**
Borrus, Amy 155
The Boston Globe 33, 40, 44, 110, 127, 138, 156, 179, 191, 281, 296
Boulton, Leyla **155**
Bovard, James **118**
Bowers, Brent 72
Bradley, Bill 141
Brady, Nicholas 21, 22, 97, 148
Brady, Rose **155**
Branigin, William **156**
Braun, Carol Moseley 295
Brazil, Federative Republic of 178, 182
Breaux, John B. 259
Bremner, Brian 155
Brimelow, Peter 28, **56**
Bristol-Myers Squibb 237
British Airways 106
Brittan, Samuel **56**
Broad, William J. **236**
Broder, David S. 31, 43, **119**, 135, 297
Broder, John M. **212**
Brokaw, Tom 12
Bronner, Ethan 33, **156**
Brooke, James **157**
Brookes, Warren T. 121
Brookhiser, Richard **119**
Brown, Edmund G., Jr. (Jerry) 8, 24, 70, 119, 122, 130, 136, 248, 253, 254, 255, 256, 262, 264, 281, 282, 286, 296
Brown, Ron 143, 247, 250, 276
Browne, Malcolm W. **236**
Browner, Carol 28
Brownstein, Ronald 213, **254**
Buchan, David **157**
Buchanan, Patrick 24, 119-122, 140, 142, 145, 150, 173, 220, 247, 251, 254, 262, 266, 267, 269, 275, 276, 280
Buchwald, Art **120**
Buckley, William F., Jr. 119, **120**, 275
Buffett, Warren 113
Burma, Ian 35
Burns, John F. 34, **158**
Bush Administration 29, 42, 117, 124, 125, 132, 143, 242, 266, 270, 297
Bush, George 6-12, 16, 24, 29, 30, 32, 40, 41, 42, 43, 50, 51, 55, 58, 61, 63, 70, 71, 75, 89, 93, 95, 97-100, 103, 104, 106, 110, 112, 115-121, 123, 126, 128-130, 133-144, 146, 147, 149, 150, 152, 169, 176, 180, 184, 204, 207, 214, 216, 220, 227, 228, 231, 238, 239, 242, 245, 248, 250-252, 255, 258-264, 266, 267, 271-274, 276, 277, 278, 280, 281, 282, 285, 286, 290, 292, 293, 294, 296, 297
BusinessWeek 25, 53, 55, 57, 58, 60, 62, 66, 70, 78, 79, 82, 87, 107, 109, 111, 155, 190, 205
Bylinsky, Gene **237**
Byrne, John A. **57**
Byron, Christopher 37, **58**

C

Calmes, Jackie **255**
Cambodia (Cambodian People's Republic) 201, 209
Campaign, Presidential 6-12, 24, 29, 117, 118, 126-128, 131, 133, 134, 137, 138, 146-148, 152, 182, 229,

302 MEDIAGUIDE

247, 251, 252, 256, 263, 266, 275, 284, 290
  Debates 120, 248, 282, 286
Canada 56, 164, 205, 257
Canham-Clyne, John **255**
Cannon, Lou **256**
Carey, John **58**
Carlson, Margaret **256**
Carnegy, Hugh **158**
Carroll, Ginny **258**
Carter, Jimmy 126, 127, 296
Carville, James 253, 267
Casey, Robert 31, **261**
Casimir, Jean **255**
Castro, Fidel 139, 151, 166, 191
CBO (Congressional Budget Office) 121
CBS (Columbia Broadcasting System) 15, 29, 260
CDC (Center for Disease Control) 239, 240
Charen, Mona **120**
Chase, Alston **121**
Chase, Marilyn **237**
Cheney, Richard B. 218, 219, 224, 226, 228, 233
Chicago Tribune 14, 17, 32, 90, 139, 142, 168, 174, 186, 188, 200, 201, 211, 250, 259, 273, 276
Chile, Republic of 190
China, People's Republic of 14, 36, 69, 85, 104, 123, 142, 151, 162, 173, 179, 182, 187, 200, 204-206, 223, 229
The Christian Science Monitor 294
Chronicles 124
Chrysler Corp. 27, 63, 68, 105
Church, George J. **158**
CIA (Central Intelligence Agency) 36, 115, 120, 160, 212, 217, 229, 231, 256, 271, 273
Cimons, Marlene **238**
Citicorp 64, 96
Civil Rights 149, 150
Claiborne, William **257**
Clift, Eleanor 24, **257**
Clines, Francis X. 24
Clinton, Bill 6-12, 13, 24, 26, 29, 31, 32, 41, 44, 50, 52, 54, 55, 61, 63, 70, 71, 78, 80, 88-90, 93-95, 97, 98, 103, 111, 112, 115-119, 121-134, 136-145, 148, 149, 159, 161, 165, 176, 182, 188, 199, 213, 215, 217, 222, 223, 228, 231, 242, 243, 245, 247-254, 257-259, 261-264, 269-278, 281, 282, 284, 286, 288-290, 292, 294, 296
Clinton, Hillary 123, 127, 141, 250, 257, 258, 262, 265, 267, 295
Clymer, Adam **258**
CNN (Cable News Network) 15, 36, 144, 174, 224, 260, 265
Cockburn, Alexander 89, **121**
Cohen, Laurie P. **59**
Cohen, Richard **122**
Cohen, Richard E. **258**
Cohen, Roger **159**
Coll, Steve 33, **159**

Collor de Mello, Fernando 182, 186
Columbia Journalism Review 274
Commonwealth of Independent States (C.I.S.) 108, 181, 183, 213, 214, 215, 220, 223, 225
  Armenia 200
  Estonia 194
  Georgia 161, 202
  Russia 11-13, 34, 36, 41, 85, 124, 138, 147, 151, 154, 155, 161, 162, 164, 169, 170, 171, 175, 192, 194, 199, 200, 202, 203, 205, 211, 215, 217, 218, 222, 226, 231, 236, 257
  Ukraine 175, 177, 200, 213
Communism 32, 34, 36, 85, 156, 163, 164, 171, 174, 175, 177, 181, 182, 188, 194, 200, 203, 291
Congress, U.S. 14, 26, 54, 56, 88, 96, 109, 121, 132, 143, 223, 226, 229, 231, 253, 255, 258, 260
  House Bank Scandal 132, 136, 249, 259, 271, 275, 287
  House Post Office 277, 284
Continental Airlines 102
Contreras, Joseph **160**
Cook, James **59**
Cooper, Henry 232
Cooper, Kenneth J. 251
Cooper, Matthew 294
Corwin, Julie 181, 203
Coughlin, Paula 254
Covault, Craig **213**
Cowan, Alison Leigh **60**
Coy, Peter **60,** 109
Creators Syndicate 120, 121, 123, 131, 148
Cresson, Edith 19, 198
Crovitz, L. Gordon 129
Crowe, Adm. William J., Jr. 115
Crudele, John **61**
C-SPAN 248
Cuba, Republic of 191
Cullison, A. E. **160**
Cuneo, Alice 25, 87
Cuomo, Mario 24, 41, 281
Czechoslovakia (Czechoslovak Socialist Republic) 153, 164

D

Dahlburg, John-Thor **161**
The Dallas Morning News 178
Daley, Steve **259**
Darlin, Damon **161**
Darman, Richard 43, 148
Dawkins, William 224
Day, Kathleen 257
de Briganti, Giovanni **213**
de Klerk, F. W. 160, 206, 208
de Soto, Hernando 118
Decker, Cathleen 266
Defense 42, 44, 52, 108, 115, 212-224, 225-227, 230-232, 236, 241, 263
  SDI (Strategic Defense Initiative) 212, 217, 218, 231, 236
Defense News 213, 215, 219, 221, 226,
227, 231
Delors, Jacques 157, 198
Delta Airlines 93
Democratic Party 26, 31, 41, 43, 118, 120, 122, 143, 144, 145, 148, 150, 247, 251, 252, 260, 263, 286
  National Convention 44, 131, 134, 251, 273, 276
Dempsey, Judy **162**
Deng Xiaoping 14, 36, 206
Denmark, Kingdom of 12, 152
Dentzer, Susan **61**
Deveny, Kathleen **62**
Devroy, Ann 251, **259**
Dewar, Helen **260**
Diamond, Edwin **260**
Digital Equipment Corp. 64
Dionne, E. J., Jr. **261**
Dobbs, Michael 13, 34, **162**
Dobrzynski, Judith H. **62**
Dolan, Carrie 238
Dolan, Maura 234
Dole, Robert 258
Dominican Republic 176
Donahue, Phil 24, 248, 272
Donlan, Thomas G. **63**
Donohoe, Cathryn **261**
Dornheim, Michael A. **214**
Dow Corning 57, 76, 239
Dowd, Maureen 254, **262**
Drew, Elizabeth **262**
Drogin, Bob **163**
Du Bois, Peter C. **63**
Duffy, Michael 132
Dukakis, Michael 118, 126, 130, 142, 146, 250, 276, 287
Dyson, Esther **64**

E

Eagleburger, Lawrence 223
Early, Gerald 39
Easterbrook, Gregg **263**
Eastland, Terry **122**
Eaton, William J. 287
EC (European Community) 18-23, 35, 104, 118, 152, 153, 157, 185, 195, 198, 214, 219, 233
  Maastricht Treaty 12, 34, 57, 92, 101, 108, 111, 125, 138, 152, 153, 157, 169, 188, 193, 196, 199, 210, 224
The Economist 14, 16, 19, 20, 23, 36
Economy, U.S. 26, 53, 61, 66, 67, 71, 73, 81, 107, 109, 111, 112, 117, 138, 171, 217, 240, 242, 266, 274, 277, 283, 289, 295, 297
  Federal Reserve 22, 23, 29, 50, 103
  Taxes 24, 32, 42, 70, 86, 89, 94, 95, 122, 132, 135, 141, 255, 258, 282
ECU (European Currency Unit) 159
Edsall, Thomas B. **263**
Education 40, 294
Edwards, Edwin 249
Egan, Jack **64**
Egan, Timothy **263**
Egypt, Arab Republic of 171, 175,

208
Einhorn, Bruce 233
El Salvador, Republic of 126, 168
Elliott, Stuart **65**
Elmer-DeWitt, Philip **238**
EMU (European Monetary Unit) 224
Energy, Department of 241
Engelberg, Stephen **163**
Environment 28, 59, 110, 123, 129, 152, 178, 187, 234, 245, 264, 265
   Global Warming 234, 238, 239, 241, 243, 244
   Rio Summit 139, 149, 178, 183, 202, 222, 234, 239, 243, 245, 263, 271, 283
EPA (Environmental Protection Agency) 28, 56, 243, 245
Erlanger, Steven **164**
ERM (European Exchange Rate Mechanism) 18-23, 27, 57, 152, 188, 204
Ethiopia (Socialist Ethiopia) 173, 192, 193
European Central Bank 185
Evans, Rowland 24, 41, **123**, 126, 142

F

Far Eastern Economic Review 172, 179, 186, 206
Farhi, Paul **65**
Farnsworth, Clyde H. **164**
Farrell, Christopher **66**
FAA (Federal Aviation Administration) 226
FBI (Federal Bureau of Investigation) 271, 281
FCC (Federal Communications Commission) 65
FDA (Food and Drug Administration) 76, 85, 237, 238, 239, 240
FDIC (Federal Deposit Insurance Corp.) 27, 52, 78, 97
Feldman, Amy 72, 103
Ferguson, Tim W. **66**
Ferraro, Geraldine 254
Fialka, John J. **214**
Fields, Suzanne **123**
Financial Times 20-23, 34, 56, 91, 95, 137, 152, 155, 157, 158, 162, 166, 167, 176, 182-185, 191, 192, 207, 208, 223, 233
Financial World 25, 113
Fineman, Howard **264**
Fineman, Mark **165**
Finnegan, Philip **215**
Fisher, Marc 165, 227
Fitzwater, Marlin 266
Flanigan, James **67**
Fleming, Thomas **124**
Flinn, Julie 109
Flint, Jerry **67**
Flowers, Gennifer 77, 131, 257, 284, 288
Foley, Thomas 253, 277, 284, 287
Forbes 27, 28, 52, 53, 55, 56, 59, 64, 67, 71, 88, 98, 100, 103, 138, 146,

166, 205
Ford Motor Co. 63, 68, 114
Fordyce, Kirk 120
Forsyth, Randall W. 27, **68**
Foreign Policy 15
Fort Worth Star-Telegram 131
Fortune 26, 28, 84, 92, 99, 105, 113, 144, 195, 237
Frady, Marshall 43
France (French Republic) 157, 169, 185, 197, 198, 203, 224
Fraser, Damien **166**
Freudenheim, Milt **68**
Friedman, Milton 64
Friedman, Thomas L. 17, **215**
Fritz, Sara **264**
Frohnmayer, John 129, 135, 249, 283
FTC (Federal Trade Commission) 119
Fuerbringer, Jonathan **69**
Fuhrman, Peter **166**
Fujimori, Alberto 151, 178, 190, 198
Fulghum, David A. **216**
Fumento, Michael **265**

G

GATT (General Agreement on Tariffs and Trade) 51, 85, 91, 98, 157, 198
Gaffney, Frank **124**
Gaidar, Yegor 155
Galen, Michele 25
Garcia, Alan 190
Gargan, Edward A. **167**
Garrett, H. Lawrence, III 232
Gates, Robert M. 212, 217
Gejdenson, Sam 231
Gelb, Leslie H. 12, 16, **125**, 130
Gellman, Barton **216**
General Electric 53
General Motors Corp. 27, 51, 55, 62, 63, 68, 80, 84, 105, 107, 112, 114
Geo. A. Hormel & Co. 55
Georges, Christopher 36, **265**
Gephardt, Richard 253
Gerber Products Co. 60
Gergen, David **125**, 145
Germany, Federal Republic of 12, 17-21, 27, 35, 51, 53, 57, 63, 64, 71, 91, 94, 101, 111, 133, 151-153, 159, 164, 165, 171, 179, 180, 185, 192, 196, 198, 203, 204, 213, 222, 227, 233
Germond, Jack W. 24, **126**
Gerstenzang, James 266, 271, 282
Gertz, Bill **217**
Geyer, Georgie Anne **126**
Ghiles, Francis 167
Gigot, Paul 24, 29, **127**
Gilder, George **69**
Gillette Co. 25
Gingrich, Newt 120, 268
Gladwell, Malcolm **239**
Glasgall, William 87, 155
Gleckman, Howard **70**, 80
Golden, Tim **168**
Goldin, Daniel 225
Gonzalez, Henry 143, 230, 231

Goodgame, Dan 132
Goodman, Ellen **127**
Goodman, John 145
Goodyear Tire & Rubber Co. 92
Goozner, Merrill **168**
Gorbachev, Mikhail S. 36, 41, 120, 124, 154, 194, 208
Gordon, Michael R. **217**
Gore, Albert, Jr. 24, 124, 134, 257, 258, 265, 269, 280, 286, 289
Gramm, Phil 248, 259
Greece (Hellenic Republic) 148
Greenberg, Paul **128**
Greene, Richard 25
Greenfield, Meg **128**
Greenhouse, Linda **266**, 274
Greenhouse, Steven **70**
Greenspan, Alan 50, 55, 97, 111
Greenwald, John **71**
Greising, David 25, 111
Grenier, Richard **129**
Grove, Lloyd **267**
Guatemala, Republic of 176
Gubernick, Lisa **71**
Gumbel, Peter **169**
Gupta, Udayan **72**
Gutman, Roy 15

H

Haas, Lawrence J. **72**
Haberman, Clyde **169**
Haiti, Republic of 33, 176, 201, 255
Hallow, Ralph Z. **267**
Harden, Blaine **170**
Harper's 39
Hart, Gary 31
Harwood, John 276
Harwood, Richard 24, **268**
Hassan II, King of Morocco 149
Havemann, Joel **170**
Hays, Kathleen **73**
Health care 26, 40, 115, 138, 141, 228, 239, 240, 242, 244, 246, 281
Healy, Melissa **218**
Hedges, Chris **171**
Hedges, Michael **268**
Helman, Gerald B. 15
Henderson, Breck W. **218**
Henriques, Diana B. **73**
Hentoff, Nat **129**, 132
Herman, Tom **74**
Hershey, Robert D., Jr. **74**
Hewlett-Packard Co. 114
Hiatt, Fred **171**
Hiebert, Murray **172**
Hill, Anita Faye 123, 247, 253, 254, 260, 273
Hilts, Philip J. **239**
Hiltzik, Michael A. 16, 35, **172**
Hitchens, Christopher **130**
Hitchens, Theresa **219**
Hoagland, Jim 16, 24, 127, **130**
Hoffman, David **173**, 216
Holley, David **173**
Holmes, Steven A. **269**
Holstein, William J. 190

Holusha, John 75
Holzer, Robert 219
Homosexuality 30, 117, 123, 136, 292
Honda Motor Co. 27, 86
Hong Kong 151, 169, 182, 185, 229
Horovitz, Bruce 75
Horwitz, Tony 15, **174**
Hughes Aircraft 52, 233
Hughes, David **220**
Hundley, Tom **174**
Hunt, Albert 122
Hurd, Douglas 224
Husarska, Anna 15
Hussein, Saddam 29, 42, 143, 147, 158, 189, 208, 210, 212, 230, 231, 268, 281

I

Iacocca, Lee 27, 81, 107
IBM 60, 84, 85, 109, 233
Ibrahim, Youssef M. **175**
Ifill, Gwen **269**
Ignatius, Adi **175**
Ihnatowycz, Roma 156
IMF (International Monetary Fund) 71, 80, 108, 147, 155, 164, 167, 170, 198, 203, 209, 277
Impoco, Jim **176**
In These Times 87, 121, 131, 255, 278
India, Republic of 167, 186
Ingersoll, Bruce **76**
Ingrassia, Lawrence 25
Ingrassia, Paul 50
Insight 153, 295
Insilco Inc. 50
Investor's Business Daily 26, 73, 86, 252, 265, 273, 277
Iran, Islamic Republic of 160, 170, 189, 192, 208, 209, 223
Iran-Contra Affair 37, 250, 269, 271, 273, 295
Iraq, Republic of 29, 41, 143, 144, 149, 165, 171, 175, 189, 210, 215, 222, 230, 231, 233, 268
IRS (Internal Revenue Service) 100, 102
Isikoff, Michael **270**
Israel, State of 42, 115, 122, 123, 149, 153, 158, 173, 175, 216, 223, 228
Italy (Italian State) 70, 203
Ivins, Molly **131**

J

Jackson, Jesse 43, 136, 139, 146, 259, 275, 277, 278
James, Canute **176**
Jameson, Sam **177**, 223
Jane's Defence Weekly 231
Japan 27, 56, 63, 68, 106, 136, 161, 168, 176, 177, 184, 190, 191, 195, 196, 199, 203, 207, 209, 210, 214, 223, 227, 276, 289
  Liberal Democratic Party 162, 195, 199

Jehl, Douglas 234, **270**, 290
Jennings, Peter 124
Johnston, David **271**
Jones, Alex S. **76**
Jordan, Vernon 253
The Journal of Commerce 80, 85, 151, 152, 160, 184, 194, 198
Judis, John B. **131**

K

Kamm, Henry **177**
Kamm, Thomas **178**
Kanner, Bernice **77**
Kantor, Mickey 251
Katz, Gregory **178**
Katz, Jon 6, 10, 24, 248, 260
Kaufman, Jonathan **179**
Kaye, Lincoln **179**
Keller, Bill **179**, 181
Kelly, John 29
Kelso, Frank 218
Kemp, Jack F. 117, 119, 120, 229, 248, 259, 267
Kempe, Frederick **180**
Kennedy, Anthony 117
Kennedy, Edward M. (Ted) 146
Kennedy, John F. 128, 130
Kennedy, William 261
Kerrey, Robert 64, 118, 133, 145, 262
Kilborn, Peter T. **77**
Kilpatrick, James J. **132**
King Features Syndicate 136
King, Larry 7, 24, 248
Kinsley, Michael 24, 32, 122, **132**
Kinzer, Stephen 15, **180**
Kirkpatrick, Jeane 133, 267
Kissinger, Henry 16, 131
Klein, Joe **271**, 292
Knight, Jerry **78**
Knight, Robin **181**
Kohl, Helmut 98, 122, 180, 185, 193
Kolata, Gina 39, **240**
Kondracke, Morton 122, 133
Kopkind, Andrew 122
Kosterlitz, Julie **240**
Kraft, Scott **181**
Kramer, Michael **134**
Krauss, Clifford **220**
Krauthammer, Charles **134**
Kristof, Nicholas D. 14, **182**
Kristol, Irving **134**
Kristol, William 248
Kriz, Margaret E. **241**
Krugman, Paul 24
Kurtz, Howard 24, **272**
Kuttner, Robert **78**
Kuwait, State of 43, 174, 175, 213, 230

L

Labaton, Stephen **79**
Laderman, Jeffrey M. **79**
Lake, Anthony 125
Lamb, Brian 24, **248**

Lamb, Christina 182
Lambro, Donald **135**
Lancaster, John **220**
Lane, Vince 134
Lawrence, Richard **80**
Lebanon, Republic of 170
Lemay, Frank 29, 143
Lenorovitz, Jeffrey M. **221**
Leo, John 30, **135**
Leopold, George **221**
Levin, Doron P. 24, **80**, 269
Levine, Joshua **81**
Levinson, Marc **81**
Lewis, Anthony 16, **136**
Lewis, Flora **183**
Lewis, Neil A. **272**
Lewis, Paul **222**
Libya (Socialist People's Libyan Arab Jamahiriya) 171
Light, Larry **82**
Limbaugh, Rush 123
Lipin, Steven 52
Lipman, Joanne **82**
Lippman, Thomas W. **83**, 297
Lloyd, John **183**
Locin, Mitchell 250
Lockheed 52
Lohr, Steve **83**
Loomis, Carol J. **84**
Los Angeles 34, 38, 150, 152, 256, 289
  King, Rodney 32, 38, 140, 141, 256, 271, 279, 288, 297
  Riots 31, 32, 59, 66, 76, 106, 116, 119, 126, 129, 132, 139-141, 145-149, 182, 187, 204, 210, 248, 260, 264, 275, 278-280
Los Angeles Times 7, 14, 16, 26, 32, 35, 38, 54, 67, 75, 93, 94, 96, 97, 100, 161, 163, 165, 170, 172, 173, 177, 181, 189, 192, 202, 209, 210, 212, 218, 223, 224, 233, 234, 238, 241, 254, 264, 266, 270, 280, 281, 282, 283, 286, 287, 289, 290
Los Angeles Times Syndicate 102, 120, 123, 128, 133, 144, 147, 148
Lublin, Joann S. 99
Lyman, Rick 16

M

MacPherson, Myra 131
Madigan, Charles M. **273**
Madison, Christopher **222**
Maggs, John **85**
Magnier, Mark **184**
Magnusson, Paul **205**
Mahar, Maggie **85**
Major, John 27, 187, 188, 194, 195, 198
Malcolm X 36
Mallet, Victor **184**
Mandel, Susan **273**
Mandela, Nelson 160
Mann, Jim **223**
Marcos, Imelda 201
Marcus, Ruth **274**, 293

Marks, John **185**, 203
Marsh, David 34, **185**
Marshall, Gen. George C. 147
Marshall, Thurgood 130
Martin Marietta 52
Marx, Gary **186**
Massing, Michael **274**
Matalin, Mary 126
Mathews, Jay **275**
Matthews, Christopher **136**
Maugh, Thomas H., II **241**
Mauthner, Robert **223**, 233
Maxwell, Robert 292
McArdle, Thomas 26, **86**, 277
McCaw Cellular Communications Inc. 51
McDonald, Hamish **186**
McDonnell Douglas Corp. 53, 231
McGough, Robert **86**
McGregor, James **187**
McGrory, Mary **137**
McGurn, William **275**
McLaughlin, John 133
McManus, Doyle **224**, 266
McNamara, Eileen 40
McNamee, Mike 80, **87**, 155
McNulty, Timothy J. 250, **276**
McQueen, Michel **276**
Mecham, Michael **224**
Medicaid 244
Medicare 246, 252
Melloan, George **187**
Mercedes-Benz 65
Merline, John 26, 86, **277**
Merrill Lynch 50
Met Capital Corp. 74
Mexico (United Mexican States) 54, 63, 125, 166, 168, 178, 188
Meyer, Michael 257
The Miami Herald 191
Middle East 128, 144, 165, 173, 174, 175, 189, 207, 209, 216, 223
Mikulski, Barbara 242
Milbank, Dana 111
Milken, Michael 59, 102
Mintz, John 297
Mitchell, George J. 242, 258
Mitra, Ramon, Jr. 163
Mitterrand, Francois 98, 130, 197, 198
Miyazawa, Kiichi 136, 176, 207
Moberg, David **87**
Moffett, Matt **188**
Morgenson, Gretchen 27, **88**
Morrison, David C. **225**
Morrocco, John D. **225**
Mortimer, Edward **137**
Moseley, Ray **188**
Moss, J. Jennings **277**, 278
Mother Jones 150
Mother Teresa 130
Motorola Inc. 25
Mufson, Steven 24, **88**, 297
Mulford, David 130
Mulroney, Brian 205, 257
Munro, Neil **226**
Murphy, Caryle **189**
Murphy, Kim **189**

Murray, Alan **89**, 276
Murray, Frank J. **278**
Muwakkil, Salim **278**
Mydans, Seth **279**

N

NAACP (National Association for the Advancement of Colored People) 30, 141
NAFTA (North American Free Trade Agreement) 12, 51, 82, 85, 104, 140, 165, 166, 168, 178, 188, 205
NASA (National Aeronautics and Space Agency) 214, 218, 225, 230, 234, 242, 246, 264
Nasar, Sylvia 24, **89**, 121
NASD (National Assoc. of Securities Dealers) 26
Nash, Nathaniel C. **190**
The Nation 121, 130, 202
National Journal 72, 103, 104, 109, 126, 144, 222, 225, 240, 241, 251, 258, 291
National Review 18, 119, 120, 275
National Security Council 131
NATO (North Atlantic Treaty Organization) 137, 213, 219, 222, 224, 233
Navy, U.S. 219, 221, 225, 226, 232, 254
Nazario, Sonia L. **279**
NBC (National Broadcasting Co.) 12, 24, 37, 58
NEA (National Endowment for the Arts) 129, 135, 140, 249, 263, 283
Neff, Robert **190**
Neikirk, William **90**
Nelson, Jack **280**
New England Journal of Medicine 235, 246
The New Republic 6, 10, 31, 32, 116
New York 37, 58, 77, 260, 292
New York Newsday 15, 102
New York Post 61
The New York Review of Books 35
The New York Times 8, 11-13, 15-17, 20, 22, 28, 34, 37, 39, 40, 44, 51, 60, 65, 68-70, 73-77, 79, 80, 83, 89, 91, 93, 96, 104, 108, 110, 115, 125, 136, 140, 142, 143, 154, 157-159, 163, 164, 167-169, 171, 175, 177, 179, 180, 182, 183, 190, 193, 197, 199, 200-204, 210, 215, 217, 220, 222, 228, 229, 232, 236, 239, 240, 243, 245, 248-250, 252, 258, 262, 263, 266, 269, 271, 272, 279, 283, 285, 286, 291, 293, 295
The New Yorker 14, 15, 36, 43, 118, 262
New Zealand 229
Newcomb, Peter 72
Newspaper Enterprise Association 149
Newsweek 7, 15, 17, 81, 95, 106, 143, 150, 154, 160, 195, 248, 257, 264, 271, 275
Nicaragua, Republic of 151

Nickerson, Colin **191**
Nigeria, Federal Republic of 192
NIH (National Institute of Health) 58
Nissan Motor Corp. 106
Nixon, Richard M. 12, 43, 83, 126, 127, 143, 294
Noah, Timothy **280**
Nolan, Martin F. **281**
Nomani, Asra Q. 92
Nordwall, Bruce D. **226**
Norman, Peter **91**
Norris, Floyd **91**
North Korea (Democratic People's Republic of Korea) 161, 196, 209, 223, 227
Norway, Kingdom of 219
Novack, Janet 40
Novak, Michael **138**
Novak, Robert 24, 41, **123**, 126, 142
NRC (Nuclear Regulatory Commission) 244
Nuclear Power 29, 110, 218, 220, 266
Nulty, Peter **92**
Nunn, Sam 232

O

Oberdorfer, Don 16, **227**
O'Brian, Bridget **92**
Oliphant, Thomas **138**
Oliver, R. Spencer 223
OMB (Office of Management and Budget) 24, 25, 117
Opall, Barbara **227**
OPEC (Organization of Petroleum Exporting Countries) 105
Oppenheimer, Andres **191**
O'Rourke, P. J. **139**
Ostrow, Ronald J. **281**
O'Sullivan, John 119
Ozanne, Julian **191**

P

Packwood, Bob 146
Page, Clarence 17, **139**
Pakistan, Islamic Republic of 186
Paltrow, Scot J. 26, **93**
Pan American World Airways 37, 58
Panetta, Leon 215
Panyarachun, Anand 201
Parks, Michael 161, **192**
Passell, Peter **93**
Pasztor, Andy **228**
Patten, Christopher 14, 152, 182
PBS (Public Broadcasting System) 129
"MacNeil/Lehrer NewsHour" 15, 125, 145
Pear, Robert **228**
Peel, Quentin **192**
Peers, Alexandra 59
Pennar, Karen 155
Peres, Shimon 120, 158
Perlez, Jane 16, **193**
Perot, H. Ross 6-12, 24, 29, 41, 55, 67, 80, 98, 103, 104, 106, 111,

115-118, 122, 126, 131, 134, 136, 143, 144, 188, 213, 229, 230, 248, 255, 257-259, 262, 264, 268-270, 274, 276, 280, 282, 284, 289, 290, 292, 293, 297
Perry, James M. 230, 276, **281**
Persian Gulf War 29, 143, 145, 147, 170, 175, 189, 196, 208, 212, 213, 217, 221, 225, 226, 250, 283
Peru, Republic of 151, 178, 186, 190
Peters, Charles 265
Peterson, Jonathan **94**
Philadelphia Inquirer 16
Philippines, Republic of 152, 163, 199
Pine, Art **282**
Pinkerton, Jim 229
Poland (Polish People's Republic) 164, 170, 171
Pollack, Andrew **193**
Pollin, Robert 122
Pope, Victoria **194**, 203
Porsche Enterprises, Inc. 28
Porter, Janet **194**
Postrel, Virginia I. 32, **140**
Pound, Edward T. 42
Pouschine, Tatiana 103
Powell, Bill **195**
Power, William **94**, 101, 102
Price, Joyce **282**
Proctor, Paul **229**
Prowse, Michael **95**
Pruden, Wesley **140**
Pryor, Dave H. 69
Puerto Rico, Commonwealth of 176

Q

Qaddafi, Muammar 171
Quayle, J. Danforth, III 25, 43, 73, 119, 120, 127, 131, 137, 248, 259, 260, 266, 272, 280, 284, 286, 297
Quiles, Paul 221
Quindlen, Anna **140**
Quinn, Jane Bryant **95**
Quint, Michael **96**

R

R. H. Macy & Co. 104, 107
Rabin, Yitzhak 154, 158, 183, 192
Race relations 30, 32, 39, 140, 141, 148, 150, 160, 279, 292
Rao, Narasimha 186
Rapoport, Carla **195**
Raspberry, William 30, **141**
Rather, Dan 132
Ratner, Steven R. 15
Reagan, Ronald 24, 29, 70, 89, 116, 117, 120, 121, 123, 133, 135, 142, 144, 251, 255, 262, 275, 281
Reason 140
Reichlin, Igor 155
Reid, T. R. **196**
Reier, Sharon **196**
Reilly, William 243

Reinhold, Robert **283**
Reischauer, Robert 24
Remnick, David 13, 36
Republican Party 26, 30, 31, 32, 61, 116, 118, 120, 121, 131, 132, 143, 144, 145, 147, 148, 260, 267, 275
  National Convention 24, 220, 248, 251, 262, 273
Rich, Spencer **242**
Richburg, Keith B. 16, **197**
Richter, Paul **283**
Riding, Alan **197**
Rifkind, Malcolm 233
Rio Summit, see Environment
Risen, James 94, **96**
Robb, Charles 251
Roberts, Paul Craig 24, 42, 86, 117, **141**
Roberts, Steven V. **284**
Robinson, Eugene **198**
Rockefeller, John D., IV (Jay) 109
Rockwell International 52
Rockwell, Keith M. **198**
Rodriguez, Paul M. 277, **284**
Rogers, David 42, 255
Rohter, Larry **285**
Rohwer, Jim 36
Rolling Stone 6, 10, 29, 139
Rollins, Edward 29
Romania, Socialist Republic of 177
Rooney, Pat 141
Roosevelt, Franklin D. 116
Rosenbaum, David E. **285**
Rosenberg, Howard 16
Rosenblatt, Robert A. **97**
Rosenstiel, Thomas B. 24, **286**
Rosenthal, A. M. 120, 123, **142**
Rosenthal, Andrew 24, **286**
Ross, Michael **287**
Roth, William V., Jr. 26
Rowan, Roy 37
Rowen, Hobart **98**
Royko, Mike **142**
Rudnitsky, Howard **98**
Russia, see Commonwealth of Independent States

S

Safire, William 24, 28, 40, **143**
Salinas de Gortari, Carlos 125, 166, 178
Salomon Brothers 59, 113
Salwen, Kevin G. **99**
Samuelson, Robert J. **143**
San Francisco Examiner 136
Sanger, David E. **199**
Saporito, Bill 28, **99**
Saudi Arabia, Kingdom of 108, 156, 189, 231
Saunders, Laura **100**
Savage, David G. **287**
Savings & Loan industry 27, 37, 106, 265
Sawyer, Kathy **242**
Scalia, Antonin 137
Schlesinger, Helmut 91

Schlesinger, Jacob M. **199**
Schmemann, Serge **200**
Schmetzer, Uli 14, **200**
Schneider, Keith **243**
Schneider, William **144**
Schrage, Michael **100**
Schwarzkopf, Gen. H. Norman 115
Sciolino, Elaine **229**
Scott, William B. **230**
Scowcroft, Brent 131, 262
Scripps-Howard News Service 146
SEC (Securities and Exchange Commission) 26, 59, 93, 99
Seib, Gerald F. **230**
Seligman, Daniel **144**
Seper, Jerry **288**
Sesit, Michael R. **100**
Sessions, William 271
Sevareid, Eric 116
Shales, Tom **288**
Shapiro, Bruce 55
Shapiro, Robert 127
Shapiro, Walter **289**
Shaw, David 38, **289**
Shenon, Philip **201**
Sheppard, Nathaniel, Jr. 32, **201**
Shevardnadze, Eduard 154
Shields, Mark 122, **145**
Shogan, Robert **290**
Shogren, Elizabeth **202**
Shribman, David 253, 282, **290**
Siconolfi, Michael 94, **101**
Sidey, Hugh **145**
Sikes, Alfred C. 65
Silverberg, David **231**
Simpson, John **202**
Singapore, Republic of 51, 184
Singer, Daniel **202**
Skinner, Samuel K. 116, 251, 259, 266
Sloan, Allan **102**
Smith Corona Corp. 54
Smith, John F. 114
Smith, R. Jeffrey **231**
Smith, Randall 94, **102**
Smith, Roger 51
Smothers, Ronald **291**
Sobran, Joseph **146**
Somalia (Somali Democratic Republic) 15-17, 35, 91, 131, 136, 141, 172, 192, 221, 218, 226, 227, 269, 282
South Africa, Republic of 160, 173, 180, 181, 206, 208
South Korea (Republic of Korea) 161, 177
Sowell, Thomas **146**
Spain (Spanish State) 159, 197
The Spectator 12, 18, 19, 202
Spencer, Leslie 56
Spencer, Peter 28
Squires, Jim 29
Stacks, John 37
Stanfield, Rochelle L. **291**
Stanglin, Douglas **203**
Starobin, Paul **103**
Starr, Barbara **231**
Steiger, Janet 119
Stempel, Robert 62

Stephanopoulos, George 257, 270
Stern, Richard L. **103**
Sterngold, James **203**
Stevens, William K. **243**
Stevenson, Richard W. **204**
Stipp, David 38, **244**
Stokes, Bruce **104**
Stout, Hillary 244
Strauss, Robert S. 220
Strom, Stephanie **104**
Sudan, Democratic Republic of the 193
Sullivan, Allanna 105
Sullivan, Andrew 265
Summers, Col. H. G., Jr. (Harry) **147**
Sun, Lena H. 14, **204**
Sununu, John 28, 132, 143, 239, 251
Supreme Court, U.S. 129, 249, 274, 287
Sweden, Kingdom of 219
Switzerland (Swiss Confederation) 167
Symonds, William C. **205**
Syria (Syrian Arab Republic) 130, 149, 208
Szymczak, Pat 203

T

Taiwan (Republic of China) 151, 169
Takayama, Hideko 195
Talbott, Strobe 13, **147**
Tannenbaum, Jeffrey 72
Tanner, James **105**
Tanzer, Andrew **205**
Taylor, Alex, III 26, **105**
Taylor, John 292
Taylor, Paul **206**
Taylor, Ronald 292
Teeter, Robert 267, 297
Thailand, Kingdom of 63, 151, 159, 184, 201
Thomas, Cal **148**
Thomas, Clarence 132, 137, 247, 253, 260, 273, 287, 296
Thomas, Paulette **106**
Thomas, Rich **106**
Thurow, Lester 126
Thurow, Roger 15
Time 10, 13, 71, 134, 145, 147, 153, 158, 238, 256, 289
Time Warner, Inc. 37, 76, 102, 159
Toner, Robin **293**
Trachtenberg, Jeffrey A. **107**
Trade 51, 85, 115, 118, 138, 151, 165, 182, 188, 212
 see also NAFTA
Transitions Research Corp. 237
Treece, James B. **107**
Tribune Media Services 115, 139, 142
Truell, Peter **108**
Truman, Harry S. 116, 119, 248
Tsongas, Paul 24, 61, 125, 138, 140, 144, 145, 234, 251, 253, 254, 255, 283, 286
Turkey, Republic of 224
Tutwiler, Margaret 131
Tyler, Patrick E. 44, **232**

Tyrrell, R. Emmett, Jr. **148**

U

Uchitelle, Louis **108**
U.K. (United Kingdom of Great Britain and Northern Ireland) 27, 57, 71, 73, 91, 174, 181, 182, 194, 198, 210, 224, 231
U.S. (United States of America) 42, 69, 106, 151, 159, 161, 165, 171, 173, 176-178, 184, 185, 187-189, 194-196, 198, 199, 201, 222, 225, 227, 252
 see also Economy, U.S.
USA Today 7, 16
U.S.News & World Report 7, 13, 30, 61, 64, 116, 125, 135, 176, 181, 185, 194, 203, 254, 284, 294
Uchitelle, Louis 108
UN (United Nations) 115, 141, 156, 159, 171, 190, 192, 201, 207, 209, 217, 222, 224, 225, 227, 230, 231, 233, 243, 273
Underwriters Laboratories Inc. 53
United Features Syndicate 132, 135
United Media Syndicate 133
Universal Press Syndicate 120, 126, 132, 146
Upjohn 240

V

Vartabedian, Ralph **233**
Vatikiotis, Michael **206**
Venezuela, Republic of 126, 151, 157, 191
Verity, John W. **109**
Victor, Kirk **109**
Vietnam, Socialist Republic of 139, 156, 172, 184
The Village Voice 129, 130
Vitzhum, Carla 208

W

Wade, Nicholas 240
Wagstyl, Stefan **207**
Wal-Mart 88
Wald, Matthew L. **110**
Waldholz, Michael **244**
Waldman, Peter **207**
Waldmeir, Patti 181, **208**
Walker, Tony **208**
The Wall Street Journal 7-9, 14, 18, 22, 23, 25, 29, 38, 42, 50, 52, 59, 62, 66, 72, 74, 76, 82, 86, 89, 92, 94, 99-102, 105-108, 111, 112, 114, 117, 127, 134, 151, 161, 169, 174, 175, 178, 180, 187, 188, 199, 207, 214, 228, 230, 235, 237, 244, 246, 247, 253, 255, 276, 279-281, 290
Wallace, Charles P. **209**
Walsh, Edward 274, **293**
Walsh, Kenneth T. **294**

Walt Disney Co. 134
Walters, Laurel Shaper **294**
Warsh, David **110**
Wartzman, Rick **111**
The Washington Monthly 7, 36, 265
The Washington Post 6, 7, 11, 13, 14, 16, 22, 30, 31, 33, 34, 41-43, 51, 54, 65, 78, 83, 88, 98, 119, 122, 128-130, 137, 141, 149, 156, 159, 162, 165, 170, 171, 173, 189, 196-198, 204, 206, 216, 220, 227, 231, 239, 242, 245, 247, 251, 253, 256, 257, 259-261, 263, 267, 268, 270, 272, 274, 275, 288, 293, 296, 297
Washington Post Writers Group 78, 127, 134, 143, 150
The Washington Times 9, 11, 42, 123, 124, 129, 135, 140, 141, 217, 249, 261, 267, 268, 277, 278, 282, 284, 288, 292
Watanabe, Teresa **209**
Waters, Maxine 129
Wattenberg, Ben **149**
Wattenberg, Daniel **295**
Weber, Vin 117, 268
Weinstein, Michael 24
Weise, Richard H. 25
Weiss, Gary **111**
Weisskopf, Michael **245**
Weld, William 149
Wells Fargo & Company 102
Wessel, David **112**
Weymouth, Lally **149**
Whitcover, Jules 126
White, David **233**
White, Joseph B. **112**
Whitney, Craig R. **210**
Wilder, L. Douglas 251
Wilford, John Noble **245**
Wilkerson, Isabel **295**
Wilkie, Curtis 44, **296**
Wilkins, Roger **150**
Will, George F. 24, 30, 127, **150**
Williams, Carol J. **210**
Williams, Daniel 192
Williams, Juan **296**
Williams, Marjorie 41
Wilson, John **296**
Wilson, Pete 283
Winslow, Ron 244, **246**
Witcover, Jules **126**
Witt, Howard **211**
Wood, Michael 129
Woodward, Bob 24, 42, 43, 119, **296**
World Bank 164, 166, 198
Worthy, Ford S. **113**
Wright, Robin 212
Wrubel, Robert **113**
Wyman, Jasper 127

X Y Z

Xerox Corp. 75
Yang, John E. **297**
Yeltsin, Boris 12, 13, 34, 36, 124, 154, 155, 164, 175, 181, 183, 192, 199, 202, 203, 224

Yugoslavia (former Socialist Federal
  Republic of Yugoslavia) 12, 14, 15,
    17, 130, 131, 136, 147, 159, 162,
    183, 189, 198, 219
  Bosnia and Herzegovina 12, 15, 34,
    125, 136-138, 142, 158, 159, 162,
    170, 174, 180, 183, 189, 190, 210,
    217, 222, 224, 227, 233
  Croatia 133, 158, 162
  Macedonia 148
  Sarajevo 130, 158, 191, 200, 233
  Serbia 34, 91, 142, 170, 174, 181,
    193
Zachary, G. Pascal **114**
Zuckerman, Mortimer 77